THE FRESHMEN

THE FRESHMEN

What Happened to the Republican Revolution?

To Joe —
Good luck with your future political career

LINDA KILLIAN

All The Best.
Linda Killian
April 9, 1998

WestviewPress
A Division of HarperCollins*Publishers*

Published in 1998 in the United States of America by Westview Press, 5500 Central Avenue, Boulder,
Colorado 80301-2877, and in the United Kingdom by Westview Press, 12 Hid's Copse Road, Cumnor
Hill, Oxford OX2 9JJ

Library of Congress Cataloging-in-Publication Data
Killian, Linda
    The freshmen : what happened to the Republican revolution? / Linda
Killian.
        p.   cm.
    Includes index.
    ISBN 0-8133-9951-3
    1. Republican Party (U.S. 1854–   )   2. United States. Congress—
Elections, 1994.   3. United States. Congress.   4. United States—
Politics and government—1993–   .   I. Title.
JK2356.K56   1998
324.2734'092'2—dc21   97-47703
                                                                                                          CIP

Text design by Heather Hutchison

10   9   8   7   6   5   4   3   2   1

To my parents,
Carl and Mary Jane Killian

CONTENTS

PREFACE

I BEGAN WORK ON THIS BOOK SHORTLY after the Republican freshmen arrived in Washington. The election of 1994 and the Republican takeover of Congress were certainly historic and more than worthy of a book. But what I found more interesting than the GOP leaders, who were already well known and receiving plenty of attention, were the party's new House members. They were the ones who in large measure made the 104th Congress different from any that had come before.

Most of the 73 Republicans elected to the House for the first time in 1994 were citizen legislators who saw themselves as temporary emissaries sent by the voters to Washington on a mission. They were brash, irrepressible, and passionately committed to the cause of balancing the budget and shrinking the size of the federal government. The freshmen were a new breed, different from the men and women who had preceded them to Congress. They were not polished, cookie-cutter politicians. They were quirky and plainspoken.

I wanted to discover who these freshmen were—how they thought, what was important to them, and what they wanted to accomplish—to understand and to explain them both as politicians and as people.

After initially interviewing nearly 50 of the freshmen, I selected roughly 25 with whom I had multiple interviews and who appear throughout the book. From this group I chose a dozen to focus on even more closely. These were the freshmen who were largely at the center of the action in the 104th Congress. I spoke to each of them dozens of times over the course of two years. I became in essence their almost constant shadow. I wanted to get inside their heads. I did this by talking to them on the way to votes and after closed-door meetings; late at night in their offices and on the road back in their districts. What resulted was a revealing, inside look at what it meant to be a freshman in the 104th Congress.

A large part of the book is told in the freshmen's own words. Many of them were extraordinarily open with me. Their frankness is one of the things that sets them apart from senior lawmakers, both Republicans and Democrats. And it is probably the thing I found most refreshing about them.

In addition to the freshmen, I interviewed hundreds of others, including senior House members and senators, congressional staffers, lobbyists, party officials, special interest activists, local officials, and constituents from the freshmen's home states. Unless otherwise noted, all of the quotes in the book are from events I witnessed or interviews I conducted either with the person speaking or with someone in attendance at the meeting or event being depicted. Some quotes are from speeches or other public statements. Many of the freshmen and other members of Congress also provided me with copies of memos, press releases, polling information, committee documents, letters, and other communications among House members, such as "Dear Colleague" letters.

I wanted the book as closely as possible to reflect the freshmen's view of what was going on in the 104th Congress and their role in it. I have also tried to convey the way that changed over the course of their first term in office. They arrived in Washington in January 1995 as outsiders, ready to take on the system and the senior members of both parties. They were going to change government and the way Congress operates. But they discovered over the next two years that it wasn't going to be as easy as they thought. Along the way they learned how Congress really works and underwent major struggles and changes, both professional and personal.

At many points I also stand back to offer my own assessment of decisions made and actions taken. As I was writing this book, people kept asking me what I thought of the freshmen, whether I was for them or against them. Occasionally, when I told people about this book, looks of horror would cross their faces, and they would say, "Oh, those extremists. Why would you want to write about them?" Others told me the freshmen were the best thing that had ever happened to Congress. The freshmen always aroused strong feelings: People either loved them or hated them, and that's another reason I wrote this book.

The freshmen's lofty ambitions, hard lessons, high drama, miscalculations, failures, and victories are all part of the journey chronicled here. I hope readers will come away with an understanding of who the freshmen were, what it was like to be in this historic freshman class, and why it's important to care, no matter what your political point of view.

I reported this book over the span of the 104th Congress both as events were happening and immediately after they took place. In many cases as well, I went back over major events in the book months later with the people involved to add another layer of reflection to their assessment of what had happened. Nearly 200 legal pads later, my notes and related materials filled a small room.

The story opens in early 1995 with Van Hilleary of Tennessee and follows the major events in the House over the course of the next two years and through the election of 1996. The epilogue follows the freshmen, by then sophomores, even further into the 105th Congress.

I talked with Van Hilleary at length during our first meeting, and through subsequent conversations I came to believe that he represented the perfect everyman of the freshmen class. He was not always at the center of the action or one of the most rebellious of the freshmen. But in political view, temperament, and background, he was typical of most of his classmates. As I attempt to illuminate the significant events of the 104th Congress and tell the individual stories of some of the freshmen, Van Hilleary serves as a touchstone throughout this book.

I had the chance to visit Van Hilleary's district several times and to travel to about 10 of the other freshmen districts, including Seattle and Washington state; Fort Wayne, Indiana; Palm Beach, Florida; Topeka, Kansas; southeastern Wisconsin; Salt

Lake City, Utah; and Tennessee. I talked with people at cafes, shopping malls, political rallies, and Fourth of July parades. I think this book is not only about politics but also about who we are as a country at the end of the twentieth century. The freshmen were part of a movement, but they were also a cross-section of America, and in reporting this book I wanted to learn about the communities they came from and the voters who sent them to Washington.

A number of people suggested I hurry up and finish this book before the freshmen were gone, defeated and sent home, relegated to the dustbin of history. But they weren't going anywhere. Most of the members of the class of '94 were reelected, and although a number of them have voluntarily term-limited themselves, they have vowed to continue fighting as long as they remain in Congress.

I hope this book is read by students of government and by political junkies—the people who closely follow and are involved in politics in their home states and in Washington. But my fondest wish and deepest desire is that *The Freshmen* will also be discovered by people around the country who don't often read books about politics. I wrote *The Freshmen* for them. They were, after all, the people who sent the freshmen to Washington.

The issues debated and the changes set in motion by the election of 1994, including what the role of government will be as we move into the next century, are too important to be left to professional politicians and journalists to consider and decide. To solve the problems this nation faces, it will take the attention and involvement of all of our citizens. If this book in any small way helps people understand how Congress functions and why it's important to care, I will be most gratified. For all of the gloom and doom spread by journalists like myself about the undue influence of lobbyists on the business of Congress, the truth is members of Congress are always influenced most by the people who elected them and who have the power to replace them. Constituent phone calls, letters, and personal questions at town hall meetings do have a major impact on members of Congress and the decisions they make.

There can be no better illustration that we live in a responsive, participatory democracy than the election of 1994. Because a lot of voters stayed home that year, the votes of those who did turn out had a profound impact. Many freshmen were elected by extremely small margins, so the votes cast by a relative handful of eligible voters resulted in major changes in Congress and in our government.

All around the country in fall 1994, close congressional races pitted Democratic incumbents against Republican newcomers. And in open seats the Republicans, even if they had previously served in government, were claiming to be the outsiders, the antigovernment candidates. Such was the case in Oklahoma, where two House members, Democrat David McCurdy and Republican James Inhofe, were vying for the unexpired Senate term of conservative Democrat David Boren, who had resigned to take over the presidency of the University of Oklahoma. I had traveled to Oklahoma to do a piece on the race for National Public Radio.

McCurdy had served in the House for 14 years and had a reputation as one of the leaders of the moderate wing of the Democratic Party. But in the 103rd Congress

McCurdy had voted for the Clinton budget (with its tax increase) and the crime bill (with its assault weapons ban). And in many districts in 1994 that kind of record was enough to ensure defeat.

Inhofe had served for 10 years in the Oklahoma House and Senate, had been mayor of Tulsa, and had unsuccessfully run for governor of Oklahoma and the U.S. House before being elected to Congress in 1986. Inhofe professed to be a strong supporter of term limits and was trying to run as an outsider even though he had been in elected office for 24 of the past 28 years. Like many GOP candidates around the country, Inhofe was running not only a local but a national campaign. His campaign themes echoed the Contract with America, including term limits, a balanced budget amendment, lower taxes, less government spending, welfare reform, and tougher crime laws.

Inhofe, one of Congress's few certified commercial pilots, had been crisscrossing the state in his 1969 Piper Aztec and managed to visit almost every town in Oklahoma before the end of the campaign. On one particular morning a few weeks before the election, I followed Inhofe on the campaign trail. He took off in his plane at 7 A.M. for Cleveland, Oklahoma, about 30 miles northwest of Tulsa, and was met at the tiny landing strip by a handful of local Republican Party activists. "Things are looking good, and what's happening here is really a very significant part of the revolution that's taking place right now in America," he told them. "All over the country liberals, insiders like Dave McCurdy, are getting defeated, and the people are taking government back. This is called the pivotal race . . . the seventh seat that would take control of the United States Senate away from Bill Clinton."

From there it was on to Hominy, where Inhofe walked up and down Main Street and stopped by the local coffee shop to shake some hands. He told the morning customers the Senate race could be summed up by the "three Gs—God, gays, and guns." Inhofe claimed Dave McCurdy was a liberal Washington insider out of touch with what Oklahomans care about, who was against prayer in schools, for gays in the military and gun control, and who voted with Bill Clinton more than 80 percent of the time.

These were hot-button issues in Oklahoma in 1994. Probably the biggest issue in the Oklahoma race, as in many races around the country, was Bill Clinton. Inhofe delighted in labeling McCurdy a "Clinton clone" and "McClinton." For his part, McCurdy was trying to convince voters how conservative he was and never mentioned the president's name on the campaign trail. Although he had campaigned hard for Bill Clinton in 1992, McCurdy had not invited the president to return the favor for him this year.

One Saturday afternoon a few weeks before the election, McCurdy campaigned at the Mid-America Stockyards in Bristow, Oklahoma. Ranchers wearing cowboy hats and chewing tobacco and snuff sat on tiered benches bidding on the young cattle that moved constantly through swinging doors leading to and from a small dirt pen at one corner of the auction hall. Styrofoam cups filled with the tobacco juice littered the floor. The last thing they had on their minds was politics. But Dave Mc-

Curdy had come here seeking votes. He stood in the back of the hall looking uncomfortable and out of place in his neatly pressed, white button-down shirt and black ostrich cowboy boots. He hung back shyly, waiting for people to approach him.

McCurdy's 1994 campaign never seemed to take off. Oklahoma was one of the worst places to be a Democrat in 1994, and McCurdy had seen a 10-point lead evaporate over the summer. By October the Senate race was a dead heat. Inhofe had been running ads that showed McCurdy as Pinocchio with a constantly growing nose. Another Inhofe ad showed large, hairy men dancing around in frilly, pink tutus while an announcer talked about McCurdy's support for a Clinton crime bill that included federal funding for programs such as dance classes for at-risk youth. McCurdy decided the only thing he could do was fight back with negative ads of his own that focused on the bankruptcy of Inhofe's business, Inhofe's claims to have graduated from college 14 years earlier than he actually did, and problems involving the financing of Inhofe's first race for Congress that resulted in a $15,000 fine from the Federal Election Commission.

A few days before the election, a Mason-Dixon poll showed Inhofe with an eight-point lead over McCurdy. In a report broadcast on National Public Radio the day before the election, I predicted McCurdy would be defeated by Inhofe and that there would be similar outcomes in races around the country. But I think few people, myself included, expected the magnitude of the next day's election results and the long-term impact they would have on this nation. Not only did Inhofe win by a decisive 15 percentage points (55–40 percent), but Oklahoma Republicans picked up the governorship and two House seats, including McCurdy's.

What happened in Oklahoma was reflective of election returns around the country, which swept Republicans into office and gave them control of both the U.S. Senate and, for the first time in 40 years, the House of Representatives. It was a truly historic election. It put Congress on the path to a balanced budget. It forced a debate about the appropriate role of government. It precipitated significant changes in the laws governing welfare.

And it brought us the freshmen.

Linda Killian

THE MAIN CAST OF CHARACTERS

Van Hilleary of Tennessee   The Class Everyman

The True Believers
Sam Brownback of Kansas
Lindsey Graham of South Carolina
David McIntosh of Indiana
Mark Neumann of Wisconsin
Matt Salmon of Arizona
Joe Scarborough of Florida
John Shadegg of Arizona
Mark Souder of Indiana

Class Presidents
George Radanovich of California
Roger Wicker of Mississippi

The Stars
Sonny Bono of California
Steve Largent of Oklahoma
J. C. Watts of Oklahoma

The Wild Bunch
Helen Chenoweth of Idaho
Wes Cooley of Oregon
Steve Stockman of Texas

The Moderates
Mark Foley of Florida
Greg Ganske of Iowa

GOP Fun Couple

Enid Greene Waldholtz
Joe Waldholtz

The Washington State Freshmen

George Nethercutt, the Giant Killer
Linda Smith, the Angry White Female
Randy Tate, the Christian Kid
Rick White, the Moderate

The Leadership

Newt Gingrich, Speaker of the House
Dick Armey, Majority Leader
Tom DeLay, Majority Whip
John Boehner, Conference Chairman
John Kasich, Budget Committee Chairman
Robert Livingston, Appropriations Committee Chairman

Bill Clinton, President of the United States

Part One

WINTER–SPRING 1995

REPUBLICAN REVOLUTIONARIES

1

PROMISES MADE—
PROMISES KEPT?

THE CELEBRATION WAS SCHEDULED TO BEGIN at 10 A.M., and the Republicans did not disappoint. Not for them the lack of punctuality and discipline they associated with Bill Clinton and the Democrats. In all things the Republicans sought to distinguish themselves from that crowd, and nowhere was the difference more apparent than in their ability to stage a spectacular display of pomp, patriotism, and self-congratulation—on time.

It was a breathtakingly beautiful day, already quite warm, as Washington can be in the early spring. The music began promptly at 9:45, and on a huge video screen flashed the images of average "Ah-murr-icans" (as Speaker Newt Gingrich liked to call them), talking about how much they liked what the Republicans were doing. At 9:50 the House members began to file down the steps of the Capitol's west front. Speaker Gingrich arrived at 9:55 and began to shake hands as he made his way to the front of the pack. Many of the members, especially those in the first row, were holding small American flags that had been handed out by young Republican staffers. The stage was awash in red, white, and blue bunting, and on the podium a sign read, "Contract with America—Promises Made—Promises Kept—Restoring the American Dream." At the bottom of the steps were dozens of reporters ready to mark the occasion, the official end of the first 100 days of the 104th Congress. On risers behind them was a bank of more than 20 TV cameras, their blank lenses pointed row after row toward the Capitol.

At 10:00 exactly, freshman J. D. Hayworth stepped up to the microphone to serve as master of ceremonies. In a deep, booming voice that recalled his previous job as a sportscaster for a Phoenix TV station, he introduced Republican National Commit-

tee chair Haley Barbour. Hayworth had one of the best voices in Congress. A 6'5"
bear of a man, Hayworth had earned the nickname "J. D. TV" from some majority
staff members because of his frequent habit of taking to the floor after the House
was out of formal session, during what is known as "special orders," to give speeches
heard only by late-night C-SPAN junkies and a few of his constituents on Pacific
time. Hayworth, who always seemed to be smiling no matter how bitter the message
he had to deliver to the American people about what the Democrats were trying to
do to them, managed in these frequent floor speeches to be rabidly partisan, slightly
goofy, and yet somehow pleasant. Behind his back, some of his own freshmen classmates referred to him as a "blowhard."

Standing next to Hayworth in the front row, somewhat dwarfed by his physical
presence, was the most famous and perhaps most maligned member of the freshman
class, Sonny Bono, undoubtedly better known for his singing career with his former
wife, Cher, than for the four years he served as mayor of Palm Springs. Bono's election to Congress had been marked by an incredible amount of media hype including
a regular "First 100 Days Bono Watch" in *Time* magazine. He had faced the snicker-
ing of political cartoonists, late-night talk show hosts, and Washington pundits who
dismissed him as a dolt and little more than a Republican publicity stunt. But Bono
was unfazed. He'd seen worse.

Haley Barbour opened the festivities by happily pointing out that the Republicans
had managed to finish work on their Contract with America not in the promised
100 days but in just 93. (He was, of course, talking about the House Republicans.
The Senate Republicans, who never signed onto the contract, would take a good
deal more time getting around to it.) Barbour touted the election of 1994 as "the
most issue-oriented campaign of [his] lifetime" as well as the "greatest midterm majority sweep in the 20th century." The rhetoric, although superheated, was fairly accurate. The election was indeed historic. The GOP's 52-seat House gain resulted in a
return to Republican control of that chamber for the first time in 42 years, ending
the longest span of one-party rule in the history of Congress.

And the men and women responsible for that change were the 73 Republican
freshmen. Congress hadn't seen that many new House Republicans since 1946,
when both Richard Nixon and a young war hero from Massachusetts named John
Kennedy were elected to the House for the first time. But Republican control of the
House lasted just two years. The party was swept out of power by Harry Truman's
campaign against the do-nothing Republican Congress and his 1948 reelection.

Gingrich, ever the history professor, was well aware of the short-lived tenure of
the 1946 Republicans, and he was determined not to repeat their fate. It had taken
him long enough to storm the palace gates and grab hold of power; he would not re-
linquish it easily. And his freshmen, the 73 storm troopers in Newt Gingrich's army,
felt the same way. They were on a mission, a crusade to save the American people
from their own government.

They were there that spring morning, dutifully smiling, waving their flags, lined
up on the steps behind Gingrich. The only African American among those 73 and

one of two African American Republicans in the House was J. C. Watts of Oklahoma, a former star quarterback on the University of Oklahoma football team. A devout Southern Baptist and an ordained minister, he led the group in prayer. "We take this time right now to say, 'Much obliged,'" intoned Watts in his Oklahoma twang.

After the Pledge of Allegiance, Bill Paxon of New York took his turn. Paxon, who served as chairman of the National Republican Congressional Committee and launched one of the smartest and most aggressive candidate recruitments on record, could reasonably claim as much credit for the Republicans' 1994 victory as just about anyone. Sure, a few GOP candidates were duds. And given the kind of year it was, a few of those duds even got elected. But on the whole the 1994 Republican candidates were a pretty impressive lot for long-shot challengers.

Many of them were small business people willing to spend a lot of their own money to get elected, even in seats where it looked pretty tough to knock off an incumbent. Sixty-five of the 73 freshmen came from districts that had been represented by Democrats in the previous Congress. Paxon was feeling pretty good about what he'd pulled off. And on this glorious, triumphant spring day, he predicted a gain of 20 to 30 seats in 1996 for the House Republicans.

Next came a video of the September 27 ceremony in which the Republicans had signed their Contract with America on these very same Capitol steps only six months earlier. The idea for a contract, an ideological compact with the American people, was not new for the Republicans. They had first tried it in the fall of 1980, when presidential candidate Ronald Reagan along with GOP candidates for the House and Senate also gathered on the Capitol steps and pledged themselves to a general policy agenda that included cutting government spending and promoting private investment. One of the organizers of that effort, labeled Governing Team Day, was a little-known Republican House freshman from Georgia named Newt Gingrich.

By 1994 Gingrich had made a name for himself as a fierce partisan who helped to bring down Democratic Speaker Jim Wright. He had become the minority whip and heir to GOP leader Bob Michel, who had announced his retirement. Gingrich thought that for the 1994 elections Republicans again needed a policy agenda that would be extremely appealing to voters. At a meeting in Salisbury, Maryland, in February 1994, House Republicans agreed on a general set of principles for their agenda: individual liberty, economic opportunity, limited government, personal responsibility, and military security. Over the next few months, the Republicans developed 10 basic principles in more detail, and the contract was drafted by Gingrich, Armey, and their staffs. Then GOP political consultants test-marketed it, using focus groups and polling to determine how and in what order the items should be presented.

They came up with catchy titles like the "Congressional Accountability Act" for a measure to require Congress to live by the same laws it had passed for the rest of the country's employers. The "Taking Back Our Streets Act" proposed changes to the Democratic crime bill. The "Personal Responsibility Act" was the Republicans' welfare reform plan. It would cut spending for welfare programs, deny benefits to women under the age of 18, and prohibit additional benefits for women who became pregnant while on welfare. The "Fiscal Responsibility Act" was another name for the balanced budget amendment and line-item veto authority for the president. The "American Dream Restoration Act" involved a $500-per-child tax credit. The "Job Creation and Wage Enhancement Act" included a 50 percent capital gains rate cut and other tax code changes as well as efforts at deregulation to help business. The "Common Sense Legal Reform Act" made changes in product liability law designed both to please business interests and punish trial lawyers, a group largely supportive of Bill Clinton and Democratic candidates. The "Citizen Legislature Act" was a promise to vote on the notion of term limits for members of Congress.

For all of the hype about their contract and all of the lockstep unity it brought about in the beginning of the 104th Congress, the contract did not prove to be terribly influential with voters in 1994. A CBS–*New York Times* poll released the week of the election showed that 71 percent of those questioned had never even heard of the contract, and another 15 percent said it would make no difference in how they voted. Seven percent said it would make them more likely to vote for a Republican House candidate, and 5 percent said it would make them less likely. But the spirit of the contract and the attempt to nationalize the off-year election did seem to make a difference, and it certainly energized the Republican candidates.

They promised to bring their contract items to the floor of the House for a vote in the first three months of the 104th Congress, and they delivered on that promise. But at the close of 100 days (or, rather, 93) only two of the contract items, those applying federal labor laws to Congress and a curb on unfunded mandates to the states, had also passed in the Senate and been signed into law by President Clinton. Many of the rest, thanks to Republican moderates in the Senate and threatened presidential vetoes, faced an uncertain future.

But on that spring day the Republicans would brook no nay-saying. There wasn't a senator in sight. Majority leader Dick Armey told the assembled group that "the birds are singing, the cherry trees are in bloom, baseball is back, and we've completed our Contract with America." Armey then proceeded through the contract item by item. "We said we'd pass a balanced budget amendment," he said, and joining him on cue, as if well rehearsed, the entire group of Republicans shouted with him, "And we did."

What followed were speeches, a lot of them, which touted the Republicans' success. Majority whip Tom DeLay, an effective party organizer but an excruciatingly bad public speaker, reminded his colleagues of something that could hardly have escaped them: "Much has been accomplished, but much remains to be done." As one after another Republican stepped to the microphone, the patience of the members, who were, after all, most used to hearing the sound of their own voices, appeared to be wearing thin. They had stood for almost an hour on the marble steps under a sun that had grown increasingly hot, and they began to yell, "Newt," "Newt," seemingly anxious both to hear from their fearless leader and to get the ceremony over with.

Gingrich stepped up to the microphone, an expansive grin on his face, and began, "Well, as I was saying last September . . ." But before he could go any further, some protesters in the crowd, obviously planted Democrats, started to blow air horns. They were quickly led away by uniformed Capitol police, but the mood was shattered. Gingrich lightly dismissed them, saying, "You can hardly have a revolution without some dissent. And if the best argument they have is to make meaningless noise, it tells you why the revolution is winning." But he was clearly bugged. Here was his moment of triumph. This photo opportunity was perhaps the single most triumphant day the Republicans would enjoy in the entire 104th Congress, and it had been marred by a few malcontents. For all his bravado and bluster, Gingrich would show himself to be quite sensitive over the next year and a half. He is anything but immune to criticism and small slights, as evidenced by his reaction to this tiny band of dissidents. He just couldn't seem to shake it off and began coughing, which forced him to stop frequently to clear his throat, and he went on with his speech rather mechanically.

"Editorial writers and pundits scoffed" at the Republicans' contract, he told the crowd, "but we did mean it. . . . We made promises and we kept promises." A contract checklist appeared on the screen behind him, and Gingrich vowed, "This is only a beginning." A young boy emerged from the crowd on the side of the steps and brought Gingrich some water. "See, this is a team effort," he quipped as he took a few sips, which seemed to help quiet his coughing. Gingrich then moved on to the real challenge the Republicans faced, balancing the federal budget and eliminating the deficit, and he challenged President Clinton to submit his own version of a balanced budget.

Standing one row behind and slightly to the right of Gingrich was freshman congressman Van Hilleary of the Fourth District of Tennessee. Throughout the event, he appeared uncomfortable, shifting his weight from one foot to another, squinting in the sun. Although he clapped and cheered at the appropriate moments, he looked relieved when Gingrich concluded his remarks and music signaled an end to the festivities.

Members, spectators, and press immediately scattered helter-skelter. Hilleary was met by his press secretary, Brad Todd, who led him to the lawn in front of the Capitol, where members were lining up to do interviews for their local TV stations back home. The National Republican Campaign Committee paid for satellite time so that small-market stations in the members' districts could lead off their nightly news reports with stories about the successful conclusion of the contract. Todd briefed Hilleary on the next stage of contract celebration, the press conferences he would be holding later that day at the Nashville and Knoxville airports. This approach was strongly recommended by the leadership, which in a memo directed members not to be bashful about talking up what they'd been doing in Washington during the three-week congressional recess that started that day.

The Speaker had been "in a great mood—jovial and joking around" until the unfortunate air horn incident, which Hilleary said "completely turned his mood." Hilleary considered the ceremony a bit excessive: "It was too long. At one point I was proud to be part of it, but most of the time I was thinking it was going too long."

Hilleary actually thought about going home early and missing the event but decided "that would kind of be like skipping graduation." Like many of the freshmen, Hilleary was skeptical of the pomp and circumstance his older colleagues considered part of being in Congress. The freshmen came with a clear agenda, and they didn't want to waste any time. They had things to get done. They didn't plan on sticking around forever and didn't have much patience for some of the niceties the more senior members took for granted.

Take, for example, being called "Congressman." Hilleary didn't much care for it. And he especially hated it when he was back in the district and someone twice his 36 years who had known him since he was in high school came up and said, "How are you doing, Congressman?" "I'm just Van; just call me 'Van,' same as you always did," he usually told them. But they rarely listened.

Hilleary is a southern boy through and through. He has spent most of his life not far from Spring City, the tiny railroad town in east Tennessee where he grew up and where his father and grandfather owned the textile mill where he worked before being elected to Congress. He is soft-spoken, has a gentle drawl, and is respectful of his elders. Manners are important where Hilleary comes from. And like one out of 10 people in his district—that's people, not men—he has served in the military. Tennessee is known as the Volunteer State, and Hilleary, who is in the Air Force Reserves, volunteered for two tours of duty during Desert Storm, a fact not lost on the voters of the Fourth District. His sandy blond hair, blue eyes, and easy, dimpled smile also give him the all-American, clean-cut good looks so helpful to politicians in the television age.

Having waited in line for a few minutes behind several other southern members, Hilleary did a little television, two interviews in quick succession. He was short and on message: The past three months had been all about "promises made and promises kept." Hilleary had to catch a 1 P.M. plane if he was going to make it to both of his scheduled news conferences back home.

Back at the office, his anxious staff readied things for his departure, making lists, gathering together what he needed back in the district, doing the so-long, farewell scramble that all congressional staffs go through to get their members out the door. This is inevitably followed by a collective sigh and the calm that descends on congressional offices when their member is back home. "They want me on that plane and gone," observed Hilleary of his staff. At 12:05, with a wave and a grin, he headed out with a garment bag and a staffer whose assignment was to go with him to the townhouse he rented a few blocks away so Hilleary could grab the rest of his things and then drive him to the airport. "I know he's forgotten something," fretted Elaine Robinson, Hilleary's personal secretary and scheduler. "Pack fast," Susan Hirschmann, his chief of staff, called out to his departing back and then muttered under her breath, "He better not miss that plane."

"It's recess. I feel like a kid on the last day of school," said Robinson, a plump, pleasant, efficient, and seemingly unflappable woman who, like Hilleary, has lived pretty much her entire life in east Tennessee. The two have known each other since they were children, and before coming to Congress with him she worked in the front office of the textile mill owned by the Hilleary family. Hilleary says the rest of the folks at the plant still haven't forgiven him for stealing her away. It is Robinson's job to be ever mindful of Hilleary's whereabouts, constantly attuned to his mood and whether he can be bothered with one more urgent phone call. She makes time for the people he needs to see and diplomatically disses those he does not. There are always many more people who want to see him, many more meetings and hearings to attend than he has time for. Hilleary says the first thing he discovered about his job on the day he was sworn in has also proven to be one of the hardest: juggling the many competing demands on his time. More than 150 of his friends, family, Air Force buddies, and most loyal supporters had traveled to Washington, some on buses, to witness his big moment, "and I had two seconds to spend with them—I didn't like it."

It wasn't until his first official day, as he was walking up the hall in the Cannon House Office Building and saw his name on a brass plate next to the door of Room 114, that Hilleary "got all excited" and it really sank in that he was actually a member of Congress. The last occupant of this office was one-term Democrat Dan Hamburg, who represented the First District of California, north of San Francisco. Hamburg, a liberal who was fond of open shirts and bolo ties, was defeated by Republican Frank Riggs, the man he had defeated in 1992. Despite his short tenure in Congress, Hamburg did have the distinction of being one of the best-looking members, picked by *People* magazine for its "most beautiful people" issue. Hilleary seems mildly amused when informed of this and does not exactly discourage a comparison. But any commonality between the two stops with their youthful good looks and office assignment.

Hilleary is staunchly conservative. He favors a repeal of the assault weapons ban that was part of the Clinton administration's 1994 crime package, and he believes abortion should be illegal except in cases of rape, incest, and to protect the life of the mother. He considers balancing the budget and passing a term-limit amendment to the Constitution to be the two most important things the 104th Congress can do; in our first interview, a month after taking office, he tells me, "If term limits and a balanced budget happen in the next two years, I might not run again." But as the weeks and months go by and the possibility of both appear less and less likely, such an idea becomes little more than the musing of someone who had not yet experienced the seduction of Washington firsthand.

Hilleary can remember the exact moment he decided to run for Congress. It was the night the House passed the Clinton budget and tax increase by one vote. He was on Air Force Reserve duty in Marietta, Georgia, and was watching coverage on C-SPAN in his room. It almost made him physically ill. As he saw it, President Clinton and the Democrats stood for "bigger government, more taxes, more regulation, and more intrusion into people's lives." If something wasn't done to stop them, we wouldn't even recognize the country in four years. "At least a Republican Congress would help keep the country from going pell-mell in that direction."

His complete lack of conviction: That was Hilleary's biggest problem with Clinton. "Clinton didn't know what he was for; he didn't know what he believed; he handled the Democratic Congress all wrong, trying to kowtow to them." And he was constantly driven by the weekly polls to find out where he should stand. Hilleary considered Clinton "passionless, rudderless, valueless, and lacking a backbone." Bill Clinton had to be stopped.

And what about that marathon, 90-minute State of the Union address in January? That had to be one of the worst speeches Hilleary had ever heard. Most of the freshmen felt the same way about Clinton. So, like an elementary school teacher warning his students not to act up during an assembly, Gingrich told them to behave themselves before they took to the House floor to hear Clinton deliver the State of the Union. Obviously mindful of how overtly partisan antics from his high-spirited youngsters might play on national television, Gingrich admonished the freshmen to have respect for the office, if not the man, and not to be chanting "Newt, Newt, Newt." But when President Clinton got to the part where he said support for the assault weapons ban had cost a number of Democrats their seats, the freshmen just couldn't help themselves. A wave of applause and cheering from the Republican side started to sweep through the chamber. Gingrich looked down from his chair behind the president and gave them "the evil eye." Although he had started to put his hands together, when he looked up at Gingrich, Hilleary knew immediately it was the wrong thing to do. His colleagues stopped clapping almost as suddenly as they had started. "They knew they were messing up."

Hilleary got to know the soon-to-be Speaker a few weeks before the election, when Gingrich made a campaign appearance for him in Tullahoma, a community of 17,000 people about 70 miles southeast of Nashville. Gingrich "vividly" remembers that night in Tullahoma and the speech he gave before a standing-room-only crowd at the American Legion Hall. He used the line that became famous during the 1994 campaign, "It is impossible to maintain a civilization with 12-year-olds having babies, 15-year-olds killing each other, 17-year-olds dying of AIDS, and 18-year-olds getting diplomas they can't read." But sensing that "people were too happy and too excited," he felt he needed to bring the crowd an even more sobering message. He told them, "Saving this country is up to every person in this audience. It's not just up to elected officials." That night Gingrich could feel the victory that was soon to come crashing like a wave across the country and was "certain Van was going to win" because people were "sick of Washington and sick of liberalism."

During freshman orientation Gingrich mentioned Tullahoma and this speech as a revelatory moment for him. Hilleary took some kidding "for being teacher's pet" and was "queen bee for a couple of days . . . but that wore off pretty quick."

What also wore off fast was the excitement over actually being a congressman. The leadership gave the freshmen no time to savor their victory and instead got right down to business. Votes were scheduled from early in the morning until after 10 P.M., and the freshmen had little time to organize their offices and learn how things get done on Capitol Hill. Many of them didn't have computers in the beginning.

Hilleary's office didn't have enough chairs, so they did what everyone else seemed to be doing: scavenged furniture that was piled up in the hallways of the House office buildings.

And when it came to scheduling, things were really a mess. "We didn't know what was important and what wasn't," Hilleary would recall. At first his staff was seeing every lobbyist that came in the door. Frequently two and three meetings or committee hearings were scheduled at the same time, and Hilleary had to make difficult choices about which to attend. He was there every night until 11 and not getting anything done. Eventually he and his staff learned by trial and error "what we could blow off and what we couldn't." Another thing he slowly figured out was voting—not how to vote but when. At first, the minute the buzzer went off for a vote he was out the door like a shot, but as time went on he figured out how late he could leave his office and still make it to the floor in time.

In a city like Washington where a lack of affectation almost seems to be an affectation in itself, Hilleary stands out. He's not afraid to be down-home; in fact he seems to revel in it. He recalls, without embarrassment but also without discernible embellishment or flourish, that he went so broke running for office—he put about $125,000 of his own money into the campaign—that he couldn't afford to buy new shoes after he was elected. So until he got his first paycheck he had to borrow a pair from one of his staff members and got sore ankles from all the walking between his office and the floor for votes. He was so happy when he got paid and could finally buy a pair of crepe-soled oxfords.

And then there was the story about his fly. He liked it so much he told it over and over, to constituents, to friends, to other members, to staffers. It happened on one of his first trips back to the district as a new congressman. He was telling a crowd, as he tends to do, that they should continue to call him just plain "Van" because he still puts his pants on just like he used to, one leg at a time. Although he noticed some odd looks, he didn't think much of it until someone came up to him after he finished speaking and said his fly was open, had been open the whole time. He felt like an idiot. An idiot congressman.

But despite a penchant for poking fun at himself, Hilleary wants very much to be taken seriously and to distinguish himself. One of the earliest indicators of clout among the freshmen involved committee assignments. Gingrich took a personal hand in making the assignments and gave unusually high priority to the freshmen because he wanted to reward them and knew he could count on them to be loyal and tough when it came to making budget cuts and holding the line on spending. They got an unprecedented number of plum seats. Republican freshmen won 16 of 30 openings on the committees with spending and fiscal authority.

Three freshmen got seats on Ways and Means, which hadn't seen a first-termer since George Bush was elected to the House in 1966. Six out of nine available seats on the Budget Committee went to Republican freshmen. They also got seven slots on Appropriations, 15 on Banking, and eight on Commerce, which all get a lot of lobbyist attention along with sizable campaign contributions for their members.

And three freshmen were made subcommittee chairs. The stars of the class, people like Sonny Bono, J. C. Watts, George Nethercutt from Washington state (who defeated former House Speaker Tom Foley), and Steve Largent (former wide receiver for the Seattle Seahawks and an NFL hall-of-famer), were all taken care of. Also given extra consideration were those who won tough districts by a narrow margin, since a prestigious committee assignment can be such a great fund-raising tool.

Hilleary wanted a seat on the Budget Committee. He wanted it bad. But instead he was assigned to the National Security, Science, and Small Business Committees. He was also placed on a freshman task force looking into dissolving the Departments of Energy, Education, and Commerce and was one of 39 assistant whips who do vote counting for the leadership.

Toward the end of his campaign, when he wasn't sure if he was going to win or not, he sold his house and used the proceeds to buy TV time. He wound up winning the race by 14 points and carrying 17 of 22 counties, but he wished the race had been closer. "If I hadn't sold my house, I'd have a better committee assignment."

Hilleary is typical of the Republican freshmen elected in 1994. He is the class everyman. He's young, extremely conservative, comes from a business rather than government background, and considers balancing the budget the most important thing the freshmen can accomplish. He's a nice guy. He knows how to get along with the other members, how to be one of the boys, and that's not exactly a bad thing when you're trying to collect votes. He doesn't rub people the wrong way. He's not one of the outspoken leaders of the class who are always being quoted in the *Washington Post*.

Gingrich says Hilleary possesses the kind of "tough-minded conservatism" that will help the Republicans succeed. But in characteristic Gingrich fashion, ever the teacher grading his pupils, he does not mince words when it comes to his assessment of how Hilleary stacks up against the other GOP freshmen: "He's in the upper third but not the upper 3 percent."

For all the talk during the campaign about how evil Washington and career politicians are, Hilleary admits the freshmen who started off the strongest were those with previous experience either on a congressional staff or in a state legislature. He says the best piece of advice he got early on was from an older member who told him to write down his first impressions of his classmates and then look at them a year or two down the road because they were bound to change dramatically. Hilleary believes it will be the hardworking, less flashy members who remain true to their words—the tortoises, not the hares—who will be the best friends to have. He clearly hopes to be that kind of congressman.

2

"JUST REGULAR FOLKS"

THESE REPUBLICAN FRESHMEN were different from any that had come before them. Not only were they different from the Democrats; they were different from the senior members of their own party. For one thing, Hilleary and his classmates were considerably younger. Almost 60 percent of them had not yet turned 45. They were a new generation. The first Republican president of their adult lives was Ronald Reagan. Reagan was a God to them, a religion. He represented a shining example of what the Republican Party should stand for. Most of them would say without hesitation that he was one of the finest presidents in history.

Never mind that they had arrived in Washington specifically to fix the mess that Ronald Reagan had begun, with his tax cuts, military spending on steroids, and unchecked government growth. It was under Ronald Reagan that the federal deficit first hit $200 billion. But never mind that. It was what Reagan represented, not what he really was, that they loved—that clean-cut, gung-ho, America-first, pro-business, shining-city-on-a-hill thing he had going. They loved it because that was who they were, too. They did seem much angrier than Reagan ever was, though. And louder.

Many of the freshmen had small business backgrounds, had started their own companies—insurance and accounting firms, construction and real estate businesses, restaurants, a winery. A lot of them made more money before they were elected than the $133,600 they would receive as members of the House. They didn't look at getting elected to Congress as a career or a promotion; they had good lives back home. They saw it as a mission.

Half of them had never before held elected office of any kind—nothing, not even a seat on the school board. They were not big believers that government was the answer to people's problems. They thought government usually was the problem. They had experience with government regulations, with the Occupational Safety and Health Administration (OSHA) and the Environmental Protection Agency (EPA), and they didn't like them.

Most, but not all of them, had attended college, state universities and schools close to home. A lot of them still didn't live too far from where they had grown up. Many had never traveled abroad. Only a handful had attended Ivy League universities, and those who did were not likely to brag about it. This crew was extremely skeptical, even downright hostile toward the East Coast cultural elite. They not only represented the average people in their districts; they claimed to be just like them. You wouldn't catch these guys at a party in Georgetown or taking in a symphony performance at the Kennedy Center. No time for that kind of hoity-toity thing. This class was full of "just regular folks." "Although when I tell people I live on Possum Trot Road in Grandview, Tennessee, they think I'm a little more regular than some of the other ones," said Hilleary.

Where they came from reflected a great deal about who they were and the way the Republican Party was changing. The largest contingent, 23 of them, came from the South. Twenty were from the West and 18 from the Midwest. The smallest number, 12, were from the Northeast and Mid-Atlantic region. The freshmen who represented the public face of the class—the bomb throwers—were smart, aggressive, committed, and extremely energetic. They seemed to be everywhere at once, holding news conferences, meeting in small groups to plot strategy, speaking on the floor. They always seemed to have 10 things going on at the same time. They called themselves the True Believers, believers in balancing the budget, smaller government, and lower taxes.

Apart from the obvious religious reference and the allusion to the conservative Christian bent of many of them, the name "True Believer" referred to their commitment to the cause, their willingness to take a bullet for it, to cast the tough votes, to go down swinging if they had to, to balance the budget no matter what, pain and sacrifice be damned. This is our children's inheritance we're spending. We're stealing from our children!

Balancing the budget was their very reason for being. Everything else flowed from that. But they did share a remarkably similar view of the world, whether they came from Fresno, California, or Tupelo, Mississippi. They were conservative, very conservative. And they were determined. They knew they were right, so it made it pretty easy not to have to worry about anyone else's point of view. It was less messy that way. "Compromise" was a four-letter word.

About 20 of the freshmen were out there constantly. You saw them all the time. People like Zach Wamp of Tennessee, Mark Neumann of Wisconsin, Linda Smith of Washington state, Joe Scarborough of Florida, Sam Brownback of Kansas, John Shadegg of Arizona, Helen Chenoweth of Idaho, Enid Waldholtz of Utah, David McIntosh and Mark Souder of Indiana. They were the ones the world identified as the freshmen. Some of the True Believers, like Hilleary, didn't say much; they just voted right. About half the class could probably be categorized as True Believers, but just about everybody usually went along with this group.

The True Believers may have prided themselves on being different from other politicians, but being a freshman in 1994 meant it wasn't easy to be different from your classmates. If Congress was like high school, then the True Believers were the in crowd, the trendsetters. It was as if the world had been turned upside down: The nerds were in charge. Those freshmen who thought a little differently kept it to themselves and usually didn't talk much at the weekly class meetings, or didn't go.

There were a dozen or so moderates in the class, most from the Northeast, people like Bill Martini of New Jersey. But they were also scattered around other parts of the country: Mark Foley of Florida, Greg Ganske of Iowa, Rick White of Washington state. Whether driven by the kind of district they came from or personal ideology, they tended to differ with their classmates on a few issues like abortion, gun control, and some social spending issues. But even the moderates could usually be counted on to vote right. They were part of the team. The Republicans were running things. At last. Dissent was frowned upon. They knew they had to stick together if they were going to lick the deficit—and the Democrats—if they were going to show the biasedliberalmedia and the know-it-all, smarty-pants crowd.

Whenever they talked about reporters, they referred to them as "the media," and that word was almost always prefaced by "biased" and "liberal." They ran it together fast like one word: "biasedliberalmedia." And they got that look on their faces. They were convinced, they were sure the media were against them, hated the conservatives. There weren't any conservatives in the media. Oh, maybe one or two on an editorial board here and there (the *Wall Street Journal* editorial page was good). But not on television, that's for sure; not at the networks.

The Republicans' long-felt distrust of the biasedliberalmedia came from their belief that they never got a fair shake from reporters. The media loved Bill Clinton and the Democrats. Just look at the way they had laughed off the contract and dismissed the idea of the Republicans' actually taking over Congress. And yet once the dust from the election had settled, they sure seemed to be getting a lot of attention from the biasedliberalmedia. Wherever two or more freshmen gathered together, you couldn't throw a stick without hitting a reporter. It had to be one of the most celebrated classes of this century, maybe ever. For a while in the beginning, it seemed as if every Republican freshmen was being followed by a network TV camera crew or a national magazine or major newspaper reporter, not to mention local reporters. They might be the "biasedliberalmedia," but they knew a good story. These freshmen were something, weren't they? Colorful. Spoke their minds. Raised hell. It drove the Republican old bulls crazy. Who were these young punks anyway? What had they ever done? What did they know? "I've been in Congress 10 years; never been on the MacNeil-Lehrer NewsHour."

Some of the moderates, like Charlie Bass of New Hampshire, Tom Davis of Virginia, and Bob Ehrlich of Maryland, were also part of another group of freshmen. Call them the "Traditional Politicians." Most of them had held elected office before, either on the local level or in state government. They didn't share the same disdain for government that many of their classmates had. They just wanted to make it work better. Many had worked in congressional offices at one time or another. They didn't think Congress was all that evil; in fact they didn't think being in Congress was half bad. Unlike the True Believers, who were motivated by the cause, circumstances just dictated that the Traditional Politicians run for Congress in 1994; they could just as easily have run two years earlier or later. About half the class fell into this group in one way or another. Ray LaHood of Illinois, for example, took the seat of his former boss, minority leader Bob Michel. LaHood knew everyone on the Hill when he was elected. For him, getting elected was almost a comedown. As Michael's chief of staff, he had more access to the leadership and knew more about what was going on than he did as a freshman.

And Roger Wicker of Mississippi, whose father was a Democratic circuit judge in that state, had worked for Trent Lott when he was in the House back in the early 1980s. Before he was elected to Congress, Wicker had been in the state senate for six years. Wicker knew how things got done in politics. He had a smooth, laid-back, slow-talking, good-ol'-boy quality. He wasn't a boat rocker, and he wasn't for term limits. He planned to be in Congress for a while. Wicker was president of the freshman class, so he was usually at the news conferences they were always having. But he also gave the impression that he was a lot more comfortable cutting backroom deals and going along with the leadership than someone like earnest, intense Mark Souder.

Souder and his fellow Hoosier David McIntosh were the most potent kind of freshmen. They were a combination of the True Believer and the Traditional Politician. Both were aggressive and smart as a whip. Souder beat Democratic incumbent Jill Long to capture a seat that had previously been held both by Dan Quayle and Senator Dan Coats. Souder knew his way around Capitol Hill. He had worked for Coats for 10 years, eight of them in Washington.

McIntosh was pegged early on as the cream of the freshman crop. He got his undergraduate degree from Yale and his law degree at the University of Chicago, where he studied under future Supreme Court justice Antonin Scalia. McIntosh was not a latecomer to the conservative cause. In law school he founded the Federalist Society for Law and Public Policy, a conservative group for lawyers and law students. He worked in the Reagan administration and then headed Vice President Dan Quayle's Council on Competitiveness. That's where he got to know the Washington conservative elite, people like Bill Kristol, Quayle's chief of staff. McIntosh was marked as a comer by this crowd early on. They paid attention to what he did. If the freshmen were forced to vote on the member of the class most likely to be Speaker of the House, or president, one day McIntosh would be at the top of the list. Of course, he acted as if he thought so, too.

McIntosh was picked by Gingrich to be part of the GOP's transition team after the election and then by his fellow freshmen to be one of two delegates from the class to the leadership. The other freshman representative to the leadership was Sue

Myrick of North Carolina. She, too, was smart and tough, but in a quiet way. She had been a city councillor and two-term mayor of Charlotte. She could get things done but wasn't flashy. The other freshmen trusted and respected her.

Myrick was one of seven women in the class. They tended to be a little bit older than the men. They'd already raised their families. Enid Waldholtz of Salt Lake City was, at 36, the youngest among them. She was soon identified as one of the stars of the class. She'd been involved in national Republican politics since she was in college and served as deputy chief of staff to former Utah governor Norman Bangerter. She had won a seat on the Rules Committee, the first freshman to be so rewarded in 80 years. These freshman women were every bit as conservative as the men. Sue Kelly, of New York's Hudson Valley, was the only pro-choice woman among them. In fact three of the Republican women, Andrea Seastrand of California, Linda Smith of Washington, and Helen Chenoweth of Idaho, banded together early in the session to try to deny federal funds for abortions for poor women in cases of rape and incest. But the effort was squelched by 40 Republican moderates, led by Connie Morella of Maryland.

If this class had a reputation for being extremist, a little off-center, maybe even a little, well, a little wacko, it was because of a handful of people like Chenoweth, Wes Cooley of Oregon, and Steve Stockman of Texas—the Wild Bunch. Cooley was a bombastic rancher who in his two years in the Oregon Senate liked to describe himself as the most conservative member of that body. Apparently the 62-year-old Cooley wanted to carry the title with him to Washington. He used to ride classmate Joe Scarborough, a fire-breathing 31-year-old, about it, getting right down in Scarborough's face on the floor and saying, "You think you're so conservative. You're not so conservative. You don't know what conservative is. *I'm* conservative," as if it were a contest.

Chenoweth preferred being addressed as "Congressman Chenoweth." Her most ardent supporters were antienvironmentalist, pro-gun, rancher types. They didn't like all the government interference they'd been suffering from the Clinton administration, especially things like restrictions of logging on federal lands and enforcement of the Endangered Species Act. "There really is a war on in the West. People in the West fight back. They're pioneer spirited," Chenoweth was fond of saying. During the campaign Chenoweth became known for fund-raisers she labeled "sockeye salmon bakes" after the endangered fish. At one of these events, she told her backers that it's "the Anglo-Saxon male that's endangered today."

Like many of the freshmen, she enjoyed support from the religious right, which was instrumental in her victory. Chenoweth was the cofounder of the conservative religious group Focus on the Family. In an April 1995 *New Republic* article about the Republican freshwomen titled "Invasion of the Church Ladies," Dennis Mansfield, the other founder of Focus on the Family, credited the leafleting of 300,000 voter guides in 1,000 evangelical and Catholic churches shortly before the election with turning the tide for Chenoweth. All over the country in the fall of 1994, the Christian Coalition distributed 33 million voter guides that favored Republican candidates and probably made the difference in a number of districts.

Chenoweth's opponent, two-term Democratic incumbent Larry LaRocco, called her "a mouthpiece for the radical right" and even aired radio ads that said Chenoweth "just seems to get crazier and crazier." But in Idaho, home to white supremacist and paramilitary groups, Chenoweth's rhetoric tapped into something. Shortly after taking office, she questioned an Agriculture Department official at a committee hearing about the use of stealth "black helicopters" over the skies of Idaho. And one of her first legislative acts was to introduce a bill that would require federal officials to receive written permission from local or state officials before carrying out law enforcement or bringing a weapon into their areas of jurisdiction. She said she'd like to eliminate all funding for the Bureau of Alcohol, Tobacco, and Firearms, the bane of conspiracy theorists and militia groups. When the tragic bombing of the federal building in Oklahoma City occurred in April 1995, Chenoweth told Idaho newspapers, "I'm not willing to condemn militias. While we can never condone this, we still must begin to look at the public policies that may be pushing people too far."

Steve Stockman of Texas was also popular with the fringe militia groups. The day of the Oklahoma City bombing, Stockman's office received a fax from a militia group in Michigan that contained references to such a bombing. And a few months after taking office, Stockman wrote a letter to the Justice Department criticizing plans for a rumored raid on militia groups he had been told about by a constituent. In an interview with a gun magazine, Stockman said federal agents had "executed" those who died at the Branch Davidian compound in Waco, Texas.

Stockman was adamantly opposed to gun control, and his number one campaign issue was a promise to fight for repeal of the assault weapons ban that was part of the Clinton crime bill. Also a conservative Christian, Stockman credited his faith and membership in the Baptist Church with helping to turn his life around. But his emphasis on religion proved a little too much for his young staff members when he arrived in Washington. Stockman required their attendance at a daily prayer session before the morning staff meeting, a policy that may have contributed to a particularly high staff turnover in his office.

Not many people thought the 37-year-old accountant who had run for the seat twice before could beat Democrat Jack Brooks, who had served in Congress for 42 years and chaired the House Judiciary Committee. This was a Democratic district. It had gone for Clinton; it had gone for Michael Dukakis; it had even gone for George McGovern. And Stockman wasn't much of a candidate. He had moved from Michigan to Texas in 1980 and had trouble finding a job. He was homeless for a while, sleeping on a bench in a downtown Fort Worth park before landing a job at an oil refinery.

But Brooks's support of Clinton and the assault weapons ban did him in—that and the anger voters felt at the Democrats. It was an awesome year for Republicans. Not a single Republican incumbent lost. Not in the House, not in the Senate, not in a single governor's mansion around the country. That meant that quite a few Republicans no one expected to win, people like Steve Stockman, got swept in with the wave. They were the Accidental Congressmen.

Michael Flanagan, who beat Ways and Means Committee chairman Dan Rostenkowski in Chicago, was another Accidental Congressman. His was not a Republican district either. No way. If Flanagan hadn't been a political novice running against a guy facing a 17-count federal indictment for defrauding the taxpayers in an overwhelmingly Republican year, there was no way he could have beaten the Chicago Democratic political machine. The 31-year-old Flanagan had no money, no organization; he didn't even have any campaign staff. The year before he decided to run, he was an unemployed lawyer who had earned a total of $6,000.

The Chicago boys didn't know what hit them. They weren't ready for it. They couldn't take precautions. Michael Flanagan was one lucky guy.

Another Accidental Congressman was Fred Heineman, the former police chief of Raleigh, North Carolina. He had no political experience, and it showed. He wasn't exactly smooth on the campaign trail. But he still managed to upset David Price, a former political science professor at Duke University who had served in the House since 1986. Heineman was able to portray Price as a tax-and-spend liberal, and he rode the anti-Washington, anti-Democratic wave to shore.

The biggest giant-killer of them all was George Nethercutt of Spokane, Washington, who beat Tom Foley. It was the first time a sitting Speaker of the House had been defeated since 1862. Nethercutt's victory was made possible by the kind of year it was and by Foley's antagonizing Washington voters by filing suit against them over their passage of a term limits initiative. Plenty of independent conservative organizations also piled on in an attempt to defeat the Speaker. But Nethercutt was a good candidate in his own right. He was intelligent, pleasant, thoughtful. He wasn't a screamer. He was different from Heineman and Flanagan and Stockman. He was no Accidental Congressman. The 50-year-old Nethercutt, a successful attorney, had been active in community affairs for years. He had headed the local Diabetes Foundation and helped start a nursery for abused children. He was the former chairman of the Spokane County Republican Party. He knew Washington and had served as chief of staff for Alaska senator Ted Stevens in the 1970s. He didn't come to Congress to tear it down. He respected the institution and wanted people to be able to respect the people who served in it.

There were also a few stars in the class. They'd been rich and famous before their election. Of course there was Sonny Bono. He kind of kept to himself once he was elected. Not that he was snobby or anything, but at 59 he just didn't have much in common with the other freshmen. And he didn't go in for all that rabble-rousing.

Steve Largent of Oklahoma, a handsome, blond, blue-eyed Seattle Seahawks hall of famer, was another star of the class. A guy's guy, a conservative Christian who married his high school sweetheart and had four children, Largent, 40, was a true golden boy. Getting elected wasn't too tough for him, and once he was in Congress he did pretty much whatever he wanted. He was a True Believer, one of the most conservative members of the class. But he didn't really need the leadership; they needed him. And he knew it. If he wanted to do something, he just did it. He didn't make a lot of noise about it, but he didn't ask permission either.

And then there were the poor freshmen Democrats. They got no attention whatsoever. If the House Democrats were looking pretty irrelevant after the 1994 election, what could be less important than a freshman Democrat? There were only 13 of them. "We can carpool to work," quipped one of them, Mike Ward of Kentucky. All but one of the freshman Democrats—Ken Bentsen of Texas, the nephew of former senator and secretary of the treasury Lloyd Bentsen—had previously held elected office. These Democrats were a hardy bunch to have survived the election of 1994. Most came from pretty safe Democratic seats, and most were on the liberal end of the ideological spectrum.

Senator Ted Kennedy's son Patrick was one of them. At 27, he was the youngest of all the freshmen, and he certainly had the most famous name. Patrick Kennedy had already served in the Rhode Island House, but in 1994 he had a tough campaign against a good opponent. He didn't say too much, and he always looked a little frightened. He had that deer-caught-in-the-headlights look. Being a politician must be a tough way for someone who seems painfully shy to earn a living. He didn't do any national interviews his whole first term in Congress. Better to stick with the friendly, local guys; the national press would always be there if he wanted it later.

*   *   *

So on January 4, 1995, the freshmen arrived to be sworn in. They gathered on the right side of the House chamber as the Republicans always did, but now there were more of them. They spilled over into the aisles. Many had brought their young children to witness this historic day. They were laughing, slapping each other on the back. It felt more like an inauguration than a simple House swearing-in ceremony. Bob Dole had come over from the Senate and was standing on the floor talking to a few of the older members. It was clear the House was where the action was.

The members were called in alphabetical order to cast their votes for Speaker. The Democrats voted for Richard Gephardt, the Republicans for Gingrich. It was strictly a formality. As the clerk got closer to Van Hilleary, calling out the members' names in alphabetical order—Hayes, Hayworth, Hefley—Hilleary was afraid he would blurt out the wrong name. He kept saying to himself, "Just don't screw this up. All he thought was, "Gingrich, Gingrich." After successfully casting his vote, Hilleary let his "mind wander a little bit." When Gingrich entered the chamber, he made an effort to be gracious. He went over to the Democratic side of the chamber and shook hands. As he climbed the steps to the Speaker's chair, someone from the Republican side of the aisle shouted, "It's a whole Newt world." It certainly was, and Gingrich and his freshmen were on top of it.

In his speech Gingrich quoted from the Contract with America (the Democrats liked to call it the Contract on America). But he also tried to sound bipartisan, invoking the spirit of Franklin Roosevelt and calling him "the greatest president of the 20th century." He said the Republicans and Democrats must work together to achieve two important goals, balancing the budget and replacing "the current welfare state with an opportunity society." He recited some of the lyrics of the "Battle Hymn of the Republic." He quoted Ben Franklin at the Constitutional Convention. "I promise each of you," he said, as he turned toward the Democrats, "that, without regard to party, my door is going to be open. I will listen to each of you. I will try to work with each of you."

The Democrats looked glum. Few applauded when Gingrich was finished. They knew it was going to be a long two years. The Republicans were clapping, hooting, hollering, stomping. Any whiff of bipartisanship evaporated by the time the oath of office was completed.

The first day was a whirlwind of activity. The Republicans accomplished more than many past Congresses had in the first week or even month. They stayed in session until nearly 2:30 A.M. They passed a measure that would require a three-fifths majority vote for any income tax rate hike. They also passed a host of rules changes that affected the way the House was run, some "Housecleaning," as it were. Most of the changes had to do with the committees; they abolished several of them right off the bat, cut the size of the remaining committee staffs, banned proxy voting, and opened committee meetings to the public. They limited committee chairs to six-year terms. They also authorized an independent firm to conduct an audit of Congress and passed a measure to require Congress to live under the same laws it had passed for the rest of the country.

*   *   *

As different as it all was, this also felt slightly familiar: a large freshman class, arriving in Washington pushing for change and congressional reform. It felt a lot like 1974, when the Watergate babies were elected to the 94th Congress. Those freshmen were Democrats, on the other end of the ideological spectrum. But in a strange way they had a great deal in common with the class that would follow them to Washington 20 years later. In their temperament and approach they were soulmates.

Both classes were big, in fact almost identical in size. Seventy-five freshman Democrats were elected to the House in 1974. Among them were many future leaders of the party—Henry Waxman and George Miller of California, Chris Dodd of Connecticut, Paul Simon of Illinois, Tom Harkin of Iowa, Paul Tsongas of Massachusetts, and Tim Wirth of Colorado. New Senate Democrats that year included Gary Hart, John Glenn, and Patrick Leahy. Michael Dukakis was elected governor of Massachusetts, Richard Lamm of Colorado. And in California Jerry Brown was elected to succeed Ronald Reagan, who had just completed two terms as governor and was returning to private life.

Newt Gingrich also ran for Congress in 1974. He lost. He tried again in 1976 and lost again. It was not until 1978, a much more favorable year for Republicans, that Gingrich won a seat in the House. A young man from Arkansas also lost a bid for Congress in 1974. Two years later he was elected attorney general of the state, and in 1978, at the age of 32, Bill Clinton was elected governor. But just two years later Clinton, like Jimmy Carter, would be turned out of office. Then in 1982, in the first of what would be several major comebacks in his political career, Clinton won re-election to the governorship.

Like the House class of '94, the class of '74 was young, and more than half of them had no legislative experience. And they had arrived in much the same way. About half of both classes had defeated incumbents. The media loved the freshmen, both sets of them, and hailed them as a new generation. The Watergate babies were certainly the last congressional freshmen to get anything like the kind of attention the Republican revolutionaries received. Both classes were elected at a time when the public's confidence in government was extremely low, and both felt they had a mandate for change.

"We had a real sense of urgency. We thought we were special. We thought we were different. We came here to take the Bastille." That could easily have been one of the freshman Republicans of 1994. But those words were spoken by George Miller for an article about the Watergate babies William Schnieder wrote for the *Atlantic Monthly* in March 1989.

One goal the Democrats of 1974 shared with the Republicans of 1994 was a desire to shake up the seniority system and make committee chairs answerable to the party caucus. As soon as they arrived, the class of '74 passed a rule requiring committee chairs to be confirmed by secret ballot in the Democratic caucus. They gave the power to make committee assignments to the party leadership, and in a move they are probably best remembered for, they dumped three powerful, southern Dixiecrats from their committee chairmanships. With the entire caucus having a say in who got the chairmanships, it meant the older members had to woo the freshmen to win their votes. They obviously didn't care much for it. One of the chairmen who was thrown out was F. Edward Hebert of Louisiana, who headed the Armed Services Committee. "Eddie Hebert came in and said, 'Now, boys and girls.' He actually called us 'boys and girls.' That was the end of him," recalled Toby Moffett of Connecticut in the *Atlantic Monthly* article.

Both groups of freshmen were more than willing to take on the establishment of their own party. They used all the press attention they were getting to push their party leaders, to help set the policy agenda, and to participate as equal partners in the business of Congress. They exerted influence not only by their willingness to stick together but also by their sheer size. The Democrats represented about 25 percent of their conference, the Republicans an even more commanding one-third. The leadership needed them to get things done.

Both groups of freshmen were sure of themselves to the point of being arrogant. They didn't know what they didn't know. And that actually made it easier for them to push ahead.

Both classes were deeply moved by the two presidents who dominated their era—as they saw it, the best and worst presidents of their lifetimes. The political views of the 1974 Democrats were shaped by their support of the civil rights movement, their opposition to the war in Vietnam, and by Watergate. Their political hero was John F. Kennedy, the president they knew and revered, the man who inspired them to public service and showed them how a president could lead the country. But the man who probably had just as much to do with their running for office was Richard

Nixon, whom they despised and believed was destroying the country. The Republicans of the 104th Congress also had their political hero and villain, the two men who moved them in the same way Kennedy and Nixon had moved the class of '74. For the Republican revolutionaries, those two presidents were Ronald Reagan and Bill Clinton.

Not too long after arriving in Washington, Hilleary and the other freshmen were invited to a White House reception. Secretary of State Warren Christopher, attempting to make conversation with Hilleary, asked the young man why he had decided to run for Congress. Hilleary, remembering where he was and ever mindful that he should be polite to his elders, tried to sidestep the question. But Christopher pressed him, and finally Hilleary's conservative zeal got the best of him. "Well, sir," he said, "I think Bill Clinton is the worst president this country has ever had." Bill Clinton had to be stopped.

3

THREE-FIFTHS

THEY WERE EXHILARATED. They were scared. They had changed the world just by getting elected. So what were the freshmen supposed to do now?

They were summoned to Washington immediately after the November election for meetings with the rest of the Republicans. They had to choose the leaders who would run the House. Of course it was obvious Newt Gingrich would be Speaker, but in their votes for some of the other officers—Dick Armey for majority leader, Tom DeLay for whip, John Boehner for conference chair—the freshmen signaled their preference for the most conservative, most aggressive candidates. They wanted people like them running things.

The freshmen also jockeyed for position among themselves, running for class office, trying to get elected to the steering group that helped make committee assignments. And the few who didn't seem to be running for something were working hard to get on the best committees. Joe Scarborough got on a bus that was taking the freshmen the few blocks from the hotel where they were staying to the Capitol. He walked to the back and sat down. Immediately Zach Wamp was on him, sticking out his hand, telling Scarborough he was running for something and wanted his vote. Scarborough had no idea who Wamp was, and already Wamp was asking for his vote. Scarborough had no idea who any of the other freshmen were.

One of the freshmen's first meetings was organized by Dick Chrysler of Michigan, the multimillionaire founder of an automobile customizing company that installed sunroofs and convertible tops. Chrysler had experience with marketing. He handed out blue pins he had made up that said "Majority Makers." After the meeting got started, Linda Smith stood up and said she didn't think Chrysler should be in charge of the meeting because he was running for class president. After Chrysler agreed to sit down, Smith announced she was also running for president. Then she put forth a motion that the freshmen should vote immediately for class president.

Vote immediately? They hadn't even met. The freshmen turned to each other, to whoever was sitting next to them. "What is she doing?" they asked each other. Scarborough stood up. A lawyer from Pensacola, Florida, who had never held public office but who led a revolt against a proposed tax increase in his hometown, Joe Scarborough was a fighter. He had a tendency to be a bit wild, to shoot from the hip. He always said what he thought, no matter the consequences. "For the first time of many times to follow, I made the mistake of saying what was on my mind. I thought her display was unseemly, a ham-fisted attempt to grab power," Scarborough recalled later.

Apparently the other freshmen thought so, too. Smith was overruled. And she was not elected president. Nobody was that day. Eventually Roger Wicker would be chosen. He wasn't a fire-breather. He could present a calm, adult face to the press and would bring the disparate freshman factions together. Smith's standing with the other members of the class never really recovered from that first impression. She was without a doubt the most unpopular member of the class. If there had been a vote among the freshmen for that honor, she would have won it hands down.

Smith had served in the Washington House and was in the middle of a state senate term when Washington's Republican front-runner dropped out of the Third District race for Congress a month before the primary. Smith won the nomination on a write-in ballot and went on to win the general election. As a member of the state legislature, she had gained notoriety by going over the heads of her colleagues directly to the voters with initiatives promoting campaign ethics and tax reform. Being unpopular with her colleagues was nothing new for Smith. Part of it had to do with being abrasive and outspoken and a woman. But that was only part of it. There were plenty of other loudmouths in the freshman class (Scarborough, for one). Smith just rubbed everybody the wrong way. She was always veering off on her own. She wasn't much of a team player. Even the mild-mannered and courtly George Nethercutt, who hardly had a bad word to say about anybody, except maybe Bill Clinton, would just roll his eyes when Linda Smith's name was mentioned.

After their first orientation program, the freshmen went directly to another orientation, a three-day session in Baltimore put on jointly by the Heritage Foundation, a conservative Washington think tank that was extremely influential with the new Republican leadership, and Empower America, Jack Kemp's political advocacy group. For the past 20 years, the orientation for incoming members of Congress had been held at the Kennedy School of Government at Harvard. But the Republicans grumbled about the sessions. They were too liberal, they were too pro-government, they were too theoretical. There were too many Democrats around. In 1992 the Heritage Foundation offered an alternative orientation program, much more conservative, much more ideological, much more popular with the Republicans. The think tank decided to continue the program in 1994. And then the Republicans won the election. Suddenly the alternative orientation became the preferred program for the incoming Republicans.

There was a handbook to help the freshmen implement the Contract with America and sessions on welfare reform, farm subsidies, congressional reform, cutting taxes, and reining in the federal government. Heritage lined up an impressive list of speakers, including Jack Kemp, Paul Gigot of the *Wall Street Journal,* Lamar Alexander, Ralph Reed of the Christian Coalition, Jeane Kirkpatrick, William Bennett, Steve Forbes, Bill Kristol, and of course Rush Limbaugh.

The freshmen had their Saturday night graduation dinner in a skybox at Camden Yards baseball field, with Rush Limbaugh for dessert. The freshmen went crazy. They loved Rush more than they loved Newt. And Rush had probably done just as much to help get them elected. A poll conducted by GOP pollster Frank Luntz showed that people who listened to 10 or more hours a week of talk radio voted three to one for the Republicans. They made Rush an honorary freshman.

The GOP freshmen had no interest in going to Cambridge, to Harvard, land of the liberal egghead, not when they could be dittoheads with their man Rush. When it became clear none of the Republican freshmen would attend, Harvard canceled its orientation. But the Democratic freshmen didn't want to go to the Heritage program. So for the first time since someone came up with the idea of trying to orient the new members of Congress, no bipartisan orientation was held.

At the time it seemed like a bold stroke for the Republicans to stage their own orientation, a chance to assert their ideological dominance right from the start. But what it really meant was that the Republican and Democratic freshmen had no chance to meet each other before the 104th Congress convened. And not even then, because by then the fighting had already started. Members sit segregated by party on the floor and in committee, and they socialize separately, too. The Democrats were pretty sore losers about suddenly being in the minority, and the Republicans were feeling pretty cocky, so things were bound to start out ugly. By skipping their joint orientation, the Republican and Democratic freshmen didn't get to know each other as people before the bell sounded and the match began. They didn't have the chance to meet members across the aisle who also had teenagers that were driving them crazy or who liked to go fishing. They didn't even know each other's names.

Personal relationships are extremely important in Congress. It's often the conversations in the elevator on the way to the floor that get things done. It's a lot easier to amend a bill with a member you know and like, even if you disagree about almost everything. Given what an extremely partisan and polarizing election it was, the orientation could have provided the only opportunity for relationships to develop across the aisle. But it wasn't going to be that kind of a Congress.

The Republican leadership thought by sending their freshmen off for three days in early December without any other distractions they would sufficiently indoctrinate them for the work ahead. But the freshmen didn't need indoctrinating; they were more conservative than their indoctrinators. One of the sessions the first day was on federal farm policy and phasing out agricultural subsidies over a five-year period. When the presentation was completed, one freshmen raised his hand. He wanted to know why the subsidies couldn't just be abolished right away. During a panel on cutting taxes, a freshman said he favored introduction of the flat tax. At another session a freshman suggested OSHA be eliminated, immediately. That got a round of applause. The mood of the freshmen was, "Let's do it all right now." Why wait? It didn't take long for word to get back to Capitol Hill. The freshmen were already developing a reputation.

They were also bonding. They didn't have much else to do. Sam Brownback suggested a bunch of the freshmen get together in the hotel lobby after Jack Kemp's dinner speech. About 30 of his classmates showed up. Mark Souder was there; so were Lindsey Graham of South Carolina and Randy Tate of Washington. But the freshmen still didn't know each other that well, and they didn't realize that sitting among them were a couple of reporters. They started talking about changing some things right away. They were all for term limits, so why shouldn't they term-limit committee chairs and even the Speaker? Newt Gingrich learned of their little idea by reading about it in the paper. Once it was out in public, he didn't have much choice but to go along. It would look bad not to. So the first day it was in session, the 104th Congress passed a rule limiting the Speaker of the House to four terms. The freshmen didn't know how Gingrich would react when he read about their comments. But when nothing did happen, it gave them courage to try something else. Every time they pushed a little further and got away with it, it just made them bolder.

In one of the first freshman meetings, John Shadegg, a lawyer from Arizona, stood up and started talking about why he had run for Congress. Shadegg had an impeccable conservative pedigree. His father, Stephen Shadegg, had managed Barry Goldwater's first Senate campaign and was a longtime adviser to Goldwater. Shadegg told his classmates he was a radical. He called himself a radical about 10 times, and Joe Scarborough decided the two probably had a lot in common. They sat down and got to talking about getting a group of like-minded freshmen together to push a conservative agenda. The idea started percolating. Sam Brownback was interested. They talked about federalism and returning more power to the states. Scarborough said they needed a name for the group and suggested "the New Federalists."

Since the original American Federalists, Alexander Hamilton, John Adams, and James Madison, advocated adoption of the Constitution and establishment of a strong central government in the *Federalist* papers, it would have made more sense for the freshmen to call themselves the Anti-Federalists. But Scarborough said that didn't have quite the same ring to it: "'The New Federalists' does sound a little like 'Up with People' or something," he admitted, slightly embarrassed. But once the name was out there, they were kind of stuck with it.

As soon as they were sworn in, the New Federalists started getting together every week, sometimes twice a week. Brownback, who had lost a bid for class president, became the head of the group. At first it was about a dozen people, including Shadegg, Scarborough, Brownback, Linda Smith, Mark Souder, Lindsey Graham, Steve Largent, Mark Sanford, Sue Myrick, and Tom Coburn. They met in each other's offices and empty committee rooms. After a while the group grew to 20 or 30 people, depending on what was going on. Their first big idea was eliminating four cabinet departments—Commerce, Energy, Education, and Housing and Urban Development. They bounced the idea off of Gingrich when he surprised them by showing up at one of their first meetings. He'd heard about this rump group of freshmen and wanted to see for himself what they were all about. He knew enough not to squelch them. Gingrich told them to float their idea with the other members to see what kind of response they got. Then he would decide whether to support them.

*   *   *

Gingrich was trying to learn how to run the House. He'd never served in the majority before; none of the Republicans had. One of his biggest challenges was keeping peace between the freshmen and the Republican moderates. Each side always thought the other got too much out of Gingrich. The first major test of Republican unity in the 104th Congress came with the balanced budget amendment vote.

The contract called for a balanced budget amendment to the Constitution that included a provision that would require "a three-fifths vote by both the House and Senate to raise taxes." The tax limitation provision would make it harder for Congress to balance the budget simply by raising taxes, and it was based on a similar provision in effect in a number of states around the country, including California and Florida. Constitutional amendments can't be passed by a simple majority of the House and Senate; they require a two-thirds vote. So the Republicans would need Democratic votes. The Democrats were feeling the heat from the election, and a lot of them wanted to vote for a balanced budget amendment. But there was no way they were going to go for an amendment that would make it almost impossible to raise taxes. Many Republican moderates were having trouble with the idea, too.

The freshmen were committed to the three-fifths provision. Majority leader Dick Armey attended a freshman class meeting and was asked whether the three-fifths requirement would be included in the balanced budget amendment. Armey said yes, but John Shadegg thought "there was too much wiggle room" in the way he said it, so he asked the question again: Would there be a single up or down vote on the balanced budget amendment with the three-fifths provision? Armey again said yes.

When GOP whip Tom DeLay did a head count of Republicans on January 4, he realized that if the three-fifths provision were included, he would lose the votes of 30 moderates, and if it weren't, he would lose the votes of 30 freshmen. The vote was postponed until the last week in January to give the leadership time to regroup. Gingrich and the GOP leaders decided they would quietly compromise and offer a balanced budget amendment without the three-fifths provision that was being put forth by Texas Democrat Charlie Stenholm and that could win the votes of enough Democrats as well as the Republican moderates. The GOP leaders figured the freshmen were so committed to the idea of a balanced budget that they would never vote against it. But they didn't bother to tell the freshmen about their change of plans. The freshmen didn't find out about the strategy change until the week before the vote. How could their leaders do this to them? Armey had promised them a vote on a balanced budget amendment *with* the tax limitation provision. It was in the contract. They had campaigned on it! They would be going back on their word. Already.

In 1992 Shadegg had led a successful referendum drive in Arizona for a similar three-fifths requirement for any tax increases by the state's legislature, and the issue had been central to his campaign for Congress. He started making calls to other freshmen. Mark Souder joined the effort. They got pledges from about 40 members that they wouldn't vote for an amendment without the tax provision; another 20 said they were leaning that way. Shadegg and Souder began distributing a "Dear Colleague" letter that urged a no vote on the balanced budget amendment. That alerted the GOP leaders, who knew they had to put a stop to this.

The Speaker's office tried to reach Souder by phone, but he managed to dodge the calls. He slipped on and off the floor quickly for votes so he wouldn't run into Armey or DeLay. But Shadegg wasn't as lucky. He got pulled aside during a vote and was told to report to Armey. It was like being summoned to the principal's office. Shadegg called Souder from his portable phone and asked him what to do. He had no choice; he had to go.

Later Shadegg would describe his being "taken to the woodshed" by Dick Armey. But Shadegg, who can have quite a temper and is not averse to raising his voice to make a point, undoubtedly gave as good as he got. Shadegg in no uncertain terms reminded Armey of his promise and told him the freshmen expected him to honor his commitment. "You made the freshmen a promise that the tax limitation amendment would be included in the balanced budget amendment. You, Dick Armey, have a personal credibility problem with the freshman class."

Armey's wife, Susan, who was doing some decorating of her husband's new office, came in at one point, but she quickly excused herself when she realized this was more than just a friendly chat between colleagues. The two men "went at it" for 40 minutes. Armey told Shadegg the only way to hold the Republican conference together was to strip off the three-fifths provision. They didn't have the votes to pass it otherwise. It would make the Republicans look pretty dumb if the freshmen brought down the balanced budget amendment, he warned Shadegg. Shadegg asked Armey to allow a vote on the entire measure, and if it didn't pass they could come back and vote on it without the three-fifths provision. Armey was not moved. "They were definitely afraid of a public relations crisis," recalled Shadegg. The meeting ended without resolution but with a warning from Shadegg to Armey that "the freshmen will revolt over this."

Then Souder was called to Armey's office. He knew Armey was personally in favor of the tax limitation and defending the decision not to include it wasn't easy for him. "I can always tell when he doesn't agree with what he has to do because he doesn't look you in the eyes," said Souder of Armey.

Armey tried to get Souder to see it his way. But Souder wouldn't budge. He asked Armey what he had said to George Bush when he came to the House Republicans and asked for their support for his 1990 budget that included a tax increase, breaking his "read my lips" convention promise, something the party's conservatives never forgave. Armey said that he had told the president to go jump in a lake, although he had used more colorful language. "Well, I'm the new Dick Armey," Souder retorted.

"We were shocked to learn they were so quick to cut the compromise. We didn't want to begin the process by compromising," recalled Shadegg. Over the weekend, back in Arizona, Shadegg decided the leadership would never change its mind, so the best they could probably get was the promise of a separate vote on the measure later. Two days before the vote, Shadegg met with Gingrich and told him the freshmen would vote no unless they got a separate vote that included the three-fifths provision. On January 26, with just an hour remaining before the scheduled vote on the balanced budget amendment, there still was no agreement between the GOP leadership and the freshmen. A dozen of the ringleaders—Souder and Shadegg, of course, and Linda Smith, Sue Myrick, Steve Largent, Tom Coburn, Mark Neumann, David McIntosh, and Randy Tate—were called to the Speaker's office. They were wearing red and white buttons that said "3/5." Gingrich won their votes by promising them they could have a separate vote on their tax limitation amendment—on April 15, 1996. The freshmen were angry and disappointed, but they knew it was the best they were going to get.

One vote Gingrich didn't win was Souder's. He and his Indiana colleague John Hostettler were the only two GOP freshmen who voted against the amendment on final passage. "I was just being stubborn because I was mad," Souder would later explain. He said if passage had been in doubt he would have voted yes. But the measure received 300 votes, 10 votes more than the two-thirds of the 435-member House required for passage.

The next day the Republicans held a press conference to announce the April 1996 date for a vote on the three-fifths measure. Because he had voted no, Souder wasn't allowed to go. He was being punished. But that didn't prevent him from talking to the *New York Times*. "We are not going to be rolled. Unless we speak up, the group of moderates in the Republican Party will control every single vote," he told the paper. And he didn't mince words about the leadership either. "They think we are spoiled children and they would like to spank us. But they know they need us back here to protect their chairmanship and majority. If we freshmen stand together, we can have continued influence."

Gingrich and Armey certainly wouldn't admit it publicly, but they knew Souder was right. There were so many freshmen that the Republicans had to have their votes to get anything done. If the freshmen wanted to stamp their feet and bang their fists, they probably would get their way much of the time.

The freshmen had not come to Washington to compromise. They didn't want to go along to get along. Shadegg said the freshmen "came of age" through the balanced budget fight. They were emboldened by their experience. It was their first lesson in their own clout. They had learned what kind of tactics they could use to get their way. "We realized the leadership had their role and we had ours," Shadegg said.

Majority leader Dick Armey would tell me a few months later that he considered an unwillingness to compromise a freshman hazard. He should know, because when he arrived with the class of 1984, he had to learn how to do it, too. "Gadflies and loose cannons": That's what he and the other freshman Republicans of '84 were called when they joined the Congress. "We were more impatient than these freshmen." Sitting behind the desk of his Capitol office just downstairs from the Speaker's suite of rooms, Armey became almost wistful as he recalled his first term in Congress with another Texas freshman. "Tom DeLay and I would grab a handful of papers and go to the floor and jump in the middle of a fight."

Armey was fond of telling the freshmen that his daddy frequently advised him, "Beware of zealots because they are humorless." But he knew the freshmen "have something they want to get done, and they have a sense of urgency about it. You expect this from freshmen. Sometimes we have to work with the freshmen on these nuances," Armey said in a fatherly but slightly condescending tone. "You never compromise on principle, but you do on the details." The freshmen arrived "with such resolve they don't understand the practical need to bend a little here and there to serve the principle."

The Republicans had 231 House members, a majority plus 13 votes. In the 103rd Congress, the Democrats had a cushion of 40 votes. Such a narrow majority made running the House more difficult and compromise more essential. On many issues the Republicans might pick up some conservative southern Democrats but also lose some of their own moderate northeastern Republicans. This was even more true in the Senate, where a handful of moderate Republicans would have a significant impact on the shape of legislation coming out of the 104th Congress.

But Lindsey Graham and many other freshmen had little patience for the idea of compromise as a legislative fact of life. "Practicality and revolutions don't go hand in hand. We have been the conscience of the election. When our leadership gets back in the politics-as-usual mode, we need to say, whoa, wait a minute; that's not why we got elected," said Graham matter-of-factly.

The struggle between the freshmen's idealism and the realism of what it takes to get things done in Washington, especially with a slim majority, would continue throughout their first year. And it would take a much bigger and more serious impasse to help them learn the necessity of compromise in governing.

Van Hilleary watched from the sidelines while the fight over the balanced budget amendment was going on. He observed that it was the members who threatened to vote against the amendment, those who made the most noise—"the squeaky wheels"—who got the most attention from the leadership and the press. "The ones who salute smartly and do what the leaders tell them" get ignored, Hilleary found. He took it all in and remembered.

4

THE PARKING LOT PETITION PROTECTION ACT

DURING HIS CAMPAIGN VAN HILLEARY, like many of the freshmen, promised that if elected he would work for passage of a term limits amendment to the Constitution. He vowed to serve no more than six terms in the House and signed a pledge that he would not vote to reverse the laws passed by 22 states limiting the terms of their congressional delegations. He did this even though Tennessee had not passed its own term limits measure.

When he arrived in Washington, Hilleary cosigned term limits legislation introduced by Republican Bill McCollum of Florida, a longtime term limits proponent in his eighth term in the House. But U.S. Term Limits, an advocacy group, called Hilleary and told him McCollum's bill violated the pledge he had made during his campaign because it would preempt state term limit laws. Hilleary told his legislative director, Roger Morse, to draft term limits legislation that would protect states' rights, but he didn't introduce it because he was assured the House Judiciary Committee would deal with the issue when it considered term limits legislation. The draft sat in a folder on Morse's desk.

On February 28 the Judiciary Committee approved a radically altered version of the McCollum measure that really wasn't a term limits bill at all. It would have allowed members who had served 12 years in the House to be eligible for another 12-year stint if they sat out one term. And it included language inserted by McCollum in committee calling for the amendment to preempt all state term limit laws.

U.S. Term Limits and other outraged groups sprang into action, contacting Hilleary and his colleagues in the House. That's when Hilleary decided to do something. Morse reached into his file and pulled out the draft. On March 1 Hilleary held an afternoon meeting with a group of freshmen including McIntosh, Myrick, and Nethercutt in a cramped room in the basement of the Capitol. He told them he had an idea: legislation that was almost identical to McCollum's that would set a national limit of 12 years of service in both the House and Senate but would still allow states to set lower limits if they chose.

The boiler room group decided to remove their names as cosponsors of the McCollum bill and start calling other freshmen to ask them to support Hilleary's bill. The next day House leaders, who had learned of Hilleary's bill, called a meeting with Hilleary, Myrick, and McIntosh. Gingrich asked how many freshmen Hilleary had onboard. Although they hadn't finished counting, McIntosh and Myrick believed Hilleary should have said there were at least 60 freshmen ready to bolt from the McCollum bill. But Hilleary, not being much of a bluffer, admitted he wasn't sure yet. The freshmen were instructed to go back and finish their count. In the next few days, Hilleary picked up 32 cosponsors and floated his bill with outside groups. It was an instant hit among staunch term limits supporters looking for a home.

Hilleary formally "dropped" his bill on Wednesday, March 8—the first legislation he had introduced in his congressional career. That same day he was summoned to a face-to-face meeting with Gingrich and Armey along with the other term limits principals. A total of nine different term limits measures had been introduced in the House. Gingrich told Hilleary he thought there should be only two Republican versions. Gingrich correctly predicted that if there were too many, the Republicans would be accused of trying to sabotage term limits by giving everybody a chance to vote yes knowing no measure would have enough votes to pass. Armey told Hilleary there would be only three measures offered on the floor: the six-year limit mentioned in the contract, the McCollum bill, and a Democratic alternative. Hilleary argued strongly that such a strategy would not protect what the voters had done in states around the country and that the Republicans, who were pushing for greater state autonomy, would be exposed to severe criticism. Hilleary was persuasive enough that Armey finally agreed to allow his bill a vote.

That night Armey wrote a letter to House members informing them that the vote on term limits, which had been scheduled for March 14, would be put off for two weeks to give the Republicans more time to build support.

In a *New York Times* story the next morning, Thursday, Heritage Foundation political analyst Dave Mason was quoted as saying, "You have a very tumultuous situation right now among members and advocacy groups about where they want to go. The great fear is that the semi-fiasco in the Judiciary Committee would be repeated on the floor, only with higher visibility, and you would see a defeat and disorganization and a lack of direction all at the same time." Mason mentioned Hilleary's bill as the one that was gathering support among outside interest groups.

But later that day Hilleary was informed that Gingrich and Armey had changed their minds and his bill would not get a vote. Hilleary wasn't ready to take no for an answer and decided to press on. He and Myrick cornered Sonny Bono on the House

floor and convinced him to become a cosponsor of the amendment, which Hilleary
had informally named the "Parking Lot Petition Protection Act."

*   *   *

Back in his office, Hilleary's press secretary, Brad Todd, fielded calls from *Time*
magazine, the *New York Times,* the *Washington Post,* the *Boston Globe,* the *Los Angeles
Times,* and the Associated Press—heady stuff for someone who had been in Congress all of two months.

Todd and Hilleary are as close as brothers, although they've known each other
only about three years. They met when Hilleary hired Todd, then just out of college,
to manage his first campaign, an unsuccessful race for the Tennessee Senate in 1992.
Todd was born and raised in Tennessee, not too far from where Hilleary grew up,
and he seems to know everything there is to know about Tennessee politics, past and
present. His round, freckled face gives him the look of a choirboy, much younger
than his 25 years, but he has the political acumen of a young Lee Atwater. Todd has
a deep affinity for and understanding of the press, somewhat unusual in a political
operative, especially one so young. It is undoubtedly because he has a graduate degree in journalism from the University of Missouri and spent five months as the
Raleigh News and Observer's Washington correspondent. He knows what reporters
need and how to give it to them. He anticipates what they're going to ask before they
ask it. Extremely intelligent, well read, and more sophisticated than his age and
background might suggest, Todd rounds out Hilleary's corners, and Hilleary re-
strains Todd's youthful exuberance. They often seem to function as one person. They
bonded during Hilleary's run for Congress, when they lived for months on a few
hours of sleep a night, eating beans out of a can. "We've been in the foxholes together," says Hilleary.

This will be another late night. Morse and Hilleary's 31-year-old chief of staff, Susan Hirschmann, will work the phones, calling interest groups. Hirschmann is the
former executive director of Phyllis Schlafly's Eagle Forum and is extremely well connected to the conservative activists who are now helping to run things on the Hill,
the kind of groups that made the phone calls, raised the money, and did the campaign legwork that put the Republicans over the top in 1994 and now have Gingrich's ear. Hirschmann and Morse win pledges of support from the American Conservative Union, National Taxpayers Union, Americans for Tax Reform, Christian
Coalition, and Heritage Foundation. Getting these groups onboard is critical to the
success of Hilleary's effort. About half an hour after Morse makes a pitch to Perot's
United We Stand, he receives a call from the majority leader's office—probably not a
coincidence. There's been another reversal: The leadership has decided to give Hilleary's bill a vote.

But between Thursday night and Friday morning, the leadership changes its mind
for the third time in as many days, and Hilleary's staff is informed their amendment
will not be offered on the floor. A press conference with the interest groups had been
scheduled for later in the day so Republican leaders could announce their term lim-

its strategy, but the groups balked; they refused to participate unless they were assured Hilleary's bill would get a vote.

A meeting is called in the Speaker's office at 2 P.M. Friday with Gingrich, Armey, McCollum, other members who have introduced term limits bills, and the interest groups—about 40 people, pretty much "everybody who had a dog in the hunt," as Hilleary would recall. The mood is extremely tense. Term limits is McCollum's issue. He is clearly angered at all the attention Hilleary and his bill are getting. McCollum begins by saying there is no way he will ever vote for Hilleary's measure and he plans to see to it that none of the other members who are pledged to his bill will either. Hilleary, sitting directly to the left of Gingrich, remains calm. His voice flat and expressionless, he lays out what his bill would do and tries to explain why it is important to vote on it, how the Republicans would open themselves up to criticism and disappoint the hundreds of grassroots people who worked to pass term limits laws if a vote on his bill were not permitted. He offers to fold his language into McCollum's bill and withdraw, but McCollum isn't interested. Several times it appears as though Hilleary has lost the fight, but with dogged determination he keeps on talking, coming back with more arguments.

By this time Gingrich has left the room and Armey is running the meeting. He says he wants to keep things simple and stick to the two-vote strategy because he thinks that will attract the most votes on the floor. "The only thing that can move members of Congress are greed and fear, and unfortunately on this issue we don't have greed at our disposal," Armey tells those in the room. At this point a representative from United We Stand raises his hand and says, "I'd like to speak to the issue of fear." He tells Armey that his group and its supporters are interested only in the Hilleary bill.

After nearly two hours, it looks as if the tide has turned. Bob Inglis, a second-term Republican from South Carolina and sponsor of a measure that would limit members to only six years in the House, asks the special interest groups how many support a vote just on his and the McCollum amendments. No one raises a hand. He then asks how many want a vote on Hilleary's amendment; hands shoot up into the air. Armey decides he has no choice but to grant a vote on Hilleary's measure. Ecstatic with his victory, Hilleary heads back to his office, bursts in, and tells his staff, "We're back in the ball game."

Because of the meeting in Gingrich's office, Hilleary has missed three planes back to Tennessee and won't make a local Chamber of Commerce dinner he is scheduled to address. It is after 7 when he finally leaves for National Airport. Hilleary checks his garment bag and heads toward the gate carrying a nylon duffel bag that contains wrapped gifts—congressional paperweights and letter openers—for supporters back home. The security guard is wary of what's in the bag. She puts the bag through the X-ray machine a second time; the letter openers look suspicious. She opens the bag and wants to know what is in the wrapped packages. Hilleary, embarrassed, tells her they are paperweights. "I don't know if this helps, but I'm a U.S. congressman," he says quietly. Either she doesn't hear him or she isn't impressed.

She wants to open the packages. Hilleary is losing his cool. He tells her in a slightly elevated tone that he is running late, that he is a congressman, and that those are congressional paperweights. She closes the bag and waves him through without expression.

Finally, at the gate, with about 10 minutes to spare, he searches for a pay phone to call the chamber dinner to apologize for his absence. A speakerphone has been rigged up so those attending the dinner will be able to hear him. Hilleary is losing his voice, but he tries to talk over departure announcements and a wailing baby. Phone call completed, he boards the plane for Nashville.

By Monday a flu that Hilleary has been battling for days is worse. So many of the freshmen and their staffs are sick that the illness has been dubbed "contractitis" because it is no doubt attributable to the late nights and long hours the House had been keeping. In its first three months, the 104th Congress was in session for a whopping 487 hours, nearly 300 more hours than the 103rd Congress during the same period. And that is almost four times the average of 123 hours for the previous 10 Congresses. The 104th had 279 roll call votes in its first three months, compared to 127 for the 103rd and 64 for the average of the previous 20 years. But the 104th's legislative output didn't match its frenetic pace. It passed 111 measures in its first three months, compared to 87 for the 103rd and an average of 86 for the previous 10 Congresses.

Despite the pace and his flu, Hilleary soldiers on, and by Tuesday, March 14, the day chosen for a rescheduled term limits press conference, he can barely talk. He still manages, however, to croak on for nearly 10 minutes about why the country desperately needs term limits, unaware that Gingrich, late for the event, has slipped in behind him and is impatiently waiting his turn to speak. "Tell him to be quiet," a leadership aide whispers to Todd. At this point a photographer from *Newsweek* snaps a photo: Hilleary at a bank of microphones, caught in midsentence, an earnest look on his face, and Gingrich just behind him with his lips pursed in an exasperated smirk. Gingrich's expression seems to say, "Kids. What can you do with them?" The photo runs a week later with the caption "Gingrich seeks political cover behind Hilleary's term limits compromise," delighting Hilleary's office and supporters back home. But right now the majority leader's staff is not amused.

After the event an Armey aide begins chewing out Todd about Hilleary's long-windedness. This being a collegial office in which nothing is kept from the boss, especially bad news, Todd relates the message to Hilleary, who, trying to be the good son, promptly calls Armey's staff member to apologize. "Problem? No problem." Armey's assistant essentially tells Hilleary. "Where did you get an idea like that?" Thus comes Hilleary's first lesson in the Capitol Hill dictum: Membership has its privileges. A staffer to the majority leader may know more than he does and may have worked on the Hill for years, but a member of Congress—even a lowly freshman—still has more juice. Members are yessed, kowtowed to, and generally stroked by everyone, even staffers who work for other members. Not a bad way to live and undoubtedly part of the reason the more senior members are so hostile to the idea of term limits.

The next day, Wednesday, March 15, only two weeks since the freshmen held their boiler room meeting and decided to introduce their own bill, the *Nashville Banner* carries a front-page story with the headline "Van's Plan" and a picture of Hilleary at the news conference with Armey on one side and Gingrich on the other. The *Washington Post* story says Hilleary's amendment "may be emerging as the most popular." And much to the surprise of Hilleary's staff, Armey decides to sign on as a cosponsor of their bill.

The Rules Committee reports out four term limits amendments: Hilleary's amendment, the six-year alternative, a cleaned-up version of McCollum's bill (a straight 12-year plan), and a Democratic alternative that calls for retroactive term limits. The Democrats' version is put forth by Representatives Barney Frank of Massachusetts and John Dingell of Michigan (who, in his 20th term, is the longest-serving member in the House). Both are admitted opponents of term limits, and their measure would require any member who has already served 12 years to step down. It doesn't have a chance. It's just an effort to embarrass the Republicans by forcing them to vote no on it.

That same day Republican strategist Bill Kristol puts out a memo praising the Hilleary amendment as "far preferable to the others." Kristol writes that Hilleary's amendment is the only approach "consistent with the promise of the Contract to advance the cause of term limits and respect the rights of the states and respect the rights of citizens to limit the terms of their elected officials." He predicts that "failure to rally behind Hilleary will open Republicans to charges of bait-and-switch hypocrisy" and asks, "Why not snatch term limits victory from the jaws of defeat?" Hilleary considers the Kristol memo a big boost. Throughout the campaign he eagerly anticipated the Kristol faxes that offered strategy and advice to conservative challengers. And Kristol has emerged as one of the most important thinkers and tacticians in the Republican Party.

Kristol gives Hilleary high marks for hiring Hirschmann, who he says could have worked for virtually any conservative Republican she chose. It was soon after the election that Hilleary made a trip to Washington to interview potential staff members. After interviewing five or six people, he knew within 15 minutes that she was the one he wanted. Hirschmann grew up in Alabama and worked with the Christian Coalition's Ralph Reed in national Republican politics while they were both still in college. She started with Schlafly's Eagle Forum in her mid-20s and worked her way up to become its executive director in just a few years. She has steely determination and ambition but wraps them in a sugarcoated package that many men, especially conservatives, find less threatening than a more obvious feminist style.

Hirschmann and Hilleary share a deep commitment to the conservative cause and an antipathy not only toward Democrats but toward moderates in their own party. At the Eagle Forum Hirschmann always supported conservatives running against moderates in Republican primaries, especially pro-life women. Hirschmann disagrees with Republicans who fear that making abortion a big issue will seriously divide and hurt the party. In Republican primaries, she contends, "abortion always cuts in favor of the pro-lifer" because the people who feel strongly about this issue, like Christian Coalition members, are the ones willing to devote time and money to campaigns. The conservatives know they have no chance of overturning the Supreme Court's *Roe v. Wade* abortion decision, but they do hope to nibble away at abortion with amendments to bills that would cut all federal funds for the procedure or require parental consent for minors.

Hirschmann says she and Hilleary come from a completely different place than moderate Republicans like Connie Morella of Maryland and Chris Shays of Connecticut. Hilleary and many other conservatives often refer to such moderate Republicans as "squishes," meaning they are "squishy" on many defining Republican issues. The freshmen believe their ideological purity not only on spending and government reform but on many social issues sets them apart from their elders. They are extremely skeptical of deal-makers like Senate majority leader Bob Dole, whom they consider all too willing to compromise.

One of the first things Hirschmann did after taking over Hilleary's office was to recruit like-minded conservative Roger Morse, 34, to be legislative director. Morse had worked on the Hill for more than a decade, six years for Tom DeLay and (just before joining Hilleary) as a policy analyst for the Republican Study Committee. Morse wanted to join the staff of one of the young, aggressive freshmen. He knew Hirschmann was an activist and figured Hilleary might be a good bet. Hirschmann and Morse are typical of the best and brightest among the Republican staffers. Some, like Morse, had been working on the Hill for years; many others, like Hirschmann, were culled from conservative interest groups and think tanks. Hilleary knows he has a good staff, and he isn't sure how long he can hold onto them. "Your most talented staff gravitate to your most talented members, so now the question is: Do I measure up? The jury's still out."

Morse is one of those like Gingrich who has been in the trenches pushing for a more conservative House and a more conservative Republican Party for years. Morse is the cofounder of a conservative Hill staff group that meets every Monday morning to float conservative ideas and talk about how to influence upcoming legislation. "A lot of our stuff is little insurrections that work to keep leadership in line and prevent bad things from happening," he explains. About 30 people usually attend the invitation-only, no-press-allowed gatherings, including a staff representative from the leadership, and the weekly meeting has gained a reputation as a must-attend for conservative staffers with clout.

For many years, both conservative GOP staffers and members in the House thought they were being shunted aside by former minority leader Bob Michel. Extremely affable and well-liked by members of both parties, Michel was no match for the bomb-throwing Gingrich. When the Republicans lost the presidency in 1992, the conservatives felt Michel was too willing to compromise and work with the Democrats. Gingrich led a quiet insurrection against Michel and refused to support many of the deals he cut with the Democrats. Gingrich also informed Michel that if he did not retire in 1994, Gingrich intended to challenge him for the leadership spot.

It is after 11 P.M. on Wednesday, March 15, and Hilleary, who has just cast his last vote of the day, throws open the door to his office and tells his staff, "I know how we can beat McCollum." McCollum claims his legislation won't preempt state term limit laws, so there is no need for Hilleary's bill. "He's just wrong and he knows it," Hilleary says angrily. McCollum had sent out a 1,000-word "Dear Colleague" letter to the rest of the House members blasting Hilleary's amendment. He called it "bad public policy" that "would lead to a hodgepodge of term limits throughout the fifty states." Such strong language in a "Dear Colleague" letter, especially in reference to a fellow Republican's bill, is somewhat unusual. But Hilleary surmises McCollum fears that Hilleary is gaining on him. "This is getting kind of touchy. Here I am, an up-start from nowhere, and I've horned in."

The next day Hilleary is asked to be on the MacNeil-Lehrer NewsHour, his first national television appearance. With him are McCollum as well as two members to speak in opposition to term limits, Democrat Barney Frank and Republican Nancy Johnson. The older members know how to filibuster, and Hilleary, soft-spoken and folksy, doesn't get much airtime. Much to the frustration of his press secretary, Hilleary hasn't learned a skill most politicians consider essential: how to turn any question around so they can give the canned answer they have prepared. Hilleary always answers the question he is asked. So when Robert MacNeil asks him what kind of support he has for his amendment, he doesn't say, "There's a groundswell moving toward my approach, which is the favorite of the freshmen and grassroots organizations"; instead, he replies that he is closing in on 50 cosponsors. Less impressive but more direct.

Hilleary still calls the appearance a "net win for us," though he admits he isn't very good at sound bites and isn't as polished as the others. "Where does smooth leave off and slick begin?" he wonders aloud, adding, "At least it came across as sincere." Hilleary says that "out of deference and respect" he felt he should "let Mr. McCollum carry the banner for term limits. I wanted to make a special effort to not act belligerent."

Such humility may have something to do with a talking-to he received from Armey earlier that day on the House floor. "He put his arm around me and said, 'Van, you've got to be careful how you're talking about McCollum's bill.' Someone had gone to him and implied that I was trashing McCollum's bill. I was sort of scared and aggravated and thinking that now in addition to everything I'm doing trying to fight term limits opponents, I'm going to have to mount a PR campaign with the leadership." But after thinking it over, Hilleary decided Armey was just trying to give him some good advice. "This is the first time I've ever done this. Sometimes the ways of Washington are not obvious. The egos are massive up here. I'm a freshman, and I've battled my way to the table." Hilleary determined to work harder not to be distracted by McCollum and to stay on message.

Back home over the weekend, no one is too interested in term limits, but Hilleary is bombarded with questions from constituents about the Republicans' welfare cuts and plans to block-grant the school lunch program. On Monday night, March 20, sitting in a leather couch in front of his desk, his shoeless feet propped up on a coffee table, Hilleary speculates on the public reaction to what the Republicans are doing. "We're taking a real beating on this back in the district." Hilleary insists the Democrats are spreading "disinformation" but says the leadership "really dropped the ball" by not responding quickly to charges that the Republicans are trying to dismantle the school lunch program. "We're going to lose the PR war if we're not careful."

At 9:45 he takes a call from Richard Cohen of the *National Journal*, who's doing a story on term limits. Hilleary spends half an hour describing how he got into this, why this is "a states' rights thing," and how his amendment would protect the wishes of the people in states that have term limit laws. When asked if it will pass, he says, "I can't say the odds are greater than 50-50, but I think we have a legitimate shot."

In less than two weeks, Hilleary has gone from having no bill in the hopper and fighting for a vote to wanting to come out on top. "Once you get in it, you want to give it everything you've got," he says. He tells Cohen he thinks his bill has the "best chance of passage." He's learning. It's impossible to tell whether or not he really believes what he's just said. And in a reference to the drubbing he's gotten as a result of taking on McCollum, he concludes, "I've learned a lot more about how this place works, and I've gotten a good dose of how politics is there in any issue. It's hard for idealism to survive sometimes."

He may not really believe his amendment has a chance, but Hilleary still hasn't given up on the idea that some version of term limits could pass the House, even though many senior Republicans, including members of the leadership, oppose term limits. Majority whip Tom DeLay, conference vice chair Susan Molinari, and a number of committee chairs, most notably Henry Hyde of the Judiciary Committee, all say they intend to vote against term limits. Gingrich and Armey have made it clear they don't consider term limits a high priority. All they promised was a vote. There would be no retribution for members who voted no. When asked about this, Gingrich nonchalantly replies, "It's a free country."

The outside term limits proponents realize that the vote isn't even going to be close and have decided that sending out mailings or airing television commercials would simply be a waste of money, especially since the leadership is expending virtually no effort on the issue. But if Hilleary knows that, too, he shows no evidence of it.

*   *   *

Tuesday night, March 21, Gingrich is hosting a $2,000-a-ticket reception at the Capitol Hill Club to celebrate his ascension to the Speakership. The invitations called it "the GOP's first Speaker's party in 40 years." That certainly is reason enough for lobbyists to pony up to attend, but not for Hilleary, for whom the event would be free. He is in his office, working on term limits. The vote is one week away.

Hilleary is still trying to attract more cosponsors to his measure. Attaching their names to bills by cosponsoring them allows members to go home and claim credit for legislation without having to do any work. But there are also benefits for the primary sponsors. Having lots of cosponsors makes your measure look serious and may sway someone who's a friend of one of the cosponsors. Being a cosponsor also puts people on record as to where they stand. It's a lot harder to back out of voting for something at the last minute if your name is on it.

Having pretty much run out of people on his side of the aisle to ask, Hilleary is approaching Democrats who are either freshmen, known reformers, or from states with term limit laws. William Luther of Minnesota, one of the 13 Democratic freshmen, had told Hilleary he was thinking of cosponsoring the amendment but needed to get clearance from the Democratic leadership first.

On Wednesday, March 22, a large chunk of the day is taken up with media interviews. The *Nashville Tennessean* is doing a profile on Hilleary, which would normally be a big deal, but he has to squeeze in *Time* and the NBC Nightly News, too. Hilleary also speaks to a Tennessee television station about welfare reform, for which he has to spend 20 minutes preparing. "We've kind of been through legislative puberty in the last three weeks. Doing something like term limits is so all-consuming that we don't have time to focus on welfare, and it's huge. He knows it, but not the intricacies of all the amendments," says Brad Todd.

The floor debate over the Republican welfare bill was a high-water mark of partisan division and ugliness during the first 100 days. Although many Democrats crossed over to vote with the Republicans on things like the balanced budget amendment, the line-item presidential veto, and barring the federal government from passing on unfunded mandates to the states, only nine Democrats voted for the GOP welfare plan. This is the kind of issue that clearly illuminates the difference in the way Democrats and Republicans see the role of government, and with the election of so many conservatives to the House, that difference has not been so sharp in many years.

The "Personal Responsibility Act" as passed by the House would give states authority over welfare, foster care, and school lunch programs and would cut benefits to legal immigrants, disabled children, and unwed teenage mothers. And although it would require welfare recipients to work, the bill would not provide additional money for training programs. The Democrats, who have taken to wearing brightly colored "Save the Children" ties and scarves with drawings by children on them, call the changes "cold-blooded and mean-spirited." Meanwhile the Republicans are getting sick and tired of being painted as heartless ogres who don't care about children.

It all reaches a crescendo on March 23, when 75-year-old Sam Gibbons of Florida, the ranking minority member of the Ways and Means Committee, tries to make an impassioned floor speech deriding the Republicans for their treatment of children and their efforts to push amendments to the welfare bill through without allowing enough time for debate. He is booed by Republican members. "Boo if you want to. Make asses out of yourselves for the American people," says Gibbons, his voice rising to a shout as Republicans attempt to drown him out. "You all sit down, sit down and shut up," he cries.

Hilleary, who has been up since 7 A.M., doesn't participate in the welfare debate, but he's starting to show the strain. He is tense and appears to be dragging as he sits down with his staff to prepare for an appearance on a national radio show that will go on the air at 10. "What's his politics?" Hilleary asks about the host, Jim Bohannon. Todd doesn't know. Hilleary will be a guest along with Becky Cain, the president of the National League of Women Voters, which opposes term limits. Todd and Hilleary go over what arguments she can be expected to use and what his best responses would be.

The show is broadcast from an Arlington, Virginia, office tower across the Potomac River from Georgetown. Bohannon, Hilleary, and Todd sit at a large, kidney-shaped, gray Formica desk in the studio. Hilleary and Bohannon wear headphones so they can hear Cain, who participates via telephone. The first portion of the program is devoted to the guests' making their points, the second to taking listener calls. Hilleary talks about the need to cut government and how easy it is to become corrupted by the system the longer you're in Washington. "If someone knows they can't be here forever, they're much more likely to do the right thing while they're here," he says. As Todd predicted earlier in Hilleary's office, Cain responds by saying, "We have term limits already, and they're called elections." It is a polite, bloodless exchange, no confrontation. This is not Rush Limbaugh.

When Bohannon asks Hilleary about term limits' forcing out seasoned senior members, Hilleary says freshmen may have to learn a lot fast, but serving in Congress "is not brain surgery either." After the show, when Todd reassures Hilleary that he did a good job, Hilleary seems surprised. It's almost midnight by the time Hilleary gets back to his office. He wonders aloud about all that has happened in just three weeks. "Who would have thought that we'd get this far?"

Five days later, Monday, March 27: The term limits vote is two days away. Hilleary is getting ready to do a call-in show on a Seattle radio station. Todd asks him whether he has his index cards with information about where the local delegations stand on term limits. The host of the show clearly has never heard of Hilleary, and before they go on the air, Hilleary is asked to spell and pronounce his name. During the show Hilleary predicts it will be a close vote. He mentions the Washington state cosponsors of his bill but not the local members who oppose term limits. After he hangs up, he tells Todd sheepishly, "I decided not to tell who the bad guys are."

Hilleary wants to make an impact, but he wants to be liked doing it. In matters of ideology he identifies with Gingrich and Armey, but when it comes to style, his role model is Howard Baker, former U.S. senator from Tennessee and chief of staff to Ronald Reagan. The politically moderate Baker, who has many friends in both parties, is the elder statesman of Tennessee Republican politics. Hilleary says the success Baker has had with his gentle, courtly, nonconfrontational style illustrates the adage that you can catch more flies with honey than with vinegar. Baker, who attended the University of Tennessee with Hilleary's father, has been a mentor to Hilleary.

Hirschmann walks into Hilleary's office and tells him he must get back on the phone and call more members. "The clock is ticking," she sings out. Both Hilleary and his staff have been working 16-hour days, but it's clear his staff is pushing him more than the other way around. "Let's face it: We're not going to win this. We're not going to get the votes," Hirschmann admits. "But it's a good experience for Van. I'm glad he took it on."

*　　*　　*

Tuesday, March 28: the day before the vote. Hilleary's day begins with an 8 A.M. appearance on "Mitchells in the Morning" on National Empowerment Television. Although very few people in Hilleary's district get cable, an appearance on this show is considered de rigueur for committed conservatives. It is hosted by the husband-and-wife team of Dan and Nancy Mitchell. He's a senior fellow at the Heritage Foundation; she's with the conservative advocacy group Citizens for a Sound Economy. Hilleary's been on the show before. And the last time, the show's attractive young female producer told Dan Mitchell she thought Hilleary was cute, something Mitchell repeated on the air, followed by a query about Hilleary's marital status. As Todd drives away from the Capitol Hill brownstone where the show is broadcast, Hilleary, uncertain how old the producer is, asks him, "Would I get put in jail for asking that girl out?"

His colleagues consider Hilleary something of a lady's man. Most of the Republican freshmen married young, and Hilleary is one of only six that have never been married. As an eligible congressman, Hilleary has taken some ribbing both from his classmates and the press. In a March story in the *Nashville Banner* headlined "Hilleary fills new role as hunk on the Hill," he was referred to as a "babe." One female lobbyist who called him a catch was quoted as saying, "Conservatives can be sexy if you like navy blue suits and boring ties." Hilleary likes to flirt; it is almost a reflex with him. And he obviously enjoys all the attention he gets. In another newspaper story on the single members of the class, Gerald Weller, 38, of Illinois, called Hilleary "the class charmer." And Lindsey Graham, 40, of South Carolina, who shares a three-story townhouse with Hilleary two blocks from the Capitol, was quoted as saying, "Hilleary's doing a lot better than I am. He kicks into second gear at midnight."

Graham, who has a dry wit and impish sense of humor, expresses frustration at his social life and told the *Hill*, a newspaper that covers Congress, "I'm changing my opinion about getting rid of the elevator operators. . . . They're about the only women I get to meet." But Hilleary seems to have no problem meeting plenty of women, many of whom probably wouldn't have paid much attention to him a few years ago. "I've never had so much opportunity and so little time," he says wistfully.

Graham and Hilleary met during orientation and found they had a few things in common—both were single, came from the South, and had military backgrounds—so they decided to rent a house together. "As far as using the place, we could just as well sleep in our office," says Graham, echoing the complaints of many of the freshmen over their crazy schedules and days that don't end until 11 or 12. Graham says there's barely enough time for "figuring out how to vote, taking care of problems back in the district, and doing your laundry." According to Graham, the most he and Hilleary usually see each other is for about five minutes in the morning.

In the car Todd and Hilleary are headed for a C-SPAN interview at the "Senate swamp," a grassy area across the parking lot from the Senate steps on the Capitol's east front. "What's my sound bite that I have to get in no matter what?" Hilleary asks Todd, who tells him he should talk about the 25 million people in 22 states who have voted in favor of term limits. "We really need one more week on this," Hilleary mutters. It is a cold, damp morning, and C-SPAN isn't ready for them, so Hilleary and Todd wait in the car. Hilleary recalls the last time he was on this side of the Capitol, the day the Senate voted on the balanced budget amendment and he and the other freshmen led a march that culminated in a press conference they held on this very spot because the Senate wouldn't let them have it on the steps.

Todd warns Hilleary not to be too technical in the interview and coaches him on the main points he should stress. The camera man calls for Hilleary and instructs him to stand on a 4-inch-high wooden platform. In his ear Hilleary has a transmitter through which he can hear the questions being put to him by a C-SPAN anchor back in the studio. He is wearing the Republican congressman's uniform—blue suit, nondescript red-and-blue-checked tie, and, because Todd has told him it looks better on TV than a white one, a blue oxford cloth shirt. He is framed in the shot with the Capitol dome behind him. During the campaign the dome was a negative image that Hilleary and other Republicans used in advertising to challenge "Washington insiders." But since the Republicans have taken over, the dome has become a symbol of the revolution.

The sky is a dull, gunmetal gray, and it is unseasonably cold for late March in Washington, but Hilleary wears only his suit jacket. It looks better on television. Behind him a group of schoolchildren file up the steps to the Capitol as he gives his C-SPAN interview. Afterward, as Todd drives over to the underground House garage, Hilleary talks about all the time his staff and some of the other freshmen have spent on the term limits fight. "They deserve that I do everything I can to make sure ours is the one that wins." He pauses for a moment. "Besides that, it's the best bill."

At 9:15 Hilleary walks into his office. His assistant, Elaine Robinson, tells him he did a good job on TV but that she isn't really sure she likes the tie. She sits at a desk just to the left of the front door. On the opposite wall is a map of Hilleary's district. There are almost no personal touches to the office. Hilleary has almost none of the photos of himself with political notables and kitsch that crowd the walls of many members' offices. He has had no time to decorate. His private office has the standard congressional-issue mahogany furniture and leather couches.

Hilleary plops down in the chair behind his desk and looks over the "whip checks"—polls of how members say they intend to vote—that his freshmen colleagues have turned in. There's good news about John Baldacci, a freshman Democrat from Maine: "Baldacci looks like a yes—whoa, baby," Hilleary says to himself. Five minutes later Todd walks in and tells Hilleary he will be doing a Memphis radio call-in show. Hilleary gets on the phone at his desk, Todd on an extension across the room. Todd carefully pronounces Hilleary's name and tells the host where he is from. Hilleary giggles softly at the seeming inanity of it all. On the air the host asks him why the Republicans are getting cold feet on term limits. Hilleary attempts to deflect the question, saying that even if all the Republicans voted yes, they'd still need the Democrats to reach the 290 votes—two-thirds of the House—required to pass a constitutional amendment. "Whether we pass this or not, we have taken a huge first step"; it is his first public acknowledgment that the measure probably won't pass.

Hilleary flips through the congressional picture book, making a list of who's for and who's against term limits. Whenever he calls members he doesn't know, Hilleary looks them up in the picture book while he's talking to them. Todd tells him a Kansas City talk show called "Friendly Fire" is next. Hilleary, who has been doing one radio show after another for days, has clearly tired of it. "Do you really think we're getting the most bang for the buck doing this? I don't." Todd patiently convinces him to do one more.

Hilleary is then informed someone from his district is outside in the reception area, a pharmacist he knows is a Democrat and not a supporter. Hilleary is not thrilled about taking time out to talk to him. "He was rude to me during the campaign. He said, 'I don't have time to talk to a politician.'" One thing a good politician never forgets is the people who voted for him. And the people who didn't. "I'll go out there for five minutes. If I let him come in here, he'll never leave," he tells Todd.

Ten minutes later Hilleary is back in the office ready to begin making calls to "whip" his colleagues. One of his first calls is to Robert "Bud" Cramer, a third-term Democrat from Alabama. Most of Hilleary's closest friends in Congress are southerners, and often he seems to have more in common with southern Democrats than northeastern Republicans. Cramer is a neighbor of sorts: His district cuts across the top of Alabama and abuts the southern portion of Hilleary's district. "This is Congressman Hilleary. Is Bud there?" he asks. In a moment Cramer gets on the line. "Bud, I appreciate your taking the call. You know I've got a term limits bill; it's the one that protects states' rights." Cramer tells Hilleary he's undecided. "We're not going to get anywhere near 290; it's going to be a free vote," Hilleary cajoles. In other words, it's not going to pass, so Cramer can vote for it, use that vote in his next campaign, and not have to worry about term limits' actually being imposed. Hilleary later explains his approach: "This is getting down to the nitty-gritty, so we're trying to use whatever political argument we think will work."

Such maneuvering has long been a popular Capitol Hill scam. Several moderate House Republicans who were opposed to aspects of the welfare reform bill used similar logic in justifying their yes votes. They were assured by Republican moderates in the Senate that items that concerned them, such as guaranteeing child care for welfare recipients required to work, would be taken care of in the Senate. So the moderates could be seen as supporting the party and know their vote had no real consequences.

Cramer says he will think about voting for the amendment. "It'd help us if you could," responds Hilleary. He's met Cramer but doesn't really know him. He wonders whether he should have gone to Cramer's office in person. "Maybe that would have given him the extra push he needed," Hilleary speculates. It proves not to be necessary. The next day Cramer votes yes on Hilleary's amendment.

Hilleary does think he should pay a brief personal visit to Terry Everett, a second-term Republican from Montgomery, Alabama, whose office is one floor up from his. But he returns without a firm commitment from Everett: "All that work for an undecided." Hilleary isn't finished, though. He decides to take Everett a copy of the letter from United We Stand endorsing his measure. Before he goes he highlights a passage. "Congressmen like big pictures and colors," he says with a smile. The personal touch seems to do the trick; Everett will turn out to be a yes vote.

At 12:30 a dozen people gather in Hilleary's office for a working lunch. Todd, Hirschmann, and staffers from other freshman offices sit around a low table in the center of the room, munching on Domino's pizza and going over the strategy for the next 24 hours. Hilleary tells them he's already gone to everyone he can think of on this, "the people who owe me a favor in my short time here—all two or three of those." The staffers laugh. Sam Brownback walks in. Like Hilleary, Brownback is enthusiastic about term limits and says he wants to speak on the floor on behalf of Hilleary's amendment. He also offers to work the door handing out flyers before the vote. "If it's there, it's there. If it's not, it's not," Hilleary says as the meeting breaks up.

By 1:30 Hilleary is back on the phone calling members. Hilleary calls the office of fellow Tennessean Bob Clement, a five-term Democrat. Clement has expressed opposition to term limits in the past, but Hilleary wants to know if he's moved to an undecided position. Hilleary is making a hard sell. He tells Clement, "The odds of Tennessee getting term limits is not great." As a result, Tennessee would be in a good position under Hilleary's amendment because its delegation could stay 12 years instead of the six or eight other delegations might be limited to. As with Cramer earlier, Hilleary stresses the Republicans are not even close to having enough votes so it's a "free ride."

Clement mentions Hilleary's picture in *Newsweek*. Hilleary, no doubt sensing the possibility of some professional jealousy on the part of the older member, does his best to play it down, "I was lucky, wasn't I? That one makes me look better than I do. . . . Even a blind squirrel finds a nut every now and then." And then veering the conversation back to business, Hilleary says, "Hey, think about this hard. Can I bug you about it again tomorrow?" Hanging up the phone, he says Clement was a "lean yes." Hilleary remarks, "I doubt that I'm on his Christmas card list, but I'm going to put him on mine."

At 3:45 Morse tells Hilleary it's time to go to the floor to make his two-minute speech in favor of the rule that will govern the debate on term limits. Hilleary walks down to the well of the House and hands a copy of his speech to the clerk. There are only about 10 members on the floor, and Hilleary makes a brief, boilerplate speech in favor of the rule, sticking to the text Morse has handed him. "The people want it;

the time has come" for term limits, he concludes. As he walks out, he notes that such a speech is essentially just form and doesn't really do anything to sway other members. "What I'm doing on the phone matters," he says. Members may have the televisions in their offices tuned to floor action, but they aren't really listening to their colleagues' speeches because they have too much else to do, Hilleary explains.

In the Speaker's Lobby, a long hallway just outside the chamber in which the press gathers to catch members on their way on and off the floor, Hilleary is stopped by a small group of reporters who ask him what kind of chance his amendment has. Hilleary tells them more members are coming onboard "because they're feeling the wrath of their constituents." Todd meets him outside the door and leads him to the Capitol lawn for an "Inside Politics" interview live on CNN.

Hilleary, who is clearly getting more comfortable with this, quickly ticks off the reasons why his amendment is the best. When anchor Jeanne Meserve says it's clear there aren't enough votes to pass term limits, Hilleary responds, "Let's not give up yet"; after all, many members will surely be thinking, "How would Tom Foley have voted on this?" When she asserts that the Republicans promised to pass term limits, Hilleary shoots back, "No, they did not"; they promised to get it to the floor for a vote. For what seems like the 100th time this week, Hilleary says the term limit vote will "flush out" the pretenders on this issue. Hilleary is especially fond of using expressions that deal with dogs and hunting—a particular favorite: "If you ain't the lead dog, the view never changes."

When Hilleary walks into the office, the staff tells him he looked and sounded great on CNN; everyone agrees that was his best television interview yet. Robinson tells Hilleary his mother was watching and called to say how proud she was and to tell him "there were tears in your father's eyes." But both Todd and Hirschmann tell Hilleary he has a five-o'clock shadow and should have shaved first. "He's getting more aggressive," Hirschmann says with a tone of pride in her voice. "He's gotten better at this just since term limits started," Todd agrees.

This has been a day full of media attention for Hilleary, and it's not over yet. The office turns on the NBC Nightly News, and at the top of the show Hilleary makes an appearance in a piece on term limits. He is shown walking across the lawn in front of the Capitol. "It is a make-or-break issue, and people who don't support it will be in trouble at the ballot box," he is heard to predict. Not much airtime, but not bad for a freshman.

Hilleary looks at his schedule for the rest of the evening. There are six or seven places he needs to be, and he has to make some decisions about where he's going to go. The leadership's whip team and the freshman Republicans will be meeting simultaneously, and Hilleary discovers he's left his most recent list of cosponsors in the cloakroom. He'll have to go back and get it, which will cost him time. Hilleary can be easily distracted and has a habit of leaving things in committee rooms, taxicabs, and airplanes. Todd jokes that USAIR has created a lost and found just for him. The staff is so used to it that they make extra copies of any piece of paper they hand Hilleary.

Hilleary decides to go first to the freshman meeting, which turns into a confrontation between Gingrich and his unruly band of revolutionaries. The freshmen are not happy with the halfhearted effort the leadership has made on behalf of term limits, and several of them tell Gingrich they're going to vote for the Democratic term limits measure even though he's directed them not to. Hilleary's housemate, Lindsey Graham, tells the Speaker he thinks the Republicans should vote for the Democrats' retroactive bill and call their bluff. "I said either the Democrats will peel off on final passage or we'll pass a term limits amendment. Me and the Speaker kind of had a disagreement over that, but I feel like that's what we should have done," Graham recalls later. Graham considers the leadership's effort on term limits "too little, too late" and says if they had worked half as hard on term limits as they did for the balanced budget amendment, it might have had a chance. Graham had no problem voting for a term limits amendment that would mean the entire GOP leadership would be prevented from running for reelection. "The country could withstand anybody in this body leaving, but I'm not sure it could withstand the effects of career politics much longer. If it means sacrificing the leadership of both parties, so be it."

When Hilleary returns from the freshman meeting, he decides to stop by a reception Howard Baker is having at his Pennsylvania Avenue condo a few blocks from the Capitol. Hilleary tells the cab driver to wait, that he'll be gone only 10 minutes. The party is being held in honor of John J. "Jimmy" Duncan Jr., from Tennessee's Second District, who has been named chairman of the Aviation Subcommittee of the Transportation and Infrastructure Committee, formerly known as Public Works and Transportation. Although not considered a particularly prestigious committee, it does afford great opportunity to provide goodies for the folks back home.

Tennessee's two new Republican senators, Bill Frist, a heart surgeon and multimillionaire who defeated three-term Democrat Jim Sasser, and Fred Thompson, a Baker protégé and rising Republican star, are there. Thompson, a lawyer, was a counsel to the Senate Watergate Committee on which Baker served but is probably better known for his part-time acting, including roles in the films *The Hunt for Red October* and *In the Line of Fire.*

On the condo's tiny balcony, which has a spectacular view of the Capitol dome, a bar has been set up. As Hilleary goes out to get a Diet Coke, his beeper goes off. There's a vote on the floor. Making his hasty good-byes, Hilleary returns to the street to find that the cab, in which he has left a folder of his term limits papers and some letters, has taken off. He runs across Pennsylvania Avenue and finally manages to flag down another taxi and makes it to the floor with just 30 seconds to spare.

Still out of breath, he slowly walks back to the office to check in. Hirschmann and the rest of the staff are eating take-out hamburgers and counting votes. She thinks they'll get between 150 and 160, well below the number they need. Hilleary steals some french fries and heads back over to the floor for one more speech. The day's regular business has ended, and the House has moved into special-order time. As he gets off the elevator, Hilleary says, "I have no idea what I'm going to say." Earlier in the day, when he spoke on behalf of the rule, he had other things on his mind. Tomorrow when he takes to the floor he will be playing for keeps, and he will be nervous, his delivery stiff. But tonight he is loose. He has nothing to lose, and no one is watching. There are only a handful of members on the floor. It's not clear to whom Hilleary is talking—maybe to himself.

Hilleary starts explaining how he got involved in the term limits fight, how it all began a month ago, when the Judiciary Committee reported out a bill that really wasn't a term limits bill at all, and how he got the other freshmen involved because they had to do something to fight for what the people in so many states had voted for. He mentions a guy named Bill Anderson who gathered signatures for a term limits petition in Missouri. He worked hard, and no other bill will protect what he did. It's for Bill Anderson and for all of the others like him, Hilleary says, that he is doing this. He holds up his voting card and says how proud he is that for the first time the House of Representatives will vote on term limits. And no matter what happens tomorrow, he says, it will be a victory for the American people.

It's a good speech, maybe even one of the best he's ever given. But not even his staff was listening. They're watching Michael Kinsley grill Bill McCollum on CNN's "Crossfire." What's wrong with letting the states have what they want? Kinsley asks McCollum. Hilleary, who has just arrived back in his office, has a sly grin on his face and utters words that in his wildest dreams he could never have imagined saying about the liberal commentator: "Michael Kinsley, my hero."

Hirschmann, however, is not amused. "I wish everybody would work rather than sitting around," she says. At 8:50 Hilleary does a telephone interview with a reporter from the *Nashville Banner*. Is it over? the reporter asks. "I'm not willing to give up yet." Hilleary acknowledges his inexperience as a legislator. "When your first bill is a constitutional amendment, the learning curve is pretty steep. I'm sure I made tactical mistakes just out of ignorance." He refers to McCollum and the trouble he's encountered: "Up here the battles you fight are never your last battle. I've tried not to make any permanent enemies." And he talks about how hard he and his staff have worked, "We've poured our heart and soul into this."

At 9:50 he does an interview on a CBS radio call-in show. Alone in his private office, the phone cradled next to his ear, Hilleary rocks back and forth in his highbacked leather chair. The TV is tuned to CNN with the sound turned down. As he listens, Hilleary scrunches up his face as if he's squinting to see something important that's just beyond his range of vision. It's his eighth interview at the end of a very long day, but he goes at it as if it's his first. He credits the work of his staff and the other freshmen, gives out the congressional switchboard number, and urges listeners to call their members and tell them they want term limits. As he has in every other interview he's given, he says this term limits vote will "flush out the pretenders."

At 10 P.M. Hirschmann calls the rest of the staff into Hilleary's office for a final meeting to talk about what needs to be done for tomorrow. They discuss the flyers they plan to hand to members on the floor. Hirschmann runs down some of the state delegations: Massachusetts—"They don't care or they're already on us"; Missouri—"It's hard to move people because of [minority leader Richard] Gephardt";

Ohio—"We're working on it." They talk about how to allot the 30 minutes Hilleary will be allowed for all members who want to speak on behalf of his amendment. "Only people who've whipped for us or helped us should get two minutes," Hirschmann decrees. She asks Hilleary if he can think of any Democrats or upper-classmen they can get to talk.

They begin to go over the different scenarios Hilleary may face and the parliamentary rules he will have to follow when he is managing his amendment on the floor. Morse assures Hilleary everything will be written down for him. Morse and Hirschmann begin firing instructions at Hilleary: "Don't vary from the script and don't yield. If people are making noise, tell the chair the House is not in order. When you recognize people who are speaking on your behalf, ad lib, say, 'my good friend from the state of Arizona, who has worked tirelessly on behalf of this effort.'" Knowing how courteous Hilleary is, his staff is worried he will get in trouble on the floor if he's pestered by the Democrats. "If Barney Frank wants to ask you a question," Morse tells him, "make him use his own time. Stay on message. They will try and interrupt you." Hirschmann tells Hilleary not to veer off the subject. Morse reminds Hilleary that he's "not changing people's minds with the debate. Whenever someone asks you a question, spin it and put it back to your message."

It's after 11 P.M. when the meeting is finally over. Hirschmann sends everyone off with a warning, "It will be a stressful day tomorrow. We don't want people making stupid mistakes." Hilleary won't leave the office until after midnight; Todd will be there until almost 2:00 A.M.

*   *   *

March 29—the big day. It's 9 A.M., and Hilleary is sitting behind his desk, already making phone calls. He didn't sleep very well. The only people left to call are Democrats, and Hilleary is trying humility as an approach: "I've just made a colossal screwup in my youthful ignorance in not getting to you all sooner," he tells a Democratic member. He's run out of time. If he had another week, Hilleary thinks it could really have made the difference. He wouldn't have got the 290 votes he needs, but he just might have come out on top.

He calls Budget Committee chairman John Kasich's office and gets his legislative director on the phone. He tries opening with small talk: "I'm sure you have an exciting life working for your boss." Then he gets down to business: "I assume he's for Mr. McCollum's bill. Is he going to vote for our bill?" He isn't. Next Hilleary plans to call Vernon Ehlers, a Republican from Michigan who serves with him on the Science Committee. Hilleary considers Ehlers to be one of the brainiest members he's met. He recalls that once after a committee hearing, impressed with Ehlers's intellect, he told him, "You're like a rocket scientist," and Ehlers retorted, "I'm a nuclear physicist. We look down on rocket scientists."

Hilleary has the TV in his office tuned to C-SPAN; the general floor debate on term limits has begun. Fellow Tennessee Republican Jimmy Duncan is blasting term limits. "Establishing arbitrary term limits—which everyone admits will force many outstanding people out of office—just does not make sense."

"Don't beat around the bush; just tell us what you think," Hilleary says to the TV screen. When Duncan finishes, Hilleary says, "Well, I'll just mark him off my list." Duncan does not vote for Hilleary's amendment. But despite his speech decrying term limits as "some radical, arbitrary gimmick . . . which corrects a problem that does not exist," he does vote yes on final passage. Call it a cover-your-backside vote.

By 12:15 the other term limits principals are all on the floor, but Hilleary is still trying to make last-minute calls. Hirschmann comes in and says she counts more than 200 votes for McCollum but the totals could be way off because the Republicans have no idea how the Democrats will be voting. "I just don't want to hemorrhage on the floor," she says, a hint of panic in her voice. Her reputation is on the line, too. If Hilleary looks stupid, he won't be the only one.

Now their attention is diverted to the television. A fracas has broken out on the floor. Second-term Republican from Ohio Martin Hoke is speaking against the Democrats' amendment, which he has called "cynical" and "hypocritical." If there's one thing members get a little touchy about, it's being called names on the House floor. Hoke, who seems to have a problem with saying the wrong thing at the wrong time, is perhaps best known for a lascivious remark he made during his first term in office. While he was waiting to do an interview with an Ohio TV station, he commented to another Ohio congressman standing next to him that a female producer setting up the equipment had large breasts, or, as he put it, "beeeg breasts." What Hoke didn't realize was that his mike was on. The incident was subsequently widely reported both in Washington and Ohio.

On the floor Hoke is saying that he had a conversation with John Dingell, who told him that although he is offering a term limits amendment, he intends to vote against term limits on final passage. "Now, if that is not a cynical manipulation and exploitation of the American public, then what is? What could be more cynical? What could be more hypocritical?" asks Hoke. Dingell, feigning a good case of moral outrage, demands that Hoke's remarks be "taken down," or stricken from the record. Hoke agrees to withdraw the word "hypocritical." Dingell asks, "What about the word 'cynical'?" Hoke further agrees to withdraw that word in direct reference to Dingell. But Dingell is not yet satisfied. He asks Hoke if he also intended to apologize. "No, I did not," Hoke responds. Dingell strongly objects.

The clerk is directed to read what Hoke has just said, so that everyone can be sure they heard it. Peter Torkildsen, a second-term Republican from Massachusetts who is presiding in the Speaker's chair, then rules that "ascribing hypocrisy to another member has been ruled out of order in the past and is unparliamentary," and he orders the remarks stricken from the record. But Dingell is still waiting for an apology from Hoke. The Democrats ask for a recorded vote on whether Hoke should be permitted to proceed with his speech on term limits unless he apologizes. The buzzer sounds, calling the members to the floor for the vote.

In Hilleary's office there is jubilation. Todd springs from his chair, claps his hands together, and screams, "Yes. All right." Several Tennessee television stations have asked to do live interviews with Hilleary at the top of their newscasts at 6 P.M., and Todd desperately wants to accommodate them. But the way things were going, it looked like Hilleary would be on the floor managing his amendment at that time. The brouhaha over Hoke's remark will bog down floor action and delay things. "This gives us a shot, but one more shenanigan ensures it," says Todd. Hilleary looks over at him and deadpans, "Should I try to get someone to pull the fire alarm?"

In the Speaker's Lobby outside the chamber, Dingell is holding court, surrounded by a circle of reporters. He is trying to suppress a mischievous smile that keeps creeping onto his face. Asked if he really thinks retroactive term limits are the best approach, he responds, "They seem like a good idea." Inside the chamber, members are swarming all over the floor, and there is a debate between the Democrats, who lost the recorded vote, and the chair over whether Hoke should be permitted to continue. Hoke is huddling with some senior Republicans who are undoubtedly encouraging him to apologize so things can move on.

Hoke asks to be recognized. He tells "the gentleman from Michigan" that what has occurred is unfortunate. "And certainly, there was no intent on my part, not now, not during the debate, not in the future, to make comments that would be taken personally by you in an offensive way, and to whatever extent you perceived them in that way, I am sorry and I apologize." There is applause from the Democratic side of the aisle, and Dingell accepts Hoke's apology. Hoke proceeds with his speech about term limits, and most of the members immediately leave the floor. The excitement over, the members head back to their offices, and the speeches for and against term limits proceed in order. A dozen or so members remain on the floor.

Hilleary, in his office, is trying to put out a small fire involving Zach Wamp, another freshman Republican from Tennessee. Despite having a fairly colorful past, Wamp managed to win the seat vacated by retiring Democrat Marilyn Lloyd, who had served in the House for 20 years. The 38-year-old Wamp admitted during his first challenge of Lloyd in 1992 that he was addicted to cocaine when he was younger. He also was arrested in 1983 for disorderly conduct at a Chattanooga bar. But as a born-again Christian, married and with two children, Wamp says he has put his reckless past behind him.

Since arriving in Congress, the colorful Wamp appears to have relished the attention he's been getting. *Newsweek* has been following him regularly during the first 100 days. There's a bit of a competition between Hilleary and Wamp, and some Tennessee political observers say they are surprised in the early days of the session that the reserved Hilleary seems to be getting more national publicity than the flamboyant Wamp.

Wamp introduced his own term limits bill, but his measure will not be getting a vote. Wamp has asked for two minutes of Hilleary's floor time to speak on behalf of Hilleary's amendment. Wamp's staff has been told that there's only one minute to spare, but they insist he has so much to say that he needs two minutes. Hilleary's staff suspects Wamp may be planning to try to upstage their boss in some way and have suggested to Hilleary that he not give Wamp any time at all. Hilleary decides that Wamp will get one minute, just like most of the others speaking on his behalf.

*   *   *

At 2:15 Judiciary Committee chairman Henry Hyde takes to the floor for what will be the rhetorical high point of the day. "I just cannot be an accessory to the dumbing down of democracy," Hyde begins his anti–term limits speech. He quotes from Saint Augustine, former Supreme Court justice Earl Warren, George Orwell, and Edmund Burke. Hyde, who has served in Congress for 21 years, dismisses term limits as a "radical distrust of democracy" that is "devoid of the hope and the optimism that built this country." He goes on, "I will not concede to the angry, pessimistic populism that drives this movement because it is just dead wrong. Our negative campaigning, our mudslinging, our name-calling has made anger the national recreation. But that is our fault, not the system's. America needs leaders. It needs statesmen. It needs giants, and you do not get them out of the phone book."

Hyde tells a story about the many appearances members of Congress are asked to make. "It is 11:30 at night, and it is January, and the snow is whirling outside the window. And I am in a banquet hall. I am at my one-millionth banquet. I am sitting there as we are honoring the mayor of one of my local towns, and they have not even introduced the commissioner of streets yet. And I am exhausted. And I look out the window at the snowstorm, and I wonder where my opponent is. He does not even know he is my opponent. He is home, stroking his collie dog, smoking a Macanudo, sipping from a snifter of Courvoisier, and watching an R-rated movie on cable. But I am at that banquet." It's not really clear what this has to do with term limits, but Hyde tells the story with great panache.

Hyde then recalls attending the 50th anniversary of D day in Normandy with other members of Congress, including Bob Dole, Bob Michel, Sam Gibbons, and John Dingell, all of whom fought in World War II. "Fifty years ago our country needed us, and we came running. I think our country still needs us. Why do you want to stop us from running? Why do you want to drive experience into obscurity?"

Hyde's passionate speech draws a standing ovation on both sides of the aisle and applause from the gallery. Hyde doesn't care much for the freshmen and their amendment and will be quoted the next day in the *Washington Post,* saying, "John Dingell is a better congressman in his little finger than any of these people."

While Hyde is finishing his speech, Hilleary heads to the floor to make a presentation. In the underground tunnel that leads from the House office buildings to the Capitol, he runs into Wamp, who tells him that he'll be speaking for two minutes on Hilleary's amendment. "You've got a minute," Hilleary says, in a tone devoid of any inflection. "Gee, I've got a lot to say; I'll have to talk fast," Wamp tells him. And looking at the reporter who is walking with Hilleary, Wamp adds, "I guarantee you what I have to say in my minute will make the national news." Hilleary says nothing to Wamp; he just keeps walking. He arrives on the floor and begins his prepared speech. Hilleary tells the members they are about to make a historic vote and even if they fall short of the votes they need, "We have still made a huge down payment on the concept of term limits." He tells fellow members, "With all due respect, I firmly believe that none of us are irreplaceable, and as proud as I am of our freshman class, none of us need to be here for the next 20 or 30 years."

At his desk Todd is drafting the press release that he will send out immediately after the final term limits vote. It begins, "Those of us who favor term limits took a big step forward tonight. Although we weren't able to pass term limits, we succeeded in flushing out the pretenders."

"The rumor running around the floor is maybe 230 for final passage," Hilleary tells his staff when he returns to the office. Hilleary appears down. "We're going to lose, and we worked night and day like dogs." But Morse and Hirschmann have a surprise they think will cheer him up: "Guess who's going to speak on your bill? Dick Armey."

"Can we get him to say Van's the first freshman to offer a constitutional amendment since 1897?" Todd says in the manner of a child who is asking his parents for a puppy: "Can we? Can we?" He has been calling Tennessee reporters all day informing them of this fact, which he dug up through an inquiry to the Library of Congress. "No, I'm not going to blow my own horn up here," Hilleary responds firmly. "You can do it back in the district if you want."

On the floor, consideration of the Democratic amendment has begun. McCollum has asked Hilleary to speak against it and sign a letter sent to other Republicans asking them not to vote for it, but as he walks over to the chamber, Hilleary still hasn't decided how he's going to vote. Hilleary makes a short and uninspired speech. "Just as retroactivity in the tax code is a bad idea, it is also a very bad idea in the term limits area," he says.

"My heart wasn't in it," he admits as he walks off the floor. "I guess I kind of have to vote against it, but I'm not sure what I'm going to do." The vote on the Democratic amendment comes 20 minutes later. Only 135 members vote yes; 54 of them are Republicans and 31 are GOP freshmen, including Lindsey Graham, who clashed with the Speaker over the issue. He has disobeyed Gingrich and voted in favor of the Democrats' retroactive amendment to prove his unswerving commitment to term limits. But Hilleary does not vote in favor of the Democratic amendment.

*   *   *

Since coming to Congress, Hilleary had not spoken on the floor of the House for more than a total of about 10 minutes, and now he's managing his own constitutional amendment. "You're doing fine" on floor speeches, Todd assures Hilleary. "I'd like to try and do a little better than fine," Hilleary responds. Shortly before 6 P.M., Hilleary, Todd, and Morse head over to the Republican National Committee communications center in the basement of a building half a block from his office to do the two local TV interviews Todd was so worried about earlier. "If it wasn't for Martin Hoke, we wouldn't have been on TV in Knoxville," says Todd with a grin.

Hilleary's campaign account is picking up the $230 tab for the satellite time. Hilleary will be shown at the top of the newscasts, being interviewed by the local anchors. As soon as the interviews are over, it's back to the office. Hilleary, Todd, Morse, and Hirschmann powwow. Hilleary's amendment will be up soon. "Let's go over possible attacks," Hilleary says. "Do not answer a Democratic question on your time; you do not have any time," Hirschmann says. "You cannot be polite," Todd reinforces. "You know this issue; you're ready," Hirschmann tells him reassuringly. Hilleary asks to be alone; he wants to focus and psyche himself up. He goes into his private office and shuts the door.

When he opens the door a few minutes later, he looks calm. "I'm ready. I'm excited," he says. Morse, carrying a large stack of papers and several large, black, three-ring binders, goes with him to the floor; Todd heads up to the press gallery to watch from there and to do a little spinning of reporters. When Hilleary arrives in the chamber, McCollum is sitting on the Democratic side of the aisle talking to Barney Frank. Something is up. Members are milling around and talking after the last vote. The chair attempts to quiet them as Hilleary stands up to be recognized: "Mr. Chairman, I offer an amendment in the nature of a substitute." The clerk reads Hilleary's amendment. "Mr. Chairman, tonight I am offering an amendment to protect the rights of individual states to impose term limit restrictions." Hilleary refers to the millions of people who fought for term limits measures around the country. "We have the opportunity either to protect the hard work of those people or turn our backs on them."

John Conyers, a Michigan Democrat in his 16th term, is managing the time for those who will be speaking against Hilleary. "Do you have any idea what kind of chaos we are suggesting under a term limitation of this nature?" Conyers asks. "This takes the cake. . . . I think it would become a nightmare that we would not want to contemplate." He suggests that states could even choose to adopt a two- or one-year limit under Hilleary's amendment.

The first to speak on behalf of Hilleary is Sue Myrick. She says the amendment would honor the promise made in the Contract with America that "House Republicans respect the rights of the states and respect the rights of citizens to limit the terms of their elected officials."

Wamp steps up to the podium. "I have some friendly advice for some of the senior members of this body from both sides of the aisle. If you think your seat in Congress belongs to you and not the people, it's time for you to go home. . . . You can vote against term limits this year, and the folks back home can vote against you next year." Whatever Wamp meant earlier about how newsworthy his speech would be is not apparent.

One after another the speeches go on, alternating between a Democrat speaking against and a Republican speaking for. George Nethercutt reminds the members that he was helped in his defeat of Tom Foley by Foley's opposition to term limits. "We freshmen have come to Washington to change the status quo, to be different than our predecessors. . . . I urge my colleagues to remember the mandate of election day 1994. Vote yes on the Hilleary amendment."

Barney Frank is next. He says he will be voting against term limits for one overriding reason: "I believe in democracy, in representative democracy, untrammeled, unrestricted, unrestrained. . . . Democracy is not simply what a given majority in a public opinion poll thinks at a given time. It is an entire structure of government."

During Frank's speech, McCollum kneels next to Hilleary. He tells him that he plans to speak against his amendment. This is what Hilleary had feared but not expected. He has to decide whether to respond to McCollum's remarks or let them go.

McCollum walks to the well of the House. "I rise here tonight reluctantly to oppose the Hilleary amendment." A murmur seems to sweep through the group of freshmen who have been sitting a row behind Hilleary for most of the debate, offering silent moral support. He is one of them, and it is unthinkable that a Republican, a Republican who has been championing the cause of term limits for years, would choose to speak against their measure, to give the Democrats ammunition.

McCollum says he will vote against Hilleary's amendment. Hilleary stands, his hands gripping the sides of a small lectern, his face expressionless. McCollum says the Hilleary amendment would create a "hodgepodge" of different limits for different states, disadvantaging those states that set lower limits and weakening members of the House in relation to senators, who would be permitted to serve 12 years. But McCollum seems to want to give himself an escape hatch, to have it both ways. He says, "If indeed the Supreme Court decides that the states currently have the right to do what they have been doing, then so be it. I am silent on it; the base bill is silent on it. But I must, as I say, oppose this now." McCollum concludes, "I urge a no vote on the Hilleary amendment."

It is clear this is no longer about term limits. This is about pride and ambition, about coming out on top, about winning. This is politics.

Morse, who is seated directly behind Hilleary, is urging his boss to fight back. "Get him, get him," he whispers loudly. There is the briefest pause, and Hilleary says, "Mr. Chairman, I yield two minutes to the gentleman from Kansas," referring to Sam Brownback. Hilleary has decided not to respond, to let it pass. But behind him the other freshmen are conferring; they cannot let this insult go unanswered. They are fiercely loyal to one another and protect their own.

"My comments will probably not be as eloquent as a number of the other people on the other side of the aisle that have been here quite a bit longer than we have. This is primarily a freshman initiative and one that we are putting forward, and so we do not, perhaps, have quite the number of years of experience that a number of other people do in this body," Brownback begins, in what appears to be an indirect response to McCollum. It's as if he were saying, "We may be new at this, but we sure put a scare in you, didn't we?" When Brownback finishes, the freshmen make their move. If McCollum thought he was going to go unanswered, he was wrong. Jon Christensen, a Nebraska insurance agent who never held political office before his election to the House, announces that although he was an original cosponsor on the McCollum bill, since the McCollum bill takes away states' rights he will be voting against it.

Matt Salmon, a freshman who served four years in the Arizona Senate before being elected to Congress, is next. He begins by saying that Hilleary "has put together a coalition, I believe, that is the envy of everybody in this body in a very, very short time." Salmon says he does not know whether the Founding Fathers would have opposed the idea of limiting the terms of members; "I was not there, did not even get the T-shirt, but I will tell my colleagues this: The Founding Fathers never envisioned a Congress like this that has plunged this country $5 trillion into debt. The American people deserve better."

A few more freshmen speak for the amendment, but as the time winds down and the vote approaches, Armey does not appear in the chamber. He won't show up as he promised he would. Hilleary begins his closing statement.

"I stand here and represent the thousands of Americans who stood out in parking lots, gathered petitions, signatures, in sweltering summer heat in Arizona, Oklahoma, and California, in the frosty weekend mornings in the Northeast and the rainy afternoons in the Pacific Northwest. Those people who have already fought and won the term limit wars in 22 states did not get involved because they were Republicans or Democrats or liberals or conservatives. They got involved because they were not happy with the government they were getting. They thought the Congress was too permanent and too arrogant. They saw a problem and were willing to do something about it. Now we have a chance to join together in a bipartisan manner to honor that work. With this freshman term limits amendment, we have a chance to tell people who voted for term limits this Congress is different. This Congress heard your concerns and respected your wishes. Or we can tell the people in 22 states that they do not know what they are doing."

When he finishes, the freshmen, who have remained on the floor, stand and applaud. They are visibly proud. Democratic whip David Bonior has been sitting on his side of the aisle taking it all in. He looks from Hilleary to the row of freshmen behind him and back again at Hilleary. The chair calls for a voice vote. All those in favor say "aye." Rules chairman Gerald Solomon, who's been in Congress for 17 years, has been pacing in the well. He screams "aye" almost loud enough to drown out all the others. All those opposed say "no." A chorus of noes. The ayes have it, the chair rules. "The ayes have it. We won," yells Solomon, who gives a little leap and thrusts his fist into the air in a gesture of victory. This is a typical Solomon move. Hilleary calls Solomon "a soulmate of the freshman class. You know how puppies run around the yard and old dogs lie on the porch? Well, he runs around. He's great."

The voice vote, however, is just pro forma. A recorded vote is called for. The buzzer sounds. The freshmen take up their positions at the doors to hand out flyers urging a yes vote. Matt Salmon is in the back; David McIntosh, Lindsey Graham, and Randy Tate of Washington stand on the Democratic side; and Hilleary and McCollum stand on either side of the door leading to the Republican side of the chamber. As the members file in, McCollum, the father of term limits, urges them to vote no on Hilleary's amendment. "This is going down," he says sharply.

The result is announced: 164 in favor, 265 opposed. Hilleary's amendment has been defeated. It's over. Members begin to come up to Hilleary to congratulate him, to tell him he did a good job. Hilleary shakes Morse's hand. They gather their papers and move to the back of the chamber.

Now it's McCollum's turn. "This is *the* term limits vote," McCollum tells the members. He doesn't want anyone to be confused. He wants to make it clear that everything until now was just preliminary; this is the main event. Several Republicans rise to speak for McCollum. And then a surprise: Salmon is introduced by Conyers. He is speaking on the Democrats' time.

"We have had three amendments so far tonight on term limits. I voted for every one of them." No one in the House is a more ardent supporter of term limits than Salmon. One of the first things he did when he was elected to the Arizona legislature was to sponsor a term limits law. But what McCollum has done has pushed Salmon too far. He mentions the Arizona term limits initiative, which passed with 74 percent of the vote. "I, in good conscience, cannot come to this body and say, 'Arizona voters, you do not know what you were doing. We know better than you. We are the font of all knowledge in this hallowed place.' . . . It is for that reason, even though I support strongly the concept of term limits, I cannot sell Arizona voters down the river on this issue." McCollum has lost both Salmon's and Christensen's votes.

Barney Frank stands to close for the Democrats. He uses all the arguments McCollum has handed him. "I congratulate the Republican leadership because they have outmaneuvered the U.S. Term Limits people. They have gotten where they wanted to be." Why did 90 Republicans vote against the Hilleary amendment? Frank asks; "because the Hilleary amendment differed from this one in one particular: It explicitly allowed the states to do what they want. . . . How are you going to claim to wrap yourself in the mantle of pure democracy and public opinion when you will be overruling the states?" Frank continues with a reference to the block grant approach so popular with the Republicans for social programs. "I have heard the gentleman from Florida [McCollum] say it: 'This is too important to be left to the states to make their own decisions. We have to state it uniformly.' . . . This is not poor people's income, some trivial subject like that. This is not whether or not kids get enough to eat. This is our careers. We cannot allow that to be done on a state-by-state basis."

Gingrich has appeared on the floor. Hilleary walks up to him and tells the Speaker, "I think what you say will turn it around." If he really believes that, he's surely the only one who does. Gingrich asks Hilleary how many votes he got and informs him that there will be a press conference upstairs after the vote before quickly moving on.

Frank, who is still speaking, acknowledges Gingrich's presence while pointing out that "the members of the leadership have been as scarce on the floor of this House as it is possible to be. . . . They were not on this floor for 12 seconds today; not one of them spoke."

But one of them is about to. Gingrich walks to the well of the House. "I believe this is a historic vote. I have been frankly surprised by our friends on the left. I would have thought, having been defeated last fall for the first time in 40 years, that paying some attention to the American people would have been useful," he says. "Everywhere in America the people say they are sick of the professional politicians; they are tired of those who use the taxpayers' money to stay entrenched, and they want to find a device to take power back from the professional political class," says

Gingrich. He promises that if the Republicans retain a majority in the House next year, term limits will be the first vote taken by the 105th Congress. "If the Democratic Party tonight defeats term limits, the contract may have been postponed in one of its 10 items, but it will be back."

The Democrats do defeat term limits. But they are helped by 40 Republicans. The McCollum amendment receives a majority, 227 votes to 204 opposed, but it is still more than 60 votes short of the two-thirds required for amendments to the Constitution.

Outside the chamber, Todd is pacing back and forth waiting for his boss. He can barely control himself. "I can't believe McCollum spoke against us. That is the lowest form of low. They were saying we weren't a team player. Well, who's a team player now?" He practically spits out the words. McCollum's move has not escaped the notice of the term limits proponents who have gathered out in the hall either. "You behaved like a real gentleman," Cleta Mitchell, head of the Term Limits Legal Institute, tells Hilleary as he comes off the floor.

The Republican leaders head upstairs for a news conference in the House radio-TV gallery. Gingrich begins by predicting that with every member of the House on record for or against term limits, it will be "a major issue in the '96 campaign. This issue is not going to go away."

But in fact it does. Hardly a peep will be made about term limits in the 1996 campaign. The voters' ardor appears to have cooled. Although opinion polls show upward of 75 percent of people like the idea of term limits, their support is not very deep. There is almost no public reaction when term limits legislation fails in the House. In fact the most reaction comes from the Democrats, who are thrilled that they can finally point to an item in the contract that the Republicans have not been able to pass.

Hilleary seems more relieved it's over than anything else. "Free at last, free at last, thank God Almighty, I'm free at last," he says as he walks through the underground tunnel back to his office after the news conference. "Y'all are the greatest," Hilleary tells his staff when he returns to his office.

"I think Van made a good impression on this. He picked up a lot of votes in a short amount of time. The Democrats didn't come around, and the senior Republicans weren't there—that's what killed us," says Todd. He is still clearly steamed over McCollum's speaking against Hilleary, which he thinks showed very bad form. "Van was magnanimous to the end. You saw two very different styles of leadership tonight," he says, his jaw tight. Todd also predicts that the freshmen will remember the move. "They're still at an impressionable stage."

Alone in his office, Hilleary reflects on what just happened. He says when McCollum came up to him on the floor and told him he was going to speak against his bill, "I said I thought that was counterproductive. I told him we don't want the spin to be Republican against Republican. The spin should be Democrats killed this measure. He can count votes as good as I can; he knew ours wasn't going to get the most. What was the point?" Hilleary thought about answering McCollum by saying,

"Well, you know, Bill, I'm just trying to protect the Florida voters" who have passed an eight-year term limits measure. "I could have said that, but what purpose would it have served? Those clips would have made the news. It's much juicier to have Republicans beating up on Republicans." So Hilleary decided to "take the bullet" and move on.

Hilleary thinks McCollum's maneuver perfectly illustrates why term limits are so badly needed. "We've got people who've been here so long, they know better than the voters." But he doesn't seem interested in dwelling on it. "We're all big boys," he says matter-of-factly.

The energetic, irrepressible, 37-year-old Salmon is not as forgiving, however. While waiting for Hilleary to finish taping a television interview in the members' recording studio a little bit later, Salmon can barely contain himself. Salmon says when he arrived in Washington he handed the clerk of the House his resignation, dated January 2001. In accordance with the wishes of the voters of Arizona, he will serve only six years, he says. "I support term limits emphatically. But when McCollum got up and spoke against Van's amendment, I decided all bets were off. If he can speak his mind, I can speak mine. I know the leadership wasn't happy with me, but they didn't elect me; my voters did," says Salmon, the words tumbling out almost faster than he can say them. Salmon says the freshmen have to stick together. "We take it personal when one of our own gets chopped up. We've been through a lot. Unlike some Republicans, we took it [the Contract with America] seriously. We haven't been here long enough to think our word is not our word."

Hilleary and Todd walk back toward the office and are stopped in the hall by John Shadegg and Steve Largent. They tell Hilleary he did a good job and comment on McCollum's speaking against his amendment. "That was low," says Largent. Both men say they can't figure out why McCollum did it.

*   *   *

When Hilleary first arrived in Washington, he thought, "If you had a good idea, you could submit a bill, talk it up, and get it passed." He soon discovered it's not that simple. "You can't just show up to the game and expect to win." Doing term limits taught Hilleary there are "all kinds of roadblocks" to getting legislation through Congress, many of which have nothing to do with the merits of the bill.

"Part of it was sheer nuts-and-bolts politics. Bill McCollum had been at it longer. He started out with 150 cosponsors; I started out with zero. We were nobody from nowhere. It was amateur hour. We were doing everything for the first time and just going by the seat of our pants." But Hilleary's youthful exuberance and inexperience were probably why he managed to get as far as he did.

When Newt Gingrich first heard about Hilleary's amendment, he told me he thought, "Here was a guy with a good idea; here was a guy who was impatient and aggressive. I wasn't tremendously helpful to him at first. I figured it was his problem to figure out how to make it work—and he did." Gingrich said Hilleary really had to keep pushing to get a vote, and that impressed him. "He's smart, and he's got guts. It wasn't easy for him to be in some of those rooms and get knocked on his tail and get back up." And Hilleary managed to do it without appearing arrogant. "He was tactful and diplomatic in his persistence. He didn't come off as stubborn and pigheaded," recalled Dick Armey.

But it's time for the spotlight to shift to someone else as the House moves on to deal with the Republican tax-cut proposal. The clock has struck midnight, the coach has turned into a pumpkin, and Hilleary is back to being just one of 73 freshmen. He senses this Wednesday night as he watches his staff reacting to all the media attention. "I hope they get their fill of it, because they won't be seeing it for a while," he says.

Back in the district over the weekend, he participates in Mule Day, an annual Tennessee Republican event, and gets a reality check. Going back home "in the afterglow of the publicity" from term limits was great at first. People mentioned his picture in *Newsweek* and seeing him on the NBC news. Then someone came up to him and said he'd written a letter to his office about a problem and wanted to know why he hadn't got a response yet. And a local Republican official admonished Hilleary to "make sure you pay attention to the mail."

Hilleary says trying to push his amendment proved to be "a monumental undertaking for our little old staff," greatly interfering with the district work, much of which he characterizes as "getting cats out of trees." That kind of stuff may be "a lot less sexy, but they're the things you've got to do to get reelected." And term limits or no term limits, he and the other freshmen are thinking about that already.

There are members who just take care of home stuff and "vote right with their district," rarely cosponsoring legislation or speaking on the floor. "It's not my total definition of being a congressman, but it is some folks', and who am I to argue with them?" he asks. He's observed that most senior Tennessee House members take this sort of approach to the job. "They cast that last vote, and they're like greased lightning to the airport, and they stay home until the last minute," says Hilleary. Then there are other members who really try to become national players and move legislation. Hilleary would like to do both, but by necessity, at least at this point in his career, it's clear he's going to have to pay more attention to the folks back home.

5

MR. HILLEARY GOES TO WASHINGTON

VAN HILLEARY'S HOMETOWN of Spring City in east Tennessee has a population of just over 2,000. Hilleary thinks it's a lot like Mayberry, Andy Griffith's fictional North Carolina hometown. Just like Mayberry, everybody seems to know everybody else in Spring City. When Hilleary was growing up, there were only one doctor, one dentist, one pharmacist, and three traffic lights, although Hilleary says the lights never all worked at the same time.

He was christened William Vanderpool Hilleary. But since both his father and grandfather were named William, his mother, Evelyn, thought one more Bill in the family would be too confusing. She simply shortened her maiden name, Vanderpool, to Van and started calling him that right from the start.

By all accounts Hilleary was a clean-cut, well-behaved youth who shunned teenage rebellion and planned for a military career. At the end of his freshman year in high school, he was first in his class but "decided being popular was more important," so he started spending more time socializing than studying and ended up 14th in a class of about 200 when he graduated from Rhea County High School.

He is the oldest of four children, three boys and a girl. His mother, who was from Nashville, sought to instill culture and a wider sense of the world in her children, and she insisted that her sons take ballet classes at Spring City's storefront dance studio. The well-meaning experiment didn't last long. It is with great fondness that Hilleary talks about his childhood and his parents, who were active in local affairs. His Republican father served on the county commission for eight years. His mother served on the school board, not because she was particularly political but because she felt the local schools needed improvement and she wanted to make sure that happened.

He is the only one among his siblings who has not married. Coming from a district where people tend to marry young—very young—Hilleary's bachelorhood has raised a few eyebrows. "If you're single and in your 30s where I come from, it's kind of an issue. It's not an automatic, 'There must be something wrong with that boy'; it's just an undertone." When he unsuccessfully ran for the state senate in 1992, he heard stories about his being "a womanizer on one end of the district and a homosexual on the other end." But when he ran for Congress, his 32-year-old Democratic opponent was single as well, so the issue disappeared.

Although he is not married, Hilleary firmly believes in the traditional nuclear family, with a father who works and a mother who stays home with the kids. And he believes that to a certain extent the federal government, through affirmative action and government contract preferences that favor firms run by minorities and women, "has artificially taken women out of the home" much faster than would have happened otherwise. Hilleary is not a proponent of affirmative action. He concedes it may have had a purpose 20 years ago, but now "to say black people should be given special privileges is wrong. I think we went too far in the other direction."

Asked for an example of something that moved him politically in college, Hilleary can think only of the court decision to force local civic clubs like the Rotary and Jaycees to admit women. Hilleary says he strongly disagreed with the decision and felt the federal government was intruding into the affairs of private institutions. He describes the court's ruling not as restoring someone's rights but taking away the rights of these groups to function as they choose. "How far do you take it? Do you force entry into someone's tree house? You've got to be careful when you start playing God and taking away someone else's individual rights."

Hilleary says this nation's welfare policies have "gone too far" and "subsidized the breakup of the family. . . . I don't think any welfare check will ever be a substitute for a parent." He is convinced welfare subsidizes illegitimacy and insists welfare has "gone from helping people who can't help themselves to buying votes" for the Democrats. He believes in discipline and rules and thinks the answers to many of this country's problems are actually quite simple, nothing a good dose of discipline and self-denial wouldn't fix. People on welfare need to pull themselves up by their bootstraps and get to work.

Hilleary considers himself a businessman, not a political theorist, and he is impatient with questions about political philosophy. He cannot point to any seminal experience or defining moment that helped to shape his views. He just is the way he is. "I grew up in a family with a basic set of principles, and it's been a guide throughout life—and politics is just life."

As Hilleary sees it, government has only about four legitimate functions: to provide a national defense; to be a referee in the business arena when it comes to things like competition and monopolies; to regulate public utilities and the stock market; and to help those who cannot help themselves (and he emphasizes that means only the elderly and people who are mentally, physically, or emotionally handicapped). "I see very little obligation for government to do anything else," he says. Hilleary thinks balancing the budget is "so much more important than anything else we're doing up here" that it will correct some of the recent excesses of government.

Hilleary recalls that in college he believed Ronald Reagan "personified everything that made America good. I remember watching Reagan's speeches and thinking he was just wonderful." Reagan was tough on the Soviets and talked about shrinking government. But Reagan did not come through on his promise to cut programs and scale back government, and the deficit grew at its fastest rate in history during his presidency. Hilleary was "very disappointed" that Reagan didn't use some of the political capital he earned through his popularity to finish the job he started. "All we ever got to was rhetoric on spending cuts," says Hilleary. His class of freshmen arrived in Congress to do what Reagan couldn't or wouldn't.

At the University of Tennessee in Knoxville, Hilleary majored in business administration but really didn't give too much thought to his future except that he knew he wanted to be an Air Force pilot. For as long as Hilleary can remember, he wanted to fly planes. He took ROTC more seriously than his studies. Although he was just an average student, he was named the outstanding ROTC squadron commander in the nation while he was in college. "Van was ROTC all the way; he was very gung ho," recalls Andy Hoover, who attended the University of Tennessee with Hilleary and was a member of the same fraternity, Sigma Chi. Hoover, too, ran for Tennessee's Fourth District congressional seat in 1994. But he ran as a Democrat and failed to win the nomination. Hoover was president of the college Democrats at UT and took a lot of ribbing for being the only Democrat in his fraternity. Hoover recalls that Hilleary was very earnest in college, his strong conservative beliefs already evident. Hilleary was "a Republican to the bone; he was to the right of Reagan," even in college. "He's the only fraternity brother that I remember who brought up abortion at the lunch table. He was strongly against it," says Hoover. For his part, Hilleary insists he was essentially apolitical in college.

After graduation Hilleary went off to pilot training school. This was his lifelong dream. He loved it. But when it came time to decide who would be staying on, Hilleary didn't make the cut. He wasn't good at juggling three things at once the way a fighter pilot must. He was shattered. To this day it remains the failure Hilleary cannot accept and cannot talk about. He is convinced he could have done it if they had just given him more time. But his learning curve was not fast enough for the Air Force. "I don't think I would have been Chuck Yaeger, but I think I would have been an adequate pilot."

What followed was the worst time of Hilleary's life. He was not going to be able to do the only thing he had ever really wanted. "It was the first time in my life I put everything I had into something and utterly failed, and it was devastating. I didn't know what to do."

He was given a choice: He could remain in the Air Force or he could leave the service. They gave him two weeks to think about it. He went back to Spring City. He had no idea what he was going to do. He didn't talk much. He was depressed. He didn't shave. That was it: That was pretty much how this extremely controlled soldier expressed his disappointment and frustration—by not shaving. At the end of the two weeks, Hilleary came up with another option. He decided to leave the Air Force but join the reserve, because a full-time career in the Air Force that did not involve being a pilot just wasn't for him. "Navigators are rarely given the opportunity for command," and it's impossible to make general unless you're a pilot, says Hilleary. He had planned to be a general.

He went to work for his father at the mill, started on a master's degree in public administration at the University of Tennessee that he never finished, then decided to go to law school at Samford University in Birmingham. But nothing quite clicked. After getting his law degree, he didn't really want to practice law, so it was back to the plant. What Hilleary recalls most about these years is a complete lack of direction.

He became a C-130 navigator and continued flying with the reserve, which is how he wound up volunteering for two tours of duty during Operation Desert Shield and Desert Storm and spending five months in the Persian Gulf. His first tour of duty was one month. He returned to Tennessee, but he knew they still needed navigators, so he volunteered to go back.

Hilleary is matter-of-fact about the decision. "I felt like the cause was just—and if something happened to me it was no big deal. If I was married and had kids, I probably wouldn't have volunteered."

Three days before Christmas, the call came. "Do you still want to go?" the officer on the other end of the phone asked. "Yes, sir," Hilleary responded. When could he leave? "Well, sir, if at all possible, I hope you can wait until after Christmas." No sooner had he hung up the phone than his mother asked, "Is that what I think it was?" "Yes, ma'am." His mother was inconsolable. "You've ruined our Christmas," she cried. "It was kind of morbid," admits Hilleary. But just the same, he was excited.

Two days after Christmas his parents drove him to the Atlanta airport. There wasn't a single dry eye at the gate. "Mom was crying. And then Dad started crying a little bit, and to see your dad cry kind of messes you up. He told me he wasn't sure I had made a good decision, but he was proud of me for going. Even the woman at the ticket counter was crying."

It was a little like a scene out of the movie *Sergeant York* about the life of Alvin P. York. In the movie Gary Cooper, who plays York, assures his mother as he leaves for the European front, "I'll be a-comin' back," then rides off on a mule. York, who won the Medal of Honor for capturing 132 German prisoners in a single battle during World War I, was born and lived his entire life on the Cumberland Plateau in northeastern Tennessee, in Hilleary's congressional district.

For four months, Hilleary flew combat support missions on a C-130, usually hauling cargo. It was "pretty boring for the most part," except for one trip, to deliver food to some Iraqi prisoners held on the Saudi-Iraqi border. It was the end of an 18-hour day and the entire crew was dead tired. The sky was dark with smoke from burning oil wells. They managed to find the airfield, but the smoke was too thick to make a safe landing. After about four attempts, the crew decided to turn around.

But then a call came over the radio. Three U.S. marines had stepped on a land mine and were critically injured. "You guys are the only ones who can take them to a field hospital." The plane turned around. Its radar wasn't working, its altimeter wasn't working, but they kept circling, getting lower and lower. It was impossible to see anything. The fifth time the smoke cleared and they could see a dirt landing strip. The only illumination came from "a guy on a motorcycle holding a light." The pilot hit the landing strip so hard it set off the plane's crash alert instruments. They "came to a halt at the far end of the runway—just like in the movies." One of the marines they picked up didn't make it, but the other two pulled through. Hilleary and the rest of the crew were named the "Air Force Reserve Crew of the Year" by the Reserve Officers Association. And like Sergeant York, Hilleary returned to Tennessee. But whereas York was met by his congressman when he returned from war, Hilleary decided to become one.

Hilleary's first political race was in 1992 for the state senate against a Tennessee institution, Anna Belle Clement O'Brien, or, as she is known by everyone, Miss Anna Belle. At 71, with a head of flaming red hair and an outspokenness to match, Miss Anna Belle is a formidable woman and definitely no stereotypical southern belle. She comes from a famous Tennessee Democratic family. Her brother Frank Clement was governor of Tennessee in the late 1950s and early 1960s. She met her husband, who was then in the state senate, while she was working in the governor's office. Charles O'Brien later became a judge and then chief justice of the state supreme court. Clement's nephew Bob has represented the Fifth District of Tennessee in Congress since 1988, and her niece Sara Kyle is on the state public service commission.

In 1974 Miss Anna Belle won her first public office when she was elected to the Tennessee House. She served one term there followed by 20 years in the state senate. Although she didn't know Hilleary when he announced his challenge to her, she knew of his family. Hilleary recalls telling people he had "less than a 50-50 chance but more than a shot in the dark." It was an uphill battle to say the least. Here was a 33-year-old nobody taking on Miss Anna Belle. "It was us against the world. I'd be shaking hands at a Wal-Mart, and I'd have people come up and want to fight me." On election day, out of 55,000 votes cast, Hilleary managed to come within 1,300 votes of defeating O'Brien. He outpolled her in three of the district's six counties, including a narrow win in her home county. The performance far exceeded expectations. But Hilleary was just "relieved it was over"; all he wanted to do was go home and go to bed. "We were so tired. I hadn't slept in two days."

O'Brien says from Hilleary's perspective it certainly worked out for the best. "If he had defeated me, he wouldn't be in Washington. He owes me a debt of gratitude. He ought to be tickled to death; in fact he ought to be one of my best friends." Point well taken, says Hilleary with a smile.

And it was during the campaign against Miss Anna Belle that Hilleary discovered something about himself: that he was actually good at politics. He can listen to strangers and make a connection. He can tell them what he thinks should be done and convince them he's the one to do it. He can make people believe he cares about what they're saying, and often he does. Although he occasionally appears stiff and awkward, this tendency shows up less often in him than in many politicians. If he had made it as a pilot, he may never have discovered this talent for politics.

Howard Baker, who went to college with Hilleary's father, thought Hilleary ran a good race against Miss Anna Belle and two years later encouraged him to try for the Fourth District House seat being vacated by Jim Cooper, who was making a run for the Senate.

In language better suited to a country singing star than a politician, Hilleary's campaign stickers declared, "I'm a Van fan." Jeff Whorley, the Democrat who faced Hilleary in the nasty congressional campaign of 1994, was certainly not one of them. Whorley grew up in the Fourth District, was a graduate of the University of the South in Sewanee, and is the great-grandson of former Tennessee governor John Price Buchanan, but he had spent a long time away from home. For eight years, he worked in Washington for Congressman Bart Gordon of Tennessee's Sixth District and at age 25 became his chief of staff.

That kind of background provided a convenient target for Hilleary, especially in such an anti-Washington year. Many of the freshmen got elected by painting their opponents as out of touch and out of step with their constituents. Before he ran for Congress, Hilleary had been to Washington only once in his life, as a child with his parents. The Hilleary campaign linked Whorley with Gordon and President Clinton. As Whorley recalls it, "They made a huge deal of me as this Washington insider—Jeff Whorley and all his liberal friends. They said if you're for gays in the military and higher taxes, then you've got Bill Clinton's candidate in the race." Hilleary's campaign sent out flyers showing the outside of the Washington condominium building where Whorley owned a studio apartment, calling it a luxury property. And in a year like 1994, even owning property in Washington was construed as somehow evil.

In addition to being tagged a Washington insider, Whorley had to contend with being considered an elitist. A year before the race, he returned home to teach creative writing at the Webb School, the prestigious prep school in Bell Buckle, Tennessee, that he had attended. The Webb School was founded in 1870 by William Robert Webb, a Confederate Army veteran who was known as Old Sawney. The school emphasized the classics, its honor code was used as a model at Princeton University, and in 1920 Webb produced more Rhodes scholars than any other secondary school in America. Woodrow Wilson, when he was president of Princeton University, once commented that "the best prepared boys we get" came from Webb. Hilleary says Webb and Sewanee are atypical of the Fourth District. He considers them to be liberal enclaves that may be physically located in middle Tennessee but are thousands of miles apart from the lifestyle and conservative attitudes of the vast majority of his constituents.

During the campaign Whorley fought back by trying to use Hilleary's background against him. Other than being in the military, the only real job Hilleary ever had before being elected to Congress was at his father's textile mill. Since Hilleary proudly pointed to his business experience, Whorley ran ads that said the Hilleary textile business had gone bankrupt. Hilleary, who was in college at the time of the bankruptcy, says his father lost control of the business in 1978 and the bank that took it over, not the family, decided to put the company into bankruptcy. Hilleary was the third generation of his family to be in the textile business. His great-grandfather was a farmer whose 150-acre farm outside of Spring City is still in the family. His grandfather started Southern Silk Mills in Spring City on the eve of the Great Depression. The mill made fabric for women's lingerie.

Hilleary's father joined the business after serving in the army in World War II. The company grew and diversified into making other fabrics, like the synthetic material used for athletic jerseys. By the early 1970s it employed 900 people. Hilleary's youngest brother, Scott, who now runs the business with his father, says just before the Arab oil embargo hit in the mid-1970s the business underwent a debt-financed expansion, and the rise in oil costs played a big part in the company's financial problems and eventual bankruptcy.

In 1982, four years after he lost the family business, William Hilleary decided to open a new company, SSM Industries. That's when Van went to work with his father. Hilleary says he's an awful lot like his tough-minded, 69-year-old father, which made their working together a bit difficult at times. The firm now has about 65 employees and $10 million in sales. It manufactures cotton and cotton-polyester fleece and jersey material used to make T-shirts and sweatshirts as well as high-performance synthetic fabric used in gloves for fighter pilots, military tank drivers' helmet linings, and survival vests.

Two years before the 1994 election, neither Hilleary nor Whorley was living or voting in the Fourth District. Whorley was still working in Bart Gordon's office in Washington, and Hilleary had moved into O'Brien's state senate district to run against her. Both candidates had to move back to the Fourth District to make the congressional race, but some Democrats tried to make this an issue, labeling Hilleary "moving Van."

The Hilleary-Whorley battle was not only ugly but expensive. Whorley spent even more of his own money than did Hilleary. Whorley personally put up half of the $800,000 he spent on the campaign, although he literally had to mortgage his farm to do it. Whorley credits Hilleary with being a tough, shrewd, dogged campaigner but insists it was the anti-Clinton, anti-Washington tide that won the race for him. "I credit him with seeing the national trend and seizing the opportunity when a dozen other Republicans in the district did not. It's either remarkably good fortune or remarkably good vision or both. Van had the courage to hitch it up and give it a go."

On election night, when he called Hilleary to congratulate him, Whorley told him, "If anyone wants me to testify that you can take a punch, I will." Hilleary's rather ungracious response: "Well, Jeff, that's fine, but you ran a deceitful campaign." He had won, but he still couldn't loosen up, couldn't let it go.

Hilleary received tremendous support from the Christian right, and Whorley contends that Christian conservatives launched a whisper campaign against him. "The

Bible incident," which became part of the lore of the campaign, took place after a debate between Hilleary and Whorley. One of Hilleary's campaign workers who was affiliated with a Christian school had brought some of the students to hear the debate. After it was over, they asked Hilleary to sign the Bibles they had brought with them. Hilleary recalls thinking the request was a little strange but protests, "What was I going to do? Tell them I wouldn't sign their Bibles?"

In a district where religion, almost exclusively conservative Protestantism, is a big factor in people's lives, it tends to intrude on politics. An emphasis on conservative values has helped the Republicans gain support from working people and former Democrats, even in an area as poor as the Fourth District.

The Fourth District of Tennessee was once represented by Cordell Hull, the congressman who greeted Sergeant Alvin York when he came home from Europe. Hull served in the House for 22 years, then briefly in the Senate before becoming Franklin D. Roosevelt's secretary of state in 1933. He served in that post for 11 years, longer than anyone in U.S. history. And as secretary of state he was instrumental in helping to establish the United Nations, for which he won a Nobel Peace Prize in 1945.

The district is 350 miles long and at one point only 6 miles wide. It snakes from the Virginia-Kentucky border in the northeast at Cumberland Gap to the Alabama-Mississippi border in the southwest, near the site where the Civil War battle of Shiloh was fought, and it spans the eastern and central time zones. It contains all three of the distinct regions of Tennessee: the flat western part where cotton is grown and that resembles Alabama and Georgia; the middle part south of Nashville, which is more economically diverse than the rest of the state; and the hardscrabble eastern region, which mostly has the farms and mountains and hollows Tennessee is known for. Many people in the district make their living farming. In the eastern hills tobacco is the number one crop. Nursery shrubs, cattle, and timber are also big in east and middle Tennessee.

There is no large urban center in the Fourth District, just lots of little towns. The largest city is Morristown, with a population of just over 21,000. Campaigning and staying in contact with constituents here involve a lot of driving, primarily on winding, two-lane roads. But these voters expect the personal touch; they want to know their congressman and to have shaken his hand at least once.

Jim Cooper, whose father, Prentice, was governor of Tennessee from 1939 to 1945, represented the Fourth District in Congress for 12 years. A Rhodes scholar with a law degree from Harvard, he was first elected in 1982 when he was 28, the youngest congressman ever to come from Tennessee. In that election he trounced Cissy Baker, the daughter of Howard Baker, who was Senate majority leader at the time. Cooper, a conservative Democrat, was popular in the district, and in 1986 and 1988 the Republicans didn't even field a candidate to run against him. In 1992 Cooper won handily with 64 percent of the vote.

Cooper is a quiet, thoughtful man who obviously considers himself a scholar of Tennessee politics. He claims that to understand what is now the Fourth District you must go all the way back to the Civil War. And he insists that reading V. O. Key Jr.'s landmark *Southern Politics in State and Nation* is essential for a nonsoutherner to achieve that understanding. To quote from the book, first published in 1949, "In 1861 East Tennessee had few slaves and was unionist; West and Middle Tennessee held slaves and Confederate sentiments. Today East Tennessee harbors many Republicans while Middle and West Tennessee are Democratic strongholds."

Cooper maintains the Civil War is still the most seminal event in Tennessee history and that east Tennessee, where Hilleary is from, represents "the most Republican part of America." No Republican candidate has ever lost a congressional race next door to the Fourth District, in the Second, which includes Knoxville and several counties surrounding it. Howard Baker, whose father and mother held that seat, says it has had the longest continuous Republican representation in Congress of any House district in the United States.

But in most of the rest of the South, and the rest of Hilleary's district, the Democratic Party dominated until recently. To many people being a southerner meant being a Democrat; it was that simple. The Republican Party was the party of Abraham Lincoln, and in the bitterness and division that followed the Civil War, southerners wanted nothing to do with it. In many local elections there often wasn't even a Republican candidate on the ballot. A number of counties in the western part of the district had never been represented by a Republican in Congress before Hilleary was elected. But Cooper says although most of the voters in the Fourth District may always have been Democrats, they have also always been extremely conservative. Hilleary appealed to those conservative sensibilities. And nowhere in the country did the Republicans do better in 1994 than they did in Tennessee. They took the governorship, picked up two House seats (giving them five of the state's nine), and won both Senate seats. In giving up his safe House seat to run for Al Gore's Senate seat, Cooper faced Fred Thompson, who already had a certain amount of star quality thanks to his movie roles. It was during Thompson's questioning as a counsel to the Senate Watergate Committee that White House aide Alexander Butterfield acknowledged the existence of secret tapes of Oval Office conversations, a revelation that led to Richard Nixon's resignation.

Although the 53-year-old Thompson had worked for years as a Washington lobbyist and had a successful legal practice there as well as in Tennessee, he was able to portray himself as an outsider with humble roots whose father was a used car salesman. At first Thompson's campaign didn't register with voters, but when he started campaigning in a pickup truck, often dressed in a flannel shirt, it took off like a shot. And Cooper, who had never faced a really tough election in his life, found himself beaten by 22 points. He wasn't only beaten, he was whomped. Cooper managed to carry only three counties in his former congressional district.

Cooper was never a back-slapping, southern pol, comfortable engaging in banter. Frank Cagle, an editor at the *Knoxville News-Sentinel* and a student of southern politics, says he thinks the Fourth District's voters always respected Cooper more than they liked him. "They thought, 'He's not a good ol' boy like me, but he's smart, and if he goes up there, he'll know what's going on.'"

For the Senate race in 1994, that didn't work. All the years Cooper had served in the House just didn't matter; in fact the voters seemed to hold that against him. "Thompson rode a horse and wore blue jeans and could be believable. If Cooper did it, he'd be laughed out of the state. It was an us-against-them election, and Fred and Van convinced everybody they were us."

In Hilleary's district personal style is as important as political ideology. The voters there want someone representing them who looks and talks like them, someone likable. In that way, Hilleary is in sync with the district. Hilleary makes no apologies for not being an intellectual. When the freshmen arrived in Washington, Gingrich instructed them to read six books, including *The Effective Executive* by Peter Drucker, James Flexner's biography of George Washington, and Alvin and Heidi Toffler's *Creating a New Civilization: The Politics of the Third Wave.* Also on the list was Alexis de Tocqueville's *Democracy in America,* which Hilleary had not only never read but had never heard of. Many freshmen, Hilleary among them, ignored the list, insisting they had no time for reading. "Does he come across as intellectual as Jim Cooper? Probably not. Can he relate to the average Tennessean and represent their needs better? Absolutely," says Randle Richardson, the chairman of the Tennessee Republican Party. "There may not be the mind of Disraeli up there, but he knows what he wants and he knows his agenda," says former college classmate Hoover. When Hilleary is told of Hoover's remark, he has no idea who Disraeli, the 19th-century British statesman and prime minister, was.

But with his aggressive effort on behalf of term limits, Hilleary has surprised a lot of people back home. One Tennessee journalist recalled her first meeting with candidate Hilleary back in 1994. "He was really stiff and uncomfortable and was clearly reading the Republican line." But since his arrival in Congress, "he really seems to have blossomed."

Like Hilleary, Fred Thompson introduced a term limits measure and pledged to serve only 12 years in Congress. Thompson, one of the most dedicated reformers among the 11 Senate freshmen, is also an activist on behalf of campaign finance reform. Unlike most of his Senate freshman classmates, Thompson is not an ultraconservative but more of a moderate in the mold of Howard Baker. And unlike Hilleary, who has expressed displeasure at the speed with which the Senate has been taking up the contract items, Thompson believes that's just the nature of his more deliberative body. "The name of the game is not the speed of legislation; it's good legislation," says Thompson. Congress is attempting to grapple with extremely difficult issues that require study and deliberation and can't be dispatched with the speed the House freshmen would like, he explains.

Even though the House was where the action was in the 104th Congress, the Senate was able to put the brakes on things. It's a different sort of institution, less hotheaded. The Founding Fathers designed it that way. George Washington is said to have told Thomas Jefferson, "We pour legislation into the senatorial saucer to cool it." The minority party has more rights in the Senate, where a single member can halt proceedings for hours. "I don't think there's anything wrong with being obstructionist. Republicans have been obstructionists in the past and will be in the future," says Thompson with a sly smile.

Sitting behind the desk of his Nashville office, Thompson chomps on an unlit cigar and reflects on what the 104th Congress has accomplished in its first three months. His familiarity and ease with the camera, his deep voice with a bit of a drawl, and his imposing physical presence have made Thompson a Republican star. Just a month after being elected to office, he was chosen to give the Republican response to Bill Clinton's first major televised address since the 1994 election.

He admits that it wasn't too rough being a Republican in 1994. "It certainly helps to run in a good year, and we all had the benefit of that." But Thompson attributes the Republicans' overwhelming success to more than Clinton's unpopularity: "People feel alienated and dissatisfied in a very fundamental way, and we represented a way to do something about that." More in the measured tones of a statesman than a politico, Thompson says it would be a mistake for the Republicans to think the election was simply a blanket embrace of their agenda. "It wasn't strictly a party deal or even a conservative deal." People are feeling frustration and anger despite a healthy economy because "working people are working harder and not getting ahead." They feel this country is losing too many social battles. It's not just the difference between Republicans and Democrats or even between liberals and conservatives; it's the failure of the entire political spectrum to come to grips with some of the problems facing the country, such as crime and the decline of the public educational system. "Republicans need to understand that's what it is and address that," insists Thompson.

Now that the first 100 days are over and the euphoria is starting to wear off, Thompson predicts the heavy lifting of actually making cuts in the budget is about to start. "It's going to take real leadership, risk taking, and strong advocacy to sell it. That's a great challenge and a great opportunity. But if it was easy, we'd have already done it. Nobody wants to give up what they've already got. What we need is some guts to do the things everyone knows we have to do."

6

THE CROWN JEWEL

It was the crown jewel of the Contract with America, according to Newt Gingrich. And indeed the disagreements among Republicans over the size and timing of the tax cut proved to be almost as costly to party unity as a fight over a rare jewel. It became the Republicans' most public disagreement during the first 100 days. And attaching the tax cut to their budget plan turned out to be a serious mistake that left them vulnerable to Democratic attacks.

But providing tax cuts was a way the Republicans thought they could pay back their core constituencies—business and pro-family conservative groups. The Republicans also envisioned tax cuts as the spoonful of sugar to help the medicine of the upcoming budget cuts go down a little easier.

The tax package included a sizable reduction in the capital gains tax and several tax breaks for businesses, but the provision that proved the most controversial was the $500 per child tax credit that would go to families with annual incomes of up to $200,000. The child credit was included in the Contract with America largely to please leaders of the religious right who thought the contract did not have enough emphasis on social issues. But the credit was criticized by a number of economists, who said it would do nothing to help stimulate investment and savings and only make it harder to deal with the deficit.

The tax cuts would be the largest since Ronald Reagan's 1981 tax legislation and were to be financed by spending cuts, reductions and cost-saving changes in welfare and Medicare, and raising federal workers' pension contributions. A Treasury Department analysis said half of the tax cut's benefits would go to people making more than $100,000 a year, although the Republicans disputed this figure.

Polls showed most Americans cared more about reducing the deficit than receiving a tax cut. But the pro-family and antitax groups that had come through for the Republicans in the election now pushed hard for the cuts, and House leaders made it clear they were committed to its passage. But some Republicans in Congress thought the $200,000 income level was too high and would make them an easy target for the Democrats, who could claim the Republicans were giving tax cuts to the wealthy while slashing programs that affected the poor and middle class, which is exactly what the Democrats did.

Freshman Greg Ganske of Iowa was sitting on the floor one day talking about the size of the tax cuts with Pat Roberts of Kansas, an eight-term incumbent and chairman of the Agriculture Committee. The two agreed to try to do something to get the income level for the child credit lowered. They approached Newt Gingrich, who said they should find out what the rest of the Republican conference thought. Ganske and Roberts put together a letter in early March saying they believed since the tax cut was supposed to be for the middle class, the income limit for the $500 per child credit should be lowered from $200,000 to $95,000. Ganske recalls that it took them only about four hours to gather nearly 100 signatures from members who felt the same way. Their effort was helped by an estimate from the Joint Committee on Taxation, which said lowering the limit to $95,000 would save the treasury $12–14 billion.

Ganske was a deficit hawk, like most of the freshmen, but he was also a moderate. He did not totally oppose the idea of a child tax credit but thought it should be limited to families that were truly middle class. The coalition he and Roberts put together included older moderates who opposed the income level and the message it sent as well as younger fiscal conservatives who wanted an assurance the tax cuts would be covered by equal budget reductions. Ganske and Roberts got ten House committee chairs, including Thomas Bliley (Commerce), Gerald Solomon (Rules), Henry Hyde (Judiciary), and Jim Leach (Banking), to sign their letter.

The freshman class was pretty much split down the middle. A faction that included Steve Largent, Matt Salmon, and David McIntosh was against lowering the limit. But nearly 40 of the freshmen, among them Joe Scarborough, Mark Neumann, Sam Brownback, Bill Martini, Sonny Bono, Lindsey Graham, Enid Waldholtz, and Roger Wicker, approved of the measure. In all, 105 Republicans, almost half the entire conference, signed the Ganske letter.

But groups like the Christian Coalition made it known they considered the $500 per child tax cut a high priority, and in return for its passage they agreed not to push for votes on controversial social issues such as abortion, gay rights, and school prayer until later in the session. Gingrich and the leadership started pressuring some of the members who had signed the Ganske letter to back down. The Coalition for America's Future, made up of business and conservative family groups, was formed to push for the tax cuts when it became clear the leadership was going to need some help. The coalition sent mail, called members, and spent $500,000 on a television advertising campaign.

Dick Armey tried to persuade Ganske to drop his effort, but the pressure from the majority leader didn't intimidate the 46-year-old doctor, who as a surgery resident had done open heart massage in an emergency room. "There isn't much that Dick Armey can say that is more exciting than that kind of situation," said Ganske.

The vote on the tax cut was scheduled for the first week in April, just before the House left for its three-week recess, but by Monday, April 3, there seemed to be so much dissension within the Republican conference that Gingrich threatened to keep the House in session beyond the start of the recess if they couldn't come to some agreement. "If we don't pass this, we're not going home," he threatened.

That same day Gingrich reached an agreement with a group of GOP moderates, including freshman Bill Martini of New Jersey, Michael Castle of Delaware, and Fred Upton of Michigan, that cleared the way for their voting for the package. Gingrich agreed to language in the bill that would ensure the tax cuts would not take effect until Congress had completed its work on a budget that would eliminate the deficit by 2002. But there was a problem on another flank, from freshman Tom Davis and senior Republicans Frank Wolf and Connie Morella, who represented areas in suburban Virginia and Maryland with large numbers of federal workers and who were concerned about the bill's provision that would increase the amount federal employees had to contribute to their pension plans.

The Democrats began their hand-to-hand combat over the tax package in the Rules Committee. Every bill that reaches the floor must pass through Rules. It is where last-minute changes are made to legislation, where it is determined how much time there will be for debate and what amendments will be allowed. There used to be nine Democrats and four Republicans on Rules. But when the Republicans took over Congress, the ratio flipped to nine Republicans and four Democrats. That kind of margin guarantees that if one or two Republicans should stray on any given issue (which would be extremely unusual), there would still be enough votes to carry the day. The committee votes are almost always along straight party lines—nine to four—and the Democrats always lose. It is understood Rules Committee members owe complete fealty to the Speaker and his wishes.

Enid Waldholtz, who was tapped by Gingrich for Rules, becoming the first freshman to serve on that committee in 80 years, insists she didn't have to swear any sort of loyalty oath to win the seat. During orientation Gingrich approached Waldholtz and asked her if she would be interested in serving on Rules. Gingrich told her it meant extra hours and extra work and suggested she talk it over with her husband, Joe Waldholtz, a former Republican operative who ran her campaign and served as her chief adviser. Of course they were interested. "The next day, I saw him in the hallway, and he said, 'Are you still interested?' and I said, 'Yes.' He said, 'OK, we'll have the press conference tomorrow,'" she would later recall. Gingrich said he picked Waldholtz because she was "smart, articulate, and tough enough to do it." She was also a loyal conservative who could be counted on to vote right. "You do have to have people [on Rules] who have a sense of the broad picture, the greater goal," Waldholtz says. Although she signed the Ganske letter, when it came time to vote in Rules she was right with the party leadership on the income limit for the child tax credit.

Putting freshmen on Rules and other key committees was just one of many ways Gingrich sought to ensure obedience. He also selected which senior Republicans would chair key committees. Rather than going strictly by seniority, Gingrich skipped over the ranking Republican when he selected a chair for Rules, Appropriations, Commerce, and Judiciary. Such a move assured Gingrich of the complete loyalty of his handpicked choices, who owed their chairmanships to him and not their own seniority.

On Tuesday, April 4, before Rules could meet on the tax cut, Gingrich had to make sure he had enough votes to pass it, so the committee did not convene until almost 3 P.M. The Rules Committee meets in a small, third-floor Capitol room, just across from the press gallery. The semicircular desk behind which the members sit spans virtually the entire width of the room. In the center sits chairman Gerald Solomon; to his right is Joe Moakley of Massachusetts, the 12-term Democrat who used to chair the committee. Behind the members at least a dozen staffers hover. Chairs that can accommodate about 40 people as well as a table for witnesses are crammed against the opposite wall of the room.

Moakley is attempting to offer an amendment. He thinks members of Congress who sleep in their offices, a practice popular with a few of the freshmen, are receiving a benefit they should pay taxes on. Republican Deborah Pryce of Ohio says she considers members "who are willing to suffer the indignities of sleeping on their sofa two or three nights a week" to be "American heroes." Moakley is trying to get a rise out of the Republicans, and Solomon jumps to the bait. When he came to Congress 16 years ago, Solomon says, he had five teenage kids in college and slept in his office "night after night to try and pay the damn bills." Democrat Martin Frost points out that members pay taxes on their parking spaces. "If we sleep in our cars, are we OK?" asks one of the Republicans.

Solomon calls for a voice vote. The amendment fails. Moakley wants a roll call. "Are you kidding?" Solomon asks in mock outrage. The vote proceeds in order from the most senior Republican to the most junior, each voting no in turn. When it gets to Waldholtz, she votes "absolutely not." Moakley, next, votes "absolutely yes." Solomon announces the failure of the amendment but tells Moakley, "I was going to invite you into my office and let you see the indentations in the couch." Moakley disappears for a moment and reappears carrying a live lobster. "I found him sleeping in Solomon's office," he says, with no further explanation.

The Democrats offer amendment after amendment, and each one is defeated in turn on a straight party vote. At 5:40 the Democrats finally give up. They haven't won a single amendment. "Everybody's hungry," says 79-year-old James Quillen, the committee's senior Republican. He wants to know if Moakley could "bring the lobster back." That reminds Moakley of a joke. Solomon looks at him sideways. "Are you sure you want to tell this?" he asks Moakley. Moakley barrels on. A guy goes into a restaurant and orders a lobster. The waiter brings it out, but it has only one claw. The guy says, "Wait a minute. This lobster has only one claw." The waiter says, "Lobsters are very cannibalistic, and when they get in fights, this happens. I guess this one lost." "Well, how about a winner?" the customer asks. "That's what I'd like: a winner," concludes Moakley. Since the 1994 election Moakley and the Democrats have been feeling like one-clawed lobsters.

*   *   *

In Hilleary's office the staff is struggling to catch up with the mountain of work that piled up during the term limits fight. At about 6, Hilleary decides to swing by some of that night's receptions. Pretty much every night Congress is in session there's a dizzying round of receptions on Capitol Hill, usually given by corporate groups, lobbyists, trade associations, or the members themselves as fund-raisers for their campaign war chests. The receptions are especially popular with the younger and single members, who often grab something for dinner at the receptions. Almost from the moment they arrived in Washington, the freshmen took to the cocktail party fund-raising circuit with a vengeance. All were assigned a "mentor" through the National Republican Campaign Committee who met with them regularly to talk about how much money they were raising and what they were doing to reduce their campaign debts.

Hilleary usually attends the fund-raisers put on by other freshmen unless he has a major conflict. There's an understanding among the members that it's good form to attend each other's fund-raisers. All but nine of the 73 Republican freshmen went into debt to win their seats. By showing up at each other's receptions, the freshmen serve as a draw for the lobbyists, who pay to get in and want their ears.

For all their talk about being different, the freshmen are very much the same as the senior members of both parties when it comes to taking money from lobbyists and political action committees (PACs). PACs can contribute up to $5,000 for the primary and $5,000 for a candidate's general election, whereas an individual is limited to donating a total of $2,000 directly to a candidate. In the first six months of 1995, the freshmen raised $5 million from PACs, almost half of their total campaign fund receipts and more than any past class of freshmen. Nine of the freshmen, including John Ensign of Nevada, Daniel Frisa of New York, Frank Cremeans of Ohio, and Jon Christensen of Nebraska, raised more than $100,000 from PACs in the first half of the year. In that same period 15 of the freshmen raised a total of more than $200,000 in campaign funds. Topping the list was Ensign, who raised nearly $450,000, followed by Tom Davis of Virginia, who brought in nearly $400,000, and Christensen, who raised $370,000. Only one Democrat was in the top tier of fund-raisers; Patrick Kennedy raised $242,411, with 32 percent of it coming from PACs.

In all of the House, fewer than 25 members refuse PAC funds. Hilleary is one of only four freshmen who does not take PAC money; fellow Tennessean Zach Wamp, Mark Sanford of South Carolina, and John Hostettler of Indiana also decline PAC money. Although Hilleary's campaign was left with $150,000 in debt, he doesn't hold many Washington receptions because he doesn't take PAC money. "All of my friends in the freshman class have held fund-raisers up here and raised $30,000 in a pop. And it takes them a lot less time than I'm going to spend raising $30,000 out of the Fourth District of Tennessee," says Hilleary.

Between 5:30 and 7:00, prime reception time, you can see the members traveling in groups between the House office buildings and popular reception spots along

First Street, SE, stopping to ask each other where the best ones are. Barbecue was especially big in 1995. Hilleary's first stop is a fund-raiser for Matt Salmon, where he makes a pass at the buffet table, shakes Salmon's hand, chats with a few staffers, and is approached by a few lobbyists. As he leaves, one of Salmon's staffers is remarking how much easier it is to get people to come to their receptions now than it was during the campaign.

Hilleary heads for the Rayburn House Office Building, where the Tennessee Funeral Directors Association is having a reception. In the hall he runs into Bob Ney, a freshman who served in the Ohio Senate for 10 years. Ney tells Hilleary the reception is over because someone collapsed in the room. At first Hilleary's not sure whether Ney is kidding or not, but Ney says he's quite serious. And Ney doesn't look like he's in a kidding mood. He says he's had "a bad press day."

Ney is one of a group of freshman Republicans stung by a hoax in which a *Spy* magazine reporter called, claiming to be from *Republican Beat,* "the GOP magazine for teens." The reporter asked questions like, "Do you think Hillary Clinton is pretty?" and "How long should teenagers date before they go 'all the way'?" (The freshmen seemed unanimous on advising teenagers to wait until they are married to have sex.)

As for their musical tastes, Joe Scarborough, who has played guitar in a number of rock bands, including one called the Establishment, and who keeps a black Alvarez guitar on a stand in his office, is definitely the hippest of the freshmen. He named Green Day, a hard rock alternative band, as his favorite group. J. C. Watts picked Boyz II Men, and Mark Neumann, perhaps the straightest arrow in a class full of straight arrows, said his favorite was the Carpenters. Sonny Bono, asked whether he or his former wife is more powerful now, replied, "Cher was, but she's slipping on the charts. She had a big lead there for a while, but she hit a banana peel, so I would say I'm out in front right now. But the contest isn't over. You never know with her."

The question about Mrs. Clinton probably elicited the most embarrassing answers from the freshmen. Bono said Mrs. Clinton wasn't his "type" and "on [his] scale she wouldn't make it." Neumann said, "She can't hold a candle to my wife, who I dated all through high school and liked in junior high." Steve Chabot of Ohio gave Mrs. Clinton "a five out of ten, which . . . is kind of average. She's not a dog . . . but she's not gorgeous." Ney told the reporter, "I think she's attractive . . . but she does have kind of big hips." The story was picked up by the *Washington Post* and papers in his district, and Ney was feeling a bit foolish. He said his wife had reprimanded him for the remark and his chief of staff lectured him, saying, "You've only been in Congress three months and already you have to write a letter of apology to the president's wife."

Ney said not only did the reporter lie about who he was, but he egged Ney on until he said something negative about Mrs. Clinton. "I've been Connie Chunged," said Ney ruefully, in a reference to Chung's interview with Newt Gingrich's mother shortly after the 1994 election in which she had encouraged Mrs. Gingrich to "whisper" to her what her son thought about Mrs. Clinton and Mrs. Gingrich said he had called her a bitch.

*   *   *

Wednesday, April 5, is the day the House will be voting on the tax cut, the last item in the Contract with America. At 11 A.M. the Republicans are still not sure they have the votes, so members are called to the floor to approve the previous day's *Congressional Record* so the leadership can do a head count and twist a few arms. Republican whip Tom DeLay finds there are at least 20 Republicans who are planning to vote no.

Outside the Capitol building Ringling Brothers has set up a sample of its act—with plenty of elephants and no donkeys—for the animal-loving, circus-loving Speaker, who once wanted to be a zookeeper. On the floor, as Democrats and Republicans go at it over whether the tax cut will help working families or is a windfall for the wealthy, there are a nauseating number of references to the show outside. "Who needs a circus outside when we have a circus on the inside?" asks freshman Democrat Lloyd Doggett of Texas. J. D. Hayworth counters, "The circus came to town 40 years ago with my liberal brethren on the other side of the aisle." Barney Frank compares moderate Republicans to the "India rubber man" of the sideshow: "The pressure that the right wing is able to generate on Republicans means we will continue to see the kind of ultimate flexibility which leads them to sign a letter saying they do not like the tax bill and then get twisted into voting for it."

"While the elephants are outside performing their tricks, the GOP elephants in this chamber are performing their tricks on the American people. . . . To paraphrase a very famous song, Mr. Speaker, where are the clowns and who are the clowns? Mr. Speaker, it looks like they are here," says Eliot Engel, a New York Democrat. "For 100 days America's children, senior citizens, and working families have watched the Republican Congress gut their school lunches, home heating assistance, and student loans. And for what reason? To pay for tax breaks for the very rich. To continue to allow billionaires to renounce their American citizenship to avoid paying taxes . . . from the mouths of babes to the pockets of billionaires," says Joe Moakley.

Budget Committee chair John Kasich takes a different view, of course. "The will of the American people is simple. . . . They want . . . this federal government downsized. They want it reduced in scope. They want it reduced in power, and they want their money given back to them so they can begin to solve problems where they live. . . . We are going to balance the budget. We are going to save the future of this country. We are going to give Americans tax relief in the process, and we are going to shift power from this city back to where we live. When it comes to deficit reduction and balancing the budget, you ain't seen nothing yet."

Sam Gibbons, the 17-term Democrat and previous chair of Ways and Means, takes the floor to recall the nation's last major tax cut and the promises that went with it. "In 1981 President Reagan was president, and his Office of Management and Budget director, Mr. Stockman, appeared before the Committee on Ways and Means, and he said this about the huge Reagan tax cut at that time: 'The combination of incentive-minded tax rate reductions and firm budget controls is expected to

lead to a balanced budget by 1984.' Does anybody remember that? That is when we
began the huge deficit."

The Republican freshmen are mindful of Reagan's failure to come through with
the promised level of budget cuts to match his tax cuts. They are committed to making the tough cuts, but that's just what the Democrats say they are afraid of, a repeat
of the Reagan years, when the wealthy benefited from government policy and bud-
getary spending at the expense of the poor and middle class. "It is déjà vu all over
again. The same rhetoric, the same people," charges Gibbons.

"Someday, when historians look back on the first 100 days of this Congress," begins minority whip David Bonior, "I think they may borrow that phrase from
Charles Dickens, 'It was the best of times, it was the worst of times.' If you are a Fortune 500 company looking for a big tax cut, if you are a billionaire Benedict Arnold
sitting on a Caribbean beach, if you are a Rupert Murdoch sitting pretty with a $38
million tax break, it is the best of times, because the Republicans are looking out for
you. But if you are a kid looking for a school lunch, if you are a senior looking for a
little heating assistance, if you are a student looking for a school loan, it may be the
worst of times, because you are not part of the Gingrich revolution." And then, in a
twist on the rhetorical device Gingrich used during the campaign, Bonior remarks,
"You cannot renew American civilization by taking Big Bird from a five-year-old,
school lunch from a 10-year-old, summer jobs from a 15-year-old, and student loans
from a 20-year-old in order to pay for a tax cut for the privileged few in our society."

Gingrich then takes the floor to close the debate on the tax cut, his crown jewel.
"Two years ago we were debating a tax increase, and all of our friends on the other
side of the aisle were saying, 'It will be OK,' and by a one-vote margin they passed it.
But the country said it was not OK to raise taxes, that government was too big, it
spends too much, and it needs to be brought under control. . . . I urge every member to look at this and ask yourself, in your constituents' lives, will not a little less
money for government and a little more money for those families be a good thing?
And is not that what this Congress was elected to do?" When Gingrich finishes, the
freshmen, along with the rest of the Republicans, rise to give him a standing ovation.

The Republicans see this as a vote they have to win. They have to hold the conference together for the last contract item. They can't let the Democrats perceive any
weakness. A week before the vote, Sam Brownback, who had signed the Ganske letter, figured he was going to vote no. He wasn't hearing from his constituents that
they wanted a tax cut. They wanted a balanced budget. But then the drumbeat of
pressure, orchestrated by the Coalition for America's Future, started. He received
nearly 1,000 phone calls organized by the Christian Coalition. Business leaders back
home were urging him to vote yes, so were the lobbyists in Washington, and the Republican leaders were leaning on him. Brownback decided to change his position
and vote yes.

Van Hilleary has reservations about the $200,000 threshold. The average income
in his district is $23,000. He is also concerned about a loophole in the bill that
would continue to allow wealthy Americans to live overseas and renounce their citi-

zenship to avoid paying U.S. taxes. But he has been onboard from the beginning. He is a solid yes vote. Like a number of Republicans, Hilleary has donned a large lapel pin that says "Do It for Our Children." He looks exhausted, and he's had enough of the all-day rhetorical slugfest that has painted the Republicans as concerned only about the well-to-do. Although he's tired of the name-calling, he admits there are aspects of the tax bill that leave the Republicans open to the charge of being "insensitive pigs."

The tax cut passes 246 to 188, and all but a handful of the 105 members who signed the Ganske letter vote in favor of the tax cut, including Ganske and Roberts. Once it was clear they weren't going to prevail, Ganske said they felt it would be better to close ranks. "We pushed it as far as we could. You can be confrontational to an extent, but you need to know how far you can go, and sometimes it's wiser to use the Chinese water torture approach rather than the charge of the Light Brigade. We never forced it onto the conference, but we kept talking about it."

Between the drip, drip, drip of Ganske and other Republicans pushing for the limit to be lowered and the firehose the Democrats were using to pound their "tax cuts for the rich" message, the size of the tax cut was eventually reduced. Seven months after the House vote, the Senate lowered the income level for the $500 per child credit to $110,000 for a two-income household and $75,000 for a single-income household. But that April, Gingrich and the House leaders, flush with success in keeping their troops together and eager to celebrate the end of the first 100 days, didn't seem to be paying much attention to the Democrats' assertions that the Republicans were cutting programs for the poor and elderly to pay for tax cuts for the wealthy. The new minority had finally found an issue that appeared to be working for them.

7

THREE WEEKS, 22 COUNTIES

BECAUSE OF THE PACE of the first 100 days, Van Hilleary wasn't able to spend much time in his district, and that's something he plans to remedy during April's three-week congressional recess. He's scheduled a "listening tour" of public meetings and sessions with local officials and civic leaders in each of the 22 counties in his district—as well as numerous private meetings, fund-raisers, receptions, and speeches.

On Saturday, April 8, one day after the ceremony marking the conclusion of the contract, Hilleary has two town meetings and two speeches scheduled. He begins in Nashville with a speech to the Tennessee Young Republicans, then drives 120 miles east to Crossville for his first public forum.

Crossville, with about 7,000 residents, is in Cumberland County. George Bush carried this county in 1992, and it's tended to be more and more Republican for the past decade. Crossville was the site of one of Franklin Roosevelt's 102 homesteading projects. In the 1930s the federal government constructed small farmhouses out of crab orchard stone, a sand-colored stone mined from a local quarry. Out-of-work coal miners, sawmill workers, people from all over the Southeast came here to start a new life and in exchange for working the land got to live in the homes. Of the 255 built, 218 of the farm cottages are still standing on the outskirts of Crossville. And the original homestead school is still being used.

Roosevelt won the hearts and votes of southerners with his creation of the homesteading project, the Tennessee Valley Authority, and other programs that lifted the region out of grinding poverty. But those Roosevelt projects represent exactly the kind of government spending that Hilleary thinks is no longer necessary. He believes government has become too big and tried to do too much. In a speech that evening, Hilleary will tell his constituents that "FDR's New Deal has become a raw deal and is on its way out." Hilleary and his fellow freshmen have made it their mission to make sure that happens.

Only about 10 people, most of them elderly men, have shown up for Hilleary's 1 P.M. forum at the Cumberland County courthouse in Crossville. Hilleary talks briefly about the end of the 100 days and refers to the budget cuts that are coming. "There's nothing worse than paddling out to the middle of the stream and losing your nerve and going back. We've just got to keep going." Then he takes a series of questions, some of which are more rambling diatribes than questions and have little or nothing to do with Congress. This is the first public meeting Hilleary has ever run as a congressman, and things kind of get away from him. One guy who describes himself as "an old, hardworking hillbilly" starts railing about the federal Bureau of Alcohol, Tobacco, and Firearms (ATF) and says, "If you want a machine gun or cannon, you should have one."

Finally, Hilleary manages to bring the meeting to a close by telling the folks he needs to get on to his next appointment. Brock Hill, a 41-year-old Republican who was born and raised in Crossville, comes up to talk to Hilleary. He owns a sporting goods store and is the county executive, an elected position. Hill says the parents of a lot of people in this area were Roosevelt Democrats, but now they feel "government has gotten out of control." He says many people down here don't like what Bill Clinton has been doing as president, especially seeing him entertaining "people of all sorts of persuasions" in the White House. "You're in the Bible Belt down here," Hill says with a broad smile.

Hilleary's next stop is Dayton, about 35 miles to the south, where for eight days in the summer of 1925 William Jennings Bryan and Clarence Darrow went toe to toe over the teaching of evolution. The infamous Scopes monkey trial held in the Dayton courthouse was the O. J. Simpson trial of its day—only much shorter. It was carried by radio, the first U.S. trial to be nationally broadcast. And more than 200 journalists, including H. L. Mencken, descended on Dayton to cover the trial.

In 1925 the Tennessee legislature had passed a bill that made it unlawful to teach any theory that denied the story of divine creation as described in the Bible, "to teach instead that man has descended from a lower order of animals." The American Civil Liberties Union ran an ad in Tennessee newspapers offering to pay the legal expenses of any teacher willing to test the law. After being approached by Dayton leaders, John Scopes, who was a mathematics teacher and coach at the local high school, agreed to go along, although he had been only a substitute biology teacher and couldn't actually remember ever teaching evolution.

Scopes was found guilty and fined $100, but the conviction was overturned by the Tennessee Supreme Court on a technicality. Bryan died in Dayton a week after the trial, and five years later William Jennings Bryan College, a fundamentalist Bible school, was founded as a legacy to the man whom Mencken dubbed "a tinpot pope in the Coca-Cola belt."

The whole idea for the trial was cooked up by several of the town fathers, with the agreement of Scopes, as a promotion gimmick. Sitting around in the town's social center, the F. E. Robinson Drug Store owned by "Doc" Robinson (the grandfather of Elaine Robinson, Hilleary's assistant and scheduler), Robinson and the others decided it would be a good publicity stunt to get tourists to come to Dayton. The idea worked, probably a lot better than they ever imagined. Evolution has been very good to Dayton, and every July there is a four-day Scopes Trial Festival, including a reenactment of the arguments by Bryan and Darrow.

The beautiful Renaissance Revival building constructed in 1891 where the trial took place still serves as Rhea County's courthouse. The huge second-floor courtroom that was used—before the trial had to be moved to the courthouse lawn because it got too hot inside and the weight of all the spectators started to crack the downstairs ceiling—looks just the way it did 70 years ago. The carved wood judge's bench and jury chairs are original, as are the spectator seats—straight-backed wooden chairs attached in long rows, with black iron arms and iron trim on the back. In the basement of the courthouse is a small museum with photos featuring the principals, one of the tables from Robinson's drugstore, and other objects associated with the trial.

The Scopes courtroom has been opened for Hilleary's public meeting, and he stands in front of a dozen or so people. Someone tells Hilleary he pays $375 a month for health insurance: "By the time I pay for the premiums, I can't afford to get sick." He wants to know what Congress is going to do about health care costs. Hilleary says he thinks the tort reform measures passed by the House will address some of the health industry's cost problems. Hilleary and his constituents don't seem aware that they are sitting in the room where a major battle over the relationship between church and state once took place. There are no questions about school prayer, although Hilleary will say later that he does think prayer should be reintroduced in schools: "I don't see what it hurts. I don't see a problem with having a prayer led by a teacher."

Religion plays a central role in public life in the Fourth District. Often public gatherings begin with a prayer. Certainly the Rhea County Republican dinner held in the William Jennings Bryan College cafeteria that night did. Dayton is less than 20 miles from Hilleary's hometown of Spring City, and his parents, many longtime family friends, and several hundred others are in attendance to cheer on their local boy. He receives a standing ovation when he steps to the podium. And he begins with his best material, the stories about telling people to call him Van while his zipper was wide open and informing Warren Christopher at the White House that he thinks Bill Clinton is the worst president we've ever had. He calls the freshmen "the conscience of the Congress" and says they have turned Washington upside down.

Hilleary reviews some of what he considers to be the Republicans' accomplishments, such as rewriting the crime bill ("We're not going to have hug-a-thug like the president's policy"). Of the Republicans' so-called National Security Restoration Act, which would restrict U.S. troops from taking part in military operations that are under foreign command, he says, "I was elected to the Congress of the United States, not the congress of the United Nations."

And he recalls the House vote on the balanced budget amendment, which he calls one of the most exciting nights of his life. Of his vote in favor, he tells his friends and neighbors, "I was thinking of y'all when I did that." Hilleary says he and some of the other freshmen acted "just like kids" as they watched the vote total go up. "We started counting down just like at a football game" and "when it went over 290, it was just phenomenal," a cheer going up in the chamber.

On March 2, the day the Senate failed to pass the balanced budget amendment, Hilleary and many of the other House freshmen led a march from their side of the Capitol over to the Senate side. They lined up in long rows and strode across the parking lot in the cold. At one point, J. D. Hayworth was chanting "BBA, BBA" (for "balanced budget amendment"), trying to get others to join him. Jim Longley, a dour freshman from Maine, told Hayworth to be quiet, that they weren't at a pep rally; what they were doing was serious business. Even before they were sworn in, when the *Washington Post* asked Longley to describe the class, he said, "We're serious as a heart attack." The freshmen held a news conference at the base of the Senate steps. Fred Thompson and several other Senate freshmen joined them. Then they marched up the steps and into the chamber.

Hilleary was standing with Steve Largent along the wall on the side of the Senate chamber right behind New York senator Daniel Patrick Moynihan. Usually during a Senate vote, the senators mill around and talk, but for this vote they sat at their desks until their names were called. The chamber was unusually quiet, and as some of the senators voted against the amendment they could hear rude remarks emanating from the direction of the freshmen. Moynihan turned his head toward the unruly band of interlopers. "You gentlemen are guests here, and welcome, but you must be-have like guests," he said, admonishing the youngsters to mind their manners before turning back to his business.

*   *   *

As Hilleary continues his speech in the Bible college cafeteria, he talks about what he calls the Republicans' school lunch public relations disaster. Hilleary says the me-dia and the Democrats are trying to paint the Republicans as "unfeeling, insensitive, Neanderthal pigs" taking food "out of the mouths of children." Hilleary vows that if block-granting the funds for school lunches proves not to be a good idea, he'll "be the first one to stand in line" to bring the school lunch program back under federal control. Hilleary concludes by telling the crowd, "I'm so proud to be from Rhea County" and promises to think of them every time he casts a vote.

The next morning Hilleary is in Shelbyville, more than 150 miles to the west, for a 10:45 service at the First Baptist Church. After greeting the parishioners for half an hour before the service, Hilleary sits in a pew near the front. The first order of busi-ness is a baptism. A young woman dressed in a white robe is fully immersed into a clear tank of bright blue water in the front of the church behind the choir. The con-gregation then joins in singing "The Old Rugged Cross" and "How Great Thou Art."

Shelbyville has a population of only 14,000, but this is clearly a thriving church. The large, new building is beautifully appointed; the choir of perhaps 50 voices is polished, almost professional. Bedford County is a Democratic stronghold that Hilleary did not carry. Even though it's Sunday morning, Hilleary can't keep his mind off politics. During a song called "There Is a River" performed by the God's Men of Praise quintet, Hilleary whispers, "All those guys will be Republicans in five years." Perhaps, if Pastor Drew Hayes has anything to do with it. Before beginning his sermon, Hayes introduces Hilleary to his congregation, telling them what a fine congressman he is, that he can be counted on to represent their interests on issues ranging from cutting the federal budget to abortion. Hayes is a bundle of energy with a cordless microphone. He does not stand behind a pulpit in a black robe but bounces around the front of the church as he delivers a message that focuses on sin, redemption, and salvation. It goes without saying that Hayes wants his parishioners to vote right, too. Conservative Christian congregations are important constituencies for the Republicans, who give them plenty of attention, especially around election time.

Over the next 20 days, Hilleary will cover nearly 3,000 miles, crisscrossing his district in an attempt to see as many people as possible and let them know what he's been up to in Washington. This is what his constituents expect, and Hilleary says it's important that "Joe at the gas station can say, 'I met Hilleary, and he's a good ol' boy.'"

When Jim Cooper first ran for this seat, he was single, just like Hilleary—probably not a coincidence, given the amount of time it takes to campaign in this district. It would be much tougher for Hilleary to keep the schedule he does if he had a family. He typically works seven days a week. He plans meetings in Washington up until the time he leaves for Tennessee late Thursday or early Friday and dovetails events back home all weekend until he heads north, usually on Sunday or Monday. He almost never gets to spend two consecutive nights at home because he's often bunking with supporters in other parts of the district so he can cram in more appearances. Hilleary has made up his mind that whoever runs against him next time will never outwork him.

On Friday, April 21, Hilleary's day begins with an 8 A.M. breakfast with supporters, followed by a public forum at the Lawrence County courthouse in Lawrenceburg, a town of about 10,000 residents. Hanging on the wall behind the judge's bench in the small courtroom is a portrait of Confederate general Robert E. Lee and a picture of a U.S. flag above the words, "This is our flag. Be PROUD of it!" Lawrence County is named for Captain James Lawrence, who commanded the *Chesapeake* in the War of 1812. After Lawrence was mortally wounded, he ordered his crew, "Don't give up the ship!"

Hilleary is spending the day in the southwestern part of the district, in three counties that border Alabama and Mississippi. Most of those who show up in Lawrenceburg want to discuss problems they are having with their veteran's and disability benefits. Hilleary has brought two staff members from his district office in Tullahoma to work with them.

His next stop is scheduled in Waynesboro, 30 miles further west. Hilleary opens that forum with his standard recounting of Republican accomplishments during the first 100 days. He holds up a chart of the 10 points in the Contract with America, the box next to each, even term limits, checked off (because they voted on it, even though they didn't pass it, Hilleary explains). Of welfare reform Hilleary says the country needs to get back to the way "it used to be—you either work or you starve—and I think you'll have some more people interested in working." Hilleary says when it comes time to vote on the tough budget cuts that lie ahead, "We'll see if this Congress is real." But when someone asks him about the Tennessee Valley Authority (TVA), created by Franklin Roosevelt to build hydroelectric dams and bring electricity and flood control to the Southeast, Hilleary responds much more like a congressman defending his district than a budget-cutting zealot. The cheap power provided by the hydroelectric dams on the Tennessee River have helped attract industry to the state and provided jobs, and Hilleary says he opposes slashing TVA's budget as much as has been suggested or privatizing the agency. He does warn them, however, that "TVA is going to take a budget cut."

After the forum he meets with local civic leaders and officials, including a representative of the elderly community, the superintendent of education, and a local law enforcement officer. Although they seem generally supportive of the Republican efforts to balance the budget, when it comes to a program they are involved with, they don't want any cuts. An elderly woman introduced as "Miss Pauline" complains about the cuts in funding for senior citizens. Hilleary tells her Meals on Wheels is an excellent program but "almost everything is going to take a little hit. . . . There's hardly any federal program that doesn't do some good, so when you cut them, you're going to do some bad."

This obviously isn't going to be as easy as it sounded. And Hilleary is talking less like a slash-and-burn budget cutter and more like, well, not quite a Democrat but certainly not someone who's enjoying dismantling the government piece by piece. "We've got to be compassionate and sensitive when we do this and not use a meat cleaver," he says. Hilleary refers to John Kasich, the House Budget Committee's blunt-speaking chairman, who in making one of his budget-cutting presentations said, "The fun's just begun." Hilleary says this kind of talk isn't helping the Republicans' image. "I don't think it's fun at all; it's just something that's necessary."

During their recess Hilleary and the other freshmen hear plenty about proposed cuts for school lunches and Meals on Wheels, along with pleas for specific programs that benefit their area, like the TVA in Hilleary's district. Part of the concern has been generated by the Democrats' successful sound bites on the school lunch issue, but part of it is just people fighting for what they're used to getting from the government. When they voted for balancing the budget and cutting welfare, a lot of Hilleary's constituents probably didn't think the TVA and student loans were going to take a hit, too.

Hilleary is on one of the freshman task forces that's looking into abolishing the Department of Education, and he asks those in attendance whether they would miss the cabinet agency that he characterizes as a "multibillion-dollar bureaucracy" if it were gone. No one speaks up. "How did we ever educate kids before it was created?" he asks rhetorically; "Don't you think Tennessee parents and Tennessee teachers and Tennessee administrators know enough to educate Tennessee kids?"

After the meeting a retired small businessman named Kevin Kinhl comes up to Hilleary to tell him he's doing a good job. Kinhl says he grew up a Democrat but now he's a Republican. Although he voted for Jimmy Carter, he says he couldn't bring himself to vote for Bill Clinton for president. Later Hilleary predicts that "in 10 years it'll be hard to find any southern white males who are Democrats."

Although Clinton carried Hilleary's district and the state of Tennessee in 1992, helped by his native son running mate, Al Gore, he beat George Bush by only three points, with 46 percent of the vote to Bush's 43 percent. Two years later, when Hilleary was elected, Clinton was extremely unpopular in the Fourth District, and not many people think he can carry Tennessee again, even with Gore on the ticket. Many conservative Tennessee Democrats voted for Clinton but felt he moved too far to the left after taking office. His positions on gun control and gays in the military hurt him badly in this district full of conservative Christians and veterans. Hilleary, referring to his military experience, says "I wouldn't want homosexuals in my tent."

In his first two years in office, Clinton alienated the Reagan Democrats and much of the Perot constituency. Exit polling showed that in 1994 Clinton's approval stood at an extremely low 27 percent among southern white males. Among all southerners his approval rating was only 37 percent, lower than in any other region of the country. Forty-four percent of southern white males said their House vote was a vote against Bill Clinton. Nationally, the Republicans gained 11 percent more of the white male vote than they had in 1992, and Perot voters who split their House votes evenly in 1992 voted Republican two to one in 1994. And making things worse for the Democrats, their turnout was extremely low, with many traditional Democratic voters staying home in 1994.

The last nonsouthern Democratic presidential candidate to carry the South was Harry Truman. Ever since Richard Nixon won the South in 1968, people have been predicting the region was lost to the Democrats. For many years, though, its representation in Congress still remained largely Democratic. But the Republican gains of 1994 made it clear that the southern "yellow dog Democrats," so named because they would rather vote for a yellow dog than a Republican, appear to be either dying off or converting. In 1960 the Democrats held an overwhelming 94 percent of the House seats from the 11 states of the former Confederacy. By 1994 that figure had dropped to 49 percent. In the U.S. Senate southern Republicans had gone from almost no presence to a majority; in 1995 there were 13 Republican and nine Democratic senators from the South.

The first step in separating southerners from the Democrats was the civil rights movement of the 1960s. Then came the Vietnam War protests, and the national Democratic Party came to be identified in the minds of many southerners as the party of minorities, feminists, and special interest groups that were not in tune with their conservative Christian values. "What came out loud and clear in 1994 is that the average Tennessean didn't believe that the Democratic Party represented working-class folks," says Randle Richardson, the chairman of the Tennessee Republican Party. He says his father was a sharecropper in west Tennessee and a Republican. His parents, who believed in hard work and self-reliance, opposed the New Deal because they thought it was a handout and represented too much government control. Richardson says he just got a call from a guy who wanted to volunteer for the GOP and who told him, "I've been a Democrat all my life. I didn't leave the Democratic Party; it left me."

Demographic changes in the South are another factor in the Republicanization of the region. The South used to be almost totally agrarian, with wealthy and poor but almost no middle class. But over the past 50 years, industrialization and economic development have exploded here. There are many more large urban centers with new suburban residents who vote Republican. And the region's pleasant climate and low cost of living have also attracted retirees from other parts of the country who have brought their Republican Party affiliation with them to the area.

By emphasizing his conservative Christian values and lack of any connection to Washington during his campaign, Hilleary was able to take advantage of the antigovernment, anti-Democratic, anti-Clinton sentiment. And in a district with extremely strong Democratic traditions, he was able to win the votes of people who had never before voted for a Republican. Hilleary's election was a dramatic reflection of the way the South's political alignment is changing.

Tennessee Democratic Party chairman Will Cheek knows the Democrats have their work cut out for them. "If the Republicans can deliver on tax cuts, budget cuts, and deficit reduction," he admits, they'll be hard to beat. But he is trying to remain optimistic about 1996. "Tennessee is conservative, but you can elect the right kind of Democrats." He says both Hilleary's and Zach Wamp's seats will be highly targeted by the Democrats.

*   *   *

An hour after he finishes his meeting in Waynesboro, Hilleary is standing before 20 people in Savannah, near the Mississippi border, less than 100 miles from Memphis. The Hardin County courthouse where Hilleary is holding the meeting was built in 1950, but its white walls, dark wood, chandeliers, ceiling fans, and curving staircase give it the look and feel of the pre–Civil War South. Hilleary tells these people he believes they have sent him to Washington for two reasons: to clean up Congress and make internal reforms and to cut government because it's become too big and too intrusive. "Enough is enough. This country was founded on personal responsibility, not the government waking you up in the morning and tucking you into bed at night."

Jim Osburn, a retired foreign service employee, tells Hilleary he thinks the Contract with America is "a beautiful public relations gimmick, but that's all it is." He says Congress didn't do the tough things, like tackling campaign finance reform. "It is a public relations thing, that's true. But it's not all gimmick," Hilleary responds.

Hilleary wants to give people an example they can relate to about how out of control Washington is. "Y'all know how much I pay in rent in Washington? I have a roommate; I split it because I couldn't afford it, but I pay $1,800." There's a gasp in the back of the room. Now Hilleary talks about the president's decision to bail out Mexico and says it was designed to help Wall Street bankers who have invested there. "I don't know of a single Wall Street banker that lives in my district. . . . The only people I know that are for it are the higher-ups. President Clinton is for it; Newt Gingrich is for it; Bob Dole is for it. I don't know a single freshman who's for it."

Hilleary is loath to criticize Gingrich in Washington, but it's a little easier to do in the district, especially when he hears constituents like Osburn telling him, "I elected you. I didn't elect Newt Gingrich." Osburn says he realizes in order to get a good committee assignment and get help with campaign financing the freshmen have to go along with the leadership. "You're his slave; we don't want you to be his slave. You need to lead a freshman revolt," he says. Hilleary says he can already imagine next year's campaign commercials. Just as the Republicans linked the Democrats with Bill Clinton in 1994, "the Democrats must be already talking about morphing our faces on Gingrich."

Vicki Dimond, a librarian at the county high school, says she has come today to represent some of the teachers at her school who couldn't be there. She mentions that the school uses funding from the National Endowment for the Humanities (NEH) to buy library books and take students on cultural excursions. She makes a pitch for the NEH and for continued funding for National Public Radio and public television. Hilleary goes into his "this is no fun but it's necessary" speech, telling her, "It's hard to justify those things as a need rather than a nice thing to have."

It is a need, especially in rural areas that have so little access to cultural activities, she counters. "How did kids get raised before the NEH and the NEA were created?" Hilleary asks. He has no problem cutting funding for these programs, and he has no problem telling his constituents about it either. "If it costs me, it costs me, but we're going to have to make some of these cuts, I'm afraid." Dimond wants to get in one last word. "If something as worthwhile as public television has to be cut, then some of these pork barrel things ought to be cut," she says. Outside in the hall she says she's a Democrat who voted for Bill Clinton. She does agree with some of the things in the contract but is "afraid that the good things will get cut but something in Newt's district or some other powerful person's will be left alone, that the cuts will be uneven." Hilleary and the Republicans claim they are trying to protect future generations of children so they will not be faced with a mountain of national debt, but Dimond says, "I'm worried about the children I teach now; I'm worried about my kids."

Hilleary is not in the best of moods when the meeting concludes. Although generally he's been getting a warm reception throughout the district, he is bothered whenever he encounters opposition. He hasn't been doing this long enough to be completely comfortable in the knowledge that such criticism is just part of the territory. Social convention is a little different down here. Differences of opinion are expressed in a much more subtle fashion, and speaking one's mind is considered to be more bad manners than the personal right and virtual responsibility to self-expression that it might be up North. People here won't tell you to go to hell; they'll tell you to go to heck, and they'll do it with a polite smile on their faces, although it still means the same thing. These people haven't exactly told Hilleary to go to heck, but the meeting wasn't a warm embrace either.

The following Monday Hilleary begins in Pulaski, a town of about 8,000 people that looks a great deal like many of the county seats in Hilleary's district. The Giles County courthouse, a large brick and granite building with a green copper dome, is in the center of the town square, surrounded on four sides by small businesses that make up the hub of the town. There are several antique stores, a number of dress shops, two drugstores, two jewelry stores, several dry goods shops, and a large furniture store. Unlike many small cities in the Northeast, whose vacant and boarded-up storefronts symbolize the death of Main Street thanks to the competition from malls and discount chains, these small southern towns are thriving. In the middle of the day it's hard to find a parking space downtown.

Pulaski was occupied by the Union Army for most of the Civil War. It has long been a crossroads for the rail lines from Nashville to Decatur, Alabama, and Memphis to Chattanooga that are still used to haul freight. But the town probably derives its greatest notoriety as the birthplace of the Ku Klux Klan, founded here in 1869. And much to the consternation of many local residents, Klan members from around the country gather in the town square every year around Martin Luther King's birthday to mark that founding.

For the most part, Hilleary's district is remarkably homogeneous—white and Protestant. Only 4 percent of the district's residents are African Americans. There are no synagogues in the district, and although there are hundreds of Baptist churches, most communities don't have a single Catholic parish. The most visible sign of any problem with race relations is probably reflected in a concern over crime.

Robert E. Lee Jr., the county's 73-year-old general sessions, juvenile, and probate judge, attributes much of the problem to declining parenting standards and a lack of discipline. Lee, who is a distant cousin and descendant of the Confederate general, won national notoriety in 1994 when he ruled that a teenage girl who had been drinking and disorderly deserved "a whipping." The punishment was carried out by her parents; as Lee describes it, "They gave her a switching, and I agreed to observe it." Lee—who sports a small, white Errol-Flynn-style mustache and is nattily attired in a gray linen jacket; a gray and white striped shirt with a starched white collar; a tie with bright, geometric designs; a Rolex watch; and black iguana cowboy boots—insists that "parental control is a thing of the past. The government has interfered with everything parents try to do. If you spank a child or whip a child with a belt or a switch, they'll take you to court. The Bible says discipline your children."

When he was growing up, Lee says, "I knew if I misbehaved I was going to suffer for it, and if I didn't misbehave I would be praised for it." Like a great many of Hilleary's constituents, Lee was born and has lived his entire life in the town he lives in now. Over the years he's seen it change from primarily a farming area to one with more small businesses and, recently, an industrial park with light manufacturing.

Giles County is Democratic and one of the few counties in the district that Hilleary didn't carry. After his open forum, he sits around a conference table with a small group of county officials asking for feedback on "how the federal government affects you, good or bad." The officials applaud the legislation that has eliminated future unfunded mandates as well as his term limits initiative, although one says, "I guarantee you that term limits will not stop influence peddling by PACs." Again here, as he will be almost everywhere he goes on this trip, Hilleary is asked about the school lunch program.

Joe T. Parker, a farmer with 500 acres who raises dairy cattle, tobacco, and chickens, says milk price controls are killing him. "I'm getting less for my milk today than I was in 1977. We just can't survive on those prices." Parker thinks the government should get out of the milk business and let the private sector handle it. He says his family has been farming the same land for 200 years. Like many of the original settlers of Tennessee, his ancestors were given the land as a thanks for their service in the Revolutionary War. Parker is critical of the Agriculture Department and says although there are only about 100 people in the county who make their living farming, probably 30 bureaucrats at various federal agencies there deal with agricultural issues.

Parker has brought with him a check for Hilleary's campaign fund from a farm organization, but when he is informed that Hilleary does not take PAC money, he says, "I guess I'll just carry it on back." Hilleary reacts with a pained smile: "Ooh, that hurts." Less than an hour before, Hilleary told the voters of Giles County he doesn't take PAC money because "I want y'all to be sure I'm representing you, not some special interest group that gave me $10,000." But since taking office, Hilleary has begun to reevaluate his decision not to take PAC money.

Hilleary says when he made his first race for state senate, his stand on PAC money was partly a practical one. He figured his well-known opponent "was going to get 90 percent of the PAC money anyway," so he would "get some mileage" out of refusing it. But it was also a philosophical decision. "There's folks who have their vote bought by PAC money. It was very idealistic and maybe naive, but I wanted to remain above suspicion."

He did the same thing in his congressional race, even refusing money from Gingrich's GOPAC and other Republican campaign committees. Hilleary has said he will continue refusing PAC money through his first reelection campaign, but he is not promising to make this a permanent decision; "I have begun to see two sides to the story." Hilleary says he's not sure all the extra time he has to spend on the phone and raising money through much smaller individual donations is worth the purity he can claim. He has had help from Howard Baker in organizing several fund-raising events in Washington and was able to raise $10,000 from wealthy individuals at an event held at Baker's Washington residence. To raise a comparable amount back home, it took him the entire three-week recess and almost 10 events. Hilleary says that time could be better used for legislative work but admits that because he doesn't take PAC money, "I don't feel obligated to see any lobbyist that comes in" the door.

What's telling about Hilleary's crisis of conscience over this issue is that no matter how right he thinks his stand is, he is feeling the pressure to join the system and exploit it in order to keep his seat. "I've had to hand back $5,000 checks, and . . . it brings a tear to your eye," he says, only partly in jest.

Next Hilleary is the luncheon speaker at a meeting of the Rotary and Exchange Clubs at the local country club. This business crowd is one Hilleary obviously feels comfortable with, and his speech features the things he's been talking about everywhere—his votes on the balanced budget amendment, welfare reform, school lunches, and term limits. Knowing that Sonny Bono is probably the most famous member of the freshman class and possibly the only name these folks will recognize, he tells them Bono is OK, although "he's been around the block a few times—he's seen it and done it and done it a few more times." Hilleary goes on to describe Bono as neither the best speaker nor the best singer, but Hilleary says he's proud to be serving with him and with the other freshmen, who are some of the "finest folks" he's ever met.

When Hilleary takes questions from the audience, a man who identifies himself as the father of two teenagers asks about the federal student loan program. Hilleary responds that although he received federally backed student loans when he attended college, "I don't think the federal government owes people a college education." He says he will "try to keep the cuts to an absolute minimum." But Hilleary does not think the government should subsidize the interest for students while they are in school.

He takes a few more questions and then receives a standing ovation. As he is walking out, shaking hands as he goes, a young man comes up to him and says, "I served with you in Desert Storm." Hilleary is extremely pleased with his reception, since he does not consider this county completely friendly territory. But in every politician's life some rain must fall. Later that evening, in an address to a senior citizen community in another part of the district, he will be blasted for his opposition to gun control and wanting to lift the ban on the sale of automatic weapons. Hilleary will tell me later that he considers owning a gun, any kind of gun, "a Second Amendment right" and asserts that automatic weapons and assault rifles are used in a fraction of the crimes committed. "I don't have one, and I don't care to have one, but if someone was breaking into my house with a gun, I'd like to be able to have the advantage." Most of Hilleary's constituents strongly oppose any form of gun control. The few who do favor gun control, Hilleary says, are mostly retirees from up North. "Do you know the difference between a Yankee and a damn Yankee?" he asks with a mischievous smile. "A damn Yankee is someone who came down here from the North and decided to stay."

The next morning, Tuesday, April 25, Ray Smith, president of a small manufacturing company named Ilene Industries in Shelbyville, is waiting for Hilleary to pay him a visit. The company, which has 30 employees and makes ball bearing cages, is having trouble paying back a $500,000 Small Business Administration loan. Although he has never met Hilleary, Smith called the district office to ask if the congressman would stop by and talk with him about the problem. Smith says the company, which was started in 1969 by his grandfather in Michigan, moved to Tennessee in 1980 because of the lower cost of doing business here. In the first year after the move, the company saved $30,000 in workmen's compensation and other taxes.

When Hilleary arrives, Smith tells him he is a "staunch Republican" and is "ecstatic" over what the Republicans are trying to do in Washington. Smith details the problems the business has had, which center on a decline in cash flow after NASA pulled the plug on a project they were involved with. "The SBA is on my payroll for $5,000 a month," Smith says. If the company didn't have that debt hanging over it, "I could be adding jobs and I could be buying machinery." Hilleary listens but does not seem optimistic that there's anything he can do. He tells Smith that when he decided to take on the debt in order to go after the NASA contract, he "rolled the dice, and that's what makes this country great." It was a gamble that didn't pay off. "My gut feeling is the best we could do is stretch out the payments," Hilleary tells him.

Hilleary seems a little unsure of the approach he should take and how much he should say. "This is the first time I've done anything like this," he says. Now that he's their congressman, people who want help, people who want a favor, local officials who want federal funding for one project or another are all looking to him. That's always been part of the job description, and it's not clear how much Hilleary and the freshmen are going to change that.

Hilleary writes support letters and tries to help district projects through the maze of paperwork and bureaucratic hoops, but he does not issue a press release every time the district wins a federal grant. His mission is to scale back government, not to dole out money. It's not clear, however, that the district's local officials and business leaders see things exactly the same way. Hilleary and many of his classmates consider themselves more than just procurement agents for their districts because "that's what put us in this mess." But different freshmen have different views on just how far they intend to stay from the federal trough.

*   *   *

Shelbyville, in the center of Hilleary's district, is known as the home of the Tennessee walking horse, a high-stepping saddle horse bred primarily for show. There are nearly 50 farms and stables within a 4-mile radius of town that raise and train walkers. Every August the Tennessee Walking Horse National Celebration brings thousands of horse people to Shelbyville from all over the country. Since the town of 14,000 has so few motels, the people of Shelbyville rent rooms in their homes to those attending the festival. And thanks to the South's legendary hospitality, many people return to stay with the same family year after year.

The area is also one of the pencil capitals of the United States. There are four major pencil manufacturing plants in the area. Henry Hulan and his two brothers run the Musgrave Pencil Company, started by "Granddaddy Musgrave" in 1916, making it the oldest pencil company in the South. Hulan says it is also one of the few family-owned pencil companies still in existence, since most have merged with giants like Faber-Castell. Musgrave is now a fourth-generation company; Hulan's 83-year-old father still comes to the plant every day, and his 29-year-old son works there. Musgrave Pencil has about 100 employees, many of them are second and third generation at the plant, just like Hulan, and he knows them all by their first names.

The Hulans are Republicans, although Henry is not politically active. His brother Raford is a Hilleary supporter who contributed to the campaign, but he differs with Hilleary on social issues. Raford says he believes in choice when it comes to the issue of abortion, and although he applauds the fiscal aspects of the contract, he thinks social extremists are dividing the Republican Party.

What has happened in Shelbyville with the Bedford County Republicans is the same thing that's happened in the national GOP, with moderates like Raford Hulan being squeezed out by more extreme conservatives who for a long time felt shut out and now are in control of the agenda. For many years, the party here was headed by General Austin Shoffner, a distinguished veteran who was part of the Bataan death march. Bobby Lemmon, a fundamentalist Christian who owns a religious printing shop, has taken over the chairmanship and helped run Hilleary's campaign in this county. It was Lemmon who brought the young people to Hilleary's Shelbyville debate to have their Bibles signed. The Bedford County Republicans used to be able to meet in a phone booth, but in the last year the party has been energized by Lemmon and other conservatives and has grown considerably.

When Hilleary arrives at the courthouse for his public forum, he takes off his navy blue jacket and rolls up his sleeves as if to signal that he's ready to get down to business and that he's just one of the folks. Neal Moore, a former military officer and retired business executive, was the other co-chair of Hilleary's campaign in this county. Moore, a redhead with thick glasses, seems to be perpetually smiling and spinning yarns. He takes a look at Hilleary and with a sly smile says in a deep drawl, "I have to tell him he's getting a little pudgy; he needs to work out in that gym I'm paying for." Moore says Hilleary's talent for persuasion and an occasional air of innocence remind him of Tom Sawyer: "I can just see him conning someone into painting a fence for him." Hilleary does have a knack for getting people to do things for him, a handy trait for a politician.

The 20 or so people who have come to the courthouse to meet with Hilleary are fervent supporters, and he is interrupted frequently by applause. When he tells them he wants to get rid of the Department of Education, a young man who has brought his two small children to the meeting stands up and says, "The value system of some bureaucrats in Washington is diametrically opposed to the values of people here in Bedford County. They have moral values I'm opposed to—they're not going to teach my children their value system. How dare they." Another, older man stands up and tells Hilleary maybe we shouldn't cut everything "because I think we should have something to remind us how socialism works." He continues, "I'm tired of the left-wing media painting me as a right-wing radical."

The people here are upset at comments made by President Clinton the day before about the bombing of the Oklahoma City federal building. The president suggested that antigovernment sentiment, fueled by some of his critics and radio talk show hosts, led to the bombing. That kind of talk may not be popular today in Shelbyville, but Clinton's performance following the Oklahoma bombing helped his stature considerably in much of the rest of the country. The bombing gave him a chance to look and act presidential in a time of crisis. And the bombing didn't just help Clinton; it hurt the Republicans. It made people stop and think about the antigovernment sentiments being espoused by some of them.

"Christian people, according to this administration, are radical right," says Lemmon, who complains that the media have been focusing all kinds of attention on the deaths and the aftermath of the Oklahoma City bombing even though "the babies that have been aborted . . . never get any airtime on the national news." The remark is greeted by applause, and someone else shouts out, "Abortion is not abortion in my mind. It's baby killing." An older woman tells Hilleary the last thing she watches on television before she goes to sleep is Rush Limbaugh. "We desperately need God back in our country and the federal government out of our lives," exhorts Lemmon, who is wearing two lapel pins, one that says "Jesus Is Lord" and a red, white, and blue elephant. The meeting is a conservative pep rally. If people have come to ask Hilleary a serious question, they don't speak up. Outside the courthouse sits a pickup truck with a miniature Confederate flag and a bumper sticker that reads, "Real Men Love Jesus."

*   *   *

It is a very different kind of crowd that Hilleary breakfasts with the next morning. The two meetings reflect the primary constituencies of the Republican Party: the conservative Christians with a social agenda and the country club business crowd. It is not always an easy partnership. This meeting is in Winchester, about 30 miles south, where several hundred people have gathered to hear from Hilleary and Jerry Benefield, the president and CEO of Nissan USA, who's there to discuss the $30 million engine plant Nissan is building nearby. The plant will bring 200 jobs to the area.

Nissan has a $1.35 billion car and truck manufacturing plant in Smyrna, about 25 miles south of Nashville, which employs 6,000 people, and Saturn has a plant not too far away, in Spring Hill. The auto plants have helped fuel the economic boom Tennessee has experienced over the past five years, not only providing thousands of jobs directly but attracting dozens of suppliers and satellite businesses that create even more jobs.

Tennessee's lack of an income tax, right-to-work laws, absence of unions, and business-friendly tax structure have helped draw companies. The state's unemployment rate stands at 4 percent, and it's not unusual to see a McDonald's with a "Help Wanted" sign offering $7 an hour. Things have definitely turned around in Tennessee. In 1982 nearby Lawrence County had an unemployment rate of 25.8 percent, and more than half of the 22 counties in the Fourth District had unemployment rates over 15 percent that year. By 1994 the Lawrence County unemployment rate had dropped to 6.7 percent, and the district's average unemployment rate was 5 percent.

In Winchester's Franklin County, where Nissan is building its plant, unemployment is 3.5 percent. In 1994 the tax base grew 18 percent, and there were 400 new homes built there. The residents are also excited that Wal-Mart has picked Winchester for one of the seven superstores it will be opening soon in Tennessee. The county also has a new 1-acre indoor pavilion, which is used for farmers' markets, horse shows, sporting events, and concerts and which brought in $300,000 in revenue in its first year of operation.

This is a very Democratic county. Every elected county official is a Democrat, and no Republican presidential candidate has ever carried this county. Never. This was one of only five counties in the whole state that went Democratic across the ticket in 1994. But although Hilleary didn't win this county, he didn't exactly get whomped, losing by only about three points. County executive Clinton Williams thinks that shows a movement toward the Republicans and is a reflection of how much conservative Democrats are disgruntled with the national party's perceived social liberalism. Although Williams is a Democratic elected official, he voted for Hilleary. He thinks his new congressman has "done a great job so far and surprised a lot of people." Williams says shortly after the election Hilleary called him out of the blue and talked with him for an hour about what was going on in the county, something that impressed Williams.

*   *   *

Perhaps the most famous spot in all of Hilleary's district is the Jack Daniel's distillery, not far from Winchester. Hilleary has been invited for a visit by Roger Brashears, the company's chief of public relations and resident raconteur, so he stops by on Wednesday afternoon. Dating to 1866, Jack Daniel's is the country's oldest registered distillery. This home of sour mash Tennessee whiskey is located in Lynchburg, population 700. And although it is now owned by Brown-Forman Corporation, a $1.6 billion operation based in Louisville, Kentucky, with prestige diverse holdings including Korbel champagne, Bolla Italian wines, Lenox china and crystal, and Hartmann luggage, Jack Daniel's still manages to profit from its down-home image. The company's advertising campaign, which features black-and-white photos of Lynchburg and some of the distillery's longtime employees, has helped make it the best-selling premium distilled spirit in the United States.

Jack Daniel's whiskey is still made essentially the way it's always been made. The limestone water from the property's Cave Spring is considered to be one of the secrets to the whiskey. The only other ingredients are corn, rye, and barley malt. The four ingredients are combined with yeast to make a mash that looks something like oatmeal and that is cooked for four days before being pumped through copper stills so that the whiskey can be boiled out. From there the clear liquid is filtered drop by drop through 10 feet of charcoal made from local sugar maple. It is this charcoal mellowing process, which takes six to eight days, that Jack Daniel's claims sets its whiskey apart from other brands. After the process is completed, the whiskey is put into 50-gallon white oak barrels to be aged for at least four years.

Another, far less famous, but in many local people's minds superior and more mellow Tennessee whiskey is also produced in Hilleary's district just up the road from Jack Daniel's. The George A. Dickel distillery in Cascade Hollow first started making whiskey in 1870. There are only 31 employees at Dickel, which produces only 250,000 barrels a year—a drop in the bucket compared to Jack Daniel's 4 million cases. Dickel chills its whiskey almost to freezing before putting it through charcoal filters. Dickel whiskey is also aged in the barrels longer than Jack Daniel's and is slightly higher in proof. But like Jack Daniel's, Dickel is owned by a liquor behemoth based in Louisville, Kentucky, United Distillers. Of the more than 700 distilleries that existed in Tennessee in the 1890s, only these two still remain (that anyone knows about).

Despite the millions of gallons of choice Tennessee whiskey that are produced here every year, you can't buy a glass of Jack Daniel's in Lynchburg because Moore County, like every one of the counties in Hilleary's district, is dry. There are no bars, and in two-thirds of the district's counties there aren't even any liquor stores. A few private clubs serve alcohol, but many of the restaurants in the district don't. It doesn't mean that people don't drink in Tennessee; they just don't often drink in public. Such abstemiousness may in part be a reflection of Tennessee's religious fervor: Nashville, with a population of only 500,000, has 900 churches in its metropolitan area, more per capita than any other city in the United States.

The next day Hilleary is in the eastern part of his district for a round of meetings. The last stop is Rutledge, a tiny town of 900 people, where the main street is Highway 11W, which runs from Knoxville to the Virginia border. This is the most rural and the most Republican county in Hilleary's district. But these folks are more than a little exercised over a decision by the Department of Agriculture to close and consolidate a number of local USDA offices around the country. Of the 22 USDA offices in Hilleary's district, seven are slated for closure under the reorganization plan, one of them here in Grainger County. Hilleary and his staff have been working on this problem since before he took office and have been unable to get anywhere. "I've really beat my head against the wall on this," Hilleary tells a group of local officials. County executive Mickey Hammer suggests maybe agricultural subsidies should be cut to help provide funds to keep offices open. "This is the only federal presence in this county except the IRS and occasionally a federal marshall or revenue agent back when we used to moonshine a little bit," says Hammer with a smile.

Hilleary tells them that the whole thing was handled much like the base-closing commission: The individual decisions cannot be appealed, and it was all "put in concrete" before he ever arrived in Washington. But the officials aren't convinced. They suggest that if this were 17-term Republican Jim Quillen's district, their office wouldn't be closing. "I'm sure . . . lots of people with lots of seniority . . . had offices closed; that's just the way it was," responds Hilleary flatly. He suggests they consider the possibility of making space in the courthouse for some kind of satellite office, but he is met with a host of reasons why that won't work. "It seems to me y'all have an attitude that it's going to be this way or no way and you might wind up having it no way," says Hilleary, smacking his fist on the table. He's clearly getting frustrated. But the officials keep going. They simply will not take no for an answer.

Next they want to know about funding for summer youth programs and school lunch cuts. Ray McElhaney, a Rutledge councilman, says he thinks there should be restrictions on the way states can use the block grants. "You shouldn't be able to build highways with school lunch money," he says. Someone else wants to know why there can't be a transitional period for people moving off welfare and into the workforce and why welfare is being cut but corporate welfare is being left alone.

Walking out of the courthouse, Hilleary tells Hammer he thinks this is the worst meeting he's had in three weeks. It's a remark he regrets as soon as he's made it. He's tired and cranky on the drive back to his district office in Morristown and not in the mood for his final meeting of the day, with members of the AFL-CIO. Hilleary doesn't expect there will be much he and they can agree on, and he certainly doesn't look like he'll have much patience if they start giving him a hard time.

He walks into his district office and tells the group they have 20 minutes. They have eight items they want to cover. Much to Hilleary's surprise, the meeting actually goes pretty well. The union members take turns explaining issues that are important to them and asking Hilleary where he stands. They are not confrontational but just want to get a hearing from Hilleary and ask him to think about some things he may not have considered.

"If y'all don't already know, I'm a free-market person, and I think the free market ought to set the wage," he tells them. But when they ask about raising the minimum wage, Hilleary says at this point he's "kind of torn on that." When they bring up striker replacement laws, Hilleary says, "We can't agree on this. I think it should be an employer's right to replace workers." In the event of a strike, Hilleary says, "employers have to think about a lot of things," such as their suppliers and customers as well as the future of the business. "A threat of a strike is tremendous leverage. Nobody wins in a strike; an employer certainly does not," he tells them. The Hilleary family's textile company is not unionized.

*   *   *

Hilleary's had to learn fast how to be a congressman. Constituents and votes don't wait until you're ready. He is becoming more comfortable with what's expected of him. But he says there's been "an awful lot of on-the-job training." He has discovered that "about 95 percent of your time is spent in nonproductive activity to get to the 5 percent that's really important." And no matter what you're working on, you frequently have to stop to "put out fires in the district, even among your friends."

The folks in Grainger County, for example, have been raising hell about the farm bureau closing ever since it was announced, but despite his many efforts, Hilleary is convinced there's nothing he can do about the closures. "The farmers come in here and vent about their closings—they just vent, vent, vent. But we don't solve any problems," says Hilleary in obvious frustration.

He's had more than a few people mad at him over the government downsizing that's ahead—like one veterans' group from Tennessee that came to Washington to lobby for veterans' programs. Hilleary spent lots of time talking with them, but he made the mistake of telling them the truth. He informed them that in this budget climate even they were going to have to take a cut in funding. That wasn't what the veterans wanted to hear. When they got home, they started sending him letters that Hilleary dubbed "nastygrams." An item in their state newsletter claimed they had got a cold reception from him when they were in Washington. "You just can't win," says Hilleary, shaking his head.

And then there are the constituents he never hears from, the ones who read about cuts in school lunch programs in the paper and decide this isn't what they wanted when they voted for him. Hilleary got to talk to only a small number of people in his tour of the district. There are so many he'll never meet.

A number of people came to his public meetings "just to tell their problems to someone." Often there isn't anything he can do but listen. Sometimes he doesn't want to do anything. When someone "who could have qualified for the Olympic wrestling team" approaches him about getting disability supplemental security income, it confirms Hilleary's feelings about the excesses of government programs. Still, he's found the most satisfying aspect of his job has been intervening in a problem for someone and being able to make a difference ("like when someone comes up to you in the district and thanks you for helping their mother get her Social Security check").

So far Hilleary likes being a congressman. His biggest complaints are the frenetic pace, having to live in a fishbowl, and having to spend so much time fund-raising. And what does he think his constituents most want from him? "I think people want to be listened to; they just want to feel like they'll be represented. They want me to try and effect change, stand up for a conservative philosophy and provide good constituent service."

Part Two

SUMMER–FALL 1995

REALITY SETS IN

8

"DEFUNDING THE LEFT"

WHEN CONGRESS RETURNED from its April recess, Gingrich took the Republicans on a retreat. It was held at Xerox Document University, a spartan training center about an hour from Washington, in Leesburg, Virginia. At first, flush with their success in passing the contract, they were "high-fiving each other" all over the place, according to Hilleary. But the purpose of the retreat was not to celebrate; it was to organize. Gingrich wanted to make sure his troops were in line for the budget push that lay ahead. Budget Committee chairman John Kasich presented the details of the plan that would make it possible to achieve a balanced budget by 2002. When the Republicans realized how deep the cuts would have to be, they were stunned. And there was a noticeable increase in the number of members visiting the bar after the budget presentation.

There would be major cuts in funding for Medicare, science, and education programs, but the Republicans were more concerned about proposed cuts in farm subsidies, transportation and highway money, veterans' programs, and the elimination of corporate tax loopholes. Committee chairs immediately started to push for more money for their pet interests.

The freshmen had a 96 percent average of voting with the House leadership on contract items. The first 100 days and passing the Contract with America were just "spring training" compared to the long budget season ahead, Gingrich told me in an interview a few weeks before the retreat. He was well aware how hard it was going to be to hold his troops together now that the real work was starting.

He acknowledged that the Democrats scored on the school lunch issue but chalked that up largely to his own mishandling of the matter, for not answering back right away. Gingrich said he was "stunned" that out of all the items in the contract, this would be "the one place to punch us." He didn't think Americans would believe the Democrats' claims: "I think we misread the issue. We should have gone after

them very aggressively right after they said it." But the Republicans were so convinced that what they were doing was right, they didn't think they needed to stop to
put out brushfires.

The most important decisions Congress makes involve money—taxpayers'
money—who gets it and how they get to spend it. But in the 104th Congress, since
budgets were going down, not up, doling out money was a much more selective
process than it had been in the past.

Being a member of Congress used to be a lot of fun. It was about saying yes. Yes,
I'll make sure you get the funding for that dam, that missile system, that community
center. People would come into your office and you could promise to do things for
them. But all that changed with the election of 1994. In the 104th Congress it
wasn't as easy to make promises. And the freshmen were feeling the pressure. "There
will be some freshmen who will fall off the wagon this summer on various votes,"
predicted Hilleary, referring to the upcoming spending bills and whether his class
would stay true to its budget-cutting goal. "But by and large the percentage will be
less" than for more senior Republicans.

Hilleary and the other freshmen have to balance the interests of their constituents
with their commitment to downsize government. "If I can't, I won't be reelected. But
that's what I'm going to try to do. Either we turn back the direction of bigger government or we don't. We have to take all the punches and let all the blood spill, and
if we're still standing after the dust settles, then we should be the majority party for
the foreseeable future," said Hilleary.

Hilleary is convinced the Republicans are "right about what we're doing," and
even if his constituents cannot be similarly convinced, "It is so much more important than any one of our seats."

Public opinion polls showed overwhelming support for balancing the federal budget in the first half of 1995. But it was not at all clear how much Americans were
willing to give up in order to do it. Several polls, including an ABC–*Washington Post*
survey in May, showed a majority of Americans opposed the Republican plans to get
rid of the Commerce, Energy, and Education Departments, as well as many other
details of their budget plan. The Republicans wanted to eliminate dozens of federal
offices and agencies, such as the president's Council of Economic Advisors, and cut
billions from foreign aid, mass transit, and low-income home fuel assistance programs, just to name a few.

Although Gingrich knew many of his freshmen were "prepared to put their job on
the line," that's not what he wanted. He wanted to hold onto the majority and his
Speakership. His advice to the freshmen on budget cutting was, "Don't tell me you're
prepared to sacrifice your seat; tell me how we do it where you get reelected."

On June 20, with House consideration of the first appropriations bill of the 1996
budget, Hilleary had to face such a choice: $2.6 million in funding for a new out-
door shooting range for the Army National Guard in Tullahoma, Tennessee. The
military was one area where the Republicans believed they should spend not less but
more—almost 30 percent more than Clinton had requested for the 1995 budget for

military construction. This shooting range was just one of a number of pet projects the Republicans had added to the budget.

Luis Gutierrez, a second-term Democrat from Chicago, offered an amendment to eliminate funding for the shooting range, pointing out that Tullahoma already had an indoor shooting range and the Army National Guard had not even requested the funding. "The majority in this House has decided we can't precisely meet our nation's needs for more police officers on our streets or more job-training programs for our workers or more Head Start for our kids or protecting Medicare for our seniors. But they want to argue today we can find $3 million for a firing range the Defense Department doesn't want. It is a question of priorities," Gutierrez said. Voting for the shooting range "says that despite all the rhetoric, despite all the promises, despite the American voters' overwhelming desire to have us change business as usual inside the Beltway, the pork is still sizzling. Take the pork out of the frying pan today," he urged.

It was up to Hilleary to defend the shooting range. He called it a vital project that would maintain the readiness of the National Guard troops: "It is the kind of training our soldiers need to fight and win wars." But Hilleary hadn't ever done this before and wasn't too sure of himself. When Bill Hefner, an 11-term Democrat from North Carolina who was on the Appropriations Committee, tried to help him out by asking how old the existing shooting range was and what was wrong with it, Hilleary had to admit he didn't know. When Hefner asked how big the new shooting range would be, Hilleary didn't know that either. "I think it is just something that the men and women in the guard and the reserve, for that matter, deserve. From my participation in Desert Storm, I know this is the type of training we had," was the best response Hilleary could muster.

Despite his somewhat less than impassioned rhetorical effort, Hilleary and the shooting range managed to squeak by. The Gutierrez amendment was defeated by two votes. But 21 of Hilleary's fellow freshmen, most of them hard-core budget hawks like Sam Brownback, Steve Largent, Mark Souder, and Mark Neumann, as well as Budget Committee chairman John Kasich, voted against funding the project.

Neumann had made it his personal mission to ferret out waste wherever he could find it, and he had decided to take on a project that was in the home district of Barbara Vucanovich, the chair of the Appropriations Committee's Military Construction Subcommittee. Neumann offered an amendment to eliminate $6.9 million earmarked for the construction of 33 officer housing units at military installations around the country. Including the cost of demolishing the 30- to 40 year-old housing they would replace, the officers' quarters would cost an average of $208,000 a unit. "We could take care of 437 barracks spaces with the same money we are going to spend on these 33 housing units," Neumann argued.

When Jerry Lewis, a nine-term California Republican and another Appropriations Subcommittee chairman, asked Neumann if he had discussed his amendment with Vucanovich before bringing it to the floor, Neumann looked at him blankly. Neumann was a bit of a naif when it came to the political ways of Washington. He took pride in that. "No, sir, I did not. I simply looked for housing units that were going to cost in excess of $200,000 per unit. I concluded it would not be a fair or good expenditure of our tax dollars to spend the money . . . when we could, in fact, be building barracks spaces."

No Republican spoke in favor of Neumann's amendment, but many Democrats, happy to cut a little from defense and embarrass the Republicans at the same time, joined with most of the GOP freshmen to help pass the amendment 266–160.

Afterward Neumann wasn't at all sorry about what he had done. Several months later he told me, "It never occurred to me that I'm supposed to ask permission to cut out wasteful government spending." Neumann is not the type to ask permission. All through the summer he would fight his guerrilla war against items in the budget he considered wasteful. And a number of his fellow freshmen joined him in the effort.

The freshmen had a kind of competitive barometer, a pureness scale, as it were, for who in the class was the most sincere about budget cutting. And they weighed themselves against each other on votes. Neumann, Souder, Brownback, and Largent were usually at the most austere end of the spectrum. They didn't believe in cutting the kind of deals Congress had engaged in for so long—you vote for my thing and I'll vote for yours. But there were plenty of freshmen who did and who worked to protect programs that affected their districts. It was understood that if members, especially the more vulnerable freshmen, felt they had to vote against a bill for self-protection, because something in it was bad for an important group of constituents, that was OK. It was even OK with a hard-core budget hawk like Mark Souder, who understood how tough it was going to be for some of his classmates to hold onto their seats in 1996.

For Van Hilleary and Zach Wamp, protecting funding for the Tennessee Valley Authority and the Appalachian Regional Commission (ARC) was something they had to do. "I don't believe in pulling the rug out from under them, although I do think they should take their proportional cut," Hilleary would explain. Created in 1965 as one of Lyndon Johnson's Great Society programs, the ARC provides economic development assistance to 13 states from New York and Pennsylvania south to Tennessee, Mississippi, and Alabama. John Kasich and his Budget Committee had recommended its elimination, but it was saved in the Appropriations Committee by a group of southern members. But ARC's funding was cut to $142 million, 50 percent of its 1995 level. The TVA took a 28 percent cut, to $103 million.

On June 12, when the Energy and Water Development Appropriations Act came to the floor, Scott Klug, a third-term Republican from Wisconsin, proposed amendments to eliminate both programs. He pointed to certain grants that the ARC had made—$750,000 to build a new football stadium for the Carolina Panthers, money for the Alabama Music Hall of Fame, and an access road for a Pennsylvania ski resort—as projects that the federal government should not be paying for. "There was a need for this program when it was set up in the 1960s . . . but here we are 30 years later. How much longer? How many billions more? . . . The problem is this is a double-dipping and in some cases triple-dipping program that has fundamentally benefited 13 states in this country at the disadvantage of the other 37. . . . What is it to-day about a poor community in West Virginia or Georgia or Kentucky that is different from New Mexico or Wisconsin or Missouri? The answer is absolutely nothing. . . . Appalachia needed help. My friends, 30 years of help is enough," Klug asserted.

ARC supporters argued that the program did a great deal of good in job training and helping severely distressed counties and was instrumental in cutting the poverty and infant mortality rates in the region. One after another, members stood to extol the virtues of this model program. "I am firmly committed to cutting the budget and cutting programs which do not work, but ARC does work; it is a program that has proven itself," said Roger Wicker of Mississippi. "It is not a federal handout where we take money out of somebody's pocket and write somebody else a check. It develops infrastructure to create private jobs in the private sector."

Zach Wamp, who had brought his young son onto the floor with him, said local officials in his district considered the Appalachian Regional Commission one of the most effective federal programs in existence. "This is a step toward a balanced budget, a 50 percent cut in funding. This is what a conservative Republican would support, not oppose, as we seek to share this patriotic burden to balance the federal budget across the board," said Wamp.

Few people rose in support of Klug's effort. Sam Brownback of Kansas was the only freshman to do so. "The question we have to ask ourselves today, then: Is this a program worth continuing, adding more debt on our kids? . . . I think that is the central question we have to ask. Is this worth putting more debt on the kids? . . . The biggest problem we are facing as a nation today . . . is the stupid debt and the amount we keep adding to it. . . . If this is worth continuing today, what about next year, and the year after that, when we really get to the tough choices, in year three, four, five, six, and seven, to balance the budget? I would suggest that now is the time to make the tough choice. . . . We are at a point in time in history where we just cannot mortgage the kids any further."

Klug's amendment was soundly defeated, 319–108, with just 30 Republican freshmen joining Brownback to vote in favor of it. One of the few who voted to eliminate the agency even though he came from a state that received money through the program was Mark Sanford, a 35-year-old real estate developer from Charleston, South Carolina. Sanford had never held public office before being elected to Congress, and he was an equal opportunity budget cutter. He supported cuts in welfare but also in agriculture subsidies and congressional staffs, and during his campaign he had suggested the growth of entitlement programs like Social Security and Medicare should be held to 2 percent a year. Sanford, a term limits supporter and strong proponent of the idea of citizen legislators, vowed to serve only three terms in Congress. He took no PAC money and slept in his office because he said he saved time that way and because he didn't want to get too comfortable in Washington.

Klug next moved to kill the TVA. Only two other members spoke on behalf of that amendment, one of them Jim Ramstad, a third-term Republican from Minnesota. "This is pure pork. How can we justify federal tax dollars, federal taxpayers' dollars, going to such functions as boat landings, campgrounds and logger education? . . . We must, must have the political courage to shut down such programs as this or allow states to take them over. . . . The American taxpayers are sick and tired, with all due respect to my good friends from Tennessee who are here fighting hard and representing the Tennessee Valley Authority well, but with all respect to them, Mr. Chairman, this is pork barrel politics in its pure form, and American taxpayers are sick and tired of such politics. Mr. Chairman, this is a real test of whether this Congress is serious about fiscal discipline."

This was a big one for Wamp. Six thousand TVA employees live in his district. "The Tennessee Valley Authority is not perfect," Wamp began. "Neither is the Pentagon perfect, neither are the Centers for Disease Control perfect, neither is the White House perfect, and neither is this institution perfect. But I have not seen any amendments to zero those core functions out." If his colleagues found it a bit over the top to compare the TVA with Congress, the White House, and the Pentagon, no one said anything about it. And the defense of the TVA was very much bipartisan, if regional. With the exception of Harold Ford, a Democrat from Memphis, the entire Tennessee delegation, five Republicans and three Democrats, strongly opposed additional cuts to the TVA, as did Ed Whitfield, a freshman Republican from Kentucky, and three Democrats from Alabama.

Jim Quillen, the 17-term dean of the Tennessee delegation, pointed out to Klug that Wisconsin had 14 Corps of Engineers projects that cost $15 million. "I do not see any amendment offered by the gentleman from Wisconsin to cut out the Corps of Engineers projects in Wisconsin. That is what he is trying to do to seven states in the Tennessee Valley area, to cut out and rape the TVA program. I think what is good for the goose is good for the gander."

Hilleary, who had not spoken on behalf of the Appalachian Regional Commission, did speak for the TVA. "I grew up in the very shadow of TVA. From . . . the home I grew up in, you could actually see the TVA dam and the cooling tower sticking out from the trees. We actually had our best friends in the world work for TVA. Now their sons and daughters work for TVA. TVA has been a lot of good things to the Tennessee Valley. It has been some bad things. It has provided jobs, flood control, electricity, and in doing so, provided a lot of economic development in a region that sorely needed it. . . . It is a long ways from being perfect. . . . I have no problem with TVA taking a hit. We all have to take a hit to balance this budget.

"I have no problem with some federal programs' being zeroed out. I think there are some programs in the federal government that are absolutely worthless and should be zeroed out. However, that is not the case in the TVA's nonpower budget. . . . The TVA's nonpower budget goes to a large extent for flood control, navigational management, ecological and environmental stewardship. These things, once again, will have to be picked up by some other federal agency. . . . All of us are budget hawks up here. Many of us in the freshman class ran on this, and this is what we are dedicated to. However, this is a big distinction in this particular case. I urge all my colleagues in the freshman class and otherwise to vote no on the Klug amendment."

Klug and his amendment were defeated 284–144. But 42 of Hilleary's freshman colleagues were not swayed by his personal pitch and voted in favor of eliminating the TVA. That's how it went all summer: One member's essential was another member's pork. Many of the freshmen thought, probably correctly, that the only way to make a dent in the budget deficit was to rip programs out by the roots, like the cabinet agencies they were seeking to abolish. Otherwise all their hard work could be reversed by a future Congress—or even, as it would turn out, by this one the following year.

But they were not driven only by their budget-cutting penchant in choosing programs for elimination. They had other, more ideological motives as well. For example, the Legal Services Corporation, which funds legal assistance for the poor, had fallen foul of some of their supporters, including businesses and landlords who had been sued by Legal Services. And the Christian Coalition thought the government was just making it easier for the poor to get a divorce. The Christian Coalition's executive director, Ralph Reed, wrote to his group's members, "What we are complaining about is the systematic subsidy for the break-up of families in the inner cities." Critics of Legal Services complained that the agency engaged in political advocacy and wanted the group prevented from providing legal services not only in divorces but in cases involving discrimination in housing and hiring, consumer fraud, utility shutoffs, patients' rights, and adoptions.

The Republicans also wanted to eliminate AmeriCorps, Bill Clinton's volunteer program, and the Goals 2000 education reform created by George Bush. And when it came to the National Endowment for the Humanities (NEH), the National Endowment for the Arts (NEA), and the Corporation for Public Broadcasting, their feelings ran much deeper. Now that they were in charge, the Republicans intended to make life miserable for the people they considered to be their enemies, those who had made life miserable for them for so long: the liberals and intellectuals. They liked to describe this as "defunding the left."

Gingrich had started talking about privatizing the Corporation for Public Broadcasting before the session even began, but the Republicans soon realized from the phone calls and letters they were receiving that public broadcasting and the arts had loyal and enthusiastic supporters, and many of them were Republicans. Whether "country club" Republicans in suburban areas who enjoyed taking advantage of arts programs or rural residents who relied on public broadcasting as a major source of news and information, they did not want to see the agencies eliminated.

Many of the freshmen from the South and Midwest saw the NEA and public radio and television at best as elitist, liberal, East Coast institutions enjoyed largely by the wealthy, who could afford to support them without the government's help. They saw public broadcasting at worst as biased and left-wing and the NEA as an organization that funded performance art that was obscene and sacrilegious and mocked patriotic ideals—in short, it was un-American! "They don't involve a great deal of money, but they're high profile and all of them have been tools of the left for a long time," explained family values social conservative Steve Largent.

By the middle of July, the freshmen were eager to flex their muscles. They had pretty much been going along with the leadership, and they were starting to worry about getting bogged down in the system and co-opted by the porking in the appropriations process. The freshmen realized they could say no to something and stop a piece of legislation in its tracks, for without them the Republican leadership didn't have the votes. But so far all they'd done was threaten to use that power. The time had come for them to assert themselves, to keep their budget-cutting momentum rolling.

The NEA was a perfect target. As John Shadegg would recall later, by calling for elimination of the NEA they could take a strong philosophical stand and not cause any serious personal hard feelings with any other Republican members trying to protect their districts, because this wasn't a program that affected just a few states or a region.

The authorization of the NEA, which was part of the Department of the Interior appropriation, called for a 40 percent reduction in the NEA's funding to $99.5 million and a phaseout of the agency in three years. All cultural funding for 1996 was just 0.02 percent of the total budget. Each American contributed 64 cents of his or her taxes to arts funding and $1,000 to military spending that year. The total federal funds spent on the arts equaled just 10 percent of the cost of a single B-2 bomber. But the freshmen considered that still too much federal money for the arts.

The freshmen tried to get the NEA killed in committee so there wouldn't have to be a vote on the floor, but they failed thanks to the efforts of Republican moderates who were supporters of the arts agency and pushed to keep it alive at least for the next three years. The freshmen were afraid that a future Congress would reverse the decision to phase out the NEA in three years. "We really felt we were painted into a corner," said Largent, who led the freshman effort to kill the NEA. They could have offered an amendment to zero out the funding, as Klug had attempted with the TVA and Appalachian Regional Commission. But since the GOP moderates were sure to vote with the Democrats, they didn't have the votes to win, and they knew it. They wanted to force the leadership to negotiate with them and decided the only way to do it was to defeat the rule for the Interior Department's appropriation bill.

Every piece of legislation that comes to the floor must be preceded by a rule, and the vote on the rule is usually along straight party lines, in this Congress the Republicans voting yes and Democrats voting no. The NEA funding came to the floor around 7 P.M. on July 12. The Republicans knew there was a move afoot by the freshmen, and they spoke of it on the floor before the vote. Appropriations Committee chairman Robert Livingston warned the freshmen of the dire consequences should they bring down the rule: "If this rule goes down, the next rule will probably also go down, and we will not end up getting a rule passed that allows us to consider the Interior appropriations bill on the floor, which means that we will tie up the business of the House, possibly risk not having an August break, taking the whole schedule into September, . . . and causing ourselves great problems. Anybody that has an issue that they want debated on this floor of this House can bring it forward.

Anybody that wants to limit any program in the bill to zero can offer that." Rules Committee chairman Gerald Solomon was clearly angered at the prospect of losing a rule. It was a matter of pride and losing face in front of the Democrats: "Any member of this body, if they do not like the Endowment for the Arts, the Endowment for the Humanities, they have a right to bring it on this floor. Let us fight it out like men, and let us cut it. That is what I am going to help them do."

None of the freshmen spoke on the floor. They weren't even sitting together because they were trying not to tip their hand. But people were onto them anyway. Democrat Norm Dicks of Washington state referred to Steve Largent by saying, "I am surprised: My good colleague, the gentleman from Oklahoma, one of the great athletes, great competitors in this chamber—I never thought I would see the day when he would want to prevail on a technicality, would not want to come out here and get it right, talk about the National Endowment for the Arts. Let us have a fair debate. Let the Congress decide this issue." But Largent remained silent. And the Democrats were divided over what to do. They had been warned by GOP whip Tom DeLay that the Republicans didn't have enough votes to pass the rule. Some of them thought they should vote yes to foil the freshmen and support the NEA, but many others thought there was too much they didn't like in the Interior bill to go along with it. And they didn't really want to help the Republicans with their little family problem either.

The GOP freshman class was split down the middle. Thirty-seven freshmen, including all the moderates in the class, voted in favor of the rule. They were joined by nearly 20 Democrats who were attempting to keep it from failing. Thirty-six Republican freshmen, including most of the budget hawks and social conservatives, along with Budget chairman Kasich, voted no, and the rule was defeated.

What happened after the vote was pandemonium, as Souder remembers it. The Republican leadership "went berserk," with senior Republicans telling the freshmen they were trying to destroy the party. Souder believed they would be able to get a compromise in a couple of hours and come back to the floor with a new rule. But the freshmen weren't too sure whose move it was. Somebody said, "Go stand in the back, and they'll come to you.'" And that's exactly what happened. Dick Armey came over to the leaders of the group—Largent, Souder, Tom Coburn, and David McIntosh—and told them to follow him to a room in the Capitol. The freshmen and the Republican moderates went at it for a while until Gingrich came in and asked each side to describe what it thought the other side wanted. This was a technique he used frequently when the moderates and the conservative freshmen clashed on an issue. The older Republicans said the freshmen wanted a date certain for the elimination of the NEA, and the freshmen said the moderate Republicans wanted enough money and time so the agency could wean itself from the government.

After about three hours, close to midnight, Armey had worked out a compromise. The NEA funding would extend for only two years instead of three, and the agency would be terminated in 1998. The freshmen could live with that. Armey told them in exasperation, "No one has ever made me look like a friend of the NEA before."

"Last night was magical," Van Hilleary said the next day in reference to the fresh-man defeat of the rule. Hilleary considered his no vote on the rule "the best thing I've done here in a while," especially in light of his defense of the TVA and the ARC earlier that same day. "I found myself in an awkward position, defending govern-ment programs which I'm not used to, and I found my bedfellows pretty strange, so that no vote kind of exorcised the demons. There are very few programs that deserve to be zeroed out, but NEA and NEH are two of them."

The freshmen really felt good about what they had done; they felt they had made a difference. Their victory also made them more arrogant than ever. "We had to show them—'You're going to have to listen to us even if we have to vote with the Democrats on a rule,'" said Souder. "I felt it was a principled battle and an impor-tant one," said Largent. The freshmen had to "draw a line in the sand," he said. The freshmen were convinced that their agenda should be everyone's agenda, that the November election had given them a mandate. The budget had to be cut, and it had to be done their way. They had no patience for anyone, Democrat or Republican, who had the temerity to disagree with them or attempted to slow them down. "If we're forced to use more guerrilla tactics, we're not opposed to doing that, and we're proud we're capable of pulling it off," said Largent.

Largent, along with Souder, Coburn, McIntosh, Neumann, John Shadegg, and Sue Myrick, had taken to meeting for breakfast at least once a week in the Capitol's members' dining room to talk about how things were going and plot strategy. Largent, Myrick, Brownback, and Shadegg were all on the Budget Committee, so they had access to a lot of information. It was at one of these breakfasts where the plan to bring down the NEA rule was hatched.

The breakfast club also came up with an early-warning plan for monitoring spending, a little something they named the Freshman Appropriations Watch. Dif-ferent freshmen were each given their own appropriations bill to keep an eye on. They were watching to see if any of the spending bills that came out of the Appro-priations Committee increased the dollar amount set by the Budget Committee. A blue alert signaled that provisions the freshmen considered critical had been dropped. A red alert meant an appropriations bill had blown out its spending target. When an alert was issued, the freshmen were organized to spring into action.

Another freshman group, the Congressional Family Caucus, was organized by Tom Coburn, a 48-year-old Oklahoma obstetrician and deacon in the Baptist Church. The caucus was made up of like-minded conservatives who professed to be deeply re-ligious and who were eager to push a social as well as budget-cutting agenda that in-cluded opposition to abortion, support for mandatory school prayer, limitation of gay rights, and federal support for private and religious schools through the use of vouch-ers and school choice. Members of the group often prayed together before votes and met for Bible study. And when they were in Washington, Coburn, Largent, and Zach Wamp also lived together in a townhouse not far from the Capitol.

Coburn was driven by what he saw as the moral decline of this country and main-tained that the Centers for Disease Control was suppressing information about the severity of the epidemic of sexually transmitted diseases in the United States. When he arrived in Washington, Coburn gave his office staff a lecture on sexually transmitted diseases. And he also discussed the issue at public forums back in his home district, which he always began with a prayer. At one speech to a school group, Coburn even showed graphic slides of the kind of sores sexually transmitted diseases can cause.

Coburn, Souder, and Largent were becoming increasingly impatient with the leadership's decision to put off votes on social issues. They were staunchly opposed to abortion and wanted to do all they could to stop it. Even if they couldn't overturn the Supreme Court's *Roe v. Wade* decision, they could see to it that the federal budget was purged of any funding for abortions. So as each appropriation bill came to the floor, they attempted to make it harder for women—poor women, government workers, women in the military—to receive abortions. They cut overseas family-planning money and prevented federal employees from using their government health insurance to pay for abortions. And they planned to bring up amendments that would allow states to forbid the use of Medicaid funds for abortions for poor women in cases of rape and incest, restrict medical schools that receive federal money from teaching abortion procedures, prevent women soldiers stationed abroad from receiving abortions in overseas military hospitals, and withhold funding for any family-planning agency like Planned Parenthood that also provides abortion services.

Their efforts were not embraced by all House Republicans but rather threatened seriously to split the conference. A group of GOP women House members met with Gingrich in July to complain to him about the antiabortion agenda of the conservative freshmen and the increasing frequency with which they were forced to vote on the issue.

*   *   *

Despite their victory over the NEA, many freshmen, including Hilleary, were still frustrated. "Every time we vote for a cut in these appropriation bills, it's just spent somewhere else. We're bleeding all over ourselves making these tough cuts, and it's just going to be spent somewhere else." By mid-July the House had cut an additional $125 million from the already trimmed Republican budget. But as programs were being eliminated through amendments offered on the floor, the appropriations committee was reallocating the additional money to bills it was still working on. This distressed not only the freshmen but a number of moderate Democrats who were concerned about deficit reduction. They had come up with a concept called the lockbox, which would create a fund where all of the savings realized by program reductions would be placed so they could be applied to the deficit. Several members, including Michael Crapo, an Idaho Republican; Bill Brewster, the only Democrat in the Oklahoma delegation; and Jane Harman, a second-term Democrat from Los Angeles, had introduced lockbox legislation. Largent and Myrick, on behalf of many of the freshmen, had sent a letter to the Republican leadership asking for a vote on the lockbox provision.

On July 12, prior to the vote on the NEA rule, Rules Committee chairman Solomon told Harman on the floor that the Republicans were working on a lockbox they thought could also pass the Senate and as soon as they had ironed out all the details it would not only be attached to the first available appropriations bill but would be made retroactive to the beginning of the appropriations process. Once the lockbox was approved by the House, all of the reductions that had been made since the appropriations process began would go straight to deficit reduction, Solomon promised Harman. On the basis of that promise and as a sign of good faith, Harman voted with the Republicans on the rule for NEA funding.

The freshmen were also starting to think their effort to abolish at least one cabinet department was going nowhere. They had zeroed in on Commerce as the best candidate and were seeking a sign from Gingrich that everything was still on track. Gingrich wrote a letter to William Clinger, the chairman of the Committee on Government Reform, urging him to act on a bill to kill the Commerce Department that could be folded into the final budget bill in the fall. In late July, when the appropriation for the Commerce Committee came to the floor, Clinger promised that he was working "to effect a timely dismantling of this department." The freshmen agreed to vote for the Commerce funding with the understanding that it was just a matter of time before the cabinet agency was killed. There wasn't even the slimmest chance that Commerce or any other cabinet department would be eliminated by the 104th Congress. But if the freshmen had any inkling of this, they showed no evidence of it. And they pressed on.

9

CUTTING THE MINK SUBSIDY

WASHINGTON IS UNCOMFORTABLY HOT and incredibly humid in the summer. For much of the city's first 100 years, European diplomats considered it a hardship post, largely because of the climate and the somewhat uncivilized nature of the inhabitants.

Parts of Washington were in fact once a swamp, and the Potomac River flowed much closer to the White House before the land between there and the Tidal Basin was filled in. The Lincoln Memorial now stands on land that was at one time under water. But the Capitol building was always on high ground. City planner Pierre L'Enfant chose a natural hill for the location because he said it stood "as a pedestal waiting for a monument." The Capitol is located not too far from the point where the Potomac and Anacostia Rivers come together. Early in the city's history the Tiber Creek, which ran past the foot of Capitol Hill, was dammed to form the Washington Canal. It was used for cheap transportation but became a foul-smelling open sewer, its stagnant water breeding swarms of mosquitoes.

Every summer the stench and the heat drove out of the city those who could afford it, as well as the president and the Congress. Congress would convene on December 1 and work through the late spring in off years and through March 1 in election years. Only a few times, such as 1861, when Abraham Lincoln called it back into session, did Congress work through the summer. In the mid-1930s, air conditioning was installed in the Capitol and the White House, and everything changed. Congress held its first year-round session in 1940. But in 1970 members wanted to foreclose the possibility of working through the entire summer, so they passed a measure that mandated Congress could not be in session during the month of August unless both chambers OK'd the move by roll call vote. Since then the August recess has become sacred.

During the summer, which can last for nearly five months in Washington, all of the Capitol buildings are kept extremely cool, almost cold, really, on account of all the men in suits talking. The temperature is adjusted so they can keep their jackets on, keep talking, and never work up a sweat. But as the summer of 1995 wore on, no amount of air conditioning could handle the hot air in Washington. Tempers flared not only between Republicans and Democrats on the floor but also among the Republicans as they attempted to stay together on the divisive appropriations bills.

And the pace, the long hours, and the many days away from home were adding to the strain. Because they had spent the first three months of the session working on the Contract with America instead of the budget, they were now forced to move through the spending bills at breakneck speed. They were all in kind of a daze, just moving from one thing to the next. By the time they made it to Friday, they had already forgotten what they had done on Monday. The August recess beckoned like a cool, green oasis. The members wanted to be out of Washington. The time that had been picked as the start of their monthlong break—3 P.M., August 4—became their mantra. But then the leadership started saying they might not make it, and the president asked Congress to work through August if they hadn't finished the appropriations bills. Stay in Washington all summer and give up their vacation? No way. They would finish somehow. No matter what it took.

George Nethercutt of Spokane, Washington, was living in a basement apartment behind the Supreme Court and making the eight-hour flight back home every weekend. When he returned on Monday, flying from West to East and losing three hours, he would often get up at 4:15 A.M. so he could be in Washington by 4 in the afternoon for the first votes of the week. In June he decided to move his wife, 14-year-old daughter, and 10-year-old son to D.C. "I want to keep my family intact. I didn't get this job to lose my family," he said. He wanted to see his children grow up. He rented a house in McLean, Virginia.

Sonny Bono also brought his family to D.C. But he and Nethercutt were among the few freshmen who did. The freshmen, many of whom had small children, believed that moving their families to Washington would somehow make them a part of the very place they despised. They had to remain separate from Washington; they couldn't start liking it too much.

*   *   *

Washington seemed a world away from the hometowns of the freshmen—and from a place like Dodge City in southwestern Kansas, where Pat Roberts, chairman of the Agriculture Committee, comes from. Most of Roberts's constituents are farmers who grow wheat, sorghum, and corn or raise beef cattle. More wheat is grown in the First District of Kansas than in any other congressional district in the country, and some years the district even ranks ahead of most states in wheat production.

As with many crops, the Agriculture Department helps set wheat prices, makes direct payments to farmers, and tells them how much they can plant. Washington has a great deal of control over the lives of Roberts's constituents, and for a long time they had been telling him they didn't like it. Once every five years, Congress approves a new farm bill, a massive undertaking with major implications not only for America's 2 million farmers but also for hundreds of agribusiness and food-related companies. In 1990 the 750-page farm bill covered not only price supports and commodity programs but export and market promotion, soil conservation, food safety, food stamps, and the school lunch program.

In the summer of 1995 Congress was set to do it again, but in the budget-cutting climate that existed it was clear the farmers were going to suffer some cuts, too. Budget chairman Kasich originally set a target goal of cutting $16 billion out of the $40 billion farm subsidy program over five years. But after much pressure from Roberts, Kasich and the rest of the leadership agreed to reduce that figure to $9 billion and allow most of the cuts to come after the year 2000. Roberts's strongest argument involved the GOP freshmen. Half of them came from farm country, and a severe cut in agriculture programs could jeopardize their chances for reelection. Roberts argued cuts that were too deep would jeopardize the Republicans' majority.

Roberts knew even the scaled-back cuts were going to be hard to sell to the farmers. But he reasoned that if the reductions were offset by more independence from the government, more freedom as it were, the farmers might go for it. This was the cornerstone of the Freedom to Farm Act developed by Roberts and his staff. Freedom to Farm would replace the traditional subsidy programs with annual payments to farmers that declined over a period of five years. These payments would provide a transition to market-based farming. The new system would allow farmers to plant any crop they wanted and let the market decide the price rather than having the government control both, as it did under the old system.

Since the Republicans were pushing for less government control in just about every other area, getting the government out of the farming business seemed to make perfect sense. Not only had the government been telling farmers what crops to plant, it had also been telling many of them not to plant anything at all. Over the previous 10 years, the Department of Agriculture had paid farmers to keep idle more than 50 million acres, an area equal in size to the states of Ohio and Indiana combined. The reason for the policy was to drive up crop prices. But the results weren't always good for rural America. According to a study conducted by the University of Minnesota, the government's acreage-idling policy had contributed to reducing rural populations by one-third since 1950. Under a market-driven system, farmers would be free to decide for themselves which crops would be the most profitable for them to grow. And early reaction to Roberts's plan indicated many farmers supported the idea of getting the government out of their fields.

Before Freedom to Farm was introduced, the appropriations bill dealing with nonentitlement Agriculture Department spending came to the floor. This represented only 20 percent of the department's total budget and did not include entitlement spending for food stamps and subsidy payments. The recommended appropriation was $62.5 billion, $5.5 billion less than the department received in 1995. The rural development loan fund, which supported economic development in rural areas, was cut by $37.6 million, and rural housing programs were cut in half. Left in place, however, were a number of programs that many freshmen thought should be eliminated as well. The first of these to come to the floor involved tobacco. Congressman Dick Durbin, an Illinois Democrat who was 14 when his father died of lung cancer, had been fighting tobacco for years and was one of the principal sponsors of the regulation that got smoking banned from all U.S. airline flights.

On July 20 Durbin, along with Republican James Hansen of Utah and Washington freshman Linda Smith, offered an amendment to cut all federal funds for extension services and crop insurance for tobacco farmers, a move that would save taxpayers $23 million a year. "Uncle Sam ought to get out of the tobacco business. We have no business subsidizing the growth, production, and processing of a product which kills hundreds of thousands of Americans each year," Durbin argued. Smith was strongly against tobacco and even more strongly opposed to tobacco lobbyists. "I found out over the last couple of days it takes courage to go up against the tobacco industry. You not only get a lot of calls to your office, you get a lot of pressure," said Smith. "Please, folks, do what is right. Do not do what the tobacco industry wants. They were prowling the halls here yesterday and the day before. Ignore them and do what is right and vote against the tobacco subsidy," Smith urged her colleagues.

The tobacco lobbyists had some powerful help in pushing for defeat of the Durbin amendment. Only a few weeks before the vote, Republican conference chairman John Boehner had been passing out checks from tobacco PACs to Republican members on the floor of the House. Smith was one of several freshmen who were outraged and pointed to what Boehner had done as an example of why campaign finance reform was so badly needed.

It is illegal to solicit money while in the Capitol or any federal building, which is why members of Congress have to go down the street to the national committee offices to make fund-raising phone calls. At one time federal law further prohibited members from receiving campaign contributions in federal buildings, but the law was changed. It was no longer illegal to accept or hand out donations in those same buildings, even on the floor of the House.

Boehner later admitted his actions gave the appearance of impropriety and said he would not repeat them. And a year and a half later, in the first month of the 105th session of Congress, the House quietly voted to make it illegal for members to accept funds on the House floor, the cloakrooms, or the Speaker's lobby. However, they can still be handed checks in their offices, committee rooms, or anywhere else in the Capitol.

In the months leading up to the agriculture votes, tobacco PACs contributed hundreds of thousands of dollars to members of Congress. During the first six months of 1995, tobacco PACs donated more than $700,000, 80 percent of it to Republicans and $200,000 of it to freshmen. Five of the top 10 House recipients of tobacco PAC contributions were GOP freshmen.

Tobacco companies had a lot to lose if the government intervened in their business, and with President Clinton and David Kessler at the FDA talking about doing just that, the tobacco companies made sure to cover their bases. In 1995 the tobacco companies donated more than $4 million in PAC and soft money to candidates and political parties. And the country's largest cigarette companies—Philip Morris, R. J. Reynolds, and R. J. R. Nabisco—were the top overall soft money donors to the Republican Party in 1995, according to Common Cause. In the first six months of 1995, they contributed $1.5 million to the Republicans, 10 times what they had given the party in 1993. An overwhelming 82 percent of all the members of the 104th Congress had accepted some tobacco industry PAC money between 1985 and 1995, Common Cause reported.

Lewis Payne Jr., a fourth-term Virginia Republican, received $18,000 from tobacco PACs in the first half of 1995, more than any other House member. And Payne introduced a bill to prevent the Food and Drug Administration from regulating tobacco as a drug. He also voted against the Durbin amendment, which he called "a direct assault on the hardworking men and women, farmers who grow tobacco in my district and in the southern part of the United States."

Freshman David Funderburk of North Carolina received $11,500 from tobacco PACs in the first six months of 1995, more than any other freshman. Only Payne, Thomas Bliley (chairman of the Commerce Committee), and Speaker Newt Gingrich topped Funderburk in tobacco PAC receipts in the House. Funderburk also spoke against the Durbin amendment, which he called a "kick in the teeth to the 200,000 men, women, and children in my state who depend on tobacco for survival."

Freshman Walter Jones, also of North Carolina, received $9,500 from the tobacco PACs. He argued that "the denial of extension services and federal crop insurance will destroy the family farmer and the economy of rural America. In my state of North Carolina alone, the production of tobacco employs approximately 260,000 people; one in 12 people has a tobacco-related job."

Durbin's amendment lost 199–223, but 28 GOP freshmen, including Sue Myrick, voted for it. She was the only member of the North Carolina delegation to do so, and she had the even greater distinction of being the only member of either party from a tobacco-producing region to vote yes. It was a move that did not go unnoticed among her colleagues, who considered it extremely courageous. Myrick would become known among the freshmen as someone who didn't back down on tough votes. "You could always count on Sue to be with you if she thought it was the right thing to do," said Joe Scarborough. As one southern freshman commented about her on the floor to another freshman after a high-profile vote, "That woman has brass balls."

After the tobacco vote, Nita Lowey of New York offered an amendment to the agriculture bill that would disqualify anyone who earned more than $100,000 in nonfarm income from receiving federal farm subsidy payments. "Too many subsidies go to independently wealthy, nonresident farm owners who do not work their own land. This amendment affirms our commitment to those family farmers who struggle each year to keep their farms and grow a crop," Lowey told her colleagues.

Only 2 percent of all farm owners would be affected by the change, but the Congressional Budget Office estimated Lowey's proposal would save taxpayers $450 million over five years. It was supported not only by the Clinton administration but by a number of conservative groups, including Citizens Against Government Waste, the National Taxpayers Union, Citizens for a Sound Economy, and the Heritage Foundation.

Between 1985 and 1995, absentee landlords who owned farmland but who lived in the 50 largest urban areas in the country collected $1.3 billion in farm subsidies, according to the Environmental Working Group, a nonprofit environmental research group that did a computer analysis of all agriculture subsidy recipients for that 10-year period. In Beverly Hills nearly 50 individuals, partnerships, corporations, joint ventures, and trusts received a total of $1.27 million in farm subsidy payments, the study reported.

These payments reward the owning of land, not the farming of it, and benefit only the wealthy or agribusinesses. But the Lowey amendment was soundly defeated, and only 21 of the GOP freshmen voted for it. Budget hawks like Sam Brownback, Mark Neumann, and Mark Souder were not so hawkish on this vote and went along with most Republicans to continue the subsidies for the wealthy.

The next day, July 21, the House considered a bipartisan amendment offered by Richard Zimmer, a third-term New Jersey Republican, and Charles Schumer, a New York Democrat, to kill the agricultural market promotion program known as MPP. Zimmer, who came to the floor wearing a tie with a pig on it, said the program "epitomizes corporate welfare and congressional pork at its worst" and had cost U.S. taxpayers $1.25 billion in the previous 10 years. But rather than cutting the program, the Appropriations Committee had actually given it a 25 percent increase for 1996. "I am proud of what this Congress has done to get the poor off welfare. I think it's time we showed the same commitment to getting the rich off welfare. At a time when we are eliminating hundreds of federal programs for the sake of federal budget reduction, we can no longer afford this program," said Zimmer.

The purpose of the market promotion program is to help American food producers promote and advertise their products overseas. The government provides a 50 percent match to funds put up by U.S. companies for overseas marketing. The program's proponents say that foreign food and wine producers receive support from their governments, which allows them to charge less for their products, and in order to be competitive American producers need help, too. But a General Accounting Office study determined that the program had no measurable impact on the sale of U.S. agricultural products overseas. And most of the money handed out under the program goes to large corporations like Sunkist, Gallo wines, Pillsbury, M & M Mars, and McDonald's, which would undoubtedly advertise overseas with or without the government's help. "Now we know why Gallo sells no wine before its time. It is waiting for its subsidy check," quipped Zimmer.

Freshman Matt Salmon of Arizona argued that cutting the program would end corporate welfare for "people like Ronald McDonald, the Keebler elves, the dancing raisins, and the Pillsbury Doughboy." But freshmen like Frank Riggs of California, George Nethercutt of Washington, Wes Cooley of Oregon, Roger Wicker of Mississippi, and Saxby Chambliss of Georgia claimed that ending the program would hurt the farmers in their districts.

The amendment to kill the market promotion program was defeated, with the freshman class split almost evenly in its votes. A handful of budget hawks and freshmen from nonfarm states voted to cut back the program; those from the farm states voted to keep it. The failure of the 104th Congress to kill this program was a clear signal that budget cutting only went so far, even with the freshmen, especially when it might hurt constituencies that were important to the Republicans.

Agriculture is the largest industry in California. More than 2 million people, one out of six Californians, are employed in agriculture-related jobs. That is a powerful incentive to support farm programs. With 52 representatives, including five GOP freshmen, the California delegation is by far the largest in the House, and most of the California House members of both parties opposed any subsidy cuts.

Brownback was one of the few farm state freshmen willing to vote for the elimination of the market promotion program. His commitment to balancing the budget proved stronger than his desire to provide pork to the farmers, despite his lifelong ties to farming. Brownback grew up on a farm in Parker, Kansas, where his parents still raise corn, wheat, soybeans, and cattle. In high school he was a national officer of the Future Farmers of America, and he became state president of the group while attending Kansas State, where he earned a degree in agricultural economics. Between 1986 and 1993 he served as secretary of agriculture for the state of Kansas, and when he arrived in Washington he still owned land that his brother farmed for him. At one time Brownback accepted government subsidies, but when he became secretary of agriculture he decided to pull out of the program. "It was clear to me it's corporate welfare and at a time we're so broke you just can't do that."

Brownback called the tobacco vote "a sick moment" for the 104th Congress and said that while that measure was on the floor, "I hid on the Democrats' side of the aisle because I didn't want to be getting hit on" by the senior Republicans lobbying on the behalf of tobacco interests. Watching what went on surrounding that vote helped convince Brownback to join Linda Smith in pushing a measure to reform campaign financing laws. But until such a measure is passed, Brownback said he would continue to take PAC money because disarmament cannot be done unilaterally. "I think it's a corrupt system; people put money in to get your ear and influence the system." But if he had not taken PAC money in 1994, he thought he probably wouldn't be in Congress: "I don't know how I could have competed. These are the rules of the game."

Brownback was also one of 27 freshmen who voted to kill the market promotion program specifically for alcohol producers, a proposal offered by Joe Kennedy of Massachusetts. The program had cost U.S. taxpayers $24 million over the previous three years, and Kennedy contended they were paying for "a worldwide scam." According to Kennedy, "The wrongheadedness with which we subsidize alcohol exports and advertising by major alcohol corporations is compounded by the error of spending millions and millions of dollars to entice people to drink. It is a tragedy and we should put an end to it." He urged fellow members, "Let's break the back of those corporations that come in and try to jump on the back of the taxpayer in this hall and say to them that we are going to stand up to not only welfare mothers but we are going to stand up to this kind of corporate subsidy as well." Kennedy predicted, "We are going to hear a lot of yacking from people that come from wine country that tell us that this is just a program to help out the small vintners of America. That is a bunch of hogwash." Kennedy claimed the Gallo company received 50 percent of the program's total budget. Kennedy's argument should have appealed both to the social conservatism and the fiscal restraint of many of the freshmen. But he had an abrasive, arrogant style that rubbed a lot of members the wrong way. And for many conservatives, saying the name "Kennedy," with all its liberal connotations, was like waving a red flag in front of a bull.

Given the history of his family, Kennedy's move to cut the alcohol subsidy was also a bit peculiar. His paternal great-grandfather had been a saloon keeper in Boston. His grandfather and namesake became the U.S. distributor for prestige European liquor immediately after Prohibition and was even rumored to have bankrolled a bootlegging operation during Prohibition. The irony of it all was not lost either on his Democratic colleagues, who joked about it in the cloakroom during the debate, or on bombastic California Republican Bob Dornan, who told Kennedy, "You are a fourth-generation Irishman, and I am a redheaded second-generation Irishman. . . . They will not be toasting you in the champagne regions of France and the distilleries of beautiful bonnie Scotland." Replied Kennedy, "Just say no, Big Bob; just say no."

Freshman George Radanovich from Fresno opposed cuts in the subsidy programs, including Kennedy's proposal, and with good reason. Top subsidy recipient Fresno produces more farm income than any other county in the country, and Radanovich, the son of Croatian immigrants, had his own vineyard and winery, although he said he did not participate in the market promotion program.

The Kennedy amendment, like virtually all of the efforts to trim agricultural aid programs, failed, winning only 130 votes. The only successful amendment that hot July involved mink. Peter Deutsch of Florida offered an amendment to eliminate the tiny $2 million a year market promotion program for the U.S. Mink Export Development Council. There are fewer than 800 mink farmers in the whole country, and most of them are in sparsely populated states. Although they do about $100 million in annual business, the mink lobby apparently wasn't strong enough to hold off the onslaught. This was one agricultural subsidy a majority of members finally decided they could vote against.

Van Hilleary's position on federal funding for tobacco was well known. But he still had to think about how to vote on some of the other agricultural programs. There are some tobacco farmers in his district, although few for whom it is their main source of income. During the campaign he promised not to cut funding for tobacco programs, so he voted against Durbin's amendment. With Jack Daniel's a major employer in his district, he wasn't sure about the Kennedy amendment. The night before the vote, someone from Jack Daniel's called Hilleary and said "go ahead and vote for it if you want to." But he decided to vote no. He did vote in favor of cutting the mink subsidy, though. Mink isn't too important to the people of Tennessee's Fourth District.

These votes were small potatoes, so to speak, compared to what lay ahead in dealing with the major depression-era subsidy programs for commodities like sugar, peanuts, milk, cotton, rice, wheat, and corn. That was serious money—about $10 billion a year. That much money was worth protecting, and in 1993–1994, agriculture PACs gave $15.5 million to congressional candidates, according to the Center for Responsive Politics, making it the third largest source of business PAC money in the country.

Despite the public relations efforts of the program's supporters to portray subsidies as keeping family farmers afloat, Agriculture Department figures indicated the subsidy programs are not primarily helping family farmers since 70 percent of all farmers received no government subsidy payments of any kind. Just 2 percent of the program's recipients, which includes corporations and partnerships, received nearly 30 percent of the subsidies, according to a study by the Environmental Working Group. This top 2 percent collected on average more than $40,000 a year , while the average annual subsidy payment to everyone else in the program was $6,500. And USDA data showed that 10 farm companies collected between $1 and $2 million a year from the government in subsidy payments. Large payments were especially common in the rice and cotton programs. A General Accounting Office report showed that federal payments made up nearly half the income of rice farmers in Louisiana and Arkansas. So it was no surprise that the cotton and rice farmers were the loudest and most bitter opponents to scaling back the subsidies.

And as with all federal programs, there was room for abuse and fraud in the subsidy program. In a report titled "Fox in the Henhouse—Cash, Crime and Conflict of Interest in Federal Farm Subsidy Programs," the Environmental Working Group found that nearly 20 percent of the Agriculture Department employees who administered the subsidy program also received subsidies.

It was in this climate that Roberts formally introduced his Freedom to Farm legislation on August 4, the day the House left for its monthlong recess, and hoped for the best.

10

CORPORATE WELFARE

Tom DeLay was a Houston exterminator before he was elected to Congress. A self-described "bug killer" who became angered at having to get a state as well as a local license for his business, he won a seat in the Texas legislature in 1978 so he could pass a law exterminating the licensing requirement.

He was elected to the House in 1984 and launched his crusade there against government regulation. In 1989, when Newt Gingrich successfully ran for minority whip, DeLay supported another candidate, something that certainly did not help to cement their relationship. People who know DeLay describe him as extremely ambitious, and in 1994 he decided he wanted to be a major player in helping the Republicans take back Congress. DeLay raised more than $2 million for House Republican candidates, including many of the soon-to-be freshmen. Only Gingrich raised more for House Republicans in 1994. Not only did DeLay hold fund-raisers in the freshmen's districts and bring them to Washington to meet PAC donors during the campaign, but he also provided advice and made sure they knew they could always call if they had a question. The freshmen appreciated his help.

After the election, when he announced he was running for whip, a position decided by the Republican conference, he won the votes of more than 50 grateful freshmen and defeated Bob Walker of Pennsylvania, Gingrich's best friend in the House and choice for the position. Gingrich immediately cut the budget of the whip's office, but that didn't slow down DeLay, who wasted no time letting business lobbyists know they were expected to cough up for Republican campaign coffers; not only that, he urged them to stop giving money to the Democrats.

He kept a list of the largest political action committees and how much they had given to each party. After the 1994 election the business lobbyists quickly shifted their PAC contributions to the Republicans, and DeLay helped them see why this was important if they wanted to have any access to the new regime. He helped them see it in a not so subtle way that earned him the nickname "The Hammer" from the lobbyists he pounded for money. DeLay got his reputation the old-fashioned way: He earned it. He was so proud of it, in fact, that he bragged to reporters about putting the bite on corporate lobbyists.

But he did more than ask for money. He devised something he labeled the "K Street Project," so-named for the street in downtown Washington where many of the lobbyists had their offices. DeLay pushed lobbying firms to fire Democrats who worked for them and hire Republicans to be their new Capitol Hill contacts. "We're just following the old adage of punish your enemies and reward your friends. We don't like to deal with people who are trying to kill the revolution," DeLay told the *Washington Post.*

Of all the Republican leaders, DeLay may have been the least subtle about the fund-raising effort, but they all did it. And the support they sought from business PACs meshed perfectly with their pro-business, antigovernment agenda. In public the Republicans sold their efforts to cut regulations as an answer to the dissatisfaction of many Americans with the overreach and ineffectiveness of government. But their takeover of Congress meant that the business community was now a full partner in the Republicans' attempt to use the budget process to remake government in an image more to their liking. Corporate lobbyists worked closely with the leadership on matters that affected them, even helping to write legislation.

And no Republican member of Congress better exemplified the cozy relationship the party enjoyed with business interests than Tom DeLay, who came up with what he called "Project Relief" to bring together special interest groups and corporate lobbyists with the Republicans to talk about how they could lessen federal regulations on business. The Environmental Protection Agency, which DeLay called "the Gestapo of government," was his favorite target. DeLay pushed to gut clean air and water regulations. "We're only going to fund those programs we want to fund. We're in charge. We don't have to negotiate with the Senate. We don't have to negotiate with the Democrats," he declared defiantly on national television.

Republican sentiments were very clear. At a time when they were chopping programs that affected the poor and middle class, they were leaving corporate subsidies—so-called corporate welfare—virtually untouched. No less a figure than Colin Powell criticized the Republicans, saying, "You see a lot of politicians attacking welfare queens, but you see them a little reluctant to take on the welfare kings on K Street."

The Cato Institute, a conservative libertarian Washington think tank, counted 125 government programs that subsidized private business. According to the Office of Management and Budget and the Joint Committee on Taxation, the federal government spent more than $100 billion on corporate subsidies and tax breaks in 1994. That would have been enough to cut the deficit in half in 1995. But instead, the Republicans made only a 1 percent reduction in corporate welfare spending while cutting many other programs much more. And in some areas they even tried to increase corporate aid, for example, attempting to repeal the alternative minimum tax that ensures that corporations, regardless of tax deductions, exemptions, and credits, pay a minimum tax. Under the GOP plan, some corporations would pay no income taxes.

The industries that benefit the most from the federal largesse include agriculture, energy, transportation, aerospace, timber, and mining. To look at some of the most blatant corporate welfare programs:

- Nearly $100 million a year in federal money goes to a consortium of the largest U.S. computer microchip producers. The original purpose of the program was to help U.S. firms compete against foreign companies, but because only the largest firms (like Intel and National Semiconductor) receive federal money, the program is really helping them at the expense of the nation's small chip manufacturers.
- Profitable electric utility cooperatives around the country receive $2 billion a year in subsidies. The program was originally created to provide rural electrification.
- In 1994 the Forest Service spent $140 million building roads in national forests, which subsidized the removal of timber from federal lands by multi-million-dollar timber companies that usually buy the timber from the government at below-market cost in the first place. Over the past 20 years, the Forest Service has built 340,000 miles of roads, more than eight times the length of the interstate highway system, primarily for the benefit of timber companies, according to the Cato Institute.
- Cost overruns, fraud, and abuse have become almost commonplace from defense contractors, but in 1994 a House investigative team uncovered practices by the Martin Marietta Corporation that seemed outrageous even for a defense contractor. The company had billed the Pentagon nearly $300,000 for the entertainment of its employees, including a Christmas party, a concert by Smokey Robinson, and golf balls. But after the charges were made public, Martin Marietta decided not to bill the government for the concert.
- The Archer Daniels Midland Corporation, a $10 billion agribusiness based in Illinois, produces ethanol and corn sweetener, receiving generous federal subsidies for both products. The company has become the poster child of corporate welfare. A U.S. Department of Agriculture study found that the $500 million subsidy for ethanol, a corn-based gasoline substitute, was an extremely inefficient use of resources. And a study by an economist at Cornell University determined that it takes about 72 percent more energy to produce a gallon of ethanol than the energy that gallon of ethanol provides. Archer Daniels Midland has undoubtedly done so well at the federal trough because the company is a major equal opportunity campaign contributor to both the Republicans and Democrats. In 1995 the company's subsidies escaped the ax thanks to the help of not only the Republicans but Bill Clinton.
- Tax loopholes allow U.S. millionaires to live in tax havens like Belize and avoid paying U.S. income taxes and allow U.S. pharmaceutical companies to operate in Puerto Rico and avoid paying taxes on their profits.

*   *   *

A lot of pork for energy and aerospace projects finds its way through the Science Committee, which in the 104th Congress was chaired by Gingrich's close friend Bob Walker from Lancaster, Pennsylvania. Walker was acerbic and short-tempered, and there was no love lost between him and the freshmen who had voted against him for whip. Unless members had federal research labs in their districts they wanted to protect, they did not consider the Science Committee a prestige assignment, and that meant a lot of freshmen ended up there as more senior members sought seats on better committees. In the 104th Congress the Science Committee had more freshmen than any other committee in the House—14 Republicans and eight Democrats.

One reason the committee was considered irrelevant was that it never said no to anything. It usually approved whatever the president requested for science programs and added a little bit on top. In 1995 Walker decided he was going to change that. After 18 years in Congress, he was not only finally in the majority, he was a chairman. Walker, elected to Congress in 1976, had been a bitter partisan fighter from the moment he arrived in Washington. Along with Gingrich and former House member Vin Weber, he was one of the founding members of the House Republicans' Conservative Opportunity Society, which relentlessly fought the Democrats and big government. Now that he was a chairman, he would finally be able to do some of the things he had been talking about for so long. He wanted to make sure he and the Science Committee were relevant in the budget process, and he was going to do it by cutting the science budget before anyone else got a chance.

Because he was also vice chairman of the Budget Committee and Gingrich's buddy, he was given the green light to decide how much the science budget would be and how the money would be spent, rather than allowing the Budget and Appropriations Committees to make those decisions, as they did in other areas. But in his conservative zeal to show he was serious about deficit reduction, Walker cut more out of science and research programs than those committees probably would have.

Walker didn't see the need to bother much with the freshmen or even to inform them of everything he was doing. Walker ran his committee with an iron hand, and the power struggle between him and the freshmen was palpable at many of its meetings, a few of which deteriorated into shouting matches. The freshmen, even those of his own party, weren't very deferential. Usually when they started a sentence with "Mr. Chairman," it ended with something Walker wasn't interested in hearing.

When the Science Committee's Energy and Environment Subcommittee met in June to discuss Walker's proposed cuts to energy programs, Mike Doyle, a Democratic freshman from Pittsburgh, offered an alternative that would have increased energy research and development spending by $816 million over what Walker was proposing but still make a 10 percent cut from the 1995 funding level. Doyle's budget figures were in line with the Senate budget resolution, which had more spending than the House. They were also in keeping with a moderate Democratic alternative known as the coalition budget, which was introduced by Charlie Stenholm of Texas.

Doyle's alternative would put more money into fossil energy, energy conservation, and renewable energy research programs. It would also put more into the Oak Ridge National Laboratory in Tennessee.

During the subcommittee debate on the Doyle substitute, Zach Wamp was the only Republican to vote with the Democrats. There were not enough votes to pass Doyle's proposal, but Wamp had made a statement. He wanted more money for Oak Ridge, a lab that had been established in his district during World War II to help with the research for the Manhattan Project and now built nuclear weapons. Wamp's Chattanooga district depends heavily on federal largesse. Anderson County, where Oak Ridge is located, receives more federal money per capita than all but four other counties in the nation. And Oak Ridge and several other Energy Department facilities are the biggest employers not only in Wamp's district but in the entire state of Tennessee. "I'm fighting like a warrior to maintain the Energy Department," Wamp told the *Washington Post* in the spring of 1995. By that summer Van Hilleary was the only Tennessee Republican still committed to the freshman initiative to abolish the Department of Energy.

When he was in Washington, Wamp was one of the noisiest freshmen about cutting the budget, but when he was back home, he assured his constituents that he would take care of them and protect them from cuts. The disconnect was noticed by his freshman colleagues, who said that despite all his talk, Wamp was usually nowhere to be found when it came to tough votes. "The fascinating thing about Zach was that he was a true believer in deficit reduction and balancing the budget everywhere in the world except his congressional district. It was like, 'I'm a messenger from God, and I'm here to cut your budget; what's mine is mine, and what's yours is negotiable,'" said one Republican committee staffer. Several freshmen considered Wamp to be a political opportunist and did not trust the sincerity of his conservative beliefs. And a number of political observers in Tennessee felt the same way. "If the Communist Party took over this country tomorrow, Zach would be a commissar," a Tennessee newspaper editor told me.

In the two weeks between the subcommittee markup where the Doyle amendment was defeated and the meeting of the full Science Committee, the Appropriations Committee allocated additional money for energy research and development programs. Walker didn't like anyone to intervene on his turf, but he decided to take the money. He was worried about Wamp. If Wamp decided to vote with the Democrats in the full committee and just two other Republicans joined him, the Democrats' bill, not Walker's, would be reported out of committee. He couldn't risk that kind of embarrassment. He had to keep Wamp happy. By the time the full Science Committee met, Walker had put an extra $265 million into his budget, including more for Oak Ridge.

At the full committee hearing, Wamp attempted to explain his subcommittee vote and what had happened since. "I didn't come here to protect my backyard. I did come here to express the prioritization of where we spend our money and how we save money as we seek collectively to do this great patriotic challenge and balance the federal budget. But Mr. Doyle offered a legitimate alternative. You know, I don't believe that Republicans are always right and Democrats are always wrong. Some may, but I don't. In this case I thought Mr. Doyle had a better alternative. . . . I want to applaud Chairman Walker. I sat down with him. I went through these issues. I said, 'These are my concerns. I represent Oak Ridge, Tennessee, home of the best national laboratory, I think, in the entire system.' He listened to those requests. . . . 'That's why I rise to support the Walker substitute, because he addressed the concerns that I had.' There it was, plain and simple: Walker had given Wamp more money and won his vote. It was the way business had always been done in Congress. But it was not the way many of Wamp's fellow freshmen wanted to do it. They didn't like what Wamp had done. They thought it made Wamp look selfish and not like a team player.

Doyle said several Republican freshmen "complained that Wamp got taken care of because he bucked Walker. I told them, 'You should have voted with me, then you would have gotten taken care of, too.'"

At the full committee meeting, Doyle offered another, less comprehensive amendment to add $80 million to research programs for oil, gas, and coal. To pay for this, he proposed taking money out of the accounts of several nuclear laboratories. But the cuts Doyle was suggesting were all in Republican districts, something Walker wasted no time in pointing out. Doyle insisted he had not meant specifically to target Republicans, but Walker immediately offered an amendment of his own to cut $30 million from the Pittsburgh Energy Technology Center. Walker, who accused Doyle of "playing political games," had responded with his own checkmate.

No sooner had Walker offered his amendment than Steve Largent spoke up. Largent and Doyle had become friends and were in the habit of getting together with Largent's housemates, Wamp and Tom Coburn, once a week for dinner when Congress was in town. Largent, obviously irritated with Walker's move, took the chairman to task. "I think my time's more valuable than to spend it on petty things like this. And I would just tell you that I'm personally offended that my chairman would impugn the integrity of my friend, who I think came to the table with a genuine amendment. He didn't know whose district the stuff was in. . . . To spend my time doing stupid stuff like this, I think we're all too busy for that. . . . Some of this, I think, is a result of having been here too long."

It was a shot right across the bow. Largent was siding with another freshman, a Democrat, against his chairman.

Doyle repeated several times that he had not set out to target Republicans. "I think it would be wrong to assume that every time any member of this committee offers a spending priority and then offsets it with a spending cut, that the first thing we do is check whose congressional district it's in, . . . and if it doesn't happen to be of that person's party, I don't think we ought to assume that it's partisanship."

Walker apologized to Doyle and withdrew his amendment, but the damage was done. Largent, angered by Walker's move against Doyle, voted with the Democrats, and enough Republicans were out of the committee room when the vote was called that Doyle's amendment passed by two votes, much to the shock of both Walker and Doyle.

At that moment the bell sounded for a vote on the floor, and as they left the committee room in the Rayburn House Office Building, Walker and Doyle found themselves on the same elevator to take them down to the basement tunnel that leads to the Capitol. "Your staff knew exactly what they were doing; they've been laughing about it for two days," Walker angrily told Doyle. The Democratic committee staff who wrote the amendment did know which districts the projects were in. It was their job to know. But Doyle was sticking with his story that it had not been his intention to target Republican districts.

"I'm not intimidated by Bob Walker," Doyle would tell me later, explaining why he introduced his amendment. "It was the world according to Bob—you're either with him or against him, and if you're against him he tries to punish you. But that wouldn't work if all the younger members say we're not going to be intimidated. I thought the hell with him, I'm not going to withdraw my amendment. I'd have died before I withdrew my amendment."

On the House floor Largent was approached by Walker and several of the Republican committee members. Walker told Largent his fellow Republicans, including two other freshmen, could thank him for cutting projects in their districts and just because Largent was mad at him he shouldn't take it out on his fellow Republicans. Because Largent had been on the winning side and under House rules was the only one who could do it, Walker asked Largent to make a motion to reconsider the Doyle amendment so there could be another vote with more Republicans present.

In an interview later, Largent would say he "really had mixed feelings" about what to do. He agreed with Doyle's amendment, but his fellow GOP freshmen whose projects were cut "nearly had tears in their eyes, saying, 'This will kill me.'" Largent said, "I knew in my heart the most compelling reason I voted for Doyle was to spite the chairman, and that's not a very good reason." Largent went over to Doyle and told him what was going on, that Walker had asked him to make a motion to reconsider the vote. "I won't ask for this vote if you tell me not to," Largent told Doyle. But Doyle didn't think it would be right for him to ask Largent to go against his chairman and his party. "Do what you feel you have to do. It won't change my feelings for you," Doyle told Largent. "It was one of the most gut-wrenching experiences I've had in Congress because I felt in some ways I was betraying my friend," Largent would say afterward.

Meanwhile, Walker was busy rounding up Republicans and telling them to hightail it back to the committee room. When the members returned from the floor, Largent made his motion to reconsider without any explanation or comment. Largent changed his vote to no and the Doyle amendment was defeated.

But Doyle still had an ace up his sleeve. He already had a commitment from Ralph Regula, the chairman of the Interior Subcommittee of the Appropriations Committee, to put more money back into the budget for fossil fuel research, which is what ultimately happened. "We made a dramatic point, and everybody knows we won the battle," Doyle would tell me later. In the end the lowly Democratic freshman had wound up beating the bombastic committee chairman.

Largent's actions that day reflected his attitude about the Republican leadership. When he agreed with what they were doing, he voted with them, but he had no problem crossing them. Unlike most of the freshmen, who relied on the leadership for fund-raising help and a good committee assignment that would also help them raise campaign funds, Largent was a free agent. Rich and famous before he ever ran for Congress and holding a safe Republican seat, he could probably be reelected for as long as he wanted. How long that would be, though, remained uncertain, since he appeared to hold the institution of Congress in fairly low regard. "What I'm trying to do is really buck the leadership and buck the status quo. I know who I am and what I'm doing here. I'm very focused on that. I've already had a career. I'm not married to being a politician. It's a very free position to be in," said Largent.

It was this attitude that drove senior Republicans crazy and caused a Republican staffer loyal to Walker to say, "I've never been able to understand how Steve Largent made the hall of fame in a team sport. His inclination was always to go against what the team was doing." Doyle thought the whole Science Committee episode "transmitted a message to members who have been here a long time" that a lot of the freshmen thought alike, even the Democrats, and they were tired of doing things the old way. Doyle seemed to get along better with the Republicans than many of the other freshman Democrats. Doyle had switched his party affiliation from Republican to Democrat only a few years earlier and had voted for the balanced budget amendment. Doyle didn't consider himself extremely partisan and wasn't like Lloyd Doggett of Texas and some of the other Democratic freshmen who were always on the floor giving one-minute speeches attacking the Republicans. "They must watch that and want to puke," said the plainspoken Doyle of people around the country viewing the congressional action on C-SPAN. Doyle thought most Americans probably weren't crazy about either party, and he was highly critical of the extreme partisanship of both the Democrats and Republicans, which he felt was hurting Congress. "If you want to be effective in the long term, it's about building bridges, not burning them," he said.

Doyle considered himself an independent thinker who was not beholden to the Democratic Party for his victory. "I think both parties should allow for some diversity," said Doyle, a pro-life Catholic. Although he didn't go along with everything the Republicans were trying to do, he also didn't completely agree with some of the liberals in the Democratic leadership and thought the debate the Republicans were pushing on the proper role and size of government was worth having.

The 42-year-old Doyle grew up in a blue-collar neighborhood of Pittsburgh, the son of a steelworker and the grandson of Irish and Italian immigrants. Half of Doyle's high school class went to work in the steel mills after graduation and half went to college. Doyle was among the second group. After attending Penn State, he came home to sell insurance. "I have to pinch myself sometimes when I'm sitting on the [House] floor. What a great country it is when someone like me can be here. I'm the first Doyle not to work in a steel mill. My dad always used to say, 'Don't ever vote for a Republican; they're not for working people.' But then he voted for Nixon," as did a lot of blue-collar Democrats in Doyle's neighborhood.

Doyle's district voted for Michael Dukakis and Bill Clinton for president, but the previous congressman was conservative Republican firebrand Rick Santorum, who successfully ran for the Senate in 1994. U.S. Steel is located in Doyle's district, as were most of Pittsburgh's steel mills before many of them closed or moved overseas. In this district the battle over America's declining industrial base is being waged at the expense of many of the guys Doyle went to high school with. When he was growing up it was possible to raise a family on what you could earn at the mills. "That's all gone now," says Doyle.

*   *   *

If Doyle's district and its steel mills represented America's industrial past, people like Bob Walker and Newt Gingrich argued that its future was represented by the NASA space station, a project launched by Ronald Reagan in 1984. The space station was supposed to make eight missions over 10 years at a cost of $8 billion. But by 1995 the international space station project still hadn't been completed, and according to the General Accounting Office its total cost would be closer to $100 billion. The U.S. government directly spends $2.1 billion a year for the space station, about the same amount it spends on cancer research. As for the space station's scientific value, its opponents argued that it had no practical value and was good for little more than studying the effect of the lack of gravity on men and women in space. Its supporters claimed that it was a platform for valuable research.

Tim Roemer, a thoughtful, 39-year-old moderate Democrat from Indiana in his third term, offered an amendment to kill the space station in the Science Committee. Van Hilleary, a Science Committee member, didn't know how he was going to vote, but he was getting a lot of pressure from Walker, who reminded him that Gingrich was a strong supporter of the space station and wanted to see it funded. "How could I tell someone who doesn't have running water in my district" that I voted for the space station, Hilleary wondered.

Members of the GOP leadership had sent out letters urging a yes vote on the space station, and Walker had been twisting the arms of his committee people, offering them funding for things in their districts in return for a vote in favor of the space station. Some high-wattage lobbyists, including former astronauts and Tom Hanks, star of the *Apollo 13* movie that was playing in theaters that summer, were also brought in to lobby for the station. Steve Largent was also undecided about the space station but thought he would probably vote against it. One night when the House was in session late, Largent slipped away to take in a nearby showing of *Apollo 13*. "I was trying to find a reason to vote for the space station," he quipped to Hilleary about playing hooky. But the movie proved unpersuasive because Largent decided not only to vote against the space station but to cosponsor Roemer's amendment.

Hilleary was hearing from constituents who commuted to Huntsville, Alabama, to work on part of the space station project there. The aerospace contractors involved with the space station, like those connected to the B-2 bomber, had figured out the best way to ensure survival of their project was to have component parts built in hundreds of congressional districts around the country, especially in Florida, Texas, and California.

But Hilleary began to feel more and more that he couldn't justify voting for the space station. And on July 28, when Roemer offered his amendment to eliminate all funding for the space station and apply the money to the deficit, Largent, Hilleary, and Wamp all voted for it. But they were among the only 13 freshmen who did, and the amendment was soundly defeated. NASA administrator Dan Goldin, who had been lobbying hard for the space station funding, was standing outside the Speaker's Lobby just off the floor when the House voted on the Roemer amendment. After hearing the results, he announced, "I'm thrilled and proud of my Congress."

Walker and the GOP leadership were just as happy, but the House's next vote would ruin their day. It involved a series of 17 so-called riders that had been added to the appropriations bill funding environmental, science, veterans', and housing programs at the urging of Tom DeLay. The riders would gut environmental enforcement by cutting the budget of the Environmental Protection Agency and prevent the EPA from enforcing key provisions of the Clean Air and Clean Water Acts, from protecting wetlands, and licensing and controlling pesticides in food. A number of the provisions were clearly written at the behest of industries like oil refiners and cement kiln operators to prevent enforcement of pollution laws.

Seven-term Republican moderate Sherwood Boehlert of Utica, New York, was strongly opposed to what he described as the "riders from hell" and vowed to fight them. The 59-year-old Boehlert, in his seventh term in the House, had long been an environmental advocate and chaired the Subcommittee on Water Resources and the Environment of the Transportation Committee. A month earlier Boehlert had been unsuccessful in fighting Republican changes to the Clean Water Act that would make pollution compliance essentially voluntary.

Boehlert offered an amendment along with Democrat Louis Stokes of Illinois to restore the EPA funding and eliminate the riders from the bill. "Should we be weakening environmental safeguards as part of an appropriations process that prevents members from having the time to adequately understand and review the implications of their actions? Should we be subjecting the public to environmental dangers as part of an appropriations process that limits the ability of members to fully debate these issues?" asked Boehlert in arguing that the riders should be killed. "Make no mistake about it. If these riders are approved, regulations dealing with arsenic in our drinking water will be prohibited. Remember that. We are talking about the clean water supply for the American people."

But Tom DeLay saw it differently. "The EPA, pure and simply, has been one of the major clawholds that government has maintained on the backs of our constituents. These riders are about changing EPA's behavior in a way that reducing their funding doesn't," said DeLay.

Moderate Republican Chris Shays of Connecticut joined Boehlert in lambasting what DeLay and many other members of his party were trying to do and accurately predicted that public reaction would be extremely negative: "What I find particularly immoral is we have laws on the books that people have to abide by, but we are saying that EPA cannot enforce them. . . . We are gutting EPA and gutting environmental laws, and let us not call it any different than that. I am looking at Republicans because that is where it is at. We are doing it, and we are going to be held accountable, and it is not going to be pretty the next election on this issue."

Shays and other moderate Republicans, including 13 freshmen, primarily from the Northeast, Midwest, and coastal areas, as well as several committee chairs, helped Boehlert in his effort to kill the riders. A total of 51 Republicans voted yes, and as the vote total for the Boehlert amendment was announced, 212–206, a cheer went up in the House chamber. "I'm green all over," Boehlert gushed after the vote. Republican leaders immediately collected around Appropriations chairman Robert Livingston to analyze computer printouts that showed which of their members had voted for the Boehlert amendment. A meeting was called, and the Republicans gathered in Gingrich's office decided to halt action on the bill and send the members home for the weekend. They needed to regroup and didn't want to lose any more votes.

All weekend the leadership lobbied hard, pressing the Republicans who had supported Boehlert to change their vote, and on Monday, July 31, at 8 P.M., they called for a revote on the environmental riders. Boehlert urged his colleagues to stand firm. "This House sent the American public a clear, unequivocal, bipartisan message on Friday, and it was this: The Congress cares about the environment. Republicans care about the environment. Democrats care about the environment. All Americans care about the environment." When the vote was taken a second time, it was a tie— 210–210—which under House rules meant the amendment was defeated and the antienvironmental riders would stay. At least for the moment.

None of the Republicans who had voted yes with Boehlert on Friday switched their votes, despite the leadership's pressure. But there were a number of Democrats absent, and that helped change the vote total. In the end one Democrat—Calvin Dooley, a moderate from a California farming district—who switched his vote from yes to no wound up making the difference.

The outcome was demoralizing for the Democrats, who had had so little to celebrate up to that point in the session. But it would prove to be a Pyrrhic victory for the Republicans. The Senate was not ready to go along with the House action, and President Clinton vowed to veto the measure should it reach his desk. The vote also drew public attention in just the way Boehlert and Chris Shays predicted. Many Americans did not share Tom DeLay's view of the EPA; they thought the EPA was there to protect them from environmental dangers, and that was something they wanted. The House action helped the Democrats paint the Republicans as antienvironmental extremists. It was an image they were never completely able to shake, and it created a wedge issue the Democrats would use through the 1996 campaign.

*   *   *

The House still had a lot of work to do before members could leave for their summer break. The leadership wanted to move forward on the defense appropriations bill, but there were a number of problems among their own members, including the vote on the B-2 bomber. Budget chairman Kasich was leading an effort to kill the costly plane, and Republican leaders weren't sure they had the votes to defeat him. The House also had to do the Labor–Education–Health and Human Services (HHS) appropriation, the most contentious of all the appropriations bills because of the cuts the Republicans had made to many social programs. The Republicans knew the Democrats would be attacking them for their insensitivity to the poor and middle class, and even some of their own moderate members were concerned about aspects of the bill, such as cuts to education. The House also planned to move forward with one of the only major nonbudget pieces of legislation they had acted on all session: a rewrite of the nation's telecommunications laws. But time was running out. They had only four days left before their summer vacation was supposed to start.

In the midst of all of this, the House took a break on August 1 for a long-scheduled tradition, the annual congressional baseball game, which pits the Democrats against the Republicans. The game is sponsored by *Roll Call*, one of the newspapers that covers Congress, and tickets are sold to raise money for charity. Several thousand people, mostly congressional staff and lobbyists, usually show up for the evening game, which is held at a minor league baseball stadium on the outskirts of Washington.

Since politicians are by nature quite competitive, the game can get pretty rough under the best of circumstances. Bones have been broken and eyes blackened in collisions at the bases and infield. They may be middle-aged and out of shape, but they are determined to win, whatever it takes, and to show off doing it. But this year the game seemed to take on even greater significance.

For the past few years, the Democrats had won the contests, led by pitcher Dave McCurdy of Oklahoma. But McCurdy had lost his bid for the Senate in 1994 and was out of the House, along with several other former Democratic baseball stars, including Mike Synar, also of Oklahoma. Oklahoma seemed to be the fount of congressional baseball talent: In 1994 the Sooner state sent pitcher Steve Largent and catcher J. C. Watts, both former professional football players, to Washington to lead a team of new, young Republicans. They had been practicing every morning at 7 A.M. for weeks, and it showed. Largent, who pitched the entire seven innings, was awesome. He even looked like a professional baseball player on the mound. He struck out nine batters and gave up only four hits. The Democrats struggled bravely, and there were a few standouts, like David Bonior, who fought as hard on the field as he did on the floor. But the Republicans didn't just beat the Democrats; they crushed them, 6–0. The game was like a metaphor for the 1994 election; the Republicans seemed invincible, and the Democrats seemed lost, demoralized.

*　　*　　*

The morning after the Republicans' victory on the field, the House began consideration of the Labor-HHS appropriation, which offered a different sort of battle with a great deal more at stake. This was, as Republican Porter Goss of the Rules

Committee said, "the mother of all appropriations bills." The Republicans had eliminated more than 150 programs and cut spending for education, job training, Head Start programs for poor children, and programs for the elderly, including Meals on Wheels and home heating assistance. The cuts in this bill alone made up about 40 percent of the savings the Republicans needed to meet their budget targets, but the most conservative freshmen thought the cuts still weren't deep enough.

And after months of promising a vote on the lockbox concept that would apply to the deficit all the cuts made in amendments to appropriations bills on the floor, the Republicans finally decided to allow a lockbox vote to be attached to the Labor-HHS bill. The House had already completed 11 appropriations bills and cut nearly $500 million through amendments that could have gone to deficit reduction if the lockbox had been in place from the beginning. But the appropriators strongly opposed such a move because that would take away their flexibility to cut deals with their colleagues and pass out additional money as they saw fit.

Unlike most of the other appropriations bills, there were few Democratic amendments offered to the Labor-HHS bill and certainly none to cut funds. The Democrats had decided this bill was so bad they weren't even going to try and make it marginally better. They were just going to vote no. And although many Democrats supported the lockbox concept, they were cynical about the Republicans' timing. "Now, when we have the last of the major appropriation bills before us, or almost the last, all of a sudden the lockbox is attached to this bill. Why? Because our Republican friends are desperately looking for some Democratic votes for this turkey of a bill on final passage," declared Democrat David Obey of Wisconsin, the former Appropriations Committee chair. "I find it ironic that the only bill that you wind up debating this on is this bill which contains funding for the poorest people in this country and for middle-class working people. . . . You would not apply the lockbox to pork projects when we had the public works bill before us. Oh, no. You would not apply it to the transportation bill when we had transportation pork out here. Oh, no. Now that it affects education, health, labor, however, now you are going to say, well, let us save the money."

And what of Rules Committee chairman Solomon's promise to Jane Harman, made on the floor just three weeks earlier, that the lockbox when passed would be retroactive? They couldn't do that, Solomon now explained, because the money had already been spent on NASA and veterans' programs.

Steve Largent admitted he was disappointed with the timing but said passing the lockbox now would be better than nothing. "For the last month, we have been going at the annual ritual of offering amendments to reduce spending in the federal budget. As a freshman and a freshman of the Committee on the Budget, to find out only hours later that we really did not reduce spending, we merely reallocated it, was really frustrating. . . . We want to make it effective yesterday and last month. This is the best we can do."

The lockbox concept was approved overwhelmingly, 373–52. Most of those opposing it were liberal Democrats. Only eight Republicans voted against the lockbox, and seven of them were on the Appropriations Committee, including its chairman, Robert Livingston.

Obey called the Labor-HHS measure the worst appropriations bill he had seen in his 25 years in Congress. It was, in Obey's view, "the meanest and most vicious and extreme attack on women and kids and workers of any appropriations bill in the postwar era." According to Obey, the bill was also the best example of the differences between Republicans and Democrats: "Next to the fight over Medicare, this bill is the epicenter of what I call the Gingrich counterrevolution." As Obey saw it, the Republicans were cutting social programs so they could give a tax break to the wealthiest Americans. And that's not what voters in 1994 were saying they wanted.

"They wanted us to deliver a dollar's worth of service for a dollar's worth of taxes. They wanted programs that were as well managed as they were well-meaning, and I think they wanted us to weed out unnecessary spending and make government smaller and make government work better at the same time. I think they also wanted a war on special interest domination of the Congress and of the government. Now, certainly I think many of us in the Democratic Party got the message. If we did not, we would have had to be deaf. And I think many of us are willing to work to try to pursue that kind of agenda. But this bill goes far beyond that."

Appropriations chairman Livingston defended what the Republicans had done: "The debate today goes way beyond this bill. It is really about the legacy that we leave our children, about the contract we signed with the American people last September, and about the mandate the American voters gave to all of us in November. That mandate is to balance the budget, to end duplication in federal programs, and to downsize government agencies. . . . The fact is we have to rein in spending. We have to start saving and economizing. Government spending is not the be-all, end-all to all of our problems. We have thrown money for too long at too many problems and gotten too little result. Now we realize if we do not start balancing our books, just like every family in America has to do and every business in America has to do, . . . this nation will, like many other nations, go bankrupt."

But the Republicans were far from united on the Labor-HHS bill. The moderates in the party were threatening to vote no because funding for family planning programs had been put into a block grant that states could spend however they wanted. The change was made at the urging of the Christian Coalition and religious conservative members, because groups like Planned Parenthood that provided birth control and medical care to poor women also provided abortion services. Jim Greenwood, a second-term Republican from Pennsylvania, successfully offered an amendment to restore funding for the 25-year-old family planning program begun during the Nixon administration and was joined by 56 other GOP moderates and House Democrats in his effort. The Greenwood amendment carried 224–204, and a dozen moderate GOP freshmen voted in favor. But some conservative freshmen were angered by the change and now weren't sure they could support the Labor-HHS bill on final passage.

Even though they had won on the family planning issue, the moderates still had many concerns about the bill. And GOP members from districts with significant labor constituencies were worried about provisions that would affect labor organizations and reverse an executive order issued by Bill Clinton that prevented federal contractors from replacing striking workers.

Gingrich was forced to spend a great deal of time pressing his members to support the Labor-HHS appropriation, and he wasn't at all sure he could do it. He told the moderates and the conservatives the same thing: They had to stick together even though there were things neither side liked about the bill. If the Republicans lost the Labor-HHS vote, it would hurt the party, he argued. They had to show solidarity. They had to show they could get things done. "We need to keep the momentum going," he said.

After several days of debate, the final vote on the Labor-HHS appropriation came at nearly 1 in the morning on August 4 and just a few hours before the vote, Gingrich still thought he was 40 votes short. The most trouble seemed to be coming from the anti-abortion, social conservatives. The night of the vote they met in a room in the Capitol to talk things over and to pray together about what to do. They finally agreed to vote for the bill, deciding that it was important to stick together and that there were good things in the bill as well as bad. According to Van Hilleary, the Christian right groups had "called off the dogs" and told the conservative members they could go ahead and vote for the appropriation.

But Gingrich was still worried about the moderates, and he was working the floor when the vote on the bill was called. Members stood looking up at the lighted electronic scoreboard that listed all of their names alphabetically and hung over the press gallery. A green light indicated a yes vote and a red light a no vote. As the time ran out, a number of senior moderates voted yes, including Sherwood Boehlert, Chris Shays, Marge Roukema of New Jersey, and Jim Leach of Iowa. A number of moderates would say later that they were counting on the Senate to "fix" things they didn't like about the bill but felt it was important to show solidarity and to pass the appropriation. When moderate Fred Upton of Michigan voted yes, Gingrich went over and gave Upton a bear hug. Virtually the last vote to be cast was that of moderate Constance Morella of Maryland, who represented the Washington suburbs. She waited until the time had expired and, rather than voting electronically, walked to the well of the chamber to fill out a red voting card, which meant she was voting no. "Don't rush into anything, Connie," yelled pugnacious Democrat Barney Frank of Massachusetts.

The Labor-HHS appropriation narrowly passed 219–208, with 10 senior Republicans and seven GOP freshmen voting no. Freshman moderates Sue Kelly of New York and Brian Bilbray of California both voted against the appropriation. It was not the first time they had departed from most of their freshman colleagues. Neither had supported the freshman effort to terminate the National Endowment for the Arts. They also voted in favor of the Boehlert amendment to strip the antienvironmental riders from the VA-HUD appropriation. Kelly and Bilbray were both pro-choice, and one of the provisions inserted into the Labor-HHS appropriation by the religious conservatives would have taken away Medicaid funding for abortions for poor women in cases of rape or incest, something they opposed. Both came from affluent, moderate Republican districts where their voters were conservative on fiscal issues but more liberal on things like abortion and the environment.

Freshman Bob Ney of Ohio voted against the Labor-HHS appropriation for an entirely different reason. His constituents were not affluent country club Republicans but union workers employed at steel mills and industrial plants. Ney had been elected from a Democratic district and believed certain aspects of the bill, like lifting the striker replacement prohibition, "went too far against labor." Ney informed the leadership before the vote that he could not go along. Although he did not receive an endorsement from the AFL-CIO leadership in 1994, Ney said he knew that many union members voted for him: "I do what I think is right; the rank and file know where I stand." When deciding how to vote, "you look at your district, obviously," said Ney.

*   *   *

Once they finished the Labor-HHS appropriation, the House had planned to start immediately on the telecommunications bill and work through the night, but bowing to pressure from the Democrats, they agreed to adjourn and come back seven hours later, at 8 A.M. The telecommunications bill, which involved the first major rewrite of all the laws governing the nation's communications and media industries since 1934, had been years in the making. The stated purpose of the bill was to open up the entire telecommunications field to competition rather than having separate local telephone, long distance, and cable television industries. In theory this would lead to better service and lower costs to consumers. But many of the changes Congress was making would allow companies to become even more consolidated and profitable. Billions of dollars were at stake, as evidenced by the full-page newspaper ads and 30-second television spots AT&T and the Baby Bells seemed to be running constantly in the weeks before the vote.

In writing the bill, Thomas Bliley, chairman of the House Commerce Committee, had favored AT&T and other long distance carriers like Sprint and MCI for providing long distance service over the seven major regional local telephone service providers—the Baby Bells. The Baby Bells began exerting their considerable lobbying muscle with Gingrich, who intervened and directed that an amendment should be offered to change the offending language more in favor of the Baby Bells. Ultimately, it was agreed that the Baby Bells would be allowed to enter the lucrative long distance market, but only after they had shown they were in compliance with the bill's other requirement that they permit competition in the area of local phone service.

AT&T and the other existing long distance carriers opposed the change and formed something called the Competitive Long Distance Coalition. They spent $10 million on a national advertising campaign and hired Marlin Fitzwater, former press secretary to President Ronald Reagan, to help them fight the bill. They also hired a telemarketing firm that sent half a million telegrams to members of Congress, which proved to be a major public relations blunder, as the firm wasn't too careful about whose names it was putting on the telegrams.

Members started to become aggravated about the sacks of telegrams clogging their offices. Freshman Michael Flanagan of Chicago decided to investigate and put several members of his staff on the case. They called some of the people whose names the telemarketing company had signed to the telegrams. Flanagan's staffers picked out 200 telegrams and were able to reach 75 people. Of those, only three knew or cared about the telecommunications bill. A number of them did not speak English, a number were bedridden or in the hospital, and one of them was slightly too young to vote. Waving one of the telegrams, Flanagan said, "We called her, and her mom answered the phone and said, 'Well, little Andrea is eight and she is out playing now, but when she comes in, I will have her call and tell you about the bill.'" Flanagan even received a telegram from someone who had died four months earlier. "It has been said in Chicago that those who have gone beyond have a tendency to vote, but to send me a telegram is indeed truly long distance at its best," said Flanagan.

Flanagan came to the floor carrying a large bag of the telegrams and plopped it down next to him. "This sack is not the mail I have received over the past 10 days. It is not even the sack of mail I received today. . . . Every member of Congress gets four mailings a day. This arrived at 2 o'clock today. . . . AT&T would have me believe that thousands of people in my district feel so strongly about their corporate profits that they are going to send me thousands of telegrams."

Flanagan's performance caused quite a stir and prompted other members to complain about the bogus telegrams, with some even calling for an investigation. It was perhaps the most attention the Chicago Republican had received in his entire time in office.

Hilleary voted against the rule on the telecommunications bill partially "as a protest to the amount of pressure I'm getting" both from AT&T and the Baby Bells and partially at the behest of former Tennessee senator Howard Baker, whose Washington law firm was working for AT&T and the coalition of long distance carriers. "All they're fighting for is whether they're going to make a gazillion dollars or a gazillion dollars plus one," said Hilleary of the telephone companies. Hilleary said if the House did not act on the telecom bill before they left for the August recess, the members and the rest of America would be faced with a barrage of advertising all month as AT&T and the Baby Bells continued to try to convince lawmakers to see things their way.

Telecommunications companies had contributed millions of dollars to members of Congress and the two political parties. Members with seats on the Commerce Committee received especially large donations. In the last two months of 1994 alone, telecommunications PACs gave them more than $100,000. And two-thirds of the House freshmen received PAC contributions from telecommunications interests immediately following their November victory.

Thursday night, or rather in the wee hours of Friday morning, as the House finished up work on the Labor-HHS bill, dozens of reporters from specialty publications and newsletters that followed the telecommunications bill (the "sparkheads," as they were known) were waiting restlessly in the press gallery for work to begin on their bill. Among them, perhaps testament to the aggressiveness of the lobbying effort on behalf of this bill, was an AT&T lobbyist. The press gallery was considered the sanctum sanctorum. Only reporters, members of Congress, gallery staff, and the occasional press secretary were permitted to enter its doors. The lobbyist's presence was a violation of the rules that caused considerable outrage among the press.

One significant aspect of the telecommunications bill was its loosening of antitrust laws on media companies and of the regulations that limited how many media outlets—newspapers, radio and TV stations, and cable systems—a single company or individual could own either in one market or across the country. Three of the 10 largest corporate mergers that occurred in 1995 involved media companies, no doubt prompted by the changes.

The largest merger of the year and the second largest in U.S. history was the $19 billion purchase of Capital Cities/ABC by the Walt Disney Company, announced just a week before House passage of the telecommunications bill and less than a month after the Senate had passed its version of telecommunications reform. Capital Cities/ABC owned not only television and radio networks but dozens of local radio and television stations, including stations in New York, Los Angeles, and Chicago as well as magazines and newspapers. Disney owned theme parks, several cable TV channels, a movie studio, and numerous publishing and entertainment enterprises.

Another media merger announced in July was the $5 billion purchase by Westinghouse of CBS, owner of radio and television networks as well as local stations. A year later Westinghouse announced it would also acquire Infinity Broadcasting, the nation's largest independent broadcaster, which owned more than 40 radio stations around the country. And in September Time Warner and Ted Turner's Turner Broadcasting System announced a $7 billion merger. Time Warner owned a publishing empire including *Time, Fortune, Sports Illustrated,* and *People* magazines and Little, Brown publishing, as well as recording companies, Warner Brothers film studio, and the nation's second largest cable TV system group. Turner Broadcasting owned the Cable News Network (CNN), other cable networks and television stations, and several movie studios. The joint entity would become the biggest media company in the world.

In addition to relaxing the rules on ownership of multiple media outlets, the new law would have allowed a single company to own TV stations that reached as much as 50 percent of all the households in the nation, up from 25 percent under the existing law. Edward Markey, a 10-term Democrat from Massachusetts, successfully offered an amendment that would allow the saturation level to increase only from 25 to 35 percent. "In this bill we have to be very, very careful that while we open up competition on one hand, we do not shut down voices on the other hand. We all know that in America the people are supposed to be the ones who own the airwaves. But the faster we rush into this telecommunication age, the more we increase the chances that a few wealthy people will control everything that we read, that we hear, that we see, and that is indeed dangerous," said Democratic whip David Bonior, a supporter of the Markey amendment.

In the final version of the legislation, which was hammered out in December, the Republicans, under pressure from the White House and the Democrats, toned down some of the provisions to relax regulations on multiple media ownership. Markey and the Democrats also succeeded in winning approval for a provision that would require the installation of a V-chip censoring device into all new television sets larger than 13 inches and create a voluntary rating system for broadcasters that parents could use as a guide in blocking out objectionable TV programs, such as those with violent or sexual content. Although Republican leaders initially opposed the move, it proved popular with the public and was included in the final legislation.

When the House passed its version of the telecommunications law on August 4, Clinton said he might veto it because it allowed deregulation without enough protection for consumers and would result in higher telephone and cable television rates and increased concentration of media ownership.

But when House and Senate leaders agreed to a number of changes, like toning down their attempt to relax media ownership limits and leaving price regulations for cable TV systems in place for at least three years, the White House agreed to go along with the bill, and on February 1, 1996, it was passed overwhelmingly by votes of 414 to 16 in the House and 91 to 5 in the Senate.

Van Hilleary felt slightly overwhelmed and slightly disgusted by the whole process. This was legislation that affected a lot of people with a lot of money, and they were willing to spend some to ensure they would keep making it. "It was politics 101, not statesmanship 101," said Hilleary of the backroom dealing and lobbying that occurred on behalf of the telecom interests. For the most part, the freshmen were on the fringes of those discussions, watching as the big boys mixed it up.

*   *   *

The freshmen were more than ready to go home for their summer vacation, but they wanted to take a parting shot first. They called a press conference the day before they left Washington to talk about what they had accomplished so far. Zach Wamp, who seemed to be the self-appointed communications chief of the class, sent out a notice to reporters about the press conference. "The difference in this class of 73 first term representatives is that—unlike many political figures—they've demonstrated a willingness to accept cuts even in programs in their own districts in order to advance the critical goal of balancing the budget," it read. "Journalists routinely attend press conferences where officials bask in the joys of handing out federal goodies. Come hear how this group is handling a far more difficult governmental mission: asking their constituents to share in real ways in the effort to balance the budget."

The firebrands of the class stood in a committee room in the Cannon House Office Building, behind a podium hung with a banner that said "104th Republican Freshmen—Courage, Compassion, Commitment!" One by one the freshmen stepped up to the microphone to talk about how they had voted to cut programs their constituents cared about.

"I wasn't sent up here to send pork back to my district; I was sent up here to balance the budget. That's what this freshman class is all about. We're about balancing the budget and, damn it, we're going to do it," said Steve Chabot of Cincinnati.

Wamp boasted about the "significant" cuts that had been made to the Department of Energy, the Tennessee Valley Authority, and the Appalachian Regional Commission without mentioning his efforts to prevent them from being eliminated or to get more money for the Oak Ridge lab. "We are the most principled body in this institution. We are the conscience of the 104th Congress," proclaimed Wamp.

Before they left town, both the Republican and Democratic House leaders had their own news conferences to put their spin on the first seven months of the 104th Congress and to look ahead to the fall. Gingrich and the Republicans talked about wanting to avoid a "train wreck" if the president and Republican Congress could not come to an agreement on the budget. Gingrich said the struggle over the Labor-HHS bill reflected the philosophical differences of the two parties. This was an anti-regulation, antibureaucracy Congress. "We're more pro-business and less pro-union," he declared. Gingrich and the Republicans may not have realized it at the time, but their actions to cut the EPA's funding and Labor-HHS programs energized and activated their opponents more than anything else they had done so far, and environmental groups and labor unions would join together in a significant effort to try to defeat them in 1996.

In their press conference the Democrats talked a lot about Medicare. The Republicans were still putting together their Medicare reform plan and would not be releasing it until they returned in September. But the Democrats knew whatever was in it, it was going to be something they didn't like and something they would be able to use to further attempt to paint the Republicans as extremists.

That Friday night five of the freshmen appeared on the MacNeil-Lehrer NewsHour on PBS. The freshman panel had been invited to be on the show from time to time to discuss how things were going in the 104th Congress. Zach Wamp, George Nethercutt, and Enid Waldholtz represented the Republicans and Zoe Lofgren of California and Chaka Fattah of Pennsylvania represented the Democrats. "We're doing what the American people want us to do," insisted Nethercutt. But Lofgren said the Republicans had inserted an "extreme social agenda" into the appropriations bills; "I don't think that reflects where America is," she remarked.

The Republicans had also made it clear by midsummer how far they were willing to take all this budget cutting. It was OK to cut programs that affected poor people. "Poor people aren't our constituency," as one freshman told me. The Republicans honestly believed the Democrats' fondness for welfare programs was just a way to buy votes. If tough choices had to be made, the best place to start was with a group of people who didn't vote for them anyway.

But for all of their high-minded talk about discipline, taking responsibility, worrying about future generations, and balancing the budget, the Republicans weren't cutting programs that helped their friends. Corporate subsidies and tax breaks were virtually untouched. Although it was true that the Democrats had been just as favorably disposed to government largesse for corporate interests, they had always been in favor of spending more money period. Now in these leaner times the Republicans had made it clear they would not cut everyone's benefits.

This allowed the Democrats to claim the Republicans were trying to do a reverse Robin Hood—to take from the poor to give to the rich through tax cuts and by leaving corporate subsidies in place. The American people seemed to have been convinced by the Republicans that budget cuts would be necessary in order to balance the budget, but they wanted them done fairly. If the poor were going to suffer, if middle-class entitlements like Medicare and student loans were going to be cut, they felt the wealthy should have to take their hits, too. It was a matter of fairness.

The freshmen kept talking about a new way of doing things, but when it came to campaign contributions from corporate lobbyists that came pouring in to them from the moment of their victory, they were decidedly old-fashioned. And this contributed to voter skepticism about whether anything would ever change in Washington. Voters thought the Republicans were going to do things a different way, take on the system, shake things up, not just open the doors even wider for corporate lobbyists.

Whether it will be possible to do much about corporate welfare until some significant campaign finance reform is enacted is highly doubtful, however. As long as corporations are shelling out millions of dollars to candidates, they're going to want something in return, and as long as candidates know they have to collect those millions to pay for the ads they'll need to win reelection, they'll be likely to lend an ear and try to be helpful when lobbyists come knocking on their doors.

11

ELEPHANTS AND TIGERS AND RHINOS— OH, MY!

IN SEPTEMBER, WHEN THEY RETURNED from their summer vacation, the freshmen seemed eager to pick up where they had left off. If they heard many complaints from voters back home about what they were doing, they didn't let on. The freshmen insisted they were getting encouragement from their constituents to "hang in there, give 'em hell, and keep pushing."

The freshmen were still quite optimistic about what they were doing; their only worry was that they hadn't gone far enough fast enough. They felt all of their good work on the Contract with America was bogged down in the Senate. Members of the Senate weren't just dragging their feet on the contract items, they were actually reversing some of what the House had done. Moderate Senate Republicans led efforts to put money back into the bills funding the Housing and Urban Development and the Health and Human Services departments. They also added money for the Environmental Protection Agency and eliminated all but one of those controversial EPA riders that had been removed and then restored in the House.

The Contract with America was beginning to fade from memory, and soon the budget battle between the Republican Congress and Bill Clinton's White House would by far eclipse the contract in attention and importance. There was starting to be a lot of talk in Washington about something that had come to be known as the "train wreck"—what would happen if Congress and the president could not reach a budget agreement and government operations were not funded.

Congress decides how much money can be spent and how to spend it, but if the president doesn't sign the budget, the money cannot be allocated. Nothing can move forward without the agreement of both the president and Congress. If they couldn't reach agreement this year, as was starting to look increasingly likely since Clinton had already threatened to veto many of the appropriations bills passed by the House, there was a good chance all nonessential government programs would be shut down because there would be no money to fund them—in other words, a train wreck.

There were two deadlines looming. The first was the start of the government's fiscal year on October 1. The budget was supposed to be completed by that date. In past years when Congress was still working on the budget or faced a disagreement with the White House over budget details when October 1 rolled around, it usually passed something called a continuing resolution, or a CR. This allowed the government to continue spending money and operating while the budget was being worked out. Continuing resolutions were quite common; in fact there had been 56 of them since 1977. But many House Republicans, including most of the freshmen, didn't think they should pass a continuing resolution this year.

The other deadline coming up in mid- to late October had to do with the government's ability to borrow money to meet its daily obligations. This involved something called the public debt ceiling. In the summer of 1995, the debt ceiling was $4.9 trillion, and the amount of money the federal government owed was around $4.8 trillion. Yes, *trillion*. The need to raise the debt ceiling was a direct result of the government's many years of deficit spending, which had driven the national debt from $710 billion in 1980 to $3.6 trillion by 1995. Soon Congress would have to vote to increase the debt ceiling so the government could continue borrowing and the federal government could continue spending.

But many Republicans felt the debt ceiling should not be increased until there was an agreement that the government was headed toward a balanced budget by the year 2002. In June senior Republican Chris Shays of Connecticut and more than 150 other Republican members sent a letter to Clinton telling him they would not vote to raise the debt ceiling "until legislation is enacted ensuring the government is on a true glide path to a balanced budget by 2002 or sooner."

Clinton and Treasury secretary Robert Rubin warned of the potentially dire financial consequences if the debt ceiling were allowed to expire. And throughout the summer, administration officials, including White House chief of staff Leon Panetta and Alice Rivlin, the director of the Office of Management and Budget, made contingency plans for dealing with a government shutdown, including possible layoff of federal workers. Should there be a shutdown, all nonessential government workers would be furloughed, but essential services (including things like the armed forces, post office, air traffic controllers, customs agents, and meat inspections) would continue to operate.

There was a great deal of speculation about what would happen in the event of a government shutdown: Who would blink first? Would the political fallout hit Clinton or the Republicans or both? Both sides tried to second-guess how it would play out and who would be hurt worse by a shutdown. The freshmen seemed the most confident of anyone. They didn't fear a shutdown at all. They were so convinced they were right that they were sure the public, eager for smaller government and a balanced budget, would take their side. But GOP leaders weren't so sure.

In September, Newt Gingrich and some other Republican leaders started floating the idea that if Bill Clinton was willing to sign welfare and regulatory reform bills, maybe the Republicans should give up $10 to $15 billion on their budget cuts to make the deal possible. But that would mean they wouldn't be hitting the first-year budget numbers they had set and might not balance the budget by 2002. The freshmen went ballistic, especially budget hawk Mark Neumann. He thought they should just shut down all nonessential government services "and leave them shut down" until a firm budget deal could be struck.

Many freshmen, including Neumann, were concerned that "we've done all this work and somebody's going to go in and compromise it all away." After their heady experience in July over eliminating funding for the National Endowment for the Arts, the freshmen were convinced they had enough votes "to bring down bills" if necessary to ensure their leaders stood firm on budget cutting. But the freshmen weren't running things, and most people in the Clinton administration didn't believe that more senior GOP congressional leaders would really force the government to shut down. The Democrats figured in the end people like Bob Dole and Senate budget chairman Pete Domenici would prevail and come to the table and make a deal that was good for everyone. For their part, House Republican leaders, especially Gingrich, thought that when push came to shove, Clinton would back down, as he had done any number of times since taking office.

It was these misjudgments on the part of all of the major players in the budget war that would lead to the budget impasse a few months later.

*   *   *

Despite their bullish stance on budget cutting in general, the Republicans were starting to have a little trouble holding their troops together on the specifics. In September the first major rift developed over Pat Roberts's Freedom to Farm Act, the rewrite of the farm subsidy program. Midwestern farmers seemed far more willing than did southerners to give up their subsidy payments in exchange for the freedom to grow whatever they wanted. Southern cotton and rice farmers, who were heavily dependent on subsidies, balked at the change.

On Wednesday, September 20, Freedom to Farm was considered by the House Agriculture Committee, which Roberts chaired. And five Republicans, including freshman Saxby Chambliss, who came from a rural district in southern Georgia, voted with the Democrats not to report the legislation out of committee. Chambliss made it clear he wasn't anxious to reduce the payments to his constituents, who had made out extremely well under the existing subsidy program. According to a study done by the Environmental Working Group, Chambliss's district had received $616 million in farm subsidy payments over the previous 10 years. And 30 percent of those payments went to only 2 percent of the district's farmers, who received an average of $58,000 a year. In a press release explaining his stand on the farm bill, Chambliss said, "When asked why I wasn't voting with the team, I said, 'My team is my farmers and the good folks back home in central and south Georgia." Freshman class president Roger Wicker, who had similar views, also opposed the elimination of the agricultural subsidies.

GOP House leaders were counting on the savings from changes to the agriculture program to help them meet their budget targets, and they didn't know what to do when Roberts couldn't report a bill out of his committee. The only choice left to them was to fold the agriculture reform into the total budget package to be considered on the House floor and hope GOP members wouldn't vote against the budget. But since 50 GOP House members opposed the changes to agricultural subsidies and were threatening to vote against the bill, the leadership was forced to accommodate southern cotton and rice growers as well as midwestern and northeastern members who represented dairy farmers concerned about changes in milk price supports.

*   *   *

The dispute over farm subsidies, however, was relatively mild compared to the rebellion that erupted over the military appropriations bill. The defense budget accounts for about one-fifth of the total federal budget—about half of all discretionary spending, which excludes entitlement programs like Medicare and Social Security. House Republicans wanted to spend $243 billion on defense in 1996, $7.8 billion more than President Clinton and the Pentagon had requested in their budget.

When the House took up the defense appropriation on September 7, the first order of business was an amendment offered by Budget Committee chairman John Kasich to eliminate $500 million that had been added to fund new B-2 bombers. The Pentagon had requested $1 billion for the B-2 program, but the House had decided to tack on an additional $500 million to build even more B-2s than the Pentagon was asking for.

The B-2 project had been launched in 1981 as part of the Reagan administration's defense buildup. The batwing-shaped stealth bomber was designed to evade Soviet air defenses with its radar-absorbing skin so that it could deliver nuclear missiles deep into the Soviet Union. But with the end of the cold war, the "Batplane's" original mission was rendered obsolete long before the plane was even completed. That didn't stop the B-2's supporters. They created a new mission for the big, slow, strange-looking plane. It would be turned into a conventional bomber. That would have been fine except for a few minor details, such as its exorbitant price tag, major cost overruns, construction delays—and the Batplane's failure to work.

After 14 years of development and six years of flight testing, Northrop Grumman, the plane's principal contractor, still had not delivered a plane capable of performing in combat. "The Air Force has yet to demonstrate that the B-2 design will meet some of its most important mission requirements," said a report prepared by the General Accounting Office. The plane had achieved only 12 percent of its required test objectives for stealth and 7 percent for survivability. And the B-2's sophisticated radar system, designed to allow it to fly close to the ground, could not yet distinguish between a rain cloud and a mountain—in understated government lingo, "achieving acceptable radar signatures, the most critical stealth feature needed for B-2 operational effectiveness, has been a problem." Simply put, the expensive and unnecessary Batplane seemed unable to do what it had been designed to do. This was a weapon system only a mother could love.

In May 1995 the Institute for Defense Analysis released a study of the B-2 that had been commissioned by Congress the previous year. The study found that there was no need for more B-2s and it would be far more cost-effective to upgrade and improve the existing planes than to build new ones. But Congress chose to ignore the report it had commissioned. Presented with a plane that didn't work and cost far more than it was supposed to, what did Congress do? It decided to buy more of them. The plane's ardent supporters pooh-poohed the B-2's astronomical price tag and ignored its defects while continuing to tout its mythical defense capabilities.

The cost of the original 20 B-2s had climbed to more than $2 billion per plane. But now Northrop Grumman was saying it could deliver another 20 planes for a bargain $1 billion a piece or less. By Pentagon estimates it would be a lot closer to $1.5 billion. And Pentagon officials said they didn't want any more B-2s, that they couldn't afford them. They would rather have other, more useful things, like aircraft carriers and tactical strike fighters.

Newt Gingrich pretty much stayed out of the B-2 fight, but majority leader Dick Armey and whip Tom DeLay pushed hard for the plane and worked closely with Northrop Grumman to lobby their members. Republicans saw the plane not only as an important jobs producer but as a potent symbol of their link to Ronald Reagan's victory in the cold war. Support for the B-2 was very much bipartisan, however. A group of Republican and Democratic members whose districts had contractors and subcontractors involved with the B-2 was formed to discuss strategy for ensuring continued funding for the B-2.

Kasich, who had been trying to get the B-2 killed for years, liked to joke that the difference between the B-2 and Dracula was that even if you put a stake through the heart of the B-2, it wouldn't die. Since most of the freshmen were budget hawks, he figured this might be his year. But the freshmen were also defense hawks and in need of the kind of campaign donations the defense PACs were passing out, so it wasn't at all clear how many of them would join him. With his stand on the B-2, Kasich, the great budget warrior, was distancing himself from most GOP leaders. During the debate on his amendment, Kasich sat by himself on the Republican side of the aisle.

"We have no one in the Pentagon that wants this airplane. . . . I ask members how they can go home and defend the billion-dollar airplane while at the same time we are trying to squeeze savings out of this federal budget, and at a time when the mission of this airplane, which was to invade the Soviet Union in the middle of the nuclear war, is over. How the heck can we go forward and tell the Pentagon to buy more?" asked Kasich on the House floor. Democrat Ron Dellums of California was the ranking Democrat on the House National Security Committee and a cosponsor with Kasich of the move to limit funding for the B-2. His voice rising, Dellums asked, "Where on this earth do we need to fly more than 20 B-2 bombers? Against a Third World country?"

Hitting on what the B-2 was really about, Kasich said, "When the general in charge of acquisition for all the major weapon systems for the Air Force says, 'We do not want the plane; we cannot afford the plane,' folks, it is time to come to the floor and make a big chop out of the stack of wood labeled corporate welfare."

The fight over the B-2 was nominally about our nation's defense, but it was much more about government pork and defense jobs that were spread across the country into the congressional districts where thousands of B-2 subcontractors were located. It was also about campaign contributions.

In the first four months of 1995, major defense PACs contributed more than $450,000 to members of Congress, 75 percent of it to Republicans. Northrop Grumman's PAC contributed $228,000 in the first half of the year, a 60 percent increase over 1993. Appropriations chairman Robert Livingston, majority leader Dick Armey, Democrat Norm Dicks of Washington state (a member of the National Security Appropriations Subcommittee), and Martin Frost (a Texas Democrat on the Rules Committee) each received a $5,000 contribution from Northrop Grumman, and all of them fought hard for increased funding for the B-2.

Northrop Grumman left no stone unturned in lobbying for the Batplane. It launched an aggressive, million-dollar campaign, running newspaper and television ads, conducting polls and focus groups. The company enlisted retired senior Air Force officers and generals to lobby members of Congress. Seven former secretaries of defense (Kasich referred to them as the "seven wonders of the world") wrote letters to members on behalf of the B-2. Northrop Grumman also paid for members to fly out to the West Coast to see the B-2 and its production facilities and even to take a ride on the Batplane. But the strategy didn't always work. Ohio senator John Glenn, a former pilot and astronaut, flew a B-2 himself, but he was opposing funding for the bomber.

Other major subcontractors on the plane, including Boeing, General Electric, and Hughes Aircraft, also lobbied hard for the B-2, and their most potent weapon was the hundreds of subcontractors and thousands of vendors who had some connection to the plane. These businesses were organized to lobby their home state delegations and talk about the jobs the plane provided. Members were sent maps of their congressional districts showing all the B-2 suppliers located there. During the August recess, B-2 contractors fanned out to lobby members back in their districts, and at least one freshman who was wavering about additional funding was told that a fundraiser some of the defense lobbyists were planning to hold for him would be canceled if he voted against the B-2.

Freshman Frank Riggs of California told the *Washington Post* that even before his election Northrop Grumman gave money to his campaign, and after he became a member they made it a point of coming to his fund-raisers and offering to encourage others to come. "That part wasn't too subtle," said Riggs. He said the company stressed the B-2 as a jobs program for California and argued that California Republicans should present a united front in support of the B-2. Democrat Julian Dixon from Los Angeles was candid about that motivation when he spoke on the House floor: "For those of us representing regions whose economies have been driven by the defense and aerospace industry, there are certainly other factors motivating our support for the B-2. The B-2 program has been essential to California's high technology aerospace industry. Thousands of subcontractors have been involved in development of this technology. The B-2 industrial base in California and throughout the nation needs to be sustained."

But B-2 opponent Dellums pointed out that there were only about 8,000 people around the country working on the B-2 in some capacity. "I understand jobs, but to the tune of $31.5 billion to build a plane the Pentagon says they do not want, they do not need? . . . You give me $31.5 billion; I will put a hell of a lot more than 8,000 people to work."

Texas, California, and Washington state were all well represented by members defending the B-2 and the defense jobs back home that went with it. And there was a surprising lack of liberal Democratic and minority members willing to oppose the B-2. John Lewis of Georgia was one of the few who did. "We should not spend money we don't have on planes we do not need. Twenty more B-2 bombers will not help our children, our sick, our elderly, or national security. Buying more will not make our world a safer place."

When the vote was taken, the Kasich amendment failed by just three votes—210–213. A total of 147 Republicans were joined by 66 Democrats in voting against it to keep the additional funds for the B-2 in the budget. Thirty of the GOP freshmen voted with Kasich, including three from California: Riggs, George Radanovich, and Brian Bilbray. But 42 others voted not to reduce funds for the bomber. Kasich was obviously frustrated by the closeness of the vote. "Oh, man," he could be heard to say to no one in particular as he smacked his fist into his open palm as the vote was announced.

Since the Senate had not provided additional funds for the B-2 in its defense funding bill, there was a question about what would happen when the two chambers met in conference to come up with legislation both bodies could pass. Eventually, the Senate did agree to spend more on the B-2.

Other House-Senate differences over the defense bill proved to be more troublesome. The first involved abortion. The House had passed an amendment that would prohibit overseas military hospitals from providing abortions for servicewomen stationed abroad. Between 1973 and 1988, abortions were available in overseas military hospitals for military personnel who used their own money to obtain them. But in 1988 Reagan banned the procedure. One of Clinton's first acts as president in 1993 was to lift that ban. Now the House, and most of the conservative freshmen, sought to reinstate it. But the Senate did not want to include the abortion ban in the military bill.

The two chambers also differed on funding for a "Star Wars" ballistic missile defense system that the House wanted included in the military budget. Clinton threatened to and eventually did veto the defense bill over the issue, saying the costly weapons system would "waste tens of billions of dollars" and could violate an existing antiballistic missile treaty and jeopardize future arms control efforts.

The House and Senate just couldn't seem to get together on the defense bill, and on September 29 there was a House insurrection. First a number of Republicans joined with the Democrats to defeat the Interior Department appropriation. And when the defense appropriation came to the floor, 130 Republicans voted against it, sending it back to conference. The Republican members who opposed the bill ran the ideological gamut, from moderates who felt it spent too much on defense to conservatives who wanted the abortion ban included. Although nearly two-thirds of the GOP House members had voted against the measure, the freshmen seemed to bear the brunt of the leadership's anger over the defeat.

House Appropriations Committee chairman Robert Livingston took the loss of the military appropriations bill particularly hard and referred to September 29 as "Black Friday." Livingston was the descendant and namesake of Robert Livingston of New York, a member of the Continental Congress and signer of the Declaration of Independence who had administered the oath of office to George Washington and later, as ambassador to France, helped negotiate the Louisiana Purchase. The current Robert Livingston, who represents a portion of New Orleans and its most affluent northern suburbs, is a charming and courtly man. He also has quite a temper, and it flares from time to time on the floor during heated debates but even more spectacularly in private meetings with members of his own party who oppose him.

Although Livingston was only the fifth-ranking Republican on the Appropriations Committee, having first been elected to Congress in 1977, Newt Gingrich passed over more senior members and selected him to chair the committee because he believed he could count on the solidly conservative Livingston to be tough and hold the line on spending cuts. Much of the heavy lifting and tough choices in the budget process had fallen on Livingston's shoulders, and he seemed to take it as a personal challenge when his appropriations bills failed to win passage or were amended. After he had served nearly 20 years in Congress, it was Livingston's unique fortune to reach the pinnacle of power usually afforded by chairing the Appropriations Committee at a time when instead of passing out seemingly unlimited federal largesse, he was overseeing the downsizing of the federal government.

Many of the Republicans on the Appropriations Committee lobbied Livingston for continued funding for priority items in their districts. But not freshman Mark Neumann. Rather, Neumann felt Livingston and the Appropriations Committee weren't being aggressive enough on budget cutting. Neumann wanted the budget balanced, the sooner the better. That was all that seemed to matter to him.

Neumann represented the First District of Wisconsin and had barely won election to the House. He received only 49 percent of the vote and managed to defeat the incumbent Democrat by just over 1,000 votes, the smallest margin of victory of any of the GOP freshmen. But Neumann didn't act like a man who had won by the skin of his teeth; he acted like someone who had been sent to Washington with an over-whelming mandate to shake things up and change the world in his own image: con-servative, evangelical Lutheran, straight to the point of being nerdy, and obsessed with the deficit. He was a man who was mad as hell and not going to take it any-more and had had the good fortune to get elected to Congress.

The 41-year-old Neumann grew up in Wisconsin and a year after they finished high school married a girl he had first met in fourth grade Sunday school. They had three children. He taught math in high school and junior college, where he used the size of the deficit as an exercise in his classes (back when the deficit was still in the billions rather than trillions). He started his own home-building business in the mid-1980s. A few years later, during a sightseeing trip to Washington that included stops at the Lincoln Memorial and Arlington Cemetery, Neumann had his epiphany: He would run for Congress and do something about the national debt.

Unfortunately, Neumann's congressman and future opponent was Democrat Les Aspin, who had served in the House since 1970, was chairman of the Armed Ser-vices Committee, and was extremely popular in Wisconsin. In 1992 Neumann sold his business and put $1 million of his own money into a race against Aspin but lost by 17 points.

When Aspin was named secretary of defense the following year, Neumann ran again in the special election to fill the seat Aspin had left open. He lost by a much closer 1 percent margin but was $250,000 in debt after the race. He didn't have a company. He didn't have a job. Two businesses he attempted to start up after the race failed as he tried to get on his financial feet. It was "as depressing as anything you'd want to live through," he recalls. About six months later he started another land de-velopment and home-building business that took off. Neumann had no intention of running in 1994, but when other Republicans failed to mount a campaign, state party leaders, including Wisconsin governor Tommy Thompson, urged him to make one more try. "I said it would take the governor himself to get me in the race, and a couple of weeks later the governor himself called," said Neumann. This time around, though, he wasn't going to be spending any more of his own money. He decided to run the low-budget campaign himself and hire only one paid staff member—a fund-raiser. After campaign budgets of nearly $1 million in each of his two previous races, Neumann's 1994 campaign cost half that, but he still managed to ride the Republi-can wave and eke out a victory.

Tall and rail thin, Neumann had a look of bug-eyed intensity about him. When-ever he had his picture taken as a member, he never seemed to be smiling. What was there to smile about when the country was trillions of dollars in debt? You'd think after the tough time he had getting to Congress, he would enjoy it just a little once he got there, but Neumann always seemed to be angry as he strode the Capitol's marble halls: How could anyone not be angry about this huge national debt we're piling up for our children? He simply could not understand why everyone wasn't as mad as he was, wasn't as eager to chop the federal budget. "We're not going anywhere near far enough fast enough. We in the Congress are way behind the American people," when it comes to cutting the budget, he would insist with impatience in his voice.

He took a humorless, no-nonsense approach to everything. Considered a difficult, demanding employer even before he was elected to Congress, his congressional staff lived in fear of his anger. His small personal office way up on the seventh floor of the Longworth House Office Building had a flip chart on an easel with budget figures and charts and graphs that showed the size of the national debt. He was obviously more comfortable with numbers than with people and said to me once, "My idea of heaven is a wall with numbers on it." An unlikely politician, he was not a backslapper; he was an accountant.

Neumann did not see shades of gray. He saw only black and white. He was right and everyone else was wrong. He was not only happy to take on the Democrats; he'd take on his own leadership if he had to. And in his first year in Congress, he did, frequently. Because of the closeness of his race, Neumann was given a seat on the Appropriations Committee to help him raise campaign contributions and ensure his reelection. His assignments there included a spot on the National Security Subcommittee.

The first run-in Neumann had with Livingston and Gingrich started only a month after he took office. The gung-ho budget hawk opposed a $3.2 billion supplemental defense appropriations bill to pay for military operations in Haiti, Bosnia, Somalia, and the Persian Gulf because it was not offset by equal budget cuts and would increase the deficit by more than $600 million. When Neumann asked his fellow committee members where the money was coming from to pay for the appropriation, he said, "They all looked at me like I was nuts." Livingston was livid, and Gingrich was more than a little annoyed by Neumann's refusal to toe the line. "The Speaker told me if I voted against it, I would be kicked off of Appropriations. Even our governor called me and told me to vote with the Speaker." But Neumann refused to back down. When the measure came to the floor, Neumann was one of 21 Republicans who voted against it. And then—nothing happened to him. Gingrich had been making an empty threat. As Neumann saw it, that experience "inoculated" him against the fear of reprisal for any stand he might take from then on.

Neumann, who considered himself "one of the angry taxpayers," felt he did the right thing because he had promised during his campaign that he would not vote for any bill that increased the deficit. "It never occurred to me that the Speaker ought to tell me how to vote. I thought the people who sent me here ought to do that."

Next Neumann decided that well-intentioned though it was, the Republican budget plan drawn up by John Kasich and aimed at balancing the budget in seven years did not go far enough fast enough. Neumann decided to devise his own plan that would balance the budget in just four years. "America's Contract with Our Children," as Neumann dubbed his budget, was extremely detailed and comprehensive in its scope. But since the plan made only minor cuts in defense, it had to include dramatic cuts in education and social programs to meet the four-year target.

The Neumann budget proposed the total elimination of federal programs including Farmers Home Administration loans, bilingual and immigrant education funds, low-income home energy assistance, the low-income housing credit, and federal subsidies for Amtrak. Neumann also proposed significantly reducing federal spending on the Environmental Protection Agency, community development block grant programs, education and student loan programs, the Centers for Disease Control, the Substance Abuse and Mental Health Services Administration, and the National Weather Service—just to name a few. He proposed privatizing air traffic control operations and included a number of conservative goals in his budget, such as eliminating all federal money for family planning services, all arts and humanities programs, and the Corporation for Public Broadcasting.

Neumann was an equal opportunity slasher, though, and favored cutting a number of corporate welfare programs, such as agricultural subsidies and the overseas market promotion program; below-cost timber sales in national forests; and the federal fuel tax subsidy for ethanol, whose major beneficiary was the Archer Daniels Midland Corporation. He proposed increasing Federal Communication Commission fees and licenses and charging royalties for mining on federal land.

No detail was too small for Neumann's attention. He even proposed eliminating the one-dollar bill and replacing it with a coin because coins did not wear out as fast and so were more cost-efficient. And Neumann's budget was not only detailed but far-reaching. He proposed reducing total federal employment costs and federal agency overhead by 20 percent over five years and making significant changes in the welfare and Medicare programs, including cost increases for elderly Medicare recipients.

Even many of the freshmen considered Neumann's plan too extreme. He did win the cosponsorship of Rules Committee chairman Gerald Solomon, but when Neumann offered his budget on the House floor, it received only 89 votes, including those of just 30 freshmen. After that, Neumann decided to try an item-by-item approach to cutting the budget and launched a guerrilla effort he called "Operation Clean Sweep," which he said meant "sweeping out the garbage spending." Neumann would take on programs one by one, offering amendments on the floor to cut them from the budget. In some instances he prevailed, like his elimination of $6.9 million that would have paid for the construction of 33 military officers' housing units at a cost in excess of $200,000 apiece.

But Neumann bit off a little more than he could chew with the "elephant, tiger, and rhino vote" in July 1995. He wanted to cut $800,000 from an international conservation program for endangered African elephants, tigers, and rhinoceroses. The amount of money was small in relation to the rest of the federal budget. But that didn't matter to Neumann. It was the principle of the thing. It also didn't matter to him that the program he sought to eliminate was a pet project of Speaker Newt Gingrich. Gingrich informed Neumann ahead of time that if he insisted on going forward with the move, Gingrich "would have to come to the floor and make sure [Neumann] lost." And Gingrich, who kept a dinosaur skull in his office and who as a child wanted to be a zookeeper, did just that.

After joking about the obvious symbolism of supporting the elephant, the GOP party symbol, Gingrich told members of the House, "This is a very small amount of money, but it is symbolically very important." He went on: "We have done a lot to cut spending this year. I am eager to get to a balanced budget. Most of us have actually voted for a massive cut in overall spending. We have proven we are committed to fiscal conservatism. This is a very tiny, very good series of programs which are not only important for ourselves, but which I believe send a signal. . . . We do not have to cut mindlessly just because we want to get to a balanced budget."

Neumann agreed that the vote was symbolic, but he saw it slightly differently. He thought private donations should fund the conservation program. "No one is questioning the importance of maintaining and preserving endangered species. . . . What is being questioned here is whether U.S. tax dollars should be used for that purpose or whether private funding should be doing that. Our children and our grandchildren are counting on this Congress to change the practices of the past, to zero out programs that we can no longer spend money on. If we had the money to spend on this program, it might be a fine program. We do not. Our checkbook is overdrawn. It is time we stopped spending money in this country that we do not have. . . . It is time that the people in this Congress start sending a loud and clear message to the people of this country that the U.S. government cannot keep doing for others what others ought to be doing for themselves."

The vote was 132–289 against Neumann's amendment. "We had a debate on the floor, and we lost. We've had our go around, and I think we understand each other," Neumann said a few months later about his relationship with the Speaker. "I think he's a brilliant man; we just don't always see eye to eye."

And so, having become a thorn deeply embedded in the sides of Gingrich, Livingston, and many other senior Republicans and having staked out his position on domestic spending, Neumann decided to take on foreign policy. Neumann took part in a congressional visit to the former Yugoslavia during the August recess. He thought the United States was too pro-Bosnian and anti-Serb, and in September, when the defense appropriations bill came to the House floor, he successfully offered an amendment that would prohibit President Clinton from sending U.S. troops to Bosnia to enforce a peace agreement unless Congress first gave its approval.

Many of the freshmen felt as Neumann did. Quite a few of them had never traveled outside of the United States before being elected to Congress, and they were somewhat isolationist in their worldview. For example, they supported eliminating the United Nations or at least cutting U.S. funding for it.

The freshmen believed that with the end of the cold war, people wanted the United States to focus inward. That sentiment may to some extent help explain the rise of the freshmen. During the cold war, as in any war (although less intensely), the United States was concentrated and united on defeating a distant but powerful enemy. When the Soviet Union was vanquished, the country lacked an enemy and a joint purpose. It can be argued that we then turned inward to find an enemy at home. For the freshmen, government was the enemy, and their battle was to kill it or at least render it less menacing. One thing they could try to do was to keep the country out of unnecessary foreign entanglements.

The Senate, however, had passed no restriction on funding for a Bosnian peace-keeping mission, and when the bill went to conference, Neumann's amendment was watered down with nonbinding language. Neumann, a conferee, agreed to sign the conference report but added next to his name the words "except to the agreement regarding U.S. deployment in Bosnia."

Neumann let it be known he would be voting against the defense appropriation when it came back to the House floor. But a few hours before the vote on September 29, Neumann paid a not-so-social call on Livingston in his office. Neumann wanted to know if the chairman knew anything about a military contractor who had recently told Neumann he wouldn't help him with fund-raising if he voted against the defense appropriations bill. Neumann suggested Livingston was behind the threat. Livingston exploded. "Get the fuck out of my office," he screamed. He yelled the demand over and over, so loudly that the Capitol police came running to find out what the disturbance was. Livingston told Neumann this was the last straw and he was going to get him thrown off the committee. Livingston then picked up the phone and called the Speaker. Gingrich talked first to Livingston and then to Neumann, advising the freshman to apologize to the chairman. Neumann, not very contritely, did apologize and thought that would end the matter, despite his later vote against the defense bill.

The week after the defense appropriation was defeated and sent back to conference, Neumann sent around a "Dear Colleague" letter in which he urged other members to support his request that his original requirement for congressional approval before any U.S. troops could be sent to Bosnia be put back into the legislation. "We must act now or be prepared to face the consequences of our inaction when coffins containing the remains of American servicemen and women are returned to the United States," wrote Neumann.

On October 11 it was Neumann who received a letter. It was from Livingston, and it informed Neumann that he was being reassigned from the Appropriations National Security Subcommittee, which controls the Pentagon's budget, to the much less powerful Subcommittee on Military Construction.

That same day Neumann was called to the Speaker's office for a private meeting to discuss his changed status on the Appropriations Committee. Gingrich counseled Neumann about the rift that had developed between the rambunctious freshman and his chairman. Gingrich explained "how it would be important for me to accept this and move on. . . . Mostly, I listened," recalled Neumann. Gingrich acknowledged later that the "intense disagreement" between Neumann and Livingston "extended far beyond" Neumann's refusal to support the defense appropriation bill "into a matter of style and approach and everything else." Livingston was tired of Neumann's rebelliousness and frequent challenges to his authority. The disciplinary action was simply the chairman's exercising his "prerogative of assigning people to the subcommittees," according to Gingrich.

But Livingston and Gingrich didn't count on the reaction the move would elicit from Neumann and the rest of the freshmen. Livingston had issued a press release announcing Neumann's reassignment. "At the start of the new Congress, Appropriations Committee members pledged to work in support of the panel's business. We have tried very hard to address Mr. Neumann's concerns, yet he has refused to support the National Security bill. We need conferees who can get the committee's work done," the press release read in part. Neumann learned of the release from a reporter. "No way would I pledge to support anybody's agenda except that of the people of Wisconsin," Neumann said. Infuriated, he scrawled, "I voted my conscience and will continue to do so no matter what" on a copy of Livingston's press release, signed it, and had his staff hand deliver a copy to every Republican House member's office.

"This was a slap at the whole freshman class; this was a slap at the integrity of the Congress; this was a slap at the American people," fumed the self-important Neumann, who seemed to be confusing himself with the rest of the country, which neither knew nor cared about his committee reassignment. But the rest of the freshmen certainly cared. After all, more than 50 of them had voted against the defense appropriation. If Neumann could be punished for voting against the leadership, they wondered which one of them would be next.

As he was coming out of Gingrich's office, Neumann ran into fellow freshman Linda Smith and told her what was happening. She headed to the House floor for an impromptu meeting with several other freshmen, including Mark Souder and class president Roger Wicker. They didn't waste any time. First they met with majority leader Dick Armey to let him know there was a problem. Then they called an emergency class meeting in a basement room in the Capitol. There was unanimity, according to Souder, that they should do something. They considered going public or asking for a conference vote on Neumann's reassignment but instead decided first to take their case to Gingrich.

When the freshman delegation arrived at Gingrich's office, only a few hours after they had first learned of the matter, the Speaker and Livingston were there going at it over the press release that had been issued about Neumann's reassignment. In a meeting on the balcony outside Gingrich's office, which looked down from the Capitol's west front over an impressive view of the Mall and the Washington Monument, Souder and the other freshmen told Gingrich and Livingston that tensions were running high. "At this point we were trying to work out something and not blow up the place," said Souder.

Livingston was not going to back down and threatened to quit his chairmanship if Neumann were reinstated in his subcommittee spot. The freshmen didn't want to see that happen. Then Livingston had an idea. He wanted to know if the freshmen would be satisfied if Neumann got a seat on the Budget Committee. Peter Hoekstra, a Republican sophomore from Michigan and a like-minded budget-cutting conservative, magnanimously offered to temporarily give up his spot on the Budget Committee to make way for Neumann and to make peace between the freshmen and the leadership. In acting as a go-between, Hoekstra said he was just trying to avert an ugly rift in the Republican conference at a time when some of the most difficult votes of the year still remained. "This was just a bump in the road. We all wanted to get this problem behind us," Hoekstra would explain later.

It seemed to be a win-win solution for everyone, especially Neumann. Now he would have two choice assignments, on both the powerful Appropriations and Budget Committees—unusual for any member but in particular a freshman. "It's like a child's dream come true," Neumann told the *Chicago Tribune*. Livingston got to save face, the leadership quickly and quietly resolved a potentially serious problem, and the freshmen emerged with more clout than ever.

Their quick response showed that they weren't "going to get rolled," asserted Souder. By flexing their muscles, they wanted to send a signal to the leadership that they intended to vote their consciences and not be punished for it. Rising up and fighting for Neumann and then getting their leaders to bend to their will so quickly was a defining moment for the class.

Although they were publicly pleased over their victory, some freshmen were a bit jealous of Neumann's good fortune. Neumann, whom many considered self-righteous and humorless, was not extremely popular with his classmates and had few close personal friends, even among those who agreed with him much of the time. It was more out of class unity than personal affinity that the freshmen fought for Neumann, and now some of them privately grumbled about his being so generously accommodated just because he was a troublemaker who never went along with anything. They wondered what kind of mutiny they would have to engineer to get better committee assignments of their own.

The next day Livingston issued a humble, one-paragraph statement amending his previous release, which he said "incorrectly implied that at the start of the 104th Congress I had exacted the pledge of all members of the Appropriations Committee to work in support of my agenda. This is a completely false statement. Mark Neumann has never pledged to follow my agenda, nor vote in any way other than what his own conscience dictated. Congressman Neumann has always been an independent voice on the committee. Mark Neumann is a man of integrity and honor."

After the dust had settled, Budget chairman Kasich, who agreed to take Neumann on his committee, had a few words of advice for Neumann. Kasich urged him to be less of a loner: "A wise man has many counsels; it's real dangerous when the only counsel you have is yourself." As for what kind of a Budget Committee member he thought Neumann would make, Kasich told me at the time, "If he wants to be a radical or a revolutionary, he'll have to get in line behind me."

For his part, about a week after the Neumann flap Livingston quipped to the *New York Times*, "I have had a lot of freshmen tell me, 'Keep plugging, we think you are doing fine.' So there is not unanimous agreement about how the old bull Livingston is suppressing the rights of the young, vigorous proponents of freedom, liberty, democracy, and of trust, justice and community, and of, oh, the American way."

12

THE MEDICARE
PRESERVATION ACT

As CONFIDENT AS THE FRESHMEN WERE, some of them were starting to be a bit uneasy about the GOP's proposed changes for the Medicare program. They had been sent home in August with instructions to hold public meetings with their constituents to explain what the Republicans were trying to do. But they didn't have any specifics to take with them, since the Republicans were still trying to put their Medicare plan together. In the "Medicare Presentation Suggested Talking Points" handed out before they left Washington, members were told to hold up a copy of the Medicare trustees report that had been issued in April. It warned that Medicare faced bankruptcy by the year 2002 if changes weren't made in the system. The freshmen were told to stress that Medicare was going broke and the Republicans were not going to cut Medicare but rather were trying to save it. "Ask how many people knew Medicare was going bankrupt before they came to the meeting," they were advised.

But their constituents were wary. Mark Neumann had 12 Medicare meetings in his district in August. He tried to avoid talking about managed care or health maintenance organizations (HMOs). One constituent told him, "I don't want any HMO or any of that crap," and said if he voted for a plan that would force her into an HMO, "I'll vote you out." Neumann did his best to assure his constituents that despite what they might be seeing on television, Medicare as they knew it would continue to exist.

The Democrats had begun running TV ads around the country that featured Bill Clinton and talked about the "cuts" the Republicans wanted to make that would hurt elderly Medicare recipients by charging them thousands of dollars more a year. The Democrats claimed the Republicans wanted to perform open-heart surgery when a little outpatient treatment was all Medicare needed. And they continually blasted the GOP plan as an attack on older Americans and a way to come up with the money needed to balance the budget and pay for a $245 billion tax cut for the wealthy. The ads, created by Democratic media consultant Bob Squier, were part of the overall re-election strategy for Clinton that had been heavily influenced by political consultant Dick Morris. The Republicans were furious over what they labeled the "Medi-scare" ads and said the Democrats were just demagoguing the issue and ignoring the "crisis" facing Medicare that could lead to the collapse of the whole system.

When President Clinton had introduced his own 10-year balanced budget plan in June, it called for $124 billion in Medicare reductions, and he was immediately blasted by Democrats who said he shouldn't have moved toward the Republican po-sition so soon in the process, that he was caving in. The White House then prepared a 100-page briefing book for administration officials about Medicare and what was wrong with the Republican approach. The book contained fewer than 200 words about what the president would specifically do to reform the system. And backing off his earlier proposal, by the fall the president was saying $89 billion in savings was all that was needed to extend the life of the Medicare trust fund.

But neither the Republicans nor the Democrats were telling the whole truth. Most of what was going on was political posturing aimed at "scaring old people" and winning political points.

The Republicans had not campaigned on reforming the Medicare system; it was not in the Contract with America. But making changes to Medicare and Medicaid, huge and costly federal entitlements, would help the Republicans get the savings they needed to balance the budget by 2002. Since defense and Social Security, called the third rail of American politics by former House Speaker Tip O'Neill, were off the table, the Republicans had to look to Medicare for more savings. Rather than sit-ting down and determining the best changes to reform Medicare and then adding up how much those changes would save, the Republicans set a $270 billion goal first and went about targeting changes to meet that goal—not exactly the best way to make decisions on a major policy reform that would affect every senior citizen in this country.

Even some Republicans considered $270 billion in Medicare reductions too much, and they thought the kind of changes necessary to achieve that level of sav-ings in seven years would put too great a strain on the system. The amount needed simply to stave off bankruptcy through at least 2002 was significantly lower. The ac-tuaries at the Health Care Financing Administration (HCFA), which oversees Medicare, estimated the figure at about $150 billion, and the Congressional Budget Office put the figure at $165 billion.

Medicare was badly in need of an overhaul. Both Congress and the White House had known for some time that Medicare was running out of money. Since 1970 there had been 10 occasions when insolvency was projected for Medicare, and each time the Democrats made minor adjustments to the program to manage things in the short term. But things were worse this time. Beginning in 1995 the Medicare

Hospital Insurance, or Part A trust fund, which primarily funds hospital and nursing home care for elderly and disabled Americans, would for the first time in decades be paying out more in benefits than it collected in payroll taxes.

In addition to the trust fund problem, there was the issue of the expanding drain on the federal treasury. Medicare Part B pays for doctor visits and other medical expenses for recipients and is financed through premiums paid by those receiving Medicare and by general government revenue. When Medicare was created in 1965, beneficiary premiums paid 50 percent of the costs of Part B, which were matched equally by money from the general fund. But as the cost of the program climbed, that ratio started to change. In 1974 the percentage of the beneficiary contribution began falling. In 1995 Medicare's monthly premiums of $46 covered only 31 percent of the cost of the program, and taxpayers were subsidizing nearly three-quarters of the cost. That's where the Republican plan for balancing the budget intersected with Medicare: Cut costs and you come up with savings you can use to lower the deficit. Funding just for Medicare and Medicaid, the federal health program for the poor, took up more than 15 percent of the federal budget.

But that was just the short-term problem. The long-term problem was far worse. In 1995 four workers were supporting each Medicare beneficiary through their payroll deductions and the contributions of their employers. When the baby boomers began hitting age 65 in the year 2010, that number would soon be cut in half, leaving only two workers to pay for each Medicare recipient. That would put a strain on the system the likes of which would make the current "crisis" seem like a mere hiccup. If the system was not quickly brought into check, it would have a meltdown when the baby boomers retired.

No one denied that Medicare's long-term future looked bleak, but neither the Democrats nor the Republicans were proposing to deal with that except to suggest that a commission or blue-ribbon panel should be created to study the problem. The argument being waged in the fall of 1995 had to do with the short term. The Republicans had figured out they needed to convince the public there was a crisis so they could generate support for significant Medicare cost cutting. And they did that pretty well. Polls showed that people did believe there was a problem with Medicare. But they were skeptical about letting the Republicans fix it.

Republican pollsters advised Gingrich and other GOP leaders that they needed to change the language they used when they talked about Medicare reform. They were to stress that they were "preserving and protecting" Medicare, and so they called their plan the "Medicare Preservation Act." Under no circumstances were they to say "cut" in describing how they planned to slow the rate of growth of Medicare spending. They also played media watchdog, especially John Kasich, who would call reporters and chastise them for calling any part of the Republican plan for Medicare a "cut." The strategy was actually quite effective, and the Republicans were largely able to stop reporters from talking about Medicare cuts.

Early on the Republicans talked a lot about the "fraud, waste, and abuse" in the system and made it sound as if just dealing with that would get them most of the savings they needed. There were of course cases of abuse in the system and a handful of doctors did get rich practicing high-volume Medicare medicine, but it was highly doubtful the Republicans would ever achieve the kind of savings they predicted by trying to crack down on fraud, waste, and abuse. The worst fraud is easy to spot: phantom health care providers billing the government for services that were never performed on nonexistent patients. But more subtle abuses—a doctor performing three tests when one would do, putting down the billing code for a more expensive procedure than the one actually performed, or telling patients to come in for more appointments than are necessary—are not only much more costly to the system than flagrant fraud but also much harder to detect.

The first week in September the Republicans held two days of sessions they called "Medicare feedback forums" for GOP members to talk about what they had heard in their districts in August. More than 30 Republican members, half of them freshmen, took advantage of the media availability and show hearing. A number of them suggested raising the age to qualify for Medicare, others brought up means testing for affluent Medicare recipients, but almost all of them mentioned curbing waste, fraud, and abuse.

Several of them related stories they had been told. Freshman Rodney Frelinghuysen of New Jersey said, "One constituent told me about her experience after a bout with illness. For six months after her recovery, a nurse visited her every day, long after she was well. When she pleaded that the nurse stop visiting, the response was that she shouldn't worry, Medicare will pay." Freshman Brian Bilbray of California described how a patient was billed for a double mammogram. When she called about the bill, saying it couldn't be correct because she had previously had a mastectomy, she was told, "Oh, what do you care? You're not paying for it." The woman, Bilbray's mother, informed her son about the incident.

On September 14 the Republicans held a joint House-Senate pep rally to talk about Medicare and the budget. More than 250 representatives and senators attended. Bob Dole opened the unity meeting. Dole knew that many of the freshmen saw him as a symbol of the past, and he tried to reassure them that he was with the program: "We *are* going to balance the budget in seven years, make no mistake about that." Dole also made an attempt to be bipartisan, saying he expected the Senate Democrats and the president to help in the effort. It was his way. It was not, however, Newt Gingrich's way. Gingrich followed Dole to the podium. "We are attempting to lead the American people from the legislative branch," said Gingrich. "Medicare is the heart of this fight." Gingrich warned his troops about the tough days that lay ahead and how important it would be to stick together on the budget. "The left-wing Democrats will lie. . . . Outside activists are going to run terrible, nasty smear campaigns. . . . Everyone of us are going to have good, tactical reasons to vote no. . . . But together we're going to have a historic and remarkable 60 days."

The Republicans still hadn't finalized the details of their massive plan and were still attempting to placate key interest groups, especially physicians, an important GOP constituency. They remembered the disastrous experience the Clinton administration had suffered with its health reform proposal the year before by not satisfying the health care interest groups who then turned on the plan and lobbied against it.

The Republicans wanted to hold back on their plan as long as possible so it couldn't be picked to death. But their strategy backfired. They were perceived as wanting to keep everyone in the dark about their plan, as if they were ashamed of it, and to ram it through without the benefit of adequate hearings and review.

"This bill, right from the start, was written in the Speaker's office," Commerce Committee chairman Thomas Bliley told the *Washington Post*. The Republicans held dozens of hearings and invited all of the interest groups—doctors, hospitals, seniors—to testify and to help write the legislation. The one group they kept out of the room was the Democrats. The Republicans wanted to completely transform a program that affected nearly 40 million people in this country, and they thought they could do it without Democratic input. This obviously didn't sit well with the Democrats, especially those who had been actively involved in health policy in the past.

The Democrats were obviously frustrated with being in the minority and having so little say in what was going on. On Wednesday, September 20, tempers erupted during a closed-door meeting of the Ways and Means Committee. Senior Democrat Sam Gibbons stormed out of the meeting after calling the Republicans "a bunch of fascists" for refusing to allow him to speak and scheduling only one hearing on their Medicare plan, which they still had not released to the Democrats. Gibbons said the Republicans' refusal to let him speak was "the rudest I've ever been treated as a member of Congress in my life." Wadding up a piece of paper and throwing it on the table, he said, "You're a bunch of dictators, that's all you are. I had to fight you guys 50 years ago" as a paratrooper in World War II.

The incident turned into a shouting match outside the committee room. Bill Thomas, chairman of the Ways and Means Health Subcommittee and a chief architect of the Medicare plan, started heckling Gibbons about throwing a tantrum and suggested the Democrats introduce a plan of their own. Gibbons then pulled Thomas's tie. What one GOP aide labeled "the brawl in the hall" had Democrats and Republicans screaming at each other about the Medicare plan and the way the Republicans had handled it.

After numerous delays and trickling out information a little at a time, the Republicans finally introduced their Medicare reform plan on September 29 and planned a vote on it as soon as possible. They emphasized that their plan would offer seniors more choices and that they were not cutting funds for Medicare, merely slowing its rate of growth and controlling costs. The Democrats reacted predictably. Senator Ted Kennedy labeled the GOP plan a "brazen, cruel, and unprecedented assault on Medicare." When the Democrats asked for a week of hearings on the plan, they were refused, causing them to storm out of a Commerce Committee hearing. To protest the Republicans' failure to schedule hearings after the plan was released, House and Senate Democrats staged their own mock hearings.

Despite their grandstanding, the Democrats had a point. The GOP Medicare reform bill was hundreds of pages long and packed with technical details that affected virtually every aspect of this nation's health care delivery system. The Democrats, as well as the public, had the right to closely examine and comment on the details of such a major change before Congress voted.

But the Democrats were wrong in saying the GOP Medicare plan went too far. In fact it didn't go far enough. Because of the relentless attacks by the Democrats, the Republicans caved in to political pressure and came up with so-called Medicare reform that wouldn't really do much actual reforming, offering instead a Band-Aid, short-term fix that relied heavily on reducing payment rates for doctors and hospitals and trying to move patients and providers into managed care plans using economic and regulatory incentives. Many health care analysts doubted the Republican plan would save as much money or move the elderly into managed care plans at the rate they predicted. And the plan made virtually no attempt to fix problems with the existing fee-for-service system.

The only direct increase in cost to Medicare recipients contained in the House Republican plan was a proposal to keep the Part B premium at its existing 31 percent level of costs rather than letting it decrease to 25 percent, as it was scheduled to do at the beginning of 1996. Keeping the premium at 31 percent meant it would cost beneficiaries only about $7 more a month in 1996 over 1995, rather than seeing their premium decrease as it was set to do, but the Democrats bitterly opposed such a change. The Republicans also proposed means testing—relating the Medicare premium cost to a beneficiary's income so wealthy Medicare recipients would pay their fair share. The Democrats, who were decrying tax breaks for the rich, opposed Medicare means testing even though it had been part of President Clinton's health reform package in 1994.

And Senate Republicans proposed raising the age for Medicare qualification in line with what is already in place for Social Security. That would mean people born in 1960 would be the first group of beneficiaries who would have to be 67 before they could receive full retirement benefits. But the Democrats fought that change, too.

Although the Republicans had traditionally opposed the price controls on Medicare providers that the Democrats had been using for years, price controls for hospitals and doctors' services were the backbone of their plan, which failed to deal with the continuing problem of providers' increasing their volume of services to counter reductions in price. If you limit the rate doctors and hospitals receive for each procedure, they will often find a way to make up the money somewhere else, for example, with more lab tests, unnecessary office visits and procedures, and in the most egregious cases by billing for services that were not performed. Kirk Johnson, general counsel of the American Medical Association, acknowledged the problem, pointing to "an inclination on the part of providers basically to retain a certain income level."

The Republicans took great pains to make the physicians happy by giving them other things they asked for, such as relaxation of existing antitrust laws, self-referral, and antikickback rules governing doctors (rules that, for example, prevented doctors from ordering lab tests and then having the tests performed in labs they owned or had some financial interest in). The changes could open the door for more fraud and abuse, but it helped the Republicans win endorsement of their plan from the American Medical Association. Roland E. "Guy" King, who was chief actuary of the Health Care Financing Administration (HCFA), from 1978 to 1994, said the Republicans based their choices about what to include in their plan primarily on political considerations. "They asked hundreds of people for advice, and then they took that advice and weighed the political consequences and how they could sell it. They picked the solutions that seem to be the least punitive to their constituencies," said King.

The biggest problem with Medicare is that it is outdated and has not kept pace with developments in the larger health care delivery system. Medicare essentially involves "open-ended entitlements," unlike Social Security, which has a fixed payment and a fixed rate of growth. Medicare costs have been rising at a dramatic 10 percent a year, about 3 percent faster than the rest of the health care industry and much faster than the rate of inflation. Between 1 and 2 percent of that growth is attributable to longer life spans and the rising number of beneficiaries. Another 3 to 4 percent is due to inflation. But about half of the increased costs in the program are due to the growth in the use of services. Some of that increase is a result of the constant development of new, ever more sophisticated tests and medical procedures, but a great deal is thought to be sheer inefficiency—the biggest problem facing the system. Although health care analysts acknowledge this is extremely difficult to address, it is also where the potential for the greatest savings lies. Nothing can be done about the increasing number of people who qualify for Medicare benefits, but it makes perfect sense to try to make the program as efficient as possible to ensure that the government gets the most for its Medicare dollar.

A strong argument can be made for linking beneficiary costs to the cost of providing medical services, not just as a way to raise money but to induce more responsible use of the system. Currently, there is almost no reason for providers or beneficiaries to make decisions based on cost. If patients had to pay something, even a small fee, whenever they used medical services, they would probably be more aware of billing mistakes and make a greater effort to save money or forgo unnecessary services. There is a 20 percent co-payment for most Medicare services. But according to the HCFA, a whopping 89 percent of all seniors don't pay them. That's because they either qualify for Medicaid or have some type of medigap insurance. That insulates seniors even further from the true costs of the program because for a fixed-dollar premium medigap policies pick up out-of-pocket costs like deductibles and co-payments.

Many employers have tried to control health care costs by linking how much their workers pay for health care to the cost of the program they choose. Employees who select a plan that allows them to go to any doctor they want rather than participate in an HMO are usually required to pay more, because that kind of plan costs more to provide. Assuming that adequate managed care plans are available and the elderly poor are protected, seniors should have to do the same. But such a suggestion was considered too radical to win approval, even by the Republicans.

No matter how rational any increases in costs to beneficiaries might be, they will undoubtedly elicit howls of protest. The Democrats decided this was a winning political issue for them and all they had to do was keep telling people they shouldn't have to pay more for Medicare whether that was right or not. Medicare is extremely popular, perhaps the most popular of all government programs, and the political ramifications of messing with it are enormous—as both parties know. Senior citizens vote. And making changes in Medicare doesn't only affect the elderly; it has a potential impact on their children, who are worried they will be forced to pick up the bills if their parents' out-of-pocket health care costs increase dramatically.

But that's not responsible, either on the part of lawmakers or Medicare recipients. The truth is most of them are getting a lot more out of Medicare than they paid for. Average Medicare recipients who retire in 1995 will get $100,000 more in benefits over the rest of their lives than they paid into the system. And what about those seniors' children and grandchildren? Is it fair for a young working family with two children, a mortgage, and an annual income of $30,000 to pick up the tab through payroll taxes for a retired couple with an annual income of $75,000 or more—especially when the young people have no idea what kind of benefits will be left when they're ready to retire?

One of the most controversial aspects of the GOP plan and one that leaders like Newt Gingrich and Dick Armey pushed aggressively was something called medical savings accounts, or MSAs. The idea was to give people a fixed contribution that they could use to purchase a high-deductible catastrophic insurance policy. They could put the money left over into a savings account and use these funds to cover routine medical costs. They could keep whatever they didn't spend, but they would be on the hook for the insurance deductible, which could be anywhere from $3,000 to $10,000, depending on the type of policy they chose. Since the elderly tend to be extremely risk-averse, especially when it comes to their health, those who picked MSAs would probably be the wealthiest and healthiest beneficiaries, but these are not the people who are costing the system money. And as in managed care, if they experienced an illness, they could simply get back in the fee-for-service program. For those reasons, the Congressional Budget Office estimated medical savings accounts wouldn't save Medicare money but would actually cost the system $3–4 billion.

So why did the Republicans insist on including it in their plan? It undoubtedly had something to do with the Golden Rule Insurance Company of Indianapolis, which sold MSA-type policies. The company's chairman, J. Patrick Rooney, had donated more than $1 million to the Republican Party and to several political groups with ties to Gingrich and had lobbied for the idea to be included in the GOP Medicare plan.

In almost no part of the GOP's Medicare reform plan would the proposed changes be less likely to have the desired effect than in the area of home health care. Costs in this area are exploding by 20 percent a year and have tripled since 1990. There are some good reasons for the increase. People are getting discharged from the hospital sooner, and home heath care can help keep people out of hospitals and nursing homes, which are far more costly.

But there's also plenty of room for abuse. It's a lot easier to make unnecessary home health visits than, say, to do unnecessary surgery, and there's almost no oversight in this area. Currently, there is no co-payment for home health care; instituting one could be one of the best ways to control overuse and abuse of the program. But that approach was deemed politically unpalatable by the Republicans and strongly opposed by the home health care industry. Instead, the Republicans proposed a plan that looked as if it had been written by the home health care industry.

As a senior member of the Budget Committee, Connecticut Republican Chris Shays drew up a series of options for Medicare reform that were included in the Budget resolution that passed the House in the spring. But most of Shays's suggestions that had real teeth and might have resulted in true reform of the system were not included in the final proposal. Shays, one of the few Republicans who was candid about the final plan's shortcomings and willing to speak openly about its potential flaws, was concerned that it did not contain enough real reform and did not hit the beneficiaries because "the political reality wouldn't allow us to."

Freshman Greg Ganske, a 46-year-old plastic surgeon from Des Moines, Iowa, had also drafted recommendations for what he, as a doctor and a legislator, thought would be the most effective reforms for Medicare. Ganske had opposed the Clinton health reform plan, and now he had some very specific ideas about what the Republicans should do about Medicare. Ganske said Medicare recipients needed to play a more active role if the overuse and abuse of the system was to be brought in check: "The key to decreasing health care costs is to decrease overutilization of services by expanding choices and personal responsibility. . . . Under the current system, health care consumers are relatively indifferent to the cost of the care they receive. . . . When consumers pay a greater share of their health care costs, health care inflation is kept in check."

Ganske also warned against counting on managed care to solve all of the system's problems. "Unless we make major structural changes in Medicare, we are merely rearranging deck chairs on the Titanic. And to do so, we must solve the fundamental problem in health care—the disconnect between health care recipients and health care spending," Ganske warned. Ganske recommended a number of strong measures, including increasing Medicare deductibles and premiums as well as the co-payments for physicians' services. He also suggested instituting a co-payment for home health care, skilled nursing services, and laboratory fees. And he proposed limiting medigap policies and freezing physician fees for one year.

Although a great deal of money could be saved by making fee-for-service Medicare more efficient, it would involve changes neither the doctors nor the Medicare recipients wanted to make. "If your goal is to do something substantive to control the rate of health care costs, it's not going to be painless. There isn't any painless way to solve this problem. There have to be sacrifices," said Guy King, former HCFA chief actuary.

When the Commerce Committee held its markup on the Medicare bill on October 11, Ganske, a member of the committee, said he believed $270 billion was too much to wring out of the Medicare system. "If Medicare and Medicaid cuts are too deep, hospitals and doctors will shy away from serving the elderly, which could further increase the number of uninsured."

In the week between that meeting and the bill's consideration on the floor, there was a great deal of horse trading as Gingrich attempted to appease various members who had concerns as well as making a last-minute bargain with the American Medical Association over physician payments. Ganske led a group of members from rural districts who complained that the payment structure under the reform plan was too low for rural areas. The day before the vote was scheduled, GOP leaders said they would take care of the issue later during conference negotiations with the Senate, but that didn't satisfy Ganske. Only by threatening to vote against the bill were Ganske and the other rural members able to win an adjustment of the reimbursement formula.

During the nine hours of floor debate on the GOP Medicare plan on October 19, one Democrat quipped that "GOP" stood for "Get Old People." There was almost no substantive debate on the merits of the plan. The Republicans mainly insisted they were going to save the system, and the Democrats claimed the Republicans were gouging the elderly to give the wealthy a tax cut and were actually trying to kill Medicare in the long run. "There is no pride in asking our senior citizens to pay more and get less so the wealthiest Americans can have it all. But there is one thing supporters of this bill are right about. This is a historic vote. With this vote, we turn back 30 years of progress, 30 years of trust, 30 years of hope that our parents and grandparents will always have the health care that they need," said House minority whip Bonior.

"Maybe this makes us different from the politicians who used to run this place: We want to solve problems for all Americans," said Gingrich, who closed the Medicare debate for the Republicans. "We want a solution to preserve and protect Medicare for the current seniors. We want a solution to set the stage for the baby boomers to retire with safety and security. We want a solution to protect younger Americans from higher taxes, higher interest rates, crushing debt, and a bankrupt government," said Gingrich. The Medicare bill passed the House on an almost straight party-line vote.

But any public relations headway the Republicans might have made with the passage of their Medicare bill was all but erased by remarks by Gingrich and Dole only a few days later. On October 24 Dole addressed a conservative group and talked about his original opposition to the creation of Medicare. "I was there, fighting the fight, voting against Medicare, one of 12, because we knew it wouldn't work in 1965." It was all the Democrats needed to bolster their claims that the Republicans never had supported the creation of Medicare and wanted to get rid of it now. That very same day Gingrich made his famous "wither on the vine" remarks. In a speech, Gingrich called the Health Care Financing Administration a "centralized command bureaucracy" like those in the Soviet Union under the Communists. "Now we don't get rid of it in round one because we don't think that that's politically smart, and we don't think that's the right way to go through a transition. But we believe it's going to wither on the vine because we think people are voluntarily going to leave it." Although Gingrich later insisted he was speaking only of HCFA, the remarks were somewhat ambiguous and seemed to be referring to the traditional Medicare fee-for-service system. There would be no political consequences to shutting down HCFA, and people could not leave a government administrative agency, but they could leave the traditional Medicare program for an HMO.

This was just what the Democrats were waiting for. Democratic polling showed that the Republicans were extremely vulnerable on the Medicare issue, and it was something the Democrats could use to attack. They wasted no time creating a television commercial using Gingrich's "wither on the vine" statement.

Democratic objections to the GOP plan focused almost exclusively on aspects they said would force seniors into managed care plans and require them to pay more in premiums. The Democrats knew their constituents opposed paying more for Medicare, and they were holding their breath waiting for the Republicans to fall apart over the issue.

The Republicans didn't realize how pivotal the Medicare issue would become and to what extent the Democrats were willing to pound it over and over. And they totally underestimated how unpopular their approach would prove to be. By making Medicare a central aspect of their budget plan, the Republicans handed the Democrats a weapon to use against them. Instead of being about balancing the budget, the Democrats were able to shift the focus of the debate to balancing the budget on the backs of the poor and the elderly to pay for tax cuts for the wealthy.

The Republicans do deserve credit for trying to focus public attention on the problems of the Medicare system. But Medicare reform should have been separated from the budget process and handled in a bipartisan way. Because of the failure of the 104th Congress to deal with Medicare, future Congresses face a more difficult task. In April 1996 the Medicare trustees, which include the cabinet secretaries of the Treasury, Health and Human Services, and Labor Departments, issued their annual report on the condition of Medicare. The report said Medicare's hospital insurance (HI) trust fund would be depleted not in 2002 but one year earlier if no action were taken.

A year later nothing had changed, including the precarious situation of the trust fund, as the trustees plainly and emphatically stated in their 1997 report: "The HI trust fund's projected exhaustion by 2001 dictates the need for prompt, effective and decisive action. We have called for this action in the past, and the situation is even more critical today. Further delay in implementing change makes the problem harder to solve." Medicare's two public trustees, appointed by President Clinton, said in their summary to the report that "the aging of the baby boom generation will place heavy demands on both Social Security and Medicare, requiring substantial changes and sacrifices by some or all Americans. . . . There are no magic bullets for solving the problem of high rates of healthcare spending. . . . Addressing the long-run issues will be difficult and challenging . . . but Medicare cannot stay exactly as it is and it is misleading to think that any part of the program—beneficiary premiums, provider payments, controls on utilization, covered services or revenues—can be exempt from change." And the full board of trustees urged Congress to set up a national advisory group "to examine the Medicare program" and "develop recommendations for effective solutions to the long-term financing problem."

Perhaps the only way to deal with such a politically sensitive and difficult issue as Medicare is to assign the task to a blue-ribbon commission similar to those used for military base closings. It is disappointing that Congress cannot handle the Medicare problem, but that may, unfortunately, be the reality. Members of a commission would not have to worry about reelection.

*   *   *

For all the Republicans' determination to avoid with Medicare reform the mistakes the Clinton administration made with its health care reform bill, they not only committed some of the same blunders but new ones as well. The Republicans attempted to draft a plan without the input of the Democrats or the White House. Then they tried to act on it quickly before all the details could be analyzed. And they did not adequately lay the groundwork and explain to the public what they were trying to do, which resulted in their losing the public relations contest with the Democrats.

The Democrats used television ads, special interest lobbying, and opposition from political leaders to define the Republicans' Medicare plan and further alarm people who were frightened of major change to their health care, just like the Republicans did against the Clinton health plan in 1994. For the first time since their loss in November 1994, the Democrats seemed truly united—united in bashing the Republicans over Medicare. "Medicare has become a metaphor for the entire Republican revolution, and the debate over Medicare is really a values debate. It says volumes about who we are, who we're fighting for, and who they are and who they're fighting for," presidential adviser George Stephanopoulos told the *New York Times*.

The Republicans argued that they never really had the chance to make their case to the American people, but if that is true, they have only themselves to blame. A major change to a program that affects 38 million Americans requires significant leadership and preparation to convince people the approach being proposed is the correct one. But the Republicans rushed in. When it comes to fixing programs like Medicare and Social Security, polls show the public trusts the Democrats, who created those programs, much more than it does the Republicans, who largely opposed their creation. And any major change to a far-reaching program like Medicare simply is not possible without bipartisan support.

As they did when the Democrats hit them on school lunch funding in the spring, the Republicans underestimated how effective the Democrats' emotional pitch would be. The Republicans thought they didn't have to respond. They were wrong. Medicare was the first major battle in the budget war that fall and possibly the most important one. As would become increasingly evident as autumn turned to winter, the Republicans simply could not do it all on their own as they had hoped.

Part Three

FALL–WINTER 1995
THE TRAIN WRECK

13

THE TRAIN WRECK

September 12 was Sam Brownback's 39th birthday, and he was spending it in Washington, much to the disappointment of his children. His nine-year-old daughter, Abby, asked him if the Democrats had sung "Happy Birthday" to him and suggested that next year he should tell Newt Gingrich he wanted the day off.

Brownback's staff had surprised him with a cake and given him a blanket with an image of the Capitol woven into it. The blanket was for the nights when he was too tired to make the six-block trip to his basement apartment and slept on the couch in his office. The impromptu party was cut short when Brownback was called to the floor for a series of votes, and some of his staff members began talking about the first divorce of the freshman class. Thirty-eight-year-old Jim Bunn of Oregon, who had five children, was getting a divorce and planned to marry one of his young staff members. There was starting to be a good deal of talk among the freshmen about who would be next, given the pressure and strain of the pace the 104th Congress was keeping and the many days members were forced to be away from their families. Brownback, who also had a seven-year-old son, Andy, and a daughter, Liz, who had just started kindergarten, didn't like being away from his family and always tried to get on the first plane back to Kansas as soon as the House was finished voting for the week.

One of the smartest and most aggressive of the freshmen, Brownback had managed to win a three-way primary and defeat a former Democratic governor of Kansas to win his seat with a commanding 66 percent of the vote. He was one of the few freshmen who had not signed the Contract with America because of concerns over several provisions, but that did not indicate any disagreement on his part with campaign '94's fundamental principles of balancing the budget and reducing the size of government. Brownback's campaign slogan was "Reduce, Reform, Return"—reduce and reform the federal government and return government control back to the states and the people. Brownback, a devout Christian, also talked about "returning to the basic values that built this country." He was one of the freshmen who felt the revolution was about more than cutting the budget; it was about morality and conservative social values and a feeling that the country was headed in the wrong direction. Brownback received a great deal of support from religious conservatives in Kansas, who made a significant contribution to his primary and general election victories.

In addition to having served as Kansas secretary of agriculture, Brownback had been a White House fellow from 1990 to 1991, working for U.S. Trade Representative Carla Hills. Brownback says when he finished that fellowship and returned home, "It took me six months to think like a Kansan again." But undoubtedly because of the experience, he was more savvy and better at playing the Washington game than most of his fellow freshmen.

Brownback's friendliness and relaxed, soft-spoken style masked his toughness and ambition. On the way back to his office after voting, after stopping to pick up a piece of litter on the sidewalk, Brownback jokes with a security guard in the lobby of the Longworth Building about a weekend football game and chats with the elevator operator about his five-year-old daughter's recent soccer match. If there was something of the Boy Scout in Brownback's manner, it was a Boy Scout on the fast track to making Eagle Scout.

In his small personal office on the third floor of Longworth, his desk was turned sideways to face the wall on which hung one of those white boards you write on with erasable markers. Brownback had written the size of the national debt—$4.9 trillion—and the amount each American owes toward it—$18,816.38—so he saw the figures every time he sat at his desk.

He thought people back home still weren't sure the freshmen would really change anything. During his campaign, after he would speak at a rally, usually at least one person would come up to him and say, "You seem like a nice young man, and I may vote for you, but none of that is ever going to happen." Brownback and the other freshmen were determined to see that it did. "People are angry. They know how much money their government wastes. Maybe we changed something, but most of what's been done is posturing. People haven't seen any real change that affects their lives. Old cultures die hard, and we haven't killed the old culture in Washington. We're a Congress away from that."

Back in Kansas over the summer break, Brownback said he had been told by constituents to stand tough and not give in. But he said other members had heard grumbling from voters about the cuts being made. The gloss that had initially covered the freshmen appeared to be cracking. "Are you guys any different than the last bunch we threw out? Did we just trade labor and left-wing special interests for big business and special interests on the right?" some people back home were asking.

Although many of the freshmen were successful, wealthy business owners before being elected, they fancied themselves populists of a sort, and they came from districts that had voted in high percentages for Ross Perot in 1992. Perot got 28 percent of the vote in Brownback's district. Brownback called the election of 1994 "the people's revolution." He and the other freshmen had been elected by angry voters seeking reform, but it was starting to look like not much reforming was getting done.

Brownback, Linda Smith, and a number of other freshmen had met with Ross Perot in June to discuss the fate of congressional reform efforts. Perot stressed to them that limiting lobbyists and special interest contributions was just as important as balancing the budget. And when Brownback and Smith addressed Perot supporters at their Dallas convention in August and talked about campaign finance reform, they received an extremely enthusiastic welcome, much to the annoyance of some of their more senior congressional colleagues who got a lukewarm response. At that meeting Perot called for a second Contract with America to get campaign finance and other congressional reforms passed.

Early in the session Brownback and Smith had introduced legislation they called the "Clean Government Resolution of 1995," the "Clean Congress Act" for short. It sought to ban gifts, trips, meals, and entertainment to members of Congress except by family members and close personal friends and to reform campaign financing by restricting PAC contributions and requiring congressional candidates to raise all their campaign funds in their home states. With senior Republican moderate Chris Shays of Connecticut, Freshman Enid Waldholtz of Utah had also introduced gift ban legislation, which had a number of Democratic cosponsors. But like all the reform legislation that had been introduced so far that session, the bills were languishing in committee.

There had been repeated promises from GOP leaders that the House would move forward on congressional reform. But when Newt Gingrich and Bill Clinton shook hands in New Hampshire in June over the idea of setting up a commission to study campaign finance reform, Smith complained that this was just an effort to stall the reform process. And a month later Gingrich said the reforms would have to wait until 1996.

Unlike most of the other changes moving through the 104th Congress, the Senate had led the House in this area. In July the Senate unanimously passed new gift and lobbying reform rules that limited senators and their staffs from accepting any gift over $50, with an annual $100 cap on gifts from a single individual, and banning all lobbyist-paid meals, travel, and lodging—like those famous golf, tennis, and ski trips that the members were so fond of. The new lobbying rules required all professional lobbyists of both the legislative and executive branches to register with Congress disclosing who they represent, what they were lobbying for, whom they lobby, and how much they are paid.

A Republican filibuster in 1994 had killed similar legislation, and GOP Senate leaders including Bob Dole and Trent Lott tried to keep it from coming to a vote this time around. But it was pushed through by a bipartisan coalition led by Republican senators John McCain of Arizona and William Cohen of Maine and Democrats Russell Feingold of Wisconsin, Paul Wellstone of Minnesota, and Carl Levin of Michigan. And it was the support of the new Senate GOP freshmen that helped ensure the measures got a vote.

On September 7 McCain and Feingold, joined by Republican freshman Fred Thompson of Tennessee, introduced a campaign finance reform bill that would ban PAC contributions and limit soft money, provide both free and subsidized television advertising and reduced postage rates for candidates who voluntarily met campaign spending limits, and require candidates to raise a majority of money in their home states. To push the issues forward, and partly as a way to make trouble for the Republicans, House Democrats began trying to attach the Senate-passed lobbying reform and gift ban measures to other pieces of legislation being considered by the House that fall. Some of the freshmen, including Smith, threatened to join them to force a vote.

In mid-September Smith wrote an op-ed piece for the *Washington Post* that began, "Americans do not trust Congress." She urged passage of campaign and lobbying reform because the "influence of cash offered by special interest lobbyists" has to be eliminated. "We must say no to free trips, gifts and campaign checks flowing to incumbents to restore the people's confidence in the remedies we've prescribed for our country," wrote Smith.

The column elicited a call to Smith from Speaker Gingrich. Smith boasted to conservative columnist Robert Novak that the GOP leaders were "terrified" of all the noise she was making about congressional reform. Smith, comparing Congress to a sewer, said, "I see some of my freshmen friends getting used to the stink—forgetting what they came here for." These were not words that endeared her either to her freshman colleagues or the leadership. And her abrasive manner rubbed many of the freshmen the wrong way. One member of the class noted that if it had been anyone else pushing lobbying and gift reform, the measures would have had a much better chance. But Smith was getting a lot of media attention, and she wasn't about to keep quiet.

Chris Shays felt so strongly about seeing the legislation enacted that he vowed not to run for reelection if the House did not pass lobbying and gift reform in the 104th Congress. Shays met with majority leader Dick Armey and told him there had to be a vote on gift ban and lobbying reform before the end of the year. If the leadership wouldn't set a date for consideration of the bills, Shays and the freshmen would join the Democrats in seeing they reached the floor.

In addition to worrying about the budget and Medicare, it seemed Gingrich and the GOP leaders would also have to deal with congressional reform. On October 27 Armey held a news conference to announce that lobby and gift reform similar to what the Senate had passed would be brought to the floor on or before November 16. But campaign finance legislation would have to wait until 1996. The Republicans were setting up a task force made up only of GOP members to come up with a campaign finance reform proposal.

Enid Waldholtz was at the press conference, declaring that the freshman class was "completely committed to reform." Smith and Shays were there, too. Smith used the occasion to plug the Smith-Shays campaign finance reform bill, which had picked up the cosponsorship of Martin Meehan, a Massachusetts Democrat, and to blast the fund-raising receptions held virtually every night Congress is in session. "The trips

across the street where we go to fund-raise is disgusting America. . . . The public per-
ceives we're selling votes. . . . People believe they don't count, only people with money
count. . . . If we did nothing else but stop lobbyists from opening a checkbook to influence legislation, [we would have accomplished something] . . . If you keep the fund-
raisers going, you keep the members from having to go home," said Smith.

Some of Smith's colleagues thought she was laying it on a little thick and making
them all look bad. But she didn't care. She said her freshman colleagues, who ran
against the system, were getting too used to the money and didn't want to give up
their advantage over challengers.

*   *   *

The freshmen continued to meet together frequently as a class and in small
groups to bolster their resolve on budget cutting. "We say to each other, 'Let's not let
the place get us and get domesticated by Washington,'" explained Brownback. As
the head of the New Federalists, Brownback was among the freshmen who were feeling restive with the GOP leadership that fall. "There's a growing sense that we've got
to differentiate ourselves, and if we've got to make our leadership uncomfortable,
we'll do it."

As to the details of any balanced budget deal, Brownback said the freshmen were
willing to negotiate. Except for some social issues like abortion and eliminating
funding for the National Endowment for the Arts, the freshmen didn't so much care
how money got moved around in the budget as they did about the bottom line. The
issues that were beyond compromise for the freshmen were the goals of reaching a
balanced budget in seven years, having the deficit go down in each of those seven
years, and hitting the fiscal targets for the 1996 budget that had been set that spring.
These were inviolate. "There's no reason at all to give on those points," asserted
Brownback. "We're absolutely willing to go to the mat to balance the budget in
seven years." At that point he and most of the freshmen were optimistic and still
feeling that momentum was on their side. "This is the fourth quarter, we're up 35–7,
and there's four minutes to play."

After Congress returned from its August recess, Gingrich and Budget chairman
Kasich had met with the freshmen and floated the idea that if they could get welfare
and regulatory reform maybe it would be worth adjusting their seven-year deadline
just a little bit to make an agreement with the White House possible. The freshmen
recoiled at such a suggestion. "You wouldn't take seven years and two months?" Kasich asked. No, the freshmen replied. "You wouldn't take seven years and one day?"
he asked again. Not one extra day, not one extra hour, they told the Budget chairman.

The freshmen immediately fired off a letter saying they planned to hold firm on
the seven-year goal as well as elimination of the Commerce Department. Months of
seeing the way things in Washington worked had caused the New Federalists to realize they had no chance of eliminating four cabinet departments, but they were still
clinging to the idea of at least getting rid of Commerce. Members of the New Feder-

alist group also signed a pledge that they would not compromise their goal of a balanced budget in seven years, and Gingrich quickly backed off the idea.

*   *   *

On September 28 the House by voice vote passed a continuing resolution that ensured the government would continue to operate for six weeks after the October 1 start of the 1996 federal fiscal year. This, at least temporarily, averted the much-anticipated "train wreck." There was no budget agreement with the White House, and most of the spending bills weren't completed, but neither side saw any reason to shut down the government at this point, although some of the freshmen grumbled about the decision. The following day the Senate approved the measure, which would fund the government at a reduced level until a permanent budget deal could be worked out. The budget negotiators would now have until November 13 to try to reach an agreement.

After the passage of their Medicare plan the third week of October, Congress took up the entire seven-year budget, known as the reconciliation bill, the following week. Gingrich had spent weeks making deals and shoring up support among House Republicans to guarantee its comfortable passage, and when the vote was taken on October 26, he lost only 10 Republican votes and picked up four conservative Democrats. Some of the Republicans who voted against it were concerned about the reductions in Medicaid reimbursement that would cost states money. And several GOP moderates, among them New York's Sherwood Boehlert, opposed the budget because it included a provision that would open part of Alaska's Arctic National Wildlife Range to oil and gas drilling.

The massive budget bill, into which the Medicare reform plan had been folded, was a blueprint for the way the Republicans wanted to change government. It would make significant changes in welfare laws and turn the program, along with Medicaid, over to the states to run; balance the budget in seven years; abolish the Commerce Department; phase out farm subsidies; reduce funding for student loans and pass on $500 tax credits to families with children; lower the capital gains tax; and reduce the earned income tax credit program for low-income working families. "It's the most decisive vote on the direction of government since 1933," proclaimed Gingrich. Clinton declared that it was also headed for certain presidential veto.

The following day the Senate passed its version of the reconciliation bill. No Democrats voted for it, and William Cohen of Maine was the only Republican to oppose it. The Senate plan moderated a few aspects of the House bill, but it was still unacceptable to the Clinton White House because of its Medicare, environmental, and education cuts.

Senate moderates of both parties were playing a role in helping to shape the budget, but in the House the Democrats had less input since the Republican takeover of Congress, many of the moderate Democrats actually felt more relevant. When the House had been run by their own party their liberal leaders had largely ignored them. Now the Republicans were stealing and implementing some of the ideas they had tried to put forth in the last Congress, for example, not passing on unfunded mandates to the states. And the moderate Democrats were able to work with GOP moderates and provide crucial swing votes on a few issues.

The liberal Democratic leadership wasn't comfortable with the idea of balancing the budget in seven years because of the domestic spending cuts that would be necessary. But the Democratic House moderates, a group of mostly southern and midwestern Democrats known as the Blue Dog Coalition, decided to offer their own plan that would balance the budget in seven years but not cut domestic programs as deeply as did the Republican proposal.

The coalition budget's spending reductions in Medicare and Medicaid were half the size of those in the Republican plan, and Medicaid would not be block-granted to the states with no guarantee of coverage for the poor and the disabled as it would in the GOP budget. The coalition's welfare cuts were also much smaller. And instead of reducing the size of the earned income tax credit for lower-income working families by nearly $24 billion as the Republicans would do, the coalition plan took only $2 billion out of that program. And the Democratic plan even cut the federal deficit over seven years by $30 billion more than the Republican plan. The coalition budget was able to do all this partially because it made a slight adjustment to cost-of-living increases for Social Security and other federal benefits but primarily because it contained no tax cuts.

The coalition budget received editorial endorsements from the *New York Times, Washington Post, Philadelphia Inquirer,* and *Newsday.* It was also applauded by former Massachusetts senator and Democratic presidential candidate Paul Tsongas and his Concord Coalition. The *Post* called the plan "a far better solution to the deficit problem than any other in sight just now" and said it was "tougher and more credible than the president's mushy proposal, but would leave largely intact important federal programs that the Republicans would destroy." The *Times* said it was a "remarkably sensible" plan that "more fairly spread the burden" of balancing the budget than did the Republican proposal, which hit the poor much harder.

The plan was not supported by the Democratic leadership and received just 72 votes. Sixty-eight Democrats, including five of the Democratic freshmen, voted for it, as did four senior moderate Republicans. The next day a similar plan offered in the Senate by Paul Simon received 19 Democratic votes. After the House voted on the coalition's budget, Budget chairman Kasich praised the efforts of the Blue Dogs. "It's the beginning of a Civil War within the Democratic Party, and there's a fight over the heart and soul of where the Democratic Party is going to go," he predicted. The Democrats were divided over what to do about the budget negotiations, but so were the Republicans, and even more bitterly. The president planned to veto the GOP budget, which meant that at midnight on Monday, November 13, there would be no money to fund the government unless something was done.

Congress would have to pass a continuing resolution (CR) to continue funding government operations until a budget deal could be worked out. It would also have to pass a measure to raise the debt limit, which would allow the government to borrow money to pay its bills. But the freshmen balked at passing either until they could extract a promise from Clinton that he would be willing to balance the budget in seven years. The freshmen wanted to hold Clinton's feet to the fire. They didn't trust him.

House leaders believed the only way they could win freshman support for a debt limit extension and CR was to add "sweeteners," such as the elimination of the Commerce Department, but GOP moderates in both the House and Senate opposed this move. The freshmen were also pushing for the inclusion of a measure that had been introduced by conservative sophomore Ernest Istook of Oklahoma and freshman David McIntosh of Indiana to restrict nonprofit groups that received federal grants from lobbying Congress. Although it was already illegal to use federal money for lobbying, the Istook-McIntosh bill would prevent any recipient of a federal grant from spending more than 5 percent of its nonfederal money on lobbying federal, state, or local officials. The bill further included extensive reporting requirements for federal grantees.

Istook and McIntosh said the main purpose of the measure was to shrink the government and government spending by restricting those who receive federal funding from seeking more. They labeled it an attempt to stop "welfare for lobbyists." But the measure was primarily aimed at the liberal social advocacy groups the Republicans disliked. Many referred to the Istook-McIntosh measure as part of the effort to "defund the left." And the Republicans chose to exempt federal contractors, like those involved in defense contracting, from the bill, although they received a much larger share of money from the federal government than grantees and were often much more active lobbyists.

In a letter to other freshmen, McIntosh offered to provide them with a list of nonprofit groups in their districts who supported Democratic congressional candidates. And he told the freshmen that the lobbying issue had been "a winner" for him back home, telling them, "It can be a winner for you."

But that wasn't at all clear. When word of the Istook-McIntosh bill spread, a coalition of more than 500 charitable and nonprofit groups, including the YMCA, the American Red Cross, the March of Dimes, the Boy Scouts and Girl Scouts, the National Council of Churches, the American Cancer Society, and the American Heart Association, united to oppose the legislation as "extreme" and something that would hurt their organizations. The president of Mothers Against Drunk Driving wrote a letter to members of the Senate suggesting that if the Istook-McIntosh amendment passed, her organization would not be able publicly to express itself yet the alcohol industry would be "able to lobby to its heart's content." Even Elizabeth Dole, wife of the Senate majority leader and head of the American Red Cross, wrote senators that the bill would "impose unrealistic limitations and burdensome reporting requirements" on nonprofit groups.

Many moderate Republicans, whose donors and supporters were the same community leaders active in many of the organizations united to oppose Istook-

McIntosh, started getting cold feet. A number of them were part of a bipartisan group of House members who wrote a letter urging their colleagues to defeat the Istook-McIntosh amendment.

McIntosh, former executive director of Dan Quayle's Council on Competitiveness and current chairman of the Subcommittee on Regulatory Affairs of the House Government Reform and Oversight Committee, was also getting some personal criticism over his behavior in pushing for the bill, including the distribution of a "forged" document by members of his staff. During a September hearing of his committee, McIntosh's staff handed out a document with a simulated letterhead of the Alliance for Justice, a lobbying group representing about 30 civil rights and public interest groups. On it were listed a number of liberal organizations and how much they purportedly received in federal grants. "Not only was the document forged, but the amounts were incorrect, as some of the groups had never received any federal money," said Democrat Louise Slaughter of New York, who asked the House to consider taking some action against McIntosh and who filed a complaint with the Ethics Committee, which eventually dismissed it without taking any action. McIntosh apologized, and the House voted not to pursue the matter, much to the outrage of Slaughter, who said the vote "condoned forgery and sanctioned governing by fraud and deceit."

The controversy certainly didn't help the Istook-McIntosh bill. Knowing that there was opposition within their own party, not only in the Senate but in the House as well, McIntosh and Istook realized they didn't have the votes to pass their measure as a freestanding bill. After attempting to attach it to various spending measures without success, they even decided to tack it on to the CR or debt limit extension, thinking that would ensure its passage.

*　　*　　*

Tuesday, November 7, was an election day, and both parties counted on making much of the results. Since it was an off year, there were only a handful of races up for grabs, including the governorships and/or state legislatures of Mississippi, Virginia, Kentucky, and New Jersey. The Republicans hoped that GOP victories around the country would provide a reaffirmation of their 1994 win and the direction they were going. The Democrats wanted to do well enough to point to a voter repudiation of the Republican Congress, energizing them for 1996.

In Mississippi the Republicans made an all-out push to pick up the nine seats they needed to take over the state senate. Brad Todd, Van Hilleary's press secretary, had been hired by the National Republican Committee to go down to Mississippi and head up the Republican campaign. The GOP had spent more than $3 million on the campaign, including mailings and TV ads that heavily stressed racial and moral themes. They targeted white Democratic candidates, considered the most vulnerable in this racially polarized state, where Republican voters were overwhelmingly white and Democratic support tended to be heavily black.

Four years earlier Kirk Fordice had been elected the first Republican governor of Mississippi since Reconstruction, and in 1995 he easily won reelection. But Democrats swept every other statewide office in Mississippi by majorities of 60 percent or better. And turning back the well-financed GOP effort to win control of the state senate, the Democrats actually gained two seats there.

In Virginia the state's conservative Republican governor, George Allen, who was not up for reelection, pushed for GOP candidates for the legislature, asking the voters to give him a Republican majority. He emphasized the possibility of a GOP revolution in the Virginia legislature much like the one in Congress, and drawing a direct parallel to the Contract with America, Allen and Virginia Republicans ran a "Pledge for Honest Change" campaign that included building more prisons, cutting spending and taxes, reforming public schools, and restricting teen abortions. Allen was more than combative as he aggressively campaigned across the state, saying at one point the Republicans were "going to shove [the Democrats'] soft teeth down their whiny throats." The approach not only seemed to energize Democrats but even hurt his chances with moderate Republicans in the northern part of the state.

The Republicans needed to pick up only three seats in both the house and senate to win a majority in the Virginia legislature, but their effort fell short. They managed to win enough senate seats to tie the chamber 20–20, but with the Democratic lieutenant governor given the responsibility of breaking ties, the chamber remained in Democratic control.

Perhaps no contest was more of a referendum on the Republican Congress than the Kentucky governor's race, if only because during the campaign Democrat Paul Patton highlighted what the Republicans were doing in Washington and urged people in Kentucky to "say no to Newt." Kentucky Democrats targeted seniors, women, and minority voters and stressed in TV ads that the GOP Congress wanted to undo affirmative action and cut funding for Medicare, education, and child care programs. The strategy worked. Not only did Patton win, but so did all the Kentucky Democrats running for statewide office. Declaring victory, Patton gleefully exclaimed, "Kentucky has said no to Newt Gingrich and Bob Dole. . . . Kentucky has said no to cuts in Medicare. . . . Kentucky has said no to the Contract with America."

House Democrats happily pointed to Patton's victory as a sign that voters had had it with the GOP agenda. Freshman Democrat Mike Ward of Louisville, Kentucky, took to the House floor the day after the election and waved a copy of his local paper, the *Louisville Courier-Journal,* whose front-page headline declared "Patton Dashes GOP Hopes." Ward, who said he planned to give a copy of the paper to Speaker Gingrich, declared, "This Kentucky election was a sharp repudiation of the Republican contract and devastating Medicare cuts." The election results were just the boost the Democrats were looking for.

*   *   *

That evening, Wednesday, November 8, the House passed a CR that would keep the government operating until December 1 at a reduced funding level. The CR included the Istook-McIntosh lobbying measure, which had been almost unanimously supported by the freshmen, with New York moderate Sue Kelly the only GOP freshman to vote against it. House Republicans also added a provision that would increase Medicare premiums by about $7 a month beginning in January 1996. The following day the House passed a debt ceiling increase, adding several amendments, including one to abolish the Commerce Department.

In the Senate the next day, members were rebelling over the House add-ons and the uppitiness of the freshmen. "I know these new members of the Congress get quite enthusiastic about saying they have a mandate to do everything that comes to mind. But this lobbying reform provision was not in the Contract with America," declared Nebraska Democrat Robert Kerrey, who compared the House freshmen to terrorists. "This provision changing our lobbying laws does not belong on this bill. Indeed, I find it rather odd that the House has not taken up the lobbying reform legislation that this body has addressed already. . . . The House should take it up over there, take up lobbying reform. If you want to add this amendment to lobbying reform legislation, do so. . . . But I think that Republicans and Democrats here, if this body is going to function, are going to have to take a stand against 60 or 70 members of the House who are constantly saying, 'Do it our way or we are going to shut the place down,'" Kerrey said.

"What we are trying to do is compromise with a minority in the House of Representatives which is basically saying, 'We will hold our breath until we get our way. We do not care if our face turns blue. We do not care if the government shuts down. We are mad at a few organizations that campaigned against us, and we will pay them back.' . . . This is an act essentially of political terrorism, where they are saying, 'We will hold you hostage unless you give us what we want.' Give us an airplane, give us this, give us that, and we will go along. We ought to say no, don't negotiate with terrorists," concluded Kerrey.

Kerrey's characterization of the freshmen and their behavior was one that had started to pick up steam. The freshmen had gone from being seen as principled newcomers who wanted to challenge the way things had always been done in Washington to stubborn children who simply didn't understand how government worked and who were threatening to grab the steering wheel and drive the car off the road if they couldn't have the radio tuned to their favorite station.

A group of freshmen including brash J. D. Hayworth of Arizona had gone over to the Senate chamber to lobby senators for the Istook-McIntosh antilobbying measure, and their behavior annoyed several of the senior senators, especially Democrat Robert Byrd. "I wish senators would just look around this chamber. If you have not looked around, do it. I do not mean to be discourteous to our colleagues from the House. They have the privilege of the floor. . . . But it is a little disconcerting to see them down in the well, buttonholing members of the Senate. . . . All the while I have been speaking, a House member has been standing over there laughing and grinning," said Byrd, referring to Hayworth, who was standing along the wall of the Senate chamber with several other freshmen. Hayworth later attempted to approach Byrd to say he had not been laughing at him but was intercepted by Democratic senators Jay Rockefeller of West Virginia and Frank Lautenberg of New Jersey, who told him that he "lacked class."

After a lengthy debate over the Istook-McIntosh provision, the Senate Republicans passed a modified version. Next the Senate turned its attention to the extension of the debt limit. Republican freshman Spencer Abraham of Michigan, a strong advocate of killing the Commerce Department, introduced an amendment to strip the Commerce elimination from the debt extension, saying, "This is not the right time and this is not the right vehicle for us to consider this important question of the Department of Commerce." And so the debt extension passed the Senate minus the amendment to kill the Commerce Department.

The two measures were then sent back to the House, where there was a great deal of disagreement over them among Republicans. In a floor speech Democrat Charles Schumer of New York did not let the situation go unnoticed: "There is a sophomore congressman from Oklahoma [Istook] who has an idea that seems outlandish even to his Republican colleagues in the Senate. . . . The extremists on that side of the aisle have this goofy scheme, and their leadership cannot even whip them in line. . . . It is Republican versus Republican. It is those on the far right versus those on the very far right. . . . Tell the gentleman from Oklahoma that his idea is kooky, . . . that he cannot get it passed on the floor of the House alone and he cannot get it passed on the floor of the Senate alone. He should stop all these tricks, . . . and then maybe we can debate the real issue, the balanced budget."

GOP House leaders were losing patience with their unruly freshmen and called a meeting on Friday to explain why the Commerce Department elimination and Istook-McIntosh measure had to come off the bills. "We need to spend some time getting these guys in line because they're so used to getting their way. They're always overreacting," conference chairman Boehner told another senior Republican on the way to one of the many meetings held that day to work out a strategy. Istook and McIntosh agreed with House leaders that it would be better to take the watered-down Senate version of their measure off the CR entirely rather than go back and forth trying to get something acceptable to both chambers. And the freshmen also agreed to go along with dropping the Commerce Department elimination—for now.

Although the freshmen had seemed both united and adamant about wanting the additional measures attached to the CR and debt extension, a few of them were privately uneasy. "My own feeling is we have cluttered our message by getting into too many side issues. I got elected to balance the budget in seven years. Where we went awry is we've allowed our fundamental core objective of a seven-year balanced budget to be obscured by other issues. Nothing is more important than balancing the budget in seven years," freshman Jim Longley of Maine told me. Longley was a former Democrat whose father had been elected in 1974 as Maine's first independent governor, defeating Democrat George Mitchell. Longley favored abortion rights and was somewhat more moderate than most of his freshman colleagues, but he felt strongly about reducing government interference with private business and property owners, especially in the area of environmental regulations. Repeatedly during his campaign he had talked about reducing the size and scope of the federal government.

Even with the Commerce Department and Istook-McIntosh amendments gone, the increase in Medicare premiums was still a part of the CR, and that gave the Democrats and Clinton an issue to use against the Republicans. This was just the first in a series of major tactical mistakes the Republicans would make, but it was a doozy.

As insistent as they were about adding provisions to the CR and debt extension, a number of the freshmen weren't so sure about the strategy of including Medicare and thought that gave Clinton a good reason for a veto. "We were upset at that tactical decision. It didn't make sense to us," Joe Scarborough of Florida would say a few weeks later. In his weekly radio address on Saturday, November 11, the president hammered the Republicans on Medicare. Comparing the United States to a family and the Republicans to a banker who could grant additional money to fund the government only if the Medicare increase were included, Clinton said, "The banker says to the family, 'I'll give you the loan, but only if you'll throw the grandparents and kids out of the house first.' Well, speaking on behalf of the family, I say, 'No thanks.'"

The Republicans had handed Clinton a good reason to say no. The president said he wanted a CR and debt limit extension free of any additions—what he referred to as "clean bills." The government was set to shut down Monday at midnight, and the rhetoric from leaders on both sides was heating up. "It's up to the president of the United States. If the government shuts down, his fingerprints are going to be all over it," said Bob Dole. But White House chief of staff Leon Panetta countered, "Don't put a gun to the head of the president and the head of the country. That's a form of terrorism." After appearing on a Sunday morning talk show, Panetta declared, "This is the Republicans against the American people." House Budget chairman Kasich said, "It's high noon, and we're going to walk out on a dusty street and have a gunfight." Unfortunately for the Republicans, *High Noon* was reported to be the president's favorite movie.

The boys-will-be-boys joust over who had the bigger gun was exactly what had turned many Americans off about government, and it confirmed their suspicions that most everything in Washington was about politics and political advantage—winning and losing, getting gunned down in the street or being the one left standing—and not about working together to solve the nation's problems.

And the president's polling showed that standing up to the Republicans, especially on Medicare, could be a winner for him. Although the Republicans must have had access to the same kind of polling that showed they were on shaky ground in forcing a government shutdown over budget cuts, they chose not to believe it. They were convinced their supporters were with them and the American people would surely see the rightness of what they were doing. But led by Dole and the extremely unpopular Gingrich, the Republicans didn't have Clinton's rhetorical and public relations prowess.

The freshmen had become the symbol of the government shutdown, and they frankly made more than a few people nervous, including some in Congress. The two trains driven by Gingrich and Clinton were barreling down the tracks straight toward each other, and lying on the rails, where they had tied themselves, were the freshmen.

On Monday, November 13, Clinton vetoed the Republican bills to extend the debt limit and keep the government running, and at midnight the government officially shut down. Clinton cited as his reason that the Republicans were trying to "impose their priorities on our nation" and should "drop their extreme proposals." Gingrich fired back, saying, "We were elected to change politics as usual."

On Tuesday 800,000 federal employees, about half the federal workforce, were sent home. For the first time in its 76-year history, the Grand Canyon was closed, as were all other national parks and monuments. Passport offices were closed, federal grants were halted, and government contractors were not being paid. Veterans' benefit checks would not be mailed; new food stamp, welfare, and Social Security applications would not be processed. Federal courts remained open, but civil cases were postponed. Amtrak and the postal service would continue to operate, and air traffic controllers would stay on the job. Some Americans hardly noticed the shutdown, but for those who had business with the federal government it would be extremely disruptive.

The negotiations between the White House and GOP congressional leaders dragged on but seemed to get nowhere. And on Wednesday morning Gingrich did something that perhaps more than any other single action ensured that the Republicans would lose the budget standoff and be blamed for the government shutdown. At a breakfast meeting of reporters, Gingrich, appearing tired and cranky, started to complain about his treatment aboard Air Force One going to and from Jerusalem for the funeral of slain Israeli prime minister Yitzhak Rabin the previous week and the part that had played in precipitating a government shutdown.

Referring to himself and Senator Dole, Gingrich said, "Both of us got on that airplane expecting to spend several hours talking about the budget and how do we avoid the shutdown." But Gingrich said the Republican leaders had to sit in the back of the plane and Clinton barely spoke to them on the trip. "Every president we had ever flown with had us up front. Every president we had ever flown with had talked to us at length." Apparently the last straw for Gingrich was being asked to exit from the rear of the plane. "This is petty. I'm going to say up front: It's petty . . . but I think it's human. . . . When you land at Andrews [Air Force Base] and you've been on the plane for 25 hours and nobody has talked to you, and they ask you to get off by the back ramp . . . you just wonder, where is their sense of manners? Where's their sense of courtesy? . . . Was it just a sign of utter incompetence or lack of consideration, or was it a deliberate strategy of insult? I don't know which it was." And Gingrich said that "snub" was "part of why you ended up with us sending down a tougher continuing resolution," which led to the presidential veto and ultimately the government shutdown.

The complaint clearly stemmed from Gingrich's view of himself as an equal to the president and feeling slighted over not being treated as one. The remarks came off as childish and underscored the problem the Republicans faced with Gingrich as their front man. He was prone to losing his temper and popping off.

The White House wasted no time in making Gingrich look even more petty. Clinton, with much shrugging of shoulders and shaking of head, said, oh so maturely, "If it would get the government open, I'd be glad to tell him I'm sorry." The White House released several pictures from the trip that showed the president talking to Dole and Gingrich on the plane, and the Democrats pointed out that in a plane full of current and past government officials, Gingrich was the only one other than the president who was able to take his wife along on the trip. White House spokesman Michael McCurry quipped that "we can send him some of those little M & M's with the presidential seal on them" that are available on Air Force One; on a more serious note he said that Clinton had "lost a friend" with Rabin's death and probably hadn't "much felt like talking about budget politics with Speaker Gingrich."

During the trip the president did, however, have the strength for a game of hearts with Mortimer Zuckerman, publisher of *U.S. News & World Report* and the New York *Daily News,* whose newspaper promptly ran a front-page drawing of a baby Newt in a diaper, the caption reading, "Cry Baby—Newt's tantrum: He closed down the government because Clinton made him sit at back of plane." And all three major television networks prominently featured Gingrich's remarks in their evening news broadcasts. The complex issues over which the Democrats and Republicans were divided in the budget battle were difficult to follow and not that interesting to the average American, but the image of Gingrich as a crybaby trying to exact some revenge on the president and shutting down the government because of an imagined slight was something that caught people's attention.

The rest of the Republicans were fit to be tied over Gingrich's loose tongue and his allowing personal grievances to overshadow the budget issues. Van Hilleary, when asked whether he thought Gingrich was being childish, just shook his head and said, "It's not a matter of being childish; it's just not smart." And not being smart, especially at this critical juncture, was unforgivable when the Republicans had so much on the line.

Even before Gingrich's remarks about his treatment on Air Force One, polls showed that the public blamed the Republicans more than the president for the government shutdown, something an inveterate poll watcher like Clinton was well aware of and happy to use to his advantage. Many Republicans now seemed more eager than Clinton to get the government reopened. They offered to take the Medicare provision off of the CR, but Clinton said that wasn't enough. Then they announced plans for another vote on a CR that would fund the government at a reduced level through December 5 if Clinton would agree to balance the budget in seven years using the Congressional Budget Office to score any plan he submitted. Still, Clinton refused.

But some of the moderate Democrats, especially the 68 who had voted in favor of the Blue Dog Coalition's budget, were getting restive, and they were being lobbied hard by the White House to stick with the president and not vote with the Republicans to reopen the government. In a Democratic caucus meeting, House leaders argued that if they voted to reopen the government, Gingrich would be the winner. James Moran, who represented a northern Virginia district with many federal workers anxious to go back to work, was one of those who argued the Democrats should vote for the CR and declare victory because the Republicans had taken off the Medicare increase.

Freshman Democrat Mike Ward of Kentucky had voted for the coalition budget and was on the fence. First he received a phone call from minority whip David Bonior. "We really need you on this. This is a big deal. This has to do with how the whole thing ends up," Bonior told him. "You've got to support the president; we can't give Newt the upper hand." Then minority leader Dick Gephardt picked up the phone. "We really need you. We've got to support the president on this. We're winning this battle," Gephardt argued. Ward said he wasn't sure.

Then came the heavy artillery. Presidential adviser George Stephanopoulos called Ward and reminded him what an important vote this was. "I understand," Ward answered, "but I'm having real trouble with it." Ward told Stephanopoulos he felt the time had come to end the shutdown. Stephanopoulos said the funding level in the CR was just too low and would hurt important domestic programs. Agreeing to the CR would be an acknowledgment that the Republicans were right on the budget, he argued. They had been polling on the government shutdown every night, and the president was coming out ahead on it, Stephanopoulos told Ward. Standing firm against the Republicans, he said, was just as important as the Medicare issue.

Ward finally agreed to vote with the president but told Stephanopoulos it was a tough decision. "People want us to get this over. You know I'm in a tough district," said the freshman, who had won his seat by just 425 votes. Stephanopoulos asked what they could do to help Ward; the freshman said he wanted a meeting at the Pentagon about help for Louisville's Naval Ordinance Station, which had been slated for closure. "Absolutely. A meeting—I can arrange," Stephanopoulos told him.

The next call was from Treasury Secretary Robert Rubin. When Ward told him he had decided to vote with the president, Rubin asked Ward, "What arguments persuaded you? I've got to make a few more of these phone calls." All of the Democrats who were on the fence were getting calls, some of them even from the president. But when Clinton called freshman Karen McCarthy of Missouri, she told him she planned to vote for the CR. So did freshman Bill Luther of Minnesota.

The night of the vote, White House chief of staff Leon Panetta came up to the Capitol to lobby Democrats to stick with the president. The vote on the new CR was taken late Wednesday evening, November 15, a total of 48 Democrats joined the Republicans to pass it 277–151, just a few votes shy of the two-thirds needed to override a presidential veto. In addition to the two freshmen, the Democrats who voted yes included not only southern moderates and Blue Dogs but most of the members from Virginia and Maryland, who had a lot of unhappy furloughed government workers in their districts.

Gingrich closed the debate on the CR: "We say to the president, 'We offer you a contract with the representatives of the American people. We will give you the money to bring back the furloughed employees. You sign on the line that you agree to work to a balanced budget.' It is that simple. It is that direct."

The following day the Senate, too, passed the CR, with the votes of seven Democrats. But Clinton said he would veto it because a promise to balance the budget in seven years would require cuts too deep in education, health care, environment, and welfare programs. "If the American people want the budget that they [the Republicans] have proposed to be the law of the land, they're entitled to another president, and that's the only way they're going to get it," said Clinton defiantly.

Many of the GOP freshmen disagreed with the strategy of reopening the government without a budget-balancing agreement in place. They wanted to vote against the CR but were convinced by Gingrich to go along. He argued, just as the Democratic leaders were doing, that they had to stick together for the sake of their party. In the end only three Republicans voted no—Joe Barton, a six-term member from Texas, and two freshmen, Mark Souder of Indiana and John Shadegg of Arizona.

Souder was a determined conservative and budget cutter but with a quieter, less confrontational style than Mark Neumann. Souder thought the Republicans should just keep working on the 1996 spending bills for each government department and not give Clinton a platform for grandstanding by trying to pass a CR and reopen the entire government now. What was the point when Clinton had already announced he wouldn't sign it? It was all just so much politicking, Souder thought, and not very helpful to their central goal of getting a balanced budget.

"The leadership is doing all this rhetorical stuff, but they're going to surrender the details," Souder predicted. The GOP leaders had started to get pretty nervous about the press coverage and all the calls they were getting about the government shutdown. "They're too easily swayed by the media," Souder complained. The freshmen were less intimidated by a little bad press. "The fear that's driving us isn't the fear of getting beat; it's the fear of not doing something." Souder and a band of budget conservatives had been bird-dogging all the spending bills, watching for add-ons and making sure extra spending didn't get stuffed in at the last minute. "If they know you're watching, they won't try to sneak things in," said Souder, speaking of his own leadership in a way you'd think would have been reserved for the Democrats.

"I think it's safe to say we've caused as much consternation with senior Republicans who've waited for their turn at the trough as we have with Democrats," said Joe Scarborough, who thought the senior members believed when the appropriations process started the freshmen would "all start grabbing for [their] piece of the pie," too. "I heard a senior member say after one of the votes, 'Those damn Shiites don't understand how things are done around here,'" Scarborough recalled. Scarborough admitted that much of what the freshmen had done was symbolic. "On most of these cases we got rolled; we were only successful a limited number of times." But the one clear victory the freshmen felt they could point to was the Republican decision to stand firm for a balanced budget in seven years. According to Scarborough, that happened "for no other reason but that the freshman class stood up."

Having worked for Indiana Republican senator Dan Coats for 10 years, Souder knew his way around the Hill. It was fine to talk about balancing the budget by 2002, but he knew this Congress couldn't commit future Congresses to anything. It was far more important to get the numbers right in the first two years when they had some control, he thought.

On Friday, November 17, the House and Senate again passed their seven-year balanced budget, or reconciliation, bill, which the president was committed to vetoing. "Today is as important a vote as any day since 1933," declared Gingrich. Because there was still no agreement about how and when the government would reopen, Clinton asked Congress to stay in session over the weekend so that budget negotiations could continue. There was an air of informality in the House office buildings as staff members played touch football and children and family members roamed the halls. There really wasn't much to do. They were all just waiting. Members milled around in the corridor outside of Gingrich's office.

Leon Panetta told the Democratic caucus that the president could not agree to a seven-year budget plan that used Congressional Budget Office (CBO) numbers because it would allow Gingrich to control the budget process.

On the floor the mood was tense and ugly. The night before, Capitol police officers had to break up a shoving match between Republican Randy "Duke" Cunningham and Democrat Jim Moran. The Democrats blamed the Republicans for the shutdown, and the Republicans blamed Clinton as they debated a measure on Saturday to reopen a few parts of the government. "We have got to get serious on this, and we need to hold the president down. I have 25,000 federal employees in my district. There is nobody who wants to see federal employees go back to work more than I do. But what is at stake here today, and throughout this week, is making sure when they go back that we will finally have the president nailed down to a framework and a commitment to balance the budget," said Scarborough.

John Mica, a second-termer from Florida, said much the same thing but in a more colorful way: "We are really here to end the sham, the scam." Accusing Clinton of being inconsistent on how long it would take to balance the budget—five, seven, eight, nine, ten years—Mica said, "We are here to nail the little bugger down."

The Democrats immediately went crazy and demanded that Mica's words be stricken from the record. After a vote on whether he should be permitted to continue speaking, Mica, clearly showing the strain, apologized. "I guess we get emotional in this. I never went to law school, and sometimes I come up here and say things I should not say. . . . But like some of you, I missed my son's football game last night. I did not get a chance to get the house cleaned today with my wife for Thanksgiving." Mica didn't want to be there on a Saturday any more than the Democrats did, but there they were.

A few hours later a Republican motion was made to adjourn the House. The Democrats jumped up and started yelling, "Work, work, work." As the vote went on, it was clear a number of Republicans didn't want to adjourn the House while the government was still shut down. When it was obvious the Republicans were going to lose the vote, Senior Democrat Steny Hoyer started beckoning to the Republicans to "come on over," and the Democrats chanted, "Switch, switch, switch" and "Clean CR." Many Republicans did switch their votes. In the end only 32 Republicans voted in favor of adjourning. When the 32–361 count was announced, a huge cheer went up on the Democratic side of the aisle, and there was chaos on the House floor. The Republican cloakroom sent a recorded message on the members' beepers advising GOP members who had voted yes to go back to the House floor and change their votes to no so they could avoid the embarrassment of being on the losing end of such a lopsided and controversial vote.

At about 3:15 in the afternoon, the Republicans recessed the House without a vote. But when the Democrats wouldn't leave the chamber and kept speaking, the Republicans had the microphones turned off. "Let's stay 24 hours a day. I can last more than any of them can," said freshman Matt Salmon as he walked off the floor. If it was a fight the Democrats wanted, the freshmen were ready to give it to them. But they weren't so sure about their leaders. "I'm really starting to get afraid the leadership is going to cave on the seven years and the CBO numbers," said Hilleary.

On the floor, minority whip Bonior was giving his members a pep talk. About 100 Democrats were staging a sit-in in the House chamber. Barney Frank of Massachusetts, always ready with a sarcastic remark, said he thought they should make Gingrich and Armey honorary morale officers for the Democratic caucus. After a while the Democrats kind of ran out of steam and started trickling out, but a few members stayed on the floor to make sure the Republicans wouldn't sneak in and try to adjourn the House. Under an obscure rule, the House could be formally in session but remain in recess for a prolonged period of time if a handful of Republicans came in every few hours and extended the recess. So the House remained in limbo, not really in session but not formally adjourned.

In his Saturday radio address, Clinton attempted to make the partisan wrangling sound as if it had a high moral purpose. "I know that for many people across our country all this conflict and drama looks just like people in Washington are playing politics again. What every American has to realize is that this is way beyond politics. There are very profound fundamental issues involved. What's at stake is nothing less than two different visions of our country, and two different futures for our people."

To some extent he was right. The Republicans of 1994 certainly did have a different vision of government than the Democrats did. There were fundamental differences about the appropriate role and size of government that were being hashed out. But they were not going to be solved in a day or a month or even, as it turned out, a year.

Dole, just back from an appearance in Florida, where he had narrowly won a presidential straw poll of GOP voters, undoubtedly had his mind on the presidential campaign and how all of this would play with the voters. He had had enough of the shutdown. He met with House Republican leaders and told them it was time to do something. Shutting down the government had been a mistake. They were losing the PR war, and they were going to pay for it.

On Saturday night the Republicans presented Clinton with a new option. They would fund the government through December 15 if he would agree to balance the budget in seven years using CBO assumptions. The White House countered with language the administration wanted to include to protect key domestic programs. The Republicans agreed to the revisions. The final agreement stated that they would work to enact legislation "to achieve a balanced budget not later than fiscal year 2002 as estimated by the Congressional Budget Office, and the president and the Congress agree that the balanced budget must protect future generations, insure Medicare solvency, reform welfare, and provide adequate funding for Medicaid, education, agriculture, national defense, veterans and the environment."

The agreement was nonbinding and meant almost nothing. But each side felt it had won the standoff. "The president of the United States has capitulated," declared Robert Livingston. But almost immediately, the Clinton White House started to backpedal.

Republican freshman George Nethercutt was set to be on CNN's "Crossfire" that night with Democratic freshman Sheila Jackson Lee. But the show was delayed because Clinton made a brief address to the nation at 7:30 about the agreement that would reopen the government the next day. Nethercutt sat in the television studio watching the president and holding a piece of paper on which the agreement language was written.

"I have expressed strong doubts that the budget can be balanced in seven years if we use the current Republican congressional budget assumptions. But I am nevertheless committed to working in the coming weeks to see if we can reach common ground on balancing the budget. The key is that nothing will be agreed to unless all elements are agreed to," said Clinton.

Nethercutt couldn't believe what he was hearing. The deal hadn't even been signed yet, and already Clinton was trying to waffle on the details. The agreement clearly stated that any deal must balance the budget in seven years. "I looked at everybody, and I said, 'Here's the language; it says seven years.' I was just shocked at the willingness of the president to essentially falsify what the agreement was."

Then Leon Panetta appeared on NBC's "Today" show and made it sound like balancing the budget in seven years was just a target rather than a requirement, as the Republicans believed. "We can do it in seven years or eight years. . . . I don't think the American people ought to read a lot into what was agreed to last night," he said.

The Republicans were livid over the administration's cavalier attitude. "This is not a goal, this is not an objective. This is a solid contract between the House, the Senate and the president. . . . It's a sacred agreement," freshman David McIntosh told the *Washington Post*. The Republicans obviously believed the agreement meant exactly what it said. But the White House saw it as just a way to get the Republicans to agree to reopen the government. Many of the freshmen had the sinking feeling that their leaders had been had. Clinton could not be trusted. They had given up the one bit of leverage they had over the Democrats—a government shutdown—and had essentially gotten nothing in return. "From then on we realized we couldn't trust the

White House because their word was not good. That led to the era of bad feelings and mistrust in the negotiations," said Nethercutt.

The agreement was, as Democratic congressman Bill Richardson of New Mexico told the *New York Times,* "a temporary cease-fire, not a permanent truce."

* * *

The government reopened Monday, November 20, after a six-day shutdown, the longest in the history of the United States. It had cost the government $700–800 million in uncollected taxes and fees and in back salary for the federal workers who would be paid for the hours they had not been working. At a time when the Republicans were fighting to cut everything they could, the financial waste of the shutdown seemed to mock their efforts.

Mark Neumann had not been present for the budget vote. That's because he was deer hunting with his son in northern Wisconsin. The House had not originally been scheduled to be in session on November 17, and Neumann had promised his son they would make their annual deer-hunting trip same as always. Just because the president was being uncooperative and the government was shut down, Neumann saw no reason to change his plans and break his promise to his son. So deer hunting it would be. "Frankly, I've earned my paycheck and I'm not afraid to say it," Neumann told the *Milwaukee Journal-Sentinel.* "My family is more important than those silly school yard games in Washington, D.C. If the people of the state of Wisconsin decide not to re-elect me because I kept a commitment to my son, then I have to say it is OK."

Neumann talked frequently that fall about the pressures he and the other freshmen were under and how the time they were forced to spend away from home was threatening their families. In a statement issued to explain why he decided to miss votes and head back to Wisconsin, Neumann said, "With six members of my class either filing or about to file for divorce, I decided that practicing family values is more important than preaching it in Washington, D.C. So when the Speaker asked me again to break a commitment to my family, I decided to say no."

One of those who had just filed for divorce, and whose filing produced more than the usual amount of interest among his freshman classmates, was Jon Christensen of Nebraska. "I regret the fact that during our marriage I have engaged in marital infidelity" and "I was unable to remain faithful," said Meredith Christensen in a signed affidavit filed with her husband's divorce petition in Omaha. Rumors flew among freshman members and their staffs about what event or events had led to such an admission.

The couple, who met when they were both law students at the South Texas College of Law, had been married for eight years and had separated twice before Christensen ran for Congress. Christensen had rarely voted before announcing his candidacy and had not been involved in civic affairs. Many of those who knew the couple suggested that the person who was most interested in getting Jon Christensen elected to Congress was really his wife.

Meredith Stewart Maxfield Christensen came from a wealthy Texas family that owned a large title insurance company and were business associates of the billionaire Hunt family. She was a Republican fund-raiser and helped her husband raise money for his campaign through her contacts in affluent Republican circles. After the election, she even spoofed her image as the rich wife who helped buy her husband a congressional seat in a song she performed at an Omaha Press Club dinner. To the tune of "I Will Follow Him," Meredith Christensen sang, "I will follow him, follow him right on to Washington. . . . His right hand I will always be. . . . Jon will make everyone see it is his destiny. . . . He'll always have my money, my money, my money . . . as long as I'm his honey, his honey, his honey."

The 32-year-old Christensen had run as a fundamentalist Christian candidate supporting school prayer, the teaching of creationism in public schools, a ban on abortion, and "traditional family values." He even used a shot of the church he attended in one of his television ads, and he received strong support from the religious right.

His campaign against incumbent Democrat Peter Hoagland was extremely negative, with charges and countercharges flying between the two candidates, who both took the extraordinary step of submitting to lie detector tests over what they had said and done during the campaign and hiring private investigators to look into the other candidate's campaign practices.

Christensen had flunked the Nebraska bar exam twice before finally passing it. He did not work as a lawyer but rather sold insurance and fertilizer through an 800 number that spelled out EE-I-EE-I-O. His intelligence or purported lack thereof came in for a great deal of comment during the campaign. One of Hoagland's campaign consultants referred to Christensen as a "lobotomy victim." The Hoagland campaign ran ads that dealt with Christensen's failing to vote before he decided to run for Congress, and it used actual news tape of Christensen trying to explain why he had not voted: "My life is scheduled from six in the morning till midnight, and I run off a piece of paper every moment, and I'm not, uh, not laying blame anywhere, but unfortunately I didn't have, uh, anything on that piece of paper that said, 'Vote today.'" A voice-over then said, "Jon Christensen didn't vote because nobody wrote it on a piece of paper for him? . . . C'mon!"

Christensen's staff was reportedly so worried about his answering questions that he had not rehearsed that when he appeared at an Omaha High School, students who were volunteers for the campaign were given questions and told to hold pens in their raised hands so Christensen would know who they were. But somehow the rest of the students found out about the plan and the whole class held pens in their raised hands.

Despite all that, Christensen was able to ride the anti-Democratic, anti-incumbent tide to victory and narrowly defeat Hoagland by one percentage point—fewer than 2,000 votes. After the election Christensen immediately started raising money for the National Republican Congressional Committee, an effort that no doubt helped him win a seat on the Ways and Means Committee. He then wasted no time using his committee assignment to leverage major campaign dollars for himself.

By the end of his first year in Congress, Christensen had distinguished himself only for his far from discreet divorce and his prodigious fund-raising. His freshman colleagues even commented privately on his seeming inability to figure out how things worked in Congress. But Christensen had no trouble understanding how to raise money. He did it one phone call and one cocktail party at a time. He even asked a freshman classmate who represented an extremely wealthy area for the names of some potential donors he could contact because he wanted to go on a little combination golfing–fund-raising trip in that freshman's district. By the end of his first year in Congress, Christensen had raised $686,181, more than any other member of the freshman class, with $265,974 of it coming from PACs.

Although he wasn't going to need Meredith's money, money, money to run for re-election, his divorce was, for obvious reasons, getting a lot of attention from reporters in Washington and Omaha. In December the *Washington Post* reported that "someone claiming to be the freshman Republican from Nebraska called the White House" to ask that Meredith Christensen not be admitted to the president's annual congressional Christmas party to which members of Congress usually brought their spouses.

But as unseemly as Christensen's divorce was, the freshman class had an even more public and spectacular divorce that fall involving rising GOP star Enid Greene Waldholtz and her husband, Joe.

14

ENID AND JOE

AT THE SAME TIME THAT THE BUDGET NEGOTIATIONS WERE GRINDING TO A
HALT, the government was shutting down, and the Republicans wrestled with the
most important issues of the 104th Congress, the short marriage of Enid Greene and
Joe Waldholtz was coming apart in a very public, very messy way.

They had been the poster couple of the Republican revolution—meeting as members of the Young Republican National Federation, courting while working on her
first campaign together, and plotting Enid's second, successful run for Congress
shortly after their wedding. She was a lawyer, a prim, smart, serious Mormon from
Salt Lake City. He was a crude, show-offy, political operative from Pittsburgh, and a
rather large man at 300 pounds plus. Actually, he was huge—Rush Limbaugh huge,
even bigger than Rush Limbaugh. On the surface they seemed to have almost nothing in common except for Republican politics. To outsiders they appeared an odd,
hard-to-figure match. But politics and ambition were the glue that held their relationship together. What didn't become clear until that fall was that greed and deceit
were pretty big factors, too.

*   *   *

Enid was the adopted daughter of a devout Mormon couple. Enid's mother,
Gerda, was a Danish immigrant who had fled to the United States during World
War II when she was 20 years old. Her father, D. Forrest Greene, was descended
from Mormon pioneers who had helped settle Utah. He was a successful stockbroker
and investor based in San Francisco, where he and Gerda met. Greene moved his
family to Salt Lake City when Enid was in junior high school, but he continued to
maintain his business in San Francisco and to commute between the two cities.
Enid, who had older twin sisters and a younger brother and sister, was the apple of
her father's eye, a perfect child who always tried to do the right thing, to be the best.

In high school she was in the pep club, choir, and on the yearbook staff, but her number one love was politics. When she was just 18 she was elected the head of the Utah chapter of the Young Republicans. She was a political science major at the University of Utah and worked part time in a Utah congressman's district office. At 22 she was a delegate to the Republican National Convention. She insists that as a child she was shy, something she had to learn to overcome, and recalls that as a 25-year-old trial lawyer fresh out of Brigham Young University Law School, she was so nervous the first time she had to appear in court that her tongue stuck to the roof of her dry mouth and she couldn't speak. "I learned if I didn't conquer it [the shyness], I wouldn't be able to do the things I wanted to do," she would tell me later. Certainly by the time she made her coming out in national Republican circles in her early 30s she had mastered her shyness in a big way. Capable, direct, tough, smart, articulate, ambitious: These are the adjectives people who knew Enid used to describe her.

Joe was another matter. He had always been heavy and hid his insecurity about it underneath his bravado and acerbic tongue. His parents, Harvey and Barbara Waldholtz, divorced when he was five. His father, who remarried, was a dentist. The Waldholtzes lived in Squirrel Hill, an affluent Pittsburgh neighborhood, and were by all accounts comfortable but not fabulously wealthy (as Joe always described them). Like Enid, Joe was already interested in politics in high school and was elected president of his high school senior class.

He was Jewish, but by the time Enid met him in the spring of 1991 he had created an elaborate lie about being the "highborn Episcopalian" son of a rich family. He even told people his ancestors arrived on the *Mayflower*. He became the extravagant Richie Rich, always picking up the check, always throwing money around for the enjoyment and amusement of his friends. But as it would become clear later, it wasn't his money he was throwing around.

By the fall of 1990, Waldholtz had dropped out of the University of Pittsburgh without finishing a degree and become actively involved in Pennsylvania Republican politics. He was an aide to Elsie Hillman, Pennsylvania's representative to the Republican National Committee, cousin of President George Bush and the wife of Pittsburgh industrialist Henry Hillman. He had also just worked on the successful campaign to get Rick Santorum elected to the House. Enid was working as the deputy chief of staff to former Utah governor Norman Bangerter. The two met at a board meeting for the Young Republicans held in southern California. She was an officer of the group and had decided to run for national chair the following year. To do that it was important to win support from the Pennsylvania delegation, although she was at first cool to Joe, describing him to a friend as "the fat guy from Pittsburgh."

What she knew about Waldholtz was that he was independently wealthy and "something of a jokester." In typical fashion he had rented a suite of rooms with its own swimming pool for the Pennsylvania delegation and held court there during the Young Republican enclave. Perhaps with 20/20 hindsight, Enid would tell me years later that on first meeting Joe, "I wasn't overly impressed by him. We got along. But Joe subsequently told people he decided that weekend he intended to marry me."

A connection had been made, and it wasn't too much later that the long-distance telephone calls started between them. They saw each other at Young Republican meetings, and the next Memorial Day weekend Joe rented a beach house in Ocean City, New Jersey, and invited a bunch of friends, including Enid. In early June 1991 they attended a big Republican gathering held in Washington on George Bush's birthday. They went to the vice president's mansion and the White House for receptions before the dinner. Joe introduced Enid to Marilyn Quayle. Enid was impressed. Suddenly they were a couple. Enid was 32, Joe five years younger.

"He was absolutely charming. He really, truly made me feel like I was the most wonderful woman in the world. He was proud, supportive." Enid, who was sensitive about her appearance and described herself as "a little pudgy," was suddenly Cinderella instead of an ugly stepsister. Joe showered her with flowers and gifts—expensive jewelry, even a mink coat.

"I had gone through all of my life really struggling with my relationship with men. The things I was interested in and good at were not only not appreciated but were negatives. . . . I was not prepared to compromise myself away."

There had been some difficult times even before she met Joe. Hometown friends say she had bouts with depression and had taken medication to deal with it. In an interview with me, she acknowledged having seen a therapist but would not comment on whether she took any medication or antidepressants.

She dated before meeting Joe but had never been close to marriage. A smart, aggressive woman with ambition and the ability to take care of herself isn't much of a turn-on for most men but even less so in the patriarchal Mormon culture that prizes traditional family values, stay-at-home moms, and conventional female beauty. She had never really fit in. Just like Joe.

Joe was someone whose eyes did not glaze over when Enid started talking politics. "Joe understood. He was not repelled by my ambitions but was proud of me. I thought, 'Boy, he loves me and thinks I'm beautiful without my having to lose another 40 pounds.' I was overwhelmed by this feeling of acceptance and relief," Enid would explain to me. Enid says understanding what she saw in Joe is not nearly so hard "if you understand my Achilles heel. I wanted to be loved and appreciated as I was and had basically decided that wasn't going to happen." Until she met Joe, Enid wasn't sure she was ever going to have the chance to get married and have a family.

So the match was made. And in the pattern that would unite them for the rest of their time together, their first act as a couple was getting Enid elected head of the Young Republicans that summer. And Joe became treasurer of the group.

He was completely "willing to play second fiddle," and Enid considered herself "one of the luckiest women in the world." Those who knew the couple used to say that Joe "worshiped the ground she walked on and would do anything for her." Anything. Furthering Enid's political career became the driving mission of the Waldholtz marriage. But in a twist of fate of epic proportions, her ambition and the man who helped her achieve it would also become the instrument of her downfall.

*   *   *

Enid was ambitious, but she was also pragmatic. In 1992, when Wayne Owens, the Democratic congressman who represented Salt Lake City, announced he was going to make a bid for the Senate seat being vacated by the retiring Jake Garn, Enid thought about running. But there were other, better-known Republicans planning to make a run at it, and she didn't think she could win the nomination. So a group of young Republican activists including Peter Valcarce went to her and convinced her to try. Eventually, they persuaded her, and Valcarce wound up becoming her campaign manager.

After wowing the state GOP convention with her speech and winning the nomination in the crowded field, Enid had to run against Karen Shepherd, a Democratic state senator. Although he had become the executive director of the Bush-Quayle campaign effort in Pennsylvania, Joe left that job to move out to Utah to help Enid with her campaign and handle its finances. Only years later would it become clear that his parting from the Pennsylvania Republicans had not been completely amicable and that he had spent some of Hillman's money on lavish travel and meals.

As a candidate for Congress and head of the Young Republicans, Enid was chosen to address the 1992 Republican National Convention—quite a coup for a first-time congressional candidate. It proved to be the high point of her candidacy.

Enid had a bit of an image problem. A former high school debater, she was extremely articulate, but the older Shepherd had more poise and came off as more mature, less abrasive. Being a single career woman in her 30s hurt Enid in family-conscious Utah. And Shepherd, although a liberal and a feminist who 14 years earlier had started a magazine "for Utah women who were moving toward living and working in a more equal society," made a point of beginning her sentences on the campaign trail with the phrase "my experience as a wife and mother is that. . . ."

Greene ran an aggressive, nasty campaign against Shepherd and as a result acquired the nickname "Meanid." One of her most negative ads against Shepherd featured a Pinocchio doll whose nose kept growing as an announcer accused Shepherd of lying about Enid's proposals for balancing the budget. Similar ads were being used in many other races around the country, but in Utah such tactics did not go over well. Enid would later acknowledge that she was perceived by many voters as too hard-edged.

One Salt Lake City TV reporter said Enid "was seen as negative and bitchy." She obviously touched a raw nerve, crossed some sort of a cultural line for women in Utah. She was regarded as just too pushy, too driven. "Enid reminds guys of their first wife and why they got divorced. She came across as this holier-than-thou, smarty-pants lawyer . . . as defensive, sarcastic, and unlikable in every way," said David Harmer, who would become her 1994 campaign manager and the first administrative assistant of her congressional office. And it wasn't just her personality that came in for criticism. Enid's appearance—her glasses, her hair, her clothes—also drew comments from the press. One local radio station even ran a contest to solicit suggestions for how she should change her short, curly hairdo.

Enid and Joe were running the campaign together, and there was a certain adolescent quality to their relationship that spilled over into it. He was living in the basement of her parents' house with several other campaign volunteers. Although Joe and Enid had separate bedrooms, they were constantly under the watchful eye of her mother, who intensely disliked Joe. Gerda slept in Enid's bedroom with her to protect her daughter from any inappropriate advances. But during the day, at least, Enid and Joe never seemed to be apart. They became each other's confidants and best friends.

They spent hours and hours talking about Karen Shepherd and the Democrats, about their enemies in the press. It was Enid and Joe against everybody else. "The paranoia was always really high. They were two paranoid people who saw Karen Shepherd as a devil with horns," said one campaign aide. "They saw the world as a hostile place, and they were standing back to back against it and fighting it off," said Rod Decker, the host of a political show on a Salt Lake City TV station. They always seemed to be up to something: plotting dirty tricks against Shepherd, calling her names. The Shepherd campaign maintains Enid's camp somehow got the code to their voice mail system so they could listen to their messages. Joe used to refer to Shepherd, a thin woman, as "Skeletor" and do imitations of her.

Things were not going well for the Greene campaign, and tensions were running high according to campaign manager Valcarce. Once Enid was sent to give a speech to a less than friendly public employees group. When she returned, she was "stomping her feet and hitting her hairbrush against the desk—crying and screaming hysterically" about having been sent there.

In a move that would foreshadow the events of the 1994 campaign, Enid got the money to help finance her 1992 race from her well-to-do father. Her parents had given her their house, and Enid arranged to sell the house back to her parents for $300,000 and put the proceeds into the campaign. But in a questionable arrangement, although the money was used for the campaign in 1992, the transaction was not legally recorded until after the election.

However, Greene was still outspent, something she would not forget. She lost the election to Shepherd by four percentage points. Despite the infusion of cash from the sale of her house, the Greene campaign was left more than $150,000 in debt. An advertising agency and several other vendors who claimed they were never paid for their work threatened to or did institute legal action. Although Joe had been responsible for the money, he blamed the debt on Valcarce's mismanagement. Only after his disappearance in 1995 would Enid claim to have discovered that Joe had embezzled $100,000 from the campaign.

After the election Enid got a job as corporate counsel to Novell, a Utah-based computer company, and Joe became the director of the Utah Republican Party, a job for which he was willing to work for $1 a month. It was a sweet deal for everyone. The party had a director they didn't have to pay, and Joe used the position as a vehicle to attack Karen Shepherd and smooth the way for Enid's 1994 run. But problems involving Joe and money were starting to surface. Bill collectors and creditors were calling the state party office looking for Joe. And the state party would later discover Waldholtz had pocketed several thousand dollars in contributions.

Virtually from the first moment she took office, Shepherd, who was only the second woman ever elected to Congress from Utah, complained to the *Salt Lake Tribune* about a "warlike assault" launched against her by Waldholtz and the state's Republicans, who were acting as if the campaign had never ended. Joe held press conferences criticizing Shepherd's performance. He convinced the national party to pay for radio ads against her and bombarded reporters with press releases about Shepherd's voting record. Even some local Republicans expressed uneasiness over Joe's dual role as head of the party and booster of Enid. To his critics, Joe responded, "It's OK for Bill and Hillary, but it's not OK for Enid and Joe?"

What came next, the announcement of their marriage, did not come as much of a surprise, but some friends still wondered what was going through Enid's mind. She had always tried to be the good girl, the perfect girl. She strictly followed Mormon doctrine and forswore alcohol, coffee, even Coca-Cola. Yet she wound up marrying outside the faith to a man largely unacceptable to her family.

Joe knew Enid's mother didn't like him and would sometimes refer to Gerda as the "Reich chancellor." He could be extremely charming according to those who knew him well, but he could also be crude and unpleasant. It clearly depended on whether he wanted something from whomever he was talking to. He played the spoiled rich boy to the hilt, saying over and over that he had "more money than God." He was always calling Salt Lake City a hick town and a backwater. Nothing was ever right about Utah. And he also had plenty of negative things to say about the sacrosanct and all-powerful Mormon Church.

According to several campaign workers, he was known for making odd and off-color remarks, for example, "Abortion should be illegal except for rich people and Negroes." And he was far from discreet about their relationship, boasting to friends that Enid was a virgin when they married. After their marriage, he would make frequent cracks to the campaign staff about their sex life—things like "Oh, she's such an animal" or "It was a busy night last night." Enid would give him a dirty look or a small scolding when he would say something inappropriate, but there was always the air of "Oh, isn't that cute," according to campaign workers who witnessed such exchanges. Enid thought she knew the real Joe. She thought, "I can put up with some of these external idiosyncrasies because who's perfect? I'm not," she would explain to me later.

They took a trip to Pittsburgh before the wedding, and Enid stayed at a hotel. Joe, who lived with his parents until he was 29 and had moved out to Utah, told her tales of their mansion with servants. He said he was embarrassed to take her to his parents' house. When she asked to see the house, he drove her to one of the city's nicest neighborhoods and pointed out a mansion but said he didn't want to go in. That was it. She asked no questions. She accepted his explanation of being distant from his

parents, of feeling they favored his older brother, and of "hating" his father for aban-
doning Joe's emotionally fragile mother when Joe was a child. The couple had dinner
with Joe's father and stepmother at a restaurant, but Joe told her not to mention a
number of taboo subjects, such as money and religion. He told her his parents were
afraid he was going to convert to Mormonism. Enid would tell me later she did not
learn Joe was Jewish until she read it in the *Salt Lake Tribune*.

* * *

Joe and Enid were married in August 1993. Since Joe was not a Mormon, they
couldn't be married in the temple that dominates both the cityscape and the social
fabric of Salt Lake City. Instead, the ceremony and reception were held at the old
Hotel Utah, which was owned by the Mormon Church. The list of 800-plus guests
included most of the state's Republican political elite and the state legislature. Utah's
governor, Mike Leavitt, performed the ceremony. Of course, in keeping with Mormon rules, there was no alcohol. But there was lots of fancy food.

Having the wedding just so was extremely important to Joe, so important that he
helped pay for it. He wanted to make a big splash. He even picked the music, the
same used by Princess Diana and Prince Charles when they were married. This was
more than just a wedding; this was the unofficial kickoff of the second campaign.
"Clearly in Joe's mind the wedding was to be the event that launched the political
season," said Valcarce.

Enid said Joe came to her on their wedding day and told her he was making her a
wedding gift of $5 million, part of his family trust. Enid said she told Joe she would
rather talk about it later. This nonexistent trust became known as TWC Ready Assets, which is how it would be reported on her financial disclosure forms. Joe told
her they could use it to finance her second run for Congress.

The couple honeymooned in Hawaii at a posh hotel. Joe skipped out without
paying the bill, using complaints about the service and the room as his reason. It was
an early warning signal. Joe never had a job that paid anything but always seemed to
have plenty of money to fuel his extravagant lifestyle. He explained to Enid and others that he was living on family money, trust funds.

In a sense he *was* living on family money, but it wasn't money he had any right to.
His tales of family wealth were not entirely false, just wildly overblown. Joe's elderly
grandmother did in fact have over $1 million in assets that had been left to her by
her husband and increased through savings and investments. Joe, who had been
given the responsibility of managing her money and paying her living expenses, had
been embezzling from his grandmother for years. And that was not the only money
Joe was stealing. He also got money out of his father, mother, and stepmother.

It seems hard to believe the couple blew through so much money, but Joe and
Enid carried on an extravagant lifestyle. Everything always had to be the best—land-
scaping, refurbishments to their home, art, furniture, flowers, clothing, jewelry,
travel, catered and expensive take-out food (especially from one of Salt Lake City's
poshest French restaurants). Joe spent money where people could see it. And in one

of their strangest affectations, their boxer dog, Winston, whom they had received as a wedding present, drank Perrier water. Joe had frequent facials, manicures, and massages. He used Rogaine to try to halt a receding hairline. He wore Armani suits, Hermes ties, gold cufflinks, and a Rolex watch. For someone who looked like he did, or maybe because of it, he was surprisingly vain. Despite Enid's family's wealth, this was all new to her. The Greenes had always lived modestly. Her father, who had grown up during the Depression, was described by those who knew him as a shrewd businessman who was extremely "frugal" and "parsimonious" in his personal life. He was a man who rode the bus rather than taking a cab and who drove a 20-year-old car. Enid was obviously intrigued by the hedonistic lifestyle Joe, who was so dramatically different from her father, thrust upon her.

As she would protest repeatedly, Joe handled all the money. In a classic case of the fox being put in charge of the henhouse, Joe had the responsibility not only for their personal finances but also her campaign finances. After so many years of being in charge, of being in control, Enid said she was happy to turn her financial concerns over to Joe. That left her free to focus all her attention on her campaign and, later, on being a congresswoman. And Joe was obviously just as happy to be in charge of the money.

After their marriage, she took the name Enid Greene Waldholtz, and in the fall of 1993 Joe announced he was leaving his position with the state Republican Party because he wanted to avoid any conflict of interest. He told local reporters Enid planned to run against Karen Shepherd, and "I don't want there to be the appearance of any impropriety. Enid and I don't believe there should be the appearance of any deck clearing." At the end of 1993 Enid started assembling a campaign staff. Of course Joe would serve as treasurer and de facto campaign manager.

KayLin Loveland had worked on Utah governor Michael Leavitt's 1992 campaign when Enid made her first run for Congress. "I was very impressed with her. I thought she was incredibly articulate," said Loveland. Also a single, young professional woman, Loveland found Enid's success refreshing since Utah Republican politics was "dominated by your white, Mormon male in his 50s." Enid had not had anything handed to her politically. "She had to fight for everything she had," recalled Loveland, who said it was not easy for a single woman to raise money to finance a campaign in Utah. When Loveland heard that Enid was thinking of running again, she called her and told her she was available. Loveland joined Team Enid as campaign manager.

The financial problems of the 1994 campaign surfaced right from the beginning. Checks were bouncing, campaign vendors were calling demanding payment, and banks and collection agencies were calling the campaign office looking for Joe, who would always shrug it off. "It was horrible; I don't know how we functioned," remembered Loveland, who didn't receive her first paycheck until the end of January, two months after she had started work. She didn't receive another until late March.

Whenever Loveland tried to ask Enid and Joe about campaign finances, "In no uncertain terms I was told it wasn't any of my concern. They would deal with the finances." But they weren't dealing. Steve Taggart, who came onboard a few months after Loveland, was suspicious of Joe: "You knew he was a flake, you just didn't know how big a flake he was."

In January 1994 Joe approached Enid's father for money for the first time. He blamed the lack of money on his mother. She was unstable; she had been taken by a con man; she had gone on a spending spree buying from the home shopping network; she had used Joe's credit card; she had gotten into his bank accounts. And he was forbidden from using his family trust to deal with it. On January 21 Forrest Greene advanced Joe $60,000, and less than two weeks later sent along another $24,000. Throughout the following spring and summer, he loaned Joe more than half a million dollars.

But Joe also borrowed much smaller amounts from Loveland and Taggart, and they had to badger him to pay it back. "His story was he was a great, wealthy trust fund baby with millions and millions"; but if that was true, why did he have so many creditors after him? Taggart wondered. Taggart had three paychecks bounce. Joe insisted that he had transferred the money directly to Taggart's account but it had wound up in Idaho. Joe always had an excuse. He would blame it on cash flow problems. He would say that he was paying his mother's bills. He would say the banks had not made the transfers or had wired the money to the wrong account. The campaign was raising money, but there never seemed to be any available.

Then David Harmer came onboard. Harmer had impeccable Republican credentials. His father, John, was a former lieutenant governor of California who had run unsuccessfully for Congress. Like Enid, David was a graduate of BYU Law School. He had worked for Senator Orrin Hatch's Judiciary Committee and at Warren Christopher's California law firm. Harmer's first three paychecks bounced. Although he was supposed to be the finance director, Harmer was given no access to any of the campaign's financial information, such as the amount of money the campaign had raised or the amount of cash on hand.

Joe seemed to spend all his time banking. He had accounts in Pittsburgh, Salt Lake City, and Washington. "That was all he did, but he couldn't produce cash," said Taggart. Taggart's father was a banker in Idaho, and after looking at the code the banks had printed on Joe's returned checks, he told his son the banks had identified Joe as someone who might be kiting checks. Finally, suspecting what was going on (and having had six checks from Waldholtz bounce), "I walked out and said, 'I'll come back when you pay me,'" said Taggart.

To put it mildly, the "Enid '94" campaign was not a happy place. Joe kept playing the staff off of one another. Joe would tell Taggart that Loveland was incompetent and vice versa. Enid was remote. Then in late April, shortly before the state GOP convention, Joe paid all the staffers what they were owed. At the convention in early May, Enid scored a big win over three minor opponents, capturing 87 percent of the vote and thus avoiding a runoff primary.

Her convention performance buoyed the mood a bit, and the campaign staff was feeling pretty good. And then it started all over again. The bill collectors were coming out of the woodwork. Taggart and Loveland couldn't figure out why—if the Federal Election Commission (FEC) reports were correct and they had money in the bank—the printers, sign people, phone company, landlord, and campaign staff couldn't be paid.

When Harmer joined the campaign, he asked for weekly finance reports and an account statement but was always stonewalled: "The finances were a black hole," he remembered. In late May Harmer wrote a three-page memo to Enid telling her why it was extremely difficult for him to do his job. There was no campaign budget, and no one had told him how much money he needed to raise or by what deadline. Harmer proposed writing a long-range fund-raising plan. "Proceeding without a plan is like being in such a hurry to get somewhere that you race out of the house without directions," wrote Harmer. "Once written, I need one to two uninterrupted hours with you and Joe to review it. I want to make sure that I understand what you expect of me and that you understand what I plan to do." After scheduling and canceling two appointments to talk with Harmer about his concerns, Enid told him a budget for the campaign would be drafted. But three weeks later nothing had changed.

Sometimes Joe would write personal checks to cover campaign expenses; sometimes expenses would be paid out of the campaign account. Loveland and Taggart were starting to suspect that Joe was stealing money from the campaign. A year later it would be discovered that Joe had siphoned money out of the campaign funds not only for his personal use but to make payments to his father, mother, and grandmother to return some of the money he had already bilked them out of.

Loveland started looking at the FEC reports and discovered lots of problems. Money that had been paid out to ad firms and vendors was not listed under disbursements. And bills that were mounting up from the same businesses were not listed as obligations. Campaign staff salaries were also missing as disbursements in the reports. Joe told Loveland he had filed amendments to correct the discrepancies, but Loveland found that the FEC had no record of such amendments. Loveland tried to talk to Enid several times about the FEC reports and problems with the campaign. But Enid always seemed to avoid her. Whenever the campaign staff tried to talk to Enid about the problems, "her response was always hostile, blaming the messenger instead of the message," said Harmer.

In April Joe was named in a civil suit filed by American Express that claimed he owed the company almost $50,000. Waldholtz said the charges were due to the fraudulent use of his credit card over a two-and-a-half-year period by an unknown person. Although Enid and Joe both told their campaign staff it was all just a mistake on the part of American Express, court documents showed they had hired an attorney to deal with the claim. "They were both at that point lying to the staff about it; it was not just Joe," insisted Taggart.

Then in June the *Salt Lake Tribune* reported that $60,000 worth of checks Joe wrote to a Salt Lake City jewelry store for jewelry and gifts for Enid had bounced. Waldholtz blamed it on a mix-up with a Pennsylvania bank account he had transferred to Utah. He said the checks had been put through after the account was closed. Enid dismissed the newspaper's account of events, calling their stories politically motivated. As she would explain to me later, she had decided the *Tribune* was untrustworthy because of a poll it published during the 1992 campaign that indicated she was further behind in the race than she actually was. After that, she discounted anything the paper wrote.

The campaign was in chaos. "Enid and Joe would go into their office and scream and yell, and you would hear her crying—it was a real roller-coaster relationship," says Valcarce, who had become a consultant to the campaign, handling fund-raising letters and other mailings. Valcarce said he wanted to speak with Joe and Enid together about the problems. He told Joe the financial shenanigans could sink Enid's candidacy. "Joe was ranting and raving. He said she would quit the race. And then he started crying. . . . He begged me not to tell her. I said, 'I think you've learned your lesson. If anything like this happens again I will talk to her.'" Joe kept telling everybody he would take care of things and tried to keep them away from Enid.

Enid always seemed to be unavailable. For three weeks, she dropped out of sight. The campaign staff was told "she was sick; she was tired; she was taking a break." Anytime they tried to reach her, Joe would answer the phone. He kept saying she would get too upset if they told her of the campaign's financial problems. They couldn't disturb her. "He played a serious H. R. Haldeman role," says Valcarce. Campaign workers would later speculate that what happened during that period when Enid vanished was that it had finally hit her that Joe's story wasn't adding up and she was trying to sort out what to do.

Enid would tell me that she was having trouble breathing and suffering from terrible fatigue during that time. She didn't know what was wrong. Did she have chronic fatigue syndrome, Epstein-Barr? Finally the trouble was diagnosed as asthma complicated by allergies. For three to four weeks, she "felt dreadful." But she chose not to tell her campaign staff in detail what was wrong because she "didn't have confidence" that they would keep quiet about it, she would say later.

In mid-June Joe called the campaign office and said Enid had laryngitis and could not make a scheduled speech that evening in Provo to a law enforcement group. He wanted Harmer to go in her place. But Harmer declined because of a family commitment. Then Enid, who was supposed to have laryngitis, called up and started screaming and yelling and threatening to fire Harmer. She said she would hold a staff meeting the following Monday to discuss the incident and other problems with the staff. But as Harmer detailed in a memo to Enid a week later, "Characteristically, that staff meeting never materialized. All of us would have welcomed the opportunity to clear the air. Since I heard nothing further from you I assumed I still had a job, but my enthusiasm for it, already in decrescendo for some time, had diminished to the point that I felt it necessary to share my concerns with your campaign manager. KayLin seems to have the responsibility of a campaign manager without corresponding authority or access. By the time she was finally able to obtain an audience with you several days had passed and other problems loomed larger."

By now the communications problems and mistrust among the campaign staff had grown so serious they felt the only way they could communicate with Enid was in writing. Loveland decided to write Enid a memo outlining problems with the FEC filings. The memo, dated June 14, 1994, concluded with the warning, "I am concerned about these discrepancies because they are easily traceable. For example, the amount of payroll taxes we paid does not match the amount of salary disbursement listed. There are checks paid from a campaign account but not listed as disbursements." Valcarce said the first FEC filing showed they had $100,000 on hand for the same period that checks were bouncing all over the place. And the contribution list included page after page of people whose surname was Waldholtz, leading him to believe Joe was falsifying the FEC reports. Loveland recommended they have the campaign records audited and then file an amended FEC report. She thought if she could convince Enid the financial problems were serious enough, Enid would agree to an audit and would find out what Joe was doing. "We couldn't go to Enid and say, 'Your husband has no money; he's kiting checks.' It would never have flown."

When Loveland gave Enid the memo, Enid exploded. She told Loveland, "If there are problems, Joe will take care of them." But it was clear nothing was going to be taken care of. Three days later Loveland wrote a longer memo detailing all of the financial problems and bounced paychecks the campaign had been experiencing. "I was trying to build a case that he was lying constantly and I couldn't trust him." Loveland took the memo to Enid's house and handed it to her in person.

Enid then told Loveland "an incredible story—a whopper": that Joe's mother was seriously depressed and was running through money. In addition, someone was embezzling money from the family. Joe was having to put money into his mother's accounts. "She said she and Joe had been working with federal investigators trying to catch the embezzler so they had to be secretive." Enid claimed that the person who was stealing money from Joe's mother also had access to his accounts and was stealing from him as well. She even said that Joe's mother was in personal danger. "She looked me in the eye and lied to me," said Loveland. "I didn't believe her. Not for a second. But I didn't ask a lot of questions. I was disgusted. I wish now I had blurted out, 'That's not true.' But I had no proof," Loveland would tell me in an interview two years after the encounter. Instead, she told Enid that was not an acceptable explanation "and I handed her my letter of resignation."

The resignation letter, dated June 17, 1994, was clearly written as much in sorrow as in anger. Loveland promised not to speak with the press "or any other members of the public regarding confidential campaign matters." She ended the letter of resignation by saying, "I truly believe that you are the best candidate for Congress in this district and wish you the best of luck."

Loveland also delivered a letter from Harmer. He, too, had had enough. "For three months I have been asking for a cash flow report, a balance sheet and a budget, to no avail. Many campaigns find these items useful. I have no year-to-date figures for either contributions or expenditures. My only knowledge of campaign finances come from FEC reports—and, by the way, it doesn't take a rocket scientist to note that the reports look a little skimpy. I have no clue where we stand on fundraising. I have no clue where the money is going," wrote Harmer. He continued, "Even more disturbing, I have been promised some of that information several times—but the deadlines come and go, and nothing changes. Our treatment of finances is disorganized, unprofessional, and possibly irresponsible. I cannot in good conscience keep asking people for money if I don't know where it goes."

Harmer would say later he was ready to resign at that point along with Loveland, but when the Waldholtzes asked him to take her place as campaign manager, he decided to stay. Enid assured Harmer that his concerns would be addressed and that an outside treasurer would be hired for the campaign. But that never happened.

After Loveland left her house, Enid called Taggart at the campaign office as he was packing up his things. "She said she wanted to talk about a problem with KayLin. She was afraid of what had been found out," said Taggart. But Taggart told Enid he was leaving the campaign as well. "By that time it was evident they were lying to everyone. They had used me for two years and I had had enough."

Enid would tell me later she had told Loveland the story about Joe's mother because that's what Joe had told her. Enid said she did question Joe at this point about what was going on, "but he had reasons, he had excuses" for everything. "I didn't think I had problems with fraud; I thought I had family problems and problems that were out of Joe's control."

Word of the bouncing checks, the resignations, the turmoil, and financial problems with the campaign was widespread within GOP circles in Utah. Senator Hatch and Governor Leavitt talked about what to do. The last thing the Republican elders wanted was a major public embarrassment or meltdown of one of their congressional candidacies. Taggart and Loveland had asked David Jordan, the former U.S. attorney for Utah, to talk with Enid and Joe to see if they couldn't get the campaign's financial situation cleaned up. Jordan reported back to Leavitt about the meetings. It was agreed the campaign would hire Huckaby and Associates, a Virginia accounting firm that specializes in election finances. And that was pretty much the end of it. The accounting firm did try to get the campaign back on track but apparently never conducted an audit to discern what had happened up to that point. The only information they had was what Joe was giving them, so they were ineffectual in halting the problems. There was a certain see no evil, hear no evil quality to the approach senior Republicans were taking. "I think they felt, 'We're engaged in a campaign. We don't want to do anything to upset that. If we don't know, we don't have to do anything,'" said Taggart.

Enid had always been something of a micromanager, worrying about every detail of the campaign, including how the office was decorated. Valcarce found that "the inexplicable part of this whole thing" was how she could fail to see what Joe was up to, how she could "worry about the minutiae and miss the big picture." But although she had been repeatedly warned by her campaign staff that there were problems, Enid would claim after Joe disappeared that she had no information about what was happening.

Shortly before the election, in an interview with the *Salt Lake Tribune* in October 1994, Enid talked about Joe: "There are some people who have made rather rude comments about this stranger from Pennsylvania. I've heard everything from, 'He's a con man with no money' to 'He lives beyond his means.' All these ridiculous things are being said."

Throughout the summer the campaign was just scraping by financially. Looking at the FEC report, Harmer thought they had about $40,000, but then there was no money in the campaign account. He didn't know where it went. He tried to talk to Enid about it. "She slammed her hand down on the table and said it was none of my business. If you asked any questions you were crossing a line with her." Harmer recalled Enid's behavior as erratic. Sometimes she would be pleasant; at other times she could have a wicked temper.

Despite the disorder of her campaign, Enid had national momentum on her side. Democrats were not popular in the fall of 1994, especially not first-term House members like Karen Shepherd who supported gun control and had voted for the Clinton budget and tax package after promising in her 1992 campaign she would not vote to increase taxes. "The problem wasn't with Enid's ideas; the problem was people hated her," said David Owen, a political consultant who helped produce Enid's campaign commercials in the last six weeks of the campaign. "Her original TV ads—it was like having 'bitch' written across the screen. She could be really strident and know-it-all," Owen contended.

In addition to Shepherd, there was an independent candidate in the race, Merrill Cook, a slightly eccentric millionaire owner of an explosives company and a former talk radio host. Cook was a perennial candidate who had previously run for mayor, county commissioner, Congress, and governor. But Cook had a following. He was Utah's version of Ross Perot. In his last race for governor in 1992, Cook had come in second, defeating the Democratic candidate by 11 points and receiving 34 percent to the incumbent Leavitt's 42 percent.

In 1993, before he made the decision to run for the congressional seat, Enid came to see Cook. She told him, "'If you run, we both lose. So don't run.' She wasn't subtle in the least," Cook recalled. Of all the candidates he ever ran against, said Cook, "She was the smartest—a great debater. . . . She has a take-no-prisoners mentality."

In 1994 Cook spent $820,000 of his own money on the congressional race, less than half what Enid eventually spent. "Maybe, she just wanted it too much. I understand what it's like to want something very bad politically. . . . Good, honest, decent people can be tempted to cross the line. . . . If rules had to be broken to achieve the political objective, so be it," Cook speculated.

During the campaign Cook joined Shepherd in releasing a joint statement decrying some of the tactics used by the Waldholtz campaign, including hiring a private detective who reviewed their campaign donor lists. "Enid Waldholtz has set a sad and disappointing precedent. This is Utah, not Chicago or Philadelphia. . . . Cloak and dagger techniques have no place in Utah politics," said the statement.

And the Utah Democratic Central Committee filed a formal complaint with the FEC over the matter, claiming fees paid to Malcolm Shannon, the private investigator, were omitted from Waldholtz campaign reports. Legal documents filed by Enid's father two years later would reveal that he had made a $10,000 payment to Shannon in July 1994. Enid and Joe had hired Shannon between February and August 1994, ostensibly to look into alleged harassing phone calls, death threats, and attempted break-ins at their home and office. Most of the campaign staff, however, viewed this as just another of Joe's strange attempts to get attention or create high drama and intrigue. "This was their stupid little game," said Taggart.

Although the burglar alarm had been tripped nearly twenty times at the Waldholtz home and the alarm wires had been cut from the inside, police were never able to discern any sign of actual intruders, and nothing was ever taken. According to Taggart, Joe always seemed to be at the house right after it happened or to be the one discovering problems. "Everyone thought Joe was doing it—it was a running joke" with the campaign staff. Shannon had also checked the campaign office for any sign of tapped telephones or electronic surveillance. But it would never really be clear what Shannon had been hired to look into. And although he would tell me in a telephone conversation in 1997 that Enid was "lying" about her version of events, he refused to be interviewed, only hinting that he knew the truth of what had happened.

*   *   *

At the end of August, polls showed Enid not only trailing Shepherd by 10 points but also behind Cook. "She thought on Labor Day she was going to come in third; I saw it in her eyes," said Cook. Enid and Joe knew something had to be done. They had to pump more money into the campaign. "It became evident that if I was to win the campaign we needed to spend more money," Enid would acknowledge a year later. She remembered only too well what had happened two years earlier when she had let Shepherd outspend her.

Joe told Enid his trust fund account had been frozen because of fighting in his family and a cousin who was suing to get more money. In fact Joe's family had taken legal action against him to find out what had happened to his grandmother's $1 million. "As a lawyer, I know you can freeze assets. I said, 'Oh my gosh, we're sunk,'" she would later recount to me. Enid had been counting on that money to help finance her campaign. When Joe said they needed to borrow money from her father, Enid responded that based on her experience in the 1992 campaign, she knew that they couldn't simply borrow money; there had to be a transfer of an asset in exchange for cash. "What do we have that we can sell?" she asked Joe. First he suggested assigning her father a portion of his family trust, but Enid said that could be challenged since the outcome of the lawsuit was uncertain.

Then Joe, without missing a beat (as Enid would later explain many times), told her he had some Pittsburgh real estate in probate that was outside of the trust and was worth $2.2 million—Enid's half would be $1.1 million. They already had a buyer for the property, Joe said. Enid suggested an assignment of the proceeds of the real estate sale to her father in exchange for cash. That would be "a permissible legal way to give my father an asset and get liquid funds that I could then put into the campaign. . . . It seemed to me in principle it ought to work. . . . I thought it was fine—clear sailing. . . . If the property had existed, this would have been a perfectly acceptable transaction with the FEC. The hitch was there was no property," she would tell me.

That was it. Her father agreed to give them the money. But no paper changed hands, and he never asked to see the property. And although Enid's ownership stake in the fictitious property was purported to be worth only $1.1 million, Enid's father transferred more than $2 million to Enid and Joe between September and November 1994; $1.7 million of that money was put into Enid's campaign.

In late August Joe called Harmer into his office for a talk. Joe had some news. He had talked to his family and money from his trust fund was being made available, Joe told Harmer. They could use it for the campaign—"there was no limit." They went from a staff of five to 12 and started buying TV time.

Enid's campaign decided to embark on a new media strategy overseen by Eddie Mahe, a high-profile Washington campaign consultant. Mahe, a former officer of the Republican National Committee, had worked for Gingrich's GOPAC as well as Utah governor Leavitt and was working on several congressional campaigns in 1994, including that of Sonny Bono. Mahe specialized in no-holds-barred campaigning. "If you're looking to improve your image, call your public relations firm. . . . If you're in a fight and looking to save your butt, call us," Mahe said in a *Roll Call* article. For its work in the last month of the campaign, Mahe's firm was paid $20,000 plus a "win bonus." The checks to Mahe did not bounce, although he told *Roll Call* he had heard about the campaign's financial problems. "I was not out there to worry about bookkeeping. As long as the bills were getting paid, it was just, 'Screw it; let's fix it afterward.'"

Mahe ordered an image makeover for Enid: softer, more attractive clothing, hair, and makeup. She needed to speak more slowly, smile more. When they were shooting one of the commercials and it wasn't going well, David Owen would tell her, "OK, Evil Enid just said that line. Now let's have Nice Enid." The change in her manner was even more pronounced than the change in her appearance. Rod Decker, the local TV host said, "The secret she learned was Christian forbearance. She would not say a mean word about Karen Shepherd." At least not in public. "I wish she had actually grown into the person portrayed in that second campaign," said Harmer.

With the new commercials in hand, the Waldholtz campaign flooded the local airwaves. The final week before the election you couldn't turn on the television in Salt Lake City without seeing a Waldholtz ad. To ensure they wouldn't get bumped by commercial advertisers, they even paid the retail rate for advertising rather than the discount rate available to political candidates. The campaign also set up a paid phone bank and sent out direct mailings to Cook and Shepherd supporters.

The massive expenditures went neither unnoticed nor unquestioned by her opponents and by the local press. In mid-October the *Salt Lake Tribune,* using previous financial disclosure filings, reported that Enid had already put nearly $800,000 of personal money into the campaign. Asked where the money was coming from, her press secretary told the newspaper, "It's family money. It's Joe and Enid's. End of story."

During campaign debates the infusion of cash would always be brought up and the answer would always be the same. At the end of October, two weeks before the election, Dave Jones, the chairman of Utah's Democratic Party, demanded that Enid tell voters where she had gotten the personal money she had poured into the campaign. He knew that she had been working as a corporate attorney for an annual salary of around $50,000. Where had all this money come from? No one could figure it out. "If it's Enid's money, what was the original source? Have they paid taxes on it? Is there some industry or special interest they are trying to hide? And if they have all this money, why are they bouncing checks?" Jones told a *Tribune* reporter. People thought it was fishy, but nobody could prove anything.

Enid's only response was that it was "family money" raised by cashing stocks, bonds, and other assets—true as far as it went. It's just that they were her father's assets. In a famous television appearance in which Decker tried to pin her down about the money, all Enid would say was, "We've worked hard, and we're very blessed. . . . I certainly made some of it, my husband made a lot of it, and we've been very fortunate."

She knew as she said it that was not the whole truth. But after everything had become public, she claimed that she thought the transfer of property to her father in exchange for cash was "too complex a transaction to explain. . . . By that time, people are completely lost and have no idea if the money's really mine, my father's, my husband's. . . . I believed that money was legally mine, and that's what I said during the campaign."

Federal election law permits the use of personal assets jointly owned with a spouse for funding campaigns, but all other family members are limited to the same $2,000 personal limit for both the primary and general election as any other contributor. The *Tribune* concluded an article on the funding of the Waldholtz campaign with the sentence, "Money cannot be considered personal funds if any person—including a relative or friend—gives or loans the candidate money in connection with a campaign."

Just as any mention of her father's loan and the "transfer of assets" had been completely omitted from her campaign spending reports, they also did not appear on her financial disclosure reports either during the campaign or after she took office. If there was nothing wrong with the transaction, why try to hide it? And why make no mention of it during the campaign? Enid would later claim that Joe had told her he would take care of reporting the transaction. "I relied on Joe to figure out how that should be dealt with," she would say of the money that her father gave them.

There's no doubt the money made a huge difference, perhaps *the* difference. Two days before the election Enid had moved into a dead heat with Shepherd. Propelled by the Republican momentum of 1994, Waldholtz won with 46 percent of the vote to Shepherd's 36 percent and Cook's 18 percent. Shepherd contended after the election that Waldholtz had been "willing to spend whatever she had to to win."

The Waldholtz campaign wound up spending around $2 million, with only about $200,000 of it coming from outside donations. Enid spent more than both of the other candidates together. In fact, Waldholtz spent more personal money to get elected than any other successful House candidate in 1994, and hers was one of the most expensive House races in the country.

After Enid's victory, Harmer recalled that "all of a sudden she relaxes; she's sweetness and light. Joe tells me he knows his presence was difficult, he has no intention of being around in the congressional office." They convinced Harmer to come to Washington as Enid's administrative assistant to run her office. It was a "pretty tempting" offer. The Republicans had just taken over Congress. It was going to be an exciting time on the Hill. Harmer accepted.

"I thought maybe things would be normal. But Joe was in the office from day one." Joe became the de facto, albeit unpaid, manager of the office, with a desk right outside the door to Enid's private office. He was a constant presence. "It wasn't long before Joe started to use the staff for personal errands." Later it would also be revealed that he did much worse. Joe had used the office account, which was strictly for congressional business, for several airplane tickets to Utah and for personal Federal Express mailings. He also had been borrowing the credit cards of several of the staff members.

A month into the start of the 104th Congress, Harmer knew he couldn't take it but felt he had to stay at least through the first 100 days. It was the same story as the campaign. Joe was running interference and trying to keep the staff away from Enid. "I found it somewhere between difficult to impossible to communicate with her. You know things are bad when the administrative assistant has to make an appointment to talk to the member." Over the Easter recess Harmer wrote his letter of resignation, effective May 31. He was never really replaced as chief of staff, and Joe's control over the office and access to Enid increased.

The national press was largely unaware of the problems that had plagued Enid Waldholtz's campaign. But they did know she was the woman Gingrich had handpicked for a seat on the Rules Committee and was pegged as a star of the revolution. She was conservative and fiercely partisan, one of the smartest, most articulate, most aggressive members of the class. A reporter from the *Economist* dubbed her "the Mormon Maggie Thatcher."

And Joe, although slightly in the background, was never completely out of view. He was still being quoted in the Utah papers, complaining about the Democrats, who were "not telling the truth to the public" about the Republican budget-balancing efforts. Joe always made for good copy.

From the outside Enid and Joe's life looked glamorous, but in reality it was quickly becoming a nightmare. All of the financial improprieties had started to catch up with them. Both Joe's thirst for the finer things in life and his propensity for banking irregularities had continued unabated after Enid's election. They threw an elaborate party to celebrate Enid's swearing-in as a member of Congress, using one of the most expensive caterers in Washington. They rented an $800,000 Georgetown townhouse where Secretary of State Henry Kissinger once lived for $3,800 a month, but they were constantly behind in their rent. And Enid bought the furniture for the townhouse at one of the most expensive stores in Salt Lake City and had it shipped cross-country.

Enid's father again came to their aid. According to court documents filed by Forrest Greene in a later suit against Waldholtz, between January 9 and October 12, 1995, Greene transferred $1.3 million into Joe and Enid's joint bank accounts in installments ranging from $408,000 in April to $13,000 in July, which was used to pay for rental furniture. On October 12, just a month before Joe's disappearance, Greene gave them another $308,000.

When Enid became pregnant shortly after being elected, Joe and her press secretary, Kate Watson, decided to milk it for all it was worth. They dug up the fact that she was only the second member of Congress in history to be pregnant while serving (the first was Yvonne Brathwaite Burke in the 1970s). "But I will be the first Republican to have a baby in office," Enid proudly declared. After they had first quietly informed Gingrich and Rules Committee chair Gerald Solomon, they released the news of the pregnancy to her hometown paper, the *Deseret News*, which is owned by the Mormon Church. "First the wedding, then the campaign and now the baby. Life has been anything but boring," Waldholtz gushed. Watson called *USA Today* the following day. Articles in the *New York Times* and the *Washington Post* followed.

From then on Waldholtz became known as the pregnant congresswoman, and there was a seemingly endless stream of requests for interviews from newspapers, magazines, and television shows. The first congressional baby of the Republican revolution was a hot story.

Her female colleagues held a shower for her in Gingrich's office. Enid and Joe continued to commute back and forth to Utah every weekend, and Joe would tease her about going into labor on the airplane or on the House floor. "Think of the publicity," he would say. But Joe also used the pregnancy as an excuse to restrict access to Enid and to keep the staff from informing her about the creditors who were calling her office with increasing frequency. He told staff members she was having a difficult pregnancy, she couldn't be upset, and if she lost the baby it would be their fault.

On August 31, at home in Salt Lake City for the summer recess, Enid gave birth a few weeks early to a 7-pound, 7-ounce baby girl by Caesarean section. Joe convinced Enid to name their daughter Elizabeth after the reigning British monarch. Enid conducted interviews from her hospital bed while cradling her baby, her husband Joe at her side holding her hand.

A few weeks later, Elizabeth would accompany her mother to the House floor for a vote. It seemed no opportunity to use the baby for public relations or campaign purposes was wasted. When she was just two months old, Elizabeth was used as bait at a $500-per-person fund-raiser in Washington. "Baby Elizabeth Waldholtz invites you to a fundraising shower to help re-elect her mom," read the invitation.

Their financial problems had begun to surface publicly in news accounts, and Joe was beginning to crack. He was alternately threatening suicide and divorce. And Enid thought he might be having a mental breakdown. "He was falling apart. He hinted that he might disappear. He threatened not to go to the fund-raiser. I don't remember if that was a suicide night or a divorce night." Both of them went to the party. Enid shook every hand; "I plastered a smile on my face, and we got through it." Enid didn't know what to expect next.

*   *   *

In her 1992 campaign Enid had blasted the Democrats for what was going on in Congress, especially the House banking scandal. "Unpaid restaurant bills. Embezzlement. Drug dealing in the House post office. Writing bad checks. In the rest of America this is called breaking the law. In Washington, D.C. it's called Congress," one of her 1992 campaign brochures declared. It seemed an eerie prophecy of what was by then beginning to surface in Enid and Joe's own life.

Once she was a member of Congress, Waldholtz was required to file financial disclosure forms, which allowed more careful scrutiny of what she and Joe owned. In July the *Salt Lake Tribune* had reported that the Waldholtzes' financial disclosure form was $1.5 million off. The paper had hired an independent accountant to look over the form. He discovered that Waldholtz did not have enough money to cover the $1.9 million she had spent on her campaign the previous year and that the forms seemed to show she actually had more money after the election.

The *Tribune's* story on the Waldholtz finances also reported that the property Joe owned in Monroeville, Pennsylvania, although listed on the form as having a worth of $500,000 to $1 million, was assessed by Allegheny County at $89,800. The accountant told the newspaper that the errors on the form could be explained either by omissions, intentional misreporting, or "some undisclosed source of cash—possibly a large gift." Waldholtz dismissed the discrepancies as "bookkeeping errors" and said she and her husband would file "minor adjustments" to clarify the report.

Around this time Enid and Joe, along with Kate Watson, had a meeting with Ladonna Lee, the president of Eddie Mahe's consulting and public relations firm. Lee had become friends with Enid and served not only as paid consultant but personal adviser. Lee knew about the investigation into the financial disclosure forms by the Utah media, and Watson had also informed her of the other financial problems and the bill collectors who were hounding Joe.

As Lee saw it there were three problems: the amendments that had not been filed to the FEC reports, the discrepancies on the financial disclosure forms, and Joe's credit troubles. Lee went through her concerns about each problem and offered her suggestions for how to deal with the media. When she reached the issue of the bounced checks and the creditors, Enid exploded. She insisted that was not true. And Joe and Watson just sat there without saying a word, according to Lee. At that point Lee decided her company couldn't do any more for Enid and Joe Waldholtz. If they refused to turn over documents to the accountants trying to help them and if Joe refused to be honest about the extent of the problems, nothing could be done. Lee sent Enid a letter informing her that the Eddie Mahe company was terminating its relationship with her.

But apparently even that move was not enough of a wake-up call for Enid.

Joe had been responsible for preparing the financial disclosure forms and according to Enid had convinced her to sign blank forms, promising her he would fill them out properly later and submit them so they could make the deadline. When the *Salt Lake Tribune* asked for verification of his family trust, which Enid supposedly held an interest in, Joe asked a member of Enid's staff to help him falsify the document, but the staff member refused.

Enid was informed of this incident the first week in September, only a few days after giving birth to Elizabeth, during a telephone call from her press secretary. As she would describe it three months later, Enid hung up the phone, turned to Joe, and told him she had just been told that Joe had asked a member of her staff to falsify a document. Joe burst into tears. He told her he had been afraid the stress would affect her pregnancy and he did it because he did not have time to get the real document to the newspaper. "Because he was so contrite and upset and penitent, I said to him, 'Joe, are you swearing to me that the document we showed the *Tribune* is a real document?' And he said yes. When I looked at him and saw how upset he was, I believed him."

But Enid insisted she started pushing him to get all of their financial documents together and get everything straightened out. And all the while Joe continued to ask her father for money. In October he said he needed $600,000, and her father gave him $308,000. He tried to get Enid to sign their house over to him, but she refused. In October it was reported that a number of checks in their congressional credit union account in Washington had bounced. Joe blamed a thief he said stole checks from his bag at the Cincinnati airport. Enid went along with the story, telling reporters the thief was writing checks from "all over this hemisphere . . . from places like Guam."

But in fact the congressional credit union had been watching their account for months and had alerted the public corruption section of the U.S. Attorney's Office that this could be a case of check kiting between the Waldholtzes' Washington and Salt Lake City accounts. This was the same office that had investigated the financial and criminal charges against Chicago congressman Dan Rostenkowski, a scandal that in no small part contributed to the voter cynicism about Congress that helped elect freshmen like Waldholtz.

On November 1 the *Hill* newspaper, which covers Congress, reported that federal authorities were looking into the Waldholtz finances, the potential election violations, and the check-bouncing problems. But Enid remained defiant. "I've said repeatedly that we've been victimized by someone who stole checks from us and that we've had wire transfers go astray, but we pay our bills and always will . . . Any allegation of check-kiting . . . is ludicrous and defamatory." A week later the *Hill* reported that the FBI was looking into the matter. Enid had by then hired a lawyer and declined comment except to say that she was trying to "get to the bottom of the questions about my financial matters."

State GOP leaders, who had long been aware of the problems with the Waldholtz finances, started distancing themselves. Governor Leavitt told the *Salt Lake Tribune*, "Seems to me she's got some explaining to do. Hopefully, she is going to do that." Russ Behrman, the executive director of the Utah GOP, admitted, "There's a lot of unease among Republicans." Senator Orrin Hatch asked for a meeting with Enid and Joe. He told Enid to hire a lawyer and an accountant to go over the FEC reports. As Hatch would later recount for the *New York Times,* "I told him and her, he has to get the heck out of the office and have nothing to do with the finances." Hatch also told Joe he could be headed for jail.

And at this point, Enid wasn't even sure if they had filed a federal income tax return for 1994. First Joe told Enid he had filed an extension; then he told her that the tax return had been filed by his trustees in Pittsburgh. Enid did nothing about this, although she knew she had never signed a 1994 tax form.

After the financial stories broke, Joe stayed home from the office. Elizabeth's nanny told Enid that he just sat in bed all day, not moving, just staring at the television. "I thought I was going to have to have him institutionalized. Little did I know he was planning his getaway," Enid would tell me later.

*   *   *

By then Enid's Washington lawyer had informed her he would be willing to represent her but not Joe on the check-kiting charges being investigated by the U.S. Attorney's Office. On Friday night, November 10, Enid had it out with Joe. Joining in the interrogation was Jim Parkinson, her brother-in-law, a California lawyer she had asked to come to Washington to help her deal with Joe. At 3 A.M. they were still going at it. She wanted to know if there was actually a trust fund. "I was begging him to tell me what was going on." But Joe continued to insist he was telling her the truth about everything. He said the family trustees would arrive in Washington the next day and straighten everything out. At one point "he begged me not to leave him," Enid recalled. At another "he took off his wedding ring, slammed it down on the table, and said he couldn't stay married to someone who wouldn't believe in him."

The next day Enid's brother-in-law went with Joe to National Airport to pick up the phantom trustees. Joe called Enid from the car saying he became lost on the way to the airport. It was a drive he had made dozens of times. He called again once they got there. Everything would be fine as soon as the trustees arrived, he told her. After he had left the house, Enid started going through Joe's briefcase and found bills from banks she didn't even know Joe was dealing with. She asked Joe to put her brother-in-law on the phone. He refused. He had sent Parkinson to the gate to meet the trustees. Joe hung up on Enid. Then he disappeared. When Parkinson came back after failing to meet the nonexistent trustees, Joe was gone. All they could find was his car in the airport parking lot reserved for members of Congress.

At the same time Enid was pressing Joe for some answers, he was due in court in Pittsburgh to respond to a legal action filed by his family, trying to force Joe to explain what had happened to his grandmother's $1 million. Enid said she discovered this only when she called Joe's father to tell him Joe was missing. That's when she says she also discovered there was no family trust fund and no trustees.

Enid contacted federal authorities to let them know Joe was missing. Initially she thought he had gone off to kill himself. Then she discovered he had taken some of the jewelry he had given to her—a gold watch with diamonds, a diamond tennis bracelet, and a long gold chain. Only as she started to sift through the boxes and boxes of financial papers that Joe had left behind did Enid say she realized what had really been going on all this time.

When she tried to freeze all of their joint accounts, she was informed that their cash card had been used twice since Joe's disappearance. Joe had withdrawn $300 from an automatic money machine in Baltimore and another $300 in Springfield, Massachusetts. Enid thought Joe was headed for Canada and had "left her and Elizabeth to face all of this. All of a sudden it dawns on me, Joe has run away to leave me to answer all of these questions." Her fear over what Joe might do to himself quickly turned to rage over what he had done to her.

On Monday Enid's congressional office issued a statement announcing that Joe had vanished. Her brother-in-law was quoted as saying that outside law enforcement agencies had been brought in for ongoing investigations into Joe's "handling of the couple's accounts." The statement said, "The congresswoman has taken steps to remove Joe Waldholtz from involvement with any of her campaign organization [activities] and her congressional office and is now handling all of her own personal accounts."

On Tuesday, just three days after Joe's disappearance, Enid moved quickly to make it clear it was her husband, and not she, who was responsible for all that had happened. In another statement released by her office, she announced she was filing for divorce on the grounds of "mental cruelty." She also sought sole custody of Elizabeth and said she planned to change her name back to Greene. The statement read in part, "I cannot begin to describe the anger and hurt over the incredible level of deception that we have uncovered in our own investigation of Joe's activities. I want this man tracked down, arrested and punished for what he has done to me, my family and the people of Utah." Enid would tell me later that her swift action in seeking a divorce was motivated out of concern for Elizabeth, to protect her from Joe.

On Wednesday, November 15, the Justice Department issued an arrest warrant for Joe, saying he was the subject of a grand jury investigation into an alleged $2 million bank fraud and check-kiting scheme and was wanted as a material witness. By the next day Enid finally decided directly to address the serious allegations that she had broken federal election laws with the financing of her campaign. In a statement issued from her office, she insisted she "fully believed" the money had come from her personal resources in compliance with election law. "My belief was based on misrepresentations made to me by Joe Waldholtz regarding the family trust, the gift he gave me when we married, and our supposed joint ownership of property in Pennsylvania," she said in the statement.

But Joe's father, Harvey Waldholtz, told the *New York Times* that he thought Enid was "trying to blame it all on Joe. . . . They're just trying to salvage Enid's career." Waldholtz said the family would not pursue criminal charges against Joe in connection with his grandmother's missing money; they just wanted Joe back.

Enid refused to talk to reporters, but Gingrich told the *Salt Lake Tribune* that what had happened to Enid was a "great personal tragedy" and that Joe had been a

"Svengali-like" partner. "You do not blame another human being for falling in love with a scoundrel," Gingrich said. Because his wife, Marianne, managed their personal finances, allowing him to concentrate on his congressional duties, Gingrich said he could understand Enid's doing the same thing. "The intensity and long hours here leave you to find people you can lean on," said Gingrich.

Six days after he had disappeared, Joe walked into the U.S. Attorney's Office and turned himself in to federal authorities in Washington. He had spent two nights in Massachusetts and four nights in Philadelphia with a friend. He was released to the custody of his lawyer but had to surrender his passport and was directed to make daily telephone contact with the FBI.

Five days later, as Joe Waldholtz entered U.S. District Court in Washington for his next court appearance, he was served with divorce papers from Enid. Waldholtz was not asked to testify before the grand jury that day and was clearly trying to make a deal with the federal prosecutors, who requested a three-week extension for the case. As he left the courthouse, Joe told reporters, "I would just like to say that I love my wife and daughter very, very much. I hope they are doing very well."

Day after day the Enid and Joe saga was featured on the front page of Utah newspapers and on the local TV news. It was both high political scandal and tabloid fodder. It was Utah's biggest story of the year. The phone in her office never stopped ringing with interview requests. NBC anchor Tom Brokaw even sent a handwritten note asking her to be on the nightly news. But Enid wasn't talking, just issuing statements. Finally, on December 11, a month after Joe's disappearance, Enid held a news conference to tell her side of the story. Eddie Mahe's political consulting company and Ladonna Lee, whom Enid had asked for advice and help shortly before Joe's disappearance, were in charge of setting up the event, to be held in Salt Lake City three days before Enid was scheduled to testify before the federal grand jury. Mahe and Lee carefully rehearsed with Enid several times what she would say about life with Joe.

The night before the news conference, Enid met with Utah governor Leavitt and members of the congressional delegation. They wanted to know what her plans were for the next day, what she was going to say. "None of us knew what to believe," Leavitt would tell me in an interview some months later. She told them she was not going to resign but had not made up her mind about whether she would run for re-election. She first had to see how the press conference went.

*   *   *

During her marathon, five-hour news conference, Waldholtz appeared with the new men in her life: her attorney, Charles Roistacher, and her accountant. She began with an opening statement chronicling in painstaking detail the events of the previous two years. For the first hour, the news conference was broadcast live on CNN and after that intermittently on C-SPAN. The televisions in congressional offices were tuned to the show, and staffers couldn't believe what they were hearing and seeing. There was a certain creepy fascination, a little bit like looking at the wreckage of an automobile crash: You didn't want to keep looking, but you couldn't help yourself.

No one had never seen anything like it. Who would answer questions about the most intimate details of her life for five hours? Only someone trying desperately to save her political career. Enid's mother was in attendance but not her father. Although D. Forrest Greene was a pivotal figure in what had happened and had already been interviewed by the U.S. Attorney's Office, he did not appear at the news conference and avoided having to answer any questions in public.

With a completely straight face, Enid said her father, although a multimillionaire, was a frugal man who drove a 1968 Cadillac and had not wanted to spend the airfare to fly from Washington to Salt Lake City. "He is an honest man. I think he has suffered enough," she said. She also said that her 76-year-old father's recollection was not as clear as hers about everything that had happened. Her father, an investor with a net worth of tens of millions of dollars, had never been presented with any legal documents, nor had he asked for any when he was making millions of dollars in loans to Joe. "When my father agreed to loan Joe money, it was because it was family. . . . My father believed because I believed." Enid said it was the custom in her family not to talk about money. "I don't think that my mother knows to this day what my father's net worth is." But after this mess, not only her mother but the rest of the world would know a great deal more about the Greene finances.

Wearing a dark green suit and no wedding ring, Enid at first appeared somewhat shaky, but as the hours wore on, she became more combative in her responses to reporters' questions. First she laid it all out: her entire life with Joe Waldholtz. She would have to tell this throng of strangers all kinds of details about her personal life, about meeting Joe, their courtship, private conversations, family problems. The only way anyone would believe her, believe she didn't know, would be if it appeared she was telling the whole truth, no matter how painful.

And she cried. Oh, how she cried. From the very beginning of the news conference, her voice broke frequently. Sometimes she dabbed at her eyes with a tissue; sometimes she sobbed openly. If it wasn't all so strange, so ghastly, and if there weren't such serious issues at stake, the whole performance would have been almost funny.

At first she extolled Joe's good qualities, the qualities that she fell in love with. He was kind to his mother and to friends in trouble. He saved a lost dog and found its rightful owner. Joe was a "teddy bear." She said when she married Joe, she had been "weary of always being the strong one" and decided to let him be in charge of financial matters. Joe had controlled everything. She didn't even know the access code to their home phone's answering system. After years of being the intelligent, independent, capable woman, she was suddenly the wronged and deluded wife. It was a strange, ill-fitting role.

She had taken a course in campaign finance law as a student at BYU law school and been a corporate attorney for seven years. She had worked on multimillion-dollar corporate deals. As an aide to the governor of Utah, she had been in charge of trying to settle the case of a Navajo trust fund that had been looted through a series of kickback schemes and dummy companies. And as a congressional candidate, she put herself forward as capable of helping to tackle the federal budget deficit. But when it came to what happened with her finances and her campaign, it was Joe, Joe, all Joe. She had known nothing. She was unaware. He was devious. He was cunning. He was a "seamless liar" and a cheat. He may in fact have been all of those things. But what did it say about Enid that she had been deceived for so long?

Joe had waved one phony document after another in front of her, she explained—like the fake tax returns that showed he had an income of $25,000 a month from his family trust. Joe used them to obtain a mortgage with Enid for their $200,000 Salt Lake City home. Joe cooked up story after story. He said his mother had gained access to his accounts and run up bills and since he could not use funds from the Waldholtz family trust for his mother, he had to borrow money from Enid's father. "That began the string of events that I so deeply regret, that dragged my father into this nightmare," said Enid.

She had been duped. "Everything I'd known about Joseph Waldholtz, who I'd loved and trusted, was a lie."

Her lawyer and accountant then offered documents Joe had falsified as evidence of his larceny. He had even forged Enid's signature on a congressional paycheck to cash it after telling her it had been lost. After two hours of this, Enid took questions from the dozens of reporters who had shown up. She went in order around the room, calling on them in turn. She was still in charge, despite everything that had happened. She stiffed the national press, telling them she would get to them when she had answered all of the questions from the Utah reporters. After hours of not being called on and angered over having made the trip to Salt Lake City for nothing, most of them left. They could have stayed home and watched it on C-SPAN.

She flooded the reporters with mountains of detail about Joe's stories and financial double-dealings. At times she became obviously impatient with reporters who had trouble understanding all of the complicated financial details of the scam. When one reporter suggested that a con man relies on the greed of his victims and perhaps it was Enid and her father's greed to win her a congressional seat that allowed them to be susceptible to Joe, she exploded. "That's a disgusting characterization of a man who's not here [by choice] to defend himself. My father is not greedy." It was just that he loved his family and wanted Joe to be able to take care of his mother, she explained. As for herself, "It was my love for my husband that made me so vulnerable."

For five hours she was unrepentant. If people thought she was going to grovel, they were dead wrong. The only mistake she would admit to was loving the wrong man. She hadn't known. She hadn't done anything wrong. "I loved Joe Waldholtz and trusted him with all my heart. I now know . . . the person I loved and trusted never existed." She was guilty of loving unwisely and too well. That was all. Not once did she even suggest that she should have known, should have guessed, should have had some inkling of what Joe Waldholtz had been up to. "I am accepting responsibility for trusting someone who was completely untrustworthy. . . . I believe I was tricked; I don't believe I was negligent."

She did apologize to her two opponents, Karen Shepherd and Merrill Cook, and to the voters. But she said she would not resign. Instead, she would try to "be the best representative I know how to be for the rest of my term."

There was no way she would resign: That would look like an admission of guilt. Besides, she'd worked too hard to even think about resigning.

"I don't think money was the only issue in this campaign. Issues are the most important reason people get elected," Enid insisted. Merrill Cook, who attended the press conference, told her the election was like her having bought a stolen car: Even though she didn't know it was stolen, she should return it. "There's no way to return an election. I wish there were," she responded. "I am responsible, and I'm bearing the consequences for the choices that I made. But I don't believe they should be the same consequences as someone who intentionally set out to do this. . . . The fact is I did not know about these illegal activities, and I did not try to cover them up."

To those who had worked for Enid, her words rang a little hollow. She deflected questions about staff resignations and tried to downplay the warnings she had received from staff members about bounced checks and financial problems during the 1994 campaign, not mentioning that a number of them had been in writing, such as the detailed memos from KayLin Loveland and David Harmer. She insisted Loveland had resigned not because of the financial problems but "because KayLin and I just weren't a good fit as a campaign manager and a candidate."

Although she had received numerous memos from Harmer about campaign finances, during her press conference she would admit only that he had sent her "one memo . . . that said the FEC reports looked a little skimpy." She seemed to lose her patience when reporters asked her about the staff warnings of problems. She insisted she had not told Harmer to stop asking questions about the finances but at the same time admitted he was not permitted access to the books. "David's job was not to double-check what Huckaby [the accounting firm] was doing or anyone else. . . . David's role [by then he was campaign manager] was not to figure out how much money was being spent where."

Enid said she had been reluctant to tell her staff how much personal money she was willing to spend on the campaign because she was afraid that would make them spendthrifts and they wouldn't do enough fund-raising. For someone who trusted her husband so implicitly, despite some very strange goings-on, her complete lack of trust for her staff presented an interesting dichotomy.

When someone asked her why she had been so desperate to win the election, she said, "I wasn't desperate to serve in the Congress. I wanted to, I wanted to badly. . . . I decided I wouldn't let money be the issue; money is too much the issue in politics today."

Several times reporters continued to press for any acknowledgment that she had been wrong but received none. To a question about whether she had used bad judgment, Enid responded: "In my professional life I'm known as a fighter. People used to say I was tough and strident. I always believed if I took on a client, whether it was in my law firm or when I went to the governor's office and when I went to Congress, that I had an obligation to fight as hard as I could on their behalf. And sometimes that meant I fought harder than other people thought even was appropriate, but I thought that was my duty. When I got married I thought that was the one place in my life that I didn't need to fight. I relaxed every guard that I had built up in my professional life with my husband. I thought that's what marriage was about. I was as stupid, as blind, as gullible, as naive, as trusting as anyone can be with another human being. Was that a mistake? It certainly was."

There was no doubt she was a skilled litigator. She knew how to present a case and how to offer a closing argument. "I know as you sit there it's hard for you to understand how I could have let these warning flags go by," she would say. "I just ask you to do this. When you go home tonight and you're with the person you love most in the world and they're holding you as you go to sleep and they tell you that they love you and that you're their life, ask yourself if you think they're capable of what I've just told you. And if you don't think they're capable of that, then maybe you'll understand why I didn't think Joe was either, and why I believed him."

Merrill Cook thought the first hour of the press conference "played pretty well with people" but after that it got to be a little much. "It took a few days to know it wasn't going over," said Cook. "I don't think the people of the state of Utah viewed her as the total victim."

Maybe what killed Enid was, as they say in the movie business, the word of mouth. The victim defense wore especially thin with the state's Democrats, who saw Karen Shepherd and the state's voters as the real victims. "It's an embarrassment that she doesn't take responsibility for it," said Paul Svendsen, a Democratic activist who ran Shepherd's 1994 campaign. Svendsen contended that all of the state's senior Republicans had to have some idea of what was going on but decided to turn a blind eye. "It's just an utter failure of ethical and moral responsibility. They were overtaken with the all-consuming need to win. No wonder people are so turned off by politics."

*   *   *

Four days later Enid testified for three hours before the federal grand jury in Washington. And the good news just seemed to keep coming. She was informed the House Ethics Committee was looking into the false financial disclosure forms she had filed in 1994 and 1995. And the IRS wanted a 1994 tax return. When she filed amended financial disclosure forms with the House in January 1996, she estimated that she owed $50,000—$130,000 in back taxes. This had all happened because of "thousands of transactions and millions of dollars about which I had no personal knowledge," she wrote to the Ethics Committee.

In a thousand-page filing to the FEC, Enid accused Joe of 858 violations in her 1994 campaign alone, including depositing campaign contributions into his personal checking accounts, using them to pay personal bills, and inventing phantom donors.

She appeared for a second time before the federal grand jury and testified for six hours. And still Joe remained unindicted. Joe was attempting to make a deal with the federal prosecutors and had not yet been compelled to testify. He appeared relaxed and smiling on his way in and out of the courthouse. "This is a very deep personal family and political tragedy. To my wife and family, I love you and miss you very much," he told reporters. Joe may have lost touch with reality, but he hadn't lost his touch for spin.

As Utah's March 18 filing deadline for Congress approached, Enid thought seriously about making a bid for reelection, although polls showed nearly three-quarters of the people in her district thought she should not run. Utah's Republican Party leaders became increasingly nervous she might actually try it. The state's senior Republicans knew she would be a badly wounded candidate. Enough was enough. But she wasn't paying attention. "I made it very clear to them I was going to make my own decision. It wasn't their decision to make. They let me figure it out for myself. They knew I wouldn't listen to them," said Enid.

Finally, on March 5, Enid announced she would not seek reelection, citing the ongoing federal investigation as one of the biggest reasons for her decision. All of the money she had left, along with plenty from her father, was going to lawyers who were defending her against the IRS, the FEC, the House Ethics Committee, and the Justice Department.

She had wanted to run again. That's why she had held that marathon press conference. She thought that might take care of everything. She tried to go on with her congressional duties as if nothing had happened. But she knew people couldn't help looking at her, whispering. "It was an act of will to go out alone in public."

Joe was living in the basement of his parents' house. But at the end of March his family had him hauled into court to explain what had happened to his grandmother's money. First Joe said it was invested, but he couldn't produce any documentation. When the judge ordered him sent to jail until he decided to be more forthcoming, his story changed. Enid and I spent it, he said.

In May Joe was finally indicted on 27 counts of bank fraud in connection with his check kiting. But the federal investigation into other matters, including campaign funding violations and false information on Enid's federal financial disclosure forms, was not yet concluded. Enid said Joe's indictment "proves he is the one who did these things." By that time she was going by the name "Enid Greene," having dropped "Waldholtz," and both the sign on her congressional office door and her stationery had been changed. If only it would be that easy to drop Joe from her life.

In early June, 22 months after their wedding, Enid was formally granted a divorce from Joe on the grounds of irreconcilable differences and mental cruelty. That same month Joe pleaded guilty to three felonies and one misdemeanor count of bank, election, and tax fraud in U.S. District Court. Waldholtz admitted writing $250,000 in bogus checks on the couple's congressional credit union account, lying on the 1994 FEC form he filed for Enid's campaign, creating ghost contributors, and falsifying Enid's 1993 federal income tax form.

What did Joe say he had learned from the whole thing? "The ends do not justify the means. There's an absolute truth. And most importantly, always tell the truth, particularly to the people you love." Joe apologized to "the good people of Utah" as well as to Karen Shepherd for "inappropriately influencing the electoral process and the election." Part of Waldholtz's plea agreement called for him to cooperate with federal prosecutors in the ongoing criminal and civil investigations of Enid's campaign finances and taxes; in return federal prosecutors dropped 23 other charges against him. And Waldholtz, in his characteristically colorful fashion, vowed to "paint myself yellow and sing like a canary."

For her part, Enid said Joe's plea "in every way supports and validates what I told the public last December about what happened in this sorry state of affairs—the fact that I did not know what Joe was doing." It seemed there was nothing left that Joe could do to surprise people, but in the fall of 1996, shortly before his sentencing, federal prosecutors revealed he had still obviously learned nothing. Waldholtz told an FBI agent that he had developed a heroin habit and had checked himself into a rehabilitation program. He had also stolen yet more money, not only from his friends and parents but even from his lawyers by writing bad checks and using their credit cards. He had also taken a prescription pad from his dentist father to use to obtain drugs, all of which drove his father to change the locks on his house to keep Joe out.

Prosecutors would say later they were never sure whether Joe's self-professed heroin addiction was real or just a ploy to get out of doing jail time by checking himself into a treatment facility. If the latter, it was unsuccessful. When he was sentenced in October 1996 to 37 months in prison, the judge told him, "No sentence is sufficient to atone for your attempts to manipulate an election, for bank fraud, for false statement, for failure to report campaign contributions. . . . There is only one thing, Mr. Waldholtz, that is certain, and that is you abused the public trust."

U.S. Attorney Craig Iscoe said he was pleased with the sentence because it was the same Waldholtz would have faced had the matter gone to trial. But Joe's behavior prior to sentencing did not bode well for his use as a witness against his former wife. Whatever shred of credibility he might have had was gone. What jury would believe Joe? "His credibility was really low because he lied so many times. Often he doesn't tell the same story twice. He was totally unreliable in terms of presenting usable evidence in court," Iscoe would tell me.

In the end there was no proof against Enid. It was simply his word against hers. And the word of a pathological liar, con man, and admitted felon against a weepy woman wronged who happens to be a member of Congress didn't look like a very good bet to the prosecutors. After spending more than $1 million on lawyers, accountants, and political consultants, Enid was informed by the U.S. Attorney's Office that she would not be charged with any crime.

Enid's father had sued to recover the money that he had loaned to Joe. Forrest Greene had been pouring money into Enid and Joe's personal bank accounts starting only a few months after their marriage until just weeks before Joe disappeared. In court documents Greene listed each of the 24 disbursements he made primarily to Enid and Joe's joint checking accounts between January 1994 and November 1995. In that legal complaint, filed in Salt Lake City, Greene repeatedly referred to the money he gave Joe as a loan and made no mention of any transfer of assets. And although Greene's complaint outlined Joe's false claims of a $325 million Waldholtz family trust and the stories about problems with his mother, there was no mention of a $2.2 million Pittsburgh property or a transfer of assets in exchange for the $1.7 million in cash that was put into Enid's campaign.

In July Enid's father obtained a judgment against Joe for the $3.9 million he had given the couple. Enid would explain to me later that although Joe appeared to have no money, the point of the suit was to collect if and when he ever did and to prevent him from profiting on their experience through a book or by selling the rights to his story. It was essentially a preemptive legal strike. Joe's family, seeking to recover anything that might be left from the $1 million he had bilked from his grandmother, also took legal action against Joe, forcing him into bankruptcy in 1997.

Enid was approached by Lee Benson, a former sportswriter for the *Deseret News,* to collaborate on a book. Benson spent several months working with Enid in the summer of 1996, but she was apparently not happy with the manuscript, even though Benson believed her claim that she had been duped and was sympathetic to her in telling the story. Benson believed Enid failed to realize what was going on until it was too late because she refused to listen to other people.

*   *   *

There seemed to be no question about what Joe had done. He left a swath of red ink and paper a mile wide. But the question that still remained was, to borrow a Watergate phrase, what did Enid know and when did she know it?

"Was there a point where there was willful self-delusion? At what point did she say to hell with the consequences?" Enid's former political consultant David Owen wondered. "She might not have known everything. But she knew on some level. She had to have known," maintained Loveland, the manager of the first half of the 1994 campaign. Merrill Cook, who defeated Enid's second 1994 campaign manager, David Harmer, in the Republican primary and won Enid's former congressional seat in 1996, found it hard to believe the "in-charge" woman who had beat him two years earlier "wouldn't know what Joe was up to."

Was she really taken in by this man until the very end, as she insisted? Could she have it both ways? Could she be the smart, tough, aggressive politician and also the adoring wife who asked no questions and believed completely in each successive lie her husband told? Didn't she notice as the world was crashing down around her ears?

When I interviewed her in the spring of 1997, Joe was serving his sentence at the Allenwood Federal Prison Camp in central Pennsylvania, the same minimum security facility, located on 4,200 acres about three hours north of Washington, where Watergate figures Charles Colson and G. Gordon Liddy did time and where many white-collar and corporate felons are sent.

Since leaving Congress, Enid had not been working and was still trying to decide what her options were. She could go work for a law firm but would rather do something related to politics. "I don't want to go fund-raise or run a PAC, but if there was something that was issue related, I'd be interested," she told me.

She had been traveling back and forth between Salt Lake City and Washington since the election. Forced to sell her house in Salt Lake to pay her considerable legal bills, she had put her furniture there in storage and had rented a small two-bedroom apartment in a modern high-rise building in the Washington suburb of Alexandria, Virginia. It was easier to try to carry on a normal life in Washington, to go to the supermarket without being recognized, than it would have been in Salt Lake City.

The apartment betrayed almost no sign that just six months earlier its occupant had been a member of Congress. There were no congressional knickknacks or photos of her with other politicians. "When Joe ran away," Enid said, she never again slept in their former bedroom in the $3,800 townhouse in Georgetown. "I couldn't," she said with an almost imperceptible shudder. Instead, she slept on the couch. Living somewhere else altogether would probably have been preferable, but she couldn't get out of her two-year lease, she explained. She never even drove his car again or spent another night in their Salt Lake City house. "It reminded me of him, and I couldn't deal with it. Every time I started thinking about the emotional side of it, it took me several hours to recuperate." She decided it was best to put every thought of Joe out of her mind.

But much as she might like to erase any trace of Joe from her life, she was living with a constant reminder: their daughter, Elizabeth. With her rosy, round cheeks and curly brown hair, Elizabeth appeared happy and content as she played and chattered nearby while her mother and I talked over the course of several hours in the living room of their apartment.

Joe saw his daughter only a few times after he disappeared. The last time was just a few months before being sent to prison. Enid and Joe's divorce judgment granted him limited supervised visitation rights. Joe indicated he hoped to challenge that decision, but Enid believed even that was too much. "I know the prevailing thinking is that some relationship [between father and child] is better than none, but I don't see it." Since Enid said Joe's pattern was "to abuse the people he claims to love the most"—his mother, his grandmother, and of course Enid—she did not think Joe deserved access to his daughter.

"If I could pick, he would never bother Elizabeth again because I don't see anything good coming out of her relationship with him. He's not a father. There's not one thing that fits the definition of a father except DNA."

But as much as she would like to leave Elizabeth innocent of everything that has happened in her young life, Enid felt that is not an option available to her. At some point she would have to be told. "I don't want Elizabeth to go through what I went through. The only way I can protect Elizabeth against him is to tell her all the truth. . . . I can't leave her vulnerable to him. She will have to know things that I regret she'll have to know. There are a lot of things I could spare her from hearing" if Joe were removed permanently from her life, Enid said.

In addition to all of the discoveries she made about his financial situation, Enid said she discovered some other rather disturbing things after Joe's disappearance. One of the first things to turn up was a Federal Express package that contained empty cigarette packages that had been opened and wrapped with tape. It was her determination that they had been used by someone sending Joe drugs. He had had surgery on his back, and she had seen him take prescription painkillers but claimed not to have known if he was abusing them.

She also said she found gay male pornography in the house, which prompted her to have herself and Elizabeth tested for AIDS. "I don't know to this day what his sexuality is," she said. It was just one more thing she was no longer sure of about the man to whom she had been married.

Without any visible trace of emotion, she said she had come to the conclusion that Joe was a "psychopath," but just a few minutes later she said, "I hope he can turn his life around." She was willing to blame Joe for everything, to write him off as the ultimate heel. But she also seemed to want to defend her relationship with him. She still stated emphatically that she loved Joe, right up until the end.

She had lost the ability to be embarrassed by any personal question, no doubt a result of being asked so many. During the federal investigation, the FBI searched both her house in Salt Lake City and her Georgetown rental. "My underwear drawer has been rummaged through. I don't have any skeletons. I don't even have any closets," she said ruefully. "My life is more ridiculous than any plot of any soap opera could be," she said with a hint of a wan smile.

How was Joe able to deceive her for so long when obvious problems were surfacing almost from the beginning of their relationship? "Early in the marriage," Enid said in her divorce filing, "there were numerous incidents of him [Joe] leaving the marital residence during the middle of the night, being emotionally distraught and making veiled threats of suicide." Enid thought it was just the problems with his mother that were wearing on Joe, she claimed. She explained her continuing trust of Joe by pointing to her own family, her model for married life: "My parents are the most honest people I know. I had never considered having to be careful of a spouse. To me your family is the most important thing there is. I never thought Joe would do anything to hurt his family."

When Joe told her that his mother had serious psychological problems, had been duped out of money, had taken money from his accounts, had "done all these things," and he needed to borrow money from her father to deal with it, she believed him because Joe outwardly appeared so devoted to his mother, talking to her on the phone every day. Joe said he didn't want to have to tell people exactly what was going on because it would embarrass his family. "I was doing this to protect Joe's family. I thought I was being a good daughter-in-law," said Enid.

She still sticks pretty much to her original story, but it is clear that by the summer of 1995, at least several months before Joe ran away, she realized there were some serious problems. It was around the time of Elizabeth's birth that things really started to unravel. But her concerns at that point were for her husband's mental stability, she insisted. "When your husband is threatening at 2 in the morning to commit suicide, you don't say, 'Give me the tax return.' If I was in on this, don't you think I would have filed a tax return? Don't you think somebody's going to notice that? . . . Do you think I thought I could have gotten away with it?" Had she known or suspected earlier, Enid said, there were a lot of things she could have done differently to try to save her own skin: She could have hired a lawyer, she could have had Joe arrested, and she could have cooperated with the authorities against him before he disappeared.

"Joe didn't just fool me," said Enid. "Joe fooled a mortgage company" with his fake tax returns showing an annual income of $500,000. "He fooled lots of people."

Enid was convinced that the investigation into her involvement was politically motivated. "Believe me, if there had been anything, they would have indicted me. They did not not indict me out of the goodness of their hearts," she said, still defiant. "Anybody who now says, 'I don't believe her,' I challenge them to come up with one scintilla of evidence that I had anything to do with what Joe Waldholtz did. . . . I defy the naysayers to put up or shut up. . . . I'm guilty of making a very poor choice of husbands, but I'm not guilty of anything more than that."

But she would not release the letter the Justice Department sent her informing her that there would be no criminal prosecution against her. Roistacher, her lawyer, said the "uncomplimentary" letter was extremely unusual, with "a lot of gratuitous comments in it." It was "almost like an independent counsel issuing a report." Obviously, the letter said more than, Congratulations. You will not be prosecuted.

When I asked if maybe she didn't try to look the other way, try to ignore all the warning signs about Joe, Enid quickly responded as a lawyer would, saying, "If I had turned a blind eye, there's a criminal definition for that. It's called willful blindness. If I had been a basically dishonest person myself, I would have caught on to Joe much sooner. The truth is I am a Goody Two-shoes. It didn't occur to me that anyone could behave like this. It's because I am such a straight arrow myself that Joe was able to fool me."

Enid said she believes she did the right thing by not resigning. "I think I did a pretty darn good job. I don't think the people of my district were ill served by my decision to stay in office." And she admitted that she would have liked to run for re-election. "There was part of me that thought, 'Do I need to run to help me establish my innocence?' But I knew if I ran, the Justice Department would not get around to clearing its investigation until after the election. I wanted to end it. I knew if I ran, those people would not bring this thing to an end."

Her public face has always been stoic and tough. But Enid said she was profoundly depressed the first few months after it all broke. So much that she even thought about killing herself. "It was hard to imagine living with the pain. When you're that low and in that much pain, you feel like you can't take it anymore and you start to think of ways to make it go away." She saw a psychiatrist a couple of times but said when she told him everything that had happened, he told her what she was feeling was a completely normal response.

"I think Elizabeth is the only reason I'm still here. For a short period of time, if I didn't have Elizabeth, I'm not sure I would have resisted the impulse to end it. But I couldn't see leaving Elizabeth alone."

The worst thing about all of it, she said, is what she had put her family through. But even at this lowest of points, she was still thinking like a lawyer. "I thought, if I write out everything that had happened and killed myself, the prosecutors would have to admit that as evidence and my Dad would be cleared." Enid never actually got close to acting on her impulse, and she made herself a deal. If she still felt this bad by the time Elizabeth was grown, she could do it then if she wanted to. "What makes you feel better is time. You deal with it, you confront it, and you move on. A short time after that, I decided it wasn't that painful after all."

She had Elizabeth. She had her family. She would be fine.

*   *   *

It is easy to believe that Joe charmed Enid in the beginning. They shared a love for the same thing—they were both political junkies. He wasn't threatened by her ambition. He liked it. He was willing to let her be center stage. In fact, he was willing to promote her career, to take the role usually assigned to a politician's wife. She could have everything she wanted: a career and a family.

Would she have married a man who looked and behaved as Joe did if she knew he had no money, someone who was just a con man? Highly unlikely. But when things started to go bad—the bounced checks, the American Express lawsuit, the warnings from campaign workers—didn't it take a conscious act of will to look the other way? Did she just not want to know, not want to see? Had it just gone too far by that point for her to acknowledge the damage that had already been done?

And what about her father, a successful businessman who had built a fortune and was not exactly a spendthrift? Why didn't he ask for some collateral, some proof as he was handing over millions of dollars to Joe? Why didn't he ask for a single document, a single piece of paper?

Maybe Enid just couldn't face what was going on. She couldn't bring herself to figure it out. After all, Joe was helping make all of her dreams possible. Perhaps she knew nothing about his check kiting and financial scams. It seems unlikely she would have been a party to that kind of activity. But when it came to the campaign, was Joe just cutting the corners she wanted cut? The sale of her house to her parents in the 1992 campaign, not recorded until later, set the pattern.

When Joe came to her and said they would need money from her father for the campaign, why didn't she pick up the phone and talk to a lawyer who specialized in election law, just to be sure they weren't doing anything wrong? Was she too busy being the candidate to do that?

She knew. By her own admission, she knew her father had given them money to help finance the campaign. And yet she kept silent. Throughout the campaign and afterward, she insisted it was her money—hers and Joe's. Would it have been so hard to say, "My father has given us money in exchange for a piece of property Joe owns in Pittsburgh," as she said she believed? If there was nothing to hide, why try to hide it?

Even if she believed, as Joe kept saying, that the money actually existed, she knew Joe's access to it had been frozen, not only in the fall of 1994 but for the entire year thereafter. The fictional property was never sold. It had been a loan from her father to the campaign, not an asset transfer, if not by intention, then by default. Her father had received nothing in payment from her and Joe in return for his $2 million. And yet Joe continued to borrow more. She knew that. But Enid said and did nothing.

She said nothing during the campaign. She said nothing for her first year in Congress. She did not report the transaction on her financial disclosure forms, either as a loan or as an asset exchange. Why didn't she make sure she saw those forms before signing them?

She told me that she did not think she needed to be more detailed in her financial disclosure and campaign finance forms because she believed what she had spent in the campaign was her money. She insisted that she thought she was doing nothing wrong. "Whether I got it from recycling cans or from a house I owned, this was my money. Whether I found it in a gutter, or sold an asset I believed I owned, it was my money."

But it wasn't.

According to the Federal Election Commission, any financial transactions used to fund campaigns must be commercially reasonable transactions. The only kind of loans permitted, other than directly from the candidate, is from banks. Ordinarily, when people sell a house, they do not receive any money for it until the ownership is legally transferred. Candidates can sell assets to finance their campaigns, but they have to do it the way anyone else would. If someone gives a candidate money and does not receive something immediately in return, such as property, it is a loan, according to FEC spokesman Ian Stirton.

Robert Bauer, a Washington attorney who specializes in campaign law and represents Democratic clients, said he believes the Enid Greene case was "an effort on her part to generate cash for the campaign and circumvent contribution limits. . . . It was devised solely for the purpose of allowing the father to exceed his contribution limit." Bauer said the 1994 transaction between Greene and her father "doesn't satisfy any of the requirements of federal campaign finance law. It was window dressing for justifying the transfer of funds."

Jan Wietold Baran is a Washington election law specialist who represents Republicans. Perhaps his most famous client is Newt Gingrich, whom he represented during the investigation by the House Ethics Committee. Baran said in order for any transfer of assets to be permissible to finance a campaign, there would have to be something to "memorialize the transaction, such as a contract or bill of sale," even if family members were involved—especially if family members were involved. "Any purchaser would want to be sure they aren't buying a pig in a poke," said Baran.

* * *

One Salt Lake City Democrat called Enid and Joe "the Bonnie and Clyde of Utah politics." "This is a story about ambition and insanity," a former friend of the couple's told *George* magazine. "She was ambitious and he was nuts."

Even those who don't believe Enid still admit to feeling some sympathy for her situation. Here was a woman who only wanted one thing her whole life and who had achieved it. And then overnight it was all taken away from her—her political career, her husband, her future. Well, maybe not her future. Enid remains coy about her political plans. Many who know her believe it's quite possible she hopes to make another run for Congress. All she would have to do is say charges were never filed against her and it was all Joe's fault.

It was clear when I interviewed her in 1997 that she had not given up her political ambitions, just put them on hold. When I asked her if she would run for office again, she responded, "I have no idea, but I don't think I'm disqualified from it."

After a few years people forget, don't they?

Governor Mike Leavitt compared what happened to Enid to the political equivalent of being hit by a cab and left a quadriplegic. "People recover. I don't know whether she will or she won't. Time will tell."

Ultimately, this story is much more than a sordid soap opera with an uncertain conclusion. It is important because it involves major election fraud. And because it says so much about the way we finance our campaigns today, about the ever growing need for more and more millions.

Enid was the candidate. It was her name on the ballot, and it was she who was sworn in as a member of the House of Representatives after having spent about $2 million of her father's money to get there.

Fighting the temptation she must have felt to take a big swing at the woman who had thrown her out of office, Democrat Karen Shepherd remained silent after the whole fiasco became public, choosing not to comment. No one would have blamed her for loudly declaring the election had been stolen from her. Maybe Enid would have won even without the extra $2 million. It was a good year for Republican challengers. But Karen Shepherd will never know, and neither will the voters.

In mounting her congressional candidacy, Enid had declared herself above reproach. She was for term limits, a balanced budget, changing the way Congress does business, and cleaning up the system. Yet her election became the very symbol of the disconnect between campaign pronouncements and candidate behavior. As Utah Democrat Paul Svendsen stated, "No wonder people are so turned off by politics."

"Just say it was bizarre," Steve Taggart said of the Enid and Joe story as he ended one of our interviews. Indeed it was a bizarre and terribly sad chapter in the history of Utah politics and the 104th Congress.

15

GOVERNMENT SHUTDOWN II

IN LATE OCTOBER 1995, just a few days before her personal financial problems started to become public in a big way, Enid Waldholtz introduced legislation to limit the gifts, meals, and paid travel expenses that House members and their staffs could accept. It was similar to the legislation the Senate had passed in July, which prohibited gifts to members of more than $50 and set a limit of $100 a year from a single source.

But in the space of a few short weeks, Waldholtz had gone from freshman class star to class embarrassment, and hers was not the face the Republicans wanted to have out front for ethics reform. Some of her GOP colleagues snickered quietly, but others who opposed any change in the gift rules openly criticized Waldholtz's support for the legislation at a time when her personal integrity was in question, suggesting she was trying to divert attention from her own problems. As a result, when the gift legislation reached the floor, Waldholtz decided to stay in her office and watch the debate on her TV monitor rather than manage her bill on the floor.

Although the pressure to do something was great, the Republican House conference was deeply divided over how to handle gift reform. On one side, led by Chris Shays of Connecticut, were the reformers, who had been pushing for action for months. On the other, led by Dan Burton of Indiana, was a group of senior Republicans who thought a few cosmetic changes were all that was needed to deal with the issue. And although the freshmen were publicly identified with the reform movement because of people like Linda Smith and Sam Brownback, the class was far from united in favor of reform. There were plenty of business-as-usual members in the class, people like Bob Barr of Georgia and class president Roger Wicker of Mississippi.

When the gift legislation came to the floor on November 16, Burton offered an amendment to remove the bill's toughest provisions and leave in place the existing rules for gifts and travel while simply adding a reporting provision that would require members to disclose any gifts over $50. Some of the reformers referred to the members who supported the Burton approach as the "golf caucus" because of the golf, tennis, and ski trips sponsored by lobbyists that they were so fond of taking and that would be permitted to continue if the Burton amendment passed. Burton's amendment did not pass, but it did receive 154 votes, including those of 108 Republicans and 29 of the GOP freshmen.

The gift measure passed by the House was actually tougher than the Senate's legislation. Gingrich, who had helped to kill a Democratic-sponsored gift ban proposal in the previous Congress, had seemingly become a born-again gift ban proponent. Gingrich recommended that if the House was going to act on the issue, it would be better for the members if they banned gifts altogether. Gingrich suggested this would be a simpler rule for members to comply with rather than trying to keep track of small gifts and risk inadvertently violating the $100 annual limit from a single person.

And the total gift ban as recommended by Gingrich passed the House overwhelmingly, 422–6. Once the Burton amendment had been defeated and a vote on the ban was inevitable, it was destined to be virtually unanimous, since no member wanted to go on the record as being in favor of continuing to receive gifts from lobbyists.

Once enacted at the beginning of 1996, the total gift ban proved to be especially unpopular with staff members, many of whom worked long hours and received relatively low salaries. They would no longer be allowed to be taken out for a meal by a lobbyist, and they would have to refuse the small goodies that come to members, especially around Christmas, things like fruit baskets and tins of popcorn that were passed around the office.

But the members found ways around the ban, especially in regard to trips. Trips, even those sponsored by corporations and lobbyists, would still be permitted if it could be argued they had some educational or fact-finding purpose. From a lobbyist's perspective, this was even better than the old rules. Now if members accepted free trips, they would at least have to sit through a presentation rather than just hitting the golf course once they arrived. And almost anything was still OK if it involved campaign fund-raising.

Action on lobbying reform was put off until the end of November, after members returned from their Thanksgiving break. The rules governing lobbyists had not been significantly changed in 50 years, and as a result only about 6,000 people were registered as lobbyists, although it was estimated that perhaps as many as ten times that number actually lobbied Congress and the executive branch of the federal government. The proposed lobbying registration and disclosure legislation was an effort to remedy that situation. It would require individuals who spend at least 20 percent of their time lobbying and those who receive or spend $5,000 or more for lobbying over a six-month period to register with Congress as lobbyists. Any company that spends at least $20,000 for lobbying any branch of the federal government in a six-month period would also have to register. Lobbyists would be required to disclose whom they represented, whom they lobbied, what they were lobbying for, and how much they were being paid. And failure to comply with the rules would be punishable by fines of up to $50,000.

As with the gift ban, the Republicans were far from united on lobbying reform, and there were dozens of amendments that members wanted to offer. Some were seen as legitimate improvements of the bill, but many were perceived simply as an effort to kill it. Perhaps the most contentious of the potential amendments was the Istook-McIntosh measure to limit the lobbying of nonprofit groups, which had been resurrected for the umpteenth time. But after four other amendments went down and it was clear the pro-reformers had convinced a majority of members to leave the lobbying bill alone, Istook and McIntosh, as well as the rest of those hoping to amend the bill, decided not to try. On November 29, with remarkably little debate, a lobbying reform bill just like that unanimously passed by the Senate in July was passed by the House, 421–0.

The 104th Congress was now on record as approving gift and lobbying reform. These were reform measures the members could legitimately point to as accomplishments. But when it came to changes in campaign financing law, which hit much closer to home and directly affected the way members raised money and ran for reelection, reform would have to wait.

*   *   *

During consideration of the gift and lobbying reform measures, the attention of the Republican leaders remained focused on their budget negotiations with the White House and their rapidly approaching deadline.

But the possibility of a second government shutdown did not worry the freshmen as it should have. Although Clinton seemed slavishly attentive to what the polls were saying about the budget standoff, the Republicans, in particular the freshmen, seemed completely oblivious to them. The freshmen believed their course was the correct one because they believed in a mythical mandate they thought they had received from the voters when they were elected one year earlier. The freshmen arrived in Washington not to make the federal government work better but to dismantle it, to balance the budget using their priorities.

But as the end of their first year in Congress approached, it was no longer clear the country shared their vision. Had their mandate disappeared, or had it simply never been there to begin with? The 1994 election did not represent an overwhelming endorsement of the Republican agenda and all of its details, as most of the freshmen believed. Polls showed many voters did not even know what the Contract with America was. The election was far more a reflection of anger and frustration over the way Clinton and the Democrats had been handling the government. It was more anti-Democrat than it was pro-Republican. The voters were rejecting the Democrats' big government approach to health care reform and their seeming inability to get anything done. Americans did support reforming Congress. They wanted smaller, more accountable government. And a balanced budget *sounded* good. But when the details of the GOP plan started taking shape and the Republican Congress began making the cuts necessary actually to balance the budget, many Americans balked. They wanted to cut wasteful government programs, not the ones they used.

* * *

So much of what went wrong in the 104th Congress came down to the fact that the Republicans just hadn't given enough thought to how they were going to run things once they took over. They came up with a nifty campaign plan, some good slogans and buzzwords, some basic tenets about balancing the budget and cutting government. But Gingrich and company had no real game plan for what came next. They were making it up as they went along. All of Gingrich's energy was directed at taking over the House; he gave little if any thought to the actual governing, to what happened after the public relations boost of the first 100 days was over.

It's a quantum leap from minority whip to Speaker of the House. The skills and talents that make one a good warrior do not necessarily make one a good governor. As a member of the minority, Gingrich had focused for so many years on the struggle of overthrowing the Democrats that he hadn't paid too much attention to how a bill becomes a law. It isn't by one party in one house in one branch of government attempting to dictate its will to everyone else. The checks and balances the Founding Fathers put in place ensured that.

The Republican majority was painfully small. In November there were 233 House Republicans, 199 Democrats, and one independent who invariably voted with the Democrats. The Republicans had a margin of only 16 votes. It's not wise to attempt large changes, "revolutionary" changes, on the basis of such a slim majority.

The Republicans had forgotten about the Democrats and all the people they had been elected to represent. They thought they didn't have to deal with the Democrats. That they could run the government without them. In their haste to remake the world in their image, they discounted the presence of a Democratic president and plenty of Democratic members of Congress still hanging around. They forgot about the veto. Clinton may have looked ineffectual and indecisive to them in the fall of 1994; he may have looked even more so in January when even he felt compelled to declare that he was still relevant. But soon enough, in the autumn of 1995, the Republicans learned just how relevant he was.

The president became aware of how important it was for him to stand firm against the Republicans not only to counter his image as someone willing to cave in, someone who never stood up for any principle, but also because it endeared him to his core constituencies. Clinton kind of snuck up on the Republicans. They weren't counting on his standing up for principle. Or standing up period.

* * *

Clinton stood up on December 6 when he vetoed the Republicans' seven-year budget plan, the plan that contained tax cuts, welfare reform, and Medicare spending reductions. He did it using the same pen Lyndon Johnson had used 30 years earlier to sign the law that created Medicare. "With this veto, the extreme Republican effort to balance the budget through wrongheaded cuts and misplaced priorities is over. Now it's up to all of us to go back to work together to show we can balance the budget and be true to our values and our economic interests," Clinton declared. The president said the legislation he was vetoing contained "the biggest Medicare and Medicaid cuts in history, deep cuts in education, a rollback in environmental protection, and a tax increase on working families."

Gingrich's response to the veto? "The president needs to recognize that Lyndon Johnson's Great Society has failed."

That day Gingrich had bigger and much more personal concerns than Clinton's veto. He had been informed by the House Ethics Committee that after a 15-month investigation into ethics charges that had been filed against him, the committee had decided to take action on one of the charges. An outside counsel would be appointed to look into the question of whether Gingrich violated tax law by accepting tax-deductible donations to finance a college course he taught that was sponsored by a private foundation. The committee said it would take no action on any of the other complaints, although it said Gingrich had violated House rules by allowing a political adviser to use his office; promoting tapes of his college lectures and giving out an 800 number that could be used to purchase them in a speech on the House floor; and using the House floor to publicize a meeting sponsored by GOPAC, his political action committee.

Later Gingrich would tell the *Washington Post* he wept openly with his wife, Marianne, in his office when he was informed of the committee's decision. He was relieved that he had been cleared of all but one of the charges but knew the investigation would continue to hang over him into 1996, an election year. The announcement that there would be a further investigation into possible wrongdoing by Gingrich could only add to his unpopularity with the public. Gingrich's problems had begun even before the 104th Congress was sworn in with the flap over the $4.5 million deal for his book *To Renew America*. But bolstered by his new status as number one Republican, Gingrich had toyed with the idea of running for president and did not discourage speculation or rule out the possibility that he was thinking about making a run.

In the beginning of the session he seemed to be everywhere—holding news conferences, doing interviews, making inflammatory off-the-cuff statements, appearing on the Sunday morning public affairs shows. If he wasn't complaining about his seat on Air Force One, he was suggesting that the actions of Susan Smith, a South Carolina woman who had driven her car into a lake and drowned her children, was an example of how sick American society had become and how much in need of change. Then he commented on the grisly murder of a young woman in Chicago whose unborn child had been cut from her stomach. The event was part of "what the welfare system has created," Gingrich said, to which a relative of the woman responded that Gingrich should "remove our family tragedy from his political rhetoric."

Many of the freshmen had been hearing from their constituents for months that the Speaker should tone it down, and they were starting to be concerned about how he might affect their own reelection. "Tell Newt to shut up," one Republican said he heard back home.

Gingrich had gone from seeming larger than life at the beginning of the session to being a seriously wounded leader by the end of 1995. His low approval ratings in national polls reflected people's uneasiness over his personal style. By the time the government had reopened after its first shutdown, the public seemed to have had enough of him, and Gingrich seemed to have got the message. In late November Gingrich held a press conference in his Georgia district and made it clear he would not run for president, that he intended to focus on running the House.

*   *   *

The relationship between House Speaker Newt Gingrich and his freshmen was similar to that of a father and his teenage children. Like a father, Gingrich took pride in their accomplishments along with the knowledge that he gave them life. And like adolescents, the freshmen were eager to show their independence and at times distance themselves from Gingrich, especially when he did something to embarrass them.

Gingrich and the GOP House leaders were generally given credit by the national press for winning majority control of the House. That's not exactly how the freshmen saw it. Gingrich did create a national theme and message for the election and help many of the freshmen with fund-raising, campaign appearances, and strategy advice. But most of the freshmen didn't think they owed Gingrich all that much. That might appear just a bit ungrateful, but the freshmen believed they had run local races, spent a lot of their own money, and got to Congress on their own. And a few of the freshmen even openly admitted that it wasn't Gingrich or the Contract with America that got them elected but the voters' dissatisfaction with Clinton.

"Gingrich didn't get me elected. Newt Gingrich came down and campaigned for me, but he didn't win my race. Newt Gingrich didn't elect any of us. The Republican Party didn't elect any of us," Joe Scarborough of Florida told me in early December. "If George Bush had been reelected, a lot of us wouldn't have been swept into office, a lot of us wouldn't have run. We felt a sense of urgency when Bill Clinton got elected. We got pulled off the couch. We were angry with what was going on in Washington."

Gingrich alternately played the schoolmaster, drill sergeant, and team captain to the freshmen, and although they respected his political instincts and vision, he did not appear to have engendered much fondness among them. Many of the freshmen considered him a brilliant political strategist, but they also considered him arrogant and aloof. "We've all got respect for him, but he's not the warm and fuzzy type," said Scarborough. As we got on an elevator in the Capitol building, Scarborough pointed to liberal Democrat Neil Abercrombie of Hawaii, who was also riding in the elevator. "Neil probably has more affection for the Speaker than most of the freshmen,"

Scarborough quipped. With the exception of Sue Myrick and David McIntosh, the class representatives to the leadership, most of the freshmen didn't have much of a personal relationship with Gingrich. "Most of his relating to the freshmen has been when he had to have us on a vote," said Van Hilleary.

Certainly the Speaker, through his intellect and drive, was able early in the session to bring about a level of party discipline that the Democrats could only dream of. But the freshmen had proved themselves willing to rebel on several occasions throughout the year—such as defeating a rule over funding of the National Endowment for the Arts and voting against the defense appropriations bill. They were just using the same tactics Gingrich had used as a young backbencher, and angry though their leader must have been at times, it's hard to imagine he also didn't occasionally have to stifle a grin at their antics.

The Democrats and many members of the press never completely understood the relationship between Gingrich and the freshmen. At the beginning of the year, they perceived the 73 newcomers as following him blindly and referred to them as "Newt's ninnies" and "Gingrich clones." Then when Gingrich started looking a bit vulnerable, the assumption was that the freshmen would run for cover. But neither assessment was entirely accurate. Even before the 104th Congress started, the freshmen signaled they were willing to take on Gingrich when they put forward the idea of term limits for the Speakership. Even he was considered expendable to the cause.

The ultraconservative True Believers in the class frequently used religious analogies to describe what they were trying to do with their revolution. Shortly after his election, Lindsey Graham of South Carolina told *Congressional Quarterly,* "I trust Newt Gingrich to lead us to the promised land, but the Good Lord never let Moses go. We'll do to him what the Good Lord did to Moses." And Scarborough said, "We remain independent and suspicious of the entire leadership. We've got a responsibility to ask tough questions."

The freshmen's feelings about Gingrich were based primarily on whether they thought he was an asset or a liability to the cause. Shortly after the Ethics Committee announcement, the *Washington Post* ran a story in which freshman Mark Foley of Florida stated, "This ethics proceeding is a serious problem for all of us. If we're going to impose gift bans on members and require everyone to file lobbying reports, then we have to be clean ourselves. I know he must be agonizing, but everyone remembers that he attacked the ethics of [former] speaker [Jim] Wright, and now all this is just coming back to roost." In a reference to Gingrich's book deal, Foley said, "Four million dollars for someone who never wrote a book before? Come on! It's not like he's John Grisham." When asked if he thought Gingrich should step down as Speaker, Foley tepidly replied, "I don't think it's appropriate—at this point."

What was interesting about Foley's remarks was that he came from a relatively safe Republican district and did not face a tough reelection race. Nor was he one of the conservative freshmen who were the most upset with Gingrich about the compromises he was making. Foley was a moderate, an affable guy who was willing to talk to the *Washington Post.* He wasn't trying to send a message. He was just saying what he thought. If he had been trying to help himself with his constituents by distancing himself from Gingrich, he would have made the remarks to a local reporter, Foley would tell me later. After his comments appeared in the *Post,* Foley said, "Everyone was flipping out for a brief moment." But he apologized to Gingrich, and the Speaker did not appear to be visibly angry with him.

Although Foley's quotes got more attention, the words of fellow Florida freshman David Weldon were more enlightening. Weldon actually told the *Post* he wished Gingrich could be more like his low-key Democratic predecessor, Speaker Tom Foley. "The revolution to restore confidence in government transcends Newt Gingrich. He may have gotten the movement started, he may have been the engineer who got the train rolling, but now the train doesn't need him to run down the tracks. It's more powerful than him," said Weldon.

Nothing could more perfectly sum up the feeling the freshmen had about Gingrich—and the rest of the senior Republicans, for that matter. This wasn't personal. It had nothing to do with Gingrich, except for the concern that his occasional verbal missteps and willingness to cut deals detracted from their message and their mission. Even George Nethercutt of Washington, one of the older and more statesmanlike members of the freshman class, expressed frustration over some of Gingrich's remarks to the press: "There's a higher purpose here than one man. These are revolutionary times; they deserve some discipline by our leaders." Nethercutt and the freshmen encouraged Gingrich to let other GOP members serve as public spokespeople for the party. And Gingrich agreed that he would keep a lower profile.

Mark Neumann, too, was losing patience with Gingrich. "He should play poker. I don't know how to read him. Some days I think he's a liberal; some days I think he's a moderate; some days I think he's a True Believer. I'm not really sure what he is."

The freshmen were afraid Gingrich was going to cut a deal with the president and sell them out. The True Believers trusted Armey more than Gingrich. They were really conservatives first and Republicans second. Their allegiance ran just as deep to conservative groups that helped get them elected, like the National Rifle Association, small business owners, and the Christian Coalition, as it did to the Republican Party.

The biggest complaint the freshmen had about Gingrich was his willingness to compromise in the time-honored congressional tradition. Their impatience was fueled by their relative lack of political experience. Van Hilleary considered Gingrich a "classic politician" who "says he's not going to give an inch and waits until the last minute and then gives as little as he can." Hilleary thought Gingrich should stand firm more often and not give at all. "You have to work harder to do it that way, but in the end you gain more credibility." It was more important to the freshmen to be right than it was to be liked or to cut a deal. They were the very antithesis of politicians.

Gingrich may have been impatient with the freshmen's stubbornness, but he understood that he held the Speakership because of them, and he knew that to hold on to it the freshmen would have to keep their seats. If that meant they needed to take a few jabs at him from time to time, so be it. Likewise, the freshmen knew they had clout and visibility the likes of which no previous freshman class had ever enjoyed largely because Gingrich had given them a powerful role. The freshmen might get impatient now and again, but they were not about to throw Gingrich overboard—at least not yet.

Gingrich may have wondered what kind of genie he had unleashed by empowering the freshmen, but it was too late to shove them back into the bottle. When Ross Perot announced in August that he planned to start a third party, Gingrich quipped that he already had a third party in the House: "It's called the freshman class."

Just before Gingrich was named *Time*'s man of the year in mid-December, conservative George Will wrote in one of his columns that if *Time* did not name Gingrich, it should select the House freshmen, "who set the tone, and much of the agenda, for 1995." Even with all the attention they had already received, the freshmen seemed to crave more. And the national press wanted to give it to them. Reporters were pressing for end-of-the-year interviews with the "revolting freshmen," as ABC's "Nightline" called them. Zach Wamp took charge of setting up something called "tiger teams" with about 25 of the freshmen to meet with reporters from all the major national media outlets. Journalists were invited to sit down with the freshmen to hear them extol the accomplishments of the class of '94.

Wamp declared the freshmen the conscience of the Congress and said if they hadn't been there standing tough, insisting on a balanced budget, that their leaders would have already cut a deal with Clinton and everybody would be headed home early for a holiday break. The freshmen claimed that they had changed the very culture of Washington and the idea that members of Congress were simply interested in bringing as much pork back to their districts as they could.

The freshmen did not think they should give Clinton another CR to keep the government open unless he presented a real plan with real numbers that would balance the budget in seven years. They had opposed the reopening of the government in November without that. Many of the freshmen would tell me later they believed reopening the government without a firm plan from the White House was one of the biggest tactical mistakes their leaders made.

*   *   *

After Clinton vetoed the Republican budget plan on December 6, he agreed to present his own budget. It would be his third budget proposal of the year. But the plan he offered fell far short of what the Republicans said it would take to balance the budget. And Clinton knew it. Even the *Washington Post* and the *New York Times* editorial pages said so. It was not a serious offer.

The budget negotiations were going nowhere, and there seemed to be almost as much tension between Gingrich and Senate majority leader Bob Dole as there was between the Republicans and the White House. Gingrich and Dole were very different sorts of men. Dole had allowed Gingrich to take the lead on legislation and hog the spotlight for the first 10 months of the year, but by December he had clearly had enough. Dole was running for president, and the budget negotiations and government shutdowns were starting to get in the way. Maybe they would never be able to get a long-term agreement with Clinton on tax cuts and Medicare spending. But that didn't mean they couldn't finish up work on the 1996 federal budget and keep the government operating, he argued.

Dole and Clinton agreed in principle to try to avoid a second government shutdown and keep the government running while they negotiated, but the House Republicans would not go along with the deal. The temporary 30-day funding measure that had ended the first government shutdown was set to expire at midnight on Friday, December 15. And the two sides weren't close to any sort of agreement.

Although negotiators including Leon Panetta and Alice Rivlin, the director of the Office of Management and Budget, and GOP House and Senate budget chairmen John Kasich and Pete Domenici met the day the funding ran out, they got nowhere. Meanwhile majority leader Dick Armey was on the House floor saying he was "bitterly disappointed" by the president's "meager offer" and announcing that a continuing resolution to keep the government running was not going to be an option.

Late in the afternoon the Republican leaders met, Sue Myrick and David McIntosh were there representing the freshmen. Gingrich went around the room and asked everyone whether Congress should pass a CR. One by one they all said no. Gingrich wanted Dole to see what he was up against.

At 5 P.M. the entire Republican House conference met in a large hearing room on the first floor of the Longworth House Office Building, and at 5:30 Clinton appeared in the White House press room to discuss the budget talks. Clinton blamed the Republicans for the failure to reach a budget agreement and said the Republicans had refused to negotiate "unless we agreed right now to make deep and unconscionable cuts in Medicare and Medicaid."

A throng of reporters waited in the foyer of the Longworth Building for the House Republican leaders to come out of their meeting. Kasich tried to remain calm as he walked out to face them. He didn't want to call Clinton a liar, not directly, anyway. "The president didn't give the full story," Kasich began. The White House "still has not come to the table with a real plan. We've told them, 'This is our program; just lay yours down.' . . . In terms of closing the government, it's not our decision. All the president has to do is make a good-faith effort. . . . We're going to be here. He can call us at midnight, tomorrow afternoon, tomorrow night, Sunday morning, Sunday night. . . . The minute we get that call we'll voice vote a CR through on the floor."

But the president didn't call.

The next day, Saturday, December 16, government shutdown II began. Because several spending bills had been signed by the president since the November shutdown, only about 300,000 of the federal government's 2 million civilian workers would be affected this time. That meant for each day the government remained closed it would cost the Treasury $40 million in back wages that would have to be paid to federal employees who were not working.

On Monday the stock market dropped 100 points; market analysts blamed the fear of a long budget stalemate. Clinton, declaring that it was "wrong for the Congress to shut the government down just to make a political point a week before

Christmas," vetoed Republican bills to fund the Departments of the Interior and Housing and Urban Development as well as the Environmental Protection Agency. But he called Gingrich and Dole and invited them to come to the White House for a negotiating session the next day that would include Vice President Al Gore.

At the negotiating session on Tuesday, December 19, Clinton refused to offer a formal plan, but the Republicans still thought the meeting went pretty well. They even talked about passing a temporary measure to reopen the government if it looked like progress was being made in the talks and the president was headed toward offering a seven-year budget plan that would be calculated by the Congressional Budget Office (CBO). Outside, before going back up to the Hill, Gingrich stopped to tell reporters what he thought had been settled. But after watching Gingrich on television, Gore went down to the press room and ticked off the Republicans by seeming to go back on what they believed Clinton had agreed to. When Gingrich met with his troops later, not only the freshmen but a majority of the Republican conference remained opposed to passing a CR until the White House coughed up a legitimate balanced budget plan.

The next day Clinton appeared in the White House press room and blasted the freshmen. Although he didn't name names, everybody knew whom he was talking about. Clinton said he wondered whether Gingrich was in charge of his troops or whether "the tail will keep wagging the dog over there." Clinton said he and the Senate, led by Dole, had wanted to reopen the government, but "the most extreme members of the House of Representatives rejected that agreement. . . . This very conservative group, the antigovernment group, what they really want is to end the role of the federal government in our life."

That night all three major TV network news shows led with Clinton's statements and the assertion that the freshmen were holding up a budget deal. The president had called them extremists. He blamed them for the government shutdown. The freshmen were actually kind of pleased. They had blue badges made up that said, "I'm A FRESHMAN . . . and Proud of It!" that they started wearing on the floor of the House.

"In this instance demonization is the most sincere form of flattery," said Arizona's J. D. Hayworth. "If you think we're going to be Monty Hall, we're not. We're standing up for what we believe in." Washington state's Rick White used a slightly loftier analogy. He compared the freshmen to George Washington at Valley Forge.

The freshmen were now even bigger news. They were invited on the Larry King show on CNN, "Meet the Press" on NBC, and were featured on ABC's "Nightline." Scarborough told Larry King, "We have a do-nothing president who feels like he gains political advantage by trying to point at us while refusing everything. . . . This is a president who's more interested in polls than balancing the budget. We have decided to do it, and if we take heat for a couple of months, that's fine." King tried to offer some fatherly advice to the freshmen: Because the polls showed the public was with the president, they'd better try something new, he suggested.

A lot of the freshmen despised Clinton. When the annual White House Christmas party for members of Congress was held, many of the freshmen, including Mark

Souder, refused to go. Souder couldn't imagine being in the same room with Bill Clinton. And he certainly couldn't imagine going to the White House while Clinton was occupying it. But in early December Souder was part of a group of freshmen (including Scarborough, Shadegg, Neumann, McIntosh, and Wicker) who met with Office of Management and Budget (OMB) director Alice Rivlin. The freshmen wanted to try to find out what the administration's bottom line was and to let the White House know how serious they were about balancing the budget in seven years. The freshmen were tired of having all their information filtered through their leaders and the media.

All of the arguing about Medicare and who would score the budget plan (the CBO or the OMB) was just so much game playing, as the freshmen saw it. It was the old way of doing things. It was actually pretty simple, they told Rivlin. No matter what else happened, they were not willing to spend more than $12 trillion over the next seven years. "What we had to say was, 'Here's the money. Spend it however you want,'" said Souder. The Senate had added money to the budget that was passed by the House, and the freshmen decided they had already compromised enough.

But Souder said even Budget chairman Kasich was uncomfortable with a firm spending limit because he thought that would make a deal with the White House more difficult to achieve. You had to be able to play with the numbers a little bit. Souder said Kasich was "annoyed to find out we had our own separate meeting with Rivlin." Kasich was worried the freshmen would "screw up whatever is going on because we don't know what we're doing."

After the freshmen met with Rivlin, class president Wicker got a late-night phone call from Clinton. "The man wouldn't stop talking," Wicker later told Souder. During the 25-minute call, Clinton told Wicker that if they used the more generous OMB estimates, there would be more room for the tax cuts the Republicans wanted. "The president is about as smooth as I've ever seen," said the former Mississippi state legislator, who had more than a passing familiarity with the word "smooth." Clinton told Wicker it was the freshmen who had the most to gain from reaching a balanced budget agreement.

Souder speculated that Clinton's reaching out to the freshmen was an attempt to "play mind games with our leadership." If the president could figure out what the freshmen's bottom line was, then the GOP leadership couldn't lie to him about it or blame the freshmen for not being able to reach a deal. But the presidential phone call was also an acknowledgment that Washington had changed dramatically. Could anyone imagine Ronald Reagan (or even George Bush, for that matter) calling up a freshman Democrat to talk about the budget?

Clinton felt no urgency to settle the budget standoff. Instead, he was posturing, feinting, trying to drum up anxiety over what the GOP budget would do. The more he stood up to the Republicans, the better his poll numbers got. And all the while the Democratic National Committee was running ads touting Clinton as the protector of the elderly, the environment, and education programs. By year's end, the committee had spent nearly $20 million airing the ads in almost half of the nation's media markets. The election was still 12 months away. There hadn't been a single presidential primary yet. The Clinton administration had become the first presidency to be marketed on TV.

The government shutdown had broken all historical records. Since 1980 there had been nine government shutdowns because of temporary funding gaps, but most of them had been over a weekend and none had lasted more than three days. That was until the shutdown in November. Now government shutdown II was headed into its second week.

"We're going to stand for principle, the consequences be damned," Shadegg told the *Washington Post*. "Our resolve is stronger than ever, and we're solid as a rock. There's no quit in this freshman class. We're going to keep pushing," declared Randy Tate. On Friday, December 22, House Appropriations chairman Robert Livingston, in Churchillian fashion, declared on the House floor, "We will never, never, never give in. We will stay here till Doomsday." But a few hours later members of Congress headed home for the holidays.

Before the freshmen left town, Gil Gutknecht of Minnesota gave Joe Scarborough a note with a quote from a Civil War Union soldier talking about the Confederates. "They fight like men crazed, because they flat do not care." Gutknecht had written on the paper, "Great way to describe the freshmen."

16

WE GOT YOU BABE

SONNY BONO DIDN'T REALLY CONSIDER HIMSELF A PART OF THE FRESHMAN CLASS. He rarely went to freshman class meetings and didn't participate in any of the freshman groups like the New Federalists. Except for his straight party-line voting record, he didn't have much in common with his classmates. Only three other freshmen (Fred Heineman of North Carolina, Wes Cooley of Oregon, and Jack Metcalf of Washington) were older than Bono's 59 years and most were 20 years younger. Born during the Depression, he was old enough to remember World War II. But his classmates were baby boomers, just children in the 1960s, when Bono met Cher and began making records.

He was certainly more colorful than the other freshmen. Bono was on his fourth marriage by the time he was elected to Congress and had met his current wife, Mary, when she was 22 and he was 50. He had 10 gold records. He had seen and done more than most of the freshmen could even imagine. Much of it he recounts in his 1991 autobiography, *And the Beat Goes On*. The book (written without a ghostwriter) chronicles his youth, the ups and downs of Sonny and Cher's show business career, their marriage, and his life after Cher up to the point where he entered politics and became mayor of Palm Springs, California. A ghostwriter no doubt would have counseled against some of the more embarrassing personal revelations and literary excesses of the book, such as appear on the first page, where Bono describes campaigning for mayor outside a Palm Springs senior center: "The hot sun was covering the vast Cochella Valley like a first coat of paint. I sipped from a cup of coffee."

Bono happily recounts his childhood encounters with the opposite sex: "Finally, the mystery was going to be unraveled—er, revealed. . . . Nervous, I wanted to get as good and as close a look at her thing as possible when she lifted her dress." And at 10 years old, he and a neighbor girl took their clothes off under his parents' house: "Can I touch it? She reached out. Ah-huh, I said. Can I feel yours too?"

Why he included such revelations or thought they would be of interest remains a mystery. But the book is nothing if not revelatory. He holds little back and is perfectly comfortable poking fun at himself throughout. Therein lies the secret to Bono's success. He may not be the smartest guy around, but he's the first one to say so. He may be the court jester, but he's laughing along with everyone else. And he has convinced his constituents that despite his wealth and celebrity status, he's just one of them. He speaks their language because he's just an average guy. At the very beginning of his memoirs, Bono addresses head-on the two things most often said about him by mentioning the names people used to call him when he ran for mayor: "the ex–Mr. Cher" and "Sonny Bonehead."

Bono's mother was the daughter of immigrants; his father was born in Italy. He describes himself as "a hardworking guy with a strict, blue-collar Italian background." Never good in school, he dropped out before finishing high school and says his father "was convinced that I was going to be a failure." Married for the first time at 19, he worked construction, bagging groceries and delivering meat before leaving his first wife and trying to make it in the music business. He met Cher when he was 26 and she was 16, and they quickly moved in together and started working on a musical career. They lived together for several years before he was divorced from his first wife, and it wasn't until long after their hit songs "I Got You Babe" in 1965 and "The Beat Goes On" in 1967 and after their daughter, Chastity, was born that they quietly got married.

In his book Bono admits to "more affairs than I could even remember" during his many marriages, including one incident with a secretary that Cher walked in on. "Working closely with someone, especially a female someone, you develop a rapport, which is what happened between me and this secretary. I gave a few flirtatious signals and found her receptive. One night the sparks flew and it happened. We made love in the office. I thought Cher was asleep. She wasn't. In the midst of our lovemaking, Cher walked into the workroom. The air was immediately let out of that balloon. There's nothing like having your wife catch you with your pants down to ruin an illicit romance. Cher didn't scream; she just glared at me and walked out of the room. I got the cold shoulder treatment for the rest of the week, but that was it."

And as one might expect from a book of this sort, he dishes on sex with Cher: "I wish that I were able to say I saw banners and fireworks the first time Cher and I made love, but I didn't. The physical part was fine, though I wouldn't equate it with a religious experience. . . . I like physical lovemaking, but I don't think Cher and I were ever that outlandishly physical. Maybe her other relationships were different. But it never really meshed with us. In the most intimate moments, Cher was reserved and protective. There was a part of her—and it still exists—that no one can get to." Bono was divorced from Cher in 1975, but it took him many years to leave her shadow.

Although he worked on the presidential campaigns of Robert Kennedy and then, after Kennedy's death, Hubert Humphrey in 1968, Bono later decided to become a Republican and says he voted for Reagan in 1984. But he was not even registered to vote when he decided to run for mayor. As he recounted many times, his entrance into politics occurred after he had moved to Palm Springs and opened a restaurant and encountered problems dealing with city hall over issues like building permits and putting up a sign. "I was Joe Q. Citizen—an honest, ordinary, but frustrated businessman, and I was not afraid to say what I thought."

After being elected in 1988, Bono pushed tourism and economic development, starting a Grand Prix auto race and the Palm Springs Film Festival. Since Palm Springs has a city manager to handle the budget and day-to-day operations of the city, Bono used his celebrity to promote Palm Springs and became something of a goodwill ambassador. But above all else, he remained a performer.

And what was politics except performing? The same principles applied. Bono called politics "the second oldest profession."

Bono served as mayor of Palm Springs for one term, surviving a recall attempt, and in 1992 made an unsuccessful run for the U.S. Senate, coming in third in the Republican primary and receiving only 17 percent of the vote. But in 1994 he spent more than $200,000 of his own money and easily won the race for California's open 44th District, a solidly Republican district. Bono played up the idea that he was not a slick, polished politician, and that appeared to be the key to his appeal.

When he arrived in Washington, all the national press knew about Bono was his past with Cher. As the most famous of the freshmen, he was the object of ridicule, but of course that was nothing new to Bono. *Time* magazine featured him in a "first 100 days Bono watch" in which they chronicled his daily schedule, highlighting the more frivolous items. But shortly after arriving in Washington, Bono did something to tame the national media lions and go a long way toward winning them over. He did it by making them laugh. Bono was invited to speak at the Washington Press Club Foundation's "Salute to Congress," which was televised on C-SPAN. He delivered a stream-of-consciousness riff on what it was like to be a member of Congress, skewering Republicans and Democrats alike and puncturing the pomposity and phoniness of Washington. It left the all-star audience rolling in the aisles.

Bono began by telling the crowd he had been encouraged not to be serious but rather to be funny in his remarks. "Evidently, none of you know what I've gone through to be serious," he deadpanned. Without mentioning Cher's name, he said, "You remember the other woman, of course, and she wasn't easy to shake when I wanted to pursue this career."

Newt Gingrich called Bono's performance "one of the most vividly wonderful explanations of the insanity of this process by which we govern ourselves" that he had ever heard. And Gingrich told Bono he would never follow him onstage again. Bono said he found Gingrich to be "a fascinating fellow" who always seemed to be smiling. "He'll rip your head off from a smile."

"I am so pleased that we are all so dedicated to mankind, unlike show business, where . . . you have egomaniacs and you have power mongers and you have elitists. . . . Here I am now part of this wonderful institution," said Bono.

"I love this game. I think it's fascinating," he said of politics. To Bono, it was a game. It was all just show business in a different form, and this was simply the latest incarnation of a man who had reinvented himself a dozen times. Bono didn't mind if people called him "Sonny" instead of "Congressman Bono." He knew that reruns of "The Sonny and Cher Show" were running on cable TV late at night, and he knew that TV fame had a lot to do with his getting elected.

After his appearance at the press club, Bono said he knew it was important to make a good impression his first time out. "If you don't score right away, you're in trouble. I chose to go ahead and cut loose. It kind of established who I was. It changed the perception of me. I think I got a leg up by going to that event. You can tell when you score and when you don't if you're a performer, and it scored. It was an observation about what this place is all about, a parody on how serious we all think we are. There was a message there."

When Bono was running for mayor, he and Cher were invited to be on David Letterman's late-night television talk show. Cher was starring in the film *Moonstruck* at the time. It would be the first time in 10 years that Sonny and Cher had sung together, and their rendition of "I Got You Babe" that night would be a classic television moment.

After being elected to Congress, Bono continued to be invited on the Letterman show and was also occasionally featured in Letterman's opening monologue. In August 1995 Bono made an appearance on the show in which he discussed Whitewater and Bill Clinton's presidency. When Letterman asked Bono if he thought he would be reelected, he replied, "People are tired of professional politicians; they want people from the streets."

Apart from his Letterman show appearances and his willingness to do fund-raisers for his fellow Republicans, Bono distinguished himself mainly for his complaints as a member of the Judiciary Committee that the other members were using too much legal jargon for him to understand what was going on and for his rambling speeches on the House floor.

One could point to virtually any Bono floor speech for its incomprehensibility, such as a statement on November 18 during the first government shutdown. Bono offered an excellent example of how not to address the House. "I came here because I did not understand all this rhetoric that is going on. I still do not understand it. For one, you hear about education. . . . The very truth of the matter is simple: Education in this country stinks. It is that simple. Now, I do not understand why we would pour more money at a lousy educational system and get the results that we are getting. But we are saying we are taking education away. We are not. I cannot send my kids to a public school. It is so lousy, I would not dare abuse my children. So that is just a bunch of nonsense. Education, they had better reform it. So we are not doing anything on the backs of education." Bono then quickly shifted gears to address the shutdown and the budget: "Look, my colleagues, here is the issue. We have to balance the budget. Otherwise we hit a wall going 180 miles an hour. It is not as complicated as all this rhetoric that we hear by these expert politicians. It is we must balance the budget."

He may have been rhetorically challenged, but what Bono lacked in oratorical skills he made up for in entertainment value. Bono was popular with his colleagues for several reasons. Not only was he entertaining to have around, but he never made trouble. He hewed closely to the party line and voted with the leadership almost 100 percent of the time. And he was an affable, generous fellow with his time. He was always willing to appear at fund-raisers for his fellow Republicans and even sing a song or two. He was the second most requested GOP fund-raiser after Gingrich.

In fact, he did so much fund-raising for his colleagues that one of the criticisms leveled against him by political opponents back home was that he spent too much time fund-raising and not enough in his district. With a seven-year-old son and a four-year-old daughter, Bono moved his family to Washington, bought a townhouse in Georgetown, and became more a part of the local scene than any of the other freshmen, who disdained socializing with the Washington elite.

Bono told me he didn't think too much of his fellow freshmen, whom he called "kamikazes." As Bono put it, "I'm not representative of this bunch of butt-kickers. They are irritating the older members. I'm very content operating more within the structure." Bono preferred to sit back and take it all in, trying to learn how things were done in Washington. "It takes a year to find out where the bathrooms are."

When the president and vice president mentioned the freshmen and called them extremists, Bono said, "They loved it; it played right into their hand; it gave them exposure." Bono talked about the freshmen with detachment, as if he weren't really a member of the class, and said Gingrich was tired of the freshmen's shenanigans. "They make additional work that I don't think he relishes. It's fatiguing for him to always have to deal with these yipping guys."

Bono said he couldn't see too much difference between politicians and movie stars, as both were concerned with stature and power. And the biggest surprise about being in Congress was realizing how much of a game politics is. "Seeing the wheeling and dealing kind of humanizes everything," he said. "Sometimes I look at the floor of Congress and see a sitcom. . . . I don't take it as seriously as some of the members do." That was an understatement to say the least. Bono was known for making odd remarks at Republican meetings to try to lighten things up. During consideration of the appropriations bill for foreign operations, the House remained in session all night as the Democrats and Republicans argued about foreign aid. At around 4 A.M. a bleary-eyed Sonny Bono approached a small group of members who were standing on the floor talking. "I've never been up this late unless I was getting pussy," Bono said with a smile before wandering off. The members just looked at each other.

Bono insisted that he had always been a conservative, despite his flamboyant Hollywood lifestyle. "People find that hard to believe because I had long hair and wore a bobcat vest." But because he grew up in a home without much money, "I had to take care of myself. I never could buy into the notion that you could get something for nothing." When he started out writing songs and trying to make it in the music business, there were plenty of lean times, and he once had to sell his typewriter to keep going.

Even though he was a performer, Bono supported the Republican efforts to defund the National Endowment for the Arts, which he considered an elitist organization: "I would have never qualified as an artist with the NEA."

Bono was pro-choice but opposed the use of any federal funds for abortion services. "My daughter is gay, as you know. I don't love her any less. I don't condemn her. . . . She's a liberal, and I'm a conservative." Chastity, 25, had talked openly of some estrangement from her father after his election to Congress. "She vehemently hates Gingrich. She hates the revolution and the Republicans."

Bono looked at serving in Congress much the same way he looked at being an entertainer, and during the government shutdown, right before Christmas, Bono thought the Republicans were badly botching things. "These guys do not understand PR," he fretted. "Later there will be a price to pay." If the government was going to be shut down, Bono thought, they should stay in session through Christmas and try to hammer out a deal with the president because otherwise it looked like they didn't care.

Because of his entertainment background, House Republican leaders in 1996 asked Bono to help build a bridge between Hollywood and the Republicans and to work on issues such as international trade and copyright protection, with which Bono had some experience as a songwriter.

One local California journalist who had followed Bono's political career said he had a history of "a fairly short attention span," trying one thing and then quickly moving on to the next. It is not something Bono denied. On being mayor, Bono said, "That job was fun for about a month, and I had it for four years. . . . As soon as I could, I got the hell out of there." Then he decided to try a run for the Senate because "the guys who looked like they were having the most fun were the senators. . . . They had this great attitude; they could tell anyone to go to hell. . . . I thought that's what I want to be." But his dismal primary showing prevented that. As for being a member of the House, Bono said it was simple: "I ran for Congress and won, so here I am."

For the moment, Bono seemed to be having a good time playing a congressman. "To me it's like discovering a whole new world. I have never been happier in my life. I just have one regret: that I'm 60 years old." But how long before Bono got bored again remained to be seen. "This can be a springboard. . . . Sitting here being a congressman the rest of my life wouldn't appeal to me. They seem to just do it and do it forever," Bono said of some of his House colleagues. "If you're not going to go somewhere with it, I don't get the point." When he ran the first time, Bono pledged that he would serve no more than six years in the House. "When you run out of gas, you should go do something else." After winning reelection to the House, Bono thought about making a run for the Senate in 1998 against Democrat Barbara Boxer.

But despite two terms in the House and possible aspirations for higher office, Bono still insisted that he wasn't a politician. "I made a living as a singer, and I'm not a singer," he said with a smile.

On January 5, 1998, Sonny Bono's political career and his life were unexpectedly cut short. He was killed in a skiing accident in California after he crashed into a tree and suffered massive head injuries. Bono was an American original, an average Joe who made it big in both politics and show business and who always seemed just a little surprised at his good fortune.

17

WATERLOO

THE GOVERNMENT WAS SHUT DOWN over Christmas 1995, and it was not a very merry one. All of the national parks were closed, as was the Smithsonian Institution and the National Gallery of Art, disrupting the holiday plans of thousands of people. In Washington a great deal was made of the fact that a special exhibition of paintings by the 17th-century Dutch artist Johannes Vermeer would have to be closed because of the shutdown. The exhibit, which opened in mid-November, was scheduled to run through the first week of February before moving to a museum in the Netherlands. It may have seemed somewhat elitist and beside the point for the media to focus so much attention on the Vermeer exhibit when hundreds of thousands of federal workers had been furloughed and so many federal agencies were affected by the shutdown. But the Vermeer show was symbolic. These were hauntingly beautiful paintings that had been created in another place, another time. This was the first exhibition in the world ever devoted to Vermeer since his death in 1675. Twenty-one of the remaining 36 Vermeer paintings known to exist were included in the show. But because a handful of politicians couldn't get their act together, people who had waited a lifetime to see these paintings and had traveled great distances to do so would be denied the opportunity.

There were other, more practical, and very real consequences of the shutdown as well, and they were starting to pile up. Federal contractors were feeling the pressure of not being paid. Leading economic statistics were not being compiled by the Labor Department, which could have a ripple effect on financial markets and the Federal Reserve. U.S. embassies abroad faced major disruptions and could not pay foreign workers. Visas and passports could not be processed, causing major problems for many travelers. A number of states were having to close their unemployment offices and suspend the processing of claims until they received more federal money. People who were purchasing homes with federally backed loans could not go forward with their plans. Veterans and some other federal pensioners were not receiving their checks, and federal employees would receive only partial paychecks for December.

But the president and members of Congress were still receiving their paychecks.

On Tuesday, January 2, 1996, Bob Dole, declaring "enough is enough," pushed a bill through the Senate to temporarily fund and reopen the government. "I think we have made our point. People have been gone from their jobs long enough." Commenting on the difference of opinion between Republicans in the House and Senate, Dole said some House members "feel this is helpful in bringing about a balanced budget. That's not my view." It was a new year, and it was time for something new. Clinton and the Democrats applauded Dole's action.

Which left just the House Republicans still wanting to keep the government shut down. And it was not even all of the House Republicans. They were divided over the matter. Many of the moderates, especially those from Virginia and Maryland with large numbers of government workers in their districts and members whose districts were near national parks, wanted to reopen the government, and they threatened to vote with the Democrats to do so. But the conservatives and the freshmen, who outnumbered the moderates in the GOP conference, wanted to hold firm. The day after the Senate vote, the House Republicans, worried about losing the vote, would not even allow the Senate proposal to come to the floor. Whip Tom DeLay accused Dole of caving in to Clinton.

Freshman Robert Ehrlich, who represented the Baltimore suburbs, expressed sympathy for the federal workers, saying they were being used as pawns. "It's not good politics to keep these people out of work." But Ehrlich agreed with his freshman colleagues that it was the only way to push the president into offering a balanced budget. "Our dilemma is how to keep pressure on him and get these people working."

That was the question the Republicans were wrestling with. As one senior Republican admitted, the budget talks were going nowhere, the GOP had lost the PR war, but "I don't think anyone really knows how to get out of this mess"—including Newt Gingrich.

Gingrich had decided the time had come for the Republicans to cut their losses and move on; the question was how. On Thursday afternoon Gingrich and the other House leaders made the rounds talking to the various GOP House factions, the moderate Tuesday Lunch Bunch, the Conservative Action Team, the New Federalists, and then the entire freshman class. Gingrich told the freshmen it was immoral to hold the government workers hostage and not pay them. He also told them there were 30–40 Republicans ready to vote with the Democrats to open the government. But many of the freshmen didn't want to give up yet.

Like everyone else, George Nethercutt was frustrated and trying to think of a way out for the Republicans. "All we wanted to do was force the president to put some numbers on the table." He knew the Republicans were being blamed for the shutdown. "I just wanted to get this stupid thing resolved." On Thursday, January 4, while riding in a cab with his press secretary, Ken Lisaius, on the way to a taping for the "MacNeil-Lehrer NewsHour," Nethercutt had an idea. Why not make an offer to the president to reopen the government if he would in turn present a seven-year balanced budget using CBO numbers? Nethercutt was thinking out loud, and the cab driver told him it sounded like a good idea. Nethercutt thought so, too.

It was amazingly simple. It was what they had been talking about all along. They should have done it back in November. "I got to the show, and I thought, what the heck, I'll mention it." Nethercutt floated his idea on the PBS news show, and when he returned to the Capitol, he mentioned it to Gingrich before the start of the Republican conference meeting. Gingrich brought Nethercutt over to repeat his idea for Kasich, DeLay, and Armey. The leaders thought the approach might work, but they had to iron out the details.

What followed was an extremely stormy two-and-a-half-hour meeting of the House Republicans. Many of the freshmen still tenaciously opposed reopening the government. Mark Souder raised an objection to the idea of caving in, and another one of the Republicans turned to him and said, "Who cares whether it's a bad idea? They're the leaders. Sit down and shut up." The reporters were waiting outside. They wanted to know what the Republican plan was, and the GOP leaders felt the pressure to announce something. But there was no plan to announce because there was no agreement within the conference on what to do.

"We will not reopen the government," David McIntosh told the *New York Times.* "If we put these workers back to work, there never will be a balanced budget," said Steve Largent. Ray LaHood of Illinois, who had worked for former Republican minority leader Bob Michael and was not exactly one of the fire-breathers of the freshman class, said, "We got snookered once by the president, and I don't think we should get snookered twice. The best way to hold his feet to the fire is by causing a lot of anxiety and heartburn in keeping the government shut down."

At 10 the next morning, Friday, January 5, Gingrich met with the House Republicans. He told them he wasn't taking any questions. It was time for them to start acting like a team, and he was calling the plays. They were going to end the shutdown. No discussion.

Gingrich's announcement was met with stunned silence. As Steve Largent would recount several days later on "Nightline," "He basically said it's my way or the highway." Gingrich told them, "You don't like the job I'm doing as Speaker, run against me." He also told them he planned to keep a list of those who voted against reopening the government. He said he didn't want to hear any complaints later from those who voted no that another Republican wasn't being a team player on some other issue down the road. McIntosh was informed that if he didn't vote with Gingrich he would have to resign from his position as freshman delegate to the leadership.

The freshmen met together later and were divided over what to do. Many disagreed with what the Speaker was doing. But they also knew open revolt and a floor defeat at this point might jeopardize not only Gingrich's Speakership but possibly much more.

The House measure, which was approved 401–17 and then quickly passed by the Senate, funded the government for three weeks—through January 26. All federal employees could go back to work, but federal agencies would be given the money to operate only when Clinton produced a seven-year balanced budget plan using CBO numbers.

McIntosh voted with the leadership. But 15 Republicans did not. Twelve freshmen voted no, including Largent, Souder, John Shadegg, Linda Smith, Helen Chenoweth, and Lindsey Graham. Souder, who was a little nervous about his decision, still wasn't sure when he reached the floor how many people were going to join him in opposing the Speaker. After casting his vote, Souder, who had developed a reputation for voting against the leadership, glanced at the electronic tally on the wall above the House press gallery. "I looked up and it was 300 to 2, and I thought, uh-oh, here we go again."

Explaining his vote later, Souder said, "I want to at least have attempted to balance the budget. I want to run on something real. When I look in the mirror, I want to know we tried. We don't want to go back and lose with some fake budget."

One of the first acts of punishment Gingrich levied against the rebels was to cancel fund-raising appearances he had scheduled in their districts. McIntosh, who was usually quite guarded in his public statements, measuring each word for its potential impact, used uncharacteristic candor to describe Gingrich's retribution, calling it "an outrageous step." "He has to stop this crybaby attitude with people who don't agree with him," said McIntosh. Steve Largent called the Speaker's actions "petty."

But Souder was nonchalant about Gingrich's change of plans, figuring it might even turn out better for him. "You don't bring Newt Gingrich in to help your ratings. I was doing it for the money." Souder said it was never his idea for Gingrich to come to his district anyway. He had scheduled a fund-raiser for mid-January and "Bill Paxon called and said Gingrich would stop by. What am I going to say—no?" Instead, Largent offered to fill in and sign footballs at Souder's fund-raiser.

Souder had never exactly been one of Gingrich's buddies, and he knew it by the way Gingrich talked to him. "The pain-in-the-neck people like me he calls by their last names. He always calls me 'Souder,' not 'Mark.'" Maybe it was something about that name. That was Neumann's first name, too.

*   *   *

On Saturday, January 6, Clinton signed the bills to put federal employees back to work, and the 21-day government shutdown was over. Federal employees, who had been paid not to work during both shutdowns, would receive their back pay. The Office of Management and Budget estimated that this second government shutdown had cost U.S. taxpayers more than $1.25 billion. Later that day Clinton presented a seven-year budget plan so that the government would be fully reopened, but because a massive snowstorm hit Washington that night, government offices in the capital city remained closed on Monday.

Although the budget Clinton offered was technically in balance, it spent far more and cut taxes far less than the Republicans wanted. And the two sides were really no closer to an agreement than they had been two months earlier. Three days later the budget talks broke down again.

For the next two and a half weeks, the White House and the Republicans made no progress on the negotiations. The Republicans realized they had no choice. Another government shutdown was not an option. On January 25, the day before the government funding measure was set to expire, the House in a 371–42 vote approved legislation that would provide another 45 days of funding at reduced spending levels for the nine cabinet departments and other government agencies for which a permanent 1996 budget had not yet been passed. That would carry the government through mid-March. The following day the Senate passed the measure, and it was signed by the president.

The details of funding the rest of government for the remainder of the year would have to be worked out, as they always were, with horse-trading between Congress and the president. That would come. But the grand design for balancing the federal budget in seven years was not going to happen, at least not right now.

"I am pleased that the Congress avoided another partial government shutdown, and I appreciate its bipartisan approach to this bill," said Clinton after signing the short-term funding measure. House Budget Committee chairman Kasich succinctly summed up the events of the previous four months: "When the president doesn't want to do something, you really can't make him."

*   *   *

Essentially, it was over. The Republicans had nothing to show for the shutdown except a black eye. The budget battle and government shutdowns had proven to be their Waterloo. It was an especially apt metaphor, since Gingrich, who thought of himself as both a warrior and a student of military theory, was fascinated by the Duke of Wellington, who defeated Napoleon at the Battle of Waterloo. But Gingrich and his troops had not been on the winning side of this battle.

The government shutdown would prove to be the turning point of the 104th Congress. It would in fact survive as the most enduring accomplishment, if you can call it that, of the session. Long after the memory of the Contract with America had faded, people would think of the government shutdown when they thought of the 104th Congress. No other Congress in the country's history had closed down the government for three weeks. That was something worth remembering.

The Republicans had set four major goals to be achieved by the end of 1995—balancing the budget, cutting taxes, reforming Medicare, and revamping the welfare system. By January 1996 they had achieved none of these. Despite all of their hype, it had not been an especially productive year. Only 67 bills were enacted into law in 1995, the lowest number for a first session of a Congress since the end of World War II. That compared with 210 bills in the first session of the 103rd Congress and the previous low of 145 in 1981. Although the freshmen might argue that was a good thing, almost none of the agenda they had run on in 1994 had been enacted into law either.

Their battle cry of "Balance the budget" had somehow turned into "Shut down the government," diverting attention from their goal. The impression that it had been the Republicans that had shut down the government and not the president remained long after the federal employees were back at work. For the first nine months of the year, Gingrich and the Republicans had repeatedly insisted that they were driving the national agenda, not the president. So when the government shutdown occurred, it was natural for people to assume Congress was responsible. The freshmen didn't mind shutting down the government; they even said they would be happy to do it again. They made the government shutdown their own by embracing it and then wondered why people were blaming them for it.

The freshmen had always been antigovernment, had felt nobody would really miss the government too much if it was closed, so it was a little disingenuous of them to say afterward that the government shutdown had really been the president's fault. For all Clinton's refusal to deal squarely with them, he had never really wanted a government shutdown. But once he had one, he was perfectly willing to use it to his advantage.

Clinton simply outmaneuvered the Republican leaders. Several times they thought they had a deal, and then all of a sudden they didn't. And through it all Clinton succeeded in coming off as the one who prevented the Republicans from going too far. This idea was to become the centerpiece of his reelection campaign.

Most Americans thought the government shutdown had embarrassed the United States, made it look like a banana republic that couldn't handle its business. And the idea of the Republicans as revolutionaries had worn a little thin. People were starting to get turned off by all the revolution talk. There was really no significant evidence that the country had wanted a revolution in the first place. People wanted the government downsized, but they didn't want it dismantled. The disgust people felt over the inability of the government to solve problems, the feeling that had helped propel the Republicans to victory in 1994, was now being turned against them because of the shutdown. It looked like they couldn't manage things any better than the Democrats, and maybe were even worse.

Several Republican strategists, including Bill Kristol, would say that calling the 1994 election a revolution may have been a mistake, not only because it implied more than the Republicans could deliver but also because it scared people. Kristol wisely argued for more incremental change that the Republicans could build on in the 1996 elections and use to win the White House. The Republicans now had nine months to erase the memory of the shutdown from voters' minds. Or if it wasn't possible to erase it, they at least had to add something to it.

Who should get the blame for the government shutdown remained a question of much discussion in the first few months of 1996. Gingrich, Dole, and the rest of the Republican leadership had horribly miscalculated. Clinton had bested them. Gingrich had repeatedly pointed to the freshmen as the reason why he couldn't compromise with Clinton. But it was a classic negotiating tactic, blaming a third party who's not at the table for your inability to compromise further. The freshmen were doing what they were expected to do. It's an open question as to who was leading whom. There's no doubt Gingrich used the freshmen as a tool and an excuse. When he did finally decide the government shutdown strategy wasn't working, he simply informed them of that fact and told the freshmen it was time to try something else. Gingrich gave them no choice. He said they had to go along because he was in charge. The problem was, he just didn't realize it soon enough. "He's been weakened in his ability to convince us that his political judgment is always wise," said Mark Souder.

But the freshmen came in for their share of blame, too. As is true with so many people, their greatest strength also proved to be their greatest weakness. They were different from other politicians because they stuck so solidly to their principles and refused to compromise. This was the source of their self-proclaimed moral authority and a breath of fresh air in Washington. But their adamant refusal to accept anything except what they considered to be total victory, to acknowledge anyone's point of view but their own, largely led to their portrayal as narrow-minded extremists.

"Some of them still operate on the assumption that only they have been to the top of the mountain and seen the promised land," said Republican moderate and freshman nemesis Sherwood Boehlert of New York. Most of the freshmen probably considered that a compliment.

Van Hilleary campaigning in Crossville, Tennessee, in 1994. (Courtesy of the office of Van Hilleary.)

From left to right, Congressmen-elect Jim Longley, Joe Scarborough, and Sam Brownback make a point at a meeting in December 1994 before the start of the 104th Congress. (Photo by Kathleen Beall, courtesy of *Congressional Quarterly*.)

The first freshman class president Roger Wicker. To his left is Helen Chenoweth of Idaho. (Photo by Richard Ellis, courtesy of *Congressional Quarterly*.)

(right) David McIntosh at the GOP celebration marking the end of the first 100 days of the 104th Congress in April 1995. (Courtesy of the office of David McIntosh.)

(left) John Shadegg of Arizona. (Photo by Maura Boruchow, courtesy of *The Hill*.)

(right) Lindsey Graham of South Carolina was skeptical about House GOP leaders from the very beginning. (Courtesy of the office of Lindsey Graham.)

Former actor Fred Thompson with the signature red pickup truck he used during his successful 1994 campaign for a Tennessee Senate seat. (Courtesy of the office of Fred Thompson.)

Van Hilleary making an impatient House Speaker Newt Gingrich wait his turn to speak at a March 1995 press conference on term limits. (Photo by Martin Simon, courtesy of SABA.)

Senate Majority Leader Bob Dole and House Speaker Newt Gingrich, November 14, 1995, the first day of the government shutdown and the same day Gingrich complained to reporters about being "snubbed" by Bill Clinton on Air Force One on the trip to Yitzhak Rabin's funeral. (Photo by Kathleen Beall, courtesy of *Congressional Quarterly*.)

Above, Oklahoma's former football-playing freshmen. At left, Steve Largent, NFL Hall of Famer. (Courtesy of the office of Steve Largent.) At right, J. C. Watts, the only African American Republican elected to Congress in 1996. (Courtesy of the office of J. C. Watts.)

Sue Myrick of North Carolina, one of two freshman representatives to the GOP leadership. (Courtesy of the office of Sue Myrick.)

Zach Wamp was a budget cutter in Washington, a defender of federal programs back home. (Photo by Pamela Hazen, courtesy of *The Hill.*)

Democrat Mike Doyle in his hometown Pittsburgh Pirates uniform at the annual congressional baseball game. (Photo by Judi Wolford, courtesy of the office of Mike Doyle.)

Democrat Lloyd Doggett, a constant critic of the Republicans during the 104th Congress. Behind Doggett is Democratic House Minority Whip David Bonior. (Photo by Maura Boruchow, courtesy of *The Hill.*)

Wisconsin's Mark Neumann, mad as hell about the deficit and not going to take it anymore. (Photo by Scott Ferrell, courtesy of *Congressional Quarterly*.)

Sonny Bono and his former wife and singing partner Cher on David Letterman's late-night television show during Bono's campaign for mayor of Palm Springs, six years before being elected to Congress. (Courtesy of Associated Press/Wide World.)

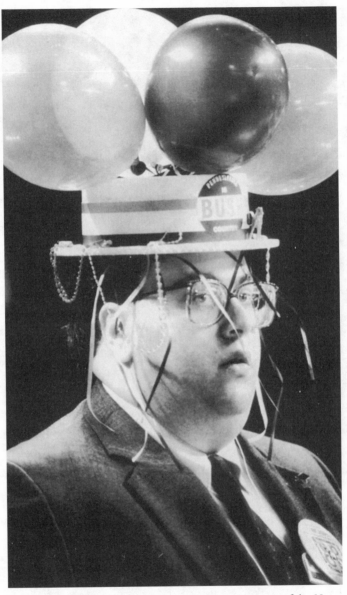

Joe Waldholtz at the 1992 Republican convention. (Courtesy of the *New York Daily News*.)

A tearful Enid Greene Waldholtz during her marathon five-hour news conference in Salt Lake City on December 11, 1995. (Courtesy of Associated Press/Wide World.)

The GOP House leadership team, from left, Majority Whip Tom DeLay, Majority Leader Dick Armey, Conference Chairman John Boehner, and at podium, Speaker Newt Gingrich at a press conference in December 1995 during the second government shutdown. (Photo by Scott Ferrell, courtesy of *Congressional Quarterly*.)

previous page:

(top) Indiana freshmen David McIntosh and Mark Souder at a meeting of the Economic and Educational Opportunities Committee. (Photo by Scott Ferrell, courtesy of *Congressional Quarterly*.)

(middle) George Radanovich, left, on February 1, 1996, the day he defeated Joe Scarborough, right, for the 1996 presidency of the freshman class. (Photo by Scott Ferrell, courtesy of *Congressional Quarterly*.)

(bottom) Florida freshman Mark Foley with one of his Everglades constituents. (Courtesy of the office of Mark Foley.)

Four of Washington state's six freshmen: above left, Linda Smith (photo by Maura Boruchow, courtesy of *The Hill*); above right, Randy Tate (photo by Maura Boruchow, courtesy of *The Hill*); below left, Rick White (courtesy of the office of Rick White); and below right, George Nethercutt (courtesy of the office of George Nethercutt).

Oregon's one-term freshman Wes Cooley salutes Sierra Club protesters on September 27, 1996, after a GOP celebration marking the end of the 104th Congress and the two-year anniversary of the signing of the Contract with America. (Courtesy of Sierra Club.)

Iowa's Greg Ganske during a '96 campaign appearance at the Iowa State Fair's Governor's Charity Steer Show. (Courtesy of the office of Greg Ganske.)

Sam Brownback, with wife Mary and three children, being sworn in to the Senate by Vice President Al Gore at the Capitol, January 7, 1997. (Photo by Maura Boruchow, courtesy of *The Hill*.)

Part Four

Winter–Spring 1996

A New Year

18

"The Era of Big Government Is Over"

In January 1996, as Clinton prepared to deliver his State of the Union address, there was still no agreement with the Republicans over balancing the federal budget. But Clinton had a more important matter on his mind: his reelection.

Clinton's status had changed dramatically since he had delivered his deadening State of the Union speech the previous year, a speech that had broken records for length of the annual presidential address but had done little else. Clinton was now the man who had faced down the Republicans and shown them what was what. Clinton was the defender of the elderly, the environment, the poor, the middle class—of truth, justice, and the American way. He had to make sure people knew that. But he also had to make sure they knew he had got the message. He had been too liberal and too much for big government the first two years of his presidency, which had not exactly been a great success and had resulted in a Republican majority in Congress. There was no way he was going to let the executive branch be next.

There had been only two Democratic presidents in the 20th century who had served more than one term in office: Woodrow Wilson and Franklin Roosevelt. Bill Clinton badly wanted to add his name to that very short list.

Clinton and his team had carefully analyzed the campaign strategies of modern presidents to determine what had worked and what hadn't. In two decades only one U.S. president had won reelection, and that was Ronald Reagan. Reagan had charted the course, had shown how it could be done. Team Clinton decided they would consciously emulate Reagan and borrow from the Reagan campaign handbook. "I think the reelection of Ronald Reagan in 1984 was just the model campaign in reelecting an incumbent. What they understood was the principal asset of this campaign. It's about the president; it's not about the campaign. Our job is to be supportive of the president, and what they did to support President Reagan was to build a seamless web from the White House to the campaign committee to the party committees. Our goal is to try and replicate that seamless web," Clinton-Gore deputy campaign manager Ann Lewis would tell me a few months after the State of the Union.

Just as Reagan's 1984 campaign was really run out of the White House, so, too, the Clinton reelection effort. Top campaign and White House staff held daily conference calls and had started meeting weekly in the private quarters of the White House with Clinton and Vice President Gore to plan strategy.

Another tactic Clinton borrowed from Reagan was to use the election-year State of the Union address as his unofficial campaign kickoff. But unlike Reagan, who formally declared his candidacy soon thereafter, Clinton never did make a formal announcement that he was seeking a second term and only became an official candidate for president when he accepted his party's nomination at the Democratic convention in August. This allowed Clinton to continue looking and acting presidential without drawing too much attention to the campaign. Like Reagan, he could use the presidency to run for the presidency. The less people focused on the election, the more natural it would seem that Clinton simply continue as president.

The State of the Union address was coming at a time of extreme partisan division. An uneasy truce between the executive and legislative branches had been arranged after the two government shutdowns. Feelings were raw on both sides, but much more so for the Republicans, who had been the losers. A few days before the State of the Union, reporters asked Gingrich what he would like to hear the president say. "Thank you and good night," Gingrich replied acidly.

Clinton wanted to seem above partisan rancor in his speech. He didn't want to focus attention on the budget negotiation problems. He wanted people to think about how well things were going for the United States, which is why there was no reason to make a change. He also wanted to lay out the major themes he planned to use for his presidential campaign.

From the very beginning of his State of the Union speech, Clinton signaled that he would not dwell on the budget bickering that had gripped Washington: "My duty tonight is to report on the state of the Union, not the state of our government but of our American community." Clinton wanted to remind people right away that things in the American community were pretty darned good: "Our economy is the healthiest it has been in three decades. We have the lowest combined rate of unemployment and inflation in 27 years. We have created nearly 8 million new American jobs. . . . The crime rate, the welfare and food stamp rolls, the poverty rate and the teen pregnancy rate are all down."

There was the rationale for keeping him on as chief executive: Things hadn't gone too bad on his watch. He did acknowledge the uneasiness some Americans felt, though: "Too many of our fellow citizens are working harder to keep up, and they are rightly concerned about the security of their families."

And then, just a few minutes into the speech, Clinton delivered his one-two punch, the most quoted, the most famous line not only of this speech but perhaps of his entire presidency, the seven words heard around the world: "The era of big government is over."

He even said it twice, repeating it toward the end of the speech, as if to make sure people heard it. People heard it all right. This Democrat, this child of the New Deal and the Great Society, was admitting the Republicans were right. But only up to a point: "We know big government does not have all the answers. We know there's not a program for every problem. We know. And we have worked to give the American people a smaller, less bureaucratic government in Washington. . . . But we cannot go back to the time when our citizens were left to fend for themselves. Instead, we must go forward as one America, one nation working together, to meet the challenges we face together."

He had stolen the Republicans' script. No one could accuse Clinton of not being flexible. "There is now broad bipartisan agreement that permanent deficit spending must come to an end. I compliment the Republicans for the energy and determination you have brought to this task of balancing the budget."

But he was not going to give the Republicans all the credit: "And I thank the Democrats for passing the largest deficit reduction plan in history in 1993, which has already cut the deficit nearly in half in three years."

Clinton quickly dispatched with the budget negotiations that had seized the Capitol: "Now it is time to finish the job and balance the budget. . . . We ought to resolve our remaining differences. I am willing to work to resolve them. I am ready to meet tomorrow, but I ask you to consider that we should at least enact these savings that both plans have in common and give the American people their balanced budget, a tax cut, lower interest rates, and a brighter future." Though "differences remain among us which are significant," Clinton said the two sides really were not that far apart and could come up with a budget that would "not undermine our obligations to our parents, our children, and our future by endangering Medicare, Medicaid, education, or the environment."

He made it all sound so easy, as if there really was no reason not to do it.

Clinton then moved on to the seven themes, or "challenges," he planned to make the focus of his reelection campaign. A number of them sounded suspiciously like Republican positions. The first challenge involved strengthening the American family. Clinton called for the passage of legislation that would require a V-chip in new television sets so parents could screen out programming they did not want their children to watch. He asked the entertainment industry to come to Washington to discuss in particular children's programming on television. Clinton also called for an end to the marketing of cigarettes to youngsters. These issues had been polled; all were popular with the public.

Next Clinton addressed welfare reform and told Congress that if they would pass "a bipartisan welfare reform that will really move people from welfare to work, and do the right thing by our children, I will sign it immediately." Clinton also said fighting crime, gangs, and drugs should be a major priority, and he announced the appointment of General Barry McCaffrey as the new head of the nation's war against illegal drugs.

Welfare and drugs and TV violence all sounded very much like Republican issues that Clinton was embracing. But he also wanted to differentiate himself from the Republicans. Clinton proposed national standards of excellence for America's schools and put forward the idea of school uniforms. He asked that the nation's student loan program be expanded and the first $10,000 of college tuition be tax deductible.

Clinton urged an increase in the minimum wage and proposed a "GI bill for America's workers" that would set aside money for people to use for community college or job training. He asked Congress to adopt legislation that had been proposed by Democratic senator Ted Kennedy and Republican senator Nancy Kassebaum that would prevent insurance companies from dropping people when they changed jobs or refusing to cover people who had preexisting health problems.

And of course Clinton mentioned Medicare. "We have all agreed to stabilize the Medicare trust fund, but we must not abandon our fundamental obligations to the people who need Medicare and Medicaid. America cannot become stronger if they become weaker."

Medicare would not be the only issue Clinton hit the congressional Republicans on. The other would be the environment. "Congress has voted to cut environmental enforcement by 25 percent. That means more toxic chemicals in our water, more smog in our air, more pesticides in our food. Lobbyists for the polluters have been allowed to write their own loopholes into bills, to weaken laws that protect the health and safety of our children."

The last issue Clinton touched on in the speech was an attempt to do the Congress one better on government reform. He applauded the Republicans for passing a gift ban and lobbying reform and urged them to pass bipartisan campaign finance reform *and* the line-item veto that was contained in the Contract with America.

And as Ronald Reagan had done so successfully in any number of speeches, Clinton introduced several people sitting in the gallery whom he considered American heroes. But Clinton's heroes were all government workers. Richard Dean, who worked for the Social Security Administration in Oklahoma City and had helped save the lives of three women by pulling them out of the rubble after the 1995 bombing of the federal building, was there. Through the two government shutdowns, Dean had continued working. "On behalf of Richard Dean and his family and all the other people who are out there working every day doing a good job for the American people, I challenge all of you in this chamber: Never, ever shut the federal government down again."

Score one for Clinton. A big one.

But he wasn't finished. "On behalf of all Americans, especially those who need their Social Security payments at the beginning of March, I also challenge the Congress to preserve the full faith and credit of the United States, to honor the obligations of this great nation as we have for 220 years, to rise above partisanship and pass a straightforward extension of the debt limit and show people America keeps its word."

It was a good speech, one of the best, if not *the* best, of his presidency. And it was only about an hour long.

Like virtually all of Clinton's speeches, the most memorable thing about it was the delivery, not the words, although there were some good lines. Clinton made a number of points at the Republicans' expense, but not in an overly partisan way. The overall tone of the speech was positive. The speech contained no soaring oratory, no rhetoric that really moved people. There were no dramatic initiatives announced or bold plan of action proposed. It was just that Clinton really knew how to give a speech. He was a good performer, in the Ronald Reagan mold.

And what followed Clinton's speech was the Republican response, delivered by Bob Dole. As Senate majority leader, Dole had chosen himself to give the response. At the time, as he faced a series of GOP primaries, it looked like a good idea. It would give him good visibility over his GOP rivals for the nomination. But compared to Clinton, Dole looked tired and old. He sounded that way, too. And he sounded a little mean, a little scary.

"President Clinton shares a view of America held by our country's elites: a nation of special interest groups united only by a dependence on government, competing with each other for handouts and held back by outdated values. Now for those who hold this view, there is only one answer to our problems—more government, bigger government, and more meddlesome government. And if you listened closely tonight, that's what President Clinton talked about. President Clinton may well be the rear guard of the welfare state. He is the chief obstacle to a balanced budget and the balanced budget amendment. He is almost the last public defender of a discredited status quo."

It was as if Dole hadn't been listening to Clinton's speech.

"Every political movement, and every public official, must locate a place in his heart where compromise ends, a core of conviction where we keep our conscience. There comes a time when even practical leaders must refuse to bend or to yield. For Republicans, and countless Democrats and independents, we have arrived at that time," Dole went on.

Clinton was talking about working together to solve the nation's problems and Dole was declaring war. Dole was out of sync with the American people. After two government shutdowns, they didn't want to hear any more about refusing to compromise. They didn't want to hear about problems; they wanted to hear about solutions. That was the key difference between the two speeches: Clinton talked about solutions, and Dole talked about problems.

It was as if Dole were speaking only to conservative Republican primary voters, not to the nation as a whole, as Clinton had done. Dole used the word "liberal," almost as an epithet, four times in his remarks.

Dole contended the nation's schools were being "run by liberals whose goal is to operate every school in America by remote control from Washington." He said the Clinton administration "has put liberal judges on the bench to war with our values, and it questions the participation of religious people in public life, treating them as fanatics out of step with America." He warned, "It is as though our government, our institutions and our culture have been hijacked by liberals and are careening dangerously off course."

Dole had to make things sound as bad as possible. If they weren't bad, why would people want to change presidents? But Americans didn't think things were as terrible as Dole was saying. And polls would show they were more than unimpressed with Dole's speech. They hated it.

Clinton, already in a good position as a result of the Republicans' botching the budget negotiations and shutting down the government, looked even better after his State of the Union performance. It was a speech that would have significant repercussions. Opinion polls showed people really liked what Clinton had to say and the way he said it—even people who hadn't voted for Clinton in 1992. They didn't like Dole. There was no ambiguity about that. Dole and the Republicans were on the ropes.

Two days after the State of the Union address, House Republicans quietly passed a measure to extend funding for government operations, even though there was no agreement with the White House on the budget. The Senate followed suit the following day. The Republicans finally knew which way the wind was blowing.

But the resonance from Clinton's speech and Dole's rebuttal would be even more far-reaching. Dole would never really recover from his performance. It hung around his neck like a millstone.

It can be argued the 1996 presidential contest never really advanced from what happened the night of the State of the Union. The difference in Clinton's and Dole's performances pretty much summed up the campaign. Dole would never be president. For all intents and purposes, it was decided that night.

19

THE FRESHMAN ADVANCE

WHEN THE HERITAGE FOUNDATION held its orientation program for the freshmen in December 1994 before they were sworn in, the conservative think tank decided to hold a follow-up, midpoint retreat to give the freshmen a chance to talk about what they had done their first year in Congress and think about where they were headed. The retreat, or "advance," as Heritage called it, was cosponsored by Jack Kemp's and Steve Forbes's Empower America group and was to be held in Baltimore in January 1996.

But the dates selected, January 25–26, would prove to be an unfortunate choice. January 25, two days after the State of the Union, turned out to be the day the House voted to extend funding to keep the government operating. The freshmen, who felt their leadership had bungled the budget negotiations and government shutdown, grudgingly voted for the funding measure because they figured they didn't have a choice. They were in no mood to follow that vote by sitting in a Baltimore hotel meeting room and "communicating" about their first year in office. They wanted to get out of Washington. They wanted to go home. Only about half of the class had even signed up for the two-day program. The freshmen who used to do everything together, who used to revel in class meetings and public pronouncements, suddenly felt like being left alone to sort things out.

The freshmen were feeling down and uncertain about what came next. Back in their districts over the holidays, they had heard from constituents who weren't too happy about the government shutdown. "What's going on up there? It seems like the Republicans have this my-way-or-no-way attitude, and I'm tired of it," one of Sam Brownback's Kansas constituents told him.

Especially angry were the government workers. One of them told Brownback, "It's like you're in a bad marriage and you're taking it out on the kids. You guys are married to Clinton, and you should be able to work it out without hurting the kids." It wasn't going to be easy, but the Republicans and Clinton *were* going to have to work it out because they were stuck with each other for at least another year.

Back in Indiana, one of David McIntosh's constituents told him, "As long as there is stalling on this, the president wins and you lose. Just get the best deal you can and get on with it." Get on with it indeed. "What are you guys doing in Washington, anyway?" As their second year in Congress began, the freshmen weren't too sure they knew the answer.

The Republicans were in a deep trough, really more like a valley. Hell, they were in the bottom of the Grand Canyon.

*   *   *

Since the January 25 vote on the government funding bill didn't come until after 7:30 P.M., and their reception in Baltimore had been scheduled to start at 6:30, followed by dinner, their evening was messed up. By the time they were finally finished voting, not many of them felt like making a one-hour trip to Baltimore in a bus.

Republican activist Bill Bennett of Empower America, who was invited to be their dinner speaker, sat around in the ballroom of the Baltimore hotel where the meeting was supposed to take place, waiting (and waiting) for the freshmen to arrive. Finally, around 9 P.M., tired and hungry, they showed up. Bennett wasted no time getting down to business. While they ate, he talked.

"You are out of control," Bennett told them with a big smile, at which he received a number of hoots and shouts from the out-of-control freshmen. "I'm a fan. You have been a tonic to this country and to this town. You have been blamed for disrupting business as usual. But business as usual was much in need of being disrupted." Bennett could sense the mood of the freshmen, and he was trying to give them a pep talk. "You made a promise, and you're trying to keep it. . . . You guys are doing the Lord's work."

Bennett told them not to worry about the media calling them extremists. "You're getting a lot of lousy press for which I think you should be congratulated." And then Bennett told them a story. It was about when he was serving as Ronald Reagan's secretary of education. At one of the cabinet meetings, Reagan said to Bennett, "You're getting horrible press." Then Reagan looked at the other cabinet secretaries and said, "What's wrong with the rest of you?"

"It's the long run, not the short run. You should hang in. You shouldn't give up," Bennett exhorted the freshmen. "Don't be mesmerized or obsessed with the daily polls." The freshmen were concerned about public reaction to the government shutdown, to Clinton's State of the Union address and Dole's response. Bennett did his best to get them not to dwell on that. He said Clinton was "certain to be both deft and shameful" in the upcoming campaign. This man who just two years earlier had proposed a national health care plan that "would have taken over one-sixth of the economy, now says the era of big government is over. . . . Did he just learn this?" Bennett asked.

He called Clinton "a perpetual graduate student," a "formidable politician but not a formidable man. . . . You're up against a very skilled orator. When you've got a showman like that, you need to put forth your best people and present your case in the most persuasive way."

The Republicans' public face hadn't been too good for the past couple of months, largely because of Newt Gingrich and Bob Dole. Bennett encouraged the freshmen to find more people who were good at talking to reporters and being on television, people like J. C. Watts and Sue Myrick.

At one of the front tables, the charter members of the Wild Bunch—Helen Chenoweth, Steve Stockman, and Wes Cooley—sat together. They had been thoroughly disgusted by Clinton's State of the Union speech and even more so by fellow Republicans who applauded, who *stood* and applauded in several places; people like New York moderate Sherwood Boehlert. They were talking among themselves about the display he had made of himself at the speech. They could hardly bring themselves to utter Boehlert's name but when they did, they made it sound like a bad word.

Bennett then gave the freshmen a warning. Nobody needed it more than the Wild Bunch. They had gone a little too far with their negative talk about government, and it had begun to backfire on them. Their anti-Washington message in 1994 had left a cloud that now hung over their heads. "Be careful with the antigovernment rhetoric. We cannot be simply critical of government," Bennett advised them, because now *they were* the government.

Bennett told them he expected the 1996 election to be a tough one for many of them, and as they began their reelection campaigns they should explain to people what they were trying to do was "restore the values and promises of this republic."

"Don't despair. Don't feel it's all hanging on you. This is a very long process. You don't have to do all the work; you just do the best you can. . . . It's now up to the American people to support you. . . . The American story will never be the same because of you. . . . You are making more of a difference to the shape of this country than anyone in recent history. . . . Have faith, have courage, cheer up."

The next day the freshmen sat through panels on issues like "government downsizing," "empowering citizens," and "strengthening America's families." But their hearts didn't seem to be in it. Dick Armey told them the revolution had not been stopped; it was just in a "pause."

The mood couldn't have been more different from that of their first retreat with Rush Limbaugh. The freshmen were just going through the motions. They weren't themselves. Virtually overnight they had been transformed into a markedly different group than that which had arrived in Washington one year earlier. They were worn out and tired, and they were sick of fighting and losing. "We've been banging our head against the wall, and everybody's feeling fairly bloody," said Mark Souder. Classmate Barbara Cubin had told him it was like the entire Republican conference had "a case of mild depression."

*   *   *

A seismic shift had taken place. The freshmen still cared about balancing the budget. But now they cared about something else just as much, maybe even more. Just like Bill Clinton, they had begun to focus on their own reelections. As Brownback put it, "The concern is getting to be, 'How do I get reelected?' rather than 'What do we get done here?'"

In the beginning of their first year, they used to talk about not caring whether they were reelected as long as they did the right thing. But with the election to determine whether they would stay or go just 10 months away, the overwhelming majority now seemed to care very much. They had not exactly been elected in a landslide in 1994. Forty-three of them had won with less than 55 percent of the vote. And the way things were going, it could be even tougher this time around.

The freshmen insisted their zeal for reelection was driven by their desire to balance the budget and cut government. If they lost, it would cost the Republicans the House majority, and those things might never get done. Party leaders were starting to be concerned about losing the majority, too, and had advised the freshmen the best thing they could do for the Republican agenda was to make sure they got reelected.

But senior Republican Chris Shays was skeptical. "They say they aren't worried about themselves, that they're worried about maintaining a Republican majority. That's a code word for worrying about themselves," Shays said. "Their strength was their willingness to lose the next election. That's what gave them the moral authority no one else could match. The irony is, if you don't worry about getting reelected, you get reelected," said Shays.

Their first year the freshmen thought they had to do everything at once because they might not get another chance. They had to prove to the voters they were serious. But they went too fast. They had frightened people. They had taken a perverse pride in being considered Visigoths. Now their own polls showed that the three words most frequently used to describe them were "mean," "extreme," and "arrogant." It was obviously time to make some changes. Their bratty, we-will-never-compromise-no-matter-what act wasn't playing well. The freshmen knew they needed to present a less scary, less strident public image. They needed a kinder, gentler reputation.

"A kinder, gentler face and accept reality, much like an alcoholic needs to accept that he has a drinking problem. We've got a president that has a veto. He vetoes what we send him. We can whine and scream about lack of direction when we sense that we're adrift, but we only have to look to Pennsylvania Avenue for the real problem," said Mark Foley of Florida. "Did we lose the PR war? Sure," said George Nethercutt. "We've realized how careful we need to be with our public relations message. We really need to work on that."

"The real place we lost steam was that second government shutdown," said Brownback. "I think we got the heck beat out of us." He said the experience reminded him of the fable about the fox who asks the goose to give him a ride across the river. Although the fox promises not to eat the goose, once they get to shore the goose is a goner. Brownback said when the Republicans agreed to reopen the government the first time on Clinton's promise that he would give them a balanced budget proposal and then he reneged on the promise, "I felt like the president was the fox and we were the goose."

"We scared too many people last year talking with such revolutionary fervor. We had too many people out there chest beating," said Brownback. "I think we showed more guts than brains at times. We did Pickett's Charge. Now we have to say, 'OK, let's be smarter this time; let's sneak around.' We need to show people we can govern."

By mid-January Mark Foley said a number of the freshmen had realized, "Maybe we are getting a little bit carried away with such inflexibility. This place doesn't operate on absolutes. That is not this process and it will never be." What they were going to have to do was compromise. 'Compromise' might be a dirty word, but it's still the only word that works," said Foley. "Compromise sounds as if you're sacrificing your principles. We should just say 'reach agreement.' You don't ever get 100 percent of what you want," said Nethercutt. "This is a change in strategy, not goals or commitments."

Joe Scarborough was among the freshman conservatives who were deeply disappointed with the way the leadership had handled the budget negotiations. "We made a commitment last fall to stare down the president, and we blinked. We turned over the agenda to the president, and that's not why we got sent up here. . . . We were sent here to force the president to balance the budget."

"I heard one colleague say that some people were running away from the Contract with America like scalded cats," Matt Salmon of Arizona told the *New York Times*. He was another of the conservative freshmen who wanted to hang tough. "We have lost our way and we need to get it back again. . . . I think that the public got a taste of what our revolution was all about during the first 100 days, but during the budget scuffle everything sort of went up in smoke."

During the government shutdowns the freshman class had been seriously divided for the first time since their election between the hard-liners and the moderates who were getting hit in their districts. Some freshmen were scornful of Bob Dole and his push to reach some sort of an agreement so that the government could be reopened. But not Foley. "I said we should be kissing Bob Dole's ring that he's making some sense out of this. Some of the freshmen were aghast. But there's a difference between backing down on principle and looking practically at the situation. We had to say, 'OK, that didn't quite work. Let's try this.'"

Since Roger Wicker had pledged to serve only one year as freshman class president, the freshmen held a new election for the position at the beginning of February. Scarborough ran, but he lost the race—according to a number of freshmen because he was considered too much of an "in-your-face bomb thrower." Instead, the freshmen selected George Radanovich, a good-looking, pleasant, soft-spoken 40-year-old from northern California who was a county supervisor and vintner before being elected to Congress. The Radanovich Winery, which he started, produced about 4,000 cases of wine a year. Radanovich was the first full-time winemaker ever elected to the House.

The district he represented, California's 19th, comprises most of the city of Fresno, the surrounding farm country in the San Joaquin Valley, and three national parks, including Yosemite and Sequoia. Radanovich, whose father was a Croatian immigrant, had won by defeating six-term incumbent Democrat Richard Lehman. Radanovich carried around a cardboard cutout of Clinton as a prop on the campaign trail and blasted his opponent's support of Clinton, even though Lehman had voted against the Clinton budget and tax increase. Although he was outspent two to one by Lehman, Radanovich still managed to win the race 57 to 40 percent.

Once elected, Radanovich was not one of the freshmen who was constantly appearing at press conferences or banging his fist on the podium while giving speeches on the House floor. In fact, he had such a low profile that some of the other freshmen weren't completely sure where he stood on certain issues.

Radanovich's chief attributes seemed to be that he was well liked by his colleagues and that he had not really distinguished himself in any way during his first year. Radanovich's election to class president symbolized the change the freshmen had undergone.

"Radanovich had not been as outspoken as Joe had on a whole range of issues. I think there was a feeling that a little softer voice would be better," said Nethercutt. Radanovich said his approach that first year was to "keep my eyes and ears open and keep my mouth shut," a novel approach for a member of this class. But now the freshmen were beginning to realize that kind of approach might work better for them. "Even though he's extremely conservative he's not an in-your-face conservative. He's a likable conservative," said Foley.

Scarborough agreed that Radanovich was probably perceived as less threatening by his classmates. "A lot of members are emotionally drained, physically drained. They didn't feel like going through three months of torture. They're tired of the siege mentality we had last year, getting knocked down every day. They said, 'Let's just not fight for a while. Let's low-key it and see if we can get things done quietly.'"

Radanovich said a big reason he had the time to be president of the class is that he took care of his reelection in 1995. He went back home every weekend; he held town meetings; he raised $450,000—"all those things that keep you from being vulnerable in your first year." As a result, he was not expecting a tough race. Instead of worrying about his own reelection, he was worrying about his classmates'. Radanovich said getting all of his classmates reelected was his number one goal.

Radanovich's second goal was coming up with a different image for the class. "We will continue to be the agents of change," Radanovich asserted, but he said the freshmen needed to do that in a more positive way. Instead of just ranting about cutting programs and saying what they were against, Radanovich said they needed to let people know what they were for.

Holding the class together was going to be harder than it had been their first year. The freshman label wasn't exactly helping them right now, and many of the freshmen decided it might be time to distance themselves from their class reputation. They started striking out on their own, trying to develop separate identities. "Being a part of the freshman class in 1996 is different than being a part of the freshman class in 1995," said Nethercutt. "The freshman class isn't running for reelection. I am. We want to be judged on our own merits, not just as a freshman class member."

The moderates, especially those who had been elected from tough, historically Democratic districts, were seeking to distance themselves from their noisy classmates. Selecting Radanovich as president was one way to address their concern about how the freshman class image was hurting them in their districts.

One moderate who had been working overtime to distance himself from his classmates ever since the government shutdown was Tom Davis, who represented Virginia's 11th District, the Washington suburbs of northern Virginia. His was a district full of angry government workers. "Any time they say 'all 73 freshmen this or all 73 freshmen that,' I just take a beating. The hardest thing I have to do is explain to my constituents that I'm not a Republican freshman," Davis told the *Washington Post* in January. Of course he was a freshman, but he insisted it was in name only.

Davis was pro-choice and more moderate on social issues than most of the freshmen. "I'm often being lumped together in the media with all these people I don't agree with," Davis told the *Hill*. "I don't like to trash my members, but frankly they were stupid to shut down the government. People like Souder and McIntosh like to whip it up, but there are plenty of freshmen who think they are extreme."

With even their own freshman colleagues calling them extreme, diehards like Souder realized they were going to have to take a few steps back. It was an election year, Gingrich and Dole had been wounded by their performance in the budget negotiations, and Clinton had renewed confidence. "We expected to be able to roll him, and we couldn't. Who thought Clinton would develop a backbone?" wondered Souder. "I believe we've hit the bottom and we're going to head up," said Souder in February.

The freshmen were losing some of their idealism and becoming more realistic about what they were likely to accomplish. "We realize now that there's a limit to what we can do," said Rick White. "There's a reality that this is not a two-year job; it's a six- or an eight-year job," said Nethercutt. And the Republicans now realized they needed a GOP president and reinforcements in Congress to finish the job. "The original GOP theme for 1996—'Promises made, Promises kept'—has been altered to read: We did our damnedest but it wasn't enough. Republicans conceded last week that it will take another election to gain a clear mandate for the changes they want to make in Medicare, Medicaid and welfare, and to enact the balanced budget and tax cuts they hoped to pass," wrote syndicated columnist David Broder at the end of January.

But victory in November was far from certain, not only in the presidential contest but in the congressional races as well. Instead of believing they were going to pick up seats in the House and Senate, the Republicans were starting to worry about holding onto what they already had. The first sign that they might have some trouble in November was a special Senate election held at the end of January in Oregon.

20

A WIN FOR THE "ECOTERRORISTS"

A SPECIAL ELECTION HAD BEEN CALLED in Oregon for January 30 to fill the U.S. Senate seat of Republican Bob Packwood, who resigned in October over charges of ethical misconduct and sexual harassment and who had served in the Senate since 1968.

Republicans and Democrats alike looked at the Oregon race as a potential harbinger of the November election results. Oregon was considered something of a swing state; its U.S. senators were Republicans, but the state had voted Democratic in the previous two presidential elections and had a Democratic governor. And the state's voters tended to be socially tolerant and fiscally conservative independents.

The special election featured a race between eight-term House Democrat Ron Wyden and Republican state senate president Gordon Smith. Wyden was a liberal with a history of working on elderly and consumer issues. He represented metropolitan Portland, the state's largest city and an area that accounted for about 40 percent of the state's voters. Smith, from much less populated eastern Oregon, was the multimillionaire owner of a frozen food company who first entered politics in 1992, when he was elected to the state senate.

Smith emphasized his support for a balanced budget, cutting taxes, and term limits. Wyden stressed his 15-year record as a member of Congress and his support for strong environmental protection and abortion rights. Polls showed the race was a dead heat.

Smith was an attractive, telegenic candidate and a polished, disciplined campaigner who was labeled the stealth candidate by Democratic activists because he shunned public appearances and interviews. The lanky Wyden was less charismatic and a bit awkward, although he came off as sincere and was extremely hardworking in the campaign. Wyden even made a quip about the difference in their appearances during a campaign debate, saying he was running on his record, not his "rugged good looks or hair."

Wyden's biggest campaign mistake occurred early in the race, during a television interview in which he could not locate Bosnia on a globe or give the price of a loaf of bread or a gallon of milk or gasoline. Smith later ran a TV ad that showed children making fun of Wyden's failure to know the answers.

Smith had a tremendous financial advantage, spending $5.5 million on the brief campaign, more than $2 million out of his own pocket and $1.3 million more than Wyden. Smith spent proportionately more per voter than did Republican Michael Huffington in his $30 million California Senate race against Democrat Diane Feinstein in 1994.

This was an expensive and extremely negative race by Oregon standards, waged largely through television ads. Smith focused his attacks on what he said was Wyden's "tax and spend" liberal record. Wyden called Smith a right-wing "extremist." The Democrats saw the race as a referendum on the GOP Congress and stressed that the extremely conservative Smith would be another vote for the Republican agenda.

The level of negative ads by both sides became an issue in the campaign, and at several joint appearances by the candidates the first question voters asked had to do with the negative tone of the race. In a decision that most people think helped him significantly, Wyden announced three weeks before election day that he was pulling all of his negative ads off the air. But interest groups supporting Wyden did not do the same. The negative ad that had drawn the most attention was run by the Teamsters Union. It mentioned worker safety violations and accidents—including amputations and the death of a 14-year-old worker—at Smith's frozen food processing plant, which employed about 800 people.

The race attracted the involvement of a number of special interest groups who saw it as a chance to try out tactics for the November campaign. Property rights activists and abortion opponents worked on behalf of Smith against Wyden. Environmentalists, abortion rights activists, and labor unions organized and campaigned for Wyden and against Smith. The AFL-CIO sent more than 30 staffers to Oregon to work for Wyden. The rise of this sort of independent activism on behalf of candidates followed the lead of groups like the National Rifle Association and the Christian Coalition, which had campaigned hard in 1994 on behalf of Republicans.

Abortion rights were a significant issue in the race. Although he was economically and socially conservative and strongly anti-abortion, Smith convinced right-to-life groups not to run ads on his behalf, playing down his pro-life position in a state where abortion rights are favored by a majority of citizens. And though Democratic candidates in many other states might shun an association with abortion rights activists, Wyden played up his pro-choice stance. On the 23rd anniversary of the Supreme Court's *Roe v. Wade* decision, Wyden appeared at a candlelight rally of abortion rights activists.

But the issue that proved to be the most important in the race was environmental protection. Oregonians take great pride in their state's natural beauty and the way they have protected it. This was the perfect place for national environmental groups to test-drive a strategy they hoped in November would help them defeat other candidates they considered to be environmentally unfriendly.

Environmentalists, who claimed that the 104th Congress was leading an assault on environmental protection laws, pulled out all the stops in Oregon. The Sierra Club and the League of Conservation Voters (LCV) sent operatives out from Washington and spent around $300,000 running radio and television ads about Smith and his environmental record. They also used membership lists, which span party affiliation, to make phone calls and send postcards to voters they identified as environmentally conscious. "We've fought for 25 years to keep our water and air safe, and in one year this Congress has started to roll back 25 years of protections, and we're not going to let that happen," said Sarah Anderson of the LCV, who spent several months in Oregon trying to make sure this particular Mr. Smith did not go to Washington.

Environmentalists claimed that as a member of the Oregon Senate, Smith voted only 4 percent of the time to protect environmental interests. Smith, who favored a suspension of the Endangered Species Act to allow logging in some old-growth forests, received major contributions from timber, oil, and gas interests. Smith provided an easy target because of his state senate record and the environmental violations that had occurred at his frozen food plant.

Although he had received more than $700,000 in federal and state grants to bring his frozen food plant into compliance with environmental laws, there had been 10 illegal wastewater spills from the plant into a tributary of the Columbia River. Four of the spills had occurred in the past three years, the most recent just four months before the election. The worst spill, in 1991, killed fish and wildlife, and Smith's company received one of the highest environmental fines in Oregon's history as a result. During the campaign the environmental groups ran ads featuring pictures of the spill.

Despite having billed himself in the GOP primary race in November and December as having one of the most conservative voting records in the Oregon Senate, Smith attempted to recast himself in January as a kinder, gentler version of his state senate alter ego. He tried to distance himself from conservative House Republicans, saying he wouldn't go along with Speaker Newt Gingrich's environmental agenda and if elected would oppose cuts in environmental protection funding. But he wasn't fooling activist Anderson: "Gordon Smith has a terrible environmental voting record. We're spending our resources to make sure that just because Gordon Smith is spending money looking into the TV saying he's an environmentalist, he's not believable. He's not an environmentalist."

Wyden enlisted the aid of Environmental Protection Agency chief Carol Browner, who made a visit to Oregon to blast the Republican Congress and predict that environmental issues would be important in the fall campaign. "The budget cuts to EPA are probably the clearest proof, the clearest evidence that what the Republican leadership in Congress wants is to roll back environmental protection and take the environmental cop off the beat," said Browner. She repeated charges made by other Democrats and by Clinton that the Republicans had "invited the special interests into the back rooms of Congress to rewrite the Clean Water Act" and said the Republicans were handing out "special deals for special interests."

The White House also dispatched Vice President Al Gore for a special trip to campaign for Wyden and highlight the environmental issue. At a rally in Portland, the Clinton administration's highest-profile environmental advocate said the Republicans had to be stopped. "We need Ron Wyden to help protect our clean air and water against the polluters who have been brought into the Congress to rewrite the environmental laws," said Gore. Gore told a crowd largely made up of college students that they had the chance to send a message to the rest of the country with the results of the Oregon election.

In addition to its timing and the attention it was drawing from national political activists, another thing that made the Oregon election different was that it was conducted entirely through mail-in ballots, making it the first ever vote-by-mail congressional election in the country. The state's 1.8 million registered voters received their ballots about three weeks before they had to be returned, on January 30. And since it was publicly recorded which voters had sent their ballots in early, the candidates used significant resources on direct mailings and professional phone banks trying to target those who had not yet voted in the days and weeks before the deadline.

Probably due to the mail balloting, voter turnout exceeded 65 percent, setting a record in the state for a special election. And Wyden defeated Smith by just over one percentage point, making him the first new Democrat to join the Senate since 1992 and the first from Oregon since 1962. Both parties immediately tried to put their own spin on the outcome. The Clinton White House called the election a repudiation of the extreme agenda of congressional Republicans. The Republican National Committee claimed that just getting that close to victory in a state like Oregon meant Clinton was in trouble.

Glen Bolger of Public Opinion Strategies, a Republican polling firm that worked for Bob Dole and handled Smith's polling, said Clinton's strong performance in the State of the Union message and Dole's lackluster rebuttal, which took place little more than halfway through Oregon's 20-day voting period, contributed to Smith's defeat. Although Smith was considered to be in the lead by several points prior to the State of the Union address, Bolger said his numbers started to go down after the speech, and Clinton's favorability rating went up five points.

Although 47 percent of Oregon voters said they approved of the way Clinton was doing his job and only 28 percent approved of Gingrich, it was still a mistake to draw too many national implications from the outcome. Only about half of the Oregon voters polled considered the election to be a referendum on either Clinton or the Republican-led Congress.

But exit polls did confirm that environmental concerns were a deciding factor in the race. Even though Smith picked up conservative Democratic votes, especially in his home area of eastern Oregon, Bolger said that wasn't enough to offset the lost votes of moderate Republicans and independents, especially women, in the Portland suburbs. Bolger said polling done in December showed that Smith had a higher vulnerability with voters on his environmental record than on any other issue, and this was the best thing the Democrats could have used to run against him.

Two-thirds of those polled after the election said the candidates' environmental positions were a more important factor in this election than in any other election they could recall. And by a 52–22 margin, those polled felt Wyden was better on the environment than Smith. A majority of those who voted for Wyden considered the environment an important issue. Of those who considered it the most important, 72 percent voted for Wyden. And among the Republican voters who rated the environment their number one concern, an overwhelming 90 percent voted for Wyden.

Daniel Weiss, legislative director of the Sierra Club in Washington, said the environmentalists spent more in Oregon than they had ever spent on a single congressional race, but he added, "We think we got our money's worth." Weiss said the message of the Oregon race was, "If you vote against the environment, this dog bites."

Environmental activists said they planned to take what they did in Oregon and try to repeat it in two dozen congressional races in November, especially targeting freshmen who were considered the most vulnerable. But their efforts in Oregon were not really the beginning. They had started a major public information campaign against Republican attempts to weaken environmental protection laws months earlier.

"The freshman class made a real miscalculation in following lockstep behind Newt Gingrich and the . . . leadership's declared war on the environment. The voters don't want that, and we're going to be there making sure the voters know just what they've done," said Anderson of the League of Conservation Voters. After the first 100 days of the 104th Congress, the LCV gave 61 of the 73 freshmen a rating of zero out of 100 on environmental votes. The LCV said the House freshmen were "the most adamantly antienvironmental voting bloc" in Congress.

Shortly thereafter, the LCV and other environmental groups started a public information and advertising push, running radio ads in members' home districts. After that resulted in calls and letters to members from their constituents, a number of House Republicans, including freshmen, began to switch their position on key environmental votes, such as cuts to the EPA. By February 1996 the number of freshmen with a zero rating on environmental votes had fallen to 36, and the LCV said 13 freshmen were now consistently supporting its environmental positions.

A memo sent to GOP members by the House Republican conference in October offered suggestions for how to deal with "the environmental lobby and their extremist friends in the eco-terrorist underworld [who] have been working overtime to define Republicans and their agenda as anti-environment, pro-polluter and hostile to the survival of every cuddly critter roaming God's green earth."

The memo encouraged lawmakers to plant a tree, adopt a highway, pass out tree saplings with their campaign brochures, tour a recycling plant, clean up a park, and definitely invite the media while they were doing it. "In order to build credibility you must engage this agenda before your opponents can label your efforts 'craven, election-year gimmicks,'" the memo advised. "The next time [Secretary of the Interior] Bruce Babbitt comes to your district and canoes down a river as a media stunt to tell the press how anti-environment their congressman is, if reporters have been to your boss' adopt-a-highway cleanup, two of his tree plantings and his Congressional Task Force on Conservation hearings, they'll just laugh Babbitt back to Washington," said the memo.

Certainly when excerpts from the memo appeared in newspapers including the *Washington Post* and the *New York Times*, no one in the Republican conference was laughing. It made the Republicans look like they *were* trying to use PR gimmicks to fool people into thinking they cared about the environment while they gutted environmental laws.

The Republicans had badly misjudged how the public would react to their environmental agenda, which included proposals to cut EPA funding; weaken EPA enforcement rules for the protection of wetlands; open up the Arctic National Wildlife Refuge to oil drilling and Alaska's Tongass National Forest to timber harvesting; close or privatize some national parks; weaken the Clean Water Act; relax some of the standards of the Superfund law and reduce federal funds for toxic waste cleanup; increase logging in old-growth forests; and prohibit any new listings under the Endangered Species Act.

But they had been able to accomplish very few of these things because of Senate and public opposition. Perhaps even more than the government shutdown, the Republicans' stand on environmental issues was hurting them badly even with their own supporters. GOP moderates, often the kind of affluent, well-educated people who donated large sums of money to the Republican Party, cared about the environment. They took advantage of the national parks. They could afford to spend time in the great outdoors. They wanted strong environmental protection continued.

A public opinion survey conducted by influential Republican pollster Linda DiVall in December emphasized the scope of the GOP's problems and provided a real wake-up call to legislators. "By greater than a 2 to 1 margin, voters have more confidence in the Democrats than Republicans as the party they trust most to protect the environment. Most disturbing is that 55 percent of all Republicans do not trust their party when it comes to protecting the environment, while 72 percent of the Democrats do trust their party," said the poll.

"The public does not agree with the GOP majority position to cut EPA spending by one-third." The poll showed that a majority of those questioned would vote against a member who voted to cut EPA funding. "Attacking the EPA is a nonstarter," warned DiVall. Only 21 percent of those responding to the poll said they felt environmental laws had gone too far, 36 percent said they had not gone far enough, and 31 percent said they were about right. And even among just Republicans, only 30 percent said they thought environmental regulations had gone too far.

"Our party is out of sync with mainstream American opinion," said DiVall in the report sent with the poll to her Republican clients. "Rather than attacking the EPA, Republicans should be clearly articulating future priorities and emphasizing the safeguarding of reasonable and balanced environmental protection done in a more efficient manner," DiVall counseled.

After the poll was released, 30 Republican moderates in the House wrote to Gingrich telling him the GOP was "taking a beating" on its environmental proposals and something had to change. And even some of the conservative freshmen were beginning to think that the Republicans' ambitious antiregulatory agenda had gone too far.

The Republicans decided to back off their efforts to weaken environmental laws, realizing this was not something they wanted to pursue in an election year. In fact they began to undertake efforts to make them look more pro-environment.

Of course Bill Clinton wanted to talk about the environment every chance he got. It was right up there with Medicare and education. He was something of a latecomer to the environmental movement. As governor of Arkansas, Clinton did little about waste dumping from chicken plants into Arkansas rivers and streams. And after being elected president, he did not give a very high priority to environmental issues during his first two years in office. He had even signed a Republican measure in early 1995 that loosened the regulations for logging in national forests, something he now said was a mistake.

But once he saw the polls that showed how unpopular the original GOP approach was and how much political mileage he could get out of the issue, he got religion in a big way. He included an environmental section in his State of the Union speech. He made a big deal of celebrating Earth Day in April. And in his acceptance speech at the Democratic National Convention, Clinton mentioned the word "environment" at least seven times and asserted, "We should make it a crime even to attempt to pollute."

The pièce de résistance was his announcement in September that he was establishing a 1.7-million-acre national monument in southern Utah's Red Rock wilderness around the Grand Staircase–Escalante National Monument to protect the area from coal mining and development. Clinton used the Antiquities Act of 1906 to make the federal decree, which did not need congressional approval. It was the same law that Republican president Theodore Roosevelt had used in 1908 to declare the Grand Canyon a national monument. Mindful of the symbolism, Clinton went to the Grand Canyon, not far from the spot where Roosevelt stood, to make his announcement.

With one stroke Clinton could make environmentalists extremely happy and deliver a "take that" to the predominantly Republican voters of Utah, which was the only state in the country where he had come in third, behind George Bush and Ross Perot, in 1992. Since Clinton wasn't going to win Utah's five measly electoral votes anyway, he might as well stick it to the state and score major points with other western voters, especially in crucial California. It was a twofer.

*   *   *

By the end of the 104th Congress, the Republicans' regulatory relief efforts had for the most part been put on hold, and almost none of their antienvironmental proposals were enacted. Unfortunately, they appeared to have learned nothing from their experience. Many Republicans yet again insisted they were the victims of biased media and a bad public relations effort in countering the information put out by the "ecoterrorists." They simply refused to accept that it might actually be the details and substance of their antienvironmental agenda that had turned voters off.

21

A $170,000 BREAKFAST

ON FEBRUARY 6, Ronald Reagan's 84th birthday, the House passed the last item from the Contract with America—a line-item veto. The measure gave future presidents the authority to veto specific parts of spending bills without having to veto the entire bill. The vote was scheduled for Reagan's birthday because he had always been a strong supporter of the line-item veto.

Since the Republicans were reluctant to give such power to Bill Clinton, the measure would not take effect until January 1997, after the election. The line-item veto could be used for specific spending programs, new or expanded entitlement programs, or narrowly targeted tax breaks. Proponents said the line-item veto would give the president a tool to use in eliminating wasteful, pork barrel spending from bills and might also discourage members from trying to put extra spending into legislation. But more than 100 Democrats who opposed the measure felt it would give the president, any president, too much power over the legislative branch.

The Senate passed the bill a few months later, and Clinton enthusiastically signed it in early April. A group of lawmakers including Democratic senators Robert Byrd and Daniel Patrick Moynihan appealed the legislation in the Supreme Court, arguing that it was unconstitutional. In 1997 the Court ruled that since the line-item veto had not yet been used, the lawmakers had not been harmed and the Court could not rule on the constitutional issue. However, the Court left open the possibility that it could rule at a later time, once the line-item veto had actually been invoked and challenged by someone affected by it.

Another issue Congress had been waiting to deal with was the farm bill. There had been months of disagreement over how to structure a rewrite of the farm subsidy program. This was not really a partisan issue but a regional matter that crossed party lines. Republican leaders endorsed the idea of moving the farm program into a more market-based system. Many Democrats as well as Republicans from some farm regions, especially the South, were skeptical of fiddling with the subsidy program.

And the nation's 2 million farmers were getting anxious. The existing subsidy program had expired, and they wanted to know what the new program would look like. Soon they would have to make decisions about spring planting.

The first week of February the Senate approved legislation that would replace most subsidy programs for crops like wheat, corn, and cotton with fixed payments for farmers that would decline over a period of seven years. Farmers would be paid a fixed amount and could grow whatever crops they wanted. The existing program, which linked government payments to market prices but which controlled what farmers could grow and how much land they could use, would be eliminated. But the new farm bill did not get rid of the dairy, sugar, and peanut price support programs, which cost consumers billions of dollars at the grocery checkout counter.

The House passed Pat Roberts's "Freedom to Farm Act" at the beginning of March, and by late that month there was agreement between the House and the Senate on a final piece of legislation. In order to attract enough votes for passage, a number of sweeteners had been added, such as additional money for rice growers (to win southern votes) and a reauthorization of the food stamp program and additional funds for conservation and rural development programs (which attracted Democratic votes). There was also $300 million added to the bill for cleaning up environmental damage to the Florida Everglades largely caused by sugar producers and to acquire Everglades land for preservation. This was part of the Republicans' new effort to improve their image on environmental matters.

In late March the House also voted on repealing the assault weapons ban that had been part of the Democratic crime bill passed in 1994. The National Rifle Association had been outraged by the measure and had worked hard against many Democrats who had voted for it, spending more than $5 million in the 1994 campaign on behalf of House candidates who opposed gun control.

The top beneficiaries among the freshmen were George Nethercutt of Washington and Mark Neumann of Wisconsin. Nethercutt had received $10,900 directly in National Rifle Association (NRA) PAC money in 1994 and 1995. But the NRA had independently spent an additional $70,000 in his district to beat former House Speaker Tom Foley. The NRA spent and donated $27,000 on behalf of Neumann. The Republicans knew the NRA had helped them win seats in the 1994 election, and they owed a debt to the organization, a debt the NRA was pushing to collect.

Although repeal of the assault weapons ban was not in the Contract with America, Newt Gingrich and Bob Dole had promised the NRA a vote on it. But after the bombing of the federal building in Oklahoma, public sentiment had shifted. Polls showed that a majority of Americans favored keeping the ban in place. This was no longer a slam dunk for the Republicans. Senate Democrats were threatening a filibuster if it came to the Senate floor, and Dole said he had no plans to schedule a

Senate vote on repealing the ban. And if the Senate did pass it, Clinton said he would veto the measure.

The House vote was strictly symbolic, a payback to the NRA.

Gingrich had created something called the Firearms Legislation Task Force and named as its chairman Bob Barr, a freshman from Georgia. Barr had worked as an intelligence analyst for the CIA and was a U.S. attorney in Atlanta before being elected to Congress. Four of the five freshmen on Gingrich's task force had received large NRA contributions. And Barr, who had accepted $10,000 in campaign funds from the NRA, was one of those pushing hardest for a vote on repealing the assault weapons ban.

The measure, which Republicans had labeled the "Gun Crime Enforcement and Second Amendment Restoration Act," would legalize semiautomatic weapons like the AK-47 and Uzi, which were banned under the 1994 crime bill, as well as gun clips that hold multiple rounds of ammunition. Barr insisted the gun ban had taken "the balance of power away from victims and toward criminals."

On March 22 the House voted 239–173 to repeal the ban after a tense, two-hour floor debate. The most emotional moments of the debate came in an exchange between Rules Committee chairman Gerald Solomon and Democratic freshman Patrick Kennedy. "Families like mine all across this country know all too well what the damage of weapons can do," Kennedy said in a pointed reference to the assassination of his uncles, President John F. Kennedy and Robert Kennedy. "And you want to arm our people even more. You want to add more magazines to the assault weapons so they can spray and kill even more people. Shame on you! . . . My God, all I have to say to you is, play with the devil, die with the devil." Kennedy, his voice rising with emotion, shook visibly as he spoke. "There are families out there, Mr. Speaker, and the gentlemen will never know what it is like, because they do not have someone in their family killed. It is not only the person who is killed, it is the whole family that's affected," said Kennedy.

Solomon angrily challenged Kennedy, saying, "When he stands up and questions the integrity of those of us that have this bill on the floor, the gentleman ought to be a little more careful. Let me tell you why."

"Tell me why," Kennedy responded.

"My wife lives alone five days a week in a rural area in upstate New York. She has a right to defend herself when I am not there, son, and don't you ever forget it," said Solomon.

Kennedy's words did not move Bob Barr. "The previous speaker on the other side speaks very loudly, if not eloquently, but some of his analogies, some of his terms are rather confusing. He talks about the devil. The devil is the person with a gun in his hand who murders anybody in this country. That is the devil. That is the person to which this legislation today is aimed," said Barr. "We must have this legislation to protect against exactly what the gentleman from Massachusetts is talking about."

Only six of the 73 GOP House freshmen voted against repealing the assault weapons ban. And only one of those six, Jon Fox of Pennsylvania, had received any PAC money from the NRA.

What the Republicans didn't foresee in pushing a vote on the assault weapons ban is that it would cost at least one of the freshmen his seat. Daniel Frisa of Long Island, New York, received nearly $6,000 from the NRA in 1995 and voted in favor of repealing the ban. The action so angered Carolyn McCarthy, a Republican, that she was moved to run for Frisa's seat. McCarthy, a 52-year-old nurse, had been widowed two years earlier when her husband was killed in a massacre by a crazed gunman on a Long Island Rail Road train. Her son was seriously wounded in the shooting, in which a semiautomatic weapon was used.

The day the House moved to repeal the weapons ban, McCarthy told the *New York Times*, "It's been two long years, and I very rarely break down. But I started crying this time because I couldn't believe that here I am defending something that most people think is needed and that I thought was safely passed. . . . It's sickening." Two months later McCarthy decided to run against Frisa as a Democrat after local GOP officials told her not to run in a primary against him. In announcing her candidacy, McCarthy said, "Since the Long Island Rail Road incident took place in this area, I truly felt Dan Frisa would vote to keep the assault weapons ban. But he didn't. . . . That's when I knew there was something wrong with our system. That is when I knew I had to run."

Another freshman who voted in favor of lifting the assault weapons ban was Mark Foley of Florida. In speaking for the measure during the floor debate, Foley said, "Guns do not kill the people; it is who is behind the trigger that kills the person. We keep trying to blame inanimate objects for crime."

The next day the *Palm Beach Post*, Foley's hometown paper, ran a story on the front page about the vote. Foley was the only one of four local representatives who had voted to lift the ban. Foley was also the only one of the four who had taken money from the NRA—more than $10,000.

The 41-year-old Foley represented Florida's 16th District, which is a true study in contrasts. It is located next to the ultrarich community of Palm Beach, where mansions, including that of Donald Trump, are located behind shrubbery and fences on the palm-tree-lined roads that run along the Atlantic coastline. On Worth Avenue, Palm Beach's main shopping street, Rolls-Royces carrying well-dressed older men and beautiful young women in very large hats and very short skirts cruise by the boutiques of Armani, Chanel, Cartier, Gucci, and Valentino. Palm Beach is an island of superaffluence where old money meets new, where the auction house Christie's has a local branch, and where the Goodwill store sells designer dress castoffs.

Palm Beach is not a part of Foley's district, but it is just a half mile over the bridge that spans Lake Worth, and its wealth spills over into Foley's district. Florida's 16th District is shaped like the letter *C* and rings West Palm Beach, a city of 70,000 people. In addition to parts of the city, it includes retirement communities; rural citrus, vegetable, and sugar farming areas; and part of the Everglades to the south and west.

Foley is one of the few moderates in the freshman class. In fact he is a former Democrat. He has a great deal more government experience than most of his classmates, and it is clear he is not as disdainful of government service as are many of the other freshmen. Foley was, at 23, the youngest person ever elected to Florida's Lake Worth City Commission. And he also served in both chambers of the Florida state legislature before being elected to Congress. He had a moderate reputation there as well and since coming to Congress had been more conservative in his voting record and followed the Republican leadership more closely than some people in his district expected.

He was one of only about a dozen of the freshmen who was pro-choice. "We are the majority, but we aren't the only people in America," Foley would say in reference to his classmates' unwillingness to compromise on many issues. Foley was much more familiar and more comfortable with compromising. Outgoing and affable, he formed friendships with older GOP moderates and with Democrats, unlike many of his freshman colleagues.

Foley was a natural politician who seemed equally at ease with the varied constituent groups he represented, whether they were wealthy donors, a senior citizens' group, or a rural chapter of the National Rifle Association. In late March, during a visit back to his district, Foley had the chance to deal with all of them.

It was especially important for Foley to be attuned to the concerns of the elderly. Only six other congressional districts in the country have more senior citizens per capita than Florida's 16th District, and Foley represented more senior citizens than any other member of the freshman class. One-fourth of all the voters in his district were over age 65. But Foley was still a supporter of the Medicare reforms the Republicans were pushing and had been holding public meetings throughout his district to talk about the proposed changes.

*   *   *

March 23, a beautiful Saturday morning. The sun is shining brightly, the temperature is in the 70s, and Foley would probably rather be at the beach. Instead, he's holding a public meeting in the dimly lit cafeteria of the Bear Lakes Middle School in his hometown of West Palm Beach, trying to explain to about 50 angry senior citizens how the Republican plans for Medicare will actually be good for them.

But they aren't buying it. Despite the warmth outside, the atmosphere in the cafeteria is definitely chilly. The older folks are peppering Foley with questions and letting him know they don't support what he's been doing in Congress for the past year. Most of those in the crowd didn't like his vote the day before on the sale of assault weapons. They're also hitting him on the Republicans' opposition to raising the minimum wage. But they're especially upset over Medicare.

"Medicare is not being cut. The growth rate is being reduced from 12 percent to 7 percent per year. . . . Do you think that's a cut, or do you think that's an increase?" Foley asks the crowd. "Absolutely it's a cut," yells a man from the audience.

Foley may not be thrilled with the reception he's getting from the senior citizens, but he doesn't show any impatience with them. He lets them talk, he doesn't bother to challenge them, and usually he doesn't even respond; he just moves on to the next person with a hand up.

Many of the people at the meeting are former union workers from the Northeast who moved down here after they retired. Seventy-seven-year-old Lou Kalb, a former machinist and union organizer from Brooklyn, is a Democrat who would like to see all the freshmen, including Foley, defeated. Kalb is carrying a copy of the National Council of Senior Citizens' newsletter, which has recently given Foley a bad report card. "So far as I'm concerned, they're first-term freshmen, and as far as I can help it they'll be last-term freshmen. . . . I would like to see them leave because I think they represent a danger to the interests and welfare and well-being of the people," says Kalb.

But a few people at the meeting feel differently. Richard Taylor, a retired small business man who owned a car wash in Palm Beach Gardens, has nothing but praise for Foley and his fellow freshmen: "I think they're the greatest thing that's happened to America in my lifetime, in my 64 years. . . . I hear these folks talking about Medicare and Medicaid, and if it wasn't for these freshmen going in and tackling this problem, these folks wouldn't have anything to worry about because we wouldn't have any Medicare or Medicaid."

Foley says most people tend to have strong feelings about the class of '94. "We have been both exalted and vilified by people who read the stories about the freshmen—'You guys are obstructionists' or 'You're the saviors of the world.' Those are the spectrums, and somewhere in the middle is probably the freshman class." Foley doesn't convince many people at his town meeting, but it doesn't seem to bother him. Later he would tell me he knew this wouldn't be a particularly friendly crowd because the school is located near a retirement community with lots of Democratic voters. "I'd get concerned [only] if there were 300 or 400 people there with signs. . . . I'm going to be truthful, I'm going to tell them about Medicare, what we hope to accomplish, and I'm going to face reality that if they don't like it they can return me home." But Foley is still running hard for reelection, even though he won in 1994 by 16 points and is not expected to have a tough race this time around.

That evening he stops by a barbecue and fund-raising auction put on by a Palm Beach County NRA group at a local shooting range, and he receives a much warmer welcome there than the one offered by the senior citizens.

George Russum, who heads the local gun group, says the previous day's House vote on assault weapons was a way to help the NRA identify its friends. "It gave us an idea of who's supporting the Constitution and who's not." The local NRA chapter definitely considers Foley a friend. "I'm supportive of Congressman Foley. I voted for him, and as long as he continues to represent my viewpoint in Congress, I'll continue to support him. I communicate with him on a regular basis to let him know what my feelings are on issues, particularly pertaining to constitutional issues. . . . You start messing with one part of the Constitution, you're messing with the whole thing. So you start screwing around with the Bill of Rights, what else is there?" asks Russum. "Are you going to take away baseball bats, are you going to take away shovels, pickaxes, take cars away from people? Where do you stop it? It's politically expedient to focus on the firearms."

Buck Kinnaird, an NRA member, is a former sports director for a local television station now handling marketing and public relations for the Atlanta Braves baseball team, which does its spring training in West Palm Beach. Kinnaird has known Foley for many years and helped with his campaign. Foley spoke to the local NRA chapter several times in 1994, and the group solidly supported him. The NRA is proud of its role in helping to elect the GOP freshmen. "They feel that they played a very important part in the '94 elections throughout the nation. On the local scene we were very happy that our candidates did quite well," says Kinnaird.

Kinnaird doesn't own an assault weapon, but he says, "I have a permit to carry a concealed weapon in Florida. . . . I do carry a .357 Magnum, and it has saved my life twice." And then, calmly and without noticeable embellishment, Kinnaird tells me how he has had to draw his gun twice in West Palm Beach to protect himself. The first time Kinnaird was set upon by four men who attempted to carjack his car. "I drew my gun, and thank goodness I didn't have to fire it. . . . They were saying, 'We're four and you're one,' and I pulled my gun and I said, 'No, I'm two.' And with that they ran."

"Another time I was coming out of a bar and two men accosted me and were going to rob me and I was able to pull my weapon and defend myself . . . I pulled my gun and stuck it in the belly of this big man and I asked him if he had prayed lately. And he said, 'Oh please mister, don't shoot me I've got a wife and two kids.' And I said, 'I'm going to count to ten and I don't want to see you here.' " And Kinnaird said the man ran away. "Thank goodness I didn't have to fire a shot. But I feel that if I had not had my weapon, I might not be here today," he says.

In the cool dark of the Florida evening, sitting at a picnic table talking with Kinnaird about his .357 Magnum while through the open door of the shooting range's clubhouse we can hear the auctioneer taking bids for rifles and gun paraphernalia, it seems a long, long way from Washington. It even seems a long way from Palm Beach.

*   *   *

It's 7:45 in the morning on Monday, March 25. About 70 people who have donated $1,000 apiece to Mark Foley's reelection campaign in exchange for the chance to meet Speaker Newt Gingrich, shake his hand, and have their pictures taken with him have gathered in a meeting room at the PGA National Resort in Palm Beach Gardens, about 15 miles north of West Palm Beach.

Foley is a little bit nervous. The event was scheduled to begin at 7:30, but the Speaker still hasn't shown up. George Bush's son Jeb, who unsuccessfully ran for governor of Florida in 1994, is working the room. A few people are munching on fruit and pastry or having a cup of coffee, but mostly they're just standing around in small clumps waiting.

Bush, an attractive and articulate conservative, says he thinks the Republican Congress has had a good first year but should have done a better job of explaining to people where they wanted to take the country. "It's critical that as Republicans advocate fundamental change that they explain that there's a lush green valley on the other side of that rocky hill, and we have not done that," says Bush. "This is not about big numbers with lots of zeros and commas; this is about ensuring that people and their children and their grandchildren have opportunity that they sense is going away from them. It needs to be put in human terms," Bush insists.

Standing nearby is Tom Lewis, the Republican who held Foley's seat in Congress for 12 years before retiring in 1994. He has admiration for what the freshmen are trying to do, but he also has the perspective and maturity of someone who's been there. "Some of them have stars in their eyes," he says of the freshmen. "They do make some pretty off-the-wall statements sometimes that cause people to start head scratching."

Lewis speaks with the candor politicians often acquire once they are out of office. "Everybody wants the budget balanced until it directly affects them. And when it affects them, they say, 'Don't do it to me; do it to the guy behind the tree.' That's one of the problems. Every agency is the most important agency in government. Every program that assists somebody is the most important, so don't cut mine. . . . That's the problem."

Lewis aptly observes that the Republicans attempted too much in 1995. "They should have just done three or four things the first year," he says. Like many senior Republicans, Lewis is a little concerned about Gingrich and his on-the-job training as Speaker. "Newt is a guerrilla fighter; he fights in the trenches. You have to give him credit for the Republican majority. Whether you like the man or dislike the man, you've got to give him credit. He had the stick-to-it-tive-ness, the ability and the drive and motivation to get a majority Republican House, and, by George, he did it. . . . He does shoot from the hip sometimes. He shouldn't draw the gun until he thinks about it a little bit."

An hour has been scheduled for this event, but Gingrich knows it won't take that long. He finally shows up around 8, a half hour late. He doesn't look awake yet, and he doesn't look very happy. He stands next to Foley in the front of the room while a small line forms. Two of Foley's staff are assigned as a "pusher" and "puller" to move people through quickly. "If everybody who's supposed to have their picture taken would please come forward so we can move through the line quickly, we'd appreciate it," one of Foley's staff members calls out.

Harold Van Arnum has been waiting in line for a few minutes. He's the chairman of a computer network company in Del Ray Beach. When it's his turn, he stands between Gingrich and Foley. The picture is snapped. Gingrich isn't smiling, but Foley has a grin so broad you'd think this was the happiest moment of his life. It takes less than 10 seconds. Van Arnum seems underwhelmed by his meeting with Gingrich. "I got a couple of grunts from him—he said 'uh-uh,' and so I guess that was, 'Hello, how are you doing?' " Gingrich would probably be the first to admit that meeting and greeting is not what he does best.

In the first few months of 1996, Gingrich seemed to be in a self-imposed public exile, rationing his press availabilities and public appearances and turning down requests for appearances on "Meet the Press" and "Nightline."

"Obviously, he made some mistakes, and he's going to try not to repeat them. The Air Force One business was not his finest hour," Gingrich's press secretary Tony Blankley told me. "Being a pretty good political strategist, he recognized that he needed to have a lower profile, and he had plenty of members who told him that, too. We had a bumpy winter," admitted Blankley.

But while Gingrich may have decided less was more when it came to sound bites at the beginning of 1996, that was not true when it came to what seemed to be his primary occupation—fund-raising.

Gingrich's unpopularity ratings rivaled those of Richard Nixon's shortly before he resigned from the presidency because of Watergate. And some of the freshmen, especially those facing tough races, were doing everything they could publicly to distance themselves from the Speaker. But when it came time to raise money, Newt was the first one they called, because no one could draw the GOP faithful like the Speaker.

The qualities that made Gingrich controversial were the same things that made him such a successful fund-raiser. He was a larger-than-life figure who always seemed to have something interesting to say. And the perception that he was under attack from the "left liberal media"—as Gingrich liked to describe reporters—just encouraged party activists to rally around him when they had the chance.

In the month of January alone, Gingrich appeared at nearly a dozen freshman fund-raising events, bringing over $1 million to their campaign coffers. Two of the biggest were for Dick Chrysler of Michigan, who raised $200,000, and George Radanovich of California, who took in $170,000. Gingrich also did a fund-raiser for Van Hilleary that earned Hilleary $45,000. Gingrich planned to do fund-raising stops in about 175 congressional districts, which worked out to about six a week, almost a fund-raiser a day.

Although Gingrich very publicly canceled some of his fund-raisers for freshmen like Mark Souder who disobeyed him and voted against reopening the government, Gingrich did not punish those who had just criticized him. If he had, the list of Republican fund-raisers would probably have been significantly smaller. Gingrich's willingness not to hold a grudge was a good thing for Foley, whose remarks to the *Washington Post* in December came off as a little snippy. As far as Gingrich was concerned, that was water under the bridge. He obviously wanted to remain Speaker, and that meant getting all of his freshmen reelected.

In less than 15 minutes, the pictures with the $1,000 donors are finished. Gingrich is quickly ushered by his small security detail through the kitchen and back corridors of the resort to another room for a news conference with Foley for local reporters. By 9 A.M. Gingrich is seated at the head table in the resort's banquet hall. When he is introduced by Foley, he receives a standing ovation from an audience of 700 who have paid either $250 to sit in the front of the hall or $150 for seats near the back. Gingrich seems to draw energy from the crowd, and for the first time this morning he looks like he's enjoying himself.

It's a 25-minute, vintage Gingrich speech. He lays out the accomplishments of the 104th Congress and the differences between the Republicans and Democrats. He

talks about Medicare reform and the president's veto of the Republicans' welfare reform plan. The professor in Gingrich can't help waxing eloquent on the creation of
the first computer 50 years ago and the technological advances, such as virtual reality
in every home, that lie in the not-too-distant future.

Then it's time for some humor with a point. The Declaration of Independence
says we have been endowed by God with the right to pursue happiness, Gingrich reminds the crowd. "The declaration does not say an entitlement to happiness, a quota
for happiness, a set-aside for happiness, a federal department of happiness. Can you
imagine Robert Reich as the federal czar of happiness? 'You at the third table—be
happy now or we will fine you.'" This gets a big laugh, as it's intended to. But Gingrich quickly gets serious. "We've gotten a lot done. The things we haven't gotten
done are almost entirely due to one person—Bill Clinton. In a few cases they're due
to the Senate." This is the most important election since 1932, Gingrich tells the
crowd. It's a clear choice between lower taxes and more local autonomy or higher
taxes and federal government bureaucrats who want to run every aspect of your life.

Gingrich wraps it up by urging the people to work hard for the GOP. "It's seven
plus one. We need seven more Senate seats and one president. . . . We need your
help. You are going to decide between now and November 5th how Florida goes.
Florida is a very important state for us. We need to reelect Mark, we need to carry
Florida, and with your help we are going to give our children a safer, a more prosper-
ous and a healthier America."

The Speaker is a hit. The crowd is on its feet, but before the applause for his
speech has even crested and as the Jupiter High School Choir prepares to launch into
"America the Beautiful," Gingrich is slipping out a back door.

Gingrich is headed for a small, private gathering at the lavish Palm Beach home of
Jose "Pepe" Fanjul, a Florida sugar baron. Fanjul's family fled Cuba when Fidel Castro came to power; Castro now lives in one of the former Fanjul homes. The Fanjuls
were the biggest sugar producers in Cuba and now, as the owners of Flo-Sun Incorporated, they are one of the biggest sugar producers in Florida.

This morning in Pepe Fanjul's living room are gathered 25 members of Team 100,
composed of people who have given $100,000 or more to the Republican Party. The
people in this room represent $2.5 million in donations to the Republicans. But
Gingrich doesn't seem impressed either with the surroundings or the company. The
donors don't seem all that impressed with him either. The mood is cordial but cool.
This is not like the crowd Gingrich just left at the PGA resort. This is a business
meeting.

After Gingrich makes a few brief remarks, the donors ask questions. They want to
know what the strategy is for winning the White House, who Dole's running mate
will be. Gingrich tells them Dole will have to focus his time in the important Midwest and the West; the South will have to be won locally.

The questions they ask reflect an interest in issues that are of concern to moderate
Republicans. These may not be the kind of people making the most noise and getting the most attention in the Republican Party. They may not represent as many

votes as the wing of the party influenced by the Christian Coalition. But this is where the money is.

These people want to know if Republican governor Bill Weld of Massachusetts can beat Democrat John Kerry in his reelection bid. Gingrich says maybe. They ask about medical savings accounts. Gingrich tells them the Republicans will probably get Clinton to veto the idea, just to prove a point, then remove it from legislation because the GOP can't win an override vote on the issue.

Gingrich is asked if the party position on abortion can be toned down at the convention. He doesn't mince words. Gingrich says they can't mess with the platform and the language calling for a constitutional amendment banning abortion because it will upset the right-to-lifers whose support they need. The best they can do, he says, is to allow pro-choice people to speak and keep Pat Buchanan and pro-life people off the stage during prime time.

Gingrich concludes by asking these people to give more, to get a friend to join. He tells them the reason the Republicans have to raise so much money is to offset the liberal media—they have to counter Dan Rather on the evening news. He shakes a few hands, and then he's gone, on to a fund-raising lunch for Florida freshman Dave Weldon, an event similar to Foley's.

Mark Foley considers the morning to have been a smash. He netted $170,000 at the breakfast, by far the most he's ever raised at a single fund-raising event.

*   *   *

The Fanjuls, who hosted the private Team 100 meeting, are very rich. *Forbes* magazine estimates their worth at more than $500 million. They have been greatly helped in amassing that fortune by the federal government's price support program for sugar, which limits foreign sugar imports to the United States and guarantees U.S. producers a high price for their sugar in the domestic market. Sugar price supports were first created in 1934 and were canceled in the 1970s when world sugar prices were high. But when world prices fell the program was revived in 1981.

In 1996 the U.S. price for sugar was around 22 cents per pound versus a world price for raw sugar of 16 cents a pound. The sugar price support program costs U.S. consumers almost $2 billion a year in higher grocery prices. But it has been remarkably resilient. The sugar program survived a challenge brought by Australia under the General Agreement on Tariffs and Trade (GATT). And when the North American Free Trade Agreement (NAFTA) was negotiated, a special exemption was included to ensure that Mexico could not import large quantities of cheaper sugar to the United States.

The General Accounting Office estimates that the program translates into a subsidy of about 5 cents for each pound of sugar produced in the United States. That means the Fanjuls and their U.S. sugar operation are benefiting by about $65 million a year. And the family is not shy about showing its gratitude.

Pepe Fanjul and his older brother Alfonso "Alfy" Fanjul Jr. carry Spanish passports; although they live in Palm Beach, they are not U.S. citizens or voters. But that does not stop them from being major contributors to U.S. political candidates. Pepe Fanjul supports Republicans and helped raise money for Dole as a member of his campaign's finance committee. His brother Alfy favors Democrats and served as a cochairman of Clinton's Florida campaign in 1992. The Fanjul family is remarkably bipartisan in their largesse to political candidates. In combination with their company, their employees, and their own political action committee, the Fanjuls donated more than $3 million to both parties from 1979 to 1996, giving new meaning to the term "sugar daddy."

In 1995–1996 the Fanjuls, their employees, and their company donated more than $400,000 to federal campaigns—$4,000 to Clinton, $28,000 to Dole, $125,000 to Democratic Party organizations, and $250,000 to the Republican Party, according to the Center for Responsive Politics, which tracks political donations. In addition, fifteen different members of the Fanjul family donated more than $275,000 directly to political candidates around the country.

The candidates the Fanjuls favored with donations ran the gamut of the American political spectrum. Liberal Democratic senators Paul Wellstone, Chris Dodd, Jay Rockefeller, and Carol Moseley-Braun all received $1,000 contributions. Tom Harkin received $2,000. Democratic House member Robert Torricelli, who was running for the Senate, was given $5,000. And House Democratic minority leader Richard Gephardt received $6,000 from various members of the family.

Among Republicans, New York's Alfonse D'Amato received $2,000. Virginia senator John Warner, running for reelection against a well-financed Democrat, received $10,000. North Carolina's Jesse Helms, also running for reelection, received $9,000. (The Democrat who was running against Helms, Harvey Gantt, got $2,000.) Massachusetts governor William Weld, a GOP moderate running for the Senate against John Kerry, received $6,000. Newt Gingrich got only $1,000.

Mark Foley received $6,000 from the Fanjuls, but he was not the only freshman to collect from the family. Van Hilleary and David Funderburk both got $1,000 contributions. Dick Chrysler got $500. And Democrat Adam Smith, who was running in Washington state against GOP freshman Randy Tate, received $14,000 from the Fanjul family.

But if the largesse the Fanjuls showed to politicians paid off handsomely for their sugar business, it did not work as well for them in another area. The Fanjuls owned 85 percent of a Miami-based financial company called FAIC Securities, which sold government, tax-exempt bonds and which, because of the Fanjuls' heritage, was able to take advantage of government programs designed to aid minority-owned firms.

Thanks to minority set-aside programs, FAIC Securities participated in numerous municipal and state bond underwritings in Florida, including issues by the Dade County Public Schools, the Florida Housing Finance Agency, the Broward County Public Schools, and the Miami International Airport.

FAIC chief executive Felix Granados told *Forbes* in 1995 that there was nothing wrong with the multimillionaire sugar family's taking advantage of the government program. "The category isn't 'economically disadvantaged.' It's 'minority.' And with a last name like Fanjul, that's just what they are," he said.

But it wasn't the Fanjuls' skillful use of minority set-aside quotas that attracted the attention of the Securities and Exchange Commission (SEC); it was their political donations and the government business they may have won as a result. In 1995 the SEC went to U.S. District Court asking the court to order FAIC securities, Alfonso and Jose Fanjul, Flo-Sun Sugar and the other business entities owned by the Fanjul family, to comply with subpoenas it had issued for documents from the financial firm. In a 65-page filing with the court, the SEC said it had reason to believe FAIC had violated the antifraud and "pay to play" provisions of federal securities laws.

The SEC cited two instances for this assertion. In November 1994 the Dade County Board of Commissioners had picked FAIC to be the senior comanaging underwriter for some county bonds. And in December 1994 the Florida Housing and Finance Authority selected FAIC to serve as comanaging underwriter for some revenue bonds. Because the Fanjuls had made donations of $7,250 to three Dade County commissioners and another $88,000 to gubernatorial, state cabinet, and state senate candidates, the SEC contended that FAIC had violated securities law that forbids underwriters from making any contributions to public officials or candidates for office in jurisdictions where they seek to participate in the underwriting of municipal securities.

A year later, in March 1996, FAIC agreed to a settlement with the SEC without admitting any wrongdoing. In exchange for the SEC's dropping the matter, FAIC had its license revoked and was ordered to pay more than $400,000 in fines and penalties.

Alfy Fanjul and his younger brother Pepe are the fourth generation of their family to grow and refine sugarcane. Their maternal great-grandfather, Andres Gomez-Mena, arrived in Cuba from Spain before the U.S. Civil War. Sugar was already Cuba's main crop, and Gomez-Mena set about building an empire, acquiring land and four sugar mills. His son, Jose "Pepe" Gomez-Mena, grew the business and served both as Cuba's secretary of agriculture in the 1930s and as the head of the country's association of sugar mill owners. By the 1950s the family's Cuban holdings had grown to include 10 sugar mills, three alcohol distilleries, and major real estate properties. But when Fidel Castro rose to power in 1959, the Fanjuls, like many wealthy Cubans, emigrated to the United States. In 1960 Alfonso Fanjul Sr. bought 4,000 acres of land near Lake Okeechobee, about 50 miles west of West Palm Beach, for $160 an acre. A sugar mill was constructed, and the first crop was processed the following year.

By 1996 the business had grown to the point where the Fanjul family and its Flo-Sun owned 340,000 acres and four sugar mills in Florida and in the Dominican Republic, processed 1 million tons of sugar a year, and employed 30,000 people. In the Dominican Republic they also owned a 7,000-acre resort and two hotels. The privately held company is now run by Alfonso Fanjul's four sons: Alfy serves as chairman and CEO, Pepe as president, and Alexander and Andres as executive vice presidents.

The 190,000 acres the Fanjuls own in Florida are to the south and east of Lake Okeechobee, where the rich, black, mucky marshland on the edge of the Everglades is perfect for growing sugarcane. The growing season runs from the late spring through the fall, and harvesting occurs from the end of October through March. For five months a year, during the harvest, the sugar mills operate seven days a week, 24 hours a day. The cutting of the cane, until fairly recently done by migrant workers with machetes brought in from Jamaica and other West Indian islands, is now done primarily by large machines.

After the cane is brought to the mill, it is chopped and fed through rollers to squeeze out the juice, which is boiled into a thick syrup. The liquid portion of the syrup, known as molasses, is then separated from the raw sugar. The crystallized sugar is refined and the molasses sold for cattle feed or rum production. Except for the mechanization of the process, sugar and molasses are still made essentially the same way they were 300 years ago in the Caribbean Islands.

Most of Flo-Sun's product is raw sugar sold in bulk to cane refineries, but the Fanjuls are expanding their own refinery operation and also market their own brand of processed sugar.

The government price supports that have kept the price of domestic sugar high and boosted the Fanjuls' profits have also encouraged cultivation on some land that at lower prices would probably be used for other crops or left fallow. Since the early 1970s the amount of Florida land cultivated in sugar has nearly doubled from 233,000 to 450,000 acres. About 40 percent of that land is owned by the Fanjuls. This has meant a continuing expansion of sugar production on land that used to be part of the Everglades ecosystem. Over the past 100 years, because of the pressure of development of all kinds, the size of the Everglades has been cut in half. The Everglades, often called the River of Grass, is a large body of slow-moving water that ranges in depth from a few inches to several feet and that serves as the filter for the aquifer that is the primary source of drinking water for much of southern Florida. It is also the habitat for a number of endangered and threatened species, such as alligators, crocodiles, manatee, and the Florida panther.

One of the biggest environmental problems with sugar production is the runoff, which is full of fertilizers high in phosphorus, cited by many environmentalists as a major cause of the degradation of the Everglades. Too much phosphorus can result in an overgrowth of algae and plants like cattails that choke off other native plants and throw the Everglades ecosystem out of balance.

The battle in Florida over what to do about cleaning up the Everglades has been intense. One proposal would have levied a 2-cent-per-pound tax on sugar growers and used the money for cleanup. In late 1995 a group called the Committee to Ensure Florida's Environmental and Economic Future began running TV ads in support of the sugar tax. The commercials showed a dead deer floating in water and charged that Mark Foley had taken "tens of thousands of dollars in campaign contributions from big sugar barons" and thought the taxpayers rather than the sugar producers should foot the bill for cleaning up the Everglades. Foley called the ad "reprehensible" and told the *Palm Beach Post,* "The ad is false and vile and seeks to destroy my family's Christmas."

In February Vice President Al Gore traveled to Everglades National Park to unveil the Clinton administration's proposal for Everglades restoration. The plan proposed a 1-cent-per-pound tax on Florida sugar along with $400 million in federal money to be used to acquire 100,000 acres of agricultural land and to pay for cleaning up damage to the Everglades ecosystem. This proposal caused Alfy Fanjul to part company with Clinton. Although Clinton might have regretted angering his formerly generous supporter, the political points he could score with environmentalists in Florida and around the country by proposing the Everglades restoration plan probably outweighed that concern.

Congress adopted its own plan for Everglades cleanup as part of the farm bill. The "Freedom to Farm Act" continued the sugar price support program and did not include a sugar tax. Foley, who was a member of the House Agriculture Committee, successfully offered an amendment that authorized spending up to $300 million in federal money to buy cane fields and take them out of production or swap them for other federal land in Florida. This former agricultural land would serve as a filtering marsh for the Everglades.

Despite all of the Republican gnashing of teeth over extra spending programs, there seemed to be no problem for Foley's amendment. It had the personal backing of Gingrich, who made a rare trip to the floor to vote in favor of it. It was seen as a good way to combat the negative press the Republicans had been getting on the environment. But that didn't mean everybody liked it. After the vote, Appropriations Committee chairman Robert Livingston came up to Foley and asked him where the $300 million had come from to pay for his amendment. "You stole that money," Livingston snapped.

When it came to the federal budget, money could indeed be fungible. Especially for the right cause.

Just a few weeks after his fund-raiser and visit to Pepe Fanjul's home, Foley took a helicopter ride with Bob Dole, who was campaigning in Florida, to take a look at the Everglades. Dole told reporters afterward that he did not favor the idea of a tax on sugar producers and touted what Congress had done in the farm bill for the Everglades.

In his first year in Congress, Foley tended to pick his battles. Although he avidly defended the sugar industry and its subsidy, he was willing to vote against the B-2 bomber, even though Northrop Grumman had a small plant in his district that employed 500 people. And in the area of the environment he showed a willingness to adapt. Foley was one of the freshmen who changed his votes on EPA funding. Although he voted with the leadership initially to cut the funding and authority of the EPA, he changed his mind after hearing from his constituents, and the last time the House voted on the EPA riders, Foley was with those who voted to restore money for the EPA.

"My allegiance is to my district first and to the Speaker second," said Foley, who had shown himself to be a fairly deft politician his first year in office.

Part Five

Summer–Fall 1996

Trying to Get Reelected

22

FINALLY: A BUDGET

Six months into the federal government's fiscal year there was still no agreement on the budget. Things were moving at a much slower pace than at the beginning of 1995. The Republicans weren't sure what to do next.

Clinton called on the Congress to finish the budget and listed the priority legislation he thought Congress should deal with before it adjourned for the year: welfare reform, a health care bill, an increase in the minimum wage, antiterrorism legislation, and campaign finance reform. What is striking about the list Clinton issued in late February is that it is so close to what the 104th Congress did eventually accomplish. And Clinton was sounding more like a Republican every day. Addressing a group of community activists, he said, "It's not like the Depression. The government is broke. . . . We've got to get rid of this deficit, so we can't go out and just hire everybody that doesn't have a job."

There were still five appropriations bills that had not been passed. Nine cabinet departments as well as dozens of federal agencies were without permanent funding. If there was going to be a permanent budget that Clinton would sign, the Republicans knew they would have to increase the funding for education, housing, environmental, and social service programs. They knew it, but they didn't like it. "The question is whether there is going to be a flank in this party that stands up for what we were elected for. . . . The killer perception among voters is that things are drifting back to normal," protested Mark Souder. Although Souder and other freshmen complained about spending too much, the GOP moderates threatened to vote against a budget deal if it spent too little.

By early March there had been nine continuing resolutions to keep the government operating, and Clinton took Congress to task for it. "We've got to stop government by continuing resolution," he said. Clinton knew he had the Republicans backed into a corner. The last thing they wanted was another government shutdown. So he was squeezing extra money out of them for some of his favorite domestic programs. Although a year earlier Republicans had boasted that they would kill his AmeriCorps volunteer program, it now looked like they would have to settle for a 15 percent cut in its funding.

On April 24 a final budget agreement was ultimately reached with the White House. But a dozen Republicans protested the additional spending that was thrown in to clinch a deal with Clinton. "It is important that the leadership remember that Republicans have made some tough compromises in the 104th Congress—and we have the scars to prove it. At the last hour, it is frustrating to concede all of our hard work to an administration whose sole goal is to increase the size and purview of the federal government," read a letter sent to GOP House members that was signed by Souder, Matt Salmon, John Shadegg, Steve Largent, and Lindsey Graham, among other freshmen.

The GOP leaders didn't care. They had a deal—finally. After seven months and two government shutdowns, the federal government would finally have a budget for 1996. The $163 billion spending plan included $5 billion of the $8 billion that Clinton had asked be put back into the budget for health, education, job, and environmental programs. And the group of antienvironmental riders that had proved so controversial were stripped from the bill at the very end.

The announcement of the final agreement seemed anticlimactic after everything that had happened.

The Republicans did not get everything they wanted, but they had achieved something significant: They had reversed a trend, taken a step forward. They were slowly reducing the size of the government and the number of federal programs. For the first time in decades, government funding for domestic discretionary programs was going down, not up. They had succeeded in cutting domestic discretionary spending by $22 billion below the 1995 federal budget level. "It's time to declare victory," declared House Appropriations Committee chairman Robert Livingston.

But the freshmen weren't so sure.

As usual, each side put its own spin on the agreement. The Republican leaders said they had won by making a major reduction in federal spending. Clinton insisted he had protected important domestic programs and prevented the Republicans from going too far with their cuts.

"Thirty years from now they won't look back and say about this that they [the Republicans] horse-traded programs with the president. They're going to say this is where the cost of government began going down," said Livingston. He was right. The president had won some political and rhetorical points. But the Republicans had won on substance. There had been a sea change.

Yet at the same time they were cutting domestic spending, the Republicans had increased spending for the military by nearly $2 billion. Domestic and military spending combined, however, represented only one-third of the $1.6 trillion federal budget. The government spent almost as much on interest on the federal debt as it did on defense. And Social Security, Medicare, and other federal entitlements cost $840 billion, a whopping half of the entire federal budget. Unless the growth of those entitlement programs was dealt with, there would be no way significantly to address the nation's debt problems. They were not part of the budget agreement. But nobody was going to take on Medicare or Social Security in an election year.

Among the freshmen there were differing views on what had actually been accomplished. "The budget was this burning issue. We had this big shutdown and we didn't get it done. It dragged on for a few months and then we passed it and it was kind of anti-climactic," said Rick White, summing it all up. He called the budget agreement "a huge step in the right direction" and said he was "thankful to have done as well as we did, and we ought to live to fight another day."

"Some people were saying, 'I'm not voting for that bill no matter what. It doesn't go far enough.' Others were saying, 'Let's pass it and move on,'" said George Nethercutt. "I like to win 21–0, but you can't all the time. If we win 21–20, I'm happy. Now we're ready for the next game. . . . I think we accomplished our objective. I felt OK about it. I didn't have any heartburn about should I vote yes or no. I didn't agree 100 percent, but I agreed enough to vote yes."

But for the purists it was not enough. It was never enough for them. "The Clinton administration got pretty much what they wanted, so they closed the deal," said budget hawk Souder. Although both sides compromised, Souder believed the Republicans had compromised more. And he was skeptical of the way the Republicans were touting the significance of the agreement. "To call it historic—it almost means you've become establishment and you believe your own hype. . . . This was just the best we could do."

Souder and some of the Republicans were angered because they were asked to vote on the plan without really knowing what was in it, in part because negotiations had gone right up until the eleventh hour, but also, he maintained, because the GOP leadership didn't want people to know all the details. "It was pretty clear the overwhelming sentiment was get it done and move on to next year. There was an attitude of resignation. People were resisting asking questions. They didn't want to know any bad news; they so desperately wanted good news."

"The people who voted no will be able to hold their heads higher than those who voted yes," Souder predicted. He was one of 20 House Republicans (including 10 freshmen) who voted against the final budget. Others were Graham, Largent, and Joe Scarborough. But freshmen budget hawk extraordinaire Mark Neumann supported the deal. Neumann was pleased that the deficit would go down under the agreement. Opponents like Souder were concerned that the budget still contained too much domestic spending and were disappointed it had no tax cuts. "Budget balancing is not the only thing; keeping spending and taxes down is the thing," said Souder. "We're at a low water mark," said the glum Souder. "I hope that somehow in the next 30 to 60 days we'll reestablish our vision."

Immediately after agreement was reached on the 1996 budget, Clinton called for a resumption of the talks on a long-term balanced budget plan. "We have a big consensus now that we ought to go ahead and balance the budget," he said without a hint of irony.

Clinton had submitted his new fiscal 1997 budget at the end of March. It would balance the budget by 2002, but more than half of its spending cuts would occur in 2001 and 2002, after Clinton had left office.

In early May it was the Republicans' turn. The House and Senate jointly offered a plan that, like Clinton's, would balance the budget by 2002 and that had most of its spending cuts in the final two years of the plan. The GOP proposal would cut $300 billion in domestic spending over six years. It included savings of $168 billion in Medicare, down from the $270 billion in the Republicans' 1995 plan, and there were also significant reductions in Medicaid and welfare programs. The Republicans also included a $500 per child tax cut for families with incomes under $110,000.

And the group of largely southern and western Democrats known as the Blue Dogs again offered their own budget in the House, which this time got 130 votes, including those of 20 Republicans. That was almost twice the number of votes they received in 1995. And the Blue Dog budget actually won 13 more votes than the Clinton budget, which got only 117. Because the Blue Dog plan had no tax cuts and proposed means testing for affluent Medicare recipients and limiting the growth in Social Security costs, it reduced the deficit by $137 billion more than the Republican plan.

Since the Republicans failed adequately to address entitlement spending in their proposal, they required disproportionate reliance on domestic spending cuts in the last years of the plan. But President Clinton called the GOP proposal "an encouraging move in the right direction." During a meeting of the House Budget Committee on which he served, Sam Brownback told me he thought it was "Republican lite."

Brownback thought the savings achieved by spending cuts should be put into reducing the deficit rather than spent on a tax cut. But it was an election year. Giving out a tax cut was the same kind of thing for the Republicans as an increase in the minimum wage was for the Democrats—it was politically popular with many of their core supporters. The Republicans, demoralized by the drubbing they took over their 1995 budget and their efforts to curb government spending, felt they had to do something to win back voters. They were nervous about their reelections and about Bob Dole's heading up the ticket. Because they had plenty to worry about, the Republicans decided two things they should worry less about were the deficit and Medicare reform.

It wasn't easy to be a congressional Republican that spring. Or as House Budget chair John Kasich said when he showed up in a Columbus, Ohio, emergency room, "Dole's down 15 points, Newt's in the witness protection program, and my own dog bit me." Kasich's 15-year-old springer spaniel, Abby, had bit his finger while Kasich was trying to separate her from some chicken bones. Kasich was just trying to do the right thing, but what he got for his trouble were three stitches on the middle finger of his right hand—an apt analogy for what had happened to the Republicans as a result of their budget efforts over the past year.

Cowed by the Democrats' distortions of their Medicare proposals and fearful of a backlash by the elderly at the polls, the Republicans scaled back their plan to reform the insolvent Medicare system. "We're not going to be as aggressive as we were in trying to deal with this problem. I can't keep walking into a buzzsaw with my troops—they won't be here to fight another day," said Kasich.

The Republicans trimmed their proposed savings for Medicare by $100 billion and did not address issues such as dramatic cost increases in the fee-for-service system or means testing for affluent Medicare recipients. They also gave up on the idea of increasing beneficiary premiums. The House budget chairman admitted he was "disappointed" with the new Republican Medicare plan: "We could have done better if this was separated from the political discussion. We were all committed to doing more, but we met a barrage of demagoguery" from the Democrats, said Kasich. Not known for mincing words, Kasich admitted that the latest Republican proposal did not come close to solving Medicare's solvency problems. "Medicare is going bankrupt. We have only inched forward. What we don't get done is left for the next group to do."

The Republicans made the political calculation that they would compromise and spend more in their 1997 budget to smooth the way for their reelections. They had to avoid another standoff with Clinton. They couldn't let a budget fight drag into the fall because they needed to get home and campaign.

As the summer wore on and the election drew closer, many of the Republicans, including some of the freshmen, were rediscovering the joys of government spending as they sought additions to the budget that would help their home districts. There was a lot more collegiality on the floor that summer as Democrats and Republicans worked together putting pet projects and extra spending into the appropriations bills.

Rather than holding their ground and saying, "Here's what we did, and here's why it was the right thing to do," the Republicans decided to give a little—in some cases to give a lot. This approach sent a message to the voters that the Republicans *had* been wrong in trying to do so much and the Democrats were right to say they were going too far.

The Republican budget narrowly passed 216–211, but 19 Republicans, including 16 freshmen, voted against the plan when it came to the floor in June. The no voters included the usual suspects—Neumann, Souder, Largent, Salmon, and Shadegg. But also voting no was freshman leadership delegate Sue Myrick.

After the vote, Gingrich appointed a task force headed by sophomore Peter Hoekstra and freshman J. D. Hayworth to look into the freshman revolt and come up with suggestions for how to avoid that kind of embarrassing display of insubordination in the future. One GOP House leader told the *Washington Post,* "The task force is along the lines of a military after-action review. We need to find out what went wrong." But the answer seemed pretty obvious: spend less.

The "Just Say No" kids wouldn't quit. Four appropriations bills had already been passed, but nine remained to be done. Freshman Gil Gutknecht of Minnesota came up with an idea. He would offer an amendment that would cut 1.9 percent from every program in every appropriations bill to make up for the $4.1 billion that was being added to the deficit in 1997. Gutknecht offered the amendment eight times, every time an appropriations bill came to the floor. A diehard group of freshmen always spoke in favor of it and always voted for it—people like Neumann, Souder,

Shadegg, Myrick, and Tom Coburn. The first time Gutknecht offered his amendment, on the Interior Department's appropriation, he received 128 votes. His all-time high, on the legislative branch appropriation, was 172 votes. The low was 45 votes on the veterans–Housing and Urban Development spending bill. The amendment never came close to passing, but Gutknecht and the other freshmen were making a point.

23

CAMPAIGN FINANCE REFORM

IT HAD BEEN MORE THAN A YEAR since Van Hilleary of Tennessee led the freshman charge in the House for a term limits amendment to the Constitution. Less than two months after the House vote, in May 1995, the Supreme Court struck down as unconstitutional the term limits laws that had been passed by 23 states. In its decision the Court ruled that the only way to limit the number of terms members of Congress could serve was to pass a constitutional amendment to do so. The court decision was a blow to the term limits movement, but its supporters vowed to press on.

In spring 1996 another Tennessean, freshman GOP senator Fred Thompson, pushed for a term limits vote in the Senate. But Senate rules made such a vote difficult. On April 23, when the Senate took up term limits, opponents of the measure threatened a filibuster. In order to force a vote on term limits, Thompson would have to win 60 votes to invoke cloture and cut off debate.

"We are not capable institutionally of dealing with the overwhelming problems facing this country under the current setup," said Thompson, arguing on the Senate floor for a vote. "We are bankrupting our country. Our Social Security system cannot survive as currently constituted. Medicare will fail. Within a few years a handful of programs and the interest on the national debt will take all of our revenues. . . . Just as sure as I'm standing here, catastrophe lies down the road, and we're fiddling while Rome burns. That's what my constitutional amendment for term limits is all about. . . . We are putting reelection above all else. Reelection requires spending. That is the way we buy votes, with taxpayers' own money. Then we give it back to them a little bit at a time. That's the cruel, hard truth."

As the Senate took the procedural roll call to determine whether there would be a term limits vote, Thompson stood in the front of the Senate chamber looking somber, his arms folded across his chest. Every Senate Republican voted to limit debate and to have a vote on term limits, including Strom Thurmond, who had served in the Senate for 40 years. Even Bob Dole, who had been in the Senate for 28 years and who admitted he had always been "lukewarm" on the idea of term limits, voted yes. But only five Democrats joined them, and that wasn't enough. Thompson and the pro–term limits forces were two votes short of being able to invoke cloture.

Immediately after the vote Thompson and several other senators appeared in the Senate press gallery to speak with reporters. "We got more votes today than anybody thought we would," said Thompson. He called it a first step. And he predicted Republicans would be able to use the term limits issue on the campaign trail in November. But in fact opposition to term limits did not prove to be much of a problem for the Democrats that fall. The issue had fallen off the voters' radar screen. They may still have liked the idea in principle, but there were a lot of things they cared about more. The Republicans had been the victims of their own success. The turnover of the House and Senate in 1994 had significantly blunted the issue. So many incumbents had been defeated and there were so many new members it was hard to stay outraged over a lack of new blood in Congress. The need for term limits just didn't seem that great anymore. Members of Congress were being term-limited—by the voters and by themselves.

But term limits or no term limits, the point Thompson was trying to make about the fever to get reelected and the race for campaign cash that it necessitated was very real, and this Congress had not addressed it. It was a vicious circle, with lawmakers chasing after campaign contributions and rewarding big donors by spending money on the programs and tax benefits they sought.

In June 1995 Gingrich and Clinton had shaken hands over the idea of appointing a blue-ribbon commission to look into campaign finance reform, but they couldn't even agree on how many members the commission should have, and nothing had happened. A year after that famous handshake, the New Hampshire man who had proposed the idea of a commission to the president and the Speaker came to Washington to try to make one more pitch. "Up in our part of the country, a handshake really means a handshake," said a frustrated Frank MacConnell.

Several members of Congress decided to take matters into their own hands. In the Senate, Republican John McCain of Arizona and Democrat Russ Feingold of Wisconsin introduced bipartisan campaign finance reform legislation that both Ross Perot and Clinton endorsed. The McCain-Feingold bill would set voluntary spending limits for congressional candidates and provide free and reduced-cost television time and mailings for those who abided by the limits. The legislation would also limit out-of-state contributions, abolish PACs, and eliminate the unregulated soft money that political parties could accept. The contribution limits would be relaxed for candidates facing wealthy opponents who either used their own money to fund their campaigns or who did not stick to the limits. Unlike many past campaign finance reform plans, this one did not include a public financing component, which was especially unpopular with Republicans. The measure had 15 cosponsors, but just three of them were Republicans, freshman Fred Thompson and two GOP members who were retiring, Nancy Landon Kassebaum of Kansas and Alan Simpson of Wyoming.

In the House, similar legislation named the "Bipartisan Clean Congress Act" was introduced by freshman Linda Smith, senior Republican Chris Shays, and Massachusetts Democrat Marty Meehan. The House bill had more Republican cosponsors than the Senate version, including freshmen Brian Bilbray, Mark Sanford, Michael Forbes, Tom Davis, Jack Metcalf, Joe Scarborough, and Sam Brownback.

Both measures were supported by Common Cause, Ross Perot's United We Stand group, Public Citizen, and the League of Women Voters. But they also had some powerful enemies, including many members of Congress. The National Right to Life Committee, the Christian Coalition, and the National Rifle Association on the right and the American Civil Liberties Union on the left all opposed the measures. And a number of PACs threatened to turn off the money tap to members who had signed on to the legislation.

McCain and Feingold argued that limiting spending would open up the system for challengers because it was so much easier for incumbents to raise money, and candidates who spend the most are invariably the winners, especially when their spending advantage is vastly disproportionate to that of their opponents. But that's just what their colleagues were afraid of—losing their edge.

"The people's cynicism about the way we seek office has grown into contempt for the way we retain office. The foundations of self government rest on the public's faith in the basic integrity of our political system. That faith is shaken today," McCain and Feingold wrote in an op-ed piece in the *Washington Post* in February 1996.

In the House Linda Smith became the most vocal proponent of campaign finance reform. This did not endear her to her colleagues but did win her a great deal of attention from reporters. She became something of a media darling for her relentless determination and her willingness to say almost anything about the venality of her colleagues and the corruption of the existing campaign financing system. "Over the last 20 years we have changed from a political system of the people to a political system of the PAC. When we sell our political system to the highest bidder, we're in deep trouble," declared Smith.

She was happy to point out that the top fund-raisers in the freshman class had used their seats on the Ways and Means and Commerce Committees to leverage bucks. Fifteen of the top 20 PAC recipients among the freshmen were assigned to one of three committees, Ways and Means, Commerce, and Banking and Financial Services. John Ensign of Nevada told the *New York Times* in February 1996 that Ways and Means was "a great committee to raise money on."

Smith was particularly opposed to the cocktail fund-raising events members held in Washington for lobbyists; she called them "purely and simply a shakedown"—of the lobbyists and of the members. "We don't tell people no around here, and we don't because of these fund-raisers across the street," said Smith. "The money comes to us at receptions from these lobbyists, from these PACs, and we don't ever have to go home even to campaign. . . . I want incumbents to have to fight for their seat, show they're worthy of the seat and go home and get their votes from real people in their district, not just from slick media campaigns."

These were fighting words to some of Smith's colleagues.

Smith had a long history of supporting campaign finance reform, going back to her time in the Washington state legislature. When she wasn't able to push a reform bill through the state senate, she took the issue directly to the voters in the form of a ballot initiative to limit campaign spending and donations from special interests, which passed in 1992. And six months after coming to Congress, Smith had the experience that convinced her to do something about fund-raising on the federal level. It happened while she was pushing for the amendment to the agriculture appropriations bill to cut federal funds for extension services and crop insurance for tobacco farmers. When Republican conference chairman John Boehner passed out checks from tobacco PACs to Republican members on the floor of the House, Smith was outraged.

The episode provided a powerful illustration for Smith to use in championing her cause. What could better illustrate the need for reform than passing out checks on the floor? Smith asked. "Why didn't they do it in the bathroom?" She was convinced the tobacco lobby had bought the votes of members, including some of the freshmen who didn't come from tobacco states and had no particular reason to vote for the federal program. "My intentions are to close the fund-raisers here. My intentions are to make sure that never again do I wonder about the checks from the tobacco lobby being passed out one night at a fund-raiser and going and losing the vote the next day to the tobacco lobby. What those checks did to the votes the next day, I don't ever want to think about again. And the American people shouldn't have to be concerned with that."

In championing her crusade, Smith could come off as pretty holier-than-thou. After all, she had taken her share of PAC money in the past. During her 1994 campaign for Congress, about a quarter of the $500,000 she spent came from PACs. And in her first year in office she took about $20,000 in PAC money before deciding to stop.

Smith claimed that her freshman colleagues were becoming addicted to the system. "The strength of the freshmen will be shown in whether or not we can put actions behind the words of our campaigns. When we ran for office, we said we're going to be different and we're going to reform Congress and we're not going to be like the other guys that were controlled by special interests. If we can take the vote and stand and change this system—close the lobbyists' checkbooks, send the campaigns back home—we will have done what we promised the American people we would do: truly be different and deliver a cleaner Congress," said Smith.

Since most of the freshmen ran against corruption and special interest control, Smith asked, "How can they not now change the system, after they promised they would be different?" The answer may have been finding out what it took to get re-elected. And what it took was money.

In 1995 the freshmen raised $24 million, with almost $10 million of it coming from PACs. They spent more time raising money than they did on legislation or taking care of constituents, Smith maintained. Every day many of the freshmen would spend hours making phone calls to potential contributors. And virtually every night they were in Washington they attended a round of fund-raisers. Some members were more conscientious about attending the fund-raisers than they were about going to committee hearings. The fund-raisers even controlled the congressional schedule, Smith insisted. "If there were a half-dozen fund-raisers on the schedule, we had to be back [in Washington] whether or not there was anything to do" on the floor, said Smith.

There were about 700 House fund-raisers held in Washington in 1995. To make it easier for lobbyists and members, the National Republican Congressional Committee (NRCC) put out a weekly and monthly calendar of events listing all the upcoming Washington fund-raisers for Republican House members. Events were most often held at the Capitol Hill Club for Republicans and the National Democratic Club for Democrats, both just a few blocks from the House office buildings and owned by the Republican and Democratic Parties. Sometimes members would have a breakfast event at a nearby restaurant, but the staple of the fund-raising circuit was the cocktail reception held between 5:30 and 8 P.M. Often members would zip over to the receptions in between votes, and many times votes would be suspended for a few hours when the House was in session late, to make it easier for the members to attend the fund-raisers.

Freshmen usually charged $250–$500, but the older members could get away with charging $1,000. It was typical for members to have about two a year; some had many more. Usually the members hired a firm that specializes in political fund-raising to organize their events. Since fund-raising has become a serious business, involving billions of dollars, there are hundreds of fund-raising companies, telemarketing firms, direct mailers, and people who sell donor lists. These firms are paid in a variety of ways. Some get a percentage of the take, some get a flat fee of about $3,000 per fund-raiser, and some are on a monthly retainer. In exchange for their fee, the firms help make phone calls, do an invitation list, arrange for the location and the caterer, handle RSVPs, do follow-up mailings, make name tags, and generally see that everything runs smoothly.

Invitations to a freshman fund-raiser typically list not only the name of the member who will benefit but the names of several senior members who are sponsoring the event. These names are printed on the invitations as bait to attract lobbyists, who know the senior members will at least put in an appearance and may even have a few words with them.

As soon as they arrived in Washington, Smith said, the freshmen were trained not on how to pass a bill but on how to raise $100,000 for their campaigns in six months. "I was immediately trained to dial for dollars." The House Republicans set up the Incumbent Retention Committee to make sure that all of the Republicans got reelected. Since the freshmen were perceived as the most vulnerable, they got the most attention. Congressional freshmen are always considered more at risk for defeat because they are generally less well known in their districts, and this class was particularly vulnerable because many of them had won seats by narrow margins in swing districts previously held by Democrats. The freshmen were assigned upper-class "buddies" who would meet with them periodically to check on their progress—how they were running their offices, handling the mail, taking care of constituent case-work, and perhaps most important, how much money they had raised.

They were encouraged to set goals, such as raising a certain amount through individual contributions, PAC donations, direct mail solicitations, and a major district fund-raiser with Newt Gingrich. And they were told to draw up budgets to determine the total amount they would need to raise.

About three months into the term, the Incumbent Retention Committee made a list of what it considered to be problem areas for the freshmen: More than 20 of them still had campaign debts of $50,000 or more; there had been a fair amount of staff turnover and turmoil in the freshman offices because many of their chiefs of staff were young and without Hill experience; a majority of the freshmen had a back-log of unanswered constituent mail; and many of the vulnerable freshmen had shut down their district campaign offices, something the leadership considered to be a mistake. When it came to fund-raising, the internal memo said, many of the fresh-men had "not learned that the member must make calls to have a successful DC PAC event." What was more serious, "There are persistent rumors from downtown [meaning the lobbyists] that some freshmen are making fundraising calls from their congressional offices," which is illegal.

But despite a few glitches, most of the freshmen were raising money hand over fist. Class president Roger Wicker ranked just 19th among the freshmen in PAC do-nations, having received $152,000, but that represented a whopping 84 percent of all the money Wicker raised in his first year in office. Twenty of the freshmen raised a total of more than $350,000 a person in 1995, but those at the very top of the list were well above that figure. Jon Christensen was at the top of the class when it came to fund-raising, having taken in more than $686,000 in just his first year. Tom Davis of Virginia raised $644,000, John Ensign raised $626,000, Greg Ganske of Iowa raised $553,000, and Frank Cremeans of Ohio raised $543,000.

By the end of the 1996 campaign, the freshmen had proven themselves to be in-credibly able fund-raisers. Twelve of the top 30 House fund-raisers were freshmen. Ensign, who raised almost $2 million for his campaign, was the top freshman fund-raiser. Ganske and Christensen each raised almost $1.8 million. Ken Bentsen of Texas wound up being the top Democratic freshman fund-raiser, bringing in nearly $1.7 million.

Ann McBride, the president of Common Cause, said the freshmen had "come to shake Washington up," but instead "they stayed to shake it down."

The freshmen were acting under strict instructions from their party leaders, who told them raising a substantial war chest would scare off challengers and help ensure their reelection. You send a message by fund-raising early, according to "Marketing Your FEC Report," a handout given to the freshmen in 1995. In nonelection years the reports were filed twice a year, but in election years they had to be filed quarterly. "The week after you have filed your FEC report, your opponent, the press, and the

DCCC [Democratic Congressional Campaign Committee] will undoubtedly have a copy of your report. Your opponent will use your FEC report to make sure you are seen as the 'fat cat' Republican; the press might use your report to show that you are a special interest congressman and the DCCC will use your fundraising report as a means to recruit a candidate against you," read the handout. "It is up to you and your campaign to plan a strategy to ensure that the most favorable message about your FEC report is reflected in the press."

Many of the freshmen took the advice to heart. In a fund-raising letter sent in June 1995, Rick White of Washington state wrote, "In a little over a week the media will give me a grade for my first six months in office. That grade won't be based on anything I've accomplished while serving in Congress. That grade will be based solely on the contribution report I filed with the Federal Election Commission June 30."

The handout provided tips for spinning the report: It advised freshmen who had raised a lot of money to turn it to their advantage by pointing out that they had raised more than their Democratic predecessors had in their first six months in office or by highlighting "what a formidable opposition you will be in the election and whoever is considering running against you should think twice about it." If, in contrast, their average dollar donation was fairly low, they could "stress the broad base of support you received throughout your district and how the 'average voter' is supporting your cause." And if they received substantial donations from major business interests in their district, they were advised to "get their permission to include their name in a press release about your FEC report. Highlight how important they are to the economic success of your district."

The Republican leadership ran seminars for the freshmen on writing a finance plan, PAC fund-raising, major donor solicitation, and direct mail fund-raising. And they kept close tabs on who was raising what.

The second floor of the NRCC was remodeled shortly after the Republicans took over. The idea was to make it as comfortable as possible to encourage the members to go there to fund-raise. There were 10 small offices that the members could use to make calls. The blue carpeting, gray walls, and gray Formica desks were modern and pleasant but fairly nondescript. All the members really need is a phone and a chair.

Some members tried to stay at arm's length from fund-raising and did not make many calls themselves but hired people to do it for them. Other freshmen were natural-born fund-raisers and actually seemed to enjoy doing it. One of the most successful Democratic freshman fund-raisers was Bill Luther of Minnesota. Having won his election in 1994 by just 550 votes after spending $1.1 million, $400,000 more than his Republican opponent, Luther wasn't taking any chances this time. Luther always seemed to be over at the DCCC making fund-raising calls. He would be there at 7:30 in the morning. He would be there at 9 at night. Luther had no problem calling people at home at night and asking them for a $100 contribution. By the end of his first year in office, Luther had raised $445,000, the ninth highest total of all the freshmen, Republicans and Democrats alike. And by the end of the campaign, Luther had raised almost $1.4 million.

The DCCC made available to members a list of what PACs had given and how much. At the DCCC there was a spiral-bound reference book, the Bible of fund-raising, that listed PACs by category so the members could relate their committee assignments or companies within their districts to the PACs. That way they could shoot for the most target-rich environment.

Unlike the NRCC, which had private cubicles with doors, there were only a few private spaces at the DCCC. Most of the Democratic members sat in an open room at desks with telephones about 3 feet away from other members who were doing exactly the same thing they were. "It's very degrading," said one freshman Democrat who spent about 10 hours a week raising money his first year but upped that to about 20 hours in 1996. Fund-raising time was built into every day's schedule. You would try to set aside 20 hours a week and hope to get in 15, what with votes and unexpected things coming up, said the freshman.

The Democratic freshman said he tried to have a major fund-raiser either in his district or in Washington about every six weeks. "You always had to have something coming up" because that's what the calls are for—'I'm having an event. Can you come? Can you be a sponsor?' 'I see you're not on the RSVP list'; 'Just calling to thank you for coming, and by the way I'm having another one next month.'" The freshman said he could see no way members of Congress would vote to change the campaign financing system because "they got elected, they have succeeded in this system, so it's absurd to think they'll change it." Another senior Democrat said, "The whole system is obscene because of how much time you have to spend fund-raising."

Mark Souder was one of the few freshmen who had a different approach to fund-raising. He did the bulk of it back in his district, and he did not see the need to collect enormous sums of money. After his first year, only four freshmen of either party had raised less than Souder's $129,000. He was able to do that for several reasons. Running a campaign in Fort Wayne, Indiana, was not nearly as expensive as in many other districts. And Souder had worked hard to cultivate his constituency, to make contacts. "If you build a local base, you don't have to do [lots of D.C. fund-raising]. I want to have the ability to say, 'I don't need your money.' I want to be able to look at myself," said Souder, who returned money sent to him by the tobacco PACs.

George Nethercutt was a reasonably successful fund-raiser, but he wasn't obsessed by it. He fell right in the middle of the class in terms of raising money, having raised $246,000 in his first year in office. By the end of the campaign, Nethercutt had raised just over $1 million. Nethercutt set a personal goal of getting two-thirds of his money from individuals and one-third from PACs, and most of it came from Washington state. He used events like coffees, lunches, and breakfasts back in his district as well as direct mail appeals and cocktail receptions in Washington. He hired a consultant to help, but Nethercutt would make his own calls before an event, although he said he didn't spend more than five or six hours a week doing it.

Van Hilleary had to spend a great deal more time than Nethercutt chasing contributions. Since he didn't accept PAC money, Hilleary had to work twice as hard as the other freshmen and had to raise most of his money at home. But Hilleary came from one of the poorest and most rural districts of any of the freshmen, including the Democrats. Hilleary's district had a median household income of just over $20,000 and a per capita income of less than $10,000. Only three other freshmen— Ed Whitfield of Kentucky, Roger Wicker of Mississippi, and Tom Coburn of Oklahoma—represented districts that were as poor.

But Hilleary's district wasn't cheap to campaign in because it was served by several major media markets. That forced Hilleary to do a lot of fund-raising in the Tennessee cities outside his district: Nashville, Knoxville, Chattanooga, and Memphis. "My goal was to get the whole state Republican Party to adopt me," said Hilleary.

Hilleary started fund-raising in earnest in the summer of 1995, and by late fall he had raised $200,000. To do that he had to spend a portion of every day fund-raising, whether he was in Washington or Tennessee. When he was in Washington, he did it by telephone. When he was back home, it usually involved personal appeals as part of his regular appearances with constituents and supporters: "Gee, I sure could use your help."

In Washington Hilleary would spend about three hours a day over at the NRCC making phone calls. But in the last six months of his first term, that amount of time increased significantly. Because he didn't take PAC money, he didn't see much point in hiring a fund-raising consultant. Hilleary raised every dime himself.

Hilleary's primary resource was a list of names of people who had helped him in the 1994 campaign. He appointed finance chairmen in charge of working to set up events and identifying donors in each of the 22 counties in his district. Each had a quota he was supposed to meet. Hilleary also developed a list of wealthy Tennessee Republicans who could help not only by giving themselves but by asking their friends to give.

"The thing I hated the most was cold calling, just calling up and asking for money," said Hilleary. Instead, he tried to leverage his time and phone calls by calling to ask people if they would host a fund-raiser for him. Then he would call people asking them to be cosponsors of the event. That meant they would not only come and contribute but convince others to do the same.

He also made direct mail appeals in Tennessee about every three weeks from a campaign file of 6,000 names. Hilleary was extremely well organized in his efforts. He used charm; he used persuasion; he used whatever worked. Mostly, he just kept doing it—over and over.

There was a kind of competition among the freshmen in terms of fund-raising. People knew how everyone was doing. Fund-raising was something that could be easily quantified. Occasionally at GOP conference meetings they would announce the names of the people who were doing well. Hilleary was one of those doing well, especially for someone who didn't take PAC money. Hilleary had raised $315,000 by the end of his first year in office, which ranked him 25th in the class in terms of fund-raising. By the end of the campaign, he had raised more than $1.2 million, more than 90 percent of it in Tennessee.

Sam Brownback told me in the fall of 1995 that although he was a cosponsor of the campaign finance reform bill, he would continue to take PAC money because otherwise he couldn't compete. "I think it's a corrupt system. People put money in to get your ear and to influence the system," Brownback said. The sheer amount of what has to be raised is what bothered Nethercutt the most about the system. "I would rather not raise money," he said, echoing the sentiments of many members. But if they wanted to be reelected, they felt they had no choice.

*   *   *

There was very little enthusiasm among members of Congress to change campaign financing. Neither party really wanted reform that would put an end to PAC contributions and cut off their money—the mother's milk of politics. They liked the edge they had over challengers. They wanted to keep their jobs.

For 20 years, congressional Democrats and Republicans had taken turns killing various campaign finance reform proposals—usually it was House Democrats and Senate Republicans. In 1992, when Congress finally did manage to pass a reform bill, it was vetoed by President George Bush, who said it favored Democrats. When he served in the minority, Gingrich had introduced campaign finance reform that would have banned PACs, but once the Republicans took over and were attracting more PAC money, Gingrich changed his feelings about fund-raising reform.

Still, McCain and the other reformers remained undeterred. After pushing for months for a vote on their legislation, McCain and Feingold were told they could bring it to the floor the last week in June. McCain was pleased but admitted he wasn't too optimistic about the chances for success. Mitch McConnell, the Darth Vader of campaign finance reform, had vowed to do everything he could, to "use all available parliamentary tactics"—in other words, a filibuster—to block consideration of the bill. The Kentucky Republican had long been totally and unabashedly opposed to any campaign finance reform. "I've handled this issue for our side for a decade. I make no apologies," said McConnell.

He obviously felt taking such a position wasn't going to cost him many votes. McConnell liked to point out that in the fall of 1994 he had led the Senate Republicans in a filibuster to block consideration of campaign finance reform and it didn't hurt the GOP one bit, since they won a huge victory in November. McConnell even seemed to take pleasure in being the front man blocking reform, charging that the McCain-Feingold approach was a limitation on free speech and public participation in the political process.

But Public Citizen, one of the groups supporting the bill, was critical of Mc-Connell's efforts and pointed out that since January 1995 he had raised more than $2.2 million in campaign cash, including nearly $700,000 from PACs. By the end of the 1996 race, McConnell had spent $4.6 million to win reelection versus the $1.7 million his Democratic opponent spent. McConnell and other Republicans claimed they had to raise more money to counter the efforts of labor unions and "the liberal media." "If you level the playing field financially for someone like me, in what way have you created a competitive situation?" McConnell said to the *Washington Post* after the election.

When the Senate finally took up campaign finance reform on June 24, 1996, it felt very much like a replay of the term limits vote. The cast of characters was different except for Fred Thompson; this time it was the Democrats pushing for a vote instead of the Republicans. But as with term limits, the bill's sponsors had to win 60 votes to prevent a filibuster. It was a long shot. Many members didn't even seem to be focused on the issue, so sure were they that it wouldn't come to a vote. At one point during the debate, with fewer than 10 senators in the chamber, Democrat Paul Simon of Illinois said, "There are more senators raising money than are here on the floor of the Senate."

Knowing that it was probably hopeless, McCain still pressed on. "This bill will not cure public cynicism for politics. But we believe it will prevent cynicism from becoming contempt and contempt from becoming utter alienation," he argued. He brought with him to the Senate floor a chart illustrating that in 1995 PACs had given $59.2 million to congressional incumbents and $3.9 million to challengers. "If the challengers were voting today instead of the incumbents, I think the outcome might be very different," said McCain.

McConnell contended that trying to limit PACs would not only be unconstitutional, it wouldn't work because politicians and campaign contributors always found a way around the rules. "Spending limits are like putting a rock on Jell-O. It oozes out the sides."

He had a point. Reforms could have unintended consequences, and it was hard to predict exactly how things would change if the McCain-Feingold measure was passed. In 1974 Congress had passed election financing reforms in reaction to the Watergate scandal and the funding abuses of the Nixon campaign. The 1974 bill created public financing of presidential elections and set contribution and spending limits for Congress, although the spending limits were later struck down by the Supreme Court as a violation of the First Amendment. Some of the reforms, such as increased public reporting requirements for candidates, had worked pretty well. Some, like the creation of political action committees, had not. The idea behind PACs was to open up the process and limit special interest influence. But the political action committees had become a big part of the problem.

Increasingly, special interests were cutting out the intermediaries of the political parties and spending their money directly to buy TV advertising for "issue advocacy" that clearly favored one candidate over another. And just as McConnell said, candidates and political parties had found ways around the system. One big loophole was "soft money," the unlimited donations made directly to political parties from corporations, unions, and special interests as well as individuals that can be used for "party-building" activities. The Republican and Democratic Parties raised almost three times as much soft money in 1995–1996 as they had in 1991–1992, according to the Federal Election Commission. The Republicans raised $50 million for 1992 and $138 million for 1996 versus the Democrats' $36 million and $124 million.

The pressure to raise huge sums of cash had led to abuses and violations on the part of both parties, but seemingly to a much greater degree by the Clinton campaign. And revelations about foreign donations to both parties and the Clinton White House's using the Lincoln bedroom for sleepovers as a reward to major givers started surfacing even before the election.

As the Senate continued its debate on campaign finance reform for a second day, Fred Thompson talked about having to raise $15,000 a week to run for reelection. "That is not why I came to the United States Senate," he complained. "The money does not flow to ideas; the money flows to power," Thompson said, arguing that the American people believe any system that costs so much and takes up so much of their representatives' time "cannot be on the level." Pointing to congressional reluctance to pass either campaign finance reform or term limits, Thompson said, "We always want to be responsive to the American people unless it affects us and our livelihood."

"Without question money is distorting democracy," asserted Democrat Bill Bradley. "People say politicians are controlled by money, and that's why this is a linchpin issue." "The incessant money chase is an insidious demand that takes away from the time we have to actually do our job here in Washington. It takes away from the time we have to study and understand the issues, to meet with our constituents, to talk with other senators and to work out solutions to the problems that face this nation," said Robert Byrd.

Linda Smith had come over from the House to watch the vote, and as the roll was called she talked with McCain and Kassebaum. The outcome was not a surprise; the proponents of campaign finance reform were six votes short of being able to invoke cloture.

After the vote Smith joined McCain, Feingold, and Thompson in the press gallery to offer an assessment of what had happened. Thompson predicted the campaign finance reform proponents would probably have to "wait until the next real good scandal to get anything done." If he had any idea how soon that would be, he didn't let on. But the Democratic fund-raising violations during the presidential campaign were of such magnitude that shortly after the start of the 105th Congress, Thompson would be charged with looking into them as chairman of the Senate's Governmental Affairs Committee.

*   *   *

The proponents of campaign finance reform in the House were disappointed by the Senate vote. Two days later, on June 27, Smith, Shays, and Meehan held a news conference to announce that they had decided to scale back their bill and push for only two reforms. They would seek to ban the unlimited soft money contributions to political parties and to prohibit political fund-raisers for members of Congress within 50 miles of Washington.

"How could anyone support soft money? It's basically crooked money. . . . How could anyone defend the endless fund-raisers?" asked Shays. "We need a 'check-free zone' to stop the shakedown of the people who ask for our votes, and we need to cut off both parties' supply of the narcotic of unlimited soft money from special interests." But this approach really didn't go anywhere. With the Senate defeat of the bipartisan McCain-Feingold bill, the House version lost its momentum and did not even have the chance to be considered on the floor.

Two weeks later, Bill Thomas, chair of the House Oversight Committee, unveiled the Republicans' version of campaign finance reform, which had essentially been written by the Republican leadership. It was clear they did not take the issue seriously. The Republican bill was a cynical and blatant attempt to heighten their party's fund-raising advantages and to disadvantage the Democrats. There was nothing even remotely bipartisan about it. They had to have known the Democrats would never vote for the bill, and there was very little likelihood of its passing. It almost looked as if they had set out to write a bad bill just to ensure it had no chance.

The Republican proposal would require that candidates raise a majority of their campaign funds in their own district. But limiting candidates strictly to their districts would generally give Republican candidates, who tended to represent more affluent areas, a tremendous advantage over Democrats, especially those who represented urban and minority districts.

The Republican bill did nothing about soft money and made no attempt to limit campaign spending. In fact, testifying before a House committee on the issue of campaign finance reform, Gingrich said he felt there wasn't enough money being spent on campaigns. Republicans tended to receive more donations from wealthy individuals, and the Republican proposal would dramatically increase the limits for individual contributions while decreasing the limit for PACs, which many Democrats tended to rely on for a greater percentage of their campaign funds.

By Common Cause's estimate, the Republican measure would increase the amount an individual could give to federal campaigns and parties from $25,000 to $3 million. Common Cause quickly put out a three-sentence press release that called the Republican bill "a phony and a sham. It is consumer fraud to call this bill 'reform.' Any member of the House who votes for this bill only can be called 'a protector of corruption.'"

Smith and Shays sent a letter to their Republican colleagues blasting the GOP proposal. "This bill is in some ways more fundamentally flawed than our current system. . . . Instead of crafting a bill that levels the playing field in elections, the Republican bill will result in greater incumbent protection." Smith said the proposal only perpetuated the image that the GOP was the party of the wealthy and called it "a slap in the face of the American people."

The House Republican leadership determined that there would be only two votes on campaign finance reform, one on their bill and one on a Democratic alternative, so the Smith-Shays-Meehan bill was shut out.

On July 25, when campaign finance reform reached the House floor, Rules Committee chairman Gerald Solomon admitted that consideration of the matter was mostly for show. "There were other members who thought we should not even take up any campaign reform bill since it was already dead, defeated in the Senate, and stood no chance of becoming law, so why waste the valuable time of the House considering what we have to accomplish here in just the next 26 legislative days?"

"What we are talking about today is a bill that does not change anything with what happens here in Washington, D.C. Every night members of Congress can still hold their fund-raisers across the street. . . . But worse yet, tobacco money still can be funneled through the parties, made legitimate by the Republican bill—funneled through in hundreds of thousands and millions of dollars, to be then funneled through to candidates," Smith said in blasting the Republican bill.

Democrat Meehan spoke of the refusal to allow his bipartisan bill, which had the support of 21 Democrats and 20 Republicans and would voluntarily limit spending and curb the influence of special interest PACs, to get a vote on the floor. Meehan called both the Republican bill and the entire debate "a sham." "Why in the world would the Republican Party submit this kind of proposal? It has been condemned by every public interest group that has been fighting for campaign finance reform in America," said Meehan.

William Thomas of California, the sponsor of the bill, argued that requiring candidates to raise 50 percent of their money at home would increase public participation in the process. "What we do is empower people back home," Thomas argued. But senior Democrat Sam Gejdenson of Connecticut said in order to believe the Republican bill was the solution, "you would have to believe that wealthy people do not have enough influence, that poor people and working people have too much influence in this institution, and there just is not enough money in politics today."

Gingrich came to the floor to speak on behalf of the Republican bill and close the debate. Pointing to the presidential system of public financing, he said limiting expenditures in campaigns does not work because money will find another way into the system. His speech seemed less a call for campaign finance reform than a partisan rant against the Democrats and their supporters, especially the labor unions. "President Clinton clearly, consciously, and systematically is getting around the law and knows it and has designed his campaign to do it because the law does not work," said Gingrich.

The Republicans' bill was defeated 259 to 162. No Democrats voted for it, and 68 Republicans voted against it, including most of the moderates and reformers and 26 of the freshmen. Even the Democratic bill won more votes than that, although it, too, was defeated, 243–177. For the 104th Congress anyway, the issue of campaign finance reform was dead.

*   *   *

There could be no doubt that money was driving the electoral system. The average cost of a House seat in 1996 was $670,000, up from $516,000 in 1994. And 160 House candidates spent more than $1 million on their campaigns in 1996. Ninety percent of all the House races were won by the candidate who spent the most.

Six months after the 1996 election, the fund-raising merry-go-round was still turning. In April 1997 more than 50 fund-raisers were scheduled for Republican House members, among them a "South Carolina fish fry" for Lindsey Graham; a defense and aerospace industry dinner for Chris Cannon, a new member of the Science Committee; a California wine reception for George Radanovich; a "first annual 39th birthday party" for Susan Molinari; a health industry breakfast for Congressman Ed Whitfield; an "ag breakfast" fund-raiser for Congressman Jerry Moran, a new member from Kansas assigned to the Agriculture Committee; an "Indy 500 warm-up" reception for Dan Burton at the American Trucking Association; and a "transportation reception" for Don Young, a top-ranking member of the Transportation Committee.

But the heightened sensitivity and increased media attention to fund-raising had caused the NRCC and its chief counsel to prepare a list of "ten tips" for members. Lawmakers were warned not to use the U.S. seal on fund-raising invitations, not to use their congressional office phone numbers for RSVPs, and not to use any official resources (such as congressional telephones, computers, or fax machines) for fund-raising. "Staffers may only perform campaign activity after completion of official duties," said the memo. It advised members that "PACs share GOP invitation letters with Democrats," saying, "The DCCC will receive and review your invitations, just as we obtain and examine their fundraising appeals. Always remember the 'Washington Post' test—everything you put on paper can and will appear on the front page of a critical newspaper." The NRCC tip sheet further instructed members, "Never promise official action in return for contributions." And the number one tip was, "No solicitations on federal property."

*   *   *

In 1995 the Center for Responsive Politics published a fascinating book called *Speaking Freely* that was composed almost entirely of interviews with 25 former members of Congress who talked about what they thought of the existing system of campaign fund-raising and the role contributions played in shaping public policy. Their assessments were remarkably candid, no doubt because the former members no longer had to stand for election or to function in the system they were criticizing.

The former members were virtually unanimous in the belief that money does indeed buy access and influence in Washington. "I think it is clear that large contributors do get a disproportionate access to members of Congress and are at least able to present their case more personally and aggressively and effectively than others," said former Senate majority leader George Mitchell.

"The brutal fact that we all agonize over is that if you get two calls and one is from a constituent who wants to complain about the Veterans Administration mistreating her father, for the tenth time, and one is from somebody who is going to give you a party and raise $10,000, you call back the contributor. And nobody likes that. There's no way to justify it. Except that you rationalize that you have to have money or you can't campaign. You're not in the game," said Democrat Wyche Fowler, who served in both the House and Senate from Georgia.

"People who contribute get the ear of the member and the ear of the staff. They have the access and access is it. Access is power. Access is clout. That's how this thing works," said Romano Mazzoli, a Democrat from Kentucky who did not take PAC money and who served in the House for 24 years.

Former New York congressman Tom Downey became a lobbyist after he was defeated in 1992 and so has a perspective on the issue from both sides of the street. "One thing you know that you'll have when you see somebody at a fund-raising event is that you're going to be there under fairly ideal circumstances. You're there because you contributed money to this person, so they're in a position to thank you. . . . When somebody is helping you win a campaign, you're going to at least certainly grant the request for a meeting . . . Money will definitely buy you some access so you can make your case."

The former members also talked about the enormous amount of time they spent fund-raising and how it took away from their legislative responsibilities. "There's hardly a day in the past six years when I've been majority leader when one or more senators hasn't called me and asked me not to have a vote at a certain time. . . . One of the most common reasons is that they are either holding or attending a fund-raising event that evening. . . . If I put all of the requests together, the Senate would never vote. I once had my staff keep a list of such requests on one day . . . and had I honored all of the requests, there could not have been a vote that day. It covered the period from 9 A.M. until midnight," said Mitchell.

"The time that you spend raising money, and the number of fund-raising events I was obliged to attend or at least stop by, gosh, you'd have five or six a night. It just wears you out doing that," said former House minority leader Robert Michel.

"I was constantly asking people for money when I was running," said Downey. "I do think that the amount of time people have to put into raising money is a serious problem in the country. . . . There's no way you can prove its impact on the quality of the Congress' work. . . . But when the members making decisions can't devote serious quality time to serious decisions, it has to [result in] a lower quality of work," said former House Republican Vin Weber of Minnesota.

"I was spending about two hours a day on the phone raising money. Minimum. Six days a week. . . . Sometimes I'd get really crackin' and I'd stay and do more. That takes away from your ability to represent your constituents, or to do your legislative work. . . . I felt like I was cheating, that I was not putting in a full day's work for what I was really elected to do. I was not elected to come back here and raise money for my next election," said Democrat Dennis DeConcini of Arizona, who served three terms in the Senate. DeConcini was one of the Keating Five, senators who were investigated for having interceded with federal regulators on behalf of Charlie Keating, the owner of failed savings and loans.

It was expected that members would raise money from interests that either had business before the committees they served on or were important in their districts, which put pressure on both the members and the lobbyists. The members thought they had to listen to lobbyists who had been generous with them and to try to do what they could to help them. And the lobbyists thought they had to donate for fear of being shut out of the process if they didn't. Most of the former members admitted that lobbyists who generously contributed could reap benefits as a result. Members thought lobbyists and special interests usually got their way on smaller, lower-profile issues that meant a lot to the company or industry involved, the sort of issues that often flew below the media's radar screen.

"There are innumerable ways for somebody to do somebody a favor . . . without attracting much attention. One of the ways became apparent to me shortly after I arrived: it is members asking questions (at committee hearings) that special interests want put to witnesses in order to frame an issue in a particular way," said Democrat Mel Levine.

"If nobody else cares about it very much, the special interest will get its way. If the public understands the issue at any level, then the special interest groups are not able to buy an outcome that the public may not want. But the fact is that the public doesn't focus on most of the work of the Congress. . . . All of us, me included, are guilty of this. If the company or interest group is . . . supportive of you and . . . vitally concerned about an issue that . . . nobody else in your district knows about or ever will know about, then the political calculus is very simple," said Weber.

*   *   *

So what should be done about all of this? There are dozens of different campaign finance reform proposals floating around and no guarantee that any of them will work. The bipartisan McCain-Feingold and Shays-Meehan reform bills were reintroduced in the 105th Congress. But House reform proponents were beginning to think they would have to take a more incremental approach to get anything passed. One idea was to try for just a soft money ban and require independent expenditure and issue advocacy groups to comply with FEC reporting and disclosure requirements.

Most of the former members said they felt public financing would be the most effective way to deal with the problems of the current campaign financing system, but polls have shown the vast majority of people do not support public financing. And, too, the soft money fund-raising excesses of 1996 in the presidential campaign, which already receives public financing, have shown there are ways around this system. It seems clear that banning soft money would go a long way toward dealing with many of the problems, but it is not the whole answer.

One thing that must be done is to give greater resources and clout to the Federal Election Commission, which is charged with the responsibility of seeing that election laws are enforced. Right now the FEC is a toothless tiger, just the way the politicians like it. The FEC cannot start a criminal investigation but must refer those matters to the Justice Department. It currently has no authority to halt illegal practices it finds out about during an election campaign. And because of a lack of staff and resources, FEC investigations take years to complete. When the FEC announced plans to look into GOPAC, Gingrich's political action committee, the Republican House retaliated by cutting the FEC's funding. The FEC needs to be truly independent and have the resources to do its job. And there's no reason why, through the Internet, candidates cannot file their campaign fund-raising data electronically so that it can be immediately made available to the public.

As another possible change, when violations are committed, the candidates as well as their campaign treasurers and donors should have to pay the price. In Great Britain if candidates for the House of Commons are found to have broken election laws, their elections are voided unless the candidates can show the violations were committed against their express orders. And if found guilty, a candidate is prohibited from running again for 10 years. Such penalties would certainly make a candidate think twice about violating election law. The U.S. Constitution probably rules out something like that, as well as some other interesting aspects of the British election system: campaigns that last only a few weeks instead of a year, candidate spending limits, providing free television time, and prohibiting paid campaign ads on television.

In *Speaking Freely* Wyche Fowler mentioned an intriguing idea worth consideration. He suggested the creation of a national lottery. The proceeds from the sale of lottery tickets would be used to finance all House and Senate races. Fowler believed such a lottery could raise as much as $4 billion, which would be more than enough to fund congressional campaigns. It would then become illegal for all candidates for Congress to accept or solicit campaign contributions. Since buying a lottery ticket would be voluntary, Americans would not have to be taxed to fund the system.

Fowler said the only place he really ran into opposition for his proposal was from the governors of states that already had lotteries and who feared the federal competition.

*   *   *

Having run for Congress as both an outsider and an incumbent, Van Hilleary had his own thoughts about possible changes to the system. He departed from many of his fellow Republicans (including Gingrich) in thinking that individual contribution limits should be increased. Hilleary thought they were fine as they were. But Hilleary did think there should be full and immediate disclosure of all money flowing into the system. "Let the voters decide if you've been bought off," he said. In order for that to work, though, he admitted the FEC would have to be given more resources.

Hilleary was torn about what his refusal to take PAC money meant both to him and to his constituents. And if he had it to do over again, Hilleary probably wouldn't have made such a pledge before running the first time. If he were able to take some PAC money, but not in an amount that exceeded individual contributions—$2,000 in an election cycle—"it would take the edge off of the amount of time I have to spend raising money." But if PAC donations were kept at $2,000, Hilleary said they probably wouldn't carry any more weight than donations from individuals.

Hilleary believed PAC contributions should be limited because he admitted they do influence lawmakers. And although he has not been publicly critical of his fellow members, Hilleary agreed with Linda Smith that the Washington fund-raisers are a bad thing.

There really should be a "disconnect between the money and legislation going through Congress," Hilleary said. The biggest problems with the system, he thought, were the amount of money candidates had to raise and the incredible amount of time they had to spend doing it.

One change Hilleary would institute immediately if he had the chance would be to require wealthy candidates who spend their own money on their races to donate the money just like everyone else does rather than loan it—this although Hilleary loaned $100,000 to his first congressional race. Such a change could be fairly significant and might slow down the spending in many cases. If candidates know that once the money is spent, it is gone forever, even the wealthy ones might think twice about investing more in their campaigns. Without such a requirement, candidates often spend more and more trying to ensure victory, partially because they know once elected they will be able to hold an unlimited amount of fund-raisers to pay themselves back.

Hilleary was not optimistic that reform would happen anytime soon. Those who had made it to Congress and succeeded in the system, which is skewed toward them, wanted to keep things the way they were, Hilleary said.

But something had to be done to keep lawmakers from spending ever more time chasing campaign dollars and then making sure the people who give them are taken care of. What a simple and logical idea it would seem to be for our representatives in Congress instead to be able to spend their time on the business of representing us and running the government.

24

KANSAS IN AUGUST

ON MAY 15, 1996, BOB DOLE MADE A SURPRISE ANNOUNCEMENT. It was an announcement that would change forever not only his life but that of another Kansan—Sam Brownback.

Dole had come to Congress in 1960, before some of the freshmen were even born. He served in the House of Representatives for eight years before being elected to the Senate. He had been Senate Republican leader longer than anyone else in history and had served as majority leader twice, from 1985 to 1986, and then 10 years later when the Republicans again gained control of the Senate.

The Senate was a job and a place that Bob Dole dearly loved. But he had run for president before, more than once. And having captured the nomination this time around, Dole had made the decision that the only way he could run for president was to get out from under the responsibilities and distractions of the Senate. He was at least 15 points behind Bill Clinton in the polls, and Dole thought leaving the Senate would jump-start his campaign. He also saw the benefit in trying to distance himself from Newt Gingrich and his freshmen. Dole had to make a clean break, had to show the American people he was serious.

But it was clear as he made his announcement that it was a painful farewell. "My time to leave this office has come, and I will seek the presidency with nothing to fall back on but the judgment of the people and nowhere to go but the White House or home," Dole said as he choked back tears.

"Giving all and risking all, I must leave Congress that I have loved, and which I have been honored to serve," Dole said. "I will then stand before you without office or authority, a private citizen, a Kansan, an American, just a man. . . . The very least a presidential candidate owes America is his full attention—everything he can give, everything he has. And that is what America shall receive from me."

Dole's announcement meant more than just the end of a long and distinguished Senate career and the impact it might have on his presidential campaign. It meant there was an opening in the Senate. And Sam Brownback wanted it badly.

Brownback and the rest of the Kansas delegation had been called to Dole's office around 1 P.M. so Dole could tell them of his plans before he made his public announcement. Afterward the *Washington Post* asked Brownback if he would like to be temporarily appointed to Dole's seat and make a run for it in November. "Well, yeah. Who wouldn't?" he responded. For Brownback, there was no hesitation. It seemed to him perfectly natural that he should be the man to take Dole's place in the Senate. But not everyone in the Kansas Republican Party was so sure.

The next day Brownback got a call from Kansas governor Bill Graves. The news was not encouraging. Graves was a moderate Republican who had been feuding for years with the antitax, antiabortion conservative wing of the state party that Brownback represented. Graves explained to Brownback that he had a number of things to consider in deciding who would replace Dole. It was pretty clear Brownback wasn't going to get the nod.

Graves sought the advice of Dole and the other senior members of the state's congressional delegation. None of them had a particularly close relationship with Brownback. The word coming back to Kansas from Washington was that Brownback and his staff had rubbed the senior members of the delegation the wrong way. The young, conservative whippersnappers hadn't asked for advice. They'd just gone ahead and done things their own way. Brownback wasn't deferential enough. Some people thought he was too big for his britches. He was also extremely ambitious. "Ambitious": That was almost always one of the first words people used to describe Brownback.

Old Kansas political hands said that Dole didn't like Brownback much, that he resented the attention Brownback, as just a lowly freshman member of the House, had received from the national media. The House had eclipsed the Senate in the 104th Congress, and Brownback was one of those leading the charge. "He's jealous of Sam," one veteran Kansas political observer said of Dole.

Senator Nancy Landon Kassebaum never publicly said anything critical of Brownback, but she told some people privately that she was getting sick and tired of hearing the freshmen constantly going on about balancing the budget and cutting programs. It was so one-note, she said. Kassebaum was a moderate who prided herself on being able to work out compromises and find a middle way between the conservatives in her own party and the liberal Democrats, an approach the new House freshmen did not particularly appreciate. She supported abortion rights, gun control, and a moderation of many of the cuts being proposed for social programs.

The daughter of former Kansas governor and 1936 Republican presidential nominee Alf Landon, Kassebaum had played a pivotal role in trying to moderate the GOP's sharpest conservative efforts during the 104th Congress. And she was in a position to do it as chair of the Labor and Human Resources Committee, which she had taken over in 1995. She had become only the second woman in Senate history to chair a full committee. But Kassebaum, 63, had announced in November that she would not be running for reelection. She had already served three terms in the Senate, although it had been her original intention to serve only two. Her decision to leave was a great disappointment to Republican moderates both in Kansas and in Washington.

The *Kansas City Star* urged Kassebaum to rethink her decision to retire and to stand for reelection because without her "Kansas could dramatically sink from one of the most powerful states to the bottom of the Senate hierarchy." But Kassebaum could not be convinced to stay on.

There was a great deal of discussion in the state party about who should run for Kassebaum's seat. Pat Roberts decided he wanted to stay in the House and retain his powerful chairmanship of the Agriculture Committee. Jan Meyers, the only other member of the state's congressional delegation who was not a freshman, had already decided to retire after 12 years in the House. That left the door open for Brownback. "I didn't know if this would fit, but I kept chewing on it," said Brownback.

The more he chewed, the better it tasted.

Brownback formed an exploratory committee. He traveled to Wichita and Kansas City talking to party people and business leaders to see if he could raise the money it would take to mount a Senate campaign. He talked to the governor, to Roberts, to his wife.

There is disagreement about just who and what it was that finally convinced Roberts to run for Kassebaum's seat. Brownback said he went back to Roberts and asked him to do it. But others within the state party suggested it was Dole and Kassebaum who urged Roberts to run so Brownback wouldn't. When Roberts finally said yes, Brownback said he thought, "Great. I'm satisfied to run for reelection."

But Dole's decision changed everything. In Brownback's mind there was no other logical person in line ahead of him, even though he had served in Congress for less than two years. He had already looked closely at making a run for the Senate and decided he could do it. "We'd been through all the decisionmaking."

Governor Graves asked Brownback to wait to do anything until he announced Dole's temporary successor. But Brownback was pretty sure Graves wasn't going to choose him. And he didn't want to wait. He wanted to get a jump on the competition. Dole made his announcement on a Wednesday. Brownback says he had been planning for some time to make his formal reelection announcement for his House seat on Friday, May 17, two days later. "We were organized to do that. We were ready to go."

But instead, on that day, Brownback told the people of Kansas he wanted to succeed Bob Dole. And one week after Dole had broken the news to Kansans that after 35 years he would no longer be representing them in Congress, Brownback started running television ads telling them he wanted to be their next senator. From the outside it looked a little fast, a little too pushy, especially for Kansans.

But once he decided what he was going to do, Brownback determined there was "no time to waste. If we were going to do it we better just go." By moving fast, Brownback lined up the support of "a lot of people we wouldn't have gotten otherwise. . . . There's an organizational advantage in getting in and moving quickly." What Brownback feared most was that another conservative would get into the race and split the conservative vote. Moving quickly prevented that.

Brownback figured he could take a moderate.

And he was going to get the chance to find out. On May 24 Graves announced he had selected his lieutenant governor, Sheila Frahm, to serve in Dole's seat through November. She was a pro-choice moderate who had been the first woman majority leader of the Kansas Senate as well as the first woman lieutenant governor in the state.

In announcing his choice, Graves said the 51-year-old Frahm had "a statewide perspective shaped by years of community and legislative experience. She is someone who has been tested both in the political arena and in public policy debates. She had conducted herself in the best interests of her Kansas constituents as her one and only priority." It was a not-so-subtle slap at Brownback. He was too young, too brash, too self-interested.

So it was decided. Brownback and Frahm would face each other in a special GOP primary to be held on August 6. The winner of that contest would go on to the November election, but it seemed clear the main event would be the primary, since Kansas had not elected a Democrat to the U.S. Senate since the 1930s.

Kansas is a Republican state. Republicans control the state legislature, the governor is a Republican, and in 1996 every member of the congressional delegation was a Republican. Because the Republican Party in Kansas is so dominant, it has a bigger tent than does the party in a number of other places. Moderates who might be registered as Democrats or independents in some other states retain their Republican affiliation in Kansas out of habit and history. It's a little bit like conservative Democrats in Louisiana.

There had been trouble brewing for some time in Kansas between the older moderates and the younger religious and social conservatives who were taking over the state party. The conservatives had risen up and seized control of the state party mechanism, and the moderates were feeling squeezed out. With his appointment of Frahm to Dole's seat, Graves was making a statement. He was taking a stand against the conservatives.

The primary contest between Brownback and Frahm became a civil war, with everyone in the state GOP taking sides. It was a microcosm of the national schism within the Republican Party, a battle between conservative antiabortion, antitax, Christian Coalition types and the more traditional, country club moderate Republicans.

Frahm was a moderate, but she was definitely not a country club Republican. She had grown up in a big family in western Kansas on a farm that didn't have running water or electricity. She had worked hard and paid her dues, moving up through the state party from her local school board to the state board of education, then one term in the state senate before becoming its majority leader. She was competent but not very charismatic.

Like Frahm, Brownback had also grown up on a farm. But he came from the eastern, more populated part of the state and now lived in Topeka, the state capital. He had been student body president at Kansas State before law school at the University of Kansas, where he met his wife, Mary. Before he was elected to Congress, the only other public office he had held was Kansas secretary of agriculture. But he had also been a White House fellow, and that had broadened his perspective. Brownback had been preparing for this campaign all his life. His attitude about seeking public office was similar to Bill Clinton's. They had both been achievers as they were growing up, and from the time both of them were old enough to think about the future, they knew they would be in politics.

Frahm stressed experience and maturity in her campaign. It sounded a lot like the strategy of the other former Senate majority leader from Kansas who was running for higher office. And neither of their campaigns would prove to be very exciting. Frahm had all of the state's GOP giants lined up behind her. Graves appeared in her television commercials. Kassebaum campaigned with her and was helping with fund-raising. And even Dole, although he had other things on his mind, had offered his tacit support. He had quietly made it clear whom he liked better.

Brownback was taking on the establishment, "the machine," as he called it. But he brought in Jack Kemp and Steve Forbes to campaign and help him raise some money. He also had the support of the conservative and antiabortion activists, and they were probably more important than the party's old guard. They volunteered. They worked hard. They voted and got their friends to vote. They donated money. This was more than politics to them.

The race was seen as a referendum on the freshmen and on the 104th Congress. Brownback was the first member of the freshman class to seek higher office. As one of the leaders of the freshman reformers in the House, Brownback had been cele-brated by the national media. He was a conservative, determined firebrand, just like most of the rest of the freshmen. But he was also smart and charismatic. He was go-ing places. You only had to talk to him for a few minutes to know that. He had a de-gree of sophistication that didn't exist in many of the other freshmen. He wasn't as one-dimensional. He was the cream of the freshman crop.

As the head of the New Federalists, Brownback had won respect and praise from his House colleagues for his hard work and leadership on a number of issues, al-though the New Federalists had not succeeded in achieving any of their major goals, such as abolishing a cabinet department. But back home the 39-year-old freshman was portrayed as an ambitious upstart and dubbed "Sam-bitious." A number of Re-publicans who supported Frahm said Brownback would have easily won reelection to the House, but because he had served only one term in Washington, they thought, he should have waited his turn for the Senate. But Brownback didn't want to wait his turn.

At the end of June, Paul Gigot wrote a flattering column in the *Wall Street Journal* about Brownback and his Senate race, calling him "arguably the most prominent of all the House freshmen." But what had won the attention of Gigot and other mem-bers of the national media had not played as well back home. The moderate wing of the state party believed that when Brownback was elected he was more of a centrist than he turned out to be. After all, he was one of the few freshmen who hadn't signed the Contract with America. Since he had arrived in Washington, they thought, he had gotten carried away with Gingrich and the revolution. Moderate Kansas Republicans also thought he had got a little too carried away with himself. As

Dole so perfectly illustrated, Kansans are generally a taciturn lot, not given to blowing their own horns.

The *Wichita Eagle* began running nasty political cartoons after Brownback announced for Dole's seat. One showed Brownback waiting around a corner for the approaching Frahm holding an enormous club labeled "Distortion of Frahm's record." But a second cartoon was much worse: It showed a tiny Brownback with a huge, scary, almost demented grin—all teeth. He was standing inside an enormous pair of wing tips labeled "Dole's shoes." And the caption read, "Man, I can't believe what a perfect fit these babies would be! Of course, I'd only need them temporarily . . . until I got the president's shoes! Then it's just a hop, skip and a jump to king of the planet! No, too small a job, ruler of the cosmos! Yeah! that's it."

Brownback clearly had a bit of an image problem and a serious uphill battle ahead of him. He would have to let people know who he was and do a careful balancing act in the primary, trying to convince the party's moderates that he wasn't as extreme as Frahm was trying to make him out to be. Unlike most candidates in other Republican primaries, he needed to move toward the center rather than the right to win. But he couldn't go so far that he alienated his conservative base. National GOP conservative leaders were watching the race closely and hoped to carry a Kansas victory into the Republican National Convention, which began a week after the primary vote.

*   *   *

Kansas lies directly in the geographic center of the United States, and many Kansans would no doubt say it represents the ideological center as well. Farming is a way of life here in what is one of the nation's leading wheat-producing states. With a population of only 2.5 million but an area of more than 82,000 square miles, Kansas is a state of many small towns. The state's largest city, Wichita, has a population of only 300,000.

Personal connections and retail politics are important here. A handshake, a personal greeting—"Hey, didn't I go to school with your cousin?"—that's what Kansans want and expect from their politicians. Brownback is good at that. He is also a skillful public speaker. But a lot of people in the state didn't know too much about him. In late June, about a month before the election, a Mason-Dixon poll gave Frahm a 23-point lead over Brownback. She also had a 19 percent advantage over him in name recognition. She had benefited from all the publicity over her appointment. And Brownback was beginning to think winning this thing might be harder than he had originally thought.

Neither he nor Frahm could campaign full time because they had to be in Washington when Congress was in session. But Congress took the Fourth of July week off, and both of them were home trying to pack as much campaigning as possible into just a few days. On July 4 Brownback is up bright and early: Independence Day meant parades and fireworks, and that meant crowds. This would be a workday for all of the candidates running in the primary.

Sam and his wife would both be on the campaign trail today, but they decided to split up so they could cover more ground. She will take their two daughters, Abby and Liz, and hit a parade in Lenexa, a Kansas City suburb. The girls are wearing white T-shirts with Brownback's name silk-screened on the front and back in blue and gold. Underneath the name is a parade of tiny elephants and the number 96.

Mary's father, John Stauffer, will be going with her. The Stauffer family is well known in Kansas as the former owners of a Topeka-based media empire that included newspapers and broadcast stations throughout the Midwest and South. Stauffer Communications was launched in 1930 by Mary Stauffer Brownback's grandfather, Oscar Stauffer, when he acquired the *Peabody Gazette* in tiny Peabody, Kansas, north of Wichita. From there it grew in 60 years to a closely held public company that owned 20 daily newspapers in Kansas, Missouri, Nebraska, Oklahoma, Michigan, Colorado, Minnesota, Tennessee, South Dakota, and Florida, its flagship publication being the *Topeka Capital-Journal*. The company also owned four radio stations, seven television outlets (including a Topeka station), and the broadcast rights to Kansas City Royals baseball games. In 1994 Morris Communications, a privately held Georgia company, bought Stauffer for an estimated $300 million.

On this particular campaign morning, it's a mad scramble to get everyone out the door and on the road. Brownback will be taking his son, Andy, and heading for a parade in Junction City, a community of 20,000 people about 50 miles west of Topeka. On the outskirts of the city is the Fort Riley Military Reservation, built in 1853 to protect settlers traveling west along the Santa Fe Trail from Indian attack. The 100,000-acre reservation is now both a historical site and a functioning army base, surrounded by farm fields.

On the drive to Junction City, Brownback talks about the split in the state party and what he's up against. "I didn't think I'd have to take on the governor," he says somewhat grimly. Frahm benefits from the organization and fund-raising support of the party, but Brownback says, "At the end of the day, I don't think it wins it for her." At least that's what he's hoping.

Upon arriving in Junction City, Brownback jumps out of the car and starts shaking hands and introducing himself to the people in the parade staging area. Some of his campaign workers are putting Brownback signs on a convertible, but he decides to walk the parade route so he can shake hands on either side of the street. His son will ride in the car and wave. It's not even 10 A.M., but it's already hot. Brownback is wearing khaki pants and a cotton pullover jersey.

Another candidate is also here today: Cheryl Brown Henderson, one of the three Republicans trying to win the nomination for the House seat Brownback is vacating. She is the daughter of Oliver Brown, the African American plaintiff named in the historic 1954 *Brown v. Board of Education* Supreme Court decision that struck down the concept of separate but equal, ending school segregation in this country. The case started in Topeka with Brown's sister, who was attending the segregated Topeka public schools.

Henderson is a newcomer to the GOP and says she first registered as a Republican only about six months earlier largely because she wanted to work on Dole's presidential campaign. "I think there need to be more moderate Republican women—those that are there need help," asserts Henderson in explaining why she decided to change her party affiliation.

Although she has virtually no political base or campaign organization, Henderson has decided to enter the GOP congressional primary, which features another famous name with no political experience: Jim Ryun, a former athlete and local hero turned politician in the mold of freshman Steve Largent. Largent and Ryun share fundamentalist Christian beliefs, and Largent encouraged Ryun to get into the race.

This may be Ryun's first run for political office, but there can be no doubt about his running ability. A three-time U.S. Olympic team member, Ryun was a silver medalist at 1,500 meters in the 1968 Olympics. In 1965, as a senior in Wichita, he became the first American high schooler to break the four-minute mile, and his time still stands as a national high school record for the mile.

After leaving competitive running, Ryun operated a summer running camp and has been a motivational speaker for corporations and Christian groups around the country. He has also written two books, his autobiography and a book titled *Chariots of Fire and a Christian Message for Today*.

The third candidate in the race is the only one with political experience, Douglas Wright, a lawyer and former mayor of Topeka. Henderson and Wright are both moderates, and their differences with Ryun mirror the ideological divisions between Brownback and Frahm. Ryun is stressing conservative, family values in his campaign and talked about the need for a "renaissance of traditional morality" in his announcement speech. He is strongly opposed to legalized abortion and says he could not support any exceptions even in cases of rape or incest. This position drew fire from Henderson, who called Ryun "an extremist."

"If Republican male candidates are going to appeal to Republican and unaffiliated women in November 1996, we better get our act together. The GOP cannot put a Band-Aid on the abortion debate and hope it will go away. The abortion debate is all about power politics and the use of Christianity as a vehicle to mold well-meaning people into political pawns," said Henderson in her announcement speech.

The former mayor, Wright, who is also a pro-choice moderate, was even more caustic in his criticism of Ryun. "He's well known by a lot of people to have extreme views," said Wright, citing an article on "courtship" Ryun wrote with his wife, Anne, for *Focus on the Family*, a Christian magazine. The Ryuns do not permit their children, who are in their 20s, to date but only to participate in courtship with potential partners who are "spiritually and financially ready for marriage." The article explained that if a young man is interested in one of Ryun's daughters, he must ask her father's permission before courtship can begin. Acceptable courtship activities include having dinner with the family, a prison ministry, or a neighborhood walk. Wright considers Ryun to be "a part of the fundamentalist Christian right" and asserts that in Kansas "a lot of people are concerned about involving religion in politics. . . . This is clearly a battle over the direction of the Republican Party in Kansas."

That may be true, but the people lined up along Junction City's main street don't seem too worked up about it. Although this city is in Brownback's congressional district, a number of people at the parade don't know much about him. With the unexpected election still a month away, nobody seems to have focused on the race yet. For the residents of Junction City, this is a day for sparklers and barbecues and military bands and fireworks.

As Brownback finishes up the parade route, he looks around anxiously for his car and driver. He is trying to make another parade that is just about to start in Wamego, about 30 miles east, and there is no time to lose. Finally he spots the car in a parking lot across the street and hops in with his son.

On the drive to Wamego, Brownback is on the cellular phone to his press secretary about an Associated Press story in that morning's paper. Brownback had held a press conference earlier that week in Wichita with several state legislators to talk about Frahm's record on taxes. But instead of writing about that, the AP ran a story on a remark made by Brownback's campaign manager. "I just read the Topeka paper. Did they even do a story on our press conference? Has anyone called the AP?" Brownback asks his press secretary. "We had a legitimate press story, and they wouldn't even cover it, and then they cover this little thing that David said. We can't get a single break," Brownback complains to the aide.

The story AP did run focused on some comments Brownback's campaign manager, David Kensinger, had made. Kensinger was talking about campaign strategy and the intention to concentrate on the eastern, more populated areas of the state. "You can't go to Phillipsburg. You have to focus your efforts on large crowds and media," said Kensinger. But in trying to make his point, Kensinger had mentioned the one town that had more political resonance for Kansas Republicans than almost any other. Phillipsburg, a town of 3,200 people in the northwestern part of the state, had been the home of the late McDill "Huck" Boyd, a newspaper publisher who had served on the Republican National Committee for two decades and who was considered to be Dole's political mentor.

It was the kind of mistake that illustrated the problems Brownback's campaign was facing. He and his campaign staff were seen as too arrogant, too Washington, too big for Kansas. Of course Brownback had apologized for his aide's imprudent remark, saying rather lamely, "I like Phillipsburg. They're good people." But Brownback's opponent wasted no time taking advantage of the misstep. Frahm immediately flew to Phillipsburg to have lunch with local residents at the town's Pizza Hut. And she issued a statement condemning the remark. "All the people of Kansas deserve to be represented in the Senate, not just those who work for television stations, radio stations and large newspapers," she said.

Having arrived in Wamego, Brownback gets out of the car, and starts looking for his campaign contingent. He has been placed near the back of the parade to give him time to get here from Junction City. One of his campaign supporters has brought a zippy little vintage convertible sportscar for Brownback to ride in, but again he decides to walk so he can cover both sides of the street.

Wamego is a town of less than 4,000 people, but it seems like all of them have turned out to watch the parade. They line the street, many sitting in folding lawn chairs. Someone in the parade is passing out popsicles to the children along the route, and Andy Brownback is eating one.

Following the parade, the Republicans have a watermelon feed in the Wamego city park. A carnival has also been set up, and a local group is sponsoring a barbecue fund-raiser in the park's open pavilion. It is the quintessential American Fourth of July afternoon.

As the watermelon is sliced, Brownback starts shaking hands, and there are plenty of them to shake. This is clearly the place to be for Republicans today. Pat Roberts, Jim Ryun, and Sheila Frahm all make appearances, as do a number of local and state officials. But Brownback outlasts them all. He stays until the last hand is shaken, the last pleasantry exchanged.

And Brownback still isn't ready to call it quits for the day yet. He wants to shake as many hands as he can. Brownback stops by his house for a few quick phone calls and to check in with Mary and the girls. Outside the garage, Andy and his sisters are setting off firecrackers, normal kid stuff. "The toughest part about campaigning is being a dad, too," Brownback says. He's torn. Part of him would like to stay here and just play with the kids. Part of him thinks he should be out there campaigning.

Brownback calls his campaign office and asks where they think he should go. Someone suggests he stop by Perry Lake just outside of Topeka. Brownback and the young volunteer who has been assigned to drive him today get back in the car. There is supposed to be some kind of event at the lake, but when Brownback arrives in midafternoon there aren't many people around. They're all out on the lake in their boats.

Brownback soldiers gamely on. There are a few people sitting on the grass listening to a country and western band perform. They aren't too interested in a conversation. They're just trying to relax and have a good time. They don't want to be bothered by a politician. "Mary was right. She told me not to come. I should have listened to her," he says mostly to himself. After about half an hour of trying to find a few people to talk to, Brownback decides it's time to go home. It's been a long, hot, tiring day, not many people's idea of a fun way to spend the Fourth of July.

Just as old soldiers like to relive past battles, politicians enjoy talking about past campaigns, especially those they won. Brownback is thinking about his 1994 race during the ride back home. He was running against Democrat John Carlin, a two-term former governor. "People didn't know me from Adam. But when they would ask me who I was running against and I would tell them, they would say, 'You've got my vote.'" It was a year when political insiders didn't have the advantage, when conservative newcomers like Brownback tapped into the zeitgeist.

Two weeks before the election, Brownback says, the tracking polls showed "we were opening up this huge, gaping lead. . . . But I didn't think the Republicans were going to take over the Congress; I thought we would win ideological control. I thought we could set the agenda and win it all in 1996."

This year Brownback isn't sensing the same kind of anger from the voters that he felt two years earlier. They aren't angry with the freshmen. They had tried. Of course they hadn't done everything they said they would. But no one had expected them to—no one, perhaps, except the freshmen themselves. They just needed more time.

Brownback is trying to figure out what kind of election this will be, not just his race, but all over the country. Five years from now, what would people remember about the 1996 election? Perhaps the most memorable thing would prove to be that there wasn't much to remember.

As for his own race, Brownback seems pretty confident. He is an optimistic person. He knows he will be strong in Topeka and Wichita, a conservative, antiabortion area. He plans to do as much talk radio as he can. This thing could go either way. Turnout is going to be the key.

If it had been up to him, maybe Brownback wouldn't have picked this as the perfect moment to run for the Senate. But it had not been up to him. "The timing's not my doing. But it's been 18 years since we've elected a new U.S. senator in Kansas, 28 in this seat. When is this going to come up again? . . . Kansas has a history of reelecting the same people."

Brownback didn't want to miss his chance. Who knew how long it would be until it came around again? So he put it all on the line, his entire political future.

That night Brownback is supposed to attend a fireworks display at Topeka's Washburn University. There will be thousands of people there. It will be a great chance to press the flesh. But Brownback has had enough for one day. He wants to spend some quiet time with his family. This will probably not go down as his favorite day on the campaign trail. But there will be better days ahead.

Tomorrow it will start all over again. He will head west for more interviews, fundraising, and handshaking. For the next month, Brownback will continue to campaign doggedly, and by the end of July, the polls will show he has drawn even with Frahm, and some even have him in the lead. The momentum shifted in his favor.

On August 6 Brownback won the primary by 11 points, defeating Frahm 53 to 42 percent. As everyone had predicted, turnout was the key. Brownback had been able to mobilize the conservatives, and the moderates did not turn out in great enough numbers for Frahm. The first thing Brownback did was to mend fences with the state's moderate Republicans. The day after the election, he appeared with Graves at a press conference at the state capitol. If either of them was holding a grudge, they didn't show it publicly.

Brownback's Democratic opponent in the general election was Jill Docking, an attractive, personable woman with a popular last name in Kansas. She was a stockbroker who was married to Tom Docking, a former lieutenant governor who had made an unsuccessful run for governor in 1986 and whose father and grandfather both had served as governor. She was a good candidate, but in a year when Dole would be at the very top of the Republican ticket, it seemed extremely unlikely that Kansas would elect a Democrat to take his place in the Senate.

Brownback spent almost $2.3 million on his campaign for the Senate, including more than $170,000 of his own money, and went on to win a decisive victory in the November election. He credited his primary and general election victories to the grassroots Republican coalition he was able to put together, especially the Christian conservatives. "They not only voted, they walked and they talked. . . . They got out and pushed hard," he told me. It was not only conservatives in his own state that mobilized to help him, but national leaders of the conservative movement as well. The Christian Coalition made phone calls and sent out hundreds of thousands of voter guides.

And after the election, information surfaced that indicated some of the conservative groups may have been motivated by more than just support for Brownback's philosophy. The *Kansas City Star* reported in front-page stories in March and April 1997 that Federal Election Commission records showed Brownback's millionaire in-laws, John and Ruth Stauffer, had contributed $37,500 to eight national conservative political action committees in the month before the Kansas primary and that those PACs had sent $36,000 in donations to Brownback's campaign.

Federal election laws limit individuals to contributions of $1,000 each to a candidate's primary and general election campaigns. But individuals can contribute $5,000 to political action committees, which in turn can give $5,000 in the primary and $5,000 in the general election directly to candidates. It is illegal for individuals to try to circumvent the federal contribution limits for a candidate by laundering money through political action committees.

The Stauffers sent $5,000 to the Citizens United Political Victory Fund the first week in July, and two weeks later the group sent $5,000 to the Brownback campaign. In mid-July the couple also made $5,000 contributions to the Free Congress PAC, the Conservative Victory Committee, and the American Free Enterprise PAC. Shortly thereafter the Free Congress PAC sent $4,500 to the Brownback campaign, the Conservative Victory Committee sent $3,000, and the American Free Enterprise PAC sent $4,500. His wife's parents also sent $2,500 to the Faith, Family, and Freedom PAC, which gave $4,000 to the Brownback campaign. Phyllis Schlafly's Eagle Forum PAC contributed $4,000 to the Brownback campaign the first week in July; a week later the PAC received a $5,000 donation from the Stauffers. Various members of the Stauffer family also contributed about $10,000 to the Brownback campaign, $10,000 to the Kansas Republican State Committee, and $25,000 to the National Republican Senatorial Committee, which was within campaign funding rules.

Brownback told the *Kansas City Star* that he was confident he and his in-laws had done nothing wrong. But the contributions raised some serious questions. The newspaper reported that campaign finance records dating back to 1987 showed no other contributions from the Stauffers to political action committees until July 1996. John Stauffer told the *Star* that he was on the mailing lists of some of the groups and that's how he became aware of their support for his son-in-law. "I don't know how it worked, but [the contributions] weren't earmarked," Stauffer said. When the paper asked him why he chose to make his contributions that July, he replied, "The political season, I suppose. . . . I really don't know that I want to discuss it."

In May a Kansas Democratic Party activist filed a complaint with the Federal Election Commission asking for an investigation into the contributions made by the

Stauffers and their possible connection to PAC donations to Brownback's campaign. The complaint accused the Stauffers of illegally funneling $36,000 to the campaign through the conservative PACs. After the complaint was filed, John Stauffer released a statement that said, "I was certain last summer and I am certain now that there was nothing illegal or improper done by my wife or myself." Brownback also issued a statement: "I am confident that the FEC will determine that my campaign operated within both the letter and spirit of the law. I welcome an FEC examination of these baseless allegations." Brownback said the complaint was part of a partisan attack against him.

As a newly appointed member of the Senate's Governmental Affairs Committee, Brownback and the campaign contributions he received came in for greater scrutiny. It was this committee, chaired by Fred Thompson, that was looking into the fund-raising abuses of the 1996 Democratic campaign. And under pressure from the Democrats, Thompson and the committee had also agreed to look into a number of conservative political organizations that may have violated campaign finance laws and that had ties to the Republican Party—some of the same groups that had ties to Brownback.

The Thompson committee subpoenaed Triad Management Services, a political fund-raising firm based in Washington that Democrats said funneled contributions from wealthy conservative donors to Republican candidates through conservative political action committees to get around donation limits. Triad also operated a tax-exempt organization called Citizens for the Republic Education Fund, which spent $420,000 on television ads against Brownback's Democratic opponent in the general election campaign. Triad and its tax-exempt organizations were able to get around election law and could accept unlimited political donations without having to reveal whom they came from.

*   *   *

Brownback had come a long way, in more ways than one, since arriving in Washington two years earlier. He had been an ardent proponent of campaign finance reform, and now his campaign was being pointed to as an illustration of some of the problems with the existing system.

He had come to Congress as a reformer. But on January 7, 1997, when he joined the 105th Congress as a member of the Senate, Brownback was one of a number of senators whose celebratory reception was paid for by corporate money. Brownback's party, which was mentioned prominently in a front-page story in the *Washington Post,* was held at the Monocle, an expensive restaurant on Capitol Hill just a few blocks from the Senate office buildings. The party was paid for by the U.S. Telephone Association, which represents local phone companies in Washington. The Baby Bells have many issues worth billions of dollars before Congress and the Federal Communications Commission. And the FCC is under the jurisdiction of the Commerce Committee, to which Brownback had been assigned.

Of course Brownback wasn't the only senator to have a reception thrown in his honor by corporate interests. Chubb and Prudential Insurance, Lockheed Martin Information Systems, and Bell Atlantic of New Jersey threw a party for newly elected New Jersey Democrat Robert Torricelli; the Chicago Board of Trade paid for a party for Democrat Richard Durbin of Illinois; the Nuclear Energy Institute sponsored a party for Republican James McClure of Idaho; and ConAgra held a breakfast for Republican Chuck Hagel of Nebraska.

But the freshmen were supposed to have been different.

The day after his swearing-in, I interviewed Brownback in Dole's former Senate office. Brownback was camping out there because he had not yet been assigned his new permanent office. With its palatial size, high ceilings, plush carpeting, and upholstered furniture, this office was far different from the cramped space he had over in the Longworth Building, where the erasable board hung over his desk, the size of the national debt written on it in Brownback's hand.

Brownback didn't think the party the Baby Bells had thrown for him the previous day was a big deal. The telephone association had asked to host a reception for him, and he had said OK. Brownback said he asked the opinion of the Ethics Committee before agreeing.

But the whole thing made Brownback look like he had gone Hollywood, like he wasn't the small-town boy from Kansas anymore. What would the Perot voters he had so earnestly addressed in Dallas about campaign finance reform think of his reception? Probably not much.

Brownback insisted he had strongly supported campaign finance reform in 1995 and 1996 and had nothing to show for it. "You know how much credit I got for that? I got zippo, none, nada, nothing." The American people just didn't care that much about campaign finance reform, even though they said they did, Brownback had concluded.

25

CLINTON AND THE FRESHMEN

THE PRESIDENTIAL CAMPAIGN and the upcoming November election had been intruding on Capitol Hill, even more so after Bob Dole wrapped up the GOP presidential nomination.

Pat Buchanan, who had won a surprising New Hampshire primary victory, seemed to reflect most closely the political philosophy of a number of the freshmen: isolationist on foreign affairs and ultraconservative on social issues. But most of them had endorsed Dole. They knew which way the wind was blowing even if they didn't think Dole was the best standard-bearer for the Republicans.

The day before the March 7 New York primary and just two weeks before Steve Forbes pulled out of the race, Jack Kemp announced that he was endorsing Forbes, leaving many Republicans scratching their heads. An earlier endorsement would have made sense—Kemp and Forbes were flat tax soulmates—but by that point in the primary season Dole was well on his way to clinching the nomination. "He must have been playing football without a helmet," Gingrich quipped to several members in the GOP cloakroom about Kemp, a former professional football player. "He is now in political exile," Gingrich predicted. It did look like a strange move on Kemp's part, and no one could have predicted that Dole would later pick Kemp as his running mate.

On March 28, two days after he swept the California primary and declared himself the Republican nominee, Dole appeared for a joint pep rally in the Longworth House Office Building with many Republicans from both the House and Senate. They wanted to hear Dole say everything would be fine, that he could beat Clinton. But Dole was laconic and lackluster. "I'll be actively campaigning—if I can help. If I can't help, just tell me and I won't show up," he told them. It was obviously meant as a joke, but the remark cut close to the bone. Dole mentioned his loss to Buchanan in

New Hampshire. "That was part of our strategy to throw everybody off," he said with a grim smile.

There were 222 days until the election. The meeting had been called to pump people up, to convince them Dole was going to be a good candidate. But it had just the opposite effect. Many of the Republicans, especially the freshmen who were considered the most vulnerable, were having their doubts about how much Dole was going to help them at the top of their ticket. They had even started to think he was going to hurt them.

In a private meeting with the freshmen, arranged by Gingrich, Dole asked for their support. Gingrich and Dole emphasized the importance of running as a team. But the freshmen weren't so sure. Their skepticism was justified when two months later Dole attempted to distance himself from them in an interview with the conservative *Washington Times*. Dole told the newspaper Gingrich and the freshmen had tried to do too much too fast. And he said their antigovernment rhetoric had led people to believe the Republicans lacked compassion. "It's got to be my agenda, not Newt's or anybody else's. [I] want to remind people the Republican party is compassionate," said Dole. And a Dole campaign aide was quoted as saying, "Any pollster would tell you that he should try to distance himself from Newt and from House Republicans, but that's not what he's doing."

It was just more evidence of the confused Dole campaign. Maybe what Dole was saying was true. But he sounded like Clinton. Criticizing the freshmen publicly just alienated him further from the conservative base of the party that loved the freshmen. In most of their districts, the freshmen were running ahead of Dole. And making comments that seemed to play into the hands of the Democrats "enraged a lot of guys," according to one of the freshmen. It may have been the last straw. If most of the freshmen had not already decided to cut themselves loose from Dole and his sinking ship, those remarks served to convince them. They were dispirited by Dole's dismal campaign and had begun to believe there was no way he was going to pull it out. They weren't about to go down with him. It was either him or them, they reasoned.

"The election in November is Bill Clinton against the freshman class. This is going to be an election where the congressional races have coattails for the presidency instead of the other way around," said Rick White of Washington state. White said voters back home were telling him, "So far you're doing OK, but you haven't convinced us you're going to get the job done."

"There's no question if Bill Clinton is returned . . . we're checkmated. We're being told no—you are too much, too radical, too extreme, too fast, too bratty, too whatever. We haven't done a good enough job explaining our positions, so if we lose the referendum, it may be our own making by failing to communicate what we hoped to accomplish and why we were doing it," said Mark Foley.

The Republican Congress had to be seen as producing, and by the spring of 1996 it had produced very little. The freshmen knew they had to have something to show the voters. They needed a record to run on. It was one thing to say, "We couldn't do everything we wanted to do because of Bill Clinton." It was quite another to say,

"We couldn't do anything." A CBS–*New York Times* poll in May showed that 66 percent of those questioned disapproved of the way Congress was handling its job.

Bill Kristol had counseled the Republicans to go all out to oppose the Clinton health care plan in 1994 and not to compromise, something many Republicans were fearful of at first. He knew the Democrats would pay a heavy price for not delivering on health care reform. It helped cost them control of Congress. Now the Republicans had to avoid putting themselves in the same position. They had to deliver at least a few of the things they had run on. A balanced budget agreement, tax cuts, term limits, welfare reform, Medicare reform, campaign finance reform—they had delivered none of them.

The Republicans were going to have to cut a deal on welfare reform. A vetoed welfare reform bill didn't help the Republicans. They'd been pointing at Clinton as the problem for six months, and he was way up in the polls. Compromising and getting a welfare bill passed helped Clinton. They knew that. But it helped them, too. They would also have to pass some things the Democrats wanted, like the minimum wage and health insurance reform. They couldn't let Clinton sound Trumanesque and point to them as the do-nothing Congress.

And so the freshmen threw their lot in with Clinton.

Likewise, Clinton had distanced himself from the congressional Democrats on more than one occasion. He wasn't running around the country saying people needed to elect a Democratic Congress because polls indicated that didn't help either him or the Democrats. They were on their own. In fact, after Ron Wyden's victory in the Oregon special election in January, Clinton had told the *Washington Post,* "The American people don't think it's the president's business to tell them what ought to happen in the congressional elections."

Not only was Clinton not campaigning for a Democratic House, one of his strongest arguments for his own reelection was that he had protected Americans from the big bad Republicans who were trying to go too far and that he would continue to do so. But that implied that the Republicans would be reelected in sufficient numbers to retain control of Congress and the Democrats would remain in the minority. Clinton sensed Americans wanted it this way.

Clinton and the freshmen now had a common goal. Their political fortunes were inextricably linked. They were interested in getting themselves reelected, and it looked like the best way to do that was together.

There had always been a strange, symbiotic relationship between Clinton and the freshmen. He had, after all, created them. His failures in 1993–1994 with a Democratic Congress had moved them to run for office and had led to their victory. But their ascension to power had revived his presidency. Clinton was at his strongest when he was battling the Republicans, especially the freshmen. It was in standing up to them during the government shutdowns that Clinton seemed to find his footing. It was as if he was really standing for something. Their hot rhetoric and relative youth made Clinton seem more presidential. He was there to tone down the youngsters. His was the calm voice of reason. The freshmen made Bill Clinton look mature.

The freshmen and Clinton had a sort of unspoken deal. They would use each other to get reelected.

*   *   *

One of the first examples of what appeared to be this new partnership involved an increase in the minimum wage. Although the Democrats did not raise this issue in the first two years of Clinton's presidency, they made it a priority after the Republicans took over Congress. The minimum wage of $4.25 an hour had not been increased since 1991, and in real dollars it was at a 40-year low. There were good reasons to raise the wage. Of the 3.6 million American workers who received the minimum wage, almost half of them were over 25 years old, which countered the argument from opponents to an increase that the minimum wage primarily affected teenagers. According to the U.S. Labor Department, 37 percent of all minimum-wage earners worked full time. And a powerful argument for raising the minimum wage was as a tool to help get people off welfare. If you could get more money on welfare than you could working, why work?

Raising the minimum wage was a big issue with labor unions, who pressed for the change, and this probably had more to do with the Democrats' sudden interest in a minimum wage increase than anything else. Opponents to the increase, primarily conservative Republicans, claimed that it would cost jobs by forcing businesses to lay off workers. But the nation's unemployment rate was at a six-year low. With the economy doing so well, it seemed the perfect time to raise the minimum wage without having it result in a significant jump in unemployment.

In March Senate Democrats began pushing for an increase to $5.15 an hour over a two-year period, but Dole and the Republicans were able to block a vote on the matter. In his radio address at the end of March, Clinton said "a member of Congress who refuses to allow the minimum wage to come up for a vote made more money during last year's one-month government shutdown than a minimum wage worker makes in an entire year."

An April CBS–*New York Times* poll showed 84 percent of those questioned favored raising the minimum wage. Opposing a wage increase was not a good move for the Republicans, despite the strong opposition from their key business supporters.

Over Congress's Easter recess the AFL-CIO started running TV ads calling for a minimum wage increase in more than 25 Republicans' districts, including those of a number of freshmen. The ads said the minimum wage hadn't gone up since 1991, although corporate profits and congressional pay had soared. The announcer mentioned the local Republican member who had voted to block a minimum wage increase and to cut Medicare and college loans "all to give a big tax break to the rich."

The ads had the desired effect. Two GOP House moderates, Jack Quinn of New York and Chris Shays of Connecticut, quickly introduced legislation to increase the minimum wage by $1 an hour and were able to attract more than 20 Republican cosponsors. Still, Republican leaders insisted they would not schedule a vote on a minimum wage increase.

For GOP freshman Phil English, aggressively supporting a minimum wage increase was part of what he needed to do to get reelected. English, who had won in 1994 with just 49 percent of the vote, represented Pennsylvania's 21st District in the northwestern corner of the state. It was a largely industrial, working-class district that not only voted for Clinton in 1992 but for Michael Dukakis in 1988. Although English had been a reliable vote for the Republican leadership in 1995, as the election approached, he saw the wisdom of distancing himself from Gingrich and the rest of the Republican leadership, and his early calls for a vote on the minimum wage increase were part of that strategy.

A number of the other freshmen, including Mark Neumann, said they were philosophically opposed to the increase but if it came to the floor for a vote they would probably have no choice but to vote yes. They considered the potential political price if they did otherwise too great.

Finally, because of pressure from their own moderate members and those facing tough races, House Republican leaders agreed in early May to schedule a vote on the minimum wage before the end of the month. The measure was sponsored by Quinn and freshman Frank Riggs of California, who said he supported the increase because "over time, by increasing the minimum wage and by implementing meaningful welfare reform, we will be moving more people from welfare to work, helping those people obtain again full employment, and, in the long term, become taxpaying, contributing members of society."

English, a cosponsor of the bill, made similar comments: "In my congressional district in western Pennsylvania, I have seen far too many families supported by one or more members working at minimum wage jobs. These hardworking folks could easily surrender and join the welfare system, but they do not."

Bill Martini, who was also facing a tough reelection campaign and came from an industrial district in New Jersey with many union members, was another cosponsor. "To me this is not an issue of politics but rather simply an issue of fairness," Martini remarked on the floor. "I do not believe this should be a partisan issue, but it is not a coincidence that this issue was raised in an election year; that, despite the fact that for two years they, my colleagues on the other side, had every opportunity to pass a minimum wage increase when they controlled both Congress and the White House, they did not. Nevertheless, we need to stop playing political games and give hardworking men and women a raise. Too often these individuals work long hours and often take second jobs, yet they feel like they are running in place."

But not all of the freshmen saw it that way. The increase had been strongly opposed by the National Federation of Independent Businesses; Steve Largent championed their cause in his floor statement: "The people who really take it in the shorts on this are small businessmen. The people that are creating 80 percent of the jobs that we have in this country, they are the ones that are going to take it in the shorts when we increase the minimum wage."

By a vote of 281–144, with 93 Republicans voting in favor of the change, the House passed a 90-cent increase in the minimum wage. On the final vote, 29 of the freshmen favored the increase, including many of those whose districts had been targeted by the union ads, such as Van Hilleary, Greg Ganske, Jim Longley, and Mark Neumann.

The Democrats were exultant. It was their first real legislative win of the year. Now they had to get the measure through the Senate. Over the Fourth of July holiday, the AFL-CIO took its advertising campaign into Maine, Pennsylvania, and New York in an effort to influence Senate votes.

On July 8 the Senate passed the minimum wage bill 72 to 24, with 27 Republicans joining all of the Senate's 47 Democrats in voting for the increase. But the Senate bill also included something for Republican supporters, $14 billion in tax relief for small businesses, including larger write-offs for equipment purchases and simplified pension rules.

By the time the measure was ready for final passage, the wage bill contained more than $20 billion in tax breaks, including a $5,000 tax credit for couples adopting a child and allowing homemakers to contribute $2,000 tax-free a year to individual retirement accounts. But there were also tax breaks targeted for large corporations, which had little or nothing to do with the minimum wage but were rewards to loyal GOP supporters. These changes allowed U.S. corporations with operations in Puerto Rico to continue to qualify for tax credits; altered pension laws to benefit both large and small companies; reduced the amount of time over which convenience stores could depreciate the cost of gasoline pumping equipment; and gave owners of pizzerias and businesses that deliver food a larger break on Social Security taxes paid on tips. In the end the minimum wage bill became an example of the dance of legislation, with each side getting something it wanted.

*   *   *

The next piece of legislation that Clinton had asked for and the Republicans delivered was the health insurance reform that had become known as the Kassebaum-Kennedy bill for its two chief Senate sponsors, Republican Nancy Landon Kassebaum, chairman of the Labor and Human Resources Committee, and Democrat Edward Kennedy, the ranking member who had also championed the minimum wage increase.

The Kassebaum-Kennedy bill guaranteed health insurance coverage for people who change or lose their jobs by prohibiting insurance companies from denying coverage to anyone because of a preexisting medical condition. It also prohibited employer-sponsored health plans from denying coverage or charging higher premiums to employees because of their health problems and increased the tax deduction for health insurance for the self-employed from 30 percent to 80 percent over 10 years.

The Senate passed the measure on April 23 by a vote of 100–0. But the bill was held up for months because of Republican leaders' insistence that a provision for the creation of medical savings accounts be included. MSAs had low premiums and would guarantee payment for all medical bills that exceeded a certain amount, such as $1,500 for an individual and $3,000 for a family. Participants would be permitted to put pretax dollars into accounts to pay their deductibles.

This was similar to a measure the Republicans had incorporated into their Medicare reform plan. And Golden Rule Insurance Company, one of the few companies that sold health insurance for people with medical savings accounts, stood to benefit significantly by the inclusion of such a provision in any federal health insurance reform plan. Golden Rule and its former chairman, J. Patrick Rooney, were major donors to Republicans and to Gingrich's GOPAC.

Finally a compromise was reached. The Kassebaum-Kennedy bill would include a small test of medical savings accounts for people who were either self-employed or worked for companies with fewer than 50 employees. With that provision as part of the measure, the House passed the Kassebaum-Kennedy bill 421–2 on August 1.

One of those who spoke in favor of the bill was freshman and doctor Greg Ganske. "This bill is long overdue. . . . We will provide genuine health care reform, expand accessibility, ensure portability, and all without a government takeover of the health care sector."

After the vote, Senator Kennedy couldn't help gloating. "Republicans have decided they need to pass Democratic initiatives before the election because their own record is too empty and too shameful to run on," said Kennedy after the House passage of his bill, which he called a "transparent insurance policy for endangered Republican candidates."

*　　*　　*

The third of the major bills Congress passed in its pre-August recess flurry of activity was the most important one for Republicans—welfare reform. The other two bills had been foisted on them by the Democrats. But they were driving the agenda on welfare reform. This was their bill, and with its passage they could finally claim credit for making good on one of their major 1994 campaign promises.

Although he had campaigned in 1992 to "end welfare as we know it," Clinton and the Democrats, much to their later regret, decided to tackle health care reform instead. Their lack of success in attempting to overhaul the health care delivery system left them no time or inclination to deal with welfare. But welfare reform, extremely popular with the public, was an issue the Republicans picked up and used with great success during their 1994 campaign.

Clinton had vetoed the Republicans' 1995 effort at welfare reform. Now there were divisions among White House advisers about whether or not he should sign a welfare bill, but it seemed clear Clinton himself wanted to do so. One hitch involved the Republican proposal to reduce funding for the Medicaid health insurance program for the poor and block-grant it to the states to administer. Clinton and the Democrats were strongly opposed to this, and the president had indicated he would veto any bill that included Medicaid.

This left the Republicans at an impasse. Should they give Clinton a bill they expected him to veto, or should they pass something they liked less but thought he might be willing to sign? A number of the freshmen, surprisingly, decided the latter course of action was preferable. They had suddenly, or not so suddenly, developed a pragmatic streak. Freshmen facing tough races could understand the benefit of getting a welfare reform proposal passed and signed, and they didn't want to jeopardize that by insisting on the Medicaid component.

On June 26 a group of House Republicans led by freshman John Ensign of Nevada sent a letter to Gingrich asking that Medicaid be taken off the welfare reform bill. "All the talk in the world about reforming the American welfare state is useless unless our reforms are signed into law or the veto of the president is overridden by Congress. We have worked too hard to bring about changes in the welfare program as a group and as individuals to risk its final passage," said the letter. It was signed by nearly 100 House Republicans, an eclectic mixture of older moderates like Amo Houghton and Connie Morella, committee chairs like Bill Thomas, and more than 25 freshmen, from moderates like Phil English, Bill Martini, Mark Foley, Charlie Bass, and Sue Kelly to conservatives like Randy Tate, Joe Scarborough, Wes Cooley, Helen Chenoweth, Matt Salmon, and Steve Largent.

Ensign, a member of the Ways and Means Committee who was in a tough reelection campaign, said he decided to push the effort to delink Medicaid and welfare reform because Medicaid was looking certain to draw a veto and he wanted to see something passed. "Anytime you do anything this major and this right it's a good election issue. . . . Sometimes good politics and good policy go together," said Ensign, sounding for all the world like a seasoned pol.

Were these the same freshmen who had insisted on shutting down the government no matter what and refused to give an inch? "Last year we thought we could get the whole pie, and we weren't ready to compromise. But if your choice is half a pie or no pie, you take half a pie," explained Ensign.

But even without the Medicaid changes, Clinton still had objections to provisions that would make severe cuts in the food stamp program and deny benefits to legal aliens. He called the GOP plan "excessively harsh and uncompromising."

The Republican bill set a five-year lifetime limit for individuals to receive welfare benefits and required the head of each household to go to work within two years of receiving benefits, although there would be some exceptions for hardship and special cases. States could withhold payments to unmarried girls under 18 unless they stayed in school and lived with an adult. And benefits would not be increased for a woman who had more children while on welfare, although this prohibition could be waived by individual states.

Even some GOP moderates were concerned with aspects of the bill, and a number of them supported a bipartisan alternative being offered by senior Republican Michael Castle of Delaware and moderate Democrat John Tanner of Tennessee. Clinton urged Congress to pass the Castle-Tanner substitute bill, which softened the food stamp and illegal alien provisions, allowed more money for job training and child care for women seeking to get off of welfare, and also included a provision for additional resources for the states during a time of recession, when more people might go on the welfare rolls. Like the Republican plan, the Castle-Tanner bill would block-grant the welfare program to individual states to run, but it would provide the possibility of vouchers for food and other necessities for children and mothers who had used all of their benefits after the five-year limit set by the Republican bill.

The bipartisan proposal, which the *Washington Post* and the *New York Times* endorsed as a more humane alternative, was beginning to pick up steam. The bill had 26 Democratic and 16 Republican cosponsors, and it was making the Republican leadership nervous.

On July 18, the day scheduled for the House vote, Gingrich sent an extremely strongly worded letter to all House Republicans urging them not to vote for the Castle-Tanner bill, which he referred to as the "Gephardt substitute" for minority leader Richard Gephardt. "I consider this to be the most important issue we will face between now and the end of the session," Gingrich wrote. He argued that if they passed the Castle-Tanner bill, which the Democrats were to offer on the floor, the Democrats would try to take credit for welfare reform and steal the spotlight from the Republicans. "It is critical that Republicans maintain the upper hand on this issue by rejecting the Gephardt substitute. . . . *Should anyone be considering a 'yes' vote for the Gephardt substitute, either Dick Armey or I would like to have the opportunity to discuss it with you prior to the vote.*" Gingrich didn't want any surprises. He wanted to know how many votes he had. And any Republicans thinking about voting for Castle-Tanner were now warned they had better think again.

When the welfare reform measure came to the floor, a food stamp amendment was successfully offered by Budget Committee chairman John Kasich and freshman Robert Ney. The measure would set a lifetime limit of three months for adults without children: After receiving food stamps for three months, people would have to hold down jobs to qualify for additional food stamps, even if it had been years since they had last received them.

"Why does Washington continue to promote a welfare system that discourages work?" asked Ney during floor debate of his amendment. "Is it extreme to want to give welfare recipients hope instead of an endless cycle of dependency? Should we not be trying to encourage work?" As Kasich described it, "Our welfare bill says at some point you have to get trained, you have to go to work. You have to get off the system and get a job. . . . If you cannot find a job, you go to work for the state in a workfare program, and maybe you whitewash the graffiti, or maybe you clean up the neighborhood, but you participate in a program where you do some work in exchange for the food stamps that you get."

But the Democrats were outraged by the provision, as well as many other aspects of the Republican plan. "I have seen some mean-spirited amendments in this place. To me this is the most mean-spirited amendment that I have ever seen on any bill that has come before this House," said Bill Hefner of North Carolina. "If this is what you have to do to get reelected to this Congress, I do not want to be a part of this body any longer if I have to vote for such mean-spirited legislation as this. . . . It is not worth it to be in this most deliberative body in the world. . . . It is degrading." Despite Hefner's admonition, the amendment passed, largely on a party-line vote.

When the Castle-Tanner amendment was ready for consideration, Gingrich was on the floor, as if to enforce discipline, and Armey was presiding in the chair. The pressure from the leadership did the trick. Although 16 Republicans had originally cosponsored the Castle-Tanner legislation, only nine Republicans voted in its favor when the vote was called, and the measure was defeated, 168–258. In addition to Castle and six other senior GOP moderates, two freshmen voted in favor of Castle-Tanner: Tom Davis of Virginia and Jon Fox of Pennsylvania.

Final House passage of the Republican welfare reform bill came on a vote of 256 to 170, with 30 Democrats supporting final passage and four Republicans voting no, including freshman Jim Bunn of Oregon.

"I was hoping we would get enough votes to have a chance [to make changes] at conference committee, and I think we got enough," said Tanner after the vote. Tanner was obviously disappointed with the falling-off of Republican support, and in a reference to some of the GOP cosponsors who had been turned by pressure from Gingrich he commented dryly, "I try to vote for bills that I sponsor."

Walking out of the chamber, freshman Matt Salmon said he was satisfied with the welfare bill and would even be willing to go along with some changes if necessary to get the president to sign it. "Eight or nine months ago we hoped for a touchdown every time we threw the ball. Now we're just happy for a first down," he said.

The Senate considered the welfare bill on July 23, the week after the House vote. The Senate passed two changes that would guarantee extended Medicaid coverage for people cut from the welfare rolls and continue the federal guarantee of food stamps for the poor. Final Senate passage of the welfare bill was on a 74 to 24 vote, with 23 Democrats supporting the bill.

Clinton said the Senate's changes made the bill better but still not good enough. "You can put wings on a pig, but you don't make it an eagle," said Clinton. "I just don't want to do anything that hurts kids. I'm going to keep working with [the Congress]. . . . We'll see if we can end up with something that is acceptable."

The GOP welfare plan, which Republicans claimed would save $55 billion over six years, was criticized by a number of social service agencies, including Catholic Charities, which called it "largely a sham designed to appease the ignorant and to pander to our worst prejudices in an election year." And studies by the Urban Institute and the federal Department of Health and Human Services, which administered the program, estimated that the changes would push 1 million children into poverty.

But despite the warnings about its potential impact, Clinton announced on July 31 that he would sign the welfare bill "first and foremost, because the current system is broken and second, because Congress has made many of the changes I sought." Clinton said he hoped to get Congress to modify provisions dealing with food stamps and legal aliens later.

New York's Democratic senator Daniel Patrick Moynihan, who had strongly opposed the bill, said, "The president has made his decision. Let us hope that it is for the best. . . . The cabinet is against the bill; the pollsters are for it. This is a defining event in his presidency. . . . This bill is not welfare reform but welfare repeal. It is the first step in dismantling the social contract that has been in place in the United States since at least the 1930s."

Clinton's decision to sign the GOP welfare reform bill disappointed many liberals in his own party, but it also deprived Dole of a powerful issue to use against him in the presidential campaign. Clinton undoubtedly made the political calculation that it was the best thing to do for his reelection. Also benefiting from Clinton's decision were the GOP freshmen and the Democrats from swing districts who had voted yes. They could now go home and say they had done something about the problem of welfare.

On August 22, the same week that he signed the minimum wage increase and health insurance reform measures, Clinton signed the welfare bill in a Rose Garden ceremony that was far less celebratory than the ceremonies held for those other bills. "Today we are ending welfare as we know it," Clinton declared. Although he criticized the provisions that reduced the food stamp program and denied aid to legal immigrants, Clinton said he decided to sign the bill because, "We can change what is wrong. We should not have passed this historic opportunity to do what is right."

Clinton was effectively ending the federal government's 60-year guarantee of federal welfare payments for poor families with children and turning the program over to the states to manage. All of the nearly 13 million people on welfare and the 26 million on food stamps as well as future recipients would be affected by the changes. The long-term impacts were difficult to predict. Maybe they would force some people off the dole and into the workforce. And maybe they would discourage some teenagers from getting pregnant and going on welfare. But the changes could also mean that eventually some women with children who were unable to find or incapable of holding a job would be left without any means of support, pushed further into poverty and hopelessness.

Marian Wright Edelman, the president of the Children's Defense Fund and a close friend of Hillary Rodham Clinton (a former officer of the organization), called the president's signing of the bill "a moment of shame." Her husband, Peter Edelman, who was an assistant secretary of the Department of Health and Human Services, along with several other HHS officials resigned in protest within a month of Clinton's signing the bill.

*   *   *

Having taken care of several substantive matters, the Republicans turned their attention to the concerns of the social conservatives, an important group of voters for them. With the exception of certain measures relating to abortion, many issues the Christian conservatives cared about had not been brought to the floor during the session because the leadership thought they were too divisive and a number of the moderates, including some freshmen, argued against it. But the Republicans still wanted to placate the conservatives, so they did so with issues that were both low priority and low controversy, that they could use to score a conservative social win without causing too much turmoil within the GOP conference.

One of these was the so-called Defense of Marriage Act, which was introduced in the House by freshman Bob Barr of Georgia. The legislation would allow states to refuse to recognize same-sex marriages performed in other states. It would also formally define marriage as the union of a man and a woman and withhold federal tax, welfare, pension, health, veteran, and Social Security benefits from the domestic partners of homosexuals.

Barr seemed a rather unlikely candidate to be introducing something called the "Defense of Marriage Act" since he had been married three times and his second wife had sued him in 1988 over payment for unpaid medical bills for his children. But he took on the task with great enthusiasm. On July 12, when the measure came to the House floor, Barr said, "As Rome burned, Nero fiddled. . . . The very foundations of our society are in danger of being burned. The flames of hedonism, the flames of narcissism, the flames of self-centered morality are licking at the very foundations of our society, the family unit." He called on his fellow members to "be resolute. This is an issue of fundamental importance to this country, to our families, and to our children. . . . Enough is enough. We must maintain a moral foundation, an ethical foundation for our families and ultimately for the United States of America."

How "fundamentally important" the American people thought it was to outlaw homosexual marriage was certainly open to debate. The burning issue that had placed the Defense of Marriage Act on the congressional agenda was a pending court case in Hawaii about whether same-sex couples could be granted marriage licenses in that state. The public hardly seemed to be clamoring for Congress to address the issue, but it offered a popular preelection boost among social conservatives as well as a chance to test the Democrats and force them to vote on the matter.

Barr was joined in support for the measure by a number of the freshmen. Largent claimed that "no culture that has ever embraced homosexuality has ever survived." Fellow Oklahoman Tom Coburn said, "We hear about diversity, but we do not hear about perversity. The real debate is about homosexuality and whether or not we sanction homosexuality in this country. . . . Homosexuality is immoral. . . . It is based on perversion. . . . It is based on lust."

According to Andrea Seastrand of California, "Traditional marriage is a house built on a rock. As shifting sands of public opinion and prevailing winds of compromise damage other institutions, marriage endures and so must its historically legal definition. This bill will fortify marriage against the storm of revisionism."

"Homosexuality has been discouraged in all cultures because it is inherently wrong and harmful to individuals, families, and societies. The only reason it has been able to gain such prominence in America today is the near blackout on information about homosexual behavior itself. We are being treated to a steady drumbeat of propaganda echoing the stolen rhetoric of the black civil rights movement and misrepresenting science," said David Funderburk of North Carolina.

Leading the opposition to the measure were the three openly gay members of the House, Democrats Barney Frank and Gerry Studds, both of Massachusetts, and Republican Steve Gunderson of Wisconsin, who had announced his retirement at the end of the year. "People talk about their marriage being threatened. I find it implausible that two men deciding to commit themselves to each other threatens the marriage of people a couple of blocks away," said Frank. Gunderson was more emotional in his plea to his colleagues: "Why are we so mean? Why are we so motivated by prejudice, intolerance, and unfortunately in some cases, bigotry? Why must we attack one element of our society for some cheap political gain? Why must we pursue the politics of division, of fear, of hate?" He went on: "Frankly, I want to ask my colleagues, Why should my partner of 13 years not be entitled to the same health insurance and survivor benefits that individuals around here, my colleagues with second and third wives, are able to give to them?"

The House voted overwhelmingly 342–67 to pass the Defense of Marriage Act, with 224 Republicans and 118 Democrats voting in favor. Gunderson was the only Republican member to vote against it.

Many moderate and even liberal members who had supported gay rights and increased AIDS research funding in the past voted in favor of the bill, including freshman Mark Foley. Quoted in *The Advocate,* a gay publication, freshman Foley criticized his colleagues who bashed gays and lesbians during the debate but said, "There were many people who voted for this legislation, myself included, because they have genuine reservations about tampering with an institution many Americans regard as sacred."

White House officials said Clinton had long opposed same-sex marriage and would sign the bill, but it was clear it was not something he was eager to do. "It's wrong for people to use this issue to demonize gays and lesbians and it's pretty clear that was the intent in trying to create a buzz on this issue. But the fact remains that if the legislation is in accord with the president's stated position, he would have no choice but to sign it," presidential adviser George Stephanopoulos told the *New York Times.* White House press secretary Michael McCurry called the legislation "gay baiting, pure and simple . . . a classic use of wedge politics designed to provoke anxieties and fears."

Passage of the legislation did have repercussions for at least one member of the House. After being informed that *The Advocate* would be mentioning him in a story about the Defense of Marriage Act, Republican Jim Kolbe, a six-term representative from Arizona who had voted in favor of the measure, announced in a written statement released on August 1 that he was a homosexual. "That I am a gay person has never affected the way that I legislate. I am the same person, one who has spent many years struggling to relieve the tax burden for families, balance the budget for our children's future and improve the quality of life we cherish in southern Arizona," read Kolbe's statement.

After Kolbe's announcement, Gunderson told the *Washington Post,* "[The Republican] party has a problem with this. Some of the rhetoric in our party has created a meanness on both sides." He said some politicians "have got to continue to foster the stereotype of gays and lesbians as irresponsible individuals consumed by illicit drugs and illicit sex to continue their political battles and raise their money. If America comes to accept gays and lesbians as mainstream Americans with the same values as the rest of America, that ends their political message."

Gunderson said he had been told that if he decided to stay in Congress, some other Republicans would oppose his taking over as chairman of the Agriculture Committee because of his homosexuality, although he had the most seniority on the committee. "Sooner or later, people are going to realize there are people all across the country, all over the Republican party, all over Capitol Hill who are gay and lesbian and accept them for the professionals and talented people they are rather than accepting them as something less," Gunderson told the *Post*.

*   *   *

As part of their effort to bolster their conservative quotient, the Republicans also passed a measure on August 1 that declared English the official language of the United States. In a 259–169 vote, largely along party lines, the House approved a measure that would require federal government agencies to conduct their business only in English. It also repealed a portion of the Voting Rights Act that required communities with large numbers of voters for whom English was a second language to print election ballots in other languages.

"Part of becoming American involves English," said Gingrich in speaking for the measure. "Is there a thing we call American? Is it unique? It is vital historically to assert and establish that English is the common language at the heart of our civilization."

As part of the legislation, it was necessary for the House to pass an exemption for certain Latin phrases, such as "E Pluribus Unum," which means "one out of many" and is the official motto and part of the seal of the United States.

26

THE END OF
THE 104TH

DESPITE THEIR SUMMER FRENZY of legislative activity, House members took time out on July 25 for the 35th annual roll call congressional baseball game. The previous year the Republicans, led by pitcher Steve Largent, had creamed the Democrats 6–0. Largent had been awesome, giving up only four hits and striking out nine Democrats. But this year was different. For one thing, the Democrats had been practicing more. And the Republicans were a little distracted. They were more concerned about reelection than baseball.

Largent was on the mound again, but he was not as overpowering as he had been the year before, and the Democrats took a 3–0 lead in the first inning. The game was marred early on by the infield collision of two Democrats who suffered cuts and fractures while attempting to catch a fly ball. There was no question these guys were playing for keeps. And after going into extra innings the Democrats pulled off a 16–14 win.

Just as the previous year's contest had symbolized the Republicans' dominance in the 1994 elections, the Democrats' surprising strength and the Republicans' many errors in this year's game seemed to be a reflection of the past eight months.

*   *   *

With passage of the minimum wage increase, welfare reform, and the Kassebaum-Kennedy health insurance bill as well as several other significant bills, Congress had enacted more major legislation in the month of July than it had in the previous 18 months of the 104th Congress.

"We're like the little engine that could," Gingrich told the *New York Times,* crediting "hard work" and "the fact that people learn from mistakes" for the late legislative productivity.

It was clearly important to the Republicans that they be seen as producing, because they had other problems to overcome, not the least their national leaders. Dole's campaign seemed to be going nowhere, and Gingrich remained the country's least popular Republican. Clinton and the Democrats were doing their best to link Dole with Gingrich. And Democratic House challengers were trying to connect their GOP freshman opponents with Gingrich as well.

To distance themselves from Gingrich, the freshmen used several strategies. One was to criticize him openly back home. Another was to vote against him when they could, for example, by voting against approving the journal of the previous day's legislative session. This was a pro forma vote, often taken by voice and not recorded. When a recorded vote was called for, it was usually because the GOP leadership wanted to bring members to the floor to do a vote count on another matter. But a no vote on approving the journal counted as a vote against the leadership, and by voting no the freshmen could attempt to increase the appearance of their independence without opposing the leaders on a significant issue.

Among those freshmen who had started making it a practice of voting no on the journal were Michael Flanagan, James Longley, John Ensign, Gil Gutknecht, Steve Stockman, Fred Heineman, and Van Hilleary, almost all of whom were expecting tough reelection races.

*   *   *

On August 3 Congress adjourned for a month so members could take some time off, attend the conventions, and most important, campaign.

Several of the freshmen who were in difficult races, such as Neumann, decided to stay home rather than attend the Republican convention. Others, such as Hilleary, cut their time in San Diego short.

The Republicans were so haunted by the specter of the 1992 convention and its divisive spirit that they were determined to be inclusive and likable this time around—so much so that the event seemed more like a group encounter session than a political convention. On opening night, Monday, August 12, the convention began with a Native American leading the Pledge of Allegiance and a young African American boy singing the national anthem. This was also the night chosen for Colin Powell to address the convention. Powell had turned down the chance to be the keynote speaker, as he had rejected the idea of running on the ticket with Dole as the vice presidential candidate.

Powell was a pro-growth fiscal conservative and a social moderate who wanted his speech to be a message of inclusion and fairness. "We are the party committed to lessening the burden of taxes, cutting government regulations, and reducing government spending, all for the purpose of generating the higher economic growth that will bring better jobs, wages, and living standards to all our people," Powell told the delegates.

"We must be firm but we must also be fair. We have to make sure that reduced government spending doesn't single out the poor and the middle class. Corporate welfare and welfare for the wealthy must be first in line for elimination. All of us— all of us, my friends—all of us must be willing to do with less from government if we are to avoid condemning our children and grandchildren with a crushing burden of debt that will deny them the American dream. . . . It is the entitlement state that must be reformed and not just the welfare state. And we must do it in a way that does not paint all of government as the enemy. Ineffective government, excessive government, wasteful government, that is the kind of government that we Republicans intend to defeat."

"The Republican Party must always be the party of inclusion. The Hispanic immigrant who became a citizen yesterday must be as precious to us as a *Mayflower* descendant. . . . It is our diversity that has made us strong. Yet our diversity has, sadly, throughout our history, been the source of discrimination that we, as guardians of the American dream, must rip out branch and root. It is our party, the party of Lincoln, that must always stand for equal rights and fair opportunity for all."

Powell said he had been asked many times why he became a Republican, and in his speech he explained: "I became a Republican because, like you, I believe our party best represents the principles of freedom, opportunity, and limited government upon which our nation was founded. I became a Republican because I believe the policies of our party will lead to greater economic growth, which is the only real solution to the problems of poverty that keep too many Americans from sharing in the wealth of this nation." But as Powell continued, "I became a Republican because I want to help build a big tent that our party has raised to attract all Americans. You all know that I believe in a woman's right to choose, and I strongly support affirmative action," he was both cheered and booed by the delegates.

After endorsing Dole, Powell ended his speech by saying that together we can overcome our differences and work to restore the American dream, and received a boisterous standing ovation. It was a terrific speech, arguably the best of the convention. But it seemed questionable whether Powell was speaking for a majority of those in the convention hall, which may explain why he left the convention early the next day and did not stay around for Bob Dole's nomination or acceptance speech.

The following night Gingrich delivered a short speech. Although as Speaker of the House he was the permanent chairman of the convention, Gingrich was keeping a low public profile, and his speech was seen by few people outside the convention hall because it was delivered before the hour the major television networks had allotted for live convention coverage. But his speech could not have been more innocuous. He opened by introducing the American gold medal winner in beach volleyball at the Atlanta Olympic Games, although what that had to do with a political convention was a complete mystery. His seven-minute speech began with a reference to Martin Luther King and went from there to compassion and volunteerism. He made no mention of the Republican revolution or the Contract with America. He didn't even mention Congress or keeping a Republican majority in the House. It was clear the strategists thought connecting Gingrich too closely with the congressional vote was not a wise move. But Gingrich's speech was so completely devoid of any substance it left one wondering why he spoke at all. The *Weekly Standard* called it "the worst and most embarrassing speech of his career."

Throughout the four days of the convention, Gingrich, new Senate majority leader Trent Lott, and other congressional leaders like Dick Armey and Tom DeLay stayed largely out of television view. The Dole campaign had decided they were not ready for prime time. Instead of talk about the contract or the revolution, it was the "common-sense Congress" that was touted whenever Congress came up, which was rare.

One member who was given a prominent speaking role was freshman J. C. Watts of Oklahoma, one of two African American Republicans serving in Congress. Watts had become the Republicans' resident folksy, storytelling, inspirational speaker of choice. His delivery had the cadence and the passion of a Baptist minister, which he was in his spare time. He was also the first black Republican to be elected to Congress from south of the Mason-Dixon line since Reconstruction. Ninety-seven percent of the delegates at the convention were white, and the party platform opposed affirmative action and called for limiting assistance to legal immigrants. But Watts told the delegates the Republicans define compassion by how few people are on welfare and food stamps rather than how many.

Watts liked to talk about his humble origins and how far he had come. "I never thought the fifth of six children born to Helen and Buddy Watts in a poor black neighborhood in the poor, rural community of Eufaula, Oklahoma, would someday be called congressman." Watts said his father had spent only two days in the seventh grade, and that's as far as he went in school, but he had a great deal of common sense: "My papa always said that the only helping hand you can rely on is at the end of your sleeve."

Watts's father raised cattle and worked as a Baptist minister and policeman to support his family. And J. C. said his adherence to tough love and pulling yourself up by your own bootstraps came from the lessons he learned from watching his father. But as a star quarterback for Oklahoma University, Watts had won the kind of notice that had opened doors for him not only in college but later, as he attempted to start a business and political career in Oklahoma. A moral conservative, African American Republican, Watts was something of a novelty and attracted a level of attention and support that he might not have received had he been white. And one could argue Watts's success had as much to do with affirmative action of a specific sort as with bootstrap pulling.

Watts's convention speech was aimed mainly at young people. "Character is doing what's right when no one's looking," he admonished them. "If you can dream it, you can do it," Watts said, because, "Friends, after all, this is America."

After Watts, House Budget chairman John Kasich spoke. Unlike Gingrich, he was not shy about touting the accomplishments of the 104th Congress. "We have worked every single day to keep our word," said Kasich. "Our budget efforts in Congress have not been about cutting and slashing" but rather about restoring the American dream for our children, Kasich insisted.

Congresswoman Susan Molinari delivered the keynote address. She was young, attractive, bright, a new mother with her beautiful baby in the audience. She was the perfect demographic—a soccer mom. Molinari's was the face the Republicans wanted to project to America. She began by telling the delegates, "This speech is a lot like a Bill Clinton promise—it won't last long, and it will sound like a Republican talking." Molinari delivered a perky but persistent attack on Clinton in combination with personal anecdotes and an endorsement of the candidacies of Bob Dole and Jack Kemp. It was a well-delivered although largely forgettable speech.

A number of other members of Congress had less visible roles at the convention, usually in the early evening hours before the three major TV networks began their coverage. George Radanovich and Sue Myrick were there representing the freshman class, and Fred Thompson spoke for the Senate freshmen.

By virtue of being from Dole's home state, the Kansas delegation was given seats at the front of the convention hall. Sitting in the front row was Senate candidate Sam Brownback, right next to Sheila Frahm, the woman he had defeated in the primary just a week earlier.

On the third night of the convention, Elizabeth Dole did her history-making, Oprah Winfrey–like walk through the audience with a handheld microphone to deliver a tribute to her husband. She was polished, personable, maybe just a little too perfect. But it was one of the convention's few memorable moments.

On Thursday, August 16, it was her husband's turn. In accepting his party's nomination, Dole described himself as "the most optimistic man in America." It was an adequate speech. There wasn't anything particularly wrong with it, but it just didn't seem that inspiring. And it really didn't explain why Dole should be president. Certainly it didn't give Dole the bounce he needed to overtake Clinton's double-digit lead.

The Democratic convention followed two weeks later. The most memorable thing about it was the very public resignation of controversial presidential adviser Dick Morris the day of Clinton's acceptance speech. The resignation came in the wake of revelations that the married Morris had been carrying on a relationship with a prostitute he met in a Washington hotel suite paid for by the Clinton campaign. Not only that, but he had let her eavesdrop on conversations with the president and told her confidential information involving the campaign. It was tawdry and beside the point, but somehow the story seemed more interesting than what was happening on the convention floor. It was certainly not the kind of news the Clinton campaign was thrilled to have sharing the front page with coverage of Clinton's acceptance speech.

The speech was vintage Clinton, a laundry list of programs and initiatives, well delivered. Clinton, unlike Dole, was eager to talk about the 104th Congress. "I could never allow cuts that devastate education for our children, that pollute our environment, that end the guarantee of health care for those who are served under Medicaid, that end our duty or violate our duty to our parents through Medicare. I just couldn't do that. As long as I'm president, I'll never let it happen. And it doesn't matter . . . if they try again as they did before to use the blackmail threat of a shutdown of the federal government to force these things on the American people. We didn't let it happen before. We won't let it happen again. Of course, there is a better answer to this dilemma. We could have the right kind of a balanced budget with a new Congress, a Democratic Congress."

Medicare, the environment, and education—that was going to be Clinton's and the Democrats' mantra. They had polled it, and it worked. They were going to say it over and over and over until even they were sick of it. It may have been about the only thing they had going for them in terms of ideas. The Democrats weren't saying, "Elect us because we'll do such and such." They didn't really have a message of their own. They were saying, "We're not the Republicans, so elect us. We'll protect you from the Republicans' extremism."

*　　*　　*

When Congress returned to Washington in September, the mood was pretty grim. The congressional Republicans had pretty much given up on Dole, and they were now starting to worry that if his candidacy looked completely hopeless, it could affect Republican turnout, which could cost their seats, maybe even the majority. "If Dole wins, we pick up seats in significant numbers. If he loses 55–45, we hold our own, winning some and losing some. Anything close to 60 percent, then we're out of power," Connecticut's Chris Shays told the *New York Times* in mid-September.

On September 11 Dole held another pep rally for congressional Republicans and attempted to assure them his campaign was on track. "Don't worry about this election. We're going to win," he told them. But few believed him. It was now every man for himself. The freshmen knew the only way they were going to combat Dole's campaign problems and what Clinton and the Democrats were saying about them was to run their own races in their own districts—to localize rather than nationalize the election as they had in 1994. To do that they had to get home and campaign. Instead they were stuck in Washington trying to finish up the budget. That meant the Republicans were willing to do "whatever we have to do," according to House majority leader Armey, to get out of the Capitol and avoid another showdown with Clinton.

George Radanovich was one of the few freshmen lucky enough not to have to be worried about his own reelection. He was facing a token Democratic challenger who had raised less than $10,000 in comparison to Radanovich's $600,000-plus. But Radanovich was worried about how Dole would do in California. There had been talk about the Dole campaign's essentially giving up on California and spending its resources elsewhere. But that could mean trouble for vulnerable California Republicans, including freshmen Andrea Seastrand and Frank Riggs.

Radanovich had recently met with Donald Rumsfeld, the national chairman of the Dole campaign, and was sharing the frustration many Republicans felt over what was happening with Dole. "He's got to convince the American people he wants to be president for reasons other than he just wants it," Radanovich fretted. Radanovich didn't even want to speculate about how many of his classmates might not be coming back. "Our goal is to get them all back. We don't want those of us who represent the revolution to be sent home."

Like Radanovich, Mark Souder of Indiana had a weak opponent and was more concerned about his fellow freshmen than about his own race. He, too, thought the Dole campaign was a mess, lacking in vision and message. Souder recounted a conversation he had with a member of the House GOP leadership about Dole's meltdown. "They said if we knew what Dole's strategy was we'd tell you, but we can't even find the person in the campaign who knows what Dole's strategy is." The realization that there was no there there had caused the freshmen to push even harder for action on the welfare bill, Souder said. "The plain truth of the matter is we said, 'Move it or we're going with the Democrats.' We didn't want to get dragged down" with Dole.

"An election year isn't where you do revolutionary things," said Souder. He admitted everything went back to the government shutdown. It always would. Now that they'd had eight months to think about it, the assessment by Souder and a number of freshmen about the government shutdown was pretty much the same as what they thought when it was happening. Gingrich should never have attached Medicare reform to the continuing resolution, and they shouldn't have reopened the government the first time without a firm deal with Clinton. If they had kept the government closed, it would have kept up the pressure. Then they could have cut a deal, reopened the government before Christmas, and looked like the good guys. And maybe they would have come a lot closer to ultimately getting what they wanted on the budget, too.

"Instead, it looked like we were a bunch of yo-yos. The government's closed. The government's open. The government's closed. The government's open. . . . We lost the PR battle and now we have no choice but to say, 'OK, how much do you need to spend to get us out of here?'" said Souder. The dismay over the way their leaders had handled the government shutdown and threatened their reelection would stay with the freshmen and later ferment into major discontent.

Steve Largent had made noises about challenging John Boehner for conference chair, but the freshmen knew they didn't have the votes. "People with pop guns shouldn't be taking on people with cannons," said Souder. But the signs of serious trouble within the House Republican conference would continue after the election and into the following year.

In the summer and fall of 1996, there were rumors about replacing Gingrich as speaker. But they were just that, rumors, because there was no one to replace him with. Over the previous year, when the going got tough there had been at least four occasions when Gingrich had told House Republicans he might have to resign as Speaker if they didn't vote the way he needed them to. "And every time he was crying wolf," according to Souder.

Much of the freshmen's dissatisfaction stemmed from a feeling that things were sprung on them at the last minute, that they weren't kept informed and weren't being told the truth by their leaders. In order to get more information about what was really going on, they formed their own groups, such as the New Federalists, the Conservative Action Team, and the freshman breakfast group. And the long hours they spent in session just contributed to their banding together. When you're sitting around until 1 A.M. waiting for votes, "You've got nothing to do but get together, nothing to do but scheme and plot and talk. The next thing you know, you've got an organized bloc," explained Souder.

"Gingrich created me. . . . We are him," said Souder of his fellow freshman revolutionaries. But they were even more lethal because they were Gingrich with much less to lose.

Before leaving for the year, the social conservatives had one more issue they wanted to push. It was a threefer. They could do something they believed in, score points with the Christian Coalition and other conservative supporters, and put Clinton and many Democrats on the spot, giving them another issue to use against Clinton in the campaign.

On September 19, House members took a vote on overturning the president's five-month-old veto of legislation they had passed to outlaw a controversial abortion procedure. The antiabortion forces had labeled it a "partial-birth abortion." The procedure, done in the later stages of pregnancy, removes a fetus feet first from the uterus and then collapses the skull so it, too, can be withdrawn. Passage of the legislation had marked the first time in 23 years that Congress had acted to ban a specific abortion procedure since the Supreme Court upheld abortion rights in *Roe v. Wade*.

The legislation would subject doctors who performed the procedure to up to two years in prison. And the only exception included in the proposed law was to protect the life of the mother. When Clinton vetoed the measure in April, he said he would sign it if an exception to protect the health of the mother were included. But supporters of the abortion ban said that would be so broad as to make the legislation meaningless.

The House vote on overriding the veto was 285–137, four votes more than the two-thirds needed. Seventy Democrats joined 215 Republicans in favor of overturning the veto. Fifteen Republicans and 121 Democrats voted no. Rodney Frelinghuysen of New Jersey and Sue Kelly of New York were the only members of the freshman class who voted to sustain the presidential veto.

But a week later, in a 57–41 vote, the Senate failed to override the presidential veto, putting an end to the legislation and the issue at least for that session of Congress.

*   *   *

On September 26 Clinton went up to Capitol Hill for a meeting with House and Senate Democrats. Clinton told them they were going to have to win their seats on their own. He was willing to appear in their districts and raise money for them, but he was not going to ask the American people to give him a Democratic Congress because he didn't think that helped them—or him. Clinton told his fellow Democrats that people seemed to like divided government and they were better off running on their own. Remarkably, there was no outrage. The Democrats were in a good mood. Clinton had a double-digit lead; his poll numbers looked terrific. Clinton told the Democrats the best thing he could do for them was to win the presidency. That seemed to make sense. A big Clinton victory had to have coattails for them, they thought. What a difference two years makes. Democrats were eager to link themselves with Clinton, quite the opposite from their attitude in 1994, when he was political poison.

A terrific illustration of the reversal of Clinton's fortunes, even just in the past six months, was the Senate race in Oregon to fill the retiring Mark Hatfield's seat. Republican millionaire Gordon Smith, who had been beaten by Ron Wyden in the January special election, was now running in this race. Smith had done his best to moderate his conservative image. There seemed little doubt Clinton would carry Oregon, and Smith was trying to link himself to the incumbent Democratic president rather than the standard-bearer of his own party. In one of his television ads, Smith said his Democratic opponent opposed "President Clinton's welfare reform bill," which Smith supported. Smith was not calling it "the Republicans' welfare reform bill" but *"President Clinton's* welfare reform bill."

*   *   *

On September 27, House Republicans held a two-year anniversary celebration of their signing of the Contract with America. The event on the Capitol steps was similar to those held the previous fall and at the end of the first 100 days. But it had a different feel to it. Everybody was more subdued and a bit apprehensive.

Many of the freshmen didn't know if they would be back after November. It was a reality Gingrich tacitly acknowledged when he said, referring to the Democrats, "Maybe they'll gain 25 seats, but they're sure not going to be a majority."

Gingrich pointed to the farm bill, welfare reform, the rewrite of telecommunications law, the line-item veto, and insurance reform as major achievements of the 104th Congress. But he seemed more in the mood for vitriol than celebration. Gingrich decried the misleading TV ads the unions and the Democrats had been running about Medicare and said the press should "stop the unions and the president from lying." "We refuse to let a handful of union bosses and their corrupt cronies buy the United States House of Representatives," Gingrich fumed.

And then Gingrich told his ice bucket story, one he had probably told more than a hundred times. Holding up a plastic ice bucket, Gingrich said, "For average, everyday, working Americans this says it all." When the Republicans took over Congress they said to themselves, "What are the dumb things Washington is doing that it doesn't need to be doing?" Refrigeration came to the Capitol building in 1937, and the last home delivery of ice in Washington was in 1951, but until the Republicans took over Congress in 1994, ice was still being delivered to members' offices by 14 full-time employees at an annual cost of $500,000. "We didn't establish a steering committee; we didn't phase it out—you know, four buckets the first year, three buckets the second year. We didn't have a retraining program for our office staffs on how to use the ice trays." The Republicans just eliminated ice delivery, Gingrich said. The Republicans also privatized the shoe shine stand, the beauty and barber shops, and turned the House post office over to the U.S. Postal Service to run.

Though symbolic, such changes seemed pretty small compared with the grandiose mission of downsizing government that the Republicans had announced when they took over Congress.

Two freshmen, J. C. Watts and Andrea Seastrand, also spoke. Seastrand, who represented an area of coastal California that included Santa Barbara and San Luis Obispo, was one of the freshmen most heavily targeted by labor unions and environmentalists. The 55-year-old Seastrand held Michael Huffington's old congressional seat and was facing the opponent she had beat in 1994 by just 1,500 votes, less than 1 percent. Democrat Walter Capps, a professor of religious studies at the University of California, Santa Barbara, was about as ideologically different from Seastrand as you could get. She was a staunch conservative both on social and fiscal matters; he was a liberal who had written a book critical of the Christian conservative movement.

Seastrand had been a loyal and constant conservative vote with the House leadership throughout the 104th Congress. Even many Republicans acknowledged privately that she was probably too conservative for the district she represented. California's 22nd District had an even split of Democrats and Republicans, but many of the Republicans were affluent moderates with whom Seastrand's environmental and antiabortion votes didn't play all that well.

Watts didn't have the same worry. His reelection was all but assured. He was there to provide his unique brand of feel-good rhetoric and inspiration. Watts said over the past two years the freshmen had frequently asked themselves, "Why on earth am I here?" and the answer, he said, was quite simple. "We're here because the American people sent us here."

Now they had to convince the American people to send them back. "It's time to get out of this crazy town and get home to the pulse of America. We might go home with our heads a little bloody, but they will be unbowed," said Watts, offering a final benediction to his fellow freshmen.

When the speeches were finished, the members broke off to do interviews with local broadcast reporters on the Capitol lawn. Jim Longley of Maine looked tired and worried as he left the rally, and he had good reason to be. Like Seastrand, the labor unions and environmentalists had targeted Longley. By the time the election was over, the AFL-CIO would spend more than $1 million on television ads against him.

Longley knew he had a good opponent, Democrat Tom Allen, a former mayor of Portland. Longley's freshman colleagues said he hadn't raised enough money and had been too focused on what was going on in Washington rather than concentrating on his own race. Longley had a tendency to be intense and blunt and was not very adept at the kind of glad-handing required of politicians.

As Seastrand and several colleagues headed toward their offices, they had to pass a group of Sierra Club protesters, not more than a dozen people. One member commented on how small the group was, and Seastrand retorted, "That's because they're all in our districts."

Wes Cooley of Oregon was not nearly so low-key in his reaction. "Bye, bye Sierra Club, you communists," Cooley shouted as he gave the protesters a middle-finger salute. When one of the Sierra Club members dared him to do it again, he did. And she snapped a photo of the memorable moment. But the Sierra Club people didn't know who Cooley was, so one of them asked him. That may not have been the wisest move. According to someone from the group who was present, Cooley went right up into the face of the person who asked him and said, "You want to get into it right here? Go ahead; push me. I'll knock your fucking head off. I'm Wes Cooley. I'm Wes Cooley from Oregon's 2nd District."

The outburst, while slightly more vulgar than others in the past, was not uncharacteristic for Cooley and was, unfortunately, a fitting end to his short tenure in Congress.

Cooley's troubles had begun six months earlier when Oregon's largest newspaper, the *Oregonian*, reported that state election officials were investigating Cooley for lying about his military service during the Korean War in the information he submitted for the state's voter pamphlet. In the wake of that story, Cooley compounded his public relations problems during a speech before a group of Northwest timber executives. Cooley cited an April Fools' Day piece in *Roll Call*, which covers Capitol Hill. The bogus story predicted that if the Democrats were able to retake the House in November, they would appoint former House Speaker Jim Wright, who left the Speakership under a cloud of financial and ethical charges, to head up a new congressional ethics office.

That's exactly why the Democrats should not regain control of the House, Cooley blustered in his speech. Cooley was apparently unaware that the newspaper story was a gag. When the *Oregonian*'s Washington correspondent, the same reporter who had written about the state's investigation into Cooley's military record, tried to get Cooley to comment on his confusion over the April Fools' story, he went ballistic. In the Speaker's Lobby, just off the House floor, Cooley started yelling at the pregnant reporter. "The only thing between you and me is jail. . . . The only thing that is keeping you from getting your nose busted is that you are a lady," Cooley reportedly shouted.

After the dustup, the 64-year-old Cooley issued a written statement in which he attempted to explain his actions. "For the last several weeks, I have been attacked by relentless assaults on my character, my record of military service and, frankly, on my duties as a Congressman. All of the scurrilous attacks have been launched by my opponents and repeated by news outlets in my district. The assault has been so constant and so untrue that it has caused me great pain and much frustration. As a result of this frustration, I inadvertently lost my temper."

Cooley also attempted to clarify his outburst, claiming he never said he would punch the reporter but rather that she should be whipped. One local newspaper publisher in Cooley's district was quoted at the time as saying, "You know Wes. He's as dumb as the day is long, but he's our chump and he votes the way we like it."

In late April things got worse. Another news story broke that concerned the date of Cooley's wedding to his second wife, Rosemary. Although the couple had been living together since the mid-1980s and had represented themselves as being married, Rosemary Herron Cooley continued to collect veteran's survivors benefits from her first husband, a marine who died in 1965. Cooley, who was a member of the House Veterans Affairs Committee, declined to disclose the date of his marriage. But the Department of Veterans Affairs said Rosemary Cooley had received a monthly benefit of nearly $900 from the death of her first husband until early 1994, when she informed the department that she had remarried. The department said it is illegal for anyone who remarries or who is living as if married to collect such benefits.

At the end of May, Cooley held a news conference in Oregon to address what he called the "baseless accusations concerning my dated personal history." Blaming the liberal media for his problems, Cooley said, "I have not lived a perfect life, free from mistakes and sometimes poor judgments." But, Cooley said, "The intense public inquiry into my distant past has blurred the distinction between my personal shortcomings and my work in representing the people of the 2nd Congressional District of Oregon."

According to Cooley, he and his wife had "kept our marriage date secret for the sake of personal privacy," and at the news conference he released a marriage certificate that was dated December 10, 1993. Cooley continued to insist that he had served with the army's special forces unit in Korea but said he couldn't prove this because his military records had been destroyed in a fire at a government building.

Cooley also said he planned to run for reelection. But local and national GOP leaders had cooled to the idea of a Cooley candidacy. Although Cooley's eastern Oregon district was solidly Republican, polls showed that Cooley was far behind his Democratic challenger, Michael Dugan, a local district attorney. Republican leaders were concerned they would lose an otherwise safe seat if they couldn't get Cooley to step aside. Bob Smith, Cooley's 65-year-old predecessor who had served for 12 years in the House before his retirement in 1994, said he was embarrassed for having helped elect Cooley. Smith publicly called on Cooley to drop out of the race and let another Republican stand in his place. Cooley's response? "I'm sorry to see we're cannibals and eat our own."

In late June Cooley appeared at a Republican gathering in his district and told party activists, "I'm in this thing to stay" unless "something really went haywire." Cooley also warned his fellow Republicans that he would remember who had refused to support his reelection bid.

By now, though, Gingrich and other House Republican leaders had started pressuring Cooley not to run. At the end of July, Gingrich wrote a letter to Bob Smith urging him to run for Cooley's seat and telling him that he would be able to keep all of the seniority he had accumulated in his previous six terms in the House if he won the seat. That meant if the Republicans stayed in the majority, Smith would be in line to be chairman of the Agriculture Committee in the 105th Congress.

Finally, in early August, Cooley decided not to seek reelection. "The chance that a liberal politician could win the 2nd District race is a risk that I am not willing to take," said Cooley in a statement announcing his decision. After Cooley's announcement, Smith agreed to run and was formally nominated at a special state convention held at the end of August. Smith called the events with Cooley "one of the most bizarre and unprecedented political situations to face Oregon."

In December 1996 Cooley was indicted by an Oregon grand jury on a felony charge of lying in the official state voter guides for the 1994 primary and general elections. And in March 1997 an Oregon circuit court judge found Cooley guilty of a felony in connection with his false claims about his Korean service in the state's voter pamphlet. Cooley did serve in the army for two years at Fort Bragg, North Carolina, but the assistant state attorney general who prosecuted the case said those who had served with Cooley, including his commanding officer, stated he never went overseas during that time.

Cooley was not sentenced to any jail time but was ordered to pay a $5,000 fine and $2,110 in prosecution expenses, do 100 hours of community service, and remain on probation for two years. In December 1997 the Justice Department officially closed its investigation and announced no criminal charges would be filed against Cooley's wife Rosemary in connection with the military widow's benefits she had received.

*   *   *

Cooley was not the only member of the freshman class Wild Bunch who had run into trouble. Helen Chenoweth of Idaho, who was in a close race and heavily targeted by Democratic supporters, had come under fire for some of her campaign and personal financial dealings, such as her failure to report on her financial disclosure forms a $50,000 personal loan she received from a former business associate shortly after being elected.

Steve Stockman of Texas had bigger problems. His 1994 victory over 21-term incumbent Jack Brooks in a solidly Democratic district was considered a fluke, and the Democrats were pulling out all the stops to defeat him. Stockman seemed to be doing what he could to help them. First it was revealed in May 1996 that Stockman had paid more than $125,000 in campaign funds to a political consulting firm called Political Won Stop that was operating out of his home, where his campaign headquarters were also located.

When a reporter from the *Houston Press* showed up at Stockman's home outside Houston and attempted to interview someone from the consulting firm or the Stockman campaign, a scuffle ensued. As a result, a campaign worker filed assault charges against the reporter, who he said pushed him. Stockman filed a trespassing charge and accused the reporter of stalking him but the district attorney took no action against the reporter who in turn filed a defamation suit against Stockman, which he later dropped.

But Stockman's rocky relationship with the media didn't end there. After *Texas Monthly* published an unflattering profile of Stockman that called him the "class clown" and the "mouthpiece of the paranoid," a Stockman aide sent an ugly letter of complaint to the female reporter who wrote the story. "Steve was elected to his job by thousands of informed voters, while you were put in your position for reasons I would refuse to speculate upon in polite society. (Hope your knees have healed up nicely)," said the letter.

The escapades of Stockman and his staff won him the moniker "maniac-in-training" from the *New Republic* and no doubt contributed significantly to his fate as a one-termer.

*   *   *

On the night of Saturday, September 28, the House planned to finish its remaining business—passing a budget for 1997. Members had been sitting around in their offices all day waiting for their leaders to finish up so they could vote and go home.

When a bunch of the freshmen went out to get something to eat, they didn't talk much about the budget. Instead they discussed the pros and cons of keeping their apartments for three months while they were back in their districts, whether to put things in storage, and what committee assignments and new offices they wanted the following year. Of course some of the members who weren't sure they'd be back were too superstitious to talk about that stuff.

Congressional negotiators and the White House had been meeting all week on the budget and had just completed a deal around 4:30 that morning. Although the White House seemed to be constantly changing its list of demands, Congress had been ever accommodating. The White House praised congressional leaders for their cooperation, and Mark Hatfield, chairman of the Senate Appropriations Committee, called the agreement "the most bipartisan in my memory."

The Republicans' seven-year balanced budget plan set a budget target for fiscal 1997 of $487 billion for all discretionary federal programs. But in the wake of the government shutdown debacle, they decided to add $10 billion to that figure to make things go more smoothly with Clinton. Then, as the pressure to get home and campaign increased, they agreed to put in another $6.5 billion that the president wanted for programs such as Head Start and Goals 2000.

"Did we add more spending than we wanted? Yes. The Democrats love spending. They never saw a spending increase they didn't worship. . . . But I think, all things considered, good work has been done," said Senate majority leader Trent Lott of the budget accord.

A number of freshmen challenged the package for spending too much, but this was the last train leaving the station, and there was really no choice but to get onboard. Although they didn't know many of the details in the 3,000-page piece of legislation, Souder said there was general agreement among the budget hawks that it had been loaded up with "lots of things we don't like." But the freshmen had lost the will to fight. They were too focused on fighting for their own reelections.

Some of them planned to vote no on final passage "but there's no intensity," not like last year. "I just want out of here, and I'm not even in a tough race," said Souder, sitting in the Speaker's Lobby as the last votes of the 104th Congress were being called inside the chamber. "My head is not here. I have no feelings about the end of the session. The session ended for us August 1. This is just mop-up. I did what I could this year," said Souder with a shrug. "I think we changed the direction of government," said Brownback, passing through on his way to vote. Brownback knew he wasn't coming back, at least not to this chamber.

On the floor senior Democrats and Republicans were engaged in what can best be described as a love fest, extolling the hard work and cooperation of the members on the other side of the aisle in finishing up the budget package. Could this really be the same Congress that shut down the government just one year earlier? What a difference a few billion dollars make.

Gingrich closed the debate by calling it "a historic evening." He paid tribute to the Founding Fathers and the government system they had created, which he had found so vexing over the past two years but which was designed to prevent sudden and dramatic changes' being wrought by a single House election. "They wanted a machine so inefficient that no dictator could make it work." And they set things up so that the Senate would "legitimately and deliberately steer" a course for the nation. And they gave the president a veto. "As our side found, it's a very powerful weapon."

Gingrich closed by saying that on November 5 the American people would choose what direction they wanted the country to go.

The spending bill was overwhelmingly approved, 370–37. A few of the budget hawks (including Scarborough, Sanford, Salmon, and Neumann) would vote no. As the time for the vote ran down, members were shaking hands and saying good-bye. And once the vote was announced, members stood and applauded.

The 104th Congress was ending not with a bang but a whimper. It was a pretty anticlimactic finish to a historic session. As she walked off the floor and through the Speaker's Lobby, Enid Greene had tears in her eyes. She knew she wouldn't be back no matter how the election turned out.

On the way back to his office after the last vote, I asked Van Hilleary how he felt. "Tired, just tired," he answered. He had been on the phone fund-raising all day. There was no sense of exhilaration at all, mostly just relief the session was over mixed with the knowledge that he had a long month of campaigning ahead of him.

"I came up here a young man, and I feel like an old man now."

Part Six

FALL 1996

THE CAMPAIGN

27

REELECT CONGRESSMAN HILLEARY

WHEN HE WASN'T IN WASHINGTON, Van Hilleary was traveling the length and breadth of Tennessee's Fourth District asking for votes, just as he had done two years earlier. But this time he wasn't the revolutionary outsider riding a wave of voter anger and anti-Clinton feeling. Now he was the congressman asking to be sent back to Washington. He was part of the system. And he could only hope that impatient voters wouldn't throw him out of office either for not changing enough or for going farther than they had wanted.

It was kind of hard to tell what people thought. They certainly weren't as angry as they had been in 1994. As he went around the district talking to voters, Hilleary got the impression they were pretty satisfied with the job he had done representing them.

He was definitely too conservative for some people. But his pleasant, nonconfrontational, aw-shucks demeanor made him seem less dogmatic than he actually was. And after two years he figured he had permanently won over some conservative Democrats who voted for him in 1994 as a protest. This time around they would be voting for him because they knew him and liked him.

Even though he had won by more than 20,000 votes in 1994, the labor unions had targeted his district for ads, which had been running for months. Because he felt he had to counter the labor spending, Hilleary was doing more fund-raising than he might otherwise have done.

Hilleary's Democratic opponent was Mark Stewart, a 36-year-old lawyer from Winchester in Franklin County, one of the most Democratic counties in the Fourth District. The red-haired, freckle-faced Stewart had served as an assistant district attorney in the county and was about as good a candidate on the issues as the Democrats were likely to find for this district. He favored term limits, welfare reform, and the death penalty. And he opposed the assault weapons ban. He also opposed legalized abortion except in cases of rape, incest, and to protect the life and health of the mother.

His personal profile was just as good. He had been born and raised in Franklin County. His father was a judge. His grandfather, Tom Stewart, not only served in the U.S. Senate but was the state district attorney general who prosecuted the Scopes monkey trial along with William Jennings Bryan. Stewart coached Little League and youth soccer, was a Boy Scout leader, and had taught Sunday school at the local Methodist church for 12 years. He was married with two children, and although that enhanced his profile as a candidate, it meant he didn't have as much time to pour into the campaign and travel this huge district as did the single Hilleary. Stewart tried to play up his image as a family man. His radio ads talked about his family and community roots. He also labeled Hilleary a "professional politician," which, after Hilleary's one term in Congress, had to be considered something of a stretch.

Like most of the Democrats running in 1996, Stewart promised to "stop Newt Gingrich and the extremists in Washington." Stewart pointed to Republican efforts to cut Medicare, to pass antienvironmental legislation, and especially to shut down the government as evidence of their extremism. "It was a clear, clear indication that they were out of touch with the voters. . . . I've had a number of Republicans come up to me and say they voted for change, but not this kind of change. This is a different year and a different time." But Stewart was fighting a serious uphill battle. He wasn't well known outside of his part of the district, and soft-spoken and serious, he wasn't exactly electrifying on the campaign trail.

Will Cheek, the state's Democratic Party chairman, thought Stewart had a chance because of the number of Democrats in Hilleary's district and because of the moderate image Stewart presented. Whatever happened, Cheek was sure it had to be a better year than 1994, when Tennessee Democrats lost the governorship, both U.S. Senate seats, and two House seats. "That was what you'd call a come-apart. . . . I knew that we were in deep trouble when I would drive out near my farm in Maury County south of Nashville and I would see Republican signs in front of shabby-looking house trailers and hardscrabble rock farms. . . . We were in deep trouble." Cheek said pocketbook issues were the best weapon the Democrats had in winning the voters who had strayed two years earlier. "We have to appeal to them on economic issues; that's the only way to get them back, for them to understand that we have their best interests at heart and the other party has the interests of money people at heart."

In districts like Hilleary's throughout the South, Democrats had been struggling for years, and the 1994 election just helped solidify the gains Republicans had been making in the region. In 1994, Republicans picked up 19 House seats and three Senate seats in the South. But it is overly simplistic to assume that there has been a permanent political realignment and the region is lost to the Democrats. Although the South is no longer firmly in the Democratic camp, it has not switched entirely to the Republican Party either. As with much of the country, it is increasingly independent, ready to be convinced election by election. And that's the way races have to be fought and won in the South.

Clinton Williams, the elected Democratic executive of Franklin County, who had voted for Hilleary in 1994, tended to vote for Democrats for local and state office. But he hadn't voted for a Democrat for president since Lyndon Johnson. "I guess I'm a pretty good example of the pragmatic part of the conservatism of the South. We tend to vote the conservative element regardless of what party affiliation it is."

As someone who was always able to attract his share of crossover voters, Democrat Ned Ray McWherter understood this well. McWherter served as Speaker of the Tennessee House for 14 years and two terms as governor, from 1986 to 1994. "In Tennessee if you're a Democrat or a Republican, you should be a conservative, but maybe a moderate conservative. . . . That is the New South, and that is the leadership of the New South," McWherter told me. He was extremely popular during his years in Tennessee politics and won reelection for governor with 61 percent of the vote, a 24-point margin of victory. McWherter was so deft at being the kind of Democrat that Republicans would vote for that his name became a byword for other Democrats on the campaign trail—as in, "I'm a Ned McWherter Democrat." "A lot of these independents today were Reagan Democrats, and I think the Democrats can get those people back if they have a good candidate," said McWherter.

McWherter was raised in rural, western Tennessee; his father was a sharecropper with only a third-grade education. McWherter rose to the state's highest office and became a millionaire by starting a trucking company and a beer distributorship. He is a large man with a deep voice; a long, slow drawl; and a down-home, good-ol'-boy manner. Most people in Tennessee know him simply as Ned, just as people knew Fred Thompson as Fred. "I had a bumper sticker that said 'Ned,' and people said, 'Yeah, Ned, he's one of us,' so I started using that in the campaign: 'He's one of us.' And I think that's what people want. There are more of us than of them."

When Thompson decided to run for the Senate the first time, he paid a courtesy call on McWherter at his "farm" in western Tennessee to seek his advice. McWherter and Thompson speak the same language and have a similar style. As governor, McWherter had appointed a former aide of his to fill Al Gore's Senate seat until an election was held, passing over Democratic congressman Jim Cooper, who badly wanted the seat. Thompson went on to trounce Cooper in 1994 and in 1996 was running way ahead of his Democratic opponent in his bid for a full six-year term.

Ned and Fred had very different styles from Newt's in-your-face attitude. But McWherter still appreciated Gingrich's political talent. "Newt Gingrich is able, brilliant, and smart as the dickens. I think he did have a vision, but I think it was his personal vision and he wanted everyone to join him in lockstep." As McWherter assessed the Republican Congress, "They got up there, and they were tough and mean, and people got down on them. They've changed their positions now, and they're trying to soften themselves up a little bit, but you can't be mean and you can't be cruel to people. . . . If they hadn't learned that pretty fast that first year or so, it would have been easy for the Democrats to take back some of those seats. It's more difficult now, I think."

McWherter, true to his roots, was nothing if not a populist. "I don't need a tax cut at the expense of someone who needs health care. . . . We need health care for the working poor men and women. . . . They get up and go to work every day and send their kids to school and come back and at the end of the year they pay their taxes. They're a majority of Americans; those are the people we need to be concerned about. Some people call them middle class. I call them the core of America. They sustain our economy. . . . Those are the people you've got to be kind to. And to give Wall Street a tax cut or give a Ned McWherter a tax cut at any expense to them, I'm opposed to and the Democrats need to sell that."

McWherter didn't know too much about Hilleary. He'd heard the young man had a personable style. And that is as important as anything when running for office in Tennessee, even more important than whether you have a "D" or an "R" after your name.

*   *   *

In Lynchburg, home of the Jack Daniel's distillery, the Iron Kettle Restaurant is located on the courthouse square. It's a popular lunchtime gathering spot for the locals, and politics, especially at this time of year, is a favorite topic.

Beauford Jennings is a retired physicist who has a farm just outside of Lynchburg. Like a number of the farmers in the area, his ancestors settled here after they were given the land by the government in exchange for fighting in the Revolutionary War. His parents were Democrats, but Jennings tends to vote Republican.

Jennings is skeptical of too much government. Most of the area's farmers don't participate in the government's farm subsidy program because they don't want people telling them what to plant and when. Jennings says he's a little disappointed in what the 104th Congress has been able to achieve. "This Congress didn't do too much. . . . I think both sides are a little bit too stubborn. There's not enough give and take."

In 1994 Jennings voted for Democrat Jim Cooper over Fred Thompson for the Senate because he had known Cooper for years. He also voted for Hilleary. Jennings is a swing voter who leans Republican but makes up his mind based on the person. He plans to vote for Dole because he considers Clinton to be "an unsavory character."

Having lunch with Jennings is another farmer, Sutton Woodard, who sells livestock feed on the side to help make ends meet. Woodard doesn't have much use for either party. "No matter who's in charge, the rich get richer and the poor get poorer. The Democrats are bad and the Republicans are worse is the way I look at it. I still think they're all for the big business people." Woodard usually votes Democratic but, like Jennings, doesn't consider himself a member of either party. "If they do a good job, I don't care if they're Republicans or Democrats," said Woodard.

Woodard thinks Hilleary's done OK, and he plans to vote for him this time around. But he'll be splitting his ticket. He'll also be voting for Clinton, largely because he thinks Dole is a bad candidate and because he likes Al Gore. Gore's favorite-son status is helping the Clinton-Gore ticket in Tennessee, and Gore has been working overtime to make sure he carries his home state: A loss here would not only be an embarrassment but an extremely bad way to start the Gore 2000 campaign. Clinton, who carried the state in 1992, has visited twice since the Democratic convention, and Gore has made at least 10 campaign trips to Tennessee, three since August.

There is not nearly the animosity toward Clinton down here that I felt in the spring of 1995 when I traveled the district with Hilleary. People who were disgusted with Clinton his first two years in office now appear ready to vote for him.

Woodard is just the kind of swing voter Hilleary is counting on. Hilleary's feeling defensive about the union ads that have been running, as well as Stewart's commercials, which talk about how mean Hilleary and the rest of the Republicans in Congress are for trying to cut things like Medicare and Meals on Wheels.

Hilleary has decided to hit back with an ad focusing on Stewart's resume as a trial lawyer. Although Stewart also served as a prosecutor, Hilleary's ad spotlights some of the clients Stewart has represented as a defense attorney: child molesters, drunk drivers, and "even a man accused of attempted murder." Of course, that is what defense attorneys do—represent people charged with crimes. But Hilleary insists this is fair game because Stewart has been stressing the crime issue, calling himself tough on crime. Says Hilleary, "You have to defend yourself; the only way you can defend yourself is with offense."

It's unfortunate Hilleary feels he has to resort to such tactics, but this is typical of the kind of campaign many of the freshmen are waging. The labor union ads have put them on the defensive, and they are using whatever they can think of to strike back, including personal attacks against their opponents. The freshmen are fighting to stay in Congress and have turned into the politicians they disdained just two years earlier.

28

THE CAMPAIGN

SEVENTY OF THE ORIGINAL 73 GOP HOUSE FRESHMEN were running for reelection. Sam Brownback was instead running for the Senate, and Wes Cooley and Enid Greene had taken themselves out of the race because of their ethical and legal problems. Mark Sanford of South Carolina was running unopposed and so was the only one of the freshmen guaranteed a second term. He was a hard-core True Believer who had frequently voted against the GOP leaders when he perceived them to be straying from the cause of a balanced budget and smaller government. And Sanford had voluntarily limited himself to three terms in office.

Although two-thirds of the freshmen weren't in any real danger of losing their seats as long as they ran a reasonably good campaign, most were expecting smaller margins of victory than they had got two years earlier. This time around they wouldn't have the benefit of a Republican wave, and they were getting no help from the top of their ticket. It wasn't clear how much Clinton's all but assured victory was going to help his party's congressional candidates, but Democratic turnout was guaranteed to be stronger than it had been in 1994.

A great deal was at stake. It was one thing for the Republicans to have won control of the House, even after 40 years. But if the election of 1994 was not to be considered a fluke, they had to hold onto the House. That was a much bigger deal.

Despite the government shutdowns and their bleak prospects just six months earlier, the freshmen had had a productive end of the session. After the summer passage of the minimum wage increase and welfare and health insurance reform, congressional approval ratings went up almost overnight by as much as 15 points in many districts. All in all, the voters seemed reasonably satisfied with the Republican Congress.

About 25 of the freshmen were in races that could go either way if the election unexpectedly turned into a blowout for the Democrats. It didn't look like this was going to be a year for a Democratic landslide, but the struggle for control of the House was close. The Democrats needed a net gain of just 20 House seats to regain the majority. Although the presidential race appeared all but decided, the House and Senate contests were far more competitive, making this one of the most exciting congressional elections in recent memory.

The biggest challenge to the freshmen as a whole came from the organized effort against them by the AFL-CIO. In spring 1996 the labor union announced a $35 million effort to wrest control of Congress away from the Republicans.

Perhaps the most notable thing about the labor campaign was its magnitude. In March the AFL-CIO's member unions endorsed a plan to take 15 cents a month for one year out of each union member's dues to help pay for the political effort. This raised $25 million, which was used primarily for broadcast advertising; another $10 million went toward on-the-ground organization. And the unions that belong to the AFL-CIO made their own, further expenditures. According to the AFL-CIO, it placed 135 paid coordinators in 102 congressional districts, 14 Senate races, and two gubernatorial races around the country. The unions also ran a major voter registration and get-out-the vote effort using thousands of union volunteers; by their calculation, they made 4 million phone calls and sent 10 million pieces of mail.

The number one labor target was freshman Republican J. D. Hayworth of Arizona, the bearish former sportscaster known for his consistent conservative voting record, booming voice, and hectoring floor speeches critical of Clinton. The AFL-CIO spent nearly $2 million in Hayworth's district trying to defeat him.

Others on the union hit list were Greg Ganske of Iowa, Dick Chrysler of Michigan, Phil English of Pennsylvania, and Bill Martini of New Jersey. Because of their early support for a minimum wage increase, English and Martini won the endorsement of several local unions in their districts. But the AFL-CIO went ahead and targeted them anyway. Both came from districts that had a major union presence and both had won in 1994 with less than 50 percent of the vote.

In Ron DiNicola, an entertainment lawyer who had moved back to his northwestern Pennsylvania district from Los Angeles and who still had a California driver's license, English did not have a particularly strong opponent. But Martini did. He was facing Bill Pascrell, the mayor of Paterson, the largest city in New Jersey's Eighth District. Pascrell began his political career by serving on the Paterson board of education and went on to the New Jersey legislature, where he still served as well as being mayor. Paterson had a $1 million deficit when Pascrell became mayor. He took a $3,000 pay cut and balanced the budget, although he had to raise property taxes to do it. Pascrell also started the city's first economic development corporation and imposed tough measures to fight drug dealing in the city. The district, which included both working-class cities and affluent suburbs, had ping-ponged between Democratic and Republican representation and had elected four different congressmen in the previous four elections.

Although the AFL-CIO decided not to challenge a few Republicans who had strong support from local unions, like freshman Bob Ney of Ohio, the union's message in 1996 seemed to be that even if you were a friend to labor on many issues, if you were a Republican, look out. AFL-CIO political director Steve Rosenthal, who had worked for the Democratic National Committee and was a Clinton appointee to the Labor Department before moving over to the AFL-CIO, told me that the targets were selected on one basis only: "If you're voting for Newt Gingrich for Speaker, you're no friend of working people."

Although the labor ads against Republicans started appearing in freshman districts in early 1996, Republican National Committee chairman Haley Barbour and other Republican officials decided not to spend money on rebuttals but to save their resources for the fall. Republicans were bitterly divided about whether this was the correct strategy, and many felt they had made a huge mistake by not responding earlier. Members who were being hit by the ads certainly felt vulnerable; some of them, like English and Ganske, decided to spend their own money for ads defending themselves against the union charges.

A number of the freshmen attacked by the labor unions were also on the hit lists of environmental groups. The League of Conservation Voters put out a "dirty dozen" list of legislators they considered to have bad environmental voting records, including freshmen Helen Chenoweth, Michael Flanagan, Steve Stockman, Jim Longley, Fred Heineman, Randy Tate, Frank Riggs, and Dick Chrysler.

Even if the Republicans could hold onto the House, about a dozen freshmen were in serious trouble and were looking like probable one-termers. There was virtually unanimous agreement between the Republican and Democratic congressional campaign committees about who the most endangered freshmen were. The parties' lists were devised with four major factors in mind: the freshman's 1994 performance and margin of victory; the kind of district the freshman came from, including its voter registration and whether Clinton had carried it in 1992; the quality of the freshman's challenger; and the kind of race the candidate was running, whether the freshman had been working hard, raising money, and had any personal weaknesses or screwups for a challenger to exploit.

By carefully considering all these factors, the Democrats had decided which districts to target most heavily and the Republicans knew which of their incumbents needed the most help. Sometimes a freshman would be weak in only one or two areas and could make up for a personal shortcoming, a tough district, or a good opponent by fund-raising and campaigning hard. Jon Christensen of Nebraska, the champion freshman fund-raiser, was one such example. For freshmen like Steve Stockman of Texas, who had low scores in all four areas, winning reelection looked pretty unlikely.

Forty-seven of the 73 GOP freshmen had won in 1994 with 55 percent of the vote or less. A low percentage of victory was always a reason to encourage challengers, but among this group were a number of freshmen who had worked so hard or distinguished themselves to such a degree in the 104th Congress that they had no reelection worries—people like David McIntosh and Mark Souder of Indiana, J. C. Watts of Oklahoma, and Tom Davis of Virginia.

A further subset was made up of those freshmen who had won with less than 55 percent of the vote and who represented districts Clinton carried in 1992. Twenty-nine freshmen fell into this category. Almost all of the freshmen who were considered the most vulnerable came from this group.

Although he was part of this group, John Ensign of Las Vegas did not seem to be facing a tough race because the Democrats had not been able to field a top-flight candidate to run against him. Ensign had won a narrow victory in 1994 with just 48 percent of the vote. But he became a crack fund-raiser, and that undoubtedly scared off a more serious challenger.

The Republicans, led by Bill Paxon, had been masterful in recruiting good candidates to run in 1994. The Democrats didn't seem quite as skillful at candidate recruitment, and in early 1995, when they were trying to line up challengers, running for the House as a Democrat didn't look quite as appealing as it would after the government shutdowns. By 1996, when it became clear Democratic fortunes were going to be better than originally thought, a lot of challengers felt it was too late to get into the race. Many of the Democrats who had been recruited to run against incumbents had a similar profile; they were lawyers who could contribute significant personal resources to their own campaigns.

In a few cases, though, the Democrats had recruited a good candidate for a district that should have been in play, and yet they weren't making much headway. Oklahoma's Second District, for example, which had belonged to the late Mike Synar for 16 years before he lost the 1994 Democratic primary. GOP freshman Tom Coburn went on to win the seat, and this time around he was challenged by Oklahoma House Speaker Glen Johnson. Coburn, who had promised not to serve more than three terms in the House, was leading in the polls and looked like a good bet for reelection.

Of the 13 original Democratic House freshmen, only a few had really tough races. Ken Bentsen in Texas was facing a long, expensive campaign because of a state court decision that had voided his and a number of other Texas primaries. The court ordered a special November election and a December runoff if no candidate won more than half the vote in November.

Democratic freshman, Mike Ward of Louisville, Kentucky, seemed to be in serious trouble. Ward had won election in 1994 by less than 500 votes and so was a target right from the start. He also had a good opponent, Anne Northup, who had served in the Kentucky legislature for 10 years. Northup was an articulate and skilled campaigner who began airing television ads three weeks before Ward started running his commercials and who also outraised Ward—nearly $1.2 million to his $880,000.

At the absolute top of the list of targeted GOP freshmen was Michael Flanagan of Chicago, who held the former seat of Dan Rostenkowski. No one really expected Flanagan to be reelected, maybe not even Flanagan. His opponent, Rod Blagojevich, was a lawyer and former prosecutor before being elected to the Illinois House of Representatives in 1992. But more important, he was the son-in-law of Chicago alderman Richard Mell. Blagojevich had worked for Mell on the city payroll before being elected to the state legislature, and Mell had thrown his considerable organizational and personal support behind his son-in-law's congressional candidacy. Blagojevich spent $1.5 million on the race (including the Democratic primary) compared to Flanagan's $724,000.

Two of the stiffest challenges to freshmen were coming from former House members who were defeated in 1994 and were trying to retake their seats. In Ohio, Democrat Ted Strickland was running against freshman Frank Cremeans. Strickland, a psychologist, had run unsuccessfully for Congress three times before winning the Sixth District seat in 1992 and then losing it to Cremeans in 1994. Cremeans had become a millionaire by starting a concrete and construction equipment business, and he spent $600,000 of his own money to get elected. After arriving in Washington, Cremeans worked overtime fund-raising to pay back the personal loans he had made to his campaign and raise enough for a second run. The 1996 race featured union ads against Cremeans and the standard charges about the Republican plans for Medicare, but there was also an extremely high level of personal animosity between the two men, and it was an ugly campaign.

The other rematch of a 1994 race was in North Carolina between Republican freshman Fred Heineman and Democrat David Price. Heineman was a former New York City policeman who had been Raleigh's police chief for 15 years. Price was a Duke University political science professor who had served four terms in Congress before losing to Heineman by 1,215 votes. Price knew almost from the moment he was defeated that he wanted to make another run for the seat and started putting out feelers in the summer of 1995. By Labor Day he had decided to do it. The government shutdown convinced him he had made the right decision.

North Carolina's Fourth District contained Raleigh and Chapel Hill, along with North Carolina State and the University of North Carolina. It also included most of the hi-tech research triangle that stretched between the two cities and Durham. This was a new South, swing district that had typical southern conservative Democratic voters, affluent Republicans, and liberal Democrats affiliated with the colleges in the area.

Heineman's 1994 win was considered something of a fluke, and many observers predicted it would be extremely difficult for him to hold this district. They thought it was going to be even tougher after he made some ill-conceived remarks to the *Raleigh News and Observer* about his income level. Heineman told the newspaper his $133,600 congressional salary and $50,000 police pension "does not make me rich. That does not make me upper-middle class. In fact, that does not make me middle class. In my opinion, that makes me lower-middle class. . . . When I see someone who is making anywhere from $300,000 to $750,000 a year, that's middle class." Since Heineman had done little to distinguish himself as a member of the 104th Congress, the remarks took on a large role in the campaign. Price ran an ad that charged that Heineman was out of touch with the concerns of the district's voters, where the median household income was less than $35,000.

A personal misstep was also a major factor in the vulnerability of another North Carolina freshman. Unlike Heineman, David Funderburk of the Second District had not been expected to have much problem winning reelection. That was until October 1995, when Funderburk and his wife were involved in an automobile accident in North Carolina in which another car was forced off the road and several people were injured. Funderburk and his wife claimed that she was driving the car, although witnesses involved said that Funderburk switched places with his wife after the accident to avoid blame. Police initially charged Funderburk with lying about what happened but reduced the charge to driving left of center when Funderburk agreed to plead no contest to that charge.

Funderburk also had a good opponent: Bob Etheridge, a tobacco farmer who had served as a county commissioner, member of the state house, and state superintendent of public instruction.

* * *

Probably the single most celebrated challenger to a freshman was Carolyn McCarthy, who was running against Daniel Frisa in New York's Fourth District.

In the spring of 1996, McCarthy was highly critical of Frisa for voting with most of the Republicans to repeal the assault weapons ban. That vote set her candidacy in motion.

Although she said she had been a Republican all her life, McCarthy was courted heavily by Democratic leaders and finally decided to make the run as a Democrat. "My feeling honestly is party labels, whether it's Republican or Democrat, don't make any difference when it comes down to the voting booth," McCarthy told the *New York Times* after she announced her candidacy.

Frisa was no stranger to intraparty challenges. He had taken on a Republican House member in a primary fight in 1994 to become the only person that year to defeat a Republican congressional incumbent. Republicans outnumbered Democrats three to two in this district, and Frisa won his race by 13 points. But no matter. McCarthy, who retained her Republican registration even as she ran as a Democrat, was formidable indeed. Frisa complained to *People* magazine, which did a profile on McCarthy, that she was a one-issue candidate running solely on gun control. He churlishly asked, "Have you heard her speak about anything else?" But McCarthy countered that gun violence was just a part of the picture, and things like fighting for drug-free schools, more education funding, and job opportunities were also important to her.

There was no doubt McCarthy would attract the votes of Republican women. Some GOP strategists had dubbed these key swing voters "soccer moms," and the media quickly picked up on the term. If 1994 had been the year of the angry white male, 1996 was the year of the soccer mom.

In fact, the 52-year-old McCarthy was a dream candidate all around—no political experience and no baggage, attractive and articulate, with a powerful, emotional message. Hers was the kind of story the national media loved, and she got more attention than any other House challenger. All she had to do was introduce herself on the campaign trail to elicit admiration and encouragement from strangers. And hundreds of volunteers lined up to work on her campaign.

This was what politics was all about: Mrs. Smith goes to Washington. By challenging one of the freshmen, McCarthy exemplified the best of the spirit of the class of '94. She was a political novice who got involved because she thought something was wrong and she wanted to change it. On election night, referring to the shooting that had taken her husband's life in 1993, she told supporters, "All we wanted to do was make something good come out of a horrible situation."

And with his behavior after McCarthy soundly defeated him 57–41 percent, Frisa may have reflected the worst of the class. He all but stopped campaigning a week before the election, did not show up at his own election-night party for supporters, and never made a concession speech. And according to his former staff members, Frisa essentially abandoned his Capitol Hill office after the election and before the start of the 105th Congress, directing that mail from constituents be thrown away.

29

WASHINGTON STATE

THERE WAS NO BETTER PLACE to assess what the voters' verdict on the GOP freshmen would be than Washington, which had elected more of them than any other state in the country in 1994.

In 1992 Washington had voted for Clinton and elected Democrats to the governorship, the U.S. Senate, and to fill eight of nine House seats. But that vote was reversed two years later when Republicans took control of both houses of the state legislature and six Republican freshmen were elected to the U.S. House. Now those freshmen were fighting for reelection as the fickle Washington voters tried to make up their minds about the 104th Congress.

A large part of the reason for the volatility of the Washington House districts was that most of them were pretty evenly balanced between Republican and Democratic voters. That's because they were created by a nonpartisan commission rather than the state legislature, which handles the task in most other states. Being politicians themselves, state legislators usually try to create safe seats for members of one party or another.

The first major signal that the Washington freshmen's reelection contests were going to be nail-biters was the state's September 17 primary. Washington's primary system has been dubbed a "jungle primary" because all of the candidates appear on the same ballot and the top Republican and Democrat vote-getters move on to the general election.

The freshman who got the biggest scare in the primary was Randy Tate, whose Democratic opponent got 1,200 more votes than he did. But several other freshmen also did worse in the primary than they had expected to. The only one of Washington's six freshmen who appeared fairly secure in his reelection bid was Doc Hastings, who represented the Fourth District of central Washington. Hastings had the lowest profile of any of the state's freshmen and spent most of his time attending to local concerns rather than grandstanding on national issues.

George Nethercutt had been targeted for defeat by the Democrats and by labor unions because he had won by only two percentage points in 1994. But he was not as vulnerable as he appeared. He did have a narrow margin of victory, but, after all, it was over a sitting Speaker of the House who had outspent him by $1 million. Nethercutt's opponent this time was Judy Olson, a wheat farmer who was receiving help from the unions and environmental groups. Nethercutt labeled their efforts "the politics of dishonesty," especially when it came to their TV ads about GOP plans for Medicare reform.

"For months, we've been getting hammered by these negative ads," Nethercutt said three days after the Washington primary, in which he won just 50 percent of the vote. With a grim laugh, Nethercutt joked that he was "scared to death" about the November election.

To counter Olson's charges that he and the Republicans were mean and extreme, Nethercutt made a series of folksy TV ads, including one with his golden retriever (who had been featured in his commercials two years earlier). Nethercutt's mother appeared in another ad about Medicare in which he said, "I resent people thinking I would do anything to hurt my own mother."

Nethercutt was proud of what he said the Republicans had been able to accomplish in the 104th Congress, and like a number of the freshmen, he was more than a little put out by Clinton's co-opting many of their issues. "He's taking credit for a lot of things we pushed. . . . He's talking like a Republican so he can get reelected."

Despite the high profile he had received as a result of beating Foley, Nethercutt had never been one of the bomb throwers of the class, partly because he was a little bit older and more mature than many of the other freshmen and partly because he was more laid-back. Nethercutt was not uncomfortable with the idea of compromise to accomplish a goal. He was well aware that was how politics worked.

Although Nethercutt's race had originally been pegged as one to watch, by the end of October a poll published in the *Spokane Spokesman Review* showed him with a 14-point lead over Olson.

*   *   *

But if Nethercutt's race was proving to be less competitive than many people had expected, Linda Smith's was surprisingly more so. Smith had long been a popular figure with religious conservatives and populist voters in the state.

Smith, 46, had certainly made a name for herself in Congress with her championing of campaign finance reform, and earlier in the year she had flirted with the idea of running for governor. Although her district was considered Democratic, because of her perceived personal strength the unions had not targeted it. But in the September primary Smith scored only a four-point lead, 52–48 percent, over her Democratic challenger, Brian Baird, the chairman of the psychology department at Pacific Lutheran University and a political unknown.

It was something of a wake-up call for Smith, although her situation didn't seem to generate much sympathy from her colleagues. In fact, some of them may have been secretly rooting for her defeat. To say Smith was not well liked in the House was putting it mildly. Staff members of other Washington House Republicans used to say Smith was not a team player. And one of them told me after her close call in the primary, "If you asked the Republican members of the Washington delegation who they would rather have out, McDermott [a contentious liberal Democrat] or Smith, they would probably say Smith."

One Seattle political writer attributed Smith's problems to the "loudmouth factor" and said voters may have thought she had been grandstanding and trying to make a national splash on campaign finance reform while not paying enough attention to her district. Smith's southwest Washington district stretched from the Pacific Ocean to the Cascade Mountains. It was a major timber-producing area and included the state capital of Olympia as well as the city of Vancouver, which was directly across the Columbia River from Oregon and was served by Portland rather than Seattle television stations.

On Sunday evening, October 27, a little more than a week before the election, Smith was trying to shore up her conservative Christian base by appearing on a conservative TV talk show on a community access channel in Longview, Washington. Smith talked about her efforts on campaign finance reform, about the Republican Congress's trying to balance the budget and passing welfare reform, and about the hits she was taking on Medicare from her opponent. She played up her independence and her efforts to cut corporate welfare and federal tobacco subsidies and recounted the story about one of her own Republican leaders' passing out campaign donations from tobacco PACs on the floor of the House. "They're leading the effort to try and get rid of me," Smith said of the tobacco lobbyists. Of the inability of the 104th Congress to pass campaign finance reform legislation, Smith explained, "The money was too good."

After the show Smith wouldn't talk about her internal poll numbers, but it was clear she knew the race could go either way.

*　　*　　*

To the north of Smith's district is the Ninth District, represented by Randy Tate, who won the seat by beating a Democratic incumbent by four points. He was the youngest of all the GOP freshmen, although he is prematurely bald and looks older than his 30 years. Tate has a pleasant but intense demeanor. He is a political junkie and something of a wunderkind, having been elected to the state legislature at the age of 22, even before he was finished with college.

A Christian conservative, Tate endorsed the 1988 presidential candidacy of Pat Robertson, and when he ran in 1994 Democrats called him "the poster boy of the radical right." Tate was ardently antiabortion. In Congress he voted against federal funding for family planning, to eliminate the National Endowments for the Arts and Humanities, and to repeal the assault weapons ban. His votes on environmental protection and opposition to an increase in the minimum wage helped draw the fire of labor unions and environmentalists. Tate received a zero rating from the League of Conservation Voters and the Sierra Club, but he scored 100 percent approval ratings from the Christian Coalition, the National Federation of Independent Business, and the National Rifle Association.

When it came to being a foot soldier in the cause of the Republican revolution, no one was more loyal or hardworking than Tate. In fact, his campaign slogan was "Working Hard. Keeping His Promises." He traveled more than 3,000 miles back to his district from Washington virtually every weekend, and a staple of his campaign involved personally ringing the doorbells of voters in the district's neighborhoods.

His was one of the most heavily targeted races in the country. Republican leaders considered Tate to be one of the best of the freshmen, and the conservatives badly wanted to keep him in Congress. Republican interest groups were pouring money into the district. The Democrats wanted just as badly to win this seat back, and labor unions and environmentalists were running TV ads against Tate.

Tate's district includes the suburbs and industrial areas south of Seattle and half of the city of Tacoma. The Ninth District was created in 1992 when Washington picked up a House seat, and it has yet to reelect an incumbent. It was the very definition of a swing seat.

Tate and his Democratic opponent, Adam Smith, had similar backgrounds but widely different political views. Smith was just five months older than Tate and, like him, won election to the state legislature in his 20s. A former Seattle prosecutor, Smith was serving in the state senate when he decided to make a run for Tate's House seat. Smith was a smart, aggressive challenger who told me he saw the key to his victory as reaching out to independent voters and moderates in both parties. "He's too partisan," Smith said of Tate. "He won by a narrow margin, and then he went back to Washington and acted like he won by 40 points."

Smith made an observation that to my mind defined the 1996 campaign better than anything else I heard as I traveled around the country that fall: "Randy Tate will do a very good job of representing the Republican Party in the Ninth District. I'll do a good job of representing everybody in the district." The challengers who were successful, like Smith, were able to convince the voters of that.

That's what the election of 1996 was really about. If the freshmen had a vulnerability, it was that they were perceived as too extreme, too unyielding, too oblivious to the views of anyone but themselves. Some of them had forgotten that once an election is over, representatives have a responsibility to represent all the people of their districts, not just the people who voted for them.

*   *   *

With so much attention focused on the fate of Washington state's freshmen, Clinton and Gore paid several visits to the Northwest on their behalf. In late September, just a few days after the Washington state primary, the president and vice president made a one-day campaign swing through the state and appeared with Democratic candidates, including Brian Baird and Adam Smith. "The country is going to be looking at Washington state because the voters of Washington state . . . bought on to Mr. Gingrich's and Mr. Dole's Contract with America. And now you have seen the results," Clinton said in his appearance.

At a rally in Centralia in Smith's district, Clinton remarked on the Republicans' 1994 victories. "They won as many seats in the state of Washington, including this one, as in any state in the country, and they said a few clear things. They said we have this Contract with America, and it will move America forward. They neglected to say they wanted to cut education. They wanted to weaken the environment. They wanted to raise taxes on the poorest working people. . . . They wanted to turn Medicare into a two-tier system. They wanted to stop Medicaid's guarantee of health care to poor children, to pregnant women, to families with people with disabilities, to the elderly in our nursing homes. They left out all the fine print in 1994. But when they took office, we saw what they wanted."

A month later, at the end of October, Gore came back to Washington to do some more campaigning. At a Seattle rally Gore told a crowd of supporters, "Washington state more than any other state among all 50 has the chance to call Newt Gingrich's bluff." Gore asked his audience "to keep fresh in your minds what happened after the Republicans gained control two years ago and embarked on an extremist course. What else can you say about someone who wants to repeal the assault weapons ban, repeal the Brady bill, eliminate the Department of Education, make Medicare wither on the vine? What are they thinking about?"

Dole didn't have a chance of carrying Washington and hadn't been to the state since late winter—not that a Dole appearance would particularly help the Republican freshmen there. The Dole-Kemp campaign wasn't spending any money on TV advertising in Washington either. But that didn't mean other high-profile Republicans were shunning the state, especially those who were looking beyond this election. On October 28, the same day Gore was in Seattle, the man he defeated for vice president, Dan Quayle, was in Washington state, too. They didn't cross paths, though. Quayle was at the Best Western Executive Inn in the industrial area of Fife just outside of Tacoma to do a fund-raiser for Randy Tate.

Tate was very much like a younger version of Quayle. Both stressed socially conservative issues in their careers and had been strongly supported by the Christian right. And both began their political careers early, Quayle having been elected to the House when he was just 28.

Quayle was a good soldier in the 1996 campaign, crisscrossing the country to raise money for Republicans running for the House, Senate, and governorships and collecting chits to cash in should he decide to run for president. At a news conference before Tate's fund-raiser, Quayle made a joke about his visit's coinciding with one by the vice president: "Al Gore chased me all over the country in 1992." Quayle made no reference to the possibility that the two of them might be running against each other again in 2000.

Quayle was grim about Dole's chances. He had been part of a losing presidential campaign, and he knew what it felt like. He knew it was over for Dole. So did most Republicans, and they were trying to salvage what they could of the election. If the presidency was lost to Clinton, they could at least hold on to Congress. And it turned out the best way they could do that was by acknowledging Clinton's all but certain victory.

The Republican Party had just launched a national TV ad campaign in support of congressional Republicans, airing what became known as the "crystal ball" ad. "What would happen if the Democrats controlled Congress and the White House?" an announcer asked as a fortune-teller gazed into a crystal ball. The ad warned voters not to give Clinton a "blank check" and reminded them of Democratic tax proposals and health care reform in the first two years of the Clinton presidency. The Republicans also ran ads on Christian radio networks recalling the worst excesses of Clinton and the Democratic Congress, such as allowing gays in the military, and claimed that if the Democrats won a majority in Congress, "Teddy Kennedy will be running the place."

"If the American people believe Bill Clinton will be reelected, they better make sure they return a Republican Congress to check Bill Clinton. Remember what the first two years [of the Clinton administration] were like" with a Democratic Congress, Quayle told his Washington state audience.

Tate was just as aware that the president was going to be reelected, and he knew he had to attract the votes of some of the same people who would be voting for Clinton. "Certainly the American people do not want to see a Democratic president and a Democratic Congress," he insisted, pledging to work with whoever was president.

After the news conference concluded, Quayle moved to another conference room in the hotel and the real reason why he had come to the state: to help Tate raise money so he could buy more last-minute TV time. First was a private reception for about 80 donors who had given $250 apiece. Quayle couldn't resist reflecting back on his last campaign, if only briefly. Of Clinton, he said, "If he had really told us what he was going to do, I'd still be vice president."

Quayle warned the donors that if people perceived the presidential race was over, it would affect turnout and could cost local candidates like Tate their seats. One donor asked Quayle why the Republicans waited so long to spend money responding to the union ads. "That's a good question. I've asked that myself. I do not know why they decided to let negative ads go unanswered for so long," Quayle answered. When Republican strategists looked back at the 1996 election, he said, that would be one of the biggest questions. "Once you're attacked, you have to respond in kind. The ads kept coming and coming, and we got behind."

When someone asked Quayle if he would run for president, he quipped, "In our party it seems you have to be 73 to run for president. I may run for president, but I won't wait until I'm 73."

One guest wondered about the liberal media and what could be done about it. "There's not a whole lot you can do about it," Quayle answered, running down a list of Washington broadcast journalists he considered to be liberals—Ken Bode, Bernard Shaw, Judy Woodruff ("who is exceedingly liberal and is married to Al Hunt"). "The whole thing is stacked against us. That's why talk radio is so important."

Another donor wanted to know why Ross Perot was in the race. "He's bored; the guy's got too much money. He's just being a gadfly. He likes the klieg lights, and he likes the attention. . . . It's an ego trip."

After about 20 minutes, Quayle and Tate moved on to the hotel's ballroom, where 400 people who had paid $50 each were gathered. Serving as master of ceremonies for the event was the conservative host of a local talk radio show, a big Tate booster. "We have a revolution to finish," he exhorted the crowd.

One of the first to speak was Jennifer Dunn, who was facing token opposition in her bid for a third House term. Dunn, who represented the district that bordered Tate's to the east, was extremely popular and received a standing ovation. "In every district Republicans are fighting hard," said Dunn, referring to the union efforts against Tate. "This is going to be the tightest race you've ever seen in this state," she predicted.

"This election is being watched by folks across the country. This campaign is bigger than Randy Tate, and it's bigger than Adam Smith," Tate told his supporters. The election was about whether the nation would return to "higher taxes, bigger government, and budgets that aren't balanced," he insisted.

Then it was Dan Quayle's turn. The audience was fired up, Quayle surprisingly animated and loose. "Are you going to let liberal special interests buy this election?" he called out. "No," the people yelled back. "Are we going to elect Randy Tate?" Quayle asked them. "Yes," they shouted.

At this point Quayle presented a story he had clearly rehearsed and performed many times. And he was actually funny, really funny. Quayle played two parts, Bill Clinton and Dick Morris. Setting the scene for his little drama, Quayle told his audience Clinton is in the White House asking the White House operator to get Morris on the phone. "I have not a clue where they found him, but they found him," said Quayle in a not-so-veiled reference to some of the phone calls Morris conducted with the president while in the presence of a call girl at a Washington hotel.

Taking on the role of Morris, Quayle asked, "Are you willing to do anything, be anything, say anything to get reelected?"

Then it was back to narrator: "And Bill Clinton says in his humble way"—Quayle paused for dramatic effect and in his best Clinton drawl, which was quite good, said, "Well, you know me."

"You've got to talk like a Republican," Quayle said as Morris advising Clinton. And so that's how Clinton came to announce in his State of the Union address that the era of big government was over, Quayle concluded.

The crowd roared. They loved it.

Having skewered the president, Quayle poked a little fun at himself and his most famous speech, which included a remark about the television character Murphy Brown (played by Candace Bergen) and her fictional out-of-wedlock baby. It was just one little line, Quayle plaintively remarked. "I put it in just to see if anyone was listening. They were listening, all right." Quayle said he took a lot of flak over that remark; Clinton even mentioned it in his 1992 convention speech. But this year, at the Democratic convention in Chicago, "Bill Clinton didn't criticize my speech; he gave it. And I want you to know no royalties come my way."

Quayle asked the Republicans if they were paying lower taxes and feeling safer in their homes or if public education was any better since Bill Clinton took office. "Do you think Bill Clinton has done a good job? Do you think he should be reelected?" If Quayle had to convince this crowd of GOP loyalists not to vote for Clinton, then things were pretty bad. Quayle had been talking for half an hour, but it was not until he closed his speech that he finally mentioned Dole's name, telling the crowd they needed to elect Dole to stop Clinton.

After Quayle finished, several signed copies of his book, *The American Family*, were auctioned off for $1,000 each, but a signed copy of the *Time* magazine issue with Newt Gingrich on the cover as man of the year drew only $375.

As the event broke up, Tate started greeting supporters. He planned to stay until every last hand was shaken. He was not about to give up.

*   *   *

The other Washington freshman under fire from the labor unions and facing a tough race was Rick White of the First District. White, who had no previous political experience, won his seat in 1994 from Democratic freshman Maria Cantwell in a 52–48 percent win.

The 42-year-old White was considered the most moderate of all the state's GOP freshmen. White grew up in Indiana and attended Dartmouth, where he campaigned for George McGovern for president. After that, he attended Georgetown Law School before moving to Seattle and taking up a corporate law practice.

White was good-looking, pleasant, intelligent, and easygoing. Unlike Tate and Smith, a Washington political reporter told me, White had developed a reputation in the state for trying "to reach out to people who disagree with him."

White and his suburban Seattle district were featured in a multiple-part series that ran in the *Wall Street Journal* during his first year in office. The First District includes a small part of Seattle as well as most of its northern and eastern suburbs and Bainbridge Island, across Puget Sound, where White and his family lived. One of White's constituents was billionaire Bill Gates and his Microsoft Corporation. And as a member of the House Commerce Committee, White had worked on a number of issues important to the hi-tech industry, including the telecommunications bill. He formed the Internet Caucus in Congress and opposed the government's regulating content on the Internet.

Like many voters in the urban areas of the Pacific Northwest, voters here tend to be fiscally conservative and socially more moderate. This is a district that gave Perot 27 percent of its presidential vote in 1992. Largely affluent and well educated, these are the kind of voters who think the government should fund the National Endowment for the Arts and the Corporation for Public Broadcasting.

From that perspective White would have seemed to be a pretty good fit with the district. He was pro-choice and sponsored a measure to restore federal funding for family planning services. Although Boeing is based in Washington, White voted against the B-2 bomber. The only other Washington Republican to do so was Linda Smith. And White was the only Republican from Washington to vote against a constitutional amendment that would have made desecration of the flag a crime.

White won the endorsement of the *Seattle Post-Intelligencer* and was the only one of the state's Republican freshmen to be endorsed by *Seattle Weekly*, an alternative newspaper. But with a greater than 90 percent voting record with the GOP leadership, he may have turned out to be too conservative for some of his constituents. He was enthusiastically onboard the efforts to cut government, including eliminating the Departments of Energy, Commerce, and Education. And his House Republican colleagues, especially Gingrich, were extremely unpopular here. Early on, White's announcement that he would vote to repeal the assault weapons ban drew fire from some in this district.

White's opponent was Jeff Coopersmith, 36, the son of Democratic fund-raiser Esther Coopersmith, who grew up in the suburbs of Washington, D.C. and moved to Seattle after law school to work in the county prosecutor's office. Coopersmith was not proving to be as strong a challenger to White as Adam Smith was to Randy Tate. For one thing, Coopersmith had to battle the image of a wealthy carpetbagger because he had moved from one area of Seattle to another in order to run against White. Coopersmith spent $1 million on his campaign, more than half of it his own money. White spent $1.5 million on the race, none of it personal funds, although he had put $100,000 into his 1994 campaign. Thanks to Coopersmith's connections through his mother, a parade of Democratic Party bigwigs had been out to Seattle to campaign for him, including Vice President Gore, House minority leader Richard Gephardt, and New Jersey senator Bill Bradley.

Coopersmith told me less than a week before the election he thought the race would depend on undecided voters. He had done his best to tell the district's voters that White was not a moderate and that the race was "a referendum on the Gingrich Congress." On issues like education, the environment, and health care, Coopersmith contended, White did not reflect the feelings of his constituents. "It's the fact that he's voted with Gingrich 93 percent of the time," said Coopersmith of White. "He promised he'd be an independent voice for the district, but he's been too extreme."

Coopersmith felt he had been helped by the union ads but admitted there had been overkill in this district by the efforts of outside interest groups. "With all the ads and counterads, it's gotten a little confusing." Coopersmith knew it was going to be a tough battle and told the *Wall Street Journal* in its last piece on White just a few days before the election, "Rick White is a nice guy. My biggest challenge is to convince people that nice guys can cast bad votes."

In the final days before the election, White was filling his days with door-to-door campaigning, fund-raising, and appearances around the district. He seemed in pretty good spirits when I caught up with him at an elementary school on October 29. Not every political candidate would take time out a week before the election to meet with a bunch of children who can't vote. But White, who had four small children, was patient and pleasant with the kids. When one of them asked him to sign an autograph for her father, White told her, "Make sure he votes."

As we left the school, he said, "This is probably the best thing I'll do all day." White was wearing a blue sport shirt and brown corduroy pants and seemed pretty relaxed for someone who was supposed to be fighting for his political survival. White said he felt pretty good about the race and believed he had convinced a majority of the district's voters that he had done the right thing for the past two years in Washington.

His next stop was for lunch with a small group of supporters and local officials at a restaurant in Shoreline, an upscale residential community. White told me Coopersmith seemed to have only one thing to say in the campaign: "He just wants to talk about Gingrich because he's so unpopular, but he doesn't want to talk about the issues. If we talk about the issues, I win." White said the union advertising "had a subliminal impact" on the race. "I'd be much farther ahead" without it, White believed. He said Coopersmith's campaign was "right out of the AFL-CIO handbook."

Like Coopersmith, White knew turnout would be the key to the race, and he knew he had to do better than Dole would in this district. Because Washington is three hours behind the East Coast and the TV networks, White was also a little concerned the presidential race would be called for Clinton before the polls closed in Washington state, which could hurt turnout even more.

After lunch White decided to shake some hands at a small strip mall across the street from the restaurant. "Hi, guys, we're out campaigning. Don't forget to vote. It's a week from today." At a Kinko's copy center he met a voter who said he was so sick of all the negative attack ads he might not vote at all.

White and a handful of campaign workers then moved on to the Lake Forest Park Town Center, another large strip mall. The first stop was one of the ubiquitous Starbucks coffee shops. A few doors down, in a greeting card store, White encountered an older woman who said she was the recently retired owner of a small construction business. The woman, who declined to give her name, was a Republican who voted for White in 1994. But she was extremely disappointed with the performance of the 104th Congress, especially the government shutdown. "You had the opportunity of a lifetime, and you blew it," she told White. "It's too bad you wanted all or nothing because you got nothing," she said, shaking her head.

White politely disagreed and pointed out what the Republican Congress had accomplished. "We definitely learned some lessons. I just hope we learned them fast enough," he told her. Outside the store White said, "I think it's fair to say the Republicans overplayed our hand. We were all at fault. We had a feeling of invincibility that first year. We kept pushing on Newt, and he didn't tell us to back off the way he should have." White thought if the Republicans held onto the House by just a razor-thin margin, there could be some repercussions for Gingrich.

As he moved on to shake another hand, White looked at me and said, "I don't know who's going to be happier to have the election over—the voters or the candidates."

30

"CAMPAIGNS ARE LIKE WAR"

In the last month of the campaign, when it had become accepted as a foregone conclusion that the presidential race was over and Clinton had won, even more attention turned to the congressional races and who would control Congress.

The Democratic and Republican congressional campaign committees, the parties' national committees, and special interest groups on both the left and the right were pouring money into key congressional districts as fast as they could. It was the most expensive campaign in history, as the groups were funneling unregulated and unlimited soft money into the congressional districts at a truly staggering rate.

A month before the election it looked as if the Democrats had a chance to win back the House. But a steady stream of news stories about foreign donations and questionable fund-raising practices by the Clinton White House and the Democrats that began in early October seemed to be eroding both Clinton's lead and the Democrats' chances for taking the House.

An NBC–*Wall Street Journal* poll taken the weekend before the election showed Clinton with a 12-point lead over Dole, down from 17 points a few weeks earlier. And for the first time in two months, the percentage of people who said they would vote for Clinton fell below 50 percent, to 49 percent. And by a 44 to 40 percent margin, voters said they preferred Congress to be controlled by the Republicans.

* * *

But Mark Neumann of Wisconsin wasn't paying attention to national polls. He had only one thing on his mind: his own reelection. His race with Lydia Spottswood, the Democratic president of the Kenosha City Council, was considered too close to call. Neumann had been in close races before. In fact, that's the only kind of race he ever seemed to be in. The first time he ran for Congress against Les Aspin, Neumann ran negative ads about Aspin and got beat by 17 points. In 1993, in the special election held to fill Aspin's seat after Aspin was appointed secretary of defense, Neumann lost by just 675 votes and then demanded a recount. In 1994 Neumann won by only 1,120 votes.

Now, in the middle of another tough race, Neumann seemed to be willing to do whatever it would take to win. Neumann's elections were characterized not only by their closeness but by their nastiness as well. He and Spottswood had been going at each other hammer and tongs.

Neumann insisted that he hadn't started it. What started it was the TV ads the labor unions began running against him almost a year earlier. Neumann liked to say they were paid for with "an endless supply of money confiscated from their members." There were plenty of union members in Neumann's blue-collar district and also plenty of Democrats, and the AFL-CIO had quickly targeted the district both for its demographics and because of the narrowness of Neumann's 1994 victory.

At the end of April, Neumann estimated the unions had already spent $350,000 running ads about Medicare cuts, school lunches, education, the environment, and tax breaks for the rich and generally "trashing my good name" even though the Democrats still hadn't found a candidate to run against him. "It's just one blatant lie after the next. You can convince anyone of anything if you spend enough money. If you give me $350,000 to spend, I can convince your mother of things about you," Neumann said, glaring at me. He took the ads very personally.

Neumann and a number of the other freshmen were angry with GOP leaders who didn't seem too concerned about the ads and weren't doing anything to respond. "They aren't aware of how serious this is. . . . That's because the ads aren't running in their districts."

One way Neumann had found to get his message out to his constituents was through taxpayer-financed radio ads promoting town hall meetings he had scheduled in his district. The ads were being used instead of mailings. But in addition to announcing the upcoming meetings, the ads touted Neumann's "work to preserve and protect Medicare and Social Security and to balance the federal budget and reduce wasteful government spending." They sounded suspiciously like political ads, though his constituents were paying for them. But Neumann said the House Ethics Committee had cleared the idea. Besides, Neumann insisted, he was saving the taxpayers money because the radio ads were cheaper than postal mailings.

Neumann's campaign was doing the mailings. One of them was a full-color, eight-page brochure that featured a picture of the Lincoln Memorial's statue of Abraham Lincoln on the cover. At the top were printed the words "Values, Principles, Integrity" and at the bottom "Re-Elect Mark Neumann to Congress."

The brochure paid for out of campaign funds was full of information about Neumann's efforts to balance the budget, protect Medicare, and stand up to Gingrich, along with a request for campaign donations. On the last page was a picture of Neumann and his family under the caption, "Mark Neumann. True to his convictions. A faith in God, a commitment to family, and a love of country are the most important values needed to serve in the United States House of Representatives."

In early May Neumann told me he thought he would win reelection. "But if I don't, I know I did what's right." What would he do if he lost? "It would be great. I wouldn't have to put up with the people in this city. . . . The worst day in Wisconsin is better than the best day in Washington."

Neumann's district, Wisconsin's First District, is a gritty collection of tightly compacted industrial cities in the southeastern corner of Wisconsin between Milwaukee and Chicago. Racine and Kenosha along Lake Michigan are the largest, with populations around 80,000. Janesville to the west, where Neumann is from, is next at about 50,000, followed by Beloit, with about 36,000 residents. This is a manufacturing center. Chrysler has a car plant here. So does General Motors, in Neumann's hometown. The Parker Pen Company is located here, too. In his office in Washington, Neumann has on display some of the products made in his district, including those by Johnson Wax, whose famous headquarters in Racine were designed by Wisconsin native Frank Lloyd Wright.

This is a district one would think naturally leans Democratic, but the Democrats had a devil of a time recruiting someone who was known districtwide to run against Neumann. For one thing, Neumann had got a lot of good press over his celebrated flaps with the GOP House leaders and Gingrich. The Democrats weren't exactly going to be able to say he had followed Gingrich blindly. In fact, Neumann could remind voters that his "punishment" for having bucked Robert Livingston, his committee chairman, was to become the only freshman ever appointed to both the Budget and Appropriations Committees.

Neumann also had been raising a great deal of money and had personal wealth he could put into the campaign.

And then there was his mean streak. When cornered, Neumann could have the fighting instincts of a pit bull. Neumann was an Evangelical Lutheran who wouldn't permit profanity in his office and who frequently cited his deeply held religious beliefs. But for someone who professed to be so religious, he didn't seem to have much Christian charity. His Boy Scout rules seemed to fly out the window when it came to campaigning. Neumann was a street fighter. He hadn't been in a campaign yet that hadn't turned ugly.

"When he feels like someone is attacking his character, he feels justified in dropping a bomb on the other person," said a Wisconsin political reporter who had covered Neumann for years. Maybe that scared off a few people who didn't have the stomach to take him on. Peter Barca, whom Neumann defeated in 1994, thought about running but decided not to, as did a number of state legislators. And with the state's July 9 filing deadline fast approaching, Democratic leaders turned to Spottswood, who agreed to get into the race. The mother of three and the wife of a doctor, she had been on the Kenosha City Council for six years.

Spottswood, 45, was pleasant and outgoing; her personality contrasted sharply with Neumann's dark, angry demeanor. "He's an incredibly aggressive man. I've seen him in three elections now, and he doesn't seem to have a problem bending the truth," Spottswood told me.

Spottswood saw government as a way to help people. Neumann saw it as something largely to be eliminated. "He makes me very uncomfortable because he has an accountant's vision of the budget. All he thinks about is, 'How can I make cuts?' He doesn't connect what he's doing to people in any way, shape, or form," she told me.

Spottswood said Wisconsin ranked 50th in the country in federal dollars returned to the state, and she was full of stories about Neumann's turning down local officials who had sought his help in winning projects for the district. "He's willing to sacrifice the people he represents to the end of balancing the budget."

One district project seeking federal funding was a research program to create a new composite material for military use. Neumann refused to help. He wouldn't "pork" for his district, he said. Eventually the decision was made to expand the program and send it to North Carolina. The money wasn't saved; it just went to someone else's district. "How counterproductive is it to chase a government project out of your district? Did the program stop being funded? No. It just went someplace else," Spottswood asserted. And when Neumann was asked to support funding for a program to combat gangs in Racine, Spottswood maintained, he "turned a completely deaf ear to that community" and that program was lost as well. "Your job as a congressman is to fight for your constituents, not sell them down the river," she said.

Spottswood also believed that Neumann had aggressively pursued an extremist conservative agenda that did not fit with what a majority of his constituents wanted when they elected him with barely more than a 1,000-vote margin. "He saw himself as having a mission statement I don't think he was really given." Neumann was able to win in 1994 by putting together a coalition of antitax and social and Christian conservatives. But Spottswood insisted they represented a minority of the people in the district. "His is not a coalition that embraces diversity. It's not about consensus; it's about exploiting differences. It's clear to me he has no depth as a legislator. He doesn't have the ability to find the center."

Of course as Neumann saw it, there was no center. There was his way and the wrong way.

Calling Neumann a "street brawler," Spottswood said, "Neumann began labeling my campaign negative before it really began." Because he objected to the ads that said the Republicans were trying to cut Medicare, give a tax break to the wealthy, and weaken environmental laws, Neumann responded by alleging that as a member of the Kenosha City Council Spottswood had voted in favor of a development project that benefited her husband financially. "This is the kind of action that put Dan Rostenkowski in jail," the ad said. When the Kenosha city attorney and the Kenosha County district attorney said there was no truth to Neumann's claims, he finally pulled the ads. "It's just an example of his creating an issue and churning it and churning it until it sounds like there's something there," Spottswood told me. "This is very typical of Neumann's style. It's pretty scary stuff."

For all his disdain for Washington, the 42-year-old Neumann seemed to be fighting awfully hard to get back to what he considered the cesspool on the Potomac.

But on October 31, just five days before the election, there seemed to be an odd lack of activity at his windowless campaign headquarters in a nondescript two-story brick office building in Janesville. Most campaign offices are on the ground floor to attract maximum visibility; Neumann's headquarters were on the second floor, without even a sign out front. The place looked more like some boiler-room operation. A few young campaign workers were making fund-raising and get-out-the-vote calls, but there were no visitors, and the workers acted as if they were doing something top secret. Neumann's Washington office had the same strangely quiet, almost paranoid feeling to it.

Neumann had a campaign manager, but she wasn't there. Neumann essentially served as his own campaign manager. He didn't trust anyone else to do things the way he wanted them done.

Neumann was in Burlington, about 45 miles to the east, shooting a last-minute commercial at a local television station. "I hope we don't have to use this," Neumann said as he sat behind a desk on the TV set. His wife, Sue, the childhood sweetheart he had been married to since college, was brushing his hair away from his face. Neumann was shooting this ad to air on Milwaukee television stations "just in case."

"Hi, folks, I'm Congressman Mark Neumann. Lydia Spottswood's Democratic attorney said it was legal for her to cast a vote that sends tax dollars to a project she has a personal interest in. Wisconsin voters know this is just plain wrong."

"You look too serious," Sue told him after one take.

"This *is* serious," Neumann responded.

He seemed tense and irritable, but she was reasonably relaxed. "We've done four campaigns in five years. We've kind of got this part down," she told me with a smile. She had curly, blond hair and a round, pleasant face.

"I am so ready for this to be over," Neumann said. "It's almost over," Sue calmly, soothingly told him.

Neumann claimed he hadn't originally planned to attack Spottswood on her council vote. "We weren't going to bring it up until she started going negative and our numbers went down by 10 points," he said. "The reason we're here cutting an ad to cut her to ribbons is we expect she's going to start running something stupid. It's not pretty, but to me to surrender this seat to someone with totally different views is something I'm not willing to do, especially when I'm getting kicked in the teeth."

Neumann's press secretary was looking over a copy of a long profile on Neumann that would appear in the *New York Times Magazine* in three days, the Sunday before the election. Neumann didn't usually read the *New York Times* or the *Washington Post* or the major news magazines. I couldn't tell if he was kidding or not when he seemed not to know what the *New Yorker* was. He read the *Milwaukee Journal*. That was it. And sometimes when he was in Washington, he'd pick up the conservative *Washington Times*.

The *New York Times* piece described Neumann as "all unsheathed edge—more intense, as Garrison Keillor might say, than the average Lutheran." Neumann was quoted as saying, "People in Washington will do anything to remain in power. Anything." It was clear that he meant everyone but him.

I asked Neumann how much the labor unions had spent running ads in his district. Without missing a beat he told me, "Eight-hundred forty one thousand, eight hundred and seventy-nine dollars." He left off the cents. Neumann knew the exact number because he went to the television stations in his district and looked up the air buys. These are the ads Neumann said forced him to go personally negative against Spottswood, the ones that talked about Medicare and tax cuts. I asked him if he thought the union ads were really personal. "Don't tell me they're not personal," he said, his voice rising angrily.

Five days to the election and Neumann was clearly on edge. I wondered what it would take to push him completely over, and I was about to find out.

Finished at the television station, Neumann, his wife, and I drove back together to Janesville in his van. He was at the wheel, and I sat in the front seat. Sue was in the back. During the trip, he did an interview with a local newspaper reporter over his cellular phone. He had just finished making a television ad in which in only slightly different form, he again accused his opponent of a possibly illegal conflict of interest, but he told the reporter he intended to be positive from that point on. "I'm making a pledge," Neumann said.

I couldn't believe what I was hearing. Was there some parallel universe I wasn't aware of in which this would be considered the truth? Had he forgotten I was sitting next to him and had just witnessed his filming another attack ad?

"These last five days I'm going to be primarily talking about our record. I'd like to lay down a challenge to Lydia Spottswood to follow our lead and do nothing but talk about her vision of the future," Neumann told the reporter.

As soon as he hung up the cellular phone, Neumann said to me, "Campaigns are like war. This is a slime-bag race; it's a street fight."

Indeed.

The first week in October Neumann's polling showed him up by 26 points. A week later his margin had slipped to 16 points. It was clearly moving in the wrong direction, and that's what had Neumann so panicked. "I understand what a thousand points of TV advertising can do to you. Nobody can withstand a million dollars' worth of pounding. This is absolutely about whether the negative ads that lie and distort the truth can convince the voters of something that's not true."

Neumann thought he had "a 60–40 chance of winning." But he knew at that point it was almost too late to change what was going to happen. "It's done. It's the massive amount of radio and TV ads that's gonna decide things." By the end of the race, Neumann had spent almost $1.3 million to Spottswood's $700,000, but that did not include the independent expenditures made for and against him.

Neumann was the incumbent. He had more money. But once again he saw himself as the underdog, the lone voice crying out the truth in the wilderness. Although he had won the endorsement of the *Milwaukee Journal,* he was convinced the media were against him.

He seemed to think his party leaders were against him, too. Dole had made a decision to pull out of Wisconsin two weeks earlier and had stopped running ads. "I don't have the time and energy to worry about Bob Dole," Neumann snapped when I asked him about this. Dole had run a miserable campaign, and the Republican leadership let Clinton steal its message, Neumann said. He was livid about this. "The issues that are ours, we let Clinton take them." He spit out the words.

Neumann had a very short fuse and a history of losing his temper—at public meetings with his constituents, with his freshman colleagues, and with House leaders. I sensed he might be on the verge of doing the same with me. But I asked him about the government shutdown. I told him voters in some other districts had mentioned it to me as something they didn't like the Republicans doing. "I'd shut it down again," he bellowed. "We were so close to balancing the budget, and then our leaders blew it."

We were sitting less than 2 feet away from each other in a closed car but Neumann was practically shrieking. His face was getting red, his eyes were bulging, and I was beginning to worry about his ability to keep the car on the road and yell at me at the same time. I could hear his wife shifting uncomfortably in the backseat and clearing her throat.

Neumann had a lot of pent-up anger, and he had decided this was the time to unleash some of it. "We're responsible for everything bad, and Clinton and the Democrats are responsible for everything good," he said in a mocking, singsong tone. Well, no, I tried to interject. I hadn't said that. I hadn't said anything like that. I was just trying to ask about the government shutdown. I tried to interrupt him, but he couldn't be stopped. "We passed welfare reform, a line-item veto, health insurance reform, but do we get any credit for that?" he shouted.

I tried to respond, tried to cut in, but this was clearly not a time for a serious discussion about what went wrong in the 104th Congress and who deserved credit for what. Neumann just wanted to vent. "That's it. This interview is over when we get to my house," he announced. Luckily, we were almost there.

When we pulled into the driveway and got out of the car, Neumann stalked off without a word. His wife came over to me and apologized for him. It was the pressure of the campaign, she explained.

31

DOWN TO THE WIRE

MARK NEUMANN AND HIS FELLOW FRESHMAN Mark Souder of Indiana are very much the same ideologically. They're both social conservatives and righteous deficit cutters who are passionately committed to downsizing the federal government. Both have proven equally willing to take on their GOP House leaders and to cast votes against them. Both were part of the vanguard of the freshman class, the most revolutionary of the revolutionaries.

They have other similarities, too. Both are somewhat nerdy and intense. Both men married young and stayed close to their hometowns to raise a family. But they offered two faces of the revolution, and their personalities and personal styles couldn't be more different. Neumann seems to be constantly angry, whereas Souder, 46, maintains a gentle tone. It's pretty hard to picture Souder raising his voice.

Whenever there was a freshman revolt because of the leadership's failure to hold firm on some issue, you could usually find Souder. But he rebelled more quietly than did Neumann. Neumann always seemed on the verge of picking a fight. Souder seemed to want to make peace. Souder could be stubborn. He could have a sarcastic sense of humor. Like Neumann, he could certainly be unyielding on points of principle. But he lacked Neumann's bitter edge. And unlike many other members of the class, Souder was comfortable talking to reporters and so was often quoted in stories about the freshmen, giving inside details about meetings and strategies.

Whereas Neumann's staff seemed cowed and a little afraid of their boss, Souder had an easy working relationship with his young staff. As a former staff member himself for Indiana senator Dan Coats, Souder was generous in sharing credit with his staff and included their pictures in his newsletters to his constituents. And his attractive press secretary, Angela Flood, appeared with him regularly on the radio and TV shows he taped to be aired on local stations and cable channels back in the district.

Souder had the benefit of coming from a much more Republican district than did Neumann, but the difference in their styles may have been reflected in the level of opposition they were facing in this election. Although there were plenty of union members in his district, Souder had not been targeted by the AFL-CIO. And he had drawn a marginal opponent, Gerald Houseman, a political novice who favored adoption of a national single-payer health insurance program and reductions in defense spending and farm programs and who seem far too liberal to attract much support in this conservative district.

Souder was a devout Evangelical Christian who grew up in the Apostolic Church and was extremely conservative on social issues, for example, supporting legal abortion only in cases where the mother's life is in danger and not even in cases of rape and incest. In spite or perhaps because of his strong religious beliefs, Souder made an effort to work with minorities and disadvantaged people in his district and develop a relationship with the African American and Jewish communities in Fort Wayne. Ever since taking office, Souder had been reaching out to those who disagreed with him. Neumann, in contrast, seemed to have done his best to alienate everyone in his district except those conservatives who had been with him from the beginning.

Souder had also done a good job of organizing his office to respond to constituent concerns. He had only one district office, in Fort Wayne, but his district staff used a small mobile home as a mobile office to reach people in the rural areas of the district.

Souder happily described himself as a policy wonk and had introduced several interesting pieces of legislation, including one that would give a 120 percent tax deduction for charitable contributions, allow nonitemizers to deduct their donations over $1,000, and exclude charitable giving from the overall limitation on itemized deductions. "As we seek to reassert fiscal responsibility in government, increased private giving and volunteer involvement can fill a need that deficit spending cannot," Souder said in presenting his proposal. Souder also introduced a 20 percent "McFlat tax," which included deductions for mortgage interest and charitable contributions.

And he pushed for more enforcement efforts to halt the flow of illegal drugs into this country, specifically into Fort Wayne, and was able to convince the Drug Enforcement Administration to open an office in Fort Wayne. He further proposed an amendment that would have limited aid to Mexico until that country does more to fight drug trafficking.

Souder's district, the Fourth District of Indiana, is in the northeast corner of the state and is centered around Fort Wayne, a city of about 175,000 people. Downtown Fort Wayne is clean and tidy. It looks the way small American cities used to. General Electric and General Motors have factories there, and the city's largest employer is the Lincoln National Life Insurance Company, which has its own museum of Abraham Lincoln memorabilia downtown. Just outside the city the landscape opens up to farmland. There are several large ice cream plants in the area; according to Souder, 10 percent of all the ice cream made in America comes from his district.

This is a Republican district, although Souder defeated a moderate three-term Democrat to win back the seat that had previously been held by Dan Quayle and Souder's former boss, Dan Coats, before both were elected to the Senate.

The area has one of the nation's largest Amish populations, and Souder's great-great-grandfather was one of the first Amish settlers in 1846. The family opened a harness shop and general store just after the turn of the century in Grabill, about 10 miles northeast of Fort Wayne. The business later became a Christian bookstore, restaurant, and furniture store that Souder had a stake in. Souder got his M.B.A. from Notre Dame and was an enthusiastic booster of the Fighting Irish.

Since he wasn't facing a tough challenge, Souder was running a somewhat low-key campaign and early on aired folksy commercials that played up his small-town, conservative image. The radio ads talked about his hometown of Grabill and his daughter's going off to college. "What if she meets someone like Bill Clinton at college?" Souder asked mischievously in the ads. Heaven forbid.

Souder won the endorsement of Perot's reform party and on Friday, November 1, the Fort Wayne *Journal Gazette* published a poll that showed him with a huge lead over his opponents. Fifty-nine percent of those responding to the poll said they planned to vote for Souder, with only 17 percent indicating they would vote for his Democratic challenger. About 20 percent were still undecided. The poll also showed that Souder led Houseman 44 to 17 percent with independent voters and 46 to 32 percent with moderates of both parties. Souder spent a great deal more money on the race than his opponent. Souder's $438,000 was modest compared to the campaigns of most of the freshmen, but it vastly exceeded the $65,000 Houseman spent.

Even though Souder appeared to be far ahead of his opponent, he was still concerned that Dole's poor showing in the presidential race could hurt other Indiana congressional candidates by depressing Republican turnout. Souder also theorized that Dole's slightly improved standing over the last few weeks of the campaign might energize the Democrats to come out and vote. This could in particular affect fellow Indiana freshman John Hostettler, who was in a much more competitive race than Souder.

Five days before the election, Dan Quayle made a visit to Fort Wayne for the annual Allen County Republican bean dinner and rally, which drew 750 people. Souder was there doing some politicking, but people seemed to have moved on from the election of 1996 to 2000 already, asking favorite son Quayle if he planned to make a run for the presidency in four years. "Of course, it's a possibility. But I just haven't focused on it, and it's not really appropriate to start talking about the year 2000 before the 1996 presidential race is concluded," Quayle told them.

*   *   *

It is Sunday morning, November 3, and Souder is visiting the Calvary Temple Worship Center in Fort Wayne. The church consists of a huge, modern complex of buildings, and the worship service is being conducted in a large hall that is more an auditorium than a sanctuary. Hundreds of people are here. Onstage is a polished 75-member choir singing "Our God Reigns," accompanied by a full orchestra, complete with electric guitars and bass. The service is half entertainment, half worship. All the music is upbeat and up-tempo. This is a stand-up-and-wave-your-arms, clap-your-hands, tap-your-feet kind of service.

The minister, Paul Paino, introduces Souder by saying, "The Lord commands us to pray for those in leadership and government. . . . As people go into their polling station, they will ask the Lord's guidance." Paino is not telling his congregation to vote for Souder, but his words are about as close as you can get to an endorsement.

Souder, who is asked to make a few remarks, delivers a religious rather than a political message. "The devil is right outside," he tells the congregation. "If we honor Jesus Christ, if we do everything we can, it's in his hands. . . . We would be going straight to hell if it wasn't for him." Souder concludes by telling the congregation, "Praise God for all of you and your commitment." He receives a standing ovation.

Next, Paino begins his sermon with a reference to a television commercial about "promises, promises, promises." "Boy, haven't we heard a lot of them in the last 90 days?" he asks the congregation as he segues into the presidential campaign. It's pretty clear where his sympathies lie. "Promises don't mean too much when they come from someone who's broken too many of them. . . . If men in leadership make promises and then those promises aren't kept, it destroys faith. . . . I heard our president say last night while I was watching TV that he wants to be the president at the end of the century and the beginning of a new one," Paino says. "I don't know if he's going to get his desire or not." Paino then moves on to the promise of Jesus Christ and eternal salvation. God "never made a promise he has not kept," Paino tells his flock.

Later that Sunday afternoon Souder hosts a fund-raiser on the outskirts of Fort Wayne. The chili cook-off and hoedown costs families just $19.96 and is really more of a feel-good rally for Souder supporters than a fund-raiser. The event is held in an enclosed pavilion behind Hilger's Farm Market, which is owned by John and Joe Hilger. The brothers have built a thriving business with a large farm, the market, a buffet-style restaurant, and a pavilion they rent out for picnics and other events. They even have a small petting zoo in the back.

The Hilgers are from a Democratic family, although both are now supporters of Souder and registered Republicans. "Don't tell Mom," John says to me with a smile.

It snowed the day before in Indiana, just flurries, but it's cold today, and people are moving around to keep warm. Souder tells them he's been frustrated with the presidential campaign: "I keep thinking in these last 48 hours as people look more at Bill Clinton and his record that it will still be possible to turn the election around." He insists that "the issues are on our side." The other day while campaigning, Souder ran into a guy who told him he wasn't sure he was going to vote, but if he did, it would be for Clinton. The man was against abortion, for lower taxes, school vouchers, and smaller government. "I said to him, 'Why are you for Clinton?' and he said, 'Because I don't like Dole.'"

Although he acknowledges the inevitable, Souder remains steadfast in his belief that his district will stay true: "Whatever else happens in America, Bill Clinton's not going to take these counties." And he didn't. Dole carried Souder's district 53 percent to Clinton's 36 percent.

Everyone is making one last push this final weekend before the election. The AFL-CIO will be making calls and doing mailings. The Republican National Committee plans to send out 13 million leaflets, and GOP state party organizations are sending out another 80 million fliers trying to persuade voters that the country can't afford to have the Democrats back in control of both the White House and Congress. The Christian Coalition will be distributing 45 million voter guides through 120,000 churches today, running radio ads on Christian stations, and making phone calls. Although Souder is happy to be supported by the group, with which he largely agrees, he tells me the Christian Coalition has received a lot of the criticism in part because "it has not adopted a Christlike tone" but rather a "we-know-the-way," judgmental attitude.

Souder tells me he's had a grueling schedule of appearances, media interviews, fund-raisers, and speeches; his son said to him the night before, "I can hardly wait until it's not an election year anymore." Souder says he has been so wrapped up in his own race he doesn't really know what's going on with the other freshmen. Everything would be different if the Republicans had won the battle over the budget and the government shutdown, he tells me.

*   *   *

That weekend in New Hampshire, Charlie Bass is out campaigning for reelection, too, but his prospects are less certain than Souder's. Bass is one of the freshmen who's been targeted by the union ads. Bass is fighting for his political future, and he's pretty sure all the revolution talk over the past two years hasn't helped him much with the voters.

"The revolution is over," Bass tells a *Washington Post* reporter. "The simple fact is there won't be any 'Contract with America.' I think Congress will be a lot more toned down. I think a lot of people will roll into Washington with a lot of different ideas about how they want to do things differently," Bass prophesies about the next Congress.

32

NOVEMBER 5

ON ELECTION DAY Van Hilleary stands outside polling places in Democratic and swing counties in his district trying to shake as many hands as possible—trying to get every last vote. At 7 P.M., when the polls close, he and Brad Todd, his campaign manager and former congressional press secretary, get in the car to drive to his campaign headquarters in Crossville. They are craving any kind of returns. They're pretty sure Clinton is going to carry the state, but they don't yet know exactly how that will affect them. They had taken a poll the day before the election but sampled too many undecided voters. The poll showed Hilleary up by only four points, and he was nervous all day.

The car radio is tuned to a talk station. The first results that are announced are from Clifty, a tiny, backwoods hamlet in Cumberland County that isn't even on a road with a route number. Clifty is Hilleary's equivalent of Dixville Notch, the tiny town in northernmost New Hampshire whose vote tallies always come in first. But it's not good news: Mark Stewart, 33 votes; Van Hilleary, 0. Hilleary has not won a single vote in Clifty. He and Todd look at each other. They can't quite believe it. They have been together on and off for nearly five years, since Hilleary made his first unsuccessful run for the state Senate. It can't be over.

"Well, man, you ran a good race," Hilleary tells Todd. "You did everything you could. You worked hard," Todd responds. It was like one of those male bonding moments from the beer commercials, the one where the guy keeps saying, "I love you, man," Hilleary would tell me later.

Around 7:30 Hilleary and Todd arrive at their headquarters, where the returns have started to come in. Hilleary is holding his own in the Republican counties, just hitting his goals, but he's actually doing better than he thought he would in the Democratic and swing counties. Clinton is going to win the state and will narrowly carry Hilleary's district by one percentage point. Fred Thompson is blowing away his

Democratic opponent for reelection to the Senate. Thompson will end up carrying the state 61–37 percent, a wider margin than any candidate has ever won in Tennessee's history.

And despite the early report from Clifty, Hilleary will be reelected, decisively. He will carry 20 of 22 counties and have a 17-point margin of victory, 58–41 percent. Like Thompson, Hilleary will do one point better than he did in the 1994 tidal wave. "I beat Fred in three counties. That's my claim to fame," Hilleary will tell me a few weeks later.

Mark Stewart, angry over the ad Hilleary ran about his defending child molesters, does not call Hilleary to congratulate him.

Although Hilleary knows pretty early that he's won, for many of his freshman colleagues it will be a very long night. In some cases races will be so close it will take days to sort out the winners.

*   *   *

It was clear very early on election night that the presidential race was over, and even in its last moments the Dole campaign was the gang that couldn't shoot straight. Just after 9 P.M. on the East Coast, the campaign faxed a concession statement to major news organizations that said, "Bob Dole has completed his last political mission with courage and honor. Even in defeat he has much to claim in the way of success." But then campaign spokesman Nelson Warfield had to retract the statement because it was "prematurely released," before all the polls had closed.

By 11 P.M. most of the House races in the eastern part of the country had been decided, and early returns showed six of the GOP freshmen had lost—Jim Longley in Maine, Dan Frisa in New York, Bill Martini in New Jersey, Fred Heineman and David Funderburk in North Carolina, and Michael Flanagan in Illinois.

At 11:25 Dole conceded but assured Republicans, "We're going to keep the Senate, and we're going to keep the House." With West Coast polls still open and many close congressional races not yet counted, the race was not completely decided, but Dole would prove to be right. For the first time in nearly 70 years, the Republicans would control the House for two consecutive Congresses.

Around midnight Clinton told supporters that the voters had spoken: "It's time to put politics aside and work together for America's future." Clinton was denied the 50 percent victory he had wanted, the 8 percent Ross Perot won keeping Clinton's victory to 49 percent of the vote. And it was obvious the country had not been too excited about this campaign. For the first time since 1924, fewer than half of all Americans voted for president.

But despite a lack of enthusiasm for the presidential campaign and low voter turnout, a great deal of deliberation was reflected in the final outcome of the election. It was determined by voters who split their tickets, voting for Clinton for president and Republicans for Congress. These voters may have been a relatively small percentage of the total electorate, but they were the ones who made the difference, who determined that Republicans would remain in the majority in Congress. These were the moderate Democrats and independents who continued to vote Republican for Congress.

Many of the congressional races were exceedingly close, decided by just a few thousand votes or less. A very small number of votes cast around the country could have made the difference between a Democratic and Republican Congress. Those kinds of margins signaled a divided electorate and one that said it wanted Democrats and Republicans to work together.

The closest race in the country in 1996 was that of freshman Jon Fox of Pennsylvania. It took more than a week for Fox to be declared the winner by an amazing 84 votes. Fox came from a tough district and had tried to be a moderate in the 104th Congress. He voted with the GOP leadership less than any of the other freshmen, although it was still 91 percent of the time. And in running for reelection Fox tried to de-emphasize his Republicanism as much as possible.

When all of the votes were finally counted, 12 freshmen were defeated, including Steve Stockman, whose race was not decided until a special Texas election was held in December. In addition to Stockman and the first six announced early on election night, the other freshmen who lost were Frank Cremeans of Ohio, Dick Chrysler of Michigan, Andrea Seastrand of California, Jim Bunn of Oregon, and Randy Tate of Washington. Six senior House Republicans were also defeated, including the ever colorful Bob Dornan of California, bringing to 18 the total number of House Republicans who lost their bids for reelection.

Two senior House Democrats and one Democratic freshman were defeated. Mike Ward of Kentucky lost his race to Anne Northup in a close contest decided by 1,299 votes, less than one percentage point. The Democrats picked up nine seats, bringing their total number of House seats to 207 to the Republicans' 227. Vermont's Independent representative Bernard Sanders invariably voted with the Democrats, which meant the Republicans had a voting margin of nine.

Of the dozen GOP freshmen who were defeated, most of them fell into the Accidental Congressman category. They had personal weaknesses or came from districts that were not nearly as conservative as they were. For the most part, these were candidates that hadn't been expected to win in 1994. The 1996 vote could be considered a correction, a realignment of the 1994 vote rather than a reversal of that election.

None of the stars of the class from the core group of True Believers were defeated, even though some of them, like Mark Neumann, faced tough races. Neumann won his race 51–49 percent. Mark Souder won with a much more comfortable 58–39 percent margin.

A great deal of attention had been paid to the money and effort the labor unions spent in an attempt to defeat the freshmen and return the Congress to Democratic control. Although labor ran campaigns in the districts of all of the freshmen who were defeated, the AFL-CIO was in a great many more districts where the freshman they targeted easily won reelection. John Shadegg of Arizona, who kept his seat by a huge 67–33 percent margin, told me shortly after the election that the "self-inflicted wounds" of members who had "goofed in some way during their term" was probably reason enough for most of the freshmen's defeats.

What did the unions really get for their money, then? They weren't able to turn over Congress and wound up spending at least $2 million a head to defeat 18 Republicans. John Sturdivant, president of the American Federation of Government Employees, joked to the *Washington Times*, "It might have been easier to just give each Republican a million dollars and ask them to go away." Shadegg said the unions could have been even more effective if they had played the game better. He pointed to the unions' "ham-handed bludgeoning" of candidates, such as running the same ad about two different candidates in the same media market, as the AFL-CIO did in Seattle with Rick White and Randy Tate. "If they had been more sophisticated," they might have been more successful, he speculated. "They spent a ton of money to accomplish an incredibly small amount," Shadegg gloated. "Their shot to win back Congress was this year, and they didn't do it."

The union money certainly made a difference in some races, but the AFL-CIO also came off looking like the big outside interloper coming in to bash the local freshman. In the Arizona race against J. D. Hayworth, the unions spent so much money and ran the same ad so many times "that organized labor became the issue in that race," according to Shadegg. Of course, part of the reason for that may have been the ads run by the Republican National Committee that claimed the "big labor bosses in Washington" were trying to buy the seat. Even though a local newspaper endorsed Hayworth's Democratic challenger and called Hayworth "bombastic," "boorish," and "an affront to his colleagues, an embarrassment for America," and even though Clinton was the first Democrat to carry Arizona since 1948, Hayworth held on to eke out a 48–47 percent victory.

Phil English, who also faced a union onslaught, was reelected 51–49 percent. "People got tired of the attacks and thought the message was being dictated from outside the district," said English, who spent $1.2 million on the race. His opponent spent $500,000. But best estimates show that outside, independent groups on both sides spent more than the two candidates did buying television time. And in one of the country's smallest competitive television markets, $1 million buys a *lot* of ads.

It was estimated that around the country Republican candidates outspent their Democratic challengers an average of five to one, yet they constantly complained about the bullying they were receiving from big labor. Ganske in Iowa spent $2.3 million to his challenger Connie McBurney's $850,000 but was still able to paint labor as a Goliath against his David. Ganske won election 52–47 percent, and on election night Ganske thanked all the Republican union members who had voted for him and exhorted them to "rise up and smite their leadership for taking their union dues."

The unions probably should have taken a page out of the Christian Coalition's strategy handbook and tried to do a little more flying below the radar screen of television and the media, as the Christian Coalition does when it sends out voter guides, calls members, and leaflets churches the Sunday before the election.

Although the unions had not achieved their goal of winning back Congress for the Democrats, they still claimed to be pleased with the impact they had on the election. A poll conducted for the AFL-CIO by Peter Hart Research immediately following the election showed that 32 percent of union members voted for Republicans for Congress in 1996, down from 40 percent in 1994. Surveys also showed that 23 percent of all voters in this election were from union households, up from 14 percent in 1994, and AFL-CIO political director Steve Rosenthal credits the union's push with the increased turnout, which he says provided the margin of victory for Democrats in a number of close races. Rosenthal pointed to freshman Andrea Seastrand's district in California. In 1994 there were an estimated 22,000 union members in that district, and about 8,000 of them voted. If 40 percent of them voted Republican, following the national trend, that was more than enough to make up the 1,500-vote margin Seastrand won the election by. The 1996 rematch went the other way, thanks to union efforts, Rosenthal claimed.

There was a lot of talk by Republicans right after the election about exacting some retribution against the unions or trying to ensure they couldn't do the same thing in future elections. "Big labor decided to create this political holy war against Republicans, and the fact is they lost," said John Boehner, head of the House Republican conference. Boehner predicted the Republicans would again attempt to introduce legislation that would require unions to inform each member how much they spend on political activities and give members the opportunity to say they don't want their dues used that way.

And the Republicans filed a complaint with the Federal Election Commission claiming the union ads violated election laws because they crossed the line into candidate advocacy. The Republicans had a point, but so did many of the ads run by independent conservative groups and by both parties. Perhaps the biggest change that could block the unions from mounting another effort like this one would be a rewrite of campaign finance laws. "I can't imagine a better argument than this election season" for campaign finance reform, said Shadegg. Many Republican freshmen who weren't too eager to tackle campaign finance reform in the 104th Congress suddenly sounded like born-again reformers after the election.

The union leaders didn't seem too concerned. Rosenthal maintained it was better to have the Republicans angry and a little fearful than complacent about the unions. AFL-CIO president John Sweeney said he didn't fear an angered Republican majority because things couldn't get much worse. Sweeney insisted the Republicans "would have done even worse if we had sat back. We're not going to sit still and let them walk all over us."

At a press conference held shortly after the election to tout the unions' accomplishments, Sweeney was asked whether the AFL-CIO would try again in the future. "You're damn right," he answered without a moment's hesitation. But later, in an interview with me, Sweeney showed slightly less bravado. "Everything we did I'm confident our members completely supported. There's nothing illegal about anything we did, and it was in the best interest of our members." Sweeney said the most important benefit of the union's effort was energizing its members. "This isn't about politics; this is about a stronger labor movement fighting for working families. This is about rebuilding the labor movement."

If that's true, one has to ask how much organizing the unions could have bought for $35 million.

Not all union members were completely happy about the strategy of going full bore against Republicans no matter who they were. Domenic Bozzotto is president of the Hotel Workers Union in Boston, which is known for its independence and which endorsed Republican governor William Weld for the U.S. Senate over Democratic incumbent John Kerry. "When we endorsed Weld, we got ostracized [by the other unions] as if we have no right to an independent thought," Bozzotto told me.

Bozzotto was critical of the AFL-CIO's decision to go after senior Republicans Peter Blute and Peter Torkildsen of Massachusetts, both of whom were defeated. Both men voted against NAFTA as members of the House. The AFL-CIO supported Kerry even though he voted for NAFTA, Bozzotto pointed out. "Blute got no credit. Blute and Torkildsen are not devils," he told me. "There are some Democrats who are bad. We're not interested in the labels; we're interested in the action. I think there are a lot of Democrats who take us for granted, who know they're going to have our support and don't give us much in return. We should be more selective," said Bozzotto.

In a few cases labor did make the difference—the Blute and Torkildsen races may be good examples. But in every case where a freshman was defeated, there was more to it than just labor ads. The one freshman that the rest of the class was the most bitterly disappointed to lose was Randy Tate. He had worked hard, gone home every weekend, raised money. He was smart and personable. He was a True Believer.

Maybe the labor expenditures made the difference in Tate's race. But he faced a good opponent in Adam Smith, and his district was poised perfectly on the edge between Republican and Democratic support. In 1996 the balance tipped Democratic, as it had tipped Republican in 1994. Tate lost 50–47 percent. And though he pointed to the labor unions' expensive campaign against him as the reason, Tate personally outspent his opponent nearly $1.6 million to $700,000. Tate had ample chance to make his case to the voters; he just didn't like their response.

The voters in Rick White's district were subjected to exactly the same labor ads run in the Seattle television market, but White won his race decisively, 54–46 percent. White's opponent was not as strong as Tate's, and White was more moderate, more in tune with his district.

Despite a couple of Washington House races that were so close they weren't decided for days, Tate was ultimately the only Washington state freshman to lose. Although it initially looked as if Linda Smith had been defeated, when the absentee ballots were counted, Smith won by fewer than 1,000 votes. And George Nethercutt's race didn't prove to be close at all. He won reelection 56–44 percent.

One freshman who could plausibly argue that the labor efforts really made the difference in his race was Bill Martini of New Jersey. Martini had tried to be a moderate, tried to push for the minimum wage. But this was a district with a Democratic tradition, and Martini faced a good opponent. The seat may just have been too hard for a Republican to hold.

Several of the freshmen were undone by their mismatches with their districts. Swept in in 1994, they were swept out again in 1996. Michael Flanagan of Chicago and Andrea Seastrand of California fell into this group. Seastrand was simply too conservative for her coastal California constituency. And Flanagan was doomed from the start.

Four of the freshmen who lost faced significant labor campaigns against them, but their defeats were due to other factors. Longley, Frisa, Cremeans, and Chrysler all had excellent opponents. Except for Frisa, all of them came from districts that were either evenly divided or leaned Democratic, and none was a terribly strong campaigner or had established a strong personal record for their first two years in the House. None of their races was close. Longley was defeated 55–45, Frisa 57–41, Cremeans 51–49, and Chrysler 54–44 percent.

Three of the freshmen who lost probably defeated themselves through their missteps or behavior. The voters do not like to be embarrassed by their representatives in Congress. They may criticize the institution, but they want to be proud of their representatives, even if they don't always agree with them. Jim Bunn of Oregon, for example, came from a competitive district and had a good challenger, Darlene Hooley, a former state legislator and county commissioner. Bunn had narrowly won his seat in 1994, by just 50–47 percent. He was also targeted by labor, but he had bigger problems.

The 39-year-old Bunn, who had five children and had run on family values in 1994, won significant support from the Christian right. But soon after coming to Washington Bunn received criticism in Oregon for the way he ran his office, including paying a 17-year-old staff member a $35,000 annual salary. And in early August, three months before the election, Bunn married his 31-year-old chief of staff, Sonja Bates Skurdal. She had been hired in January 1995 to run his Washington office, although she had no previous political or government experience except for managing his 1994 campaign. Skurdal had sought a divorce from her husband at roughly the same time Bunn filed for divorce. And at the time of their wedding, Bunn was paying Skurdal $97,500 as his chief of staff.

In the final months of the campaign, Skurdal resigned her job in Bunn's office to run his campaign, although Bunn said he didn't feel she should have had to do that. "It's wrong that she had to leave the job because she married me," Bunn told the *Oregonian* a month before the election. Apparently the voters didn't agree with him: Bunn was defeated 51–46 percent.

Both of the North Carolina freshmen who lost could look to themselves for the reason as well. Fred Heineman had been an Accidental Congressman in 1994. The man he had upset, former congressman David Price, was well known and running an aggressive, no-mistakes campaign against him. But Heineman had given him an opening. He had done little to distinguish himself in two years in office, and his comment that his six-figure salary made him only lower middle class typified his slightly goofy, out-of-touch demeanor.

The one freshman who seemed to have no one but himself to blame for his defeat was David Funderburk. Until his motor vehicle mishap and his apparent dissembling about what had taken place, there was no reason Funderburk should have been vulnerable. Funderburk was the only one of the dozen freshmen who lost who had received more than 55 percent of the vote in 1994—he'd won with a 12-point margin of victory. Funderburk also came from a pretty solidly Republican district. Funderburk and Cremeans of Ohio were the only two defeated freshmen who came from districts Clinton had not carried in 1992.

It seemed clear the voters were sending Funderburk a message. And across the country in 1996, the voters were sending another, much bigger message.

Of the 58 freshmen who won reelection, exactly half won their races in districts that Clinton carried. That is too significant a statistic to be considered anything but a deliberate and conscious decision by the voters that they liked things the way they were. Divided government kept everybody in check. It seemed to suit the voters' desire for marginalism rather than dramatic change in either direction.

Several of these 29 districts are particularly worth noting. Clinton carried Tom Coburn's Oklahoma district 47–40 percent. But Coburn was decisively reelected 55–45 percent. Coburn was about as hard right as you could get on both social and fiscal matters. His constituents clearly approved of the way he was representing them at the same time that they wanted to give Clinton another term. Coburn and his wing of the freshman class despised Clinton, but the voters said they were going to have to work together.

At the other end of the freshman ideological spectrum, Tom Davis of Virginia offered a textbook case of how a freshman from the class of 1994 who came from a moderate district with plenty of Democratic voters could survive. Early in his term, especially when the government shutdown happened, Davis attempted to distance himself from his classmates and the antigovernment Republicans and tried to look out for the interests of his constituents, many of whom were government employees. He won his race 64–35 percent, and Clinton carried the district 48–46 percent.

*   *   *

The day after the election, the two party chairmen, Haley Barbour and Senator Chris Dodd, appeared at the National Press Club in Washington for a little analysis of what had just happened. Both men claimed victory for their parties. Democrat Dodd, a liberal, said the American people were asking for less shrillness and for moderation. Republican Barbour called it a "ratifying election" of the Republican agenda. "The American people like the decision they made in 1994. This election was a victory for Republican ideals," Barbour declared.

Barbour also claimed Clinton had even campaigned "as a moderate Republican. . . . There were days it sounded like Ronald Reagan had taken over his body." Barbour was very close to the truth. In many respects Clinton was the Democrats' version of Reagan. He was an attractive and personable candidate who could communicate well and whom people seemed to like. Both were natural and gifted politicians who presented optimistic campaigns and visions for the country. Both were able to attract votes from people who didn't agree with them on many issues. Clinton presented an appealing face for the Democratic Party. Since most voters vote for people rather than ideas, it was also a winning face.

By contrast, Gingrich had presented an unappealing face for the Republicans, and it had cost some of them their seats. Gingrich sensed a new approach was in order. In interviews after the election, he repeatedly talked about trying to find "common ground" with Clinton. Gingrich said he expected the Republicans to stay away from "symbolic fights that are divisive" and instead focus on "practical things that help the American people." Declared Gingrich: "We're in a situation where we survived all of the ads; we survived all the campaigning; we survived a very strong showing by their nominee for president. And we are, for the first time in 68 years, still in the majority."

33

WHAT HAPPENED TO THE REPUBLICAN REVOLUTION?

THEY WERE THE SELF-DESCRIBED REVOLUTIONARIES, the peasants with pitch-forks who were not outside but inside the castle walls. They came to Washington to shake things up. They disdained compromise and prided themselves on their purity. They were going to slice and dice the federal budget no matter how much it hurt. In the beginning they ran around like kids who had taken over the classroom.

Largely because of their number and the historic nature of the 1994 election, the freshmen roared into town believing only they knew the truth of what was best for the country. They dismissed anyone who had the temerity to disagree with them, and they believed they had a mandate from the voters for their agenda.

One of the biggest mistakes the freshmen made was in misreading their mandate. It's true that no Republican incumbent lost in 1994. That undoubtedly said some-thing about the mood of the voters and their dissatisfaction with the way Clinton and the Democrats had been running the country. But many of the freshmen won election by just a few thousand votes. The election of 1994 had been decisive in its unanimity but narrow in its margins. The Republicans did not have the sweeping mandate for change they thought they did.

What happened to the Republican revolution is that it never existed in the first place except in the minds of Newt Gingrich and the freshmen. *Webster's* defines "rev-olution" as a "complete, radical change" or "the overthrow of a government, form of government or social system by those governed." It's doubtful that any "revolution" could be effected by a single U.S. congressional election. But that's not what Americans voted for in 1994 anyway. The American people were not looking for a revolution, just some much-needed change. But the freshmen tried to give them a revolution anyway. Using the word "revolution" to describe what they were trying to do put the freshmen at a disadvantage right from the start.

The Republicans raised the bar of expectations too high to jump over. Revolutions are not meant to happen in a democracy like ours. The dramas of the 104th Congress perfectly illustrated the brilliance of the framers of the Constitution and the system of governance they created. The House, with its two-year terms, was expected to "ever be subject to precipitancy, changeability, and excess."

The freshmen would have done well to follow the advice of Oliver Ellsworth, a delegate to the Constitutional Convention from Connecticut, who urged, "Let not too much be attempted; by which all may be lost." And as delegate Edmund Randolph, the governor of Virginia, declared, the purpose of the Senate is "to restrain, if possible, the fury of democracy." The Senate served exactly that function in the 104th Congress, to the agitation of the impatient freshmen.

The Republicans scared people with their zeal and their unwillingness to hear any voice but their own. People thought they wanted to go too fast. They had not adequately explained what they were trying to do, and they had not convinced people it was the right thing.

Voters did want a balanced federal budget and smaller, more accountable, more sensible, less intrusive government. The freshmen were asking the right questions about our government, but they didn't always offer the right answers. In cutting the federal budget, the Republicans didn't apply the ax fairly. Yes, Americans were concerned about welfare, did not want it to become a way of life for people. But Americans are not mean-spirited; they did not want children to go hungry or elderly immigrants who came to this country legally years ago to be denied health care. The Republicans made budget cuts that disproportionately affected the poor while not doing enough to reduce corporate welfare, wasteful defense spending, and other pork programs.

An analysis by the Center on Budget and Policy Priorities conducted at the end of the 104th Congress found that more than 93 percent of the budget reductions in entitlements came from programs that affected low-income people, although those programs accounted for less than a quarter of total expenditures for entitlement programs, including Medicare and Social Security. When it came to discretionary spending, more than a third of the cuts made by the 104th Congress came from programs for the poor, although they accounted for less than a quarter of overall spending on nondefense discretionary programs. To be fair, many of the freshmen did push for such cuts but were outvoted by senior members of their own party and Democrats who wanted to protect programs important to constituencies and lobbyists that mattered to them.

The freshmen also made a mistake in trying to impose their social agenda on the Congress, which drew opposition not only from the Democrats but divided their own party. Although the hard-core, conservative supporters of the freshmen fervently endorsed their social agenda, most Americans did not believe the ban on assault weapons should be lifted, environmental regulations should be rolled back, or the abortion debate should be revisited at every opportunity.

And the Republicans made a number of tactical mistakes. They tried to ignore for too long the president and his veto power, even when they did not have enough votes to override that veto. The freshmen can be excused for not immediately realizing the dangers they faced in forcing a standoff with Clinton without a veto-proof majority, but their leaders should have known better.

The two words that best describe the way the Republicans functioned for most of the 104th Congress are "centralization" and "anarchy." Power was too centralized in Gingrich, who was making key decisions and taking action on his own without discussing them with the Republican conference. And when his freshman troops thought they hadn't been adequately informed or disagreed with his actions, anarchy would often ensue.

The Republicans' biggest mistake was shutting down the government, which made them look petty and immature. They deflected attention away from what they were fighting for and handed Clinton a club to use against them. The government shutdown was a turning point and a low from which they never fully recovered. The shutdown, combined with all of their grandstanding in the first year, diminished many of their achievements. If you judge the 104th Congress against past Congresses, it was extremely productive and significant. Judged only by their own early rhetoric and goals, the Republicans didn't get most of what they were seeking.

Much of what the 104th Congress accomplished came at the end of the session, after the freshmen had learned how to govern, which meant they had learned how to compromise with the Democrats. Their constituents said they wanted it done, so they passed a minimum wage increase, even though many said privately they did not agree with it. They passed health insurance and welfare reform, which Americans also said they wanted. One could argue that at that point they became very much like the people they had replaced, part of the system. But had they not changed strategy in the spring and summer of 1996, it's a safe bet a great many more of the freshmen would not have been reelected and the Republicans could have lost the majority. By compromising to get a few things done, they lived to fight another day.

The Republican 104th Congress did make hard choices, helping to reduce the size of the deficit and beginning to control the rate of growth in government spending. The Republicans set in place a program to phase out agricultural subsidies even though many of them came from rural, farming districts. They passed the line-item veto, prevented unfunded federal mandates from being passed on to local and state governments, and reformed Congress by adopting a gift ban, revising the rules on lobbying, and requiring Congress to obey the laws it passed for everyone else. The congressional reform measures in particular never would have happened without the freshmen. They deserve credit for those things.

Clinton may have demonized the freshmen as extremists, but deep down he knew they were on to something. And so he stole their message. In many respects during the campaign he hewed to the freshman message more closely than did Dole. Clinton signed on to welfare reform, a balanced budget, smaller government, and a tax cut. The Democrats had no real message of their own. They had no vision of what they would do if they took Congress back. They simply said they were not the extremist Republicans.

It is no coincidence that Bill Clinton won decisive margins of victory in the same districts that reelected the freshmen. The voters believed that with a Republican Congress and Bill Clinton in the White House, they would get more or less what they wanted—that the Republican Congress and the Democratic president would moderate each other, pulling both toward the middle.

Many of the freshmen were inspired to run for office by Clinton, by the tax increase and big-government approach of his first two years. Many voters also thought Clinton was going too far to the left. And though the 1994 election looked like a repudiation of his administration, the Clinton presidency started to become a success only when he stood up to the freshmen during the government shutdown, when voters thought the Republicans were moving too far to the right. Clinton took the freshmen on, but he also got their message. He stood before the country and acknowledged that the era of big government was over. Likewise, the freshmen won the most approval from the public when they started working with the president to pass legislation.

Americans didn't want the federal government dismantled. They just wanted it to work better, to do what it is supposed to do. Government can't do everything, but it must do some things, and in many cases it can do them better than it's doing them now. That's what people elect politicians to do: to make government work better and to find solutions to national problems.

The freshmen and the 104th Congress expended most of their energy trying to balance the budget but left many serious problems unaddressed. What to do about the long-term future of Medicare and Social Security remains a significant national problem that must be dealt with on a bipartisan basis. This is a job too hard for one party to do alone. Congress must also address our largely failing public education system and the problems of our inner cities along with the lack of jobs for urban minorities, which has contributed to the problems of crime and drugs. And the failure of the freshmen and the 104th Congress to deal with campaign finance reform resulted in an election in 1996 that exemplified the worst excesses ever of the existing campaign financing system and its soft money loopholes.

*   *   *

The most important contribution the freshmen and the Republicans made in 1994 and through the 104th Congress was to change the national debate and the national agenda. Suddenly it was no longer a matter of whether the budget would be balanced but when. Their efforts were fundamental in changing the way we view government and its role in our lives as we head into the 21st century. Rather than believing government can address any problem through the creation of yet another program, Americans now see the limits of government and of what we can afford. What the freshmen produced was not a revolution but an evolution, in thinking.

The election of the freshmen and the Republican House majority did signal the biggest change in American government in half a century. Whether it will be a lasting change is not yet clear.

To what extent have the freshmen reshaped American politics? They have certainly made it more popular to tell the truth. The freshmen were willing to tell it like it is. Even many people who didn't agree with them respected their candor and commitment. But did they permanently change Congress? They weren't able to eliminate anything big, like a cabinet department. And because of the closeness of the 1996 election, pressures were mounting before their second term began to push Congress back to the old way of doing things.

The freshmen realized about halfway through their first year in Congress that what they wanted to do was going to take longer than two years to accomplish. And in their reelection campaigns the freshmen asked the voters to let them finish the job they started. Having won reelection, they were a little older, a little wiser, and a lot more politically savvy. And while they may have derided the way Congress does its business when they arrived, they grudgingly learned respect for the power of the system's checks and balances.

When the freshmen returned to Washington shortly after the 1996 election for some organizational meetings, they seemed to be experiencing a strange mixture of euphoria, exhaustion, and disappointment. "I went up to my colleagues and started hugging them. 'It's great to have you back,' I told them. We really went through something. It's been a truly remarkable experience. We've been waging a political war and for two years there's been a siege mentality," Joe Scarborough told me.

They were back. And the ones who survived were both different and curiously the same. Many of the freshmen were never revolutionaries, just Republican politicians who happened to get elected in 1994. But after the 1996 election, a core group of about two dozen True Believers remained, united by the goals of reducing government spending and balancing the budget. Having been called Nazis, fascists, and radicals for two years, some of the freshmen were ready to give up the fight, but others were more determined than ever. "We won the idea war," Sam Brownback told me. "If we hadn't yelled so hard we wouldn't have gotten as far as we did. You have to give the war cry."

After the election many of the freshmen were feeling rather used by Gingrich. "We were the shock troops," said John Shadegg. The Republicans should have picked three or four things and pushed all the way to get them done rather than trying for everything and then caving in, he said. Their leaders should have known better. "Somebody should have been the adult. Somebody should have known you can't do it all at once."

*   *   *

Early in the 104th Congress, Steve Largent said he would like his political career to be "brilliant but brief." Some of the members of his class, like Mark Sanford and Matt Salmon, voluntarily term-limited themselves to six years in the House when they ran for election the first time. Others, like Lindsey Graham and Van Hilleary, set their limit of service at 12 years. Is it possible to make a lasting impact on something as enormous and intractable as the federal government in just a few terms in Congress? The freshmen feel they have to try.

Lindsey Graham said he thinks there is a tendency for people the longer they serve in Congress to forget where they came from, "to get comfortable with your surroundings, make new friends, and believe your own press. Eventually our class will be part of the problem if we stay here long enough."

After Van Hilleary won his election in 1994, Howard Baker sat him down and told him a story. It was something that happened to Baker shortly after he arrived in the Senate almost 30 years earlier. Norris Cotton, a New Hampshire senator whom Baker described as a fierce-looking, pipe-smoking, hardheaded New Englander, took him aside and asked him if he could smell the marble. "I didn't know marble had a smell," Baker replied innocently. "Well, white marble, the kind around here does," Cotton told him. "And when you can smell it, you'll like it. And you'll be ruined for life."

It's not clear whether Hilleary and the other freshmen can smell the marble yet.

EPILOGUE

THE REPUBLICANS HELD ONTO CONTROL of the House in 1996, but only by the slimmest of margins. Their narrow majority coupled with their failure to recapture the White House had a dramatic impact on the agenda they were able to pursue in the 105th Congress. Another factor was Newt Gingrich's problems.

Many of the freshmen blamed Gingrich and his tactical and public relations mistakes for the losses they suffered in the election. They were also acutely aware that Gingrich's ethical problems and extremely low poll numbers, showing him to be the least popular major political figure in the country, were still hurting them. The Sunday after the election, Steve Largent appeared on the Fox News Sunday television interview program and said maybe it would be better if Gingrich stepped aside as Speaker until his ethical problems were cleared up. A number of House Republicans felt the same way, but few were willing to say so publicly.

A week later the House Republicans met in Washington to organize and unanimously reelected Gingrich as their leader in an informal vote. But the Republicans were not nearly as unified as they appeared. It was a seemingly humbled Gingrich who spoke to his conference and to the press that day. "I made a few big errors. I was both the Speaker of the House and our leading advocate, and some days I didn't do it very well," he admitted to reporters. Gingrich predicted, "This will be a different Congress. Therefore as Speaker, I'll probably function a little differently. . . . This will be a slower Congress" than the 104th.

Gingrich said he wanted to work with Bill Clinton and the Democrats and to have a closer working relationship with the Senate. He was going to have to. He simply didn't have the votes to do it any other way if he wanted to pass any significant legislation. "We find ourselves here with a Democratic president and a Republican Congress, and we have an absolute moral obligation to make this system work. If the last Congress was the 'Confrontation Congress,' this Congress will be the 'Implementation Congress,'" Gingrich asserted. There would be no more government shutdowns. That much seemed clear.

In December, after two years of saying he had done nothing wrong, Gingrich essentially agreed to a plea bargain with the Ethics Committee and admitted to having violated House rules in funding the college course he had taught that was financed with tax-exempt donations. Gingrich also acknowledged giving the Ethics Committee "inaccurate, incomplete, and unreliable information."

As a result of these developments, Gingrich found himself having to shore up support within the GOP conference to ensure he had the votes to be reelected as Speaker when the 105th Congress convened the first week in January. "It's like night and day compared to two years ago," former freshman Ray LaHood told the *Washington Post*. "All the euphoria about his ability to win a House majority, the willingness to support his agenda, that's all gone. . . . Newt has been damaged, his effectiveness has been damaged."

The House Republicans met behind closed doors two days before Congress convened. The meeting featured screaming by several members angry at Gingrich over the position he had put the party in and one member even suggesting that he had lied to his fellow Republicans. There were also penitent tears from Gingrich. It was stunning how often Gingrich seemed to be moved to tears since becoming Speaker, usually over his own problems and predicaments. He had cried on a number of occasions and had spoken about it with reporters.

Gingrich told his fellow Republicans that if his problems persisted and he continued to remain as unpopular with the public as he was at that moment, he would step down as Speaker and not endanger the rest of the Republican conference and their legislative agenda. "He told us all kinds of things to get our votes," Mark Souder would tell me several months later. "Some of us naively believed he would put [the] party above himself."

The House swearing-in on January 7, 1997, was quite different from the ceremony that had taken place in the House chamber two years earlier. Missing was the riotous air of celebration that had been a part of the opening of the 104th Congress. Now there was a feeling of anticipation but also of uncertainty. Because he had spent days telephoning and buttonholing members, it was presumed Gingrich had enough votes to secure the Speakership. But the question remained how many Republicans would defect and vote against him. Sam Brownback, now a member of the Senate, was on the floor receiving congratulations from his former House colleagues. He was curious about what would happen. "I wanted to get a feel for that baby. I'm glad I wasn't voting. I think it was a tough one. I don't know how I would have voted," Brownback would tell me the next day when we talked in his Senate office.

At 12:30 P.M. GOP conference chairman John Boehner addressed the House: "Two years ago we began a new chapter in American history. We began to change America by reforming Washington." Boehner then placed Gingrich's name in nomination for election as House Speaker.

The first Republican to vote against Gingrich was moderate Tom Campbell of California, who voted for fellow GOP moderate Jim Leach. Former freshman Michael Forbes of New York also voted against Gingrich and for Leach. When his name was called, Leach, who had called Gingrich "ethically damaged," voted for former Republican House leader Robert Michel, a move that won a round of applause from the Democratic side of the aisle. And former freshman Linda Smith of Washington state voted for retired House member Robert Walker of Pennsylvania, a close friend of Gingrich's. Five Republicans—former freshmen John Hostettler and Mark Neumann and senior members Scott Klug, Constance Morella, and Frank Wolf—voted present instead of voting for Gingrich.

At 2 P.M. the clerk finally announced that Gingrich had been elected speaker, with just 216 votes to Richard Gephardt's 205. But the vote was even closer than it looked, Souder would tell me later, because many Republicans were deeply conflicted about voting for Gingrich and did so with serious reservations.

Addressing the House after the vote, Gingrich said, "For those who agonized and ended up voting for me, I thank you. Some of this difficulty, frankly, I brought on myself. To the degree I was too brash, too self-confident, or too pushy, I apologize. To whatever degree and in any way that I brought controversy or inappropriate attention to the House, I apologize. It is my intention to do everything I can to work with every member of this Congress," Gingrich told his colleagues.

A few weeks later the House would vote 395–28 to follow the recommendation of the Ethics Committee and to reprimand Gingrich and order him to pay a $300,000 penalty for ethics violations. It was the first time in the history of the House that a sitting Speaker had been disciplined for ethical lapses. The size of the penalty stunned a number of members. It was pretty hard for GOP members to tell people back home this was the equivalent of a speeding ticket when Gingrich was being forced to pay a $300,000 fine. Following the release of the Ethics Committee report, a number of the former freshmen said if they had known what was in the report, they probably would not have voted for Gingrich as Speaker. "Some of us wished we had our first vote back," Souder would tell me.

In defiant appearances back in his home district in Georgia in late January, Gingrich seemed to blame everyone but himself for what had happened. Gingrich said he had "trusted" the Washington lawyers who prepared his material for the Ethics Committee. "They didn't do the job right and I didn't catch them," Gingrich contended. But his lawyer, Jan Baran, an election law specialist, said Gingrich had reviewed all of the documents submitted to the committee.

The "liberal media" also came in for its share of the blame from Gingrich, who contended that journalists allow liberal politicians to get away with things, whereas they hold conservatives to a different standard: "Somehow on the left . . . you can do anything you want and nobody seems to notice. But if you are a conservative and you want to follow the law and you hire lawyers and you do what you can—if you make a single mistake, you better plan to be pilloried because you're politically incorrect."

Gingrich's outbursts didn't play too well with many of his GOP House colleagues, especially the former freshmen. They saw this as just another example of his refusing to tell the truth and to take responsibility for his actions. "A lot of freshmen think he's hurting the cause," Van Hilleary would tell me in January. "He's not this visionary that is irreplaceable; he makes mistakes." Hilleary and his classmates were doing quite a bit of reappraisal. The former freshmen, who were now sophomores, were realizing how much they hadn't known two years earlier and how many mistakes they made while trying to learn how to govern. Fifty-eight of the original 73 remained in the House, but they were a far less cohesive group than they had once been.

There was a surprising amount of competitiveness and backbiting among the sophomores. It was apparent in the lobbying that was taking place for new and more prestigious committee assignments. The most sought-after plums were two seats on the Ways and Means Committee, which oversees all tax legislation and is a huge boon for fund-raising. Several of the former freshmen were after the seats, including Jerry Weller, John Shadegg, and Mark Foley. The competition was so intense that Weller had started lobbying for Ways and Means the day after the 1996 election with a phone call to majority leader Dick Armey. "For me, from Election Day on, it was the sole focus," Weller told the *Wall Street Journal* in January.

Weller had a few things going for him. He had formed his own PAC and raised more than $100,000 for the 1996 campaigns of fellow Republicans, including many of his classmates who were in tough races. That kind of party loyalty tended to be rewarded. In addition, along with J. D. Hayworth and Zach Wamp, Weller had served in the 104th Congress on the Steering Committee, which makes the committee assignments for Republicans. Weller, Hayworth, and Wamp would all manage to improve their committee assignments in their second terms.

Hayworth, who had been reelected by the skin of his teeth with 48 percent of the vote and who had been a loyal and loud supporter of the Republican leadership in the 104th Congress, also wanted on Ways and Means. He and Weller wound up winning those coveted seats. And Wamp managed to score a slot on the Appropriations Committee, the perfect place for someone who had talked tough about cutting the budget in Washington but who promised to protect programs for his district when he was back home in Tennessee.

There was a great deal of grumbling among the sophomores about the assignments. Shadegg said he thought Hayworth was being a tad ungrateful in seeking a Ways and Means seat since Shadegg had said early on he wanted a seat on the committee and had tried to help raise money for Hayworth's campaign. Shadegg believed he was passed over because he had voted and spoken out against the leadership a few too many times. A number of sophomores felt this was also part of the reason Matt Salmon didn't win the Commerce Committee seat he had been seeking. Weller and Hayworth were party men, not boat rockers.

Another thing that may have hurt Salmon's chances for a better committee assignment was that, like Sanford, he had voluntarily limited himself to serving only three terms in the House. Some of their classmates assumed Salmon and Sanford were stuck on less prestigious committees because the Republican leaders considered it a waste to give better assignments to members who would be leaving the House in just four more years and would not have the chance to move up on their committees. (That, and because they weren't "butt-kissers," one freshman told me.)

But Hilleary, for one, was extremely happy with his committee reassignment. He had managed to secure the Budget Committee seat he had been wanting for two years.

Now that he had won his first reelection, Hilleary toyed with the idea of making a future bid for governor of Tennessee or for the Senate should Fred Thompson be a part of a successful GOP presidential ticket in 2000. For a class that had disdained career politics and Washington, a surprising number of the freshmen had already started talking about seeking higher office, including two of the most obstreperous. Linda Smith of Washington had formally declared her candidacy for a 1998 race against Democratic senator Patty Murray, and Mark Neumann had all but announced his intention to run against Wisconsin Democratic senator Russ Feingold. John Ensign of Nevada also announced he would make a Senate bid and Jon Christensen of Nebraska was running for governor.

* * *

The 105th Congress began at a snail's pace compared to the 104th. After being sworn in, the members immediately left town for two weeks and were in session for only two more days in January.

And there were other differences that made this session of Congress look far more like traditional past Congresses than like the 104th. Since Gingrich seemed to have his hands full managing his image restoration, he had less time for top-down management of legislation. That meant committee chairs had more autonomy and bills were moving through the committee system as they had before the 104th Congress.

And the new GOP members elected in 1996 were a pale imitation of the previous freshman class. They were older and more moderate and had more traditional political experience than the class of '94. "They don't have the fervor we had. . . . I see the reform aspect of our agenda getting blunted pretty bad," Hilleary told me. There was also a lot less lockstep unity among the Republicans; party leaders were having trouble holding their troops together. Since their margin was so small, the defection of just a handful of Republicans could doom a piece of legislation. Not that the 105th Congress actually seemed to be doing that much.

They had managed to win reelection and to hold the majority, but they were acting like losers instead of winners. Feeling that they had been beaten over the head on Medicare and some other issues by the Democrats and the labor unions, the Republicans seemed unwilling to attempt anything too difficult or ambitious in the 105th Congress. The 1996 election had "scared the bejesus" out of the GOP moderates, according to one member. Their ranks had been thinned, especially in the Northeast. In Massachusetts two moderates had been defeated, leaving the state's 12-member congressional delegation without a single Republican.

From the very beginning of the 105th Congress, the moderates made it clear they planned to assert themselves and would not be forced into voting for things they didn't agree with for the good of party unity. "They feared for their political lives, and they told the Speaker to back off," as one member put it. This just exacerbated the already existing tensions between the GOP moderates and the conservatives.

The most conservative of the former freshmen figured there was strength in numbers and they needed to stick together, so a dozen of the True Believers decided to get offices on the same floor of one of the House office buildings. That way they could be near each other for late-night plotting sessions. A couple of hallways on the fourth floor of the Cannon House Office Building became their clubhouse. The list of former freshmen with offices on the floor read like a who's who of the class malcontents: Mark Souder, John Shadegg, Steve Largent, Tom Coburn, Mark Neumann, and John Hostettler. Altogether, 16 of the Republican freshmen of 1994 located their offices there—more than one-quarter of those who remained in the House.

Hilleary kept his office on the first floor of Cannon. But he had become part of the group of rebels. He was no longer the good soldier who saluted smartly and followed orders. Hilleary thought the True Believers' core, conservative principles and goals were being ignored and something had to be done about it.

Part of the reason for all the tiptoeing around was that Gingrich was badly wounded and no longer dealing from a position of strength but from one of weakness. The True Believers had lost confidence in his judgment, his management, and his ability to continue to pursue their conservative agenda. Gingrich was clearly not a man of moderation. He always seemed to be overreacting. First he overreacted in the 104th Congress by trying to go too far; now he was overcompensating and seemed afraid to do anything. "The Newt Gingrich that was the fire-eater changed into Newt Gingrich the compromiser," Salmon remarked.

The Republicans were suffering from a severe loss of momentum. The heady early days of the 104th Congress seemed like a distant memory.

*   *   *

The first significant act of defiance by the former freshmen came in March, when a group of 11 House members—the Gang of Eleven—opposed the appropriations bill that included the funding for Congress. It contained a significant increase in the budget for congressional committees and their staffs, exactly the kind of spending increase the Republicans never would have considered in the 104th Congress.

After that vote, Newt Gingrich insisted that the insurgents (nine sophomores— Lindsey Graham, Matt Salmon, Mark Souder, Mark Sanford, Mark Neumann, Joe Scarborough, Steve Largent, Steve Chabot, and Tom Coburn—plus two Republicans in their third term, Peter Hoekstra and Bob Inglis) explain themselves in front of a meeting of the House Republican conference. Largent, who had never been afraid to stand up to Gingrich, made it clear the Speaker didn't scare him. Largent talked about playing professional football and told Gingrich if he hadn't been intimidated by the huge linebackers he had faced on the football field, he certainly wasn't going to be intimidated by Gingrich.

Things got pretty quiet at that point. Nobody knew exactly how to react. Graham was next. He decided to lighten things up and go for the laugh. "Well, I can be intimidated," Graham said with a smile but added on a more serious note, "Not over this issue, though."

Matt Salmon told me several months later that Gingrich's attempt to humiliate those who had voted against him backfired because "it created an immense amount of solidarity" among the 11. "All of a sudden we became the bad guys," said Graham. "Newt tried to run us over and belittle us." That, as Gingrich would soon discover, turned out to be a mistake.

The next major rebellion came over Gingrich's handling of something called the disaster relief bill. This should have been a fairly routine legislative matter. Congress regularly passes emergency supplemental funding bills to take care of needs that arise unexpectedly, such as the flooding in the Midwest and South that occurred in the winter and spring of 1997. Since the president was certain to sign the bill, the Republicans decided to attach a few extras.

But the extras the Republicans attached to the disaster relief bill made them look blatantly partisan. One provision would have prevented a future government shutdown if Congress and the president could not agree on a budget; it was clearly designed to avoid a repeat of the shutdown that had turned out so badly for the Republicans in the fall of 1995. The other involved the 2000 census and Republican efforts to block the Commerce Department from using a sampling technique to compensate for the undercounting of inner-city blacks and Hispanics that the Republicans worried would benefit Democrats in future congressional elections.

In early June President Clinton pulled out his veto pen, the weapon that had worked so successfully for him in the previous Congress. In vetoing the disaster relief bill because of the GOP provisions, he claimed the Republicans were "playing politics with the lives of Americans in need." As during the government shutdowns, public sentiment was not with the Republicans, and they had not worked out an exit strategy for what to do after a presidential veto.

The Democrats in Congress immediately jumped on the issue and started to do everything they could to make the Republicans look bad, such as holding an all-night vigil for the flood victims in the office of Senate minority leader Thomas Daschle. Even though the bill under consideration was simply to replenish what was being spent and aid continued to flow uninterrupted to the flood victims, the Republicans were taking a public relations pounding on the issue. The disaster relief bill had turned into a major disaster for them.

Only three days after the presidential veto, the Republicans backed down and removed the two offending provisions, and Clinton quickly signed the bill. Although the Republican conference held a meeting before the vote and members were instructed to vote yes on the bill, most of the GOP leaders, including Senate majority leader Trent Lott, House majority leader Dick Armey, majority whip Tom DeLay, and conference chairman John Boehner, voted against it on final passage.

That was the last straw for Lindsey Graham. "I was as mad as I've ever been since I've been in Congress. I went home and told people I'm not going to take this crap anymore." The sophomores were upset over a number of things. They considered the census and government shutdown provisions worth fighting for, but the issues involved were larger than those two specifics. Once again Gingrich and their leaders had bungled the public relations effort and allowed themselves to be outmaneuvered by Clinton and the Democrats. Once the decision had been made to attach the two provisions to the bill, the sophomores thought their leaders should have stood their ground and fought rather than giving up at the first sign of trouble. And when Gingrich decided to back down, he did it quickly and by making a unilateral decision, without first discussing it with his fellow House Republicans, just as he had done at crucial moments in the 104th Congress. "When it got tough, Newt cut and ran. . . . After leading us up the hill, he went down the other side without us," said Graham.

It was the government shutdown all over again. Gingrich had chosen the wrong strategy from the start, certain to be unpopular with the public, and picked both the wrong time to fight and the wrong time to cave in, as the sophomores saw it.

"In pushing legislation to avoid an embarrassment of two years ago, we have created an embarrassment of this year," House Appropriations chairman Robert Livingston told the *Washington Post* the day after the president signed the disaster relief bill. Livingston had cautioned against trying to take on the president regarding the census and government shutdown provisions. "They have ended up with the worst of all worlds because they have compromised on other issues of real principle (such as the budget and tax cuts) but decided to fight on a trivial issue and lost. It was silly," Bill Kristol, the conservative activist and editor of the *Weekly Standard,* was quoted as saying in the same *Post* story.

Many of the sophomores agreed with Kristol's assessment that Gingrich was too willing to compromise with Clinton, too eager to cut a deal to make himself look like a more reasonable person and to improve his public approval ratings. The funny thing was no matter what Gingrich tried, his job approval rating never seemed to get much above 30 percent.

Gingrich's handling of the episode exacerbated the frustration many Republicans were feeling over his leadership. He was forced publicly to deny that members of his own party were trying to throw him overboard and claimed rumors of insurrection were just figments of the media's imagination. But denial or not, one month later it would all boil over into an aborted attempt to oust him from the Speakership.

After Gingrich botched the disaster relief bill, the small group made up mostly of sophomore Republicans who had been meeting off and on since March (when they had voted against the increase for committee funding) were joined by even more dissidents. Graham hosted a meeting in his office that nearly 40 people attended. The main topic of discussion was what to do about Gingrich. "Everybody there didn't trust him anymore and half wanted him out," Graham said.

The group of dissidents included Graham, Hilleary, Neumann, Coburn, Largent, McIntosh, Sanford, and Sue Myrick. There were two notable aspects to the group's makeup. The first was that McIntosh and Myrick had been the class representatives to the leadership throughout the 104th Congress and probably knew Gingrich better than almost any of the other former freshmen. The other was that two of the group's leaders were the roommates—Graham and Hilleary—who had not been among the chief rebels who had routinely voted against the leadership since 1995. Now even they had finally had enough.

The dissidents started meeting privately on a regular basis to talk about the direction the House Republicans seemed to be headed in and how they could get back on track. They thought the party was drifting, and they were hearing complaints from conservative activists back in their districts. "We believed too much in what was said on the Capitol steps three years ago [when the Contract with America was unveiled]. We didn't want the revolution of '94 to stop. We came here believing we could slay any dragon, and this year when we couldn't even kill a butterfly, we got discouraged," Salmon told me. "The 105th Congress has been a big left turn for us," asserted Graham. "We've been sucked back into the political system that most of us ran against. . . . We've lost our political stride." Graham said Republican leaders were "worried about maintaining power rather than using power."

The dissidents also believed that time and time again Gingrich and other House leaders had misled them about what was in specific pieces of legislation, what the strategy would be for handling a particular issue, about any number of things. The bottom line was that they had lost faith in Gingrich and his ability to tell the truth, even to them. "Most of our leaders lie with reckless abandon. They lie when telling the truth would be easier," one of the sophomores remarked. "He'll say something on Monday, and it's different on Tuesday," said Graham of Gingrich. "I think the Speaker has a problem with keeping his word," said Souder.

The group talked about how they could get through to Gingrich and convince him that things weren't working. Gingrich just didn't seem to be listening; that was another big part of the problem, as the dissidents saw it.

The insurgent Republicans were portrayed in the press as fanatical, hard-right conservatives who would never be satisfied whenever their leaders compromised. But the situation was more complicated than that. Several members of the group were senior moderates, such as Tom Campbell of California, one of those who had voted against Gingrich for Speaker back in January. "Gingrich has made mistake after mistake. It's not only about ideology; it's about competence," said one of the sophomores. The only image Gingrich seemed able to cultivate for the Republicans was a negative one—"sort of mean and disorganized," in Graham's words.

The dissidents decided there had to be a change either in who was leading the party or in the way things were being done. They talked about the best way to accomplish that and considered a number of options, including confronting Gingrich directly at a private meeting of the House Republican conference. But they also drafted a resolution that could be offered on the House floor to force a vote on whether Gingrich should be replaced as Speaker. The way they saw it, according to Graham, "if there was another major screwup," they would have to confront the Speaker.

There had been several signals from the top House leaders that they supported the effort to overthrow Gingrich. For one thing, Armey had let the dissidents use one of his conference rooms for a meeting, although he was not present. And Armey, DeLay, Boehner, and Bill Paxon met several times to talk about the Gingrich issue before deciding to make an overture to the rebels in an effort to figure out how serious the rebels were about wanting to overthrow Gingrich. There were signals that each of the four men privately considered himself to be a potential successor to Gingrich. As Graham would later describe it, the frustration of the rank-and-file Republicans and the ambition of the GOP leaders collided to set in motion the near-coup.

On the evening of July 10, DeLay approached Graham and told him he wanted to meet with the dissidents. Nearly 20 Republicans attended the late-night meeting with DeLay in Graham's office. They talked about the different ways they could try to force Gingrich out, including approaching him in private, challenging him in a conference meeting, or calling for a vote on the floor. Only once in the history of Congress had there been a vote on the House floor to declare the Speaker's office vacant. It happened in 1910, when progressive Republicans unsuccessfully challenged conservative Republican Speaker Joseph Cannon.

The group of dissidents couldn't agree on a course of action or on a successor to Gingrich. Probably the biggest thing Gingrich had going for him was the leadership team he had surrounded himself with. They were almost no threat. There simply was no logical successor to Gingrich who could do a better job of managing the House, planning long-term strategy, and most important, dealing with the press and being the public face of the House Republicans. The person who seemed to have the most support for the job was Paxon. He was not only popular with the sophomores, but they believed both the conservatives and moderates in the party could accept him.

DeLay wanted to know how far the rebels were willing to go. Souder in turn asked DeLay whether he would go down in front of the well of the House with them if they did call for a floor vote to remove Gingrich from the Speakership—in other words, whether he would vote with them. DeLay said he would, but "he immediately regretted saying yes once he was out of the room," according to Souder. DeLay would later attribute his response to the lateness of the hour and the stress of the situation.

DeLay had been pressing the dissidents to move quickly because he said several reporters were starting to get wind of the coup and were working on stories about it. They had to act before Gingrich learned of their plans through news accounts, DeLay argued. In fact, the House leaders themselves had been talking to reporters about the potential coup, fueling the speculation. Rather than remaining passive observers or acting as intelligence agents for Gingrich, whom they had not yet informed of what was happening, DeLay and the other GOP leaders were egging the dissidents on.

Well after midnight, when DeLay left the dissidents, he met with Armey and Paxon to make a report. He told Armey that it looked like Paxon had more support than he did as the choice to succeed Gingrich. Many believe that's what really crumbled the coup, that Armey decided to back out when he determined he did not have the votes and would not be the one to replace Gingrich. Whatever the reason, Armey and the other leaders got cold feet sometime between Thursday night and Friday morning, and the coup was over before it even began.

On Friday morning Armey met with Gingrich to inform him of the plot against him. Then the entire leadership team met. The sophomore dissidents also sent a small delegation to meet with Gingrich. The leaders, especially Armey, blamed the dissidents for what had happened, denying their own role in the coup plotting. Armey would later go to the length of issuing a statement that said, "Any and all allegations that I was involved in some ridiculous plot to oust the speaker are completely false and, in fact, ludicrous."

The freshmen felt profoundly used by their leaders. They had not wanted to act so quickly; their leaders had pushed them to go forward with the coup. "We were not ready to move; we were not expecting to move until fall," one of the sophomores told me. Although Souder was just as frustrated as the rest of the insurgents, he had been on the fringes of the coup plotting because he thought all along the effort was doomed to failure: "It was dumb, which is why it didn't happen." Until the leaders got involved, Souder said the scheme "was like a loaded gun no one intended to fire."

Once the plot fizzled, there were numerous quips by talk show pundits about the "kindergarten coup" and the insurgents armed with Nerf bats trying to bring Gingrich down. One editorial cartoon showed Gingrich with several knives stuck in his posterior and an aide telling him, "Their aim was low, so it's not fatal, but sitting will be a lot trickier from now on." David Letterman even devoted a top 10 list on his late-night television show to the reasons why the Republicans wanted to overthrow Gingrich. The whole thing was a major embarrassment for the Republicans and just highlighted the disarray within the GOP conference.

The following week the Republicans held a stormy conference meeting. When Armey stood up and denied any involvement in the aborted effort to oust Gingrich, Graham lunged for the microphone to challenge Armey but was restrained by several colleagues and did not speak. That night Paxon met with Gingrich and the other GOP House leaders and resigned his leadership position, saying he had lost Gingrich's trust. But Paxon's resignation alone didn't satisfy moderates and other House Republicans who were loyal to Gingrich. They pushed for another conference meeting at which Armey, DeLay, and Boehner would be forced to explain their hand in the coup plot. For their part, the dissidents were eager to see the leaders take responsibility for their role instead of blaming everything on them.

On Wednesday night, July 23, the House Republicans held a three-hour, closed-door session in a basement room of the Capitol. Before the meeting a group of the dissidents met in Graham's office. They were feeling pretty grim about what might happen and expected Gingrich to try to humiliate them, as he had done in the past when they had challenged him. They also thought he might try to force out the members of his leadership team who appeared to have thrown in with the dissidents, especially DeLay. They "were not going to let DeLay take the fall," according to Salmon. If Gingrich wanted to oust DeLay, they would go to the floor and call for a vote on whether he should remain Speaker, said Salmon. "We were not going to let him exact his pound of flesh."

But Gingrich surprised them. At the meeting, which was part therapy session, part revival meeting, he appeared "very humble and conciliatory," according to Salmon. Gingrich said he would not seek retribution against anyone. And so the dissidents decided to put down their weapons: "The daggers fell to the floor," according to Salmon. In deciding against a purge, Gingrich was no doubt mindful of the axiom to keep your friends close and your enemies closer.

After Gingrich spoke, DeLay, his voice cracking with emotion, addressed his fellow Republicans and read from a prepared statement about what had happened and his role in the would-be coup. Armey and Boehner were more restrained and continued to deny any complicity with the dissidents, although they apologized to their colleagues and to Gingrich for discussing the possibility of Gingrich's ouster. Prior to the meeting, Armey's office had confirmed reports that he had mused with the other leaders about his becoming Speaker if Gingrich were overthrown. When it was Paxon's turn, he told his fellow Republicans, "If you want a head on a platter, you've got mine." Paxon had indeed lopped off his own head by voluntarily resigning his leadership post.

But when none of the young dissidents had been heard from, moderate Sherwood Boehlert of New York challenged them to come forward and explain themselves. Graham was the first to step up to the microphone. He told the conference he was the first Republican to represent South Carolina's Third District in 120 years. Graham said he'd like to hold onto the seat for the party, but Gingrich's missteps were making it kind of tough, especially since Gingrich was even less popular in his district than Clinton.

But Graham also called for reconciliation, and many of his colleagues were moved by what he had to say. The dissidents received more support than they expected. Even members who had nothing to do with the coup stood up to say that they, too, were frustrated with the way things had been run in the House. "We expressed a lot of tough love," said Salmon.

The comedic relief was provided by Sonny Bono, who in his characteristic, rambling manner, related a story about the low point of his entertainment career after breaking up with Cher and having to do a guest spot on "Fantasy Island"—the point being that he bounced back and so would the Republicans.

*   *   *

In the short term Gingrich was strengthened by the coup that wasn't. But his long-term future remained hard to predict. The meeting may have cleared the air, but it did not solve the fundamental problems facing the Republicans—not only Gingrich but their narrow majority, their lack of a clear direction, and the division between the conservatives and the moderates.

"It was not just, 'Let's kiss and make up.' Things are not completely well. Things have got to be different around here. We need an agenda," Salmon told me after the meeting. "A small minority in the conference was dictating how we were going to act. We shouldn't have to come in and compromise to the last on everything. This year all the compromise has been one-sided."

"There's still a lot of frustration. We've got a deep problem," said Souder. The general consensus was that Gingrich would remain Speaker until his next major mistake. And since "he tends to be mistake prone," as Souder put it, there was no telling how long that would be.

Heading into the election year of 1998, many House Republicans were worried about the campaign ahead and the thin record they had to run on. They seemed to be almost more fearful than they were in 1996 and even thought there was a serious chance they could lose the majority. "We prevailed in '96 because people knew we tried, and they were proud of us," said Graham. He thought the Republicans were in danger of losing their base, the party activists he described as "the people who stand out in the rain" for GOP candidates. "They ain't going to want to stand out in the rain" if the Republicans kept going as they had been, Graham told me. Graham still saw Gingrich and his negative poll numbers as a major liability for the Republicans: "That's a cloud over us in '98 that's hanging as thick as it can be."

As a Speaker of the House, Gingrich had been something of a disappointment. It looked as if Gingrich's legacy as Speaker would never equal his role as a revolutionary—as the man who led the Republicans out of 40 years of wandering in the desert— from the minority to majority control of the House. Said Graham, "His shining moment may forever remain the day that the polls closed in November 1994."

*   *   *

The most substantive legislative action of the first year of the 105th Congress was the budget deal between the congressional Republicans and Clinton. The deal was a departure from the budget-balancing struggle of the previous Congress. The agreement included significant increases in domestic spending for education and children's health benefits, which Clinton wanted. And there was a package of tax cuts that Republicans sought. It was the kind of incremental, something-for-everyone deal that the Republicans would never have considered at the beginning of the 104th Congress. In many ways it also signaled a return to business as usual.

Thanks to a strong economy, as well as the spending cuts and tax increases passed by Clinton and the Democrats in the 103rd Congress, the deficit shrank dramatically between 1993 and 1997. In 1992 the budget deficit had been $290 billion. For all of the Republicans' chest pounding about budget cutting and deficit reduction, it turned out that the 103rd Democratic Congress actually did more to reduce the deficit than both the Republican 104th and 105th Congresses combined. The Democrats made more than $255 billion in spending reductions and $250 billion in tax increases over fiscal 1994–1998, according to the Office of Management and Budget. That reduced the 1997 deficit by $116 billion, according to the Congressional Budget Office. In contrast, the spending reductions made by the 104th Congress reduced the deficit by just $21 billion. And the 105th Congress was responsible for only $2 billion in immediate deficit cutting, primarily because of an extension in airline ticket tax, according to the CBO. But the healthy economy, which resulted in increased tax revenues, meant that by the end of fiscal 1997 the deficit stood at just $23 billion, the lowest since 1974.

Perhaps inspired by such good news, Congress and the president decided in 1997 that deficit reduction wasn't such a big deal anymore and agreed to spend more and cut taxes. Their 1997 budget deal included a $12 billion increase in spending and $9 billion tax cut, which would actually cause the deficit to increase by $21 billion in 1998, according to CBO. And the bulk of the spending reductions from the 1997 budget balancing legislation were targeted to occur after 2000.

Cutting taxes and increasing spending were the same approach Reagan had taken, which had created the deficit the freshmen had been elected to eliminate. "We're repeating that same pattern," said Graham, who along with a number of the sophomores had voted against the spending increases in the budget. "Cutting taxes and at the same time increasing spending is not a good marriage. This has short-term political appeal, akin to the honeymoon, but unfortunately presents a financial mess that people will soon get tired of picking up after," Graham warned.

*   *   *

The freshmen of 1994 knew that their legacy was tenuous. It would depend not only on the congressional election of 1998 but the presidential contest of 2000. What happened in the first year of the 105th Congress made it clear that the achievements of the 104th Congress could easily be reversed, especially if the Republicans lost control of the House and failed to recapture the presidency. As Graham told me, "We could be a footnote, or we could be fundamental change. That's not decided yet."

ACKNOWLEDGMENTS

WHILE I WAS WRITING THIS BOOK, two former members of Congress whom I knew and respected passed away, and I would like to acknowledge them here. Both were men of honesty, integrity, and courage and this nation is a better place for their having served it.

Paul Tsongas, from Lowell, Massachusetts, was first elected to the House in 1974, one of the "Watergate babies." I met Tsongas when he was serving in the Senate and I was a young reporter right out of college, covering the Massachusetts congressional delegation for the Griffin-Larrabee News Service. Over the years I interviewed Tsongas many times, and he was always thoughtful and straightforward. He also had a dry wit and could be extremely funny. I always looked forward to talking with him, and I always knew I would learn something.

Some people, most of them his political adversaries, thought he could be a bit self-righteous. But I remember him as someone who set high standards both for himself and for the rest of us. He thought Americans were smart and mature enough to hear the truth. His 1992 campaign for the presidency was mostly about truth telling. He focused on the federal budget deficit and even bravely addressed the issue of Social Security and entitlement reform. His tough-love message did not win many votes, but he did manage to win the New Hampshire primary. And he emerged from the presidential campaign a national figure of greater stature.

In December 1995, at the height of the second government shutdown, I spoke with him about the budget fight and the freshmen. He was sympathetic to their goal but disagreed with them on a number of details. Tsongas felt that he represented the "passionate center" of Americans who are fiscally conservative, socially tolerant, supportive of environmental protection, and sickened by the existing campaign financing system.

When he discovered that he had cancer, Tsongas left the Senate to return home to his family and to Massachusetts. He underwent painful bone marrow replacement and for some years it appeared he had beaten the cancer. Until his death in January 1997 at 55, Paul Tsongas continued to speak out on issues that were important to him and continued to make a difference.

Mike Synar also wasn't afraid to go his own way, but he was no centrist. Synar was an unabashed, unreconstructed liberal. Whereas Tsongas was understated to the point of being accused by some of having no charisma, there was nothing understated about Mike Synar. He grabbed life with both hands and shook it. He was irrepressible, pushy, exasperating, irreverent, smart, funny, and always outrageous, not to mention one of the best dancers I have ever known.

Mike came from an Oklahoma ranching family and was first elected to the House in 1978 at the age of 28. Mike was always sure he was right, no matter what the subject. He often began a sentence with, "You're wrong, and here's why you're wrong." He loved to infuriate his enemies, and he had lots of them. He took on the NRA, the ranchers by favoring higher grazing fees on federal land, and the tobacco companies by pushing for tighter regulation of tobacco. All this while representing a farming district that was full of tobacco-chewing ranchers who drove pickup trucks with gun racks.

He viewed politics as being about good guys and bad guys, the powerful versus the powerless. And he considered himself one of the good guys. Unlike so many members of Congress who weigh each vote for its political consequences back home, he always voted his conscience and was fond of saying, "If you don't like voting, don't be a congressman." He felt he owed his constituents his best judgment even if they often disagreed with him. He loved being in Congress, but with every vote he was willing to risk losing his seat if he thought what he was doing was right.

People thought Mike was too liberal for his district but for 16 years he managed to hang on, finally losing the 1994 primary. He was able to do this largely because he remained an Okie from Muskogee in manner if not in political outlook. "I've had a darn good run. I never thought I would be here this long. When I was asked by my folks, 'What do you want to do when you grow up?' I told them I wanted to be in the United States Congress," Mike would tell me shortly after his defeat.

He had always been an ardent supporter of campaign finance reform and took no PAC money for his own campaigns. After leaving Congress, he decided to head the Campaign for America Project, a nonprofit group organized to push campaign finance reform and he hoped the 104th Congress would be the one to pass campaign finance reform—with his help, of course.

But it was not to be. He started getting intense headaches in early 1995. A brain tumor was diagnosed that summer, and he lived only six months more. He died in January 1996 at the age of 45.

About a year before he died, Mike Synar was awarded the John F. Kennedy Profile in Courage Award. In accepting that award at the JFK Library in Boston, he said, "I believe that to be courageous is to be guided by your own internal compass rather than popular decisions and the madness of crowds."

By that or any other definition, Mike Synar was a courageous public servant.

In his political views, he was the exact opposite of the freshmen. And had he remained in Congress, he surely would have helped lead the Democratic charge against what they were trying to do. But in many ways Synar and the freshmen were very much alike: committed to their own political vision and to a take-no-prisoners, direct approach in trying to achieve it. Nine times out of 10 they would have battled on the issues, but they would have done so with equal passion. As Mike, who had a sense for the theatrical, once told me, "It would have been great drama." And a lot of fun to watch.

This book would never have been possible without the cooperation of many of the freshmen. I am grateful to those who worked with me, most of all to Van Hilleary and his staff, especially Elaine Robinson. They showed incredible generosity of time and spirit in participating in this project. It took a leap of faith for Van to get involved, and I know I have Brad Todd to thank for convincing him this would be worth doing. As the weeks stretched into months, and then years, with ever another last interview requested, I know that Brad took some grief over his original recommendation. I hope they believe the effort was worth it.

Other freshmen and their staffs who were extremely helpful to me include Joe Scarborough and David Stafford; Mark Foley, Michele Famigletti, and Kirk Fordham; Mark Souder, Angela Flood, and Ziad Ojakli; Barbara Levering in Greg Ganske's office; Sam Brownback and his staff, especially Emily Wellman; Mike Ward and his staff; Lindsey Graham and Kevin Bishop; Brad Hunt; Rick White and Connie Correll; and George Nethercutt and Ken Lisaius, who always went above and beyond the call of duty, even risking his Library of Congress borrowing privileges for me.

There were also many senior members of Congress of both parties as well as their personal and committee staff whom I spoke with many times and whose assistance I relied upon. For special help along the way, I want to thank Dan Maffei in Daniel Patrick Moynihan's office; Bruce Cuthbertson in John Kasich's office; Chris Shays and his staff, especially Peter Carson; and Sherrod Brown, who listened from time to time while I vented about everything that was going wrong.

Hundreds of people agreed to be interviewed for this book, and I am thankful to all of them and hope that I have been faithful to their words and ideas.

While I was researching and doing my own reporting for this book, I was informed by reading the work of dozens of reporters who cover Congress. The *Washington Post*, the *New York Times*, the *Los Angeles Times*, and the *Wall Street Journal* as well as *Roll Call*, the *Hill*, *Congressional Quarterly*, and the *National Journal* all were invaluable sources of information. I also read and learned from *Time*, *Newsweek*, *U.S. News & World Report*, the *Weekly Standard*, and the *New Republic*. And my work was made much easier by *The Almanac of American Politics* by Michael Barone and Grant Ujifusa. I don't know what I would have done without both their 1996 and 1998 volumes.

Richard Fenno at the University of Rochester, Burdett Loomis at the University of Kansas, and Gary Jacobson at UC San Diego read the manuscript as I was writing it and offered excellent suggestions. They are the best when it comes to congressional study, and I was honored to have their input.

Roy Norton read an early draft of the first few chapters, and as always offered brilliant observations. Allen Houston at the *San Jose Mercury News*, a dear friend and the best editor I have ever had, was a frequent source of advice and counsel, and I know the book is better for his suggestions.

I like to flatter myself that in 1993, early in my tenure as editor of National Public Radio's "All Things Considered," I launched Bill Kristol's journalistic career by asking him to be a commentator for the show. We became friends as a result of that endeavor, and I value his opinion enormously. Several small sections of this book first appeared in the *Weekly Standard*, and I know they are better for the editing I received there. I am also thankful to Matt Rees at the *Weekly Standard* for his thoughts as I was writing this book.

There are many friends and colleagues who were patient with me through this seemingly endless process. Ken DeCell and Howard Means at *Washingtonian* shared their own stories of authorship and assured me I could do it.

David Gergen provided good advice along the way. The ever charming Chris Buckley saw the earliest chapters of this book and offered encouragement and help more than once.

I thank Mary Beth Grover and Lynne Tolman for their friendship. Paula Stout knew what I was going through and gave me many good suggestions.

Ellen and John Giannuzzi and their three wonderful children reminded me there is life outside the Beltway when I ventured north to Boston.

And Bill Ballou helped give me the final push I needed to finish.

My travel budget for this book was nonexistent, and a number of people offered me shelter during my reporting. In Tennessee I especially want to thank Tom Wood in Nashville; Andrew Hoover; Will Cheek; John Seigenthaler; Henry and Lynne Hulan; Penny and Jon Frere, who were gracious hosts on several occasions; and Ned McWherter, who was a charming and very entertaining host. In Indiana, John and Joe Hilger fed me wonderfully and gave me my first and what will probably be my only ride on a combine.

I will always be thankful to Scott Winder for his enduring friendship and for shouldering a burden for me that he should never have had to take on. In more ways than one, I owe him an enormous debt. I am also grateful to know his mother, Barbara Rees, and Rex and Julie Winder and their family, who opened their home to me whenever I passed through Portland.

Many political reporters at newspapers around the country were helpful in sharing their thoughts about their own freshmen. I especially want to thank Frank Cagle and Harry Moskos at the *Knoxville News-Sentinel.*

Richard Fahle at C-SPAN provided me with a number of tapes that were extremely useful to the project.

Bob Kazdin got me started on Medicare and Rick Foster at the Health Care Financing Administration made sure I knew what I was talking about.

Many people helped me with the chapter on Enid and Joe Waldholtz, but I am especially grateful to Peter Valcarce, KayLin Loveland, Steve Taggart, and David Harmer. Lee Benson shared his thoughts and his manuscript. Charles Sherrill generously volunteered to loan me the tapes of the Salt Lake City news conference and was extremely patient in waiting for me to return them. I also thank Enid Greene for agreeing to spend several hours with me telling me her side of the story.

Donald Ritchie in the Senate historian's office was always helpful with yet another historical detail.

Without the help of Scott Ferrell at *Congressional Quarterly* and Pamela Hazen at the *Hill,* this book would probably not have had pictures.

Jack Beatty at the *Atlantic Monthly* first suggested that the freshmen might be worth a book, and it is he that set me on this path.

I am thankful to everyone at Westview Press but most especially to my editor, Leo Wiegman, who always remained patient.

I absolutely could not have done this book without my agent, Philippa Brophy, and her able assistant, Nichole Britton. Flip refused to give up on this project, and her perseverance and belief in it kept me going on more than one occasion. I will always be grateful to her.

L. K.

APPENDIX:
FRESHMEN ELECTED IN 1994

TABLE A.1   The 1994 House Freshmen

	Vote Percentage in 1994	Vote Percentage in 1996
Arizona		
Matt Salmon—1st District	56	60
John Shadegg—4th District	60	67
J. D. Hayworth—6th District	55	48
California		
Frank Riggs—1st District	53	50
George Radanovich—19th District	57	67
Andrea Seastrand[a]—22nd District	49	44
Sonny Bono—44th District	56	58
Brian Bilbray—49th District	49	53
Florida		
Joe Scarborough—1st District	62	73
Dave Weldon—15th District	54	51
Mark Foley—16th District	58	64
Georgia		
Bob Barr—7th District	52	58
Saxby Chambliss—8th District	63	53
Charles Norwood—10th District	65	52
Idaho		
Helen Chenoweth—1st District	55	50
Illinois		
Michael Flanagan[a]—5th District	54	36
Jerry Weller—11th District	61	52
Ray LaHood—18th District	60	59
Indiana		
David McIntosh—2nd District	54	58
Mark Souder—4th District	55	58
John Hostettler—8th District	52	50

(continues)

TABLE A.1   *(continued)*

	Vote Percentage in 1994	*Vote Percentage in 1996*
Iowa		
Greg Ganske—4th District	53	52
Tom Latham—5th District	61	65
Kansas		
Sam Brownback[b]—2nd District	66	
Todd Tiahrt—4th District	53	50
Kentucky		
Ed Whitfield—1st District	51	54
Maine		
James Longley[a]—1st District	52	45
Maryland		
Robert Ehrlich—2nd District	63	62
Michigan		
Dick Chrysler[a]—8th District	52	44
Minnesota		
Gil Gutknecht—1st District	55	53
Mississippi		
Roger Wicker—1st District	63	68
Nebraska		
Jon Christensen—2nd District	50	57
Nevada		
John Ensign—1st District	48	50
New Hampshire		
Charles Bass—2nd District	51	51
New Jersey		
Frank LoBiondo—2nd District	65	60
Bill Martini[a]—8th District	50	48
Rodney Frelinghuysen—11th District	71	66
New York		
Michael Forbes—1st District	53	55
Daniel Frisa[a]—4th District	50	41
Sue Kelly—19th District	52	46
North Carolina		
David Funderburk[a]—2nd District	56	46
Walter Jones—3rd District	53	63
Fred Heineman[a]—4th District	50	44
Richard Burr—5th District	57	62
Sue Myrick—9th District	65	63

(continues)

TABLE A.1   (*continued*)

	Vote Percentage in 1994	Vote Percentage in 1996
Ohio		
Steve Chabot—1st District	56	54
Frank Cremeans[a]—6th District	51	49
Robert Ney—18th District	54	50
Steven LaTourette—19th District	48	55
Oklahoma		
Steve Largent—1st District	63	68
Tom Coburn—2nd District	52	55
J. C. Watts, Jr.—4th District	52	58
Oregon		
Wes Cooley[c]—2nd District	57	
Jim Bunn[a]—5th District	50	46
Pennsylvania		
Jon Fox—13th District	49	49
Phil English—21st District	49	51
South Carolina		
Marshall (Mark) Sanford Jr.[d]—1st District	66	96
Lindsey Graham—3rd District	60	60
Tennessee		
Zach Wamp—3rd District	52	56
Van Hilleary—4th District	57	58
Ed Bryant—7th District	60	65
Texas		
Steve Stockman[a]—9th District	52	47
William (Mac) Thornberry—13th District	55	67
Utah		
Enid Greene Waldholtz[c]—2nd District	46	
Virginia		
Thomas Davis—11th District	53	64
Washington		
Rick White—1st District	52	54
Jack Metcalf—2nd District	55	49
Linda Smith—3rd District	52	50
Richard (Doc) Hastings—4th District	53	53
George Nethercutt—5th District	51	56
Randy Tate[a]—9th District	52	47
Wisconsin		
Mark Neumann—1st District	49	51
Wyoming		
Barbara Cubin	53	55

(*continues*)

TABLE A.1   (*continued*)

	Vote Percentage in 1994	*Vote Percentage in 1996*
The Democrats		
Zoe Lofgren—California, 16th District	65	66
Mike Ward[a]—Kentucky, 3rd District	44	50
John Baldacci—Maine, 2nd District	46	72
Lynn Rivers—Michigan, 13th District	52	57
William Luther—Minnesota, 6th District	50	56
Karen McCarthy—Missouri, 5th District	57	67
Chaka Fattah—Pennsylvania, 2nd District	86	88
Mike Doyle—Pennsylvania, 18th District	55	56
Frank Mascara—Pennsylvania, 20th District	53	54
Patrick Kennedy—Rhode Island, 1st District	54	69
Lloyd Doggett—Texas, 10th District	56	56
Sheila Jackson Lee—Texas, 18th District	73	77
Ken Bentsen—Texas, 25th District	52	57

[a]Defeated in 1996.
[b]Elected to the Senate.
[c]Did not seek reelection.
[d]Unopposed for reelection.

TABLE A.2   The 1994 Senate Republican Freshmen

	Vote Percentage in 1994	Vote Percentage in 1996
Arizona		
Jon Kyl	54	–
Maine		
Olympia Snowe	60	–
Michigan		
Spencer Abraham	52	–
Minnesota		
Rod Grams	49	–
Missouri		
John Ashcroft	60	–
Ohio		
Mike DeWine	53	–
Oklahoma		
James Inhofe	55	57
Pennsylvania		
Rick Santorum	49	–
Tennessee		
Bill Frist	56	–
Fred Thompson	61	61
Wyoming		
Craig Thomas	59	–

NOTE: No Democrats were newly elected to the Senate in 1994.

INDEX

Abortion, 9, 17, 38, 96, 113, 277, 361
    for servicewomen, 151
Abraham, Spencer (Mich.), 186, 445(table)
Accidental Congressmen, 18–19, 407
AFL-CIO. *See* American Federation of
    Labor-Congress of Industrial
    Organizations
Agribusiness, 126
Agriculture, Department of (USDA), 92,
    98, 116–117
Alaska, 180, 281
Alcohol subsidy, 121–122
Alexander, Lamar, 26
Allen, George, 184
Alliance for Justice, 183
"All Things Considered" (National Public
    Radio program), 437
Almanac of American Politics, The (Barone
    and Ujifusa), 437
American Civil Liberties Union, 309
American Conservative Union, 34
American Federation of Government
    Employees, 408
American Federation of Labor-Congress of
    Industrial Organizations (AFL-CIO),
    277, 343, 345, 363, 377–378, 394,
    407–410
American Free Enterprise (PAC), 337
Americans for Tax Reform, 34
AmeriCorps, 109, 302
Amish, 401
Anderson, Bill, 49
Anderson, Sarah, 278, 280
Antiquities Act (1906), 282
Antitrust laws, 141
Appalachian Regional Commission (ARC),
    106, 107
ARC. *See* Appalachian Regional
    Commission

Archer Daniels Midland Corporation, 126
Arctic National Wildlife Refuge, 281
Arizona
    Republican Freshmen Representatives. *See*
        Hayworth, J. D.; Salmon, Matt;
        Shadegg, John
    Republican Freshman Senator. *See* Kyl,
        Jon
Armey, Dick, 5, 6, 28, 29, 30–31, 42, 111,
    178, 357, 424
    and B-2, 149, 150
    and disaster relief bill, 427
    and the Freshmen, 242, 271, 429,
        430–431
    majority leader, 24
    and Medicare, 167
    and tax cuts, 74
    and term limits, 33, 35, 37, 39, 57
    and Van Hilleary, 61
Ashcroft, John (Mo.), 445(table)
Aspin, Les, 153, 394
Assault weapons ban, xii, 9, 10, 18, 284,
    286, 288–289, 416
AT&T (company), 139, 140
ATF. *See* Bureau of Alcohol, Tobacco, and
    Firearms
Atlantic Monthly, 22, 439

Babbitt, Bruce, 280–281
Baby Bells, 139, 338, 339
Baird, Brian, 384, 386
Baker, Cissy, 69
Baker, Howard, 42, 48, 67, 69, 70, 92, 419
Balanced budget amendment, xiii, 6, 9, 13,
    28–31, 41, 64, 80, 85, 104, 161,
    179–180, 181, 191, 194, 237, 238,
    258, 304, 417
Baldacci, John (Mo.), 44, 441–444(table)
Ballistic missile defense system, 152